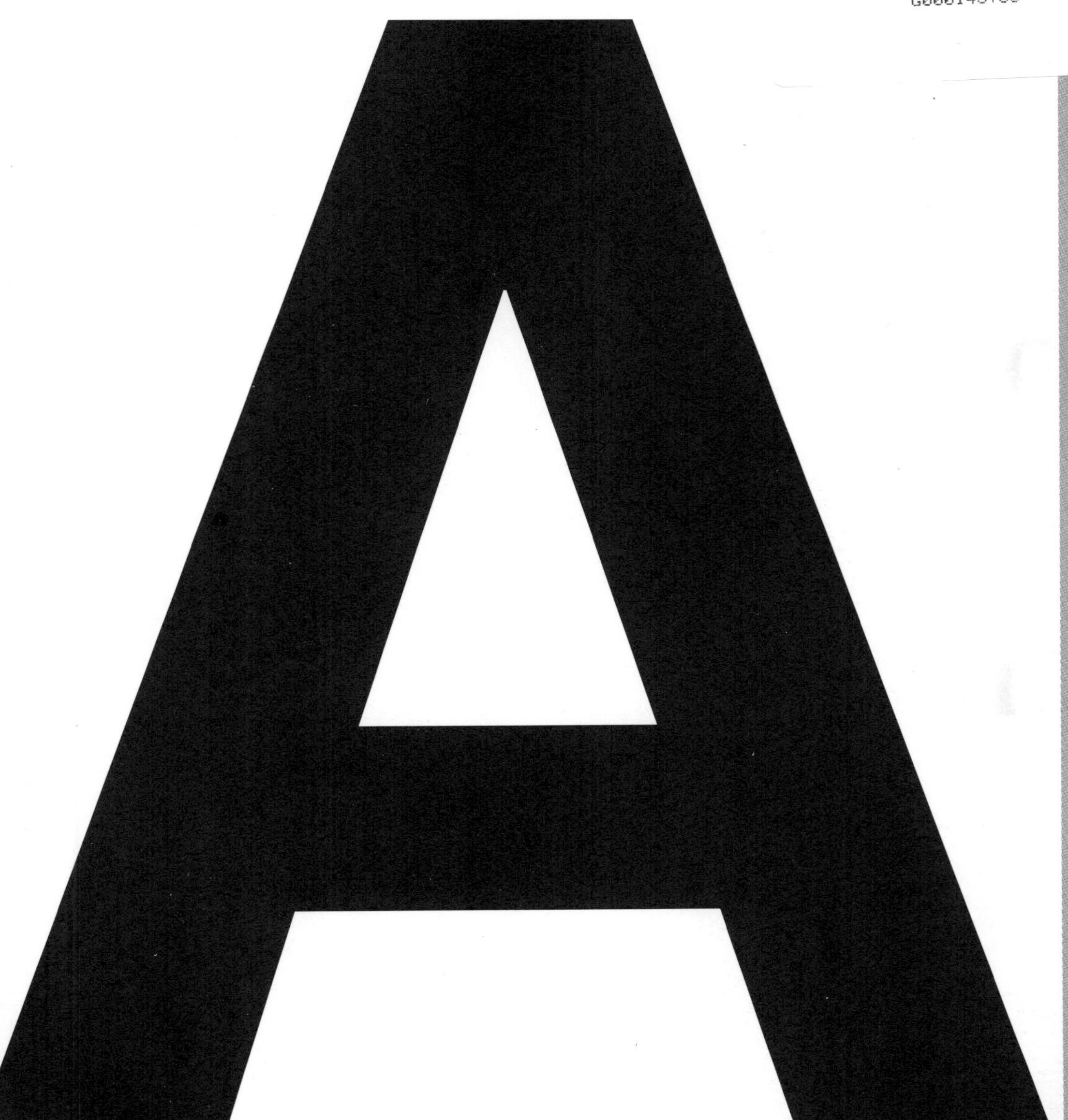

Projects Review 01/02 Architectural Association
www.aaschool.ac.uk/projectsreview2002

Contents

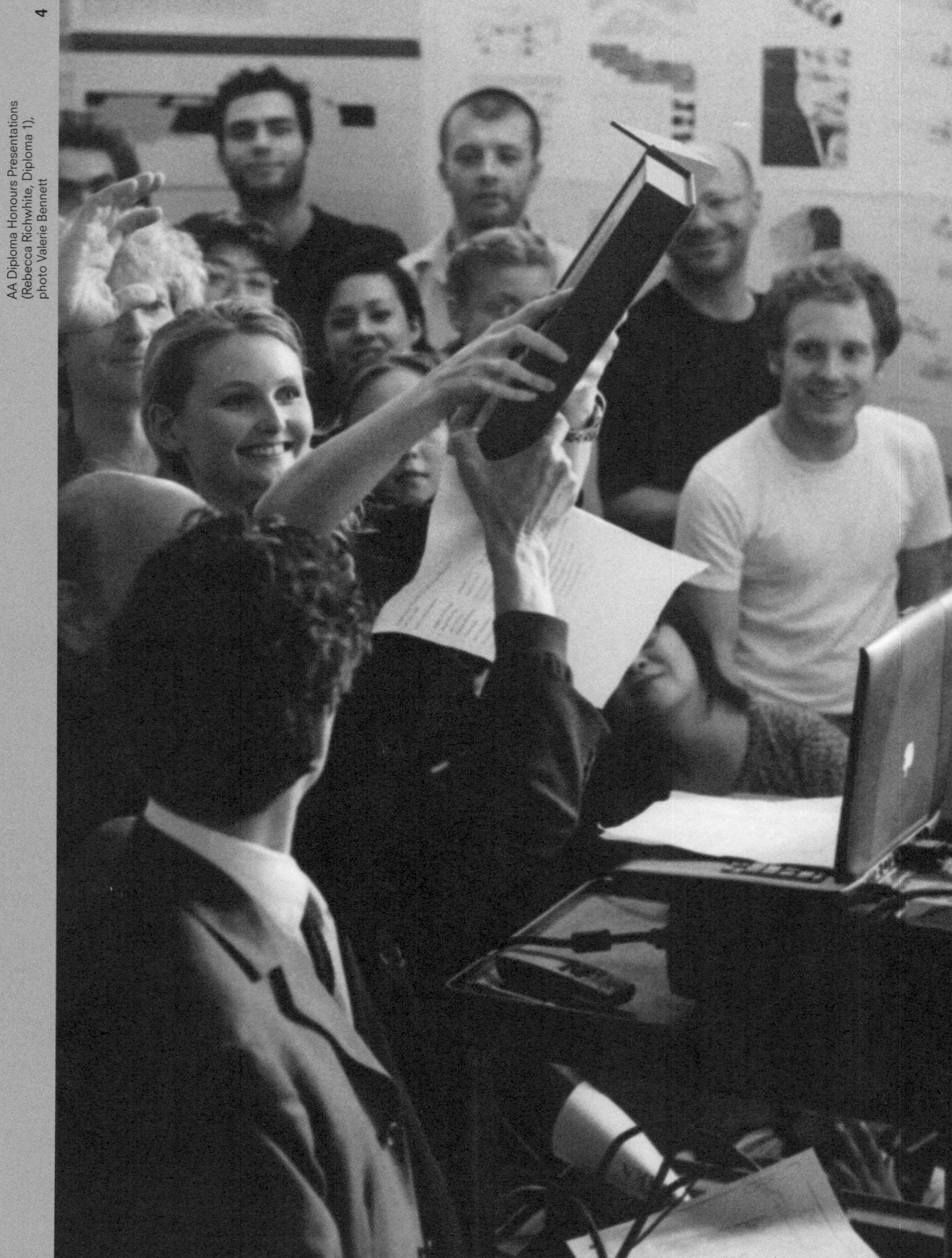

AA Diploma Honours Presentations (Rebecca Richwhite, Diploma 1), photo Valerie Bennett

It has been an unusual year. Even before it began, the events of September 11 had not only marked the lives of most people around the world but, in many respects, had also affected, if not changed, many of our conceptions about architecture and urbanism. Beyond the nightmare of such a terrible loss of life, some thought those events revealed the beauty of Yamasaki's architecture, while others used them to express their hatred of the alienating qualities of the World Trade Center. What was striking was that people took an interest in the structure of the towers and were amazed at their self-destructive capacities. Architecture and engineering became subjects of everyday conversation. And once taxi drivers start talking about structural engineering, you know it is a topic that has entered the public consciousness. The annihilation of one of the key icons of modernism – the skyscraper – by another – the aeroplane – was surely the final nail in the coffin of modernism. One had to pause, even if momentarily, and think afresh.

The attacks on the Twin Towers led, in turn, to the systematic destruction of the rubble of Afghanistan and to the production of even more rubble. One has to assume that with all that has happened so far this year there is an assumption being made somewhere that links architecture, and more specifically its physical erasure, to our conceptions of justice.

The practices and projects presented in this book address the relationship between architecture and justice in a different way. They are, without exception, although with varying degrees of success, engaged in the construction of new places, territories and spaces, and of architectures that prepare the spaces in which the conflicts of democracy can take place. Accordingly, therefore, the School has developed specific programmes, units, courses, lectures and exhibitions that help present the divergent forces of our material culture. The establishment of such components is in many respects anticipatory. The School not only provides a ground for debate but must also set up the intellectual frameworks that will help construct future visions, inventive solutions and innovations. This year, the AA has established a new postgraduate programme in Emergent Technologies & Design, from which the first group of students will graduate in September 2002. In many ways, this programme reflects some of the recent interests and tendencies within the School as a whole, such as, for example, the latent potential in the relationship between architecture and engineering.

Technology plays an increasingly dominant role in everyday life. It is therefore crucial that architects not adhere solely to old conventions but that they engage with working procedures that help bring about previously unforeseen conditions of spatial practice, all the while seeking to improve those that are current. Articulating the potential exchange between emergent technology and design challenges the predictability of standard linear design methodologies. Moreover, it utilises emergent technology's performative qualities as the instigator of new and different spatial situations.

The role and ambitions of the Emergent Technologies & Design programme is supplemented by the work that has started to be carried out at Hooke Park. These woodlands and workshops in Dorset (which the AA is now acquiring) give various groups of students the opportunity to explore additional aspects of architectural and design fabrication, in particular as they relate to issues of sustainability.

When looking at the work of the various parts of the School, it is often hard to communicate in a publication such as this the sense of preparation, or the temporal aspect of the work. It is also hard to reflect student and staff encounters across the boundaries of their courses, units or programmes. Yet these remain important, because it is the intensity of such encounters that helps both to articulate the real differences that exist within the School and to consolidate our commitment to an ever-changing model of architectural education, one in which justice is not an act of destruction but of construction.

Mohsen Mostafavi

The end-of-year exhibition takes over the AA's entire Bedford Square premises for just over a month, but this publication – and the accompanying website – provides a more lasting record of the work produced by AA students during the past academic year. Projects Review **encompasses every course offered by the School, from Foundation to the Graduate School. In the texts on these pages, the Academic Advisors for the Intermediate and Diploma school provide their views of the year.**

The Intermediate School is a time in which students begin to formulate more precisely their own particular intellectual positions on architecture and the ways of mediating them. While First Year and Foundation initiate an understanding of some of the basic tools of architectural discourse – usually centring upon larger-scale objects of fabrication and spaces with relatively defined programmes – the Intermediate School emphasises the synthesis of visual and verbal material in projects of greater complexity. It is expected that at the close of the third year students will exhibit confidence in the articulation of an architectural question as well as be able to communicate it through various media – whether digital, analogue, models or writing. At the Final Review Tables, in the last week of June, tutors assess students' work according to its maturity and ability to handle the more specific and complex architectural projects the students will face in the Diploma School. Likened more to the construction of an argument than the mere compilation of a year's work, the portfolio is the primary device in a process of synthesis.

This work, always in concert with research topics initiated by the unit tutors, has been particularly diverse. Questions into the inherent qualities of materials and techniques were made manifest in small-scale interventions along Kingsland Road in London and a hotel in the Swiss Alps. Contemporary issues of popular culture were investigated in two units exploring the Big Brother **and Guggenheim phenomenons. Two units grounded their work in the development of an installation questioning the relationship of the individual and collective space in Hoxton and Leicester squares. Another unit has continued its longstanding exploration of off-the-shelf materials for the fabrication of mobile living units and the architecture of flat-packing. Two units extended upon existing structures but in radically different ways and scales. One, with techniques of the digital skin, extended the Smithsons' Economist Building with a photo library and exhibition space while the other explored the large-scale structure of the multizoned space of the airport. Finally, one unit considered the development of architectural fragments through abstract, urban, gamelike systems. The one-year sequence affords students the opportunity to engage in a dialogue with the tutors and to manifest the depth of that dialogue in a final design project, a process that recognises the important link between the exploration of an idea and its means of representation. Generally, the phase of research and experimentation is developed during the first term and part of the second, and emphasises the understanding of the intentions of the unit, the development of an idea, and the skills required in order to conclude a more advanced project based on the year's work. The Intermediate School encourages students to join different units between their second and third years. As a result, more often than not, it is the student rather than the tutor who synthesises the diversity of work across the School. It is remarkable to witness those Third Year students who have uniquely integrated the particularities of three distinct years of education.**

Between a tendency towards greater integration of TS, GS, and CS into the unit portfolios and the desire of tutors to pursue their own interests, there is at times conflict. That such struggles are critical to discussions within the School and the development of individual disciplines is made manifest through joint workshops, seminars and juries. At present, discussions continue to evolve among the academic staff to find a formula that manages to successfully balance the diversity of work and the specific desires of each of the courses.

Upon entering the Intermediate School, students must make the critical but often difficult choice – especially for Second Years and those new to the School – about which unit to join. Many are not yet sure of their interests and future directions, and choose a unit largely as a result of an intuitive response to the prospectus, the unit presentation or word of mouth. This year, an evening event at the beginning of the year was introduced to enable students to further inform their decisions by speaking directly with the tutors. A clear indication of the compatibility between the diverse student body and the various units on offer this year was evident in the very small differences in the number of applicants per unit.

The Open Jury, held at the end of February, marks a critical turning point, as student work shifts from more research-based projects and exercises towards a final project. It is a public event at which students and tutors assess their positions relative to the rest of the School. This is often the first time students are asked to organise their work and present it publicly. A formalised Final Jury Week was also introduced this year. Here, emphasis was placed upon the connections among the different units in Intermediate School, as well as with those of the Diploma School. The AA proves to be a dynamic institution. Not only are there the exciting moments as the work achieves fruition during the third term, but each new academic year poses new questions and ways of evaluating them.

Charles Tashima

Four new members have joined the teaching staff of the Diploma School this year. Martine de Maeseneer is the unit master of a new Diploma 12. She is teaching with Ines Geisler. Caroline Voet is now acting as tutor with Christian Kieckens in Diploma 5 (last year's Unit 15), and Thomas Durner, a former student of Diploma 3, has joined forces with Pascal Schöning.

Beyond unit work, there are ongoing links between the Diploma School and other parts of the AA. Michael Hensel and Mike Weinstock are collaborating on the new Graduate School programme in Emergent Technologies and Design. A recently published issue of Architectural Design**, 'Contemporary Techniques in Architecture', includes research articles related to their work. Ciro Najle has continued to divide his teaching between Diploma 14 and the Landscape Urbanism programme in the Graduate School. Carlos Villanueva Brandt continues his collaboration with Housing & Urbanism, with a workshop in Mexico City, and Shin Egashira continues to teach both in Diploma 11 and First Year 1.**

There have been a number of special projects and joint workshops this year. Just a few examples: Diploma 4 started the year with a short competition project for the Royal Opera House in Copenhagen, which was completed in a very intensive few weeks. Diploma 2 and Diploma 11 held a joint workshop on sustainable forms of building construction, led by Bill Dunster, architect of BedZed, the new supergreen housing development in south London. Sandra Denicke and Torange Khonsari, former students of Diploma 10, have held an extended workshop with current students in Hamburg and London. Diploma 14 held a joint workshop with Mark Hemel and the students of First Year 2 on catenary structures and 3D modelling. Diploma 13 ran a 'sandbox' workshop, looking at issues of foundation and structural form. Shin Egashira travelled to Taiwan in December with Diploma 11 and First Year Unit 1 for a workshop with students from Tunghai and Donghai universities. Martine de Maeseneer arranged a unit workshop in Berlin with Kai Volker, an architect and teacher from the Bauhaus in Dessau.

The open jury, which gives students and tutors the opportunity to see work in progress at the midpoint in the year, was held a little later than usual, so that it would coincide with the visit from the RIBA/ARB joint validation board. The event occurred over two days, with a mixture of internal and visiting critics including Ulrike Karlsson, Lars Spuybroek, Richard Wentworth and Sarah Wigglesworth. We were also joined by various members of our External Examiners panel: – Peter Carl, Leslie Gill Tim Macfarlane, Eva Jiricna and Marcel Meili.

The joint validation board were highly complimentary about the range of programmes running in the Diploma School. A total of 16 General Studies seminar courses are offered, in addition to one course run jointly by Communications and General Studies, six lecture programmes within Fourth Year Technical Studies and the still relatively new Future Practice course.

Alongside the Fourth Year Review Tables and the Diploma Committee, the annual visit by an international group of External Examiners provides an opportunity to reflect on the current direction of the teaching programme. Work produced within the confines of a unit is brought into the collective debate of the School.

Looking at the range of programmes offered in the Diploma School, is it possible to identify any clear collective thematic in the work? Or to put it another way: what is the current shape of the Diploma School? At least two units this year have taken on topics dealing explicitly with agricultural and landscape issues: Diploma 4 have been addressing residential and office construction on former farmland in Holland, while Diploma 8's year started with a proposal for a farm in Dorset. Another group of units have worked with strategic urban issues – Diploma 2 in East Manchester, Diploma 6 in Shoreditch, Diploma 10 on the A13, also in east London, and Diploma 14 in a whole range of different locations. Diplomas 1, 5, 7 and 13 have all pursued projects around quite specific individual building proposals – opera house, city block, art house and holistic centre respectively. Diplomas 3, 11 and 12, on the other hand, have all dealt in different ways with issues of dwelling and identity in the city and beyond. As the programmes of units shift from year to year, it is possible to see themes introduced in one context and taken up in another. It is this process, of something like a long-term conversation, that gives the Diploma School its special character, and a depth that goes beyond simple diversity.

Peter Beard

Opposite page, above: Antoni Malinowski installation, photo Nicola Bailey; centre: Laban Dance Centre, showing polycarbonate cladding, photo Hélène Binet; below: Pasmore Pavilion at Peterlee

Throughout the academic year, the AA organises and hosts a number of lectures, seminars and exhibitions that are open to the public as well as to members and students. These events attract leading architectural practitioners and theorists from around the world; they also provide a platform for the discussion of the work of innovative but lesser known practices and individuals, and of people from related fields. The following pages highlight some of the public events held this year.

A number of exhibitions took as their theme the meeting of art and architecture in works as diverse as Victor Pasmore's concrete pavilion at Peterlee and Antoni Malinowski's colour installation in the Front Members' Room.

Paul Usherwood wrote about the Pasmore Pavilion in Building Design:
'Painter Victor Pasmore's pavilion at Peterlee New Town, Co. Durham, is at once both architecture and sculpture. A two-storey abstract structure composed of interlocking triangles, the pavilion is today scarred and neglected, a sad illustration of the kind of problems that public art so often encounters. The exhibition at the AA documents the artistic process behind the pavilion, which, almost from the day it was completed in the 1970s, has been a battleground among different groups. First, there are Pasmore's art world admirers. They have always seen the pavilion as a kind of arty pergola, or as Alan Bowness and Luigi Lambertini say in their book on Pasmore, a piece of "purely abstract form through which to walk, in which to linger, and on which to play ... a free anonymous monument which, because of its independence, can lift the activity and psychology of an urban housing community on to a universal plane". That the community in question has shown little inclination to view it in the same way is supposedly of little account.... Then there is the architectural community, which has often been somewhat suspicious of the pavilion. In the 1960s, the Newcastle architect Harry Faulkner-Brown summarily dismissed Pasmore's pretensions to any kind of authority in architectural matters with the statement that "the person best qualified to create a building with strong sculptural qualities is an architect with sculpture sympathies and abilities". Thirdly, there are the local teenagers who have always made the pavilion their meeting place. And last but not least, there are those one might describe as indignant local residents. Predictably, the latter are unimpressed by talk of the pavilion's artistic qualities or its role in some kind of turf war between artists and architects. In their view, the pavilion should be demolished without further ado, because it is a "dirty old bit of concrete", as a local councillor puts it, but mostly because it has come to be the venue for graffiti, sex and drug-taking. In practice, though, demolition would be an expensive option. As the artist himself once remarked, the concrete structure would take 'an atom bomb' to blow it up. So what should be done? Pasmore himself would probably say there is no need to do anything. In 1982, he was shown the graffiti that had replaced his original, elegant biomorphic abstractions and impishly claimed that he was delighted with the decoration of the interior: "The children have done what I couldn't do; they have humanised the place and made it a social centre"'.
The Developing Process: The Pasmore Pavilion at Peterlee was shown from 8 November to 5 December.

Sarah Kent of Time Out was positively lyrical about Antoni Malinowski's work:
'Traversing the elegant, Adams-style Georgian ceiling of the Front Members' Room of the AA, a swarm of small black marks and spindly black lines make their way across the wedding-cake mouldings and travel down the wall towards a swathe of rich cochineal. Dipping beneath the dado rail and smothering the skirting board, a looping arc of luscious crimson hides the white emulsion beneath a glistening skin that looks as sticky as syrup and as seductive as honey. Between the tall windows where the wall is darker, a deep blue film of lapis lazuli sucks in the light and enhances it with a velvety richness.

For Antoni Malinowski colour is palpable substance as well as visual effect. His installation may be subtle, but it demonstrates beautifully how limited is our understanding of colour and consequently how banal our usage and application of it. He is currently trying to instill the idea into students at the Architectural Association. Let's hope he succeeds.'

Antoni Malinowski teaches the Communications courses Drawing: From 4D to 2D & Back Again and Colour Me Moves. His exhibition, Echoing the Pavilion, ran from 5 October to 2 November 2001.

Colour in architecture was again the subject of discussion in an evening lecture in November, in which the artist Michael Craig-Martin discussed the development of his work and ideas, with particular emphasis on projects with architects. These include the Laban Dance Centre in Deptford, where he has been working with Herzog & de Meuron.

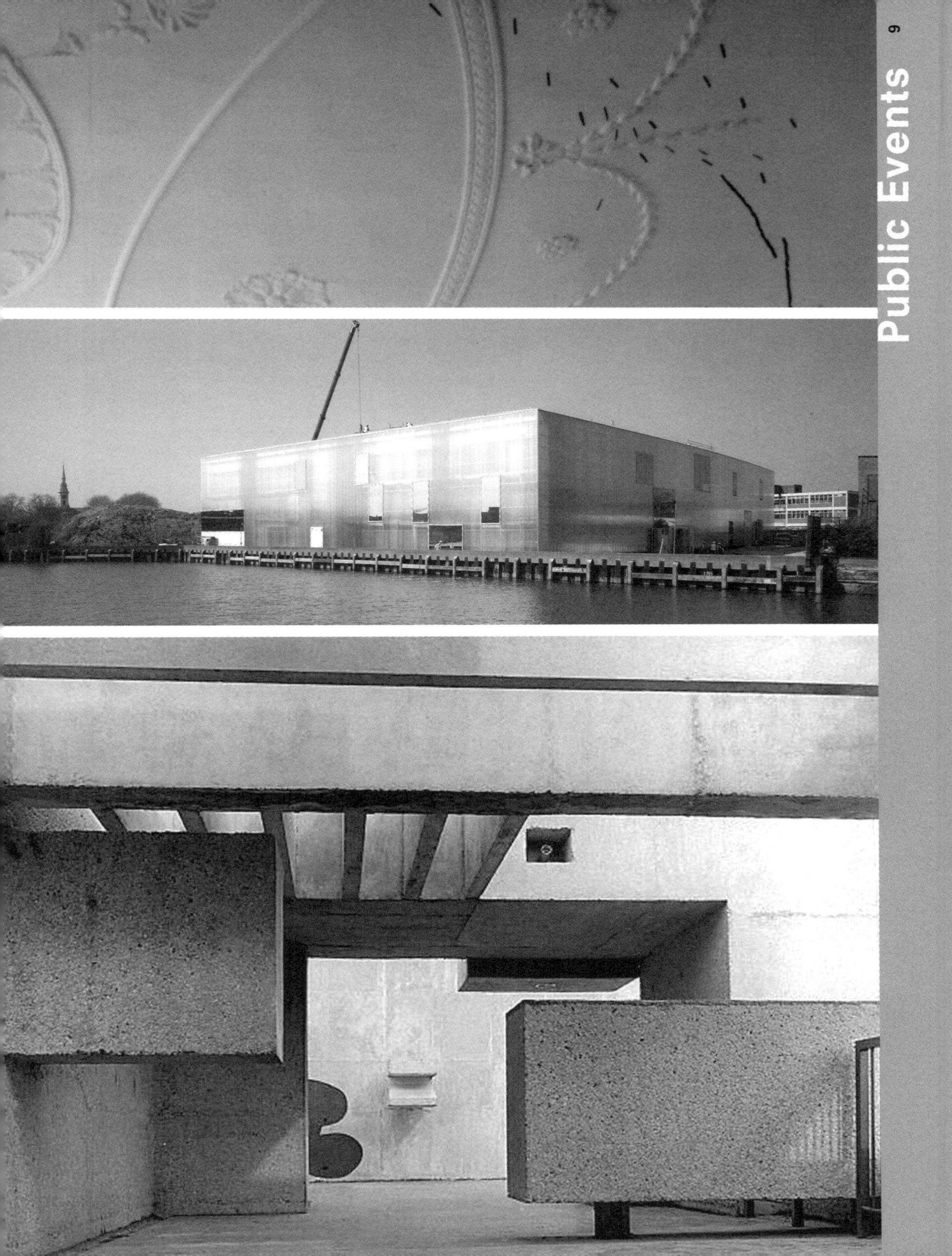

This page: Nigel Henderson, Stressed photograph of a street scene in Italy, from the exhibition Nigel Henderson: Parallel of Life and Art. Opposite: Parallel of Life and Art exhibition, photos by Sue Barr

In 1953, the Parallel of Life and Art exhibition, organised by Nigel Henderson with his friends from the Independent Group, was heralded as the beginning of Brutalism in British art and architecture. Almost half a century later, the show was reconstructed at the AA.

Tom Dyckhoff reviewed the work of Nigel Henderson in The Guardian Weekend:

'For all his reticence, Henderson was the unwitting catalyst behind the resurgence in British culture after 1945. He was, said David Sylvester, the late authority on the period, a "seminal figure", the older brother to a more pushy, attention-seeking band of British artists, architects and sculptors which emerged, shell-shocked, into the drab, shabby years of austerity and tried to patch itself up....

Henderson was the "image finder", the archaeologist, for Eduardo Paolozzi and Alison and Peter Smithson, who formed a kind of gang within the Independent Group's gang. He'd take them on his walks around Bethnal Green, scavenging out the qualities worth salvaging for the radical future the Independent Group thought would rise, phoenix-like, from the bomb sites.... The Smithsons used Henderson's images to argue against the postwar rebuilding that was wiping out the life of the street. They proposed repairing Blitzed streets with a scalpel, not a sledge-hammer; not clearing the slums, but learning their "natural" qualities, and creating a modern, humane version – "streets in the sky" – to snake across the city, and knit into people's innate attachment to where they lived.... Henderson was never really interested in all this.... He hankered for "the marvellous, the thing that you can never quite achieve except in dreams – the super-real". His camera was used not so much to reflect reality, like standard photojournalism, but, like those Victorian early photographers with their images of faeries at the bottom of their garden, to expose a reality behind the reality of ordinary life, the fundamental order of things'.'

In October, Peter Smithson gave a talk about the Patio and Pavilion project, first shown in the Independent Group's This Is Tomorrow exhibition at the Whitechapel Gallery in 1956. Consisting of a shelter-pavilion within a 'patio', the structure was 'inhabited' by Eduardo Paolozzi and Nigel Henderson, who scattered objects and imagery, mostly gleaned from the East End. It represented for its creators, Alison and Peter Smithson, the fundamentals of architecture, and is revisited in the forthcoming AA Files 47**.**

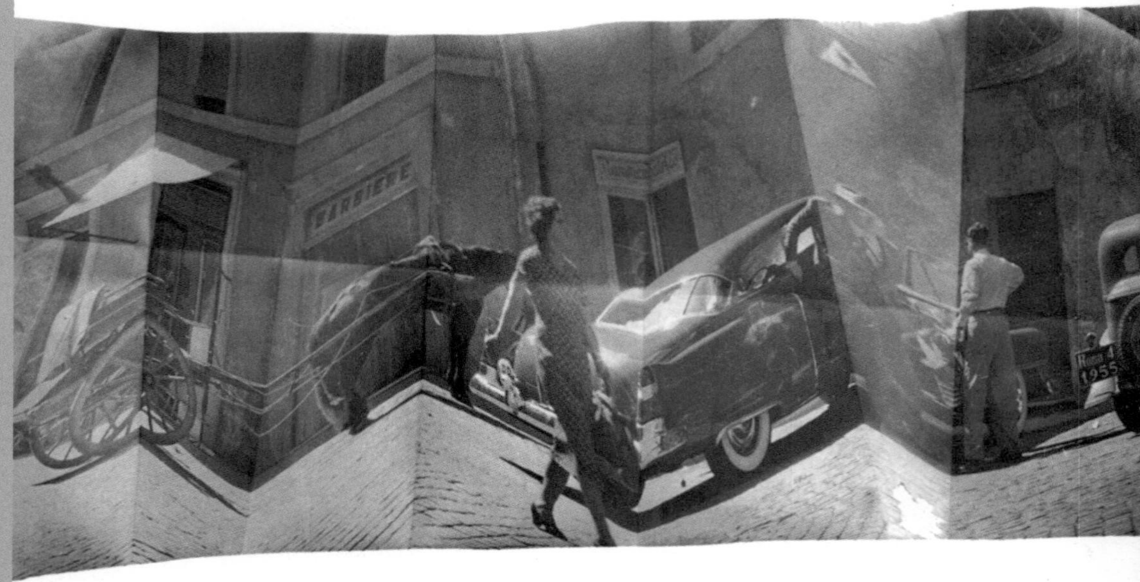

P Is for Perec and Paris

A double issue of AA Files**, published in April 2002, was centred around the reality of ordinary life in Paris as recorded by the French writer Georges Perec.**

In a review of the journal in The Daily Telegraph, Tom Payne wrote:

'Last month was the 20th anniversary of Perec's death; it is fitting, and fittingly odd, that the Architectural Association has published an excellent tribute.

The central texts are four fragments of a project designed to take Perec 12 years, of which even he tired (and this is saying something of the man who wrote Draft Inventory of Liquid and Solid Provisions I Ingested throughout the Year 1974). The plan was to visit 12 places, one a month, describe them 12 times each, and for each piece of field observation to produce a companion description written from memory. The sequence of these descriptions was determined by a mathematical sequence too complicated to explain here.... An extract shows the process taking its toll on the author.

"Over the road, no. 33 is a shop called 'EsthétiCHien' (dog grooming, etc.) General impression? (rue de l'Assomption bores me shitless) A beautiful girl at the wheel of a Morris." But after a while the listing process can take on its own music.... Perec finds a voice, quite flat, quite un-French, with which to amaze us.

Joyce once expressed the hope that, if Dublin should vanish, you could reconstruct it from reading Ulysses.... In his street-notes, [Perec] is documenting houses doomed to demolition. It leads the contributors here to contemplate their own Paris and their own sense of place'.

The publication of Perec and Paris **was celebrated with launch events at the French Institute and the AA, with contributions from artists, filmmakers, writers and poets. Also published this year:** AA Files 43**, which documents the first three years of the Maeda Visiting Artist programme at the AA, featuring projects by Richard Wilson, Krzysztof Wodiczko and Tadashi Kawamata, and** AA Files 44**, which includes work by de Blacam & Meagher, David Ward and Constant, star of this year's** Documenta **exhibition in Kassel.**

Another Paris, Another Time: **Tableaux for the Cinema**

In 1998 the filmmaker Eric Rohmer asked the painter Jean Baptiste Marot to create a set of views of Paris at the time of the Revolution for his film L'Anglaise et le Duc.

Marot described this work in an article in AA Files:

'The idea of using paintings for the exteriors in the film derived, above all, from the wish to escape the typical alternatives available to makers of historical films: building huge sets, shutting oneself in one of those eternal period enclaves, or going to film a Paris of the past in Bordeaux or Provins. Painting has often been used in the cinema, either openly, in the fashion of stage sets (as in Rohmer's 1978 film, Perceval le Gallois), or to produce special effects ..., such as the paintings used in early science fiction films. What is original in Rohmer's project is the prominent place he gives to paintings in the very conception of the film, and to the search for an equilibrium – and even a real ambiguity – between cinema and painting. And this is in order to tell a story in which the setting (Paris during the Revolution) belongs to a period of which the only remaining colour images are painted views....

The immobility of the picture frame leads to a scenography that is devised from the point of view of the ideal spectator, as it would be at the theatre. The only difference is that in the exterior shots of the film the actions are brief and the set changes instantaneous. Consequently the composition of all these views ... has been conceived so that the spectator immediately understands everyone's position and their field of vision. It was a matter of producing frames which could deal with the geometry of people's gazes and glances, and with their bodies. One sees this, for example, in Hopper's paintings'.

The exhibition was shown from 25 January to 22 February 2002. Jean Baptiste Marot was this year's Maeda Visiting Artist at the AA. The Fellowship, generously sponsored by the Maeda Corporation of Japan, provides an opportunity to bring into the School people who are engaged in fields other than architecture, but whose work can nevertheless make a significant contribution to architectural ideas. Marot worked with AA students at a site in Paris. A thorough invesigation of the site, the Promenade Plantée, resulted in the construction of a series of nonperspectival devices that capture a fragment of the city, producing a 'portable' Paris.

This page, from left: Constant, New Babylon (detail), drypoint etching, private collection; Jean Baptiste Marot, Rue de Vaugirard, from L'Anglaise et le Duc. Opposite: Jun Aoki, façade material from Luis Vuitton Omotesando, featured in the forthcoming AA Files 47

Workshops ranging from modelmaking to object fabrication and prototyping were carried out by First Year and Intermediate units at Hooke Parke, the AA's Dorset outpost, approximately three hours from London. The 350-acre site consists of a series of workshops and residential buildings amidst a young woodland. The buildings, designed by Frei Otto, ABK and Ted Cullinan Architects, demonstrate an innovative use of thinnings technology in their construction. Photo shows work by First Year Unit 3

This page: photo by Frank Baron; opposite: Alex Caterall and Alex Trimboli on the Silk Route

AA students Alex Caterall and Alex Trimboli, recipients of the Peter Sabara Travel Scholarship, journeyed much farther than Dorset and chose an ancient trade path, the Silk Route, as their departure point for an exotic excursion. An exhibition of quirky, often beautiful photographs offered an intimate insight into the lives and architecture they encountered on their journey from Hong Kong to Stockholm.
Travelling the Silk Route was on show from 8 November to 5 December.

From old lines of communication to new: the performance Work, Place, on 20 June, was the culmination of an experimental wireless internet project led by Communications tutor Pete Gomes. A small group emulated a working office by connecting to the internet using the AA's wireless node, 802.11 technology and mobile phones, but within the artificial confines of an office plan chalked on the pavement.

Sean Dodson of The Guardian was there to witness the event:

'… A group of six students and their lecturer march out of the AA at lunchtime, carrying chairs and their laptop computers. A man in a pinstripe suit stops and stares as all seven sit down within the chalked markings, open their laptops and switch on…. "You have to totally rethink the internet when you encounter a wireless network like this", says Pete Gomes…. "We want to demonstrate that it is possible to build simple, cheap, wireless networks and that anyone with a laptop can connect within the radius of the antenna we have on the roof of the AA"…. Most of the technology for wireless is hand built. "Low-tech copper wire and coffee cans make directional antennae with the ability to transmit DVD-quality video direct to computers in the local area using a designated public frequency". Ironically, the biggest problem with casting a data cloud outside the AA is the sun. When it shines, the pavement networkers struggle to read their computer screens. James Stevens, a pioneer in this sort of thing, resorts to covering his laptop and his head with his jacket'.

Opposite: Off the Shelf installation, photo by Sue Barr

The work of the Intermediate Unit taught by Alex de Rijke, Philip Marsh and Sadie Morgan was a central part of the exhibition Off the Shelf: dRMM Practice and Unit Projects.

Jeremy Melvin reviewed the show in The Architects' Journal:

'The term "off the shelf" is both a metaphor which describes dRMM's propensity for materials from standard builder's catalogues, and a literal description of the exhibition display, laid out on rolling track-fixed library shelves. Even the exhibition title [spelled out on the ends of the shelves] can be driven in opposite directions to wildly contradictory conclusions, and the various projects oscillate between knowing literalness and conscious surrealism....

One piece of furniture shows how dRMM and the unit they teach can fashion a poetry from this strategy: a Z-shaped chair with a thoughtful footrest, made from copper water pipes. It is a functional (and not very comfortable) object, but the copper pipes raise very different expectations from the act of sitting, which are only dispelled by the practicality of the chair. It has something of a conjuror's trick....

The most far-reaching application of these ideas is in the modifications to the Kingsdale School in Dulwich. Playful inventions in form and material – a pod-like auditorium within an ETFE-roofed atrium – bring a new dimension to the monocular Modernist heroics of Leslie Martin's original design. Modernism, in form and social programme, dRMM seems to be saying, is something whose pretensions can be toyed with, flipped in the air and reconstituted; but never wholly ignored.'

The exhibition ran from 14 November to 4 December and was accompanied by the AA publication Off the Shelf.

Two other AA publications initiated this year incorporate student work.

(+RAMTV) negotiate my boundary!

RAMTV.org is a platform for design research founded by recent graduates of the AADRL. (+RAMTV) negotiate my boundary! **investigates how today's changing social systems and domestic organisations suggest the potential for a new and highly responsive form of urban residential architecture. This research is developed through a design project about mass-customisation. The book simulates a design process whereby clients customise their dwellings by accessing a website.** (+RAMTV) negotiate my boundary! **is available in Summer 2002.**

Landscape Urbanism: The Machinic Landscape

As well as illustrating projects from the AA's postgraduate programme in Landscape Urbanism, the book includes essays and projects by Abalos & Herreros, Larry Barth, Peter Beard, Florian Beigel, James Corner, Michel Desvigne, Keller Easterling, Michael Hensel, Chris Hight, Detlef Mertins, Mohsen Mostafavi, Ciro Najle, Reiser + Umemoto and Alejandro Zaera-Polo. The exhibition of work from the LU programme was held from 1 to 22 March. The publication will be available in Autumn 2002.

Other AA publications this year looked at contemporary practice in Switzerland. Approximations was the first book to analyse for an international audience the work of Peter Märkli. John Bancroft in The Architects' Journal marvelled at the result: 'We are faced here with a greatness which does not need to shout to convey its message.' Steven Spier, in World Architecture, mused on why Märkli should now be receiving the wider attention he deserved: 'Could it be that the world has had its fill of a fast-food architecture based on cynical realism and lifestyle and is ready to embrace something more enduring and ultimately more nourishing?'

The House of Stone was devoted to a new project by the Zurich-based practice Meili + Peter. This is the kind of project that happens only rarely – a house built to the highest standards of craftsmanship with the full support of the client, who acted as a patron of architecture in almost a Renaissance sense.
The publication is available in Summer 2002. See www.aaschool.ac.uk/publications for details.

Marcel Meili,
Markus Peter
Architects
Zurich
The House
of Stone

AA

...ge: Meili & Peter Architects, House ...e, photo by Heinrich Helfenstein; ...te: Peter Märkli exhibition ...graphed by Sue Barr

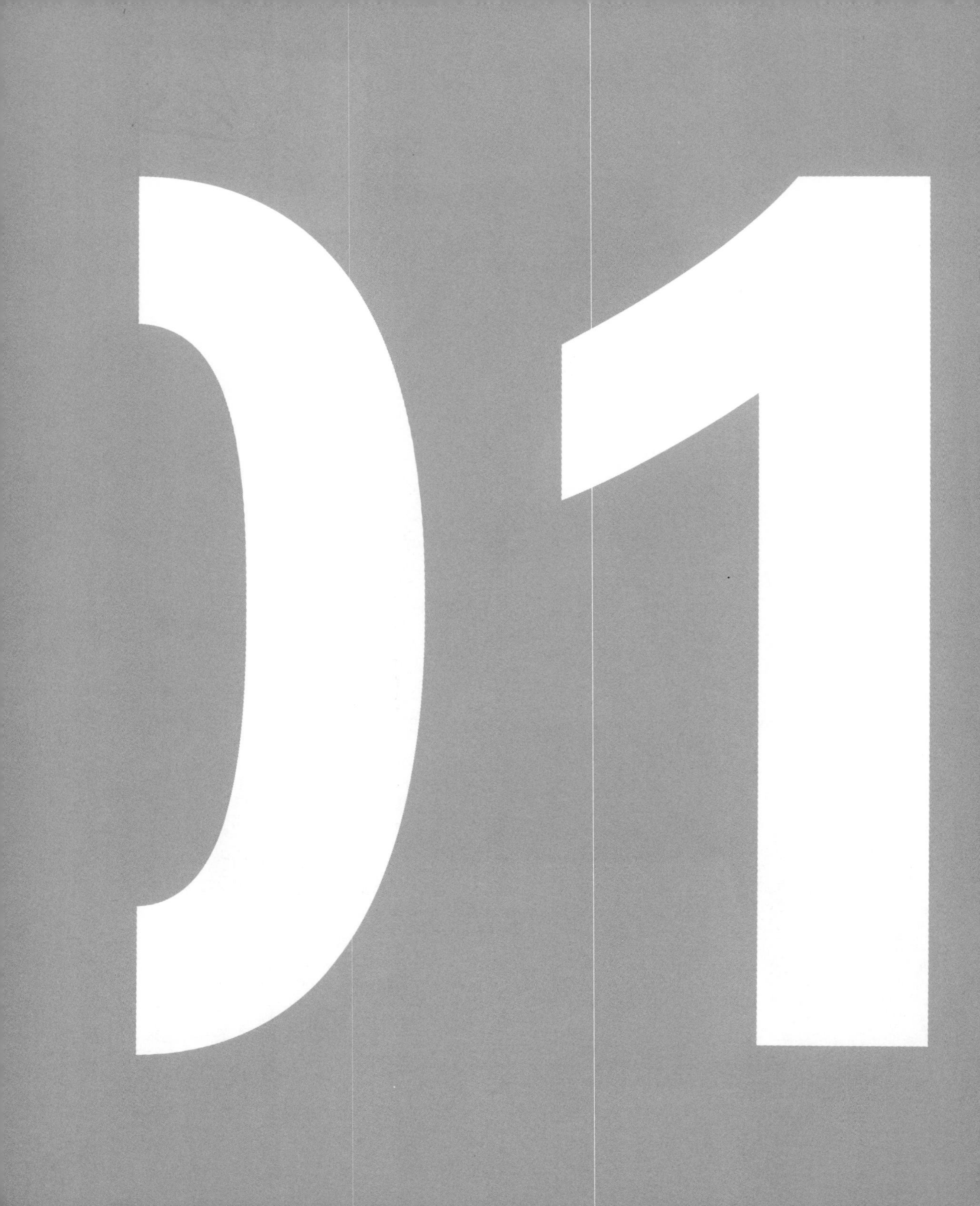

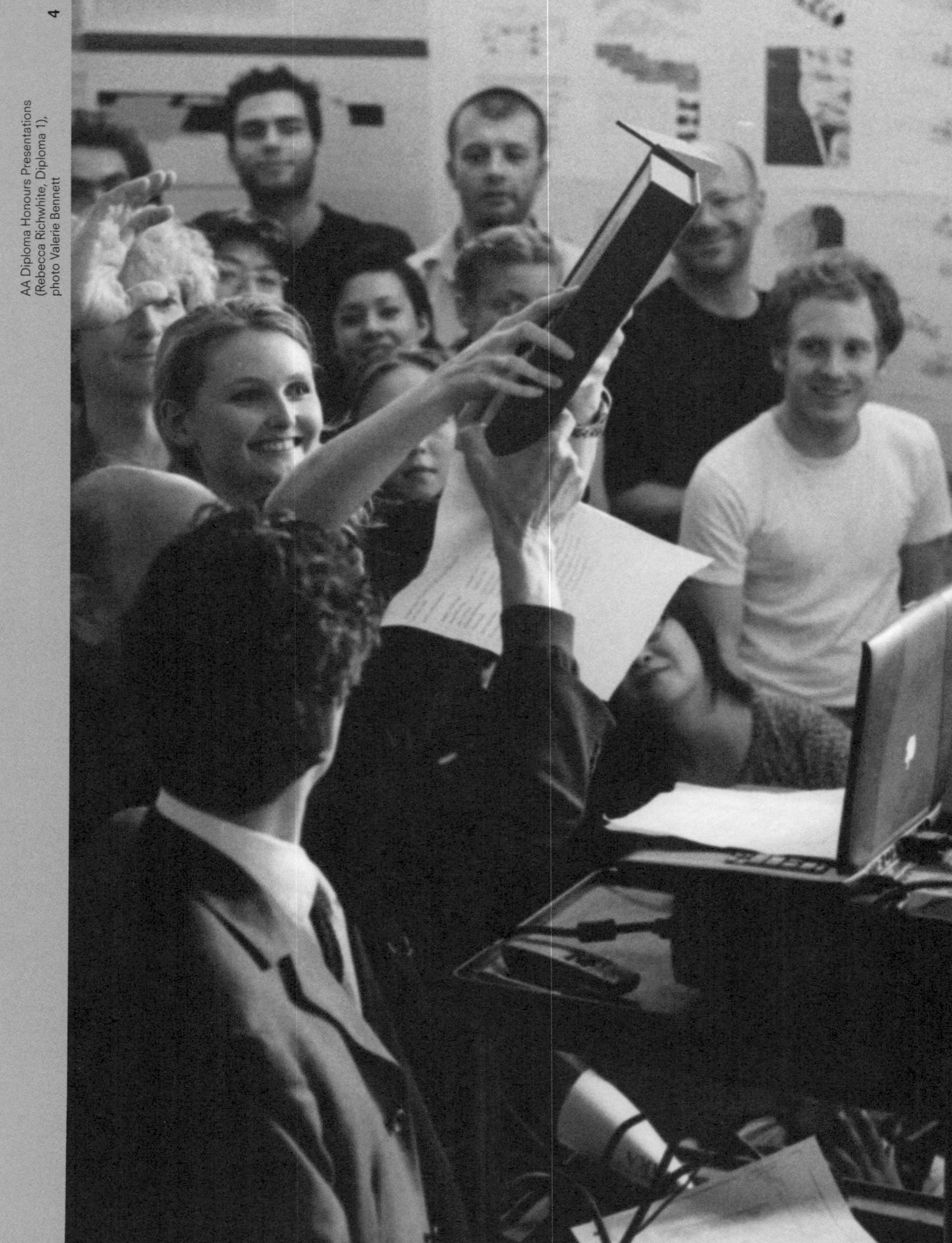

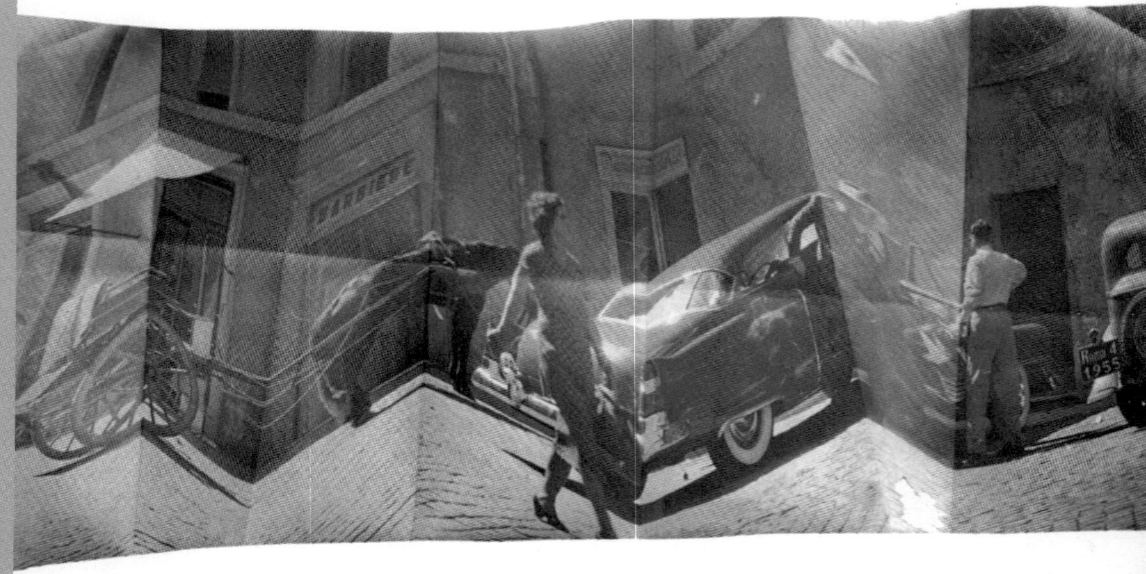

The Guardian Thursday June 20 2002

The following text is an extract from Mohsen Mostafavi's essay in Approximations

'Manlio Brusatin has defined the discourse on colour as having been connected to the effect of changing light conditions on objects. This, he says, leads to two different senses of colour: "... first, colour as material; second, colour as sensation and sign". Märkli's architecture reveals that he is well aware of the subtleties of this distinction. His work is particularly attuned to the qualities and sensations of architecture during moments when light fades or disappears.

Unlike Le Corbusier, who used primary colours – in projects such as the Salvation Army hostel – to add a supplementary life to the building, Märkli's intentions with regard to colour are less directly obvious to the viewer, but perhaps this makes their effect longer lasting. For Le Corbusier the use of both white and coloured paint on the surfaces of buildings conveyed specific associations. White in particular was linked by him with morality and justice and had the power to erase the weakness of the equivocal. "The perfect object", he said, "is a living organism, animated by the sense of truth". And for him the smoothness of "ripolin" and the white of whitewash were the objects of truth.

Even though Märkli feels a close affinity with both Le Corbusier and Mediterranean culture, his choice of colours acknowledges that the light in Switzerland is not the same as in the Mediterranean, which seems to have been Le Corbusier's preferred model for the effects of sunlight. Where Le Corbusier's buildings are surfaces which reveal their objective truth in the brightness of daylight, Märkli's buildings work best when seen in fainter light – what Kircher referred to as opaque light, lumen opacatum, locating colour as a degree of darkness. Märkli's buildings respond to their specific light conditions in the same way as altarpieces in dimly lit churches, where "shadows [are] soft – conditions all agreeing with the character of their colouring ..."'

The publication was accompanied by an exhibition from 28 February to 22 March 2002

This page: Wandel, Hoefer, Lorch + Hirsch, synagogue in Dresden, photo by Norbert Miguletz; opposite page, centre: projects by Blue Architects and John Lonsdale, from Winners exhibition; below: Plasma Studio, silversmith's workshop, live/work refurbishment, 2001

The recently completed synagogue in Dresden by Wandel, Hoefer, Lorch + Hirsch was the subject of an exhibition held in January and February. One of the synagogue's architects, Nikolaus Hirsch, is Diploma 7 Unit Master.

'To walk around Dresden today is to see architecture destroyed and reconstructed. Although 1950s socialist system building still dominates, it is in places being superseded by banal contemporary commercial developments. Meanwhile, in the core of the city, heritage enthusiasts are recreating the buildings of historic Dresden. The centrepiece of this effort is the spectacular reconstruction of the Frauenkirche, the giant 18th-century cathedral that lay in ruins for 50 years after the Second World War ... This tendency to reconstruct buildings as facsimiles, and to erase evidence of the socialist era where possible, reflects the prevailing desire to avoid explicit symbolic reference to an era that destroyed the urban fabric of the city. This can be broadly characterised as a Christian liberal reaction to the secular socialist legacy, but Judaism, such as it is in Dresden, faces different problems. Wolfgang Lorch says: "Jewish history is different from Christian history. Christian history has gone for continuity, as with the reconstruction of the Frauenkirche. We are saying that in the special case of the Jewish history of Dresden there is only destruction, no continuity. We must start with a new building, a building for the future."
The synagogue complex is deliberately and strikingly hermeneutic. A simple plan places two blocks at either end of a raised plot, described by the architect as a "piece of topography". At one end sits the three-storey multipurpose community hall ... At the other is the main event: the elegant twisted temple ... The twisted form of the temple is subtle until you stand close to it, when the full drama of the shifting planes of concrete becomes evident. The twist is a brilliant move, symbolically and in terms of the context and setting. It means that while the base of the temple fits in with the city's grid, the roof of the building and the pews inside face east – Jews face east to pray ...'
(From Kieran Long's building study in World Architecture)

The Prix de Rome is Holland's oldest and most prestigious art and architecture award. It is awarded every five years to two outstanding proposals in the fields of architecture and urban landscape architecture. The winners in 2001 were Blue Architects (Gianni Cito, Thomas Hildebrand) and Big House Architects (John Lonsdale), all former AA students. An exhibition in October, 'Winners', presented their proposals. The AA also had a strong presence in the 2002 BD/Corus Young Architect of the Year Awards. The winner was Plasma Studio, otherwise known as Eva Castro and Holger Kehne. Eva Castro is a graduate of the AADRL course. Ciro Najle and Sebastian Khourian, who teach Diploma Unit 14, were joint second place winners (in their incarnation 'Meta Infrastructural Domain').
Intermediate Unit 4 student Ema Bonifacic was the winner of the Circle 33 Innovation in Housing competition. Her project, Open Castle, turned the massiveness of the traditional castle wall into a series of open volumes – stairwells, passages and rooms – that house a diverse community.

A selection of the architects, writers, engineers and artists to visit the AA in the past year and participate in its varied programme of events (clockwise from top left): Alejandro Zaera Polo and Farshid Moussavi; Ian Buruma; Peter Märkli; William Curtis; David Adjaye; Peter Smithson; Kisho Kurokawa; Herbert Dreiseitl; Zeynep Celik; Merrill Elam; Kazuyo Sejima. Photos by Valerie Bennett

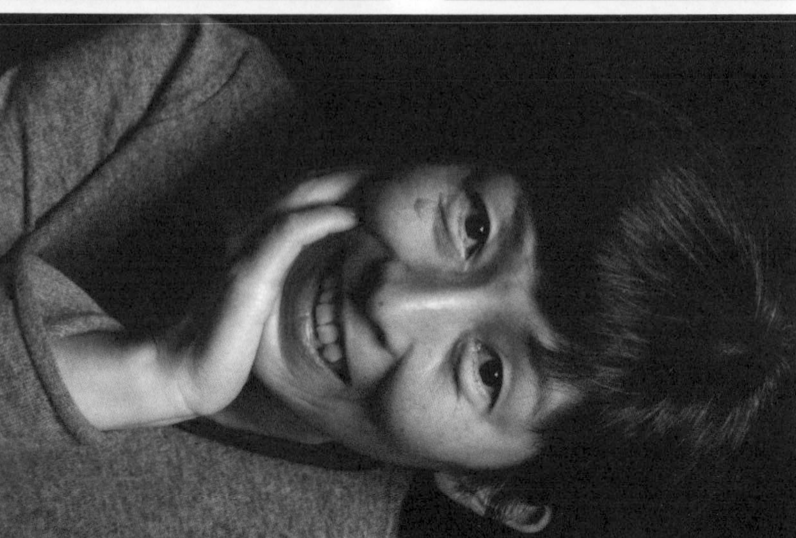

Evening Lectures not only serve as a platform from which practitioners can introduce new work, they also provide an important space for theoretical debate, reflection on the past and projections of the future. The following extracts give something of the flavour:

12 November: Zeynep Celik

'Photographic images communicate meaning by referential and phenomenological strategies. In the former, the image recalls what it represents by way of resemblance or association. In the latter, the image addresses the viewer and offers an experience which shapes the viewer's understanding of the subject. Photography played an important role in the service of colonialism by providing images, "objective documents", that carried credibility and authority. It reduced colonies to visual codes, and shaped the ways in which they should be understood.

The early history of photography has a particularly intertwined relationship with France's most important possession: Algeria. To use Roland Barthes's terminology, photography contributed a "stock of signs" and "cognitive connotations" that enabled the colony to be identified in a quick and easy way.

Starting with the work of the nineteenth-century French photographer Félix Moulin, I will concentrate on two interrelated and prominent categories in photographs of Algiers: houses and women. The French obsession with the houses of Algiers had begun immediately following Occupation. Taking different turns at different historical moments, the Algerian house remained at the centre of the colonial discourse. Many factors contributed to this phenomenon. Foremost among them was a resistance to colonisation that caused people to turn away from the occupied public spaces of the city and made the house a place of refuge, based on the sanctity of the realm of women and family in Islamic cultures. The closing up of the Algerian people led the French to argue that entering the Algerian house would mean conquering the nucleus of this closed society.'

17 January: Saskia Sassen

'What interests me is this mix: microsites and global spans. The new network technologies allow any building to connect with, and become part of, a global space. Any resource-poor organisation in any city that has cheap connectivity can now become part of global networks that connect other such resource-poor organisations. I think this means something both politically and socially, and the question I have for you is this: What does it mean for architecture? What does it mean for urbanism, and for how we think about the city, about urban space?

We can think of an urban spatiality today that actually connects multiple fragments in many different cities, creating an incredible connectivity, if you like, but at the same time fragmenting each of the cities within which it is located. Sometimes, when I'm in my most extreme mode, I think that urban space in certain kinds of places (the financial centre of the City of London, to give just one example) is actually a multiplicity of fragments located on multiple global circuits. What kind of urban spatiality does that constitute? And if you add the political dimension – that multiple small organisations can become connected in this global effort – what does that do to the specific fabric of the city? Do we need to rethink some of the basic categories with which we have understood the city?'

Work by Mario Gottfried Hesketh of First Year 2 installed on the terrace of the AA. Photograph Chris Fenn

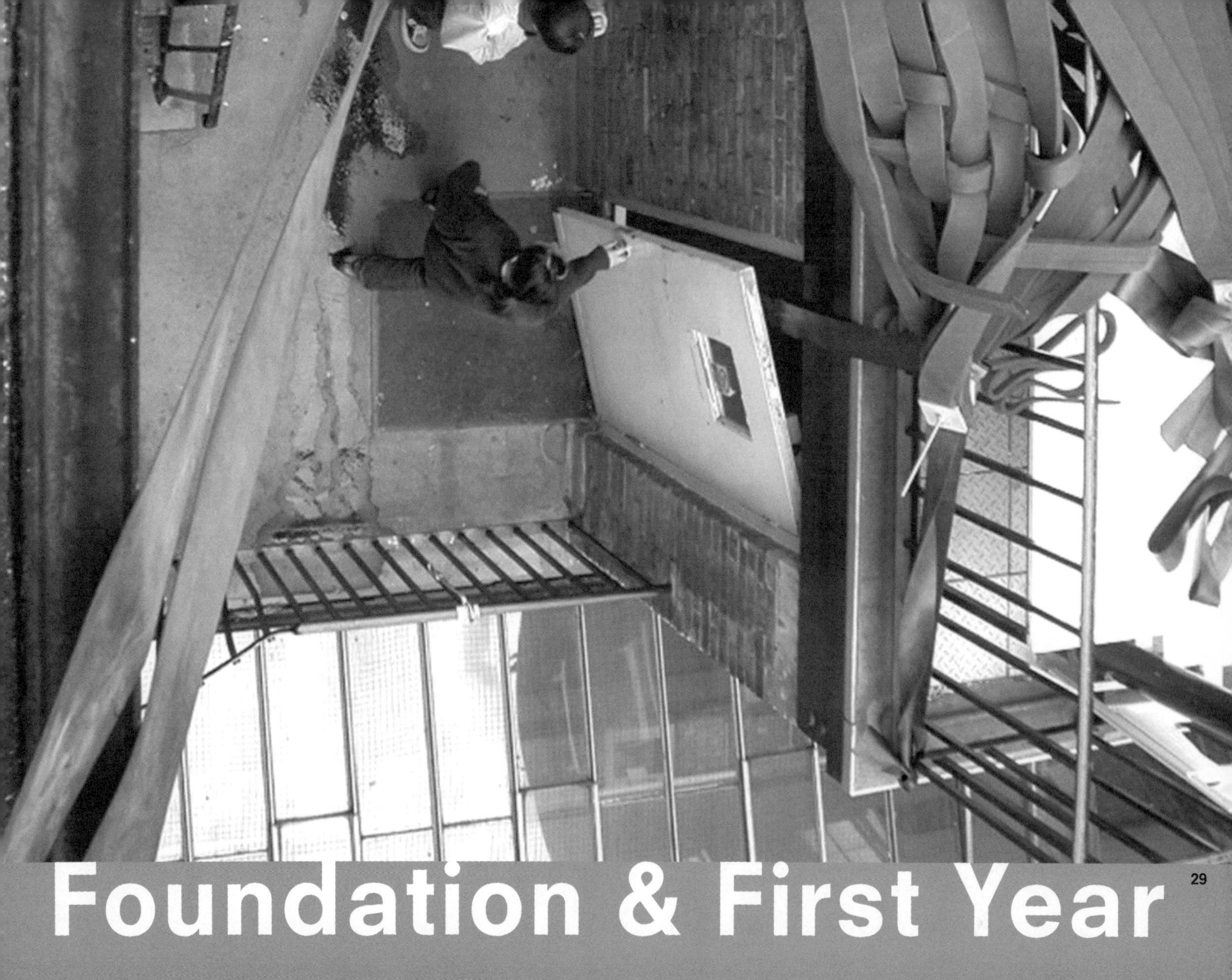

Foundation & First Year

The Foundation of Exotic Studies (FES)

A bird of paradise, absinthe, the smell of jasmine on a moonlit summer's night, phosphorescence in the Gulf of Siam, bare feet on fine warm sand, the sound of mandolins, Danzón, night-time in Veracruz, stepping on fresh snow, Manhattan at night, shooting stars, ironed white cotton sheets, a new pair of shoes, slipping a new vinyl record out of its sleeve, feeling a plane leave the surface of the earth, the yellow light of a taxi on an empty street, an orchestra warming up, an unsolicited smile, twilight, silk, the smell of coriander, of mint, of wild garlic. The markets of Fes, the bazaars of Istanbul, the Blue Mosque, Hagia Sophia, Uluru, Maori tattoos, bell birds, tango, a fresh hot almond croissant, siestas, fire, giant Buddhas, palm trees, ships, opera houses, heavy cutlery, hillside towns, a mariachi serenade.

The experience of travel has influenced much of the source research of the FES, as has the influence of travel on literature, anthropology, painting, mapping world architecture, film and music. Leisure, adventure, conversation, food and event theory/practice have also contributed to the body of knowledge embodied in our ethos.

In formulating the subject of exoticism within an academic context, we chose to focus our investigations specifically on London. This, we believed, would harness our work in a precise manner, enabling observations to be evaluated against a physical framework: the city. Projects, lectures, seminars, workshops, trips in London and abroad were the interface between imagination and materiality. In choosing London as a 'laboratory' for our research it was understood that for all of us it was a new experience and one that contained positive mystery and anticipation. Newness, freshness, the alien, the first time – these are the keystones to FES. We propose that immense cities such as London are saturated with exoticism; that they have the capacity for infinite intrigue, pleasure and terror equal to the jungle, the deep ocean, the desert and the cosmos.

'Nothing here is natural; everything is transformed – forced – from the earth and mankind to the light and air. But the sheer enormity of such human accretion and creation makes one forget the distortion and artificiality; instead of a noble, healthy beauty, there is life, swarming and grandiose; the gleam on the brown waves, the diffusion of light trapped in vapour, the gentle highlights and traces of pink playing over the whole colossal spectacle bestow a sort of grace upon the monstrous city, like a smile on the face of a swarthy, bristling Cyclops.' (Hippolyte Taine 1862)

It would be impossible to study London without considering the inert poetry that resides within its soul, but it would also be foolish to ignore its social cruelty, retail tackiness, violence, injustice and costliness. The memory of London fog may be an appropriate metaphor with which to approach this contradiction. The by-product of industrialisation and progress, fog was a common atmospheric element from the early nineteenth century up to the early 1960s, when the Clean Air Act abolished its sources. Some artists, writers and social commentators regarded the fog as a satanic veil – a disease brought on by a modern world controlled by greed and power. Others regarded it as an aesthetic catalyst inspiring romantic visions, blurring reality with dreams. Fog blemished detailed urban form and replaced it with a spectre's silhouette.

The same contradictions persist today. Having survived the bleak 1980s and nervous 1990s, London is once more a leading and desirable city. The work and ideas formulated this year are indications and reflections of living in London now, but more than observations, they are proposals for a city driven by personal experience and vision.

Course Master
John Andrews
Tutor
Teresa Stoppani
History Lecturer
Alan Powers
Contemporary Theory
Brian Hatton
Technical Consultant
Lee Dalby

Students
Can Sinan Aksoy
Maria Fernanda Arrillaga
Ivana Bocina
Marcus Brett
Tom Brooksbank
Marie-Isabel De Monseignat
Sedoo Gemade
Rosanna Gould
Anna Gromovik
Justin Kim
Yoo Na Lee
Eric Mak
Chimwando Ngulube
Caroline Notari
Mei Lin Ong
Aya Shimozuma
Aurelia Teneze
Bianca Thelmo
Piotr Topinski
Yusra Zulkifli

Special thanks
AA Maintenance Staff
AA Workshop Staff
Miraj Ahmed
Domenico Ambrosino
Franco Ambrosino
Peter Beard
Valentin Bontjes van Beek
Alessandra Como
Mark Cousins
Jean Michel Crettaz
Tim Dodds
Shin Egashira
Simon English
Michael Hensel
Hugo Hinsley
Johannes Käferstein
Nikos Koronis
Pablo Leon de la Barra
George Liaropoulos-Legendre
Antoni Malinowski
Sheila Marshall
Mohsen Mostafavi
Mark Prizeman
Natasha Sandmeier
Goswin Schwendinger
Ban Shubber
Tony Swannell
Ivana Wingham

Aurelia Teneze Communications, featuring Piotr Topinsky and Caroline Notari **Caroline Notari** Invisible London

Anna Gromovik Urban portrait
Introducing the individual, the group, the AA and London; the Urban Portraiture project exposed an intimate perception of London based on personal observation.

Group work Bamboo project

Construction: a three-dimensional interpretation of the map where point, space and line were combined to produce a facsimile of architecture. Bamboo, PVA, scalpel and splitting knives.

Yusra Zulkifli **Yoo Na Lee**

Map project
A subjective memory map making the journey to the location of the portrait. Ideas contained within the text were also used to generate the form of the map.
Watercolour paper, 6H, 4H and 2H pencils.

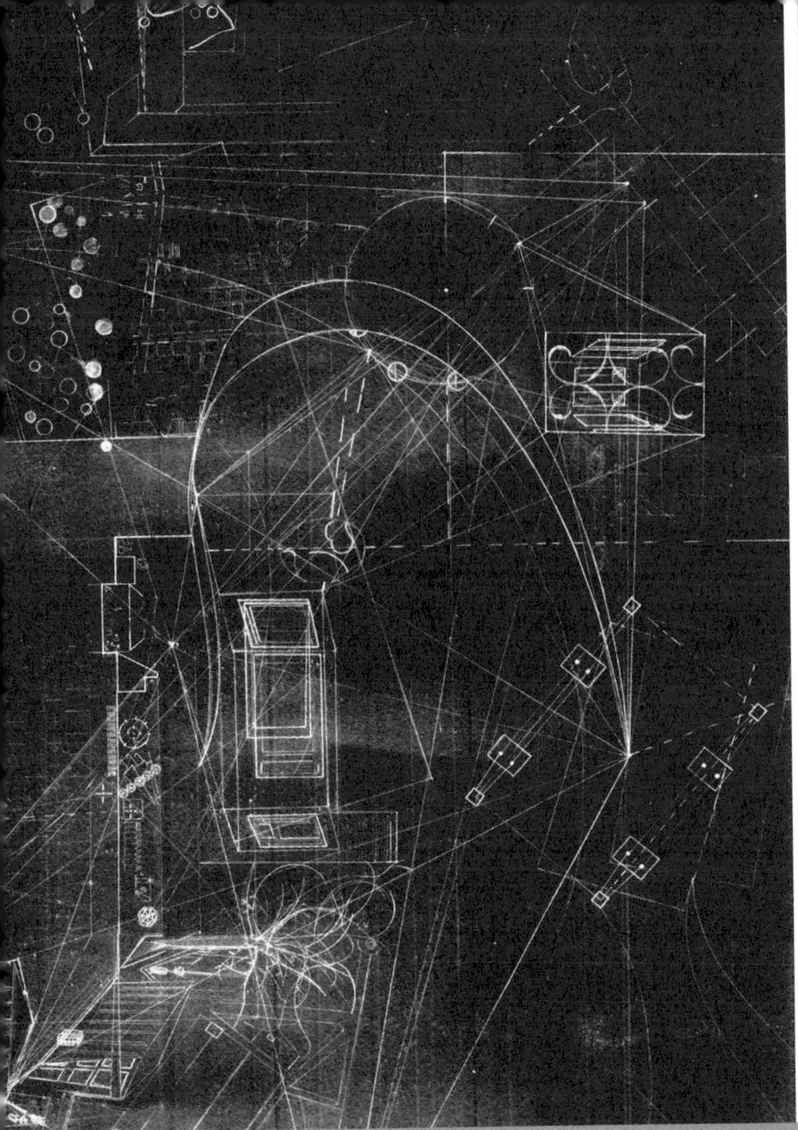

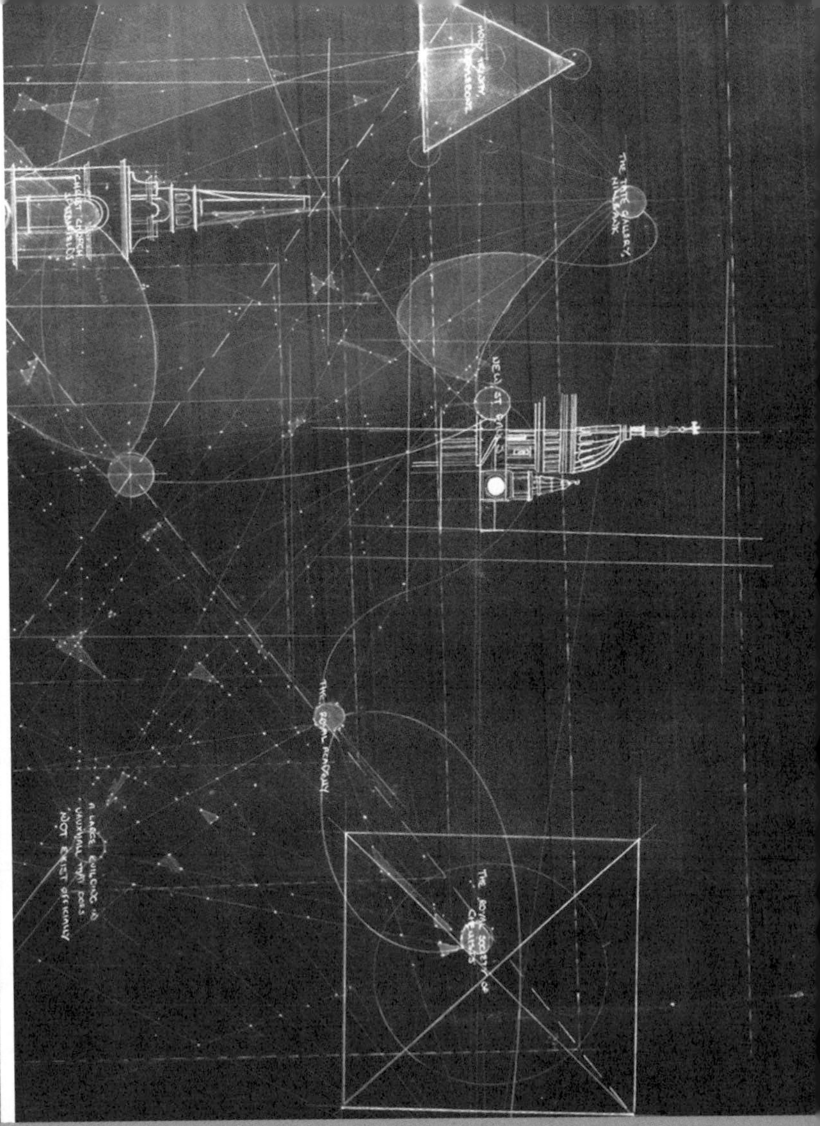

THE TATE GALLERY, MILLBANK

HOLY TRINITY, MARYLEBONE

NEW ST PAULS

THE ROYAL SOCIETY OF CHEMISTS

THE ROYAL ACADEMY

CHRIST CHURCH SPITALFIELDS

A LARGE BUILDING IN VAUXHALL THAT DOES NOT EXIST OFFICIALLY

Museum project
The design of a museum for the Foundation of Exotic Studies, London.
Drawing, models, film, photography, text, CAD, 1:1 construction.

A

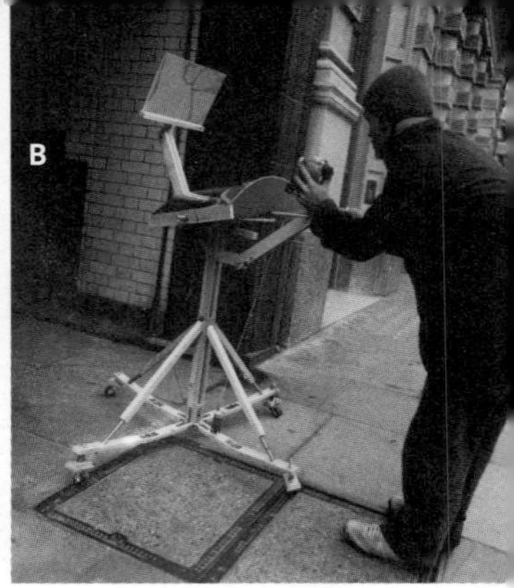

B

C

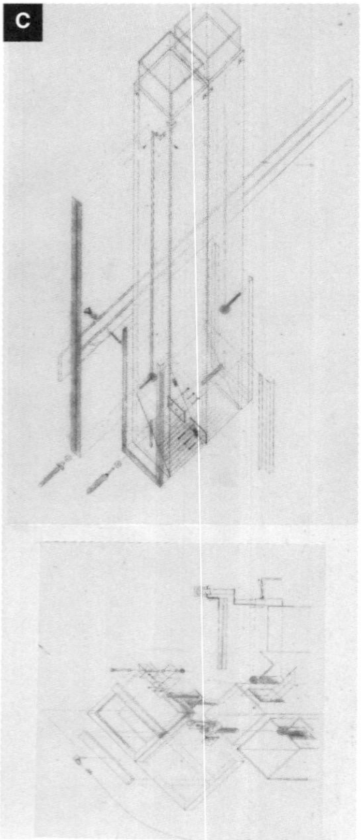

C

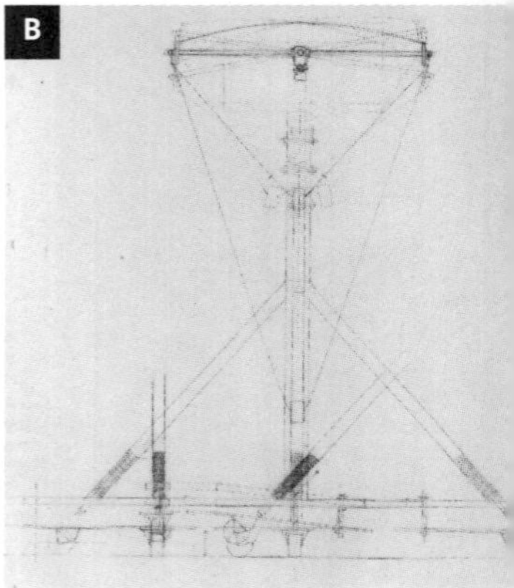

B

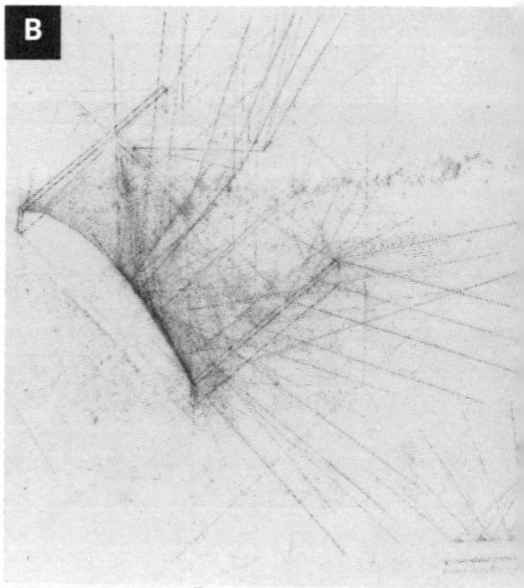

B

D

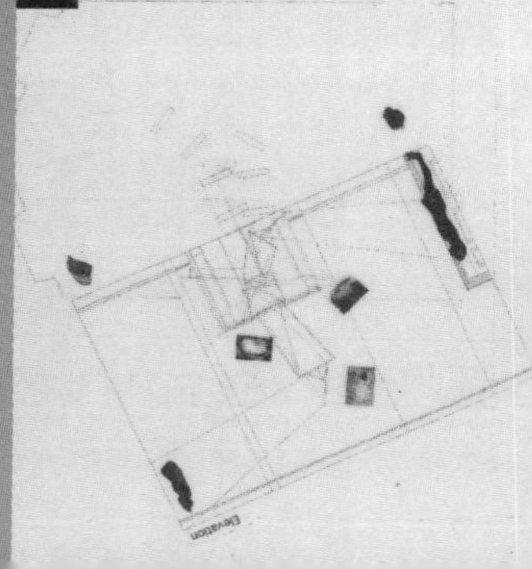

D

D

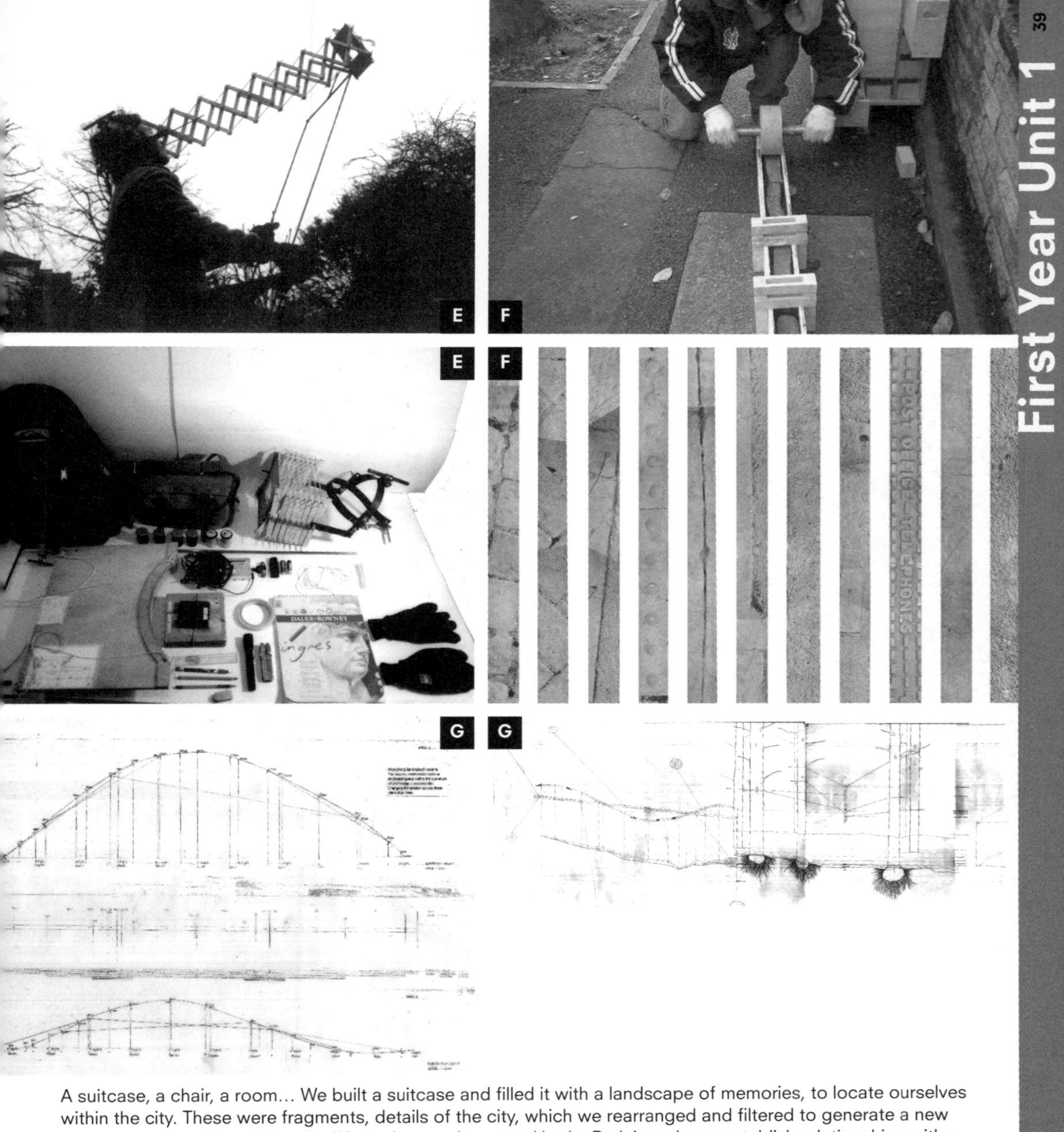

A suitcase, a chair, a room… We built a suitcase and filled it with a landscape of memories, to locate ourselves within the city. These were fragments, details of the city, which we rearranged and filtered to generate a new space, a new reading of the city. We took our suitcase to Hooke Park in order to establish relationships with a different topography. Reinventing our suitcase to relate to and inform us about the new surfaces and textures of the forest. To map our bodies and represent the landscapes around us, we constructed chairs – chairs that enabled us to fit our body into the details of the forest, so as to establish positions and specific viewpoints within its landscape. We built chairs to experience the forest and we carried a suitcase of memories from the city, combining and developing both in order to design two rooms: a room within the forest and room inside the city. Each different landscape, its phenomena and experiences led to different but nevertheless related outcomes.

Suitcases

A Julia King Transferring suitcase of the city into musical notation. **B KeitaTajima** Suitcase for mapping the sky. **C Jake Choi** Double periscope suitcase. **D Takamasa Kikuchi** Dark box for collaging views. **E Jze Yi Kuo** Set of instant details and impressions of the city. **F Joo-han Baek** Casting the texture of the city into strips of plaster. **G Andrea Marini** A curved frame mediating the space between the bridge and ground, capturing sunlight.

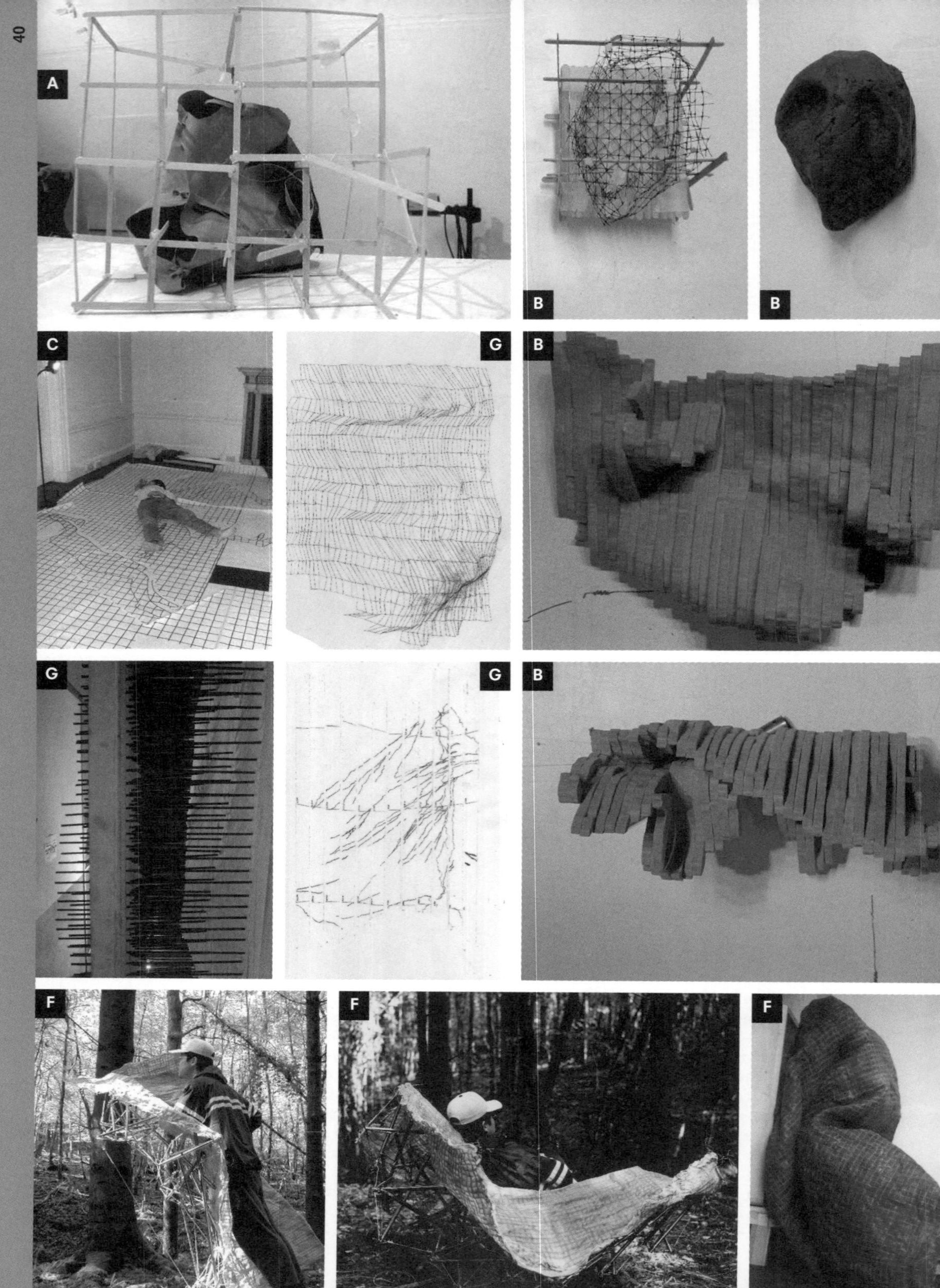
A
B
B
C
G
B
G
G
B
F
F
F

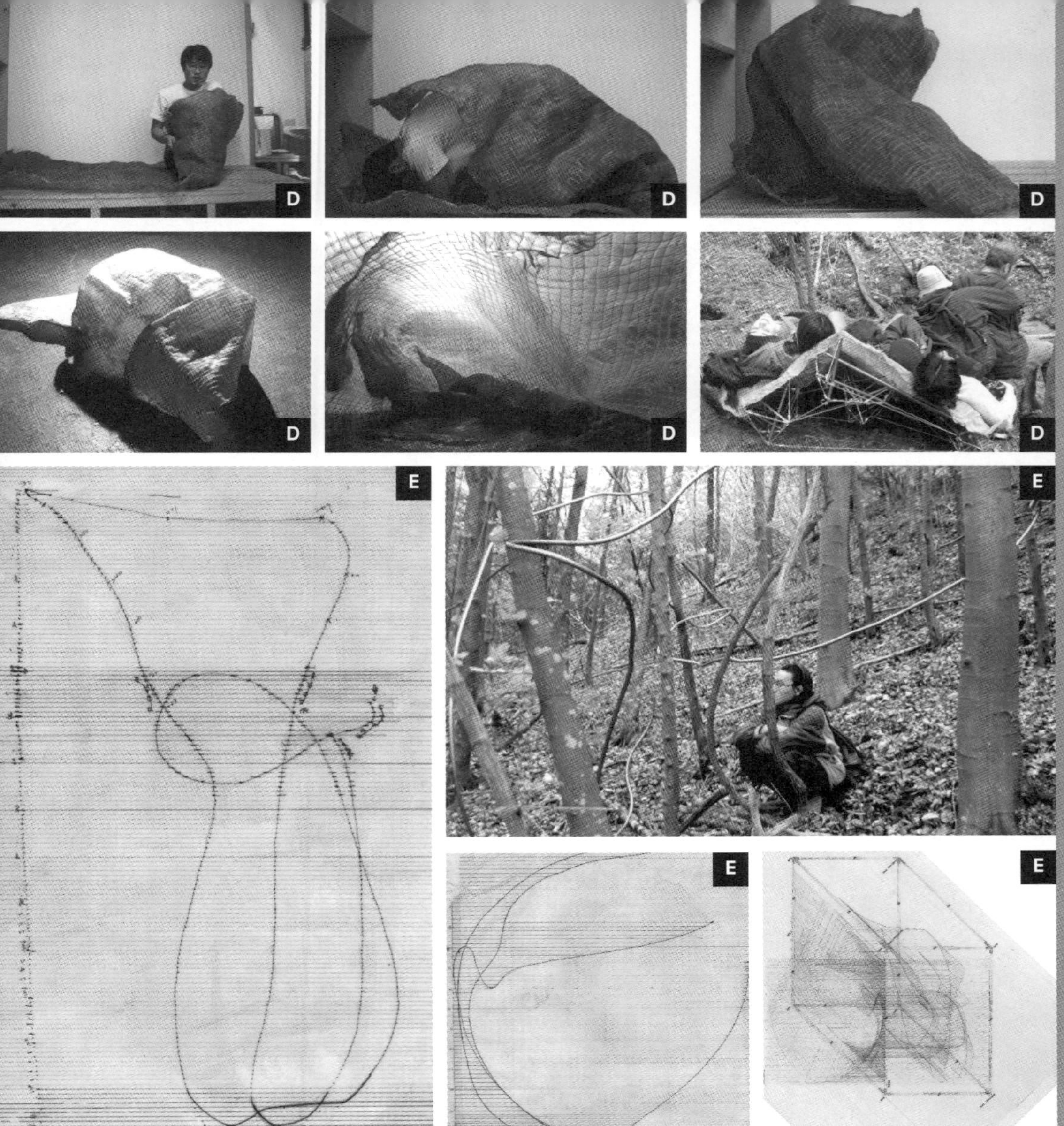

Body Mapping
A Roberto Marsura Conceptual models showing the transformation of solid to skin. **B Mo Woon-yin Wong** Using the negative spaces as a means of reconciling the movements of the hand. **C Jze Yi Kuo** Using a projected grid as a way to draw 1:1 drawings. **D Joo-han Baek** A latex material that encloses the body, keeping its form. **E Jake Choi** Metal pipes defining volumes of space occupied by the body in movement. **F Joo-han Baek** Tensegrity Skin: latex skin and supporting structure enabling the formation of different landscapes. **G Andrea Marini** and **Keita Tajima** Suspended plaster body shell.

A

A

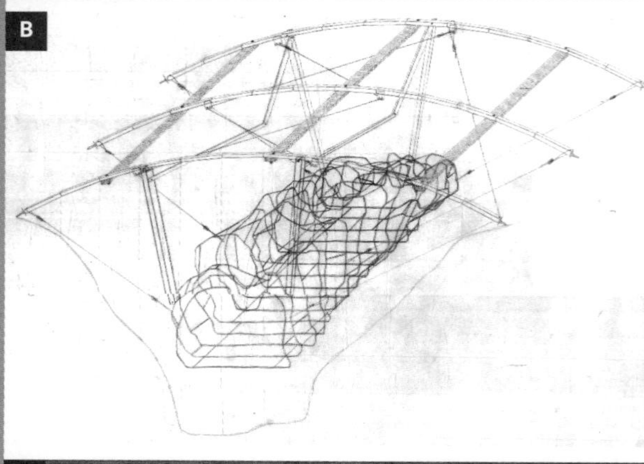
B

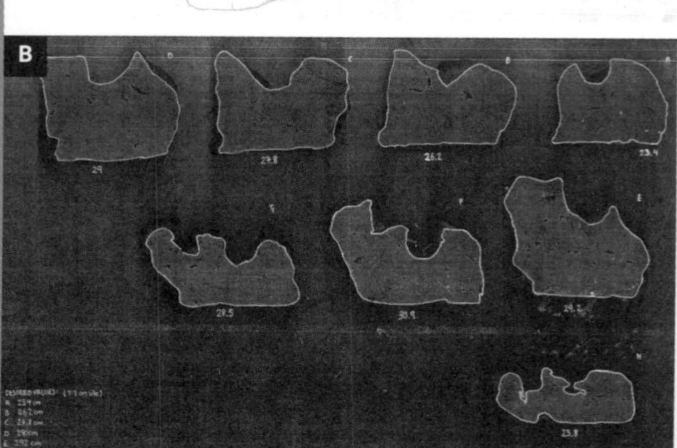
B
29
29.8
26.2
23.4
28.5
30.9
23.8

B

A Mo Woon-yin Wong Broken Landscape: assortment of clay panels supported by a steel frame profiles the body. **B Julia King** Sound Observatory: a bridge spanning a stream, with suspended steel furniture holding space sensitive to sound. **C Takamasa Kikuchi** Device for Twisting Reality: an enclosed space containing a series of mirrors providing simultaneous views of the forest. **D Roberto Marsura** Wind Catcher: a structure allowing the user to experience the wind shifting one's view of the landscape.

A
A
A
B
C
C
C

A Andrea Marini Folded Skin: structure enabling the experience of shifting horizons.
B Jze Yi Kuo Extended Landscape Surface: a woven structure creates an enclosed space between itself and the land. **C Jze Yi Kuo** Conceptual model of room derived from the rotating, unfolding and refolding of chair around site. **D Keita Tajima** Surface Between the Ground: a cut into the ground creates a contained space and a new surface in the landscape. **E Keita Tajimi** conceptual model showing the furniture as a room using a similar dialogue between the surface and the land.

Hingeing, Weaving, Pleating, Stretching, Sliding, Folding....

In the unit we are particularly interested in developing design from the potential latent in systems and materials. Students are asked to focus on an 'architectural system'; for example, to investigate hingeing, weaving, folding, pleating, vacuum-forming, etcetera.

Objective

The aim of the unit is to develop a consistent and intrinsic link between the development of ideas and the organisation of materials.

Stages

Generally we divide the year into three stages. In the first, students develop an architectural idea according to an individual brief. In the second, they explore the relationship between architectural concept, structure and material. In the third stage they focus on the consistency between material construction and the underlying architectural idea.

Workshops

We started the year with a workshop exploring complex spatial organizations. Our subject matter was a range of different knots used in sailing or weaving, knitting and similar systems. The aim of the workshop was to build up an understanding of how these processes are ordered in space and time, what purpose they fulfil, and how they can be seen as spatial systems.

In a second workshop in collaboration with Diploma Unit 14 we focused on the issue of internal connectivity within a large structural system. We subjected a hanging model to a sequence of transformations, analysing and documenting our findings at each stage. The aim of the workshop was to explore a consistency in the process of construction and material organisation.

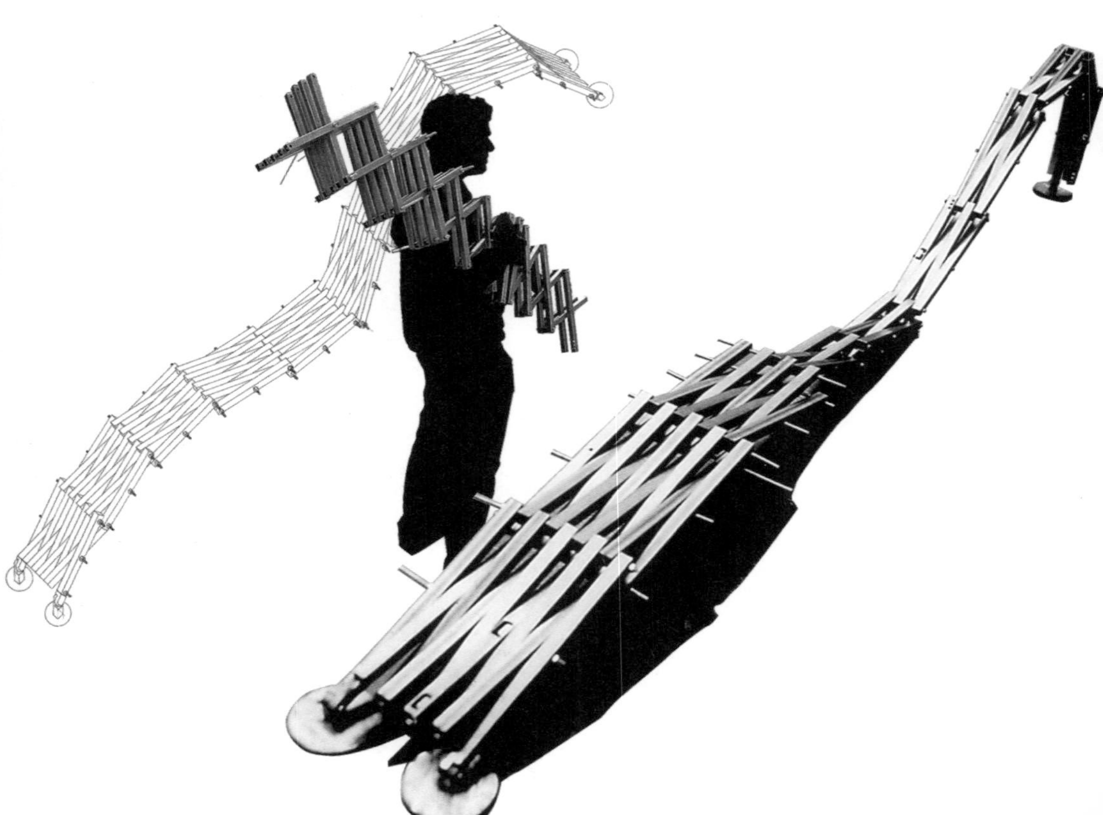

Main Project

The main study involved the development of a mobile object for temporary use by the modern metropolitan citizen. After gathering the information that would describe their brief, students defined the activities they wished their furniture to cater for. They described their activities in the form of drawings, and deconstructed existing designed objects into distinct elements that were active or productive. Subsequently they developed the activities into a proposal while at the same time defining their design language – the technique and material that would form the essential set of tools for building their project. The final phase required them to translate each project into a full-size prototype while remaining sensitive to their personal design language.

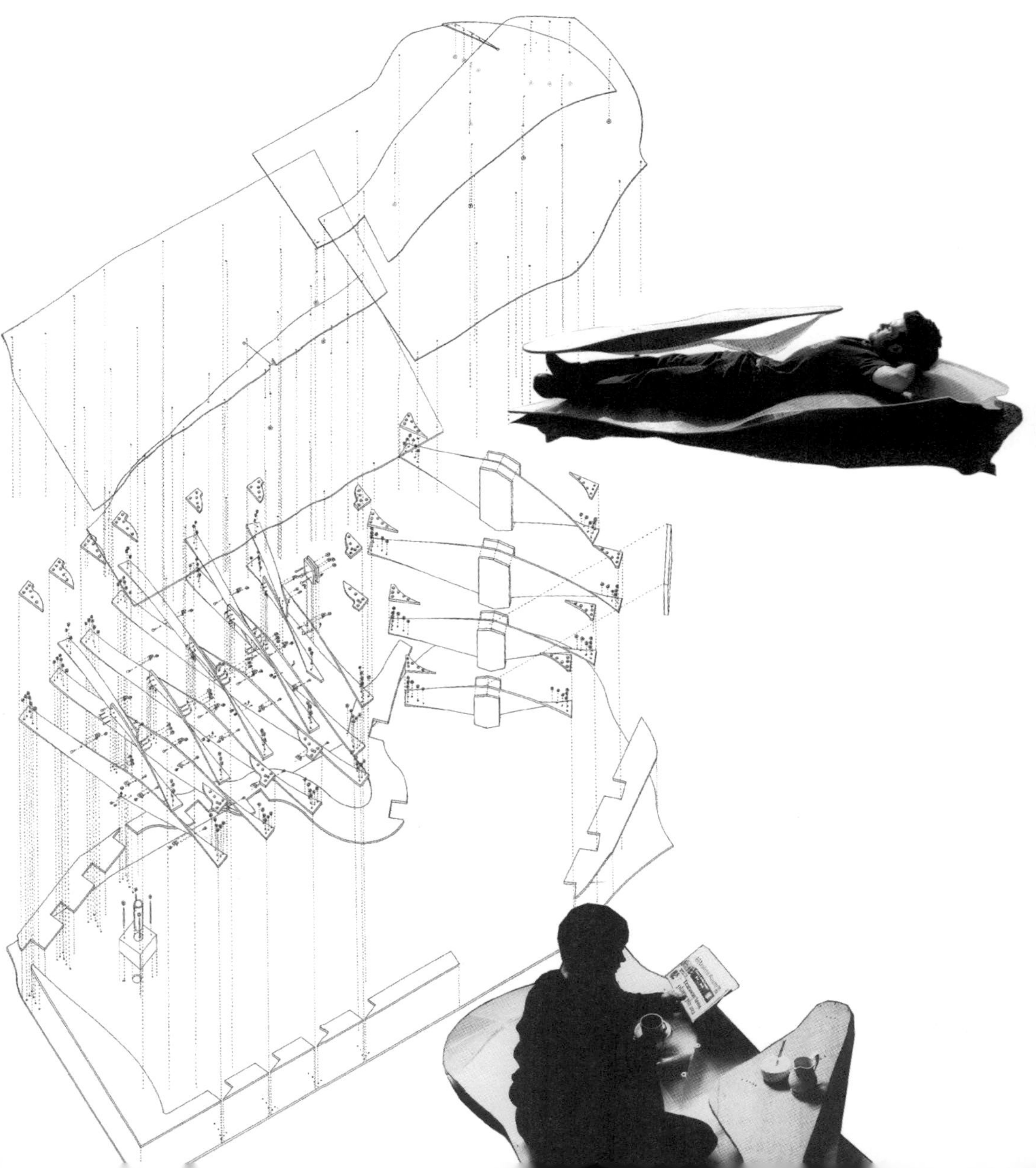

Erik Brett Jacobsen

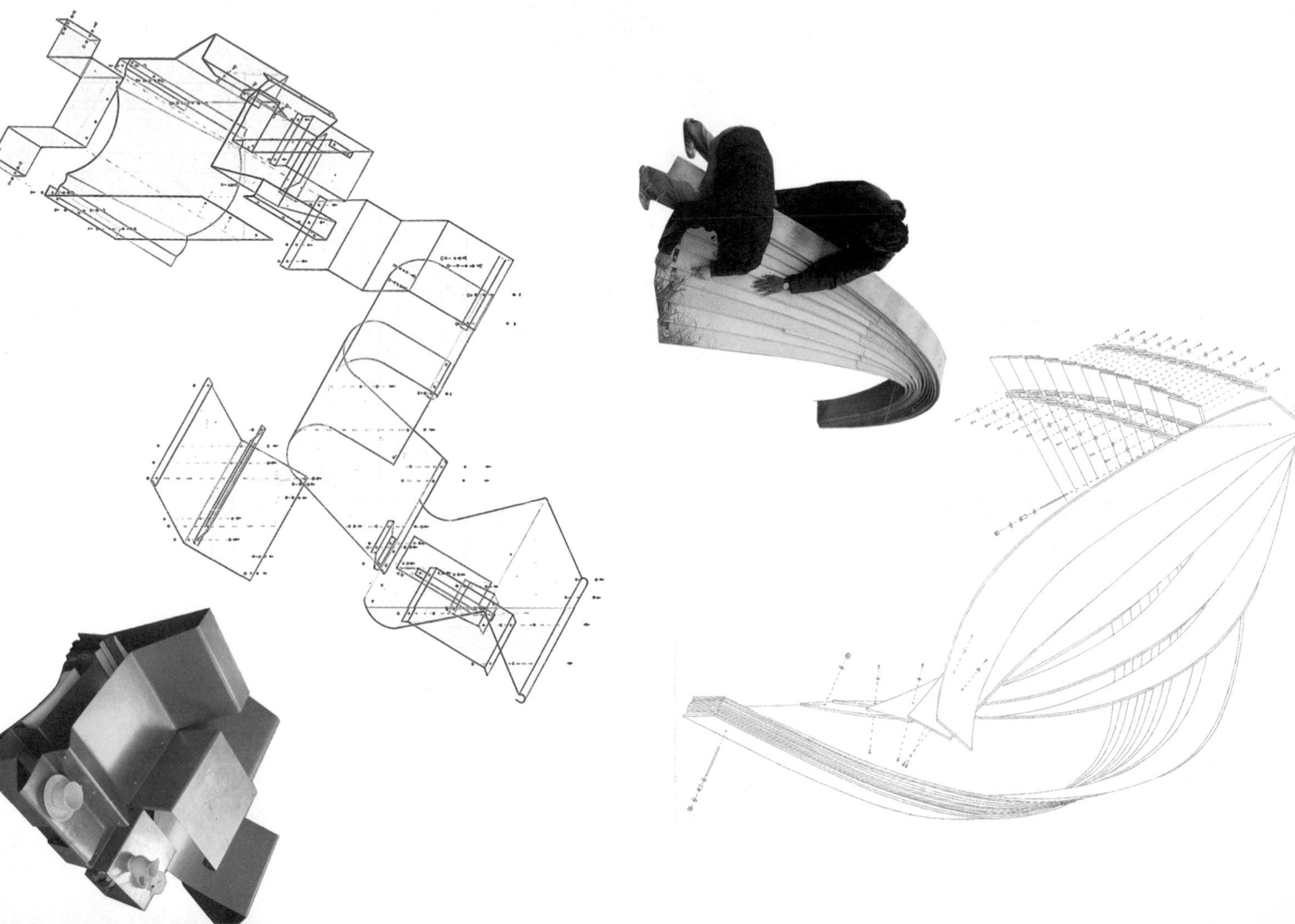

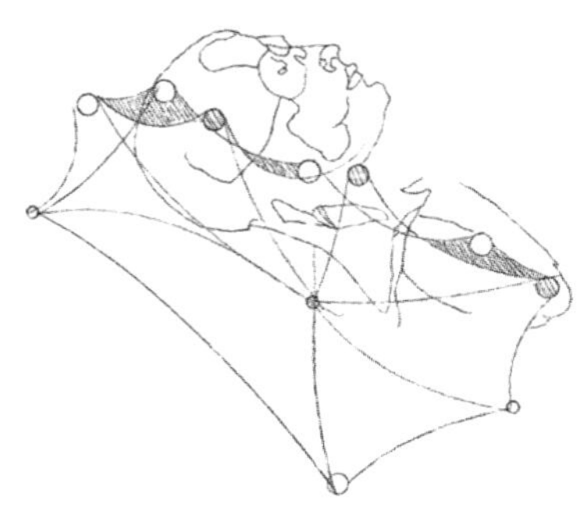

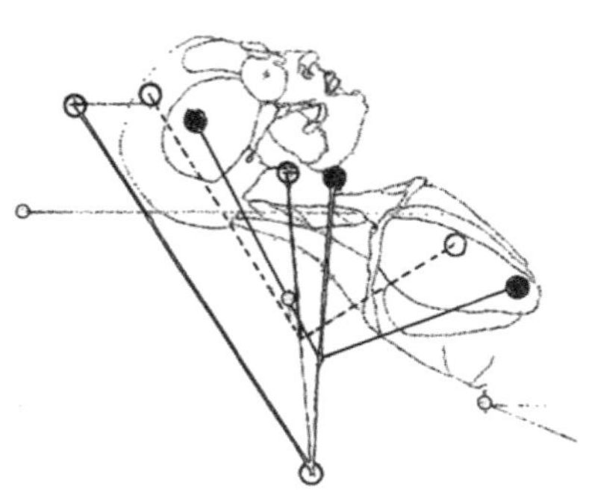

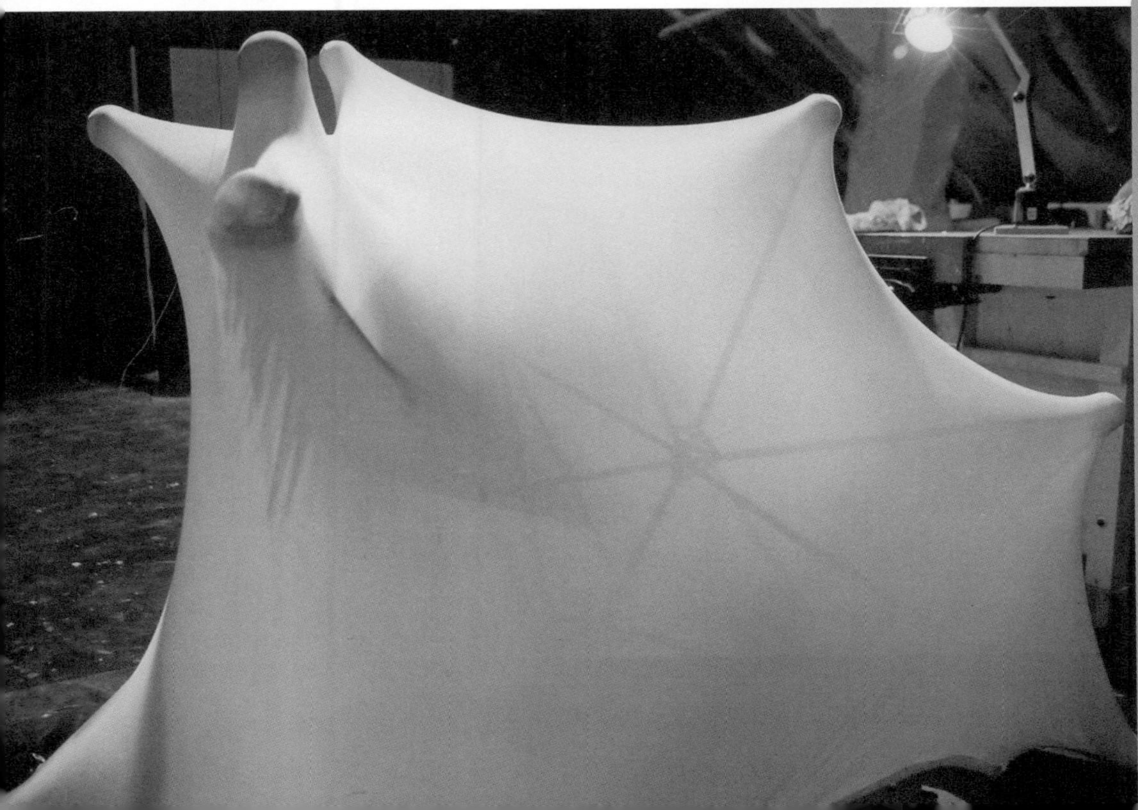

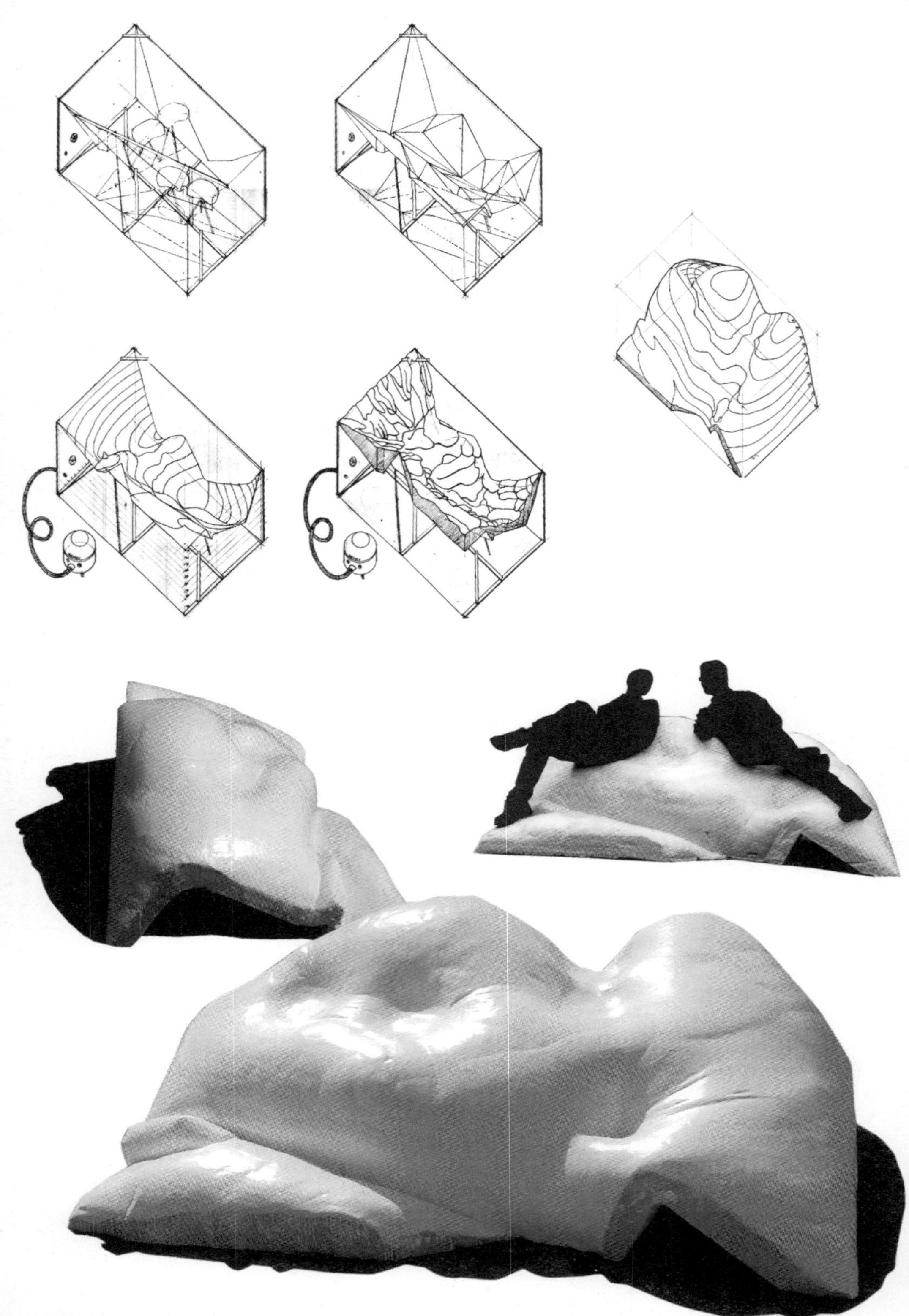

In addition to our project work we went on a unit trip to Pankese, a small village in Ghana. Students built a 20-metre bamboo structure as a shadow-producing surface, to be used by the local community during and after football games and as a playground for the adjacent primary school.

Unit Staff
Mark Hemel
Nate Kolbe

Students
Alexander Abolwahabi
Renata Dantas
Tim Den Dekker
Farah Ghanim
Mario Gottfried Hesketh
Erik Brett Jacobsen
Jade Keung
Aida Mahmodova
Danny Marks
Beza Mbeboh
Chris Thorn

The unit would like to thank
Denis Balent
Valentin Bontjes Van Beek
Gianni Bottsford
Jason Bruges
Luigi Centola
Tom Emerson
Francesca Hughes
Hanif Kara
Holger Kehne
Barbara Kuit
Andreas Lang
Quintin Lake
George Liaropoulos-Legendre
Chris Lee
Ciro Najle
Garin O'Avazian
Antonio Ramirez
Lluis Viu Rebes
Max de Rosee
Makoto Saito
Lola Sheppard
Benedikt Schleicher
Tony Swannell
Charles Tashima
Mike Weinstock
Brendan Woods
Kris van Veert
Caroline Voet
Mason White

The unit focused on movement and settlement in relation to 'town and country'. We began the year by mapping journeys from home to the AA, exploring them in terms of time and distance as well as in relation to the physical and non-physical forces operating in the urban environment. This mapping revealed topographies and spatialities that form the backdrop of daily trajectories. Some fragments or moments of action and inaction became sites on which to test and measure precisely the relationships of the body to a point of contact in the city. Measuring fences, the bus-stop bench, phone-box cards or the reflections in a tube train led to proposals for alternative interfaces.

As we travelled from the city to the country, individuals compiled inventories of ideal things to take away – not necessarily objects, but tastes, routines, words, numbers, emotions, ideas. Hooke Park, Dorset was the destination. Again, we embarked on a process of information-gathering and measuring so as to locate ourselves. Three short films explored and documented the place and the particular conditions and forces operating within Hooke Park. These films, which explored the themes of Points, Lines and Spaces, became vehicles with which to reveal certain realities behind the notions of the countryside and its relationship to the city – the countryside as a manufactured and manufacturing place.

We were drawn to locations on account of particular interests or observed conditions that might enable temporary occupation. Measuring devices were invented, constructed or improvised to record levels, distances, heights and edges in order to understand the 'lie of the land'. The physicality of measuring the land became the raw material for drawn documentation and the design of a 'groundwork'. Research into casting techniques was carried out in London, exploring materiality and a form of construction that would allow for repetition and prefabrication or construction in situ. Interventions which were to remain on site had to be biodegradable and have a short lifespan. The casting experiments reflected this in their use of compacted soil and vegetation. Alternatively, some used prefabricated concrete to be installed and then removed. The logistics of construction was a vital part of the groundwork proposals – the design of the formwork, the ease of handling and reuse was a key consideration for the in-situ pieces. The experiments produced markers or modules for each site which became prototypes for the final groundwork.

As part of our research into casting, we made a journey to the Unité d'Habitation in Marseille. We mapped concrete surfaces in and around the building, retracing the formwork.

The unit returned to the site with formworks, prefabricated castings, tools and materials with which to construct the groundworks for temporary inhabitation. In all cases the process of construction revealed the sheer physicality involved in working with the land. As well as the idea and intent of design there is the task of building – the labour. This direct confrontation with the reality of the land caused a shift in our understanding of the projects – the final piece of work was informed by the labour required to make the groundwork, and the body's negotiations with the site. The pieces cast in situ required constant labour that was directly connected to the site throughout the process of making, while the prefabricated pieces made without context were suddenly transformed as they were adjusted to their final position.

The projects brought to the fore issues that are implicit in the programme but are not necessarily a part of its rhetoric. The groundwork project in Hooke Park revealed not only our intentions for inhabitation and settlement but also the way in which the physical process of measuring the land became, in many cases, the project itself. No part of the process is neutral.

Special thanks to

in London
Marilyn Dyer
Edouard Le Maistre
Marcellus Letang
Antonia Loyd
Trys Smith
at Hooke Park
Charlie & Georgie Corry Wright
Bruce Hunter-Inglis
Jonathan Forest
Chris Sadd
in Marseille
Laura Binder
Frederic Blanc-Rejne
Anne-Marie & Yves Bousquet
Remy Marciano
Carina Richards

Visiting Critics
Peter Beard
Valentin Bontjes van Beek
Carlos Cottet
David Emerson
David Grandorge
Nasser Golzari
Takako Hasegawa
Mohsen Mostafavi
Diana Periton
Greg Ross
Susanne Schmelcher
Tony Swannell
Brendan Woods

Students
Madeleine Adlercreutz
Maya Carni
Caroline Grubel
Yoon Jeong Han
Raphaelle Heaf
Samuel Tze Yeung Lam
Seung Joon Oh
Elida Cing Geo Ong
Catherine Saethre
Nikolay Shahpazov
Martin Strom

Unit Staff
Miraj Ahmed
Pierre d'Avoine
Tom Emerson

London: Movement in the City
Journey
Fragment 1 - action / site
Fragment 2 – interface

Things to Take Away
An inventory

Hooke Park: Settlement
Reconnaissance / Finding the site
Measuring Devices

Unité d'Habitation, Marseille
Retracing formwork

Groundworks
Marker / Module; Formwork and Casting
Construct
Inhabitation, Occupation, Performance

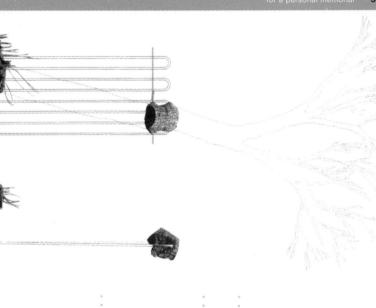

Nikolay Shahpazov Rubber overlay of prostitute cards in phone box on Queensway – a confrontational device to attract or deflect the potential user

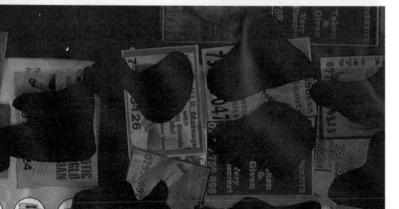

Caroline Grubel Hybrid image of park railing and tree stump – the catalyst for an investigation of the railings as a site for a personal memorial

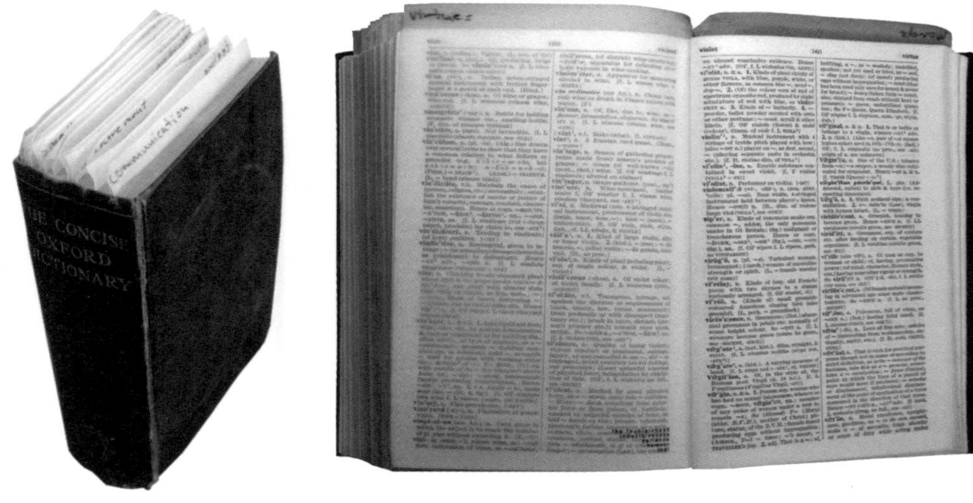

Martin Strom The Concise Oxford Dictionary is reconfigured with personal erasures and insertions to provide a menu of 'things to take away'

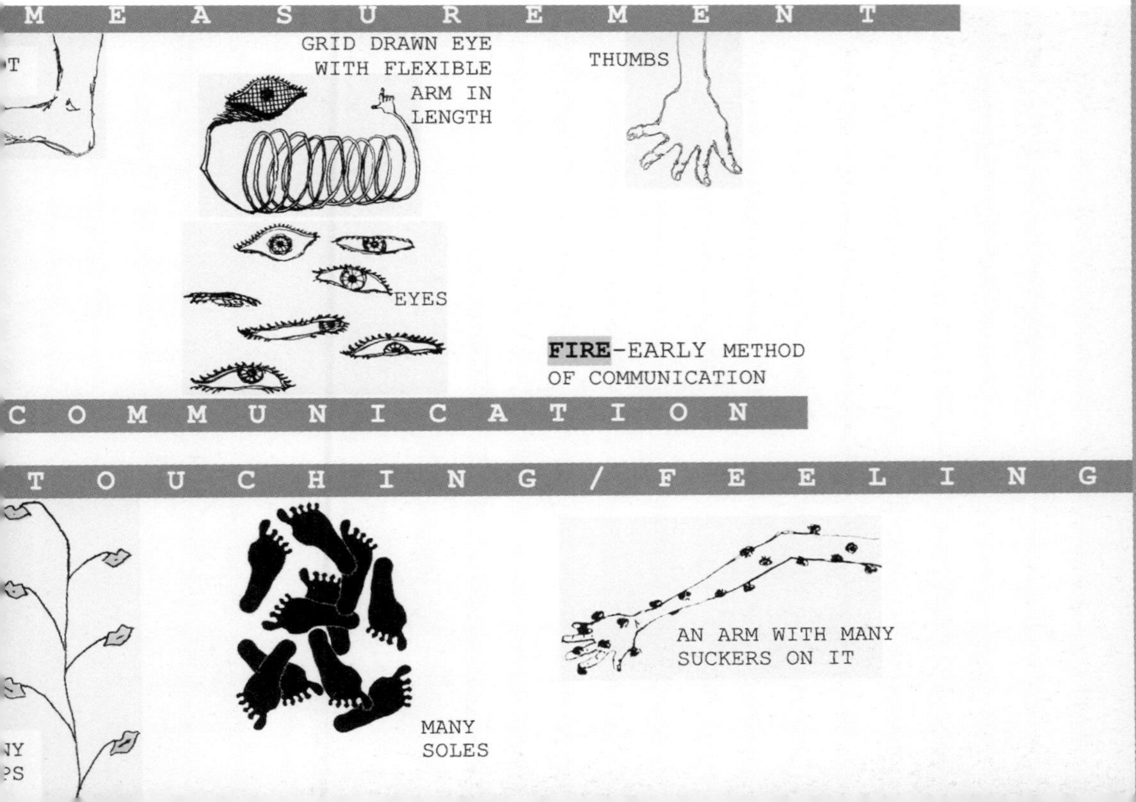

M E A S U R E M E N T

T

GRID DRAWN EYE WITH FLEXIBLE ARM IN LENGTH

THUMBS

EYES

FIRE-EARLY METHOD OF COMMUNICATION

C O M M U N I C A T I O N

T O U C H I N G / F E E L I N G

AN ARM WITH MANY SUCKERS ON IT

MANY SOLES

NY
PS

Yoon Jeong Han Inventory of essential measuring devices is compiled for later use on a woodland site. Hardness and softness become topography

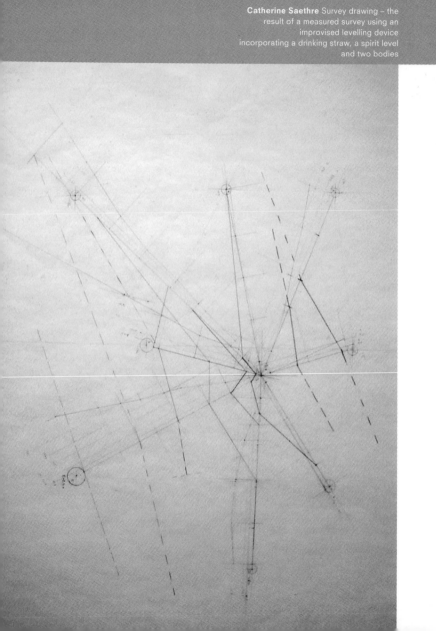

Catherine Saethre Survey drawing – the result of a measured survey using an improvised levelling device incorporating a drinking straw, a spirit level and two bodies

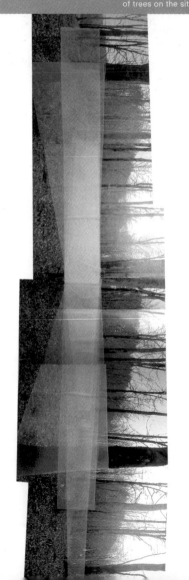

Elida Cing Geo Ong Drawing that demonstrates principle of a measuring device – a datum set above the ground using string tensioned between a group of trees on the site at Hooke Park

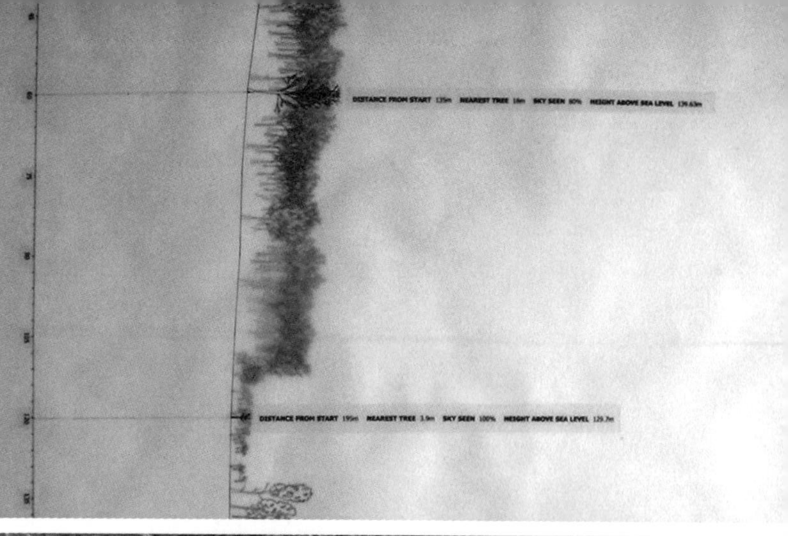

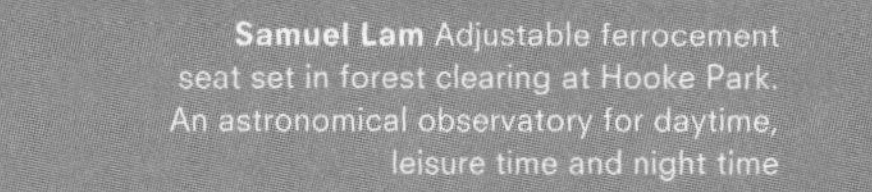

Samuel Lam Adjustable ferrocement seat set in forest clearing at Hooke Park. An astronomical observatory for daytime, leisure time and night time

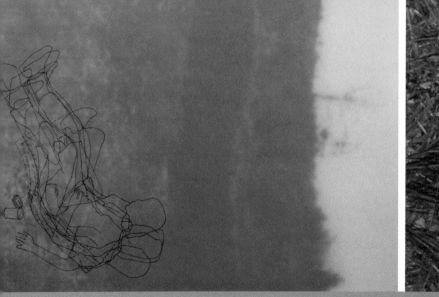

Raphaelle Heaf Local and global data inscribe marble dust cylindrical milestones that mark a place and make a route

Joon Oh An underground heating chamber, formed with coppice structure, supports a new heated earth platform

Madeleine Adlercreutz Performance testing the limits of six rammed earth and cement posts formed in a ditch. The line of posts establishes a pathway in the bluebell woods

Maya Carni Edge: meeting line of two surfaces.
Merge: join or blend gradually (concrete to earth)

1 Jason Cheung
Apollo's Leg, from which the unfolded representation originates

2 Mai Al Sudari
The suspended jewel with qualities of fragility and jaggedness

3 Carl Fraser
Fluidity Jig

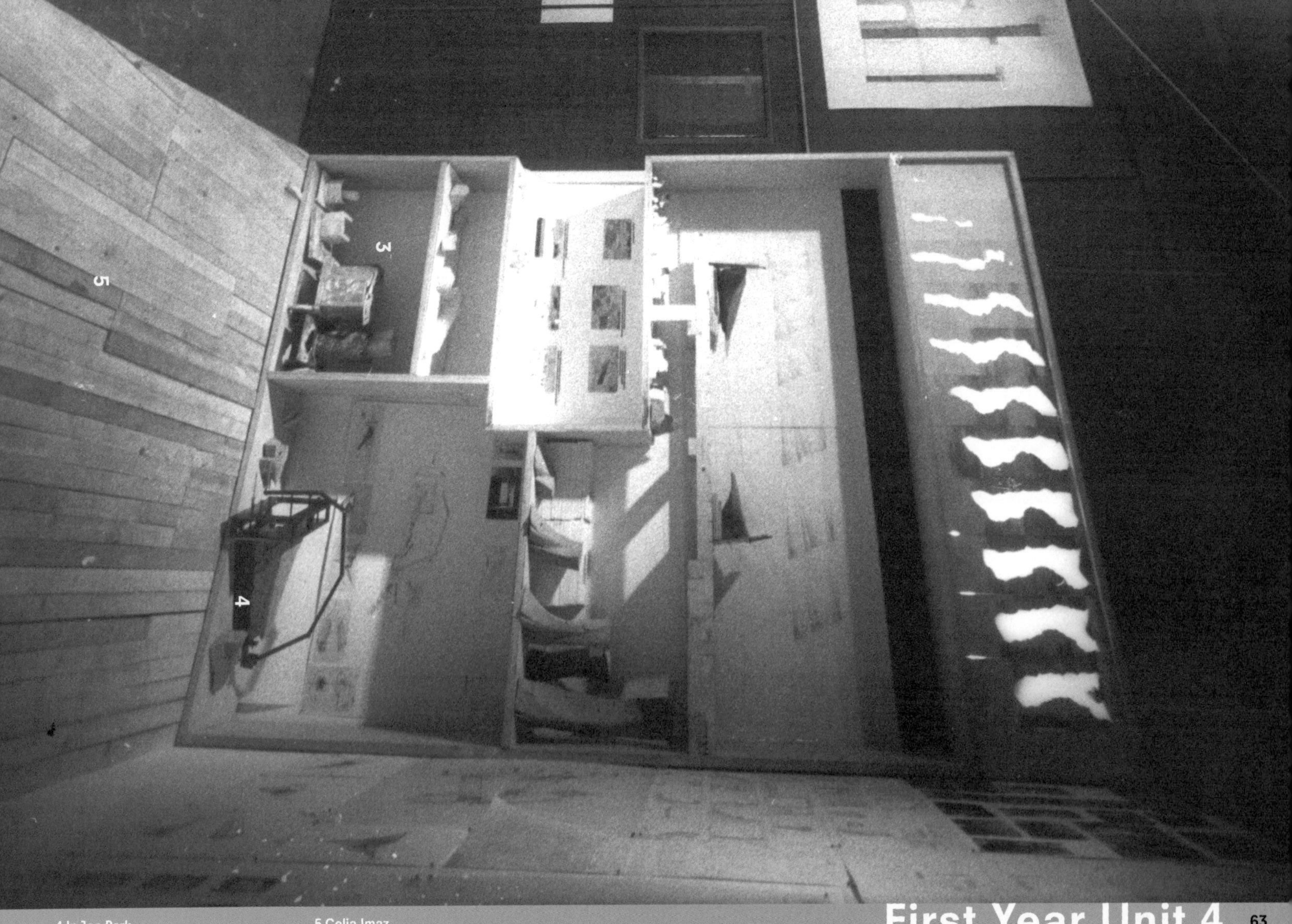

4 In Joo Park
Secret door, opened with knots in the wood, where damage becomes functional.

5 Celia Imaz
Clay-cutter

Celia Imaz
Clay-cutter that solidifies cavities found in the Soane Museum

Chieng Ming Ng
View detector: laser beam indicates where the gaze lands given a particular eye position

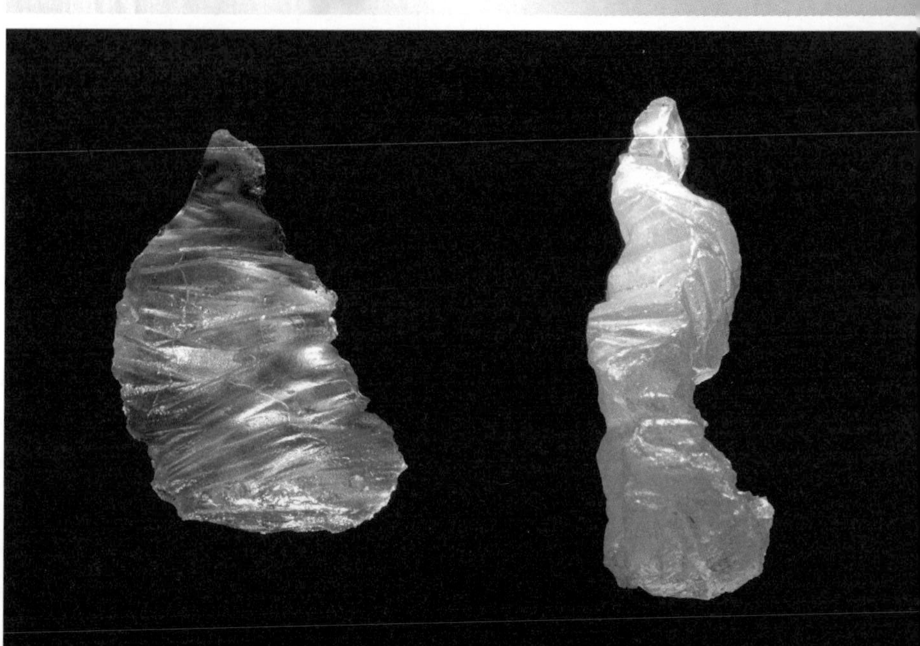

Mai Al Sudairi
The suspended jewel in its resin form

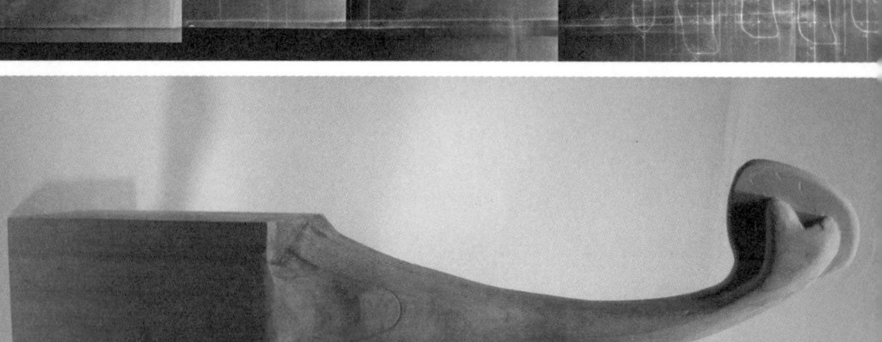

Mika Iwazaki
The vehicle for a visual journey through the glass window, off the mirror and back through the glass again

Carl Fraser
Mr Fraser testing the perfect angle for contemplation

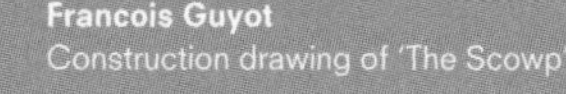

Francois Guyot
Construction drawing of 'The Scowp'

The Scowp, a climbing step that allows recreational activities to take place on a wall

Jason Cheung & Marilena Rizou
Escape – a bench to create a 'Moment of Relief' after a tedious climb up the hill

Mika Iwazaki & Chieng Ming Ng
'The Angel's Wing': a view discovered by accident is hidden to allow others to discover it with the same intensity of surprise

Simon Sung-Jae Lee & In Joo Park
A dam that contains dye to create a painting in the snow: the 'Continuous Moment'

Celia Imaz & Carl Fraser
A fragment of the fusion of snow and frozen river accentuating the 'Blue Moment' – at which the snow reflects the blue of the gradually darkening sky.

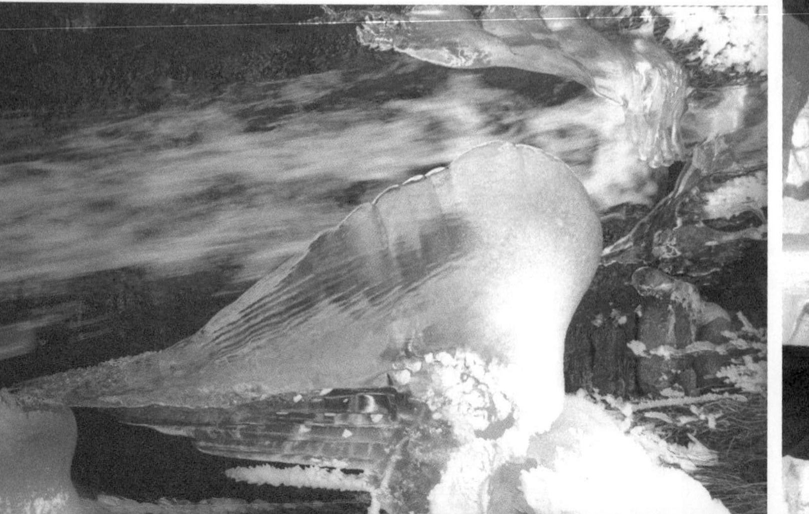

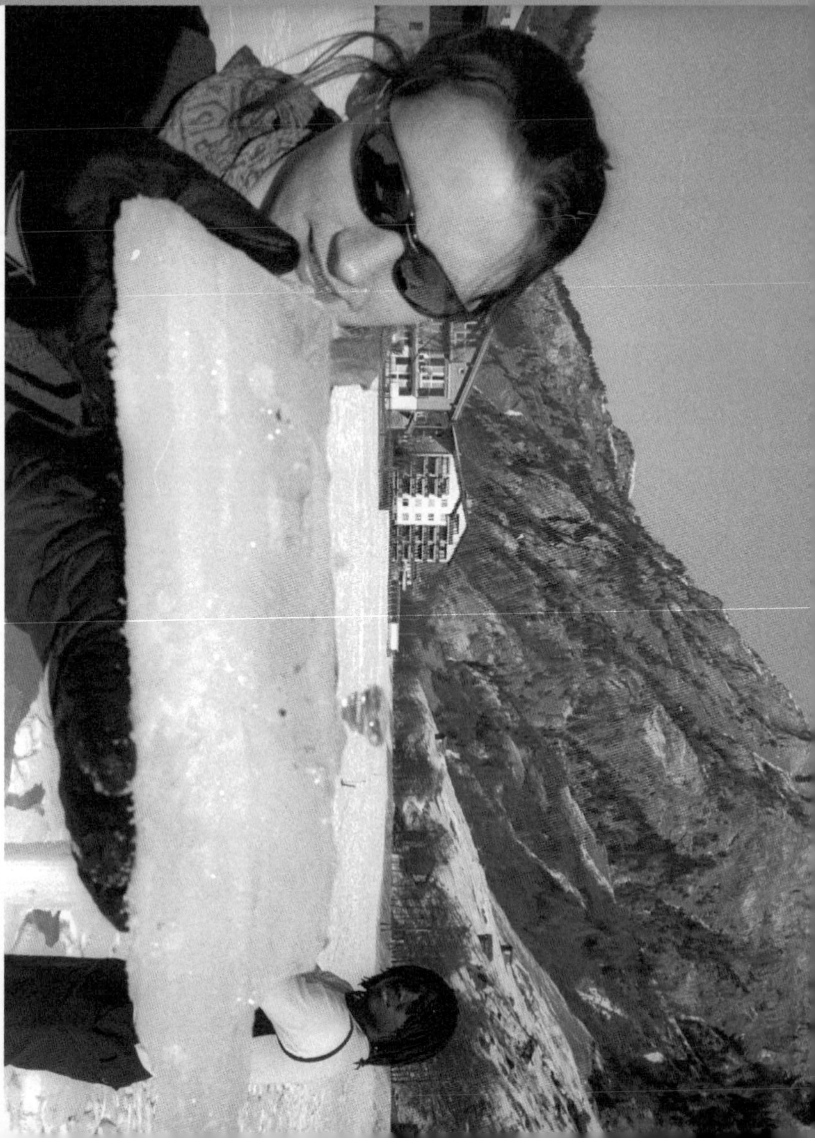

Celia Imaz
A 1:1 prototype of 'Steps to the Water' generated by wire-cutting clay allong two profiles

Celia Imaz
'Steps to the Water': a proposal to break through the present boundary fence in order to allow people to get closer to the water

In Joo Park
The bench–trolley evolves according to the way Chinatown changes throughout the course of a day

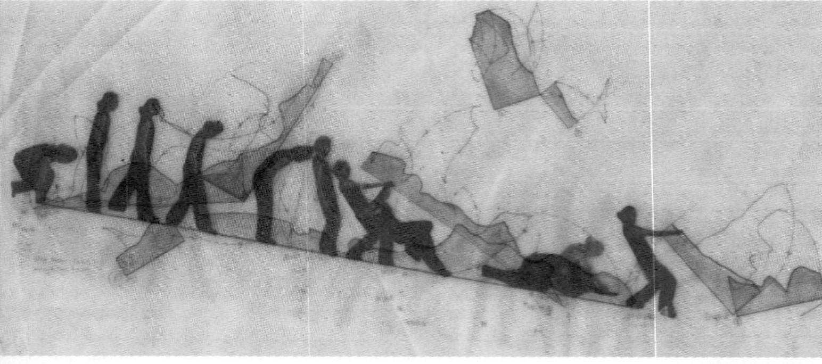

Mai Al Sudari
Silhouettes of frozen body positions evolving into a sectional pathway that generates a landscape

Chieng Ming
The gyroscope, an urban 'toy' that allows people waiting for their vehicles to engage with the visual distortions provided by a transparent block.

Unit Master
Valentin Bontjes van Beek

Students
Mai Al Sudari
Jason Cheung
Carl Fraser
François Guyot
Celia Imaz
Mika Iwazaki
Simon Sung-Jae Lee
Chieng Ming Ng
In Joo Park
Marilena Rizow

Visiting Critics
Miraj Ahmed
John Andrews
Sam Britton
Liz Campbell
Louis Colombo
Celine Condorelli
Fergus Comer
Pierre d'Avoine
Marco Djermaghian
Shin Egashira
Tom Emerson
Mark Hemel
Takuro Hoshino
Alex Hurst
Johannes Käferstein
Katrin Lahusen
Andreas Lang
Sandra Morris
Mohsen Mostafavi
Diana Periton
David Phillips
Mark Prizeman
David Racz
Irénée Scalbert
Veronica Schmid
Mark Shepard
Greg Sheng
Suzanne Song
Teresa Stoppani
Toni Swannell
Lluís Viu Rebés
Eiffel Wong
Julia Wood
Brendan Woods
Peter Zelner

Special thanks to
Artist Space NY
Diego Cortes
Mark Cousins
Michael Kennedy
Bernard Tschumi
Joan Waltemath
AA Workshop/Modelshop

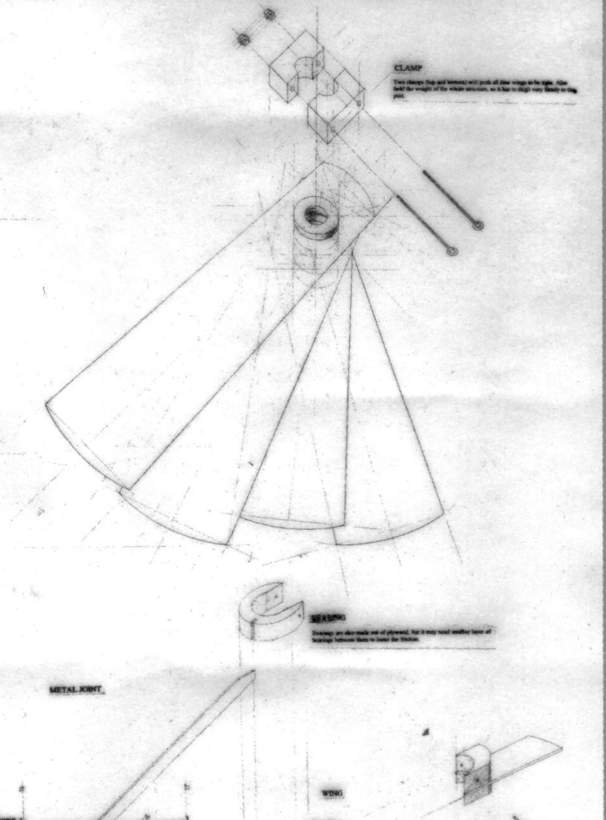

Simon Sung-Jae Lee
Parasitic roof and bench structure that docks onto a lamppost to create concentrations of people

Construction drawing of roof

The unit's interest is in the moments that make spaces and the spaces that make moments. We looked at three types of site – domestic, rural and urban – each time focusing on the personal and working at a 1:1 scale within a public space.

The house of Sir John Soane, now a museum, provided a springboard for our investigations and for the creation of 'Moment–Spaces'. On our first visit we went to two locations of our choice and remained at each of them for between 7 and 20 minutes. During this time no recordings or notes were taken. Relying solely on memory, we returned home and wrote a short text about our observations. This became an entry guide to the place and provided a brief for reading the museum in a new way. The drawings resulting from this new reading became the basis for the fabrication of several physical models.

The rural site was located in Vals, Switzerland, an alpine village that we visited in the middle of January. Here our relation to place and time was tested more directly: our material was snow, and our time-frame was 48 hours. Each team designed, scripted and built a 'moment in the snow' that was subject to a site, an activity and a duration.

The final test was at the urban site. In New York we focused on two locations, Chinatown and the Westside waterfront. The results obtained in New York complemented and re-informed data collected in London's Chinatown and South Bank. On our return we fabricated models, or 'baits', and released them onto our London site. The baits incorporated the readings of the Soane Museum, the scripting at Vals, and the specificities of the urban sites. Their ability to dock-on and attract moments gave us pointers towards our final proposals. Finally, each student developed a proposal for an intervention – a trap to catch a moment – that commented on the site in which it was set, the moment it was set to catch or create, and the space in which it would come to exist.

Intermediate 4 staged an exhibition in the Bar of their entries to the Circle 33/Architecture Foundation National Housing Competition (won by unit member Ema Bonifacic)

Intermediate School

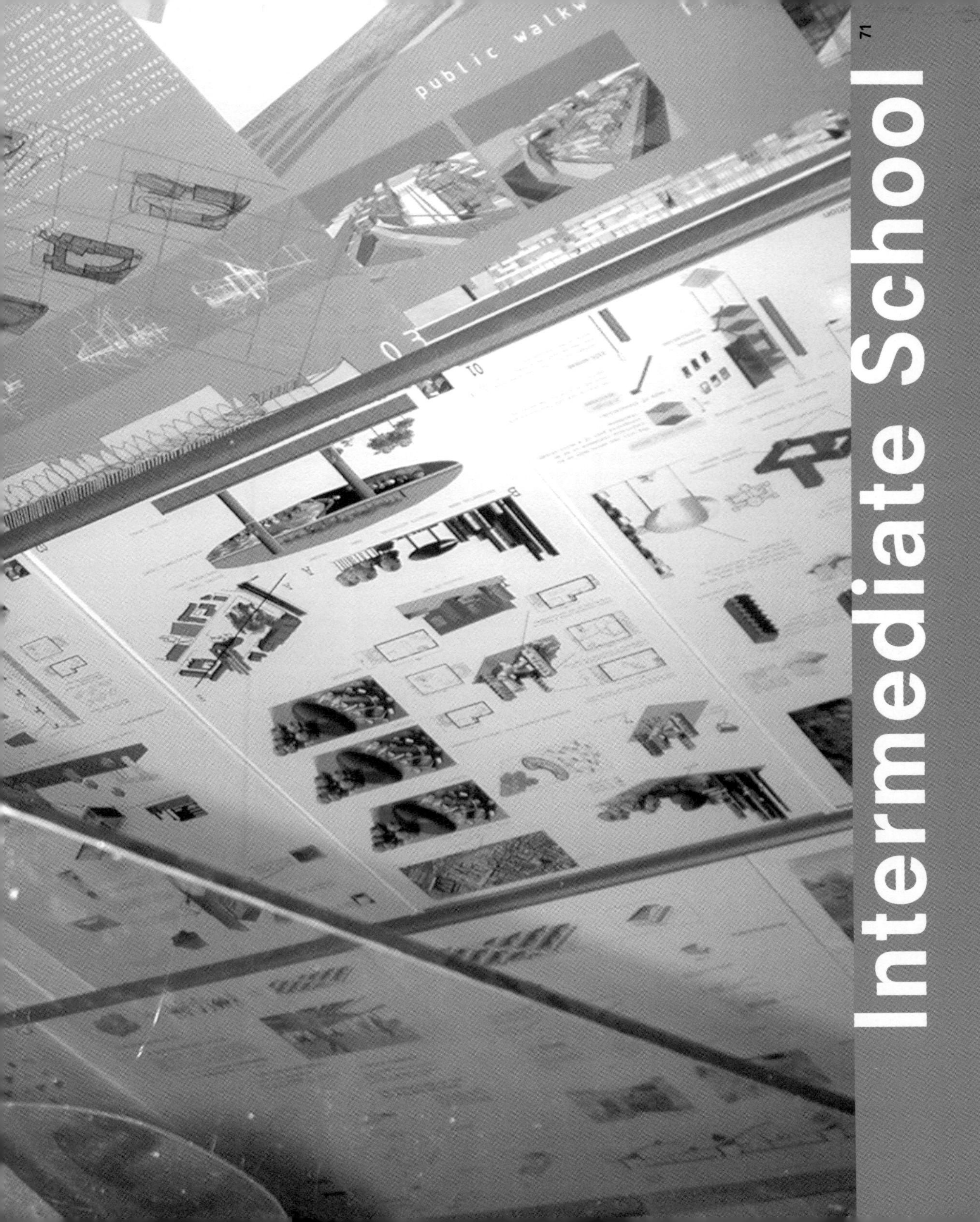

The work of Inter 1 is primarily concerned with place-making and our methodology, as such, combines looking, thinking and making. This year we have been working in Hoxton Square, London EC1. A decade ago, this was a forgotten, uninhabited remnant of London's industrial past, a place that provided cheap accommodation for artists. Now its warehouses have been colonised as 'loft-style apartments', galleries, design offices and trendy bars. Inter 1 has been looking at the phenomenon of urban regeneration and asking these questions:
How do the various strains of Hoxton life encounter each other?
What could sustain and support social life there?
Where is it appropriate to engage with the economic and social processes of refurbishment and change?
Can architecture be an active participant in a situation in a state of flux and transformation?

Urban Parlour Hoxton

Our involvement with the site began with a very short project in the first week of the autumn term. Students worked in groups of two or three to fabricate urban furniture in response to initial impressions of Hoxton Square. These pieces encouraged and amplified some of the situations which occur there in an ad hoc and unacknowledged manner. They included external timber bar counters, enthusiastically appropriated by the drinkers in the Square, fabric bean bags, cardboard drinks trays that doubled as folding seats and flyers, and steps which opened the square to nocturnal use. Following this, individual projects were developed as site-specific 1:1 proposals. This work critiqued the 'as-found' conditions of the place, challenging the constraints of the closed English 'Square' and making the activities of Hoxton available within the setting of an 'urban parlour', an outside room. During the Christmas vacation, students photographed their family homes. We compared the ways inhabitation occurs in different places and examined the diversity of climate and cultures as well as the similarities between distant ways of life. The unit trip to New York in February allowed us to extend this comparison, and to consider the peculiar and idiosyncratic qualities of London and Manhattan as well as the ubiquitous and universal aspects of urban existence.

Autonomy & Contingency

Students' building proposals consider the site as a space of transition, both physically and culturally, from the lush extravagance of Hoxton Square towards the working-class housing of Hoxton Street. We worked with local photographic artist Rut Blees Luxemburg, who took us on walks to look at unexamined parts of the city. The 'visual attune-ment' she encouraged became a means to frame thinking about the places we observed. Subsequent research in Hoxton revealed certain spaces of possibility. Our photographs became a way of looking at what can be missed in casual observation and revealed sites for architectural investigation in which the imagination can wander. The development of particular ways of looking at particular things led to proposals for certain modifications to the place. Spatial boundaries were challenged in the design of thresholds which articulate some of the conflicts between public and private life in Hoxton. Threshold studies led to the establishment of spatial programmes which comment upon the cultural and temporal structures of Hoxton. These spatial propositions developed as formal configurations that established a loose framework of territories, volumes and building mass. The final stages of work combine 1:1 studies built in order to examine the material aspects of the imagination, 1:20 models which locate the moments of transition within a spatial context of inhabitation, light, orientation, views, etc., as well as 1:200 'conceptual models' which attempt to express a temperament towards the reconfiguration of the grounds for architecture as a social art. We begin with responses to the particular qualities of a site, in order to allow what is common to appear.

Unit Masters
Andrew Houlton
Stephen Taylor
Patrick Lynch

Students
Daniel Koo
Krasimir Kotsinov
Lucienne Leung
Asako Mogi
Hideki Oka
Eir Saemundsdottir
Megumi Sakamoto
Mariko Sakuma
Takao Shimizu

Visiting Critics
Peter Beard
Rut Blees Luxemburg
Tony Fretton
John Glew
Regine Leibinger
Martine de Maesener
Mohsen Mostafavi
Peter St John

Special thanks to
Rut Blees Luxemburg
Kenneth Frampton
Alun Jones

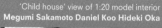

Mariko Sakuma
'Child house' view of 1:20 model interior
Megumi Sakamoto Daniel Koo Hideki Oka

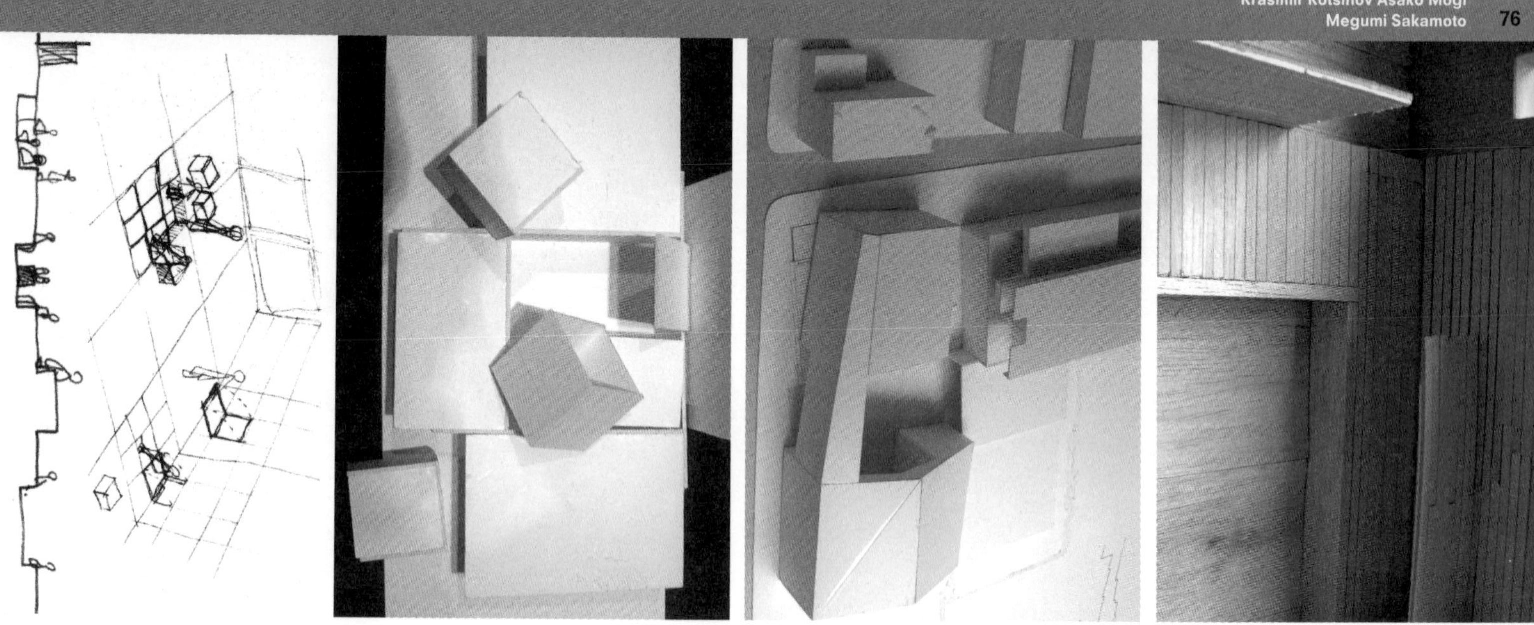

Mariko Sakuma 'Child house' models
Takao Shimizu Eir Saemunsdottir
Daniel Koo Lucie Leung
Krasimir Kotsinov Asako Mogi
Megumi Sakamoto

'The site in its absolute particularities dictates to me the possibilities of response.' **Robert Irwin**

Asako Mogi
Key-worker housing 1:1 threshold study
1:200 & 1:100 site models & 1:50 model

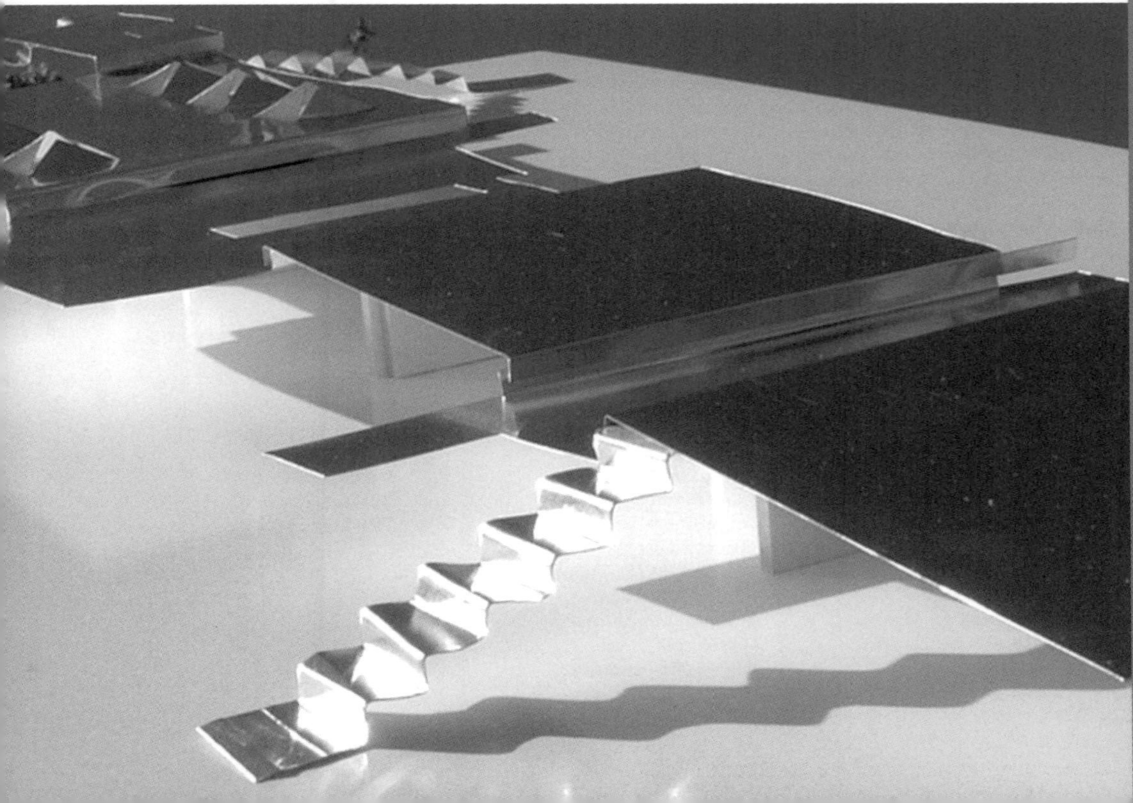

This year Intermediate Unit 2 conducted a structured exploration of surface, in order to tap the potential – and push back the limitations – of curvilinearity in architecture. The three-term exploration followed a technical and critical agenda. Our process involved descriptive drawing, the production of material models by analogue means, the use of custom-written modelling software and a selective access to numerically controlled fabrication.

Death Mask

The year began with a project on a microscale that engaged with a familiar but elusive surface – the human face. To produce on paper the sinuous lines that best describe it, the participants took on the challenge raised by Robin Evans in relation to Piero della Francesca's *De Prospectiva Pingendi*: how can one submit to delineation that which has features but no discernible lines?

Digital Skin

The term continued with a project on the body and the microscale of a formidable artificial creation, computer-generated meshes. Inverting the course of the discovery process, the group inherited a ready-made network of edges and polygons and worked their way back to the production of a physical artefact.

The site of the Digital Skin lies somewhere between the human physique and the cyberbody of virtual worlds. Its raw material came in the form of various anatomic or character-based meshes put together by the computer-gaming community. These meshes brought forth an assorted array of associations: physical, emotional, medical, morbid and even sensual.

Soft Room

The third and conclusive experiment investigated the mysterious sightings of surface within the domestic context of 36 Bedford Square. The group produced several conceptual blueprints for a full-scale installation made of four pliant walls with various physical configurations and degrees of material definition. Parts of the project were realised at full scale – though the scope of the experiment was generally restricted to the actualisation of a model at 1:5.

Stranded House

Stranded House is not a house in the literal sense, but a place – like Mansion House, Manor House, Customs House or even the Court of Chancery of Dickens's fictional *Bleak House*. Stranded House is a place in Paris or London whose name is evocative of duration and continuity.

Part original structure and part addition, Stranded House is a Siamese building type. Like the Digital Skin, it is half-new and half-old, a centaur form that combines two separate programmes and formal types (and occasionally brings about flares of conflict between them).

Stranded House was sited in the Smithsons' Economist Building on St James Street. The perceived regularities of the building served as underlay and counterpoint to the deployment of an addition relying on the formal and programmatic languages explored in the previous experiments.

The story of Stranded House is rooted in the confrontation between old and new, but it also expresses a state of continuity – between curvilinear and straight, soft and hard, temporary and permanent, classical and contemporary.

Unit Staff
George Liaropoulos-Legendre
Lluis Viu Rebes

Students
Edouard Cabay
Kelvin K.W. Chu
Daniel Coll I Capdevilla
Josh I. Goh
Ho-Min Kim
Leonidas Lazarakis
Nazila Maghzian
Beatriz Minguez de Molina
Dan Narita
Alexia Petridis
Bart Schoonderbeek
Pavlos Sideris

Jurors
George Arvanitis
Valentin Bontjes Van Beek
Stephan Buerger
Javier Castañon
Shin Egashira
Martin Hagel
Mark Hemel
Johannes Käferstein
Dimitra Katsota
Martine de Maeseneer
Michel Mossessian
Mohsen Mostafavi
Ciro Najle
Annabelle Perdomo
Charles Tashima
Jeff Turko
Tom Verebes
Julian Varas
Megan Yakeley

Special thanks to
Antonia Loyd
Mohsen Mostafavi
Charles Tashima
Ciro Najle

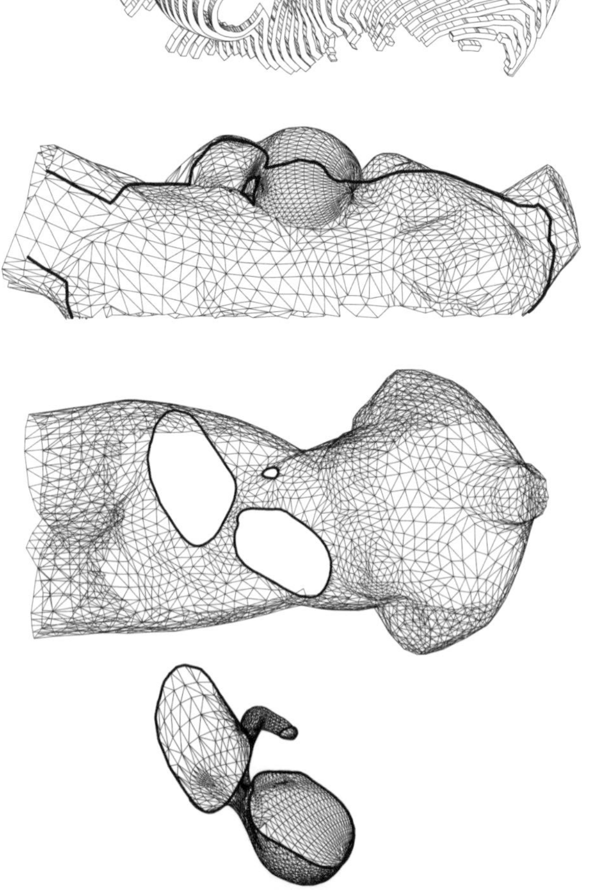

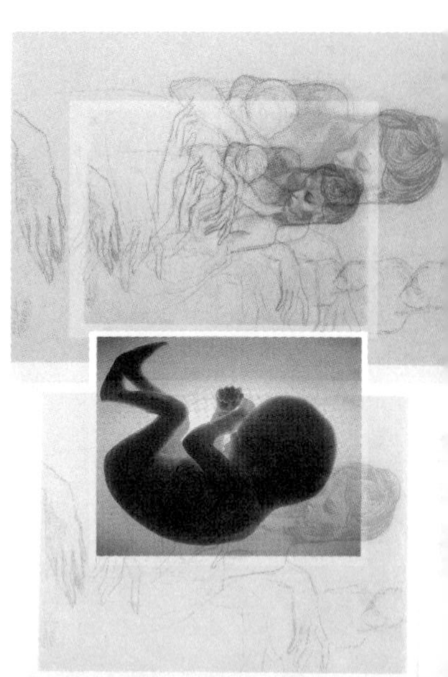

Nazila Maghzian Digital Skin

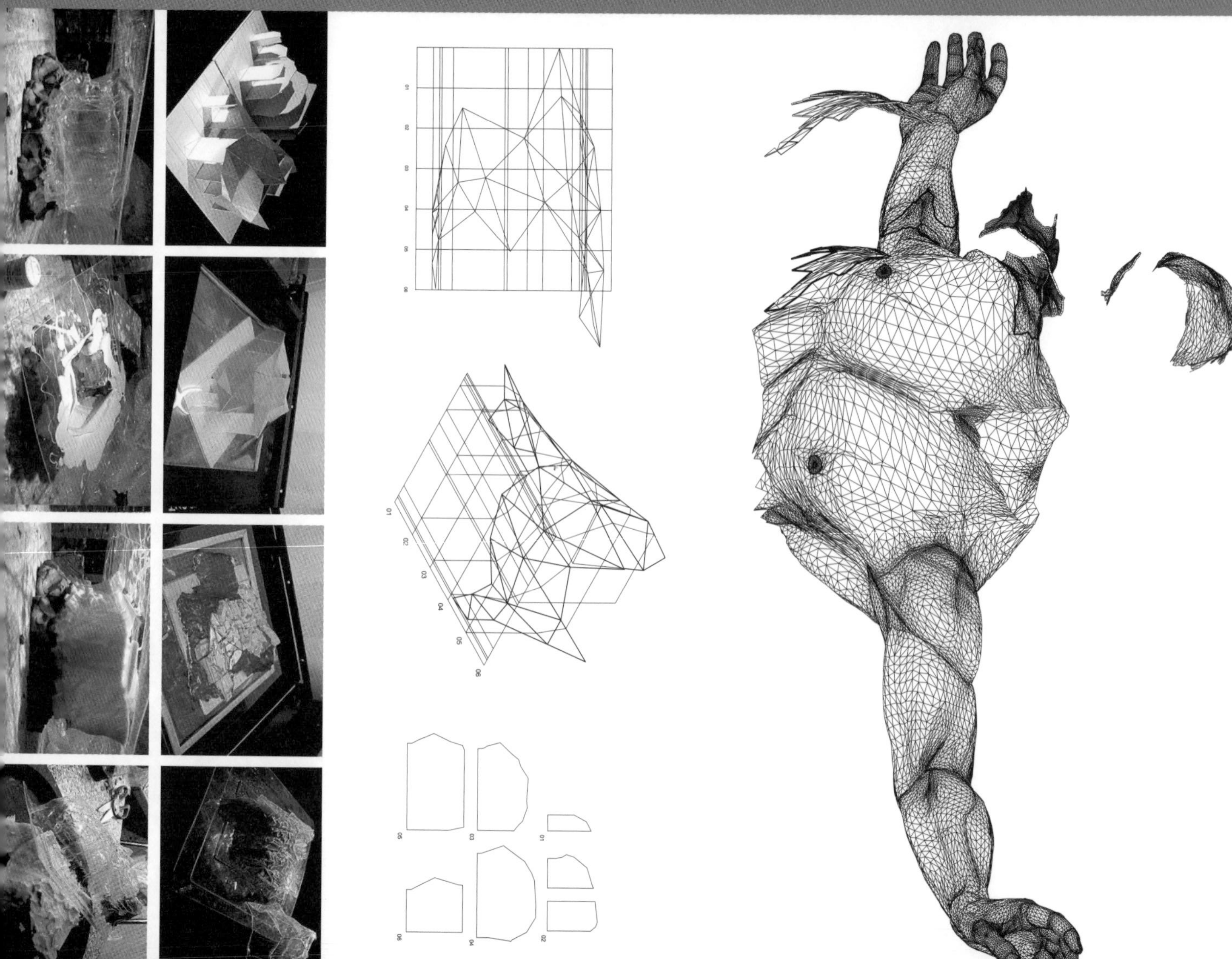
01
02
03
04
05
06

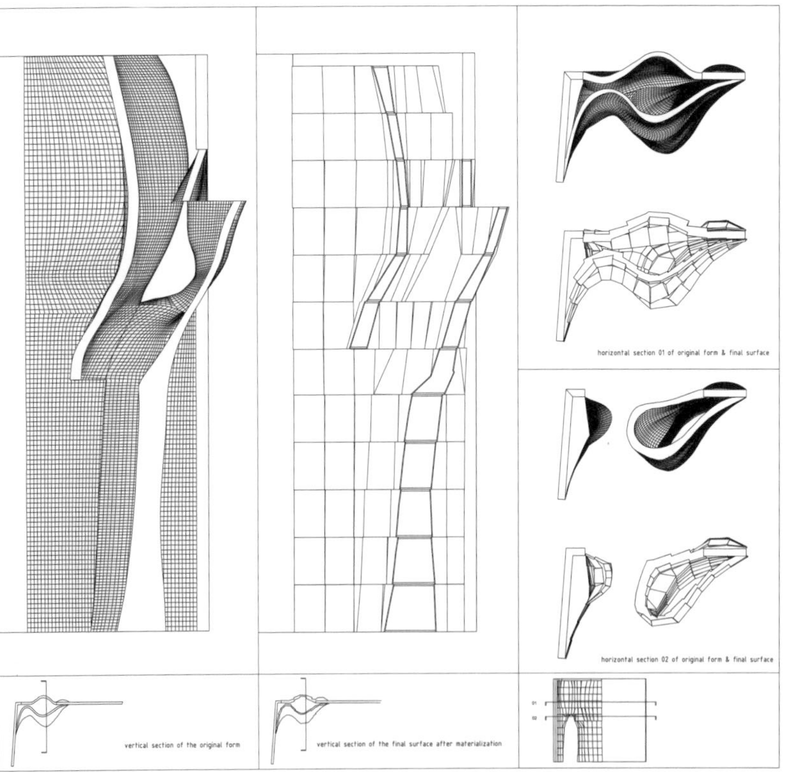
horizontal section 01 of original form & final surface
horizontal section 02 of original form & final surface
vertical section of the original form
vertical section of the final surface after materialization
01
02

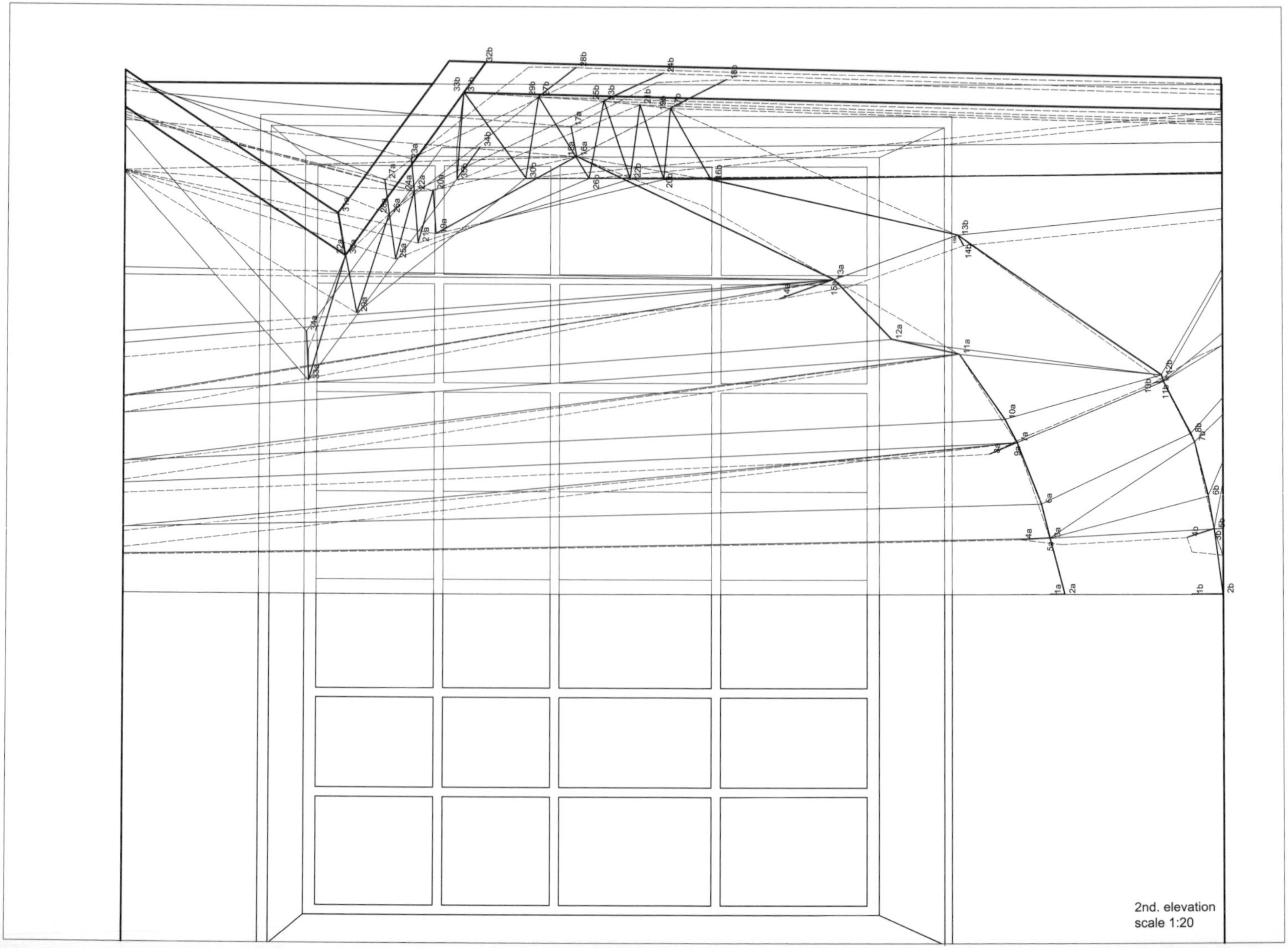

2nd. elevation
scale 1:20

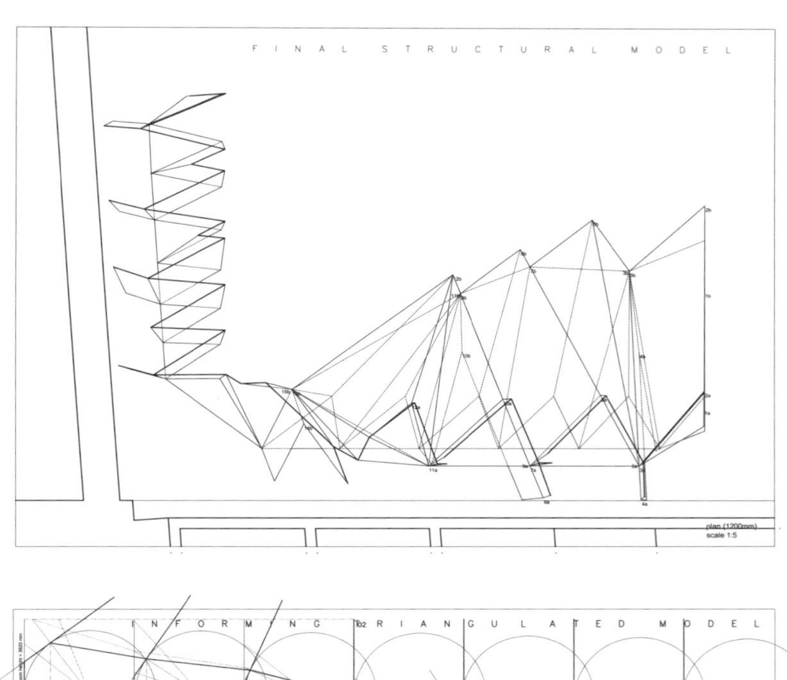
FINAL STRUCTURAL MODEL
plan (1200mm)
scale 1:5

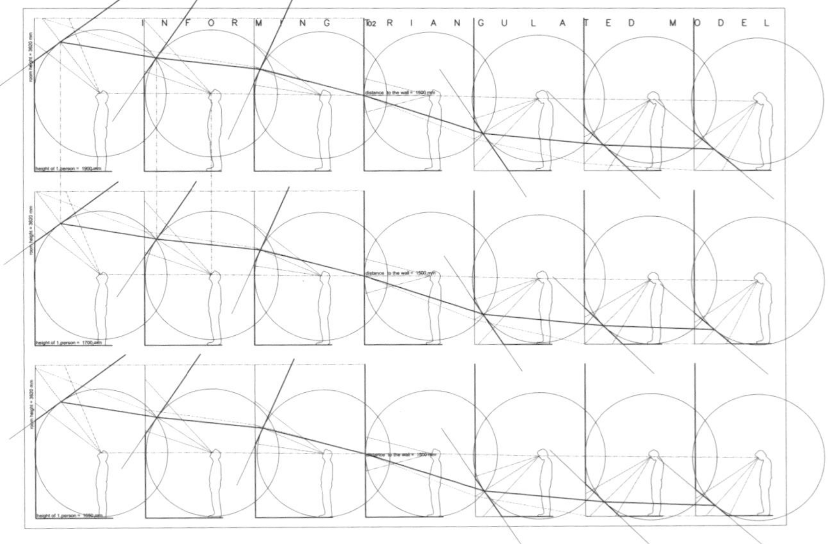
INFORMING TRIANGULATED MODEL

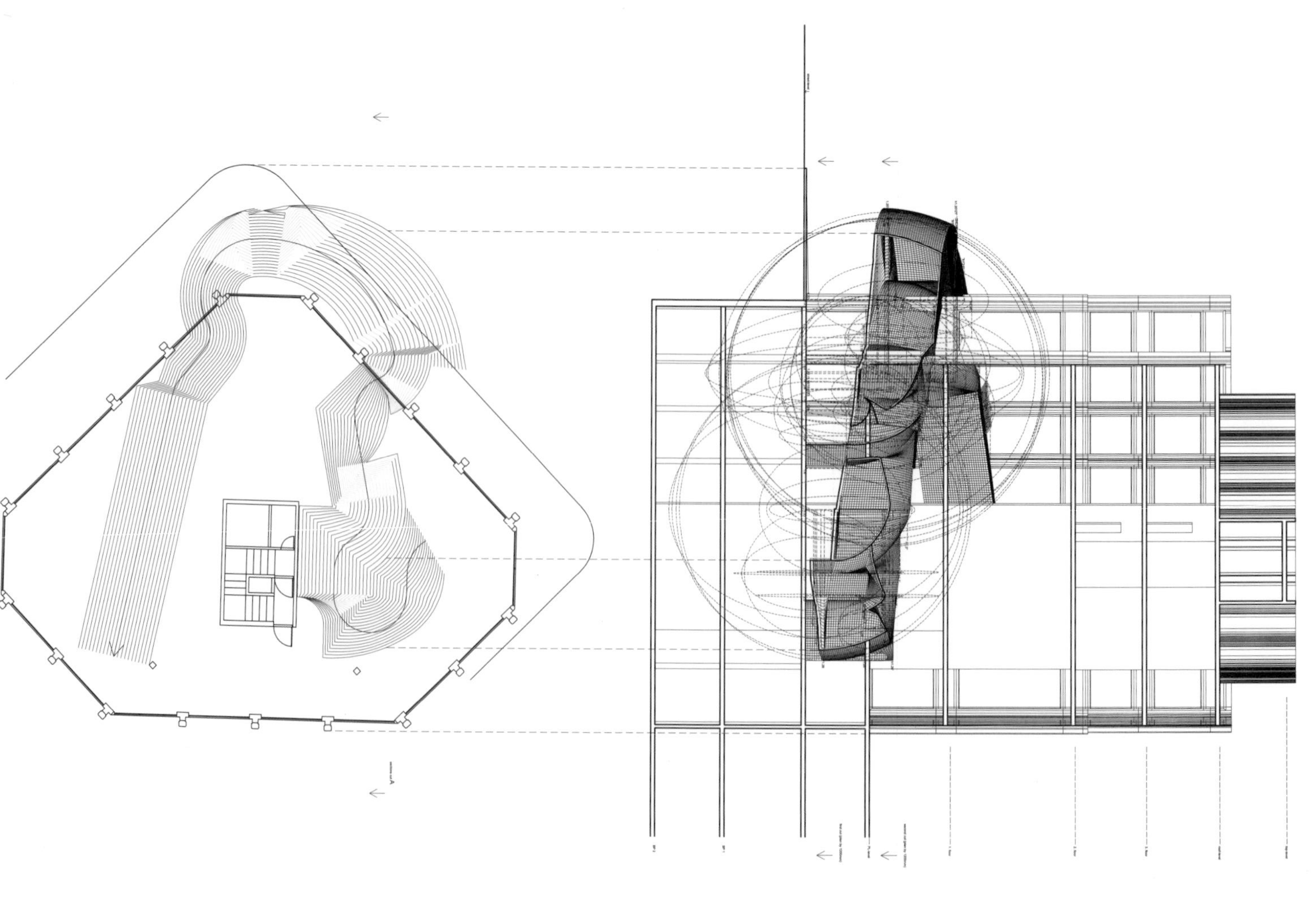

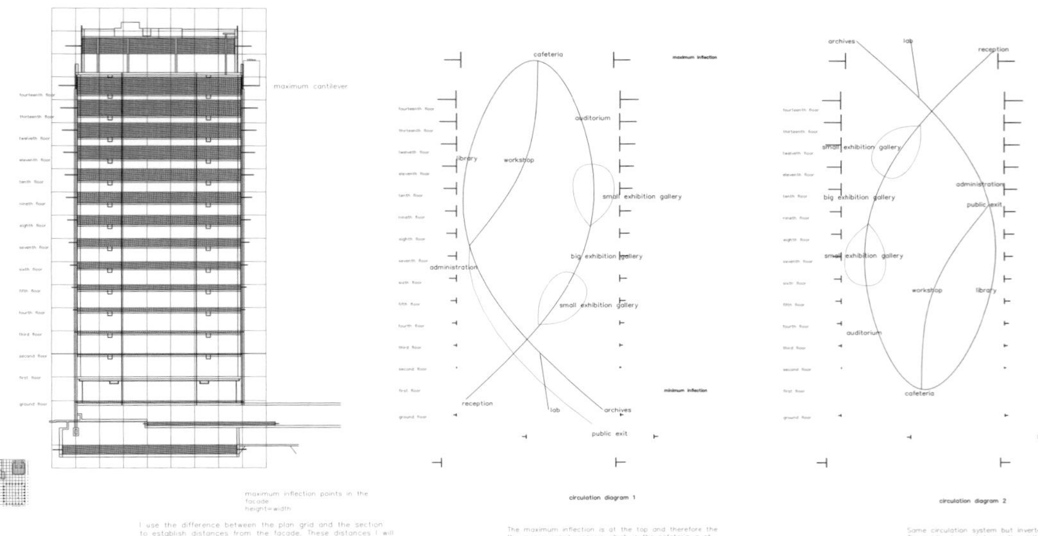

maximum inflection points in the facade height=width

I use the difference between the plan grid and the section to establish distances from the facade. These distances I will use to inflect the facade and therefore vary the density between the lines.

circulation diagram 1

The maximum inflection is at the top and therefore the the more opened program which is the cafeteria is at the top.
Problem: the public must go up during the visit.

circulation diagram 2

Same circulation system but inverted.
The public descend during the visit.

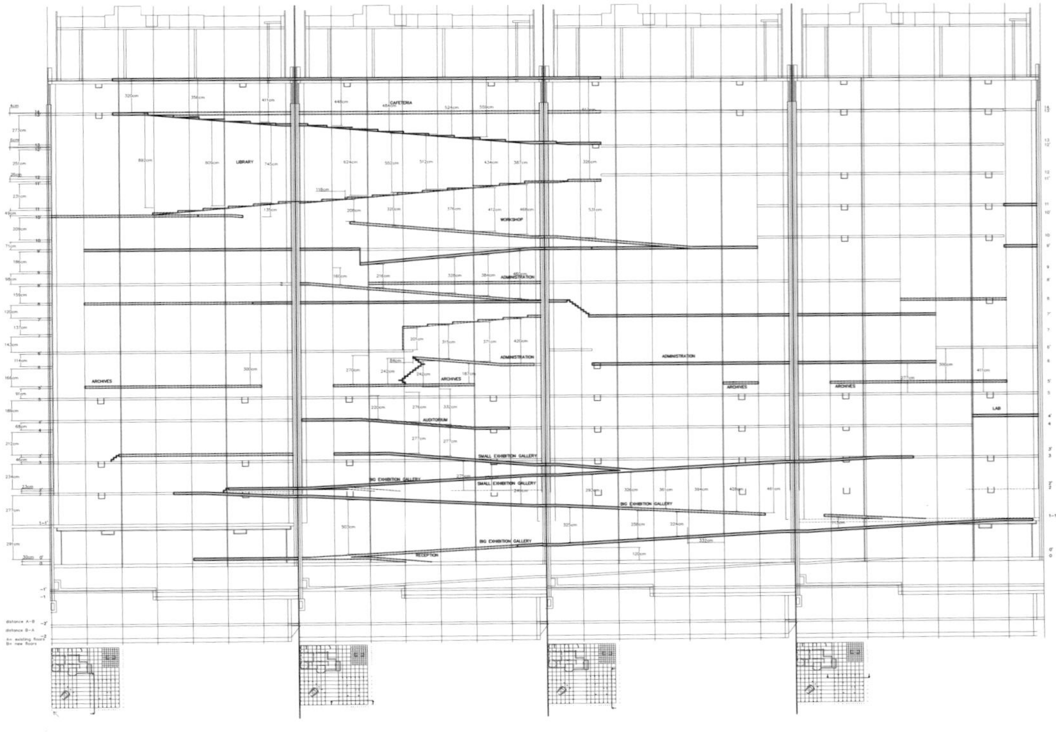

Unit Agenda

This year's brief stipulated the development and engineering of an architecture of inhabitation that could effect change and respond to behavioural forces or environmental shifts. Through the year it became evident that Inter 3's 'Big Brother House 3' – a micro-environment that responds to the shifting demands of changing inhabitants and an audience – was developing from an elaborate machine for living into a machine for viewing. Through multiple analyses of domestic space, surveillance systems and, above all, responsive mechanisms and architecture, students developed a new thread of thinking. At its simplest it is this: Domesticity + Surveillance = Interaction.

Interactive architecture became a base from which to extend the interactive experience that accounts for the popularity of the Big Brother show among viewers. Students developed a body of work that became coherent and thorough in its negotiation of boundaries between public and private, interior and exterior, digital and analogue, transparency and opacity, viewer and viewed, contestant and audience, recorded and live.

Project 1 **Domestic Space**

The first project of the year called for the analysis of a selection of twentieth-century houses that were key to the establishment of new forms of domestic space and inhabitation. These examples exhibit fundamental responses to the ongoing search for new strategies for living and to the need for variable levels of publicness within a private territory. The unit related the findings of formal compositional analysis to organisational and operational patterns of domestic living, and speculated on new patterns of domestic use, the complexities of social interchange, and emergent models for an architectural response.

Project 2 **Transformation**

Taking a primary effect or technique that was observed and analysed in each exemplary house, students were required to produce an intervention into the existing house that would intensify and transform it. Thus, instead of simply documenting an existing project, students generated a new domestic space. Consequently, the project served to bridge analysis and design work.

Project 3 **Site**

By siting our 'Big Brother House 3' in the middle of Leicester Square, at the centre of London's entertainment district, the unit could take advantage of a hyperactive location in order to work towards a greater integration of media, public interaction and intimate space – to force the development of responsive systems that can negotiate the boundaries between them.

Project 4 **Big Brother House 3**

One of the driving forces for the Big Brother House brief is the potent way in which it externalises an interior. Students assimilated the information and ideas gathered in the early part of the year to generate projects that were at once highly specialised (in terms of resolving domestic space and its relation to a media-saturated physical environment), and sufficiently broad to address the larger issue of the format of the show and its reliance on audience interaction.

Unit Masters
Natasha Sandmeier
Jenny Jones

Students
Sara Castilho
Adam Cossey
Nausica Gabrielides
Noe Golomb
Antonis Karides
Jun Kawamata
Christina Liao
Nan-Kuei Lin
Ashley Littlewood
Christos Malekos
Mitsuhiro Tokuda
Mark Tynan

Visiting Critics
Javier Castañon
Oliver Domeisen
Johannes Käferstein
George Liaropolous-Legendre
Mohsen Mostafavi
Mike Weinstock
Brett Steele
Shumon Basar
Charles Tashima
Manuela Gatto
Vasilis Stroumpakos
Robert Sedlak
Anna Liu
Mike Tonkin
Peter Beard
Masoud Golsorki
Juergen Mayer

Special thanks to
Antonia Loyd
Chris Leubkeman @ OAP
Tony Sheehan @ OAP
Helen Hawken @ Bazal

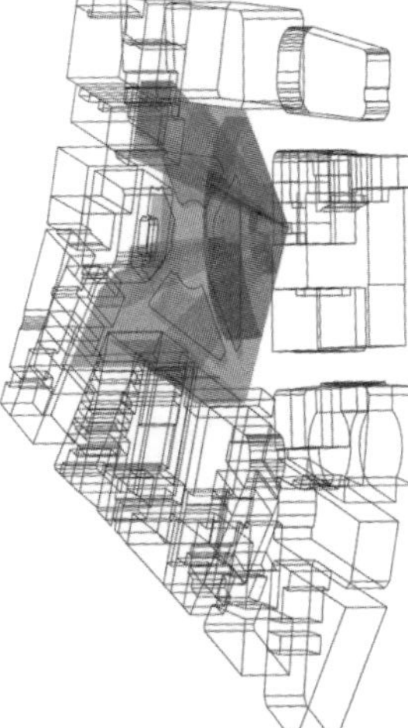

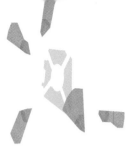

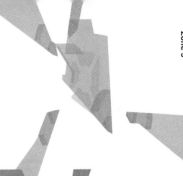

Ashley Littlewood Leicester Square Surveillance
The 187 surveillance cameras in operation in Leicester Square – from multiple webcams to the police CCTV camera – were exhaustively documented to determine the extent of surveillance and reveal blind spots for covert actions.

Adam Cossey Deployable Surface

Accelerated population change and the loss of privacy within the Big Brother house place enormous demands on the performance of the house as well as its efficiency. The proposal offers the inhabitants a kinetic interior surface that has the ability to adapt to constantly changing demands. Not only is the house an active participant in the show, it also becomes the broadcasting medium.

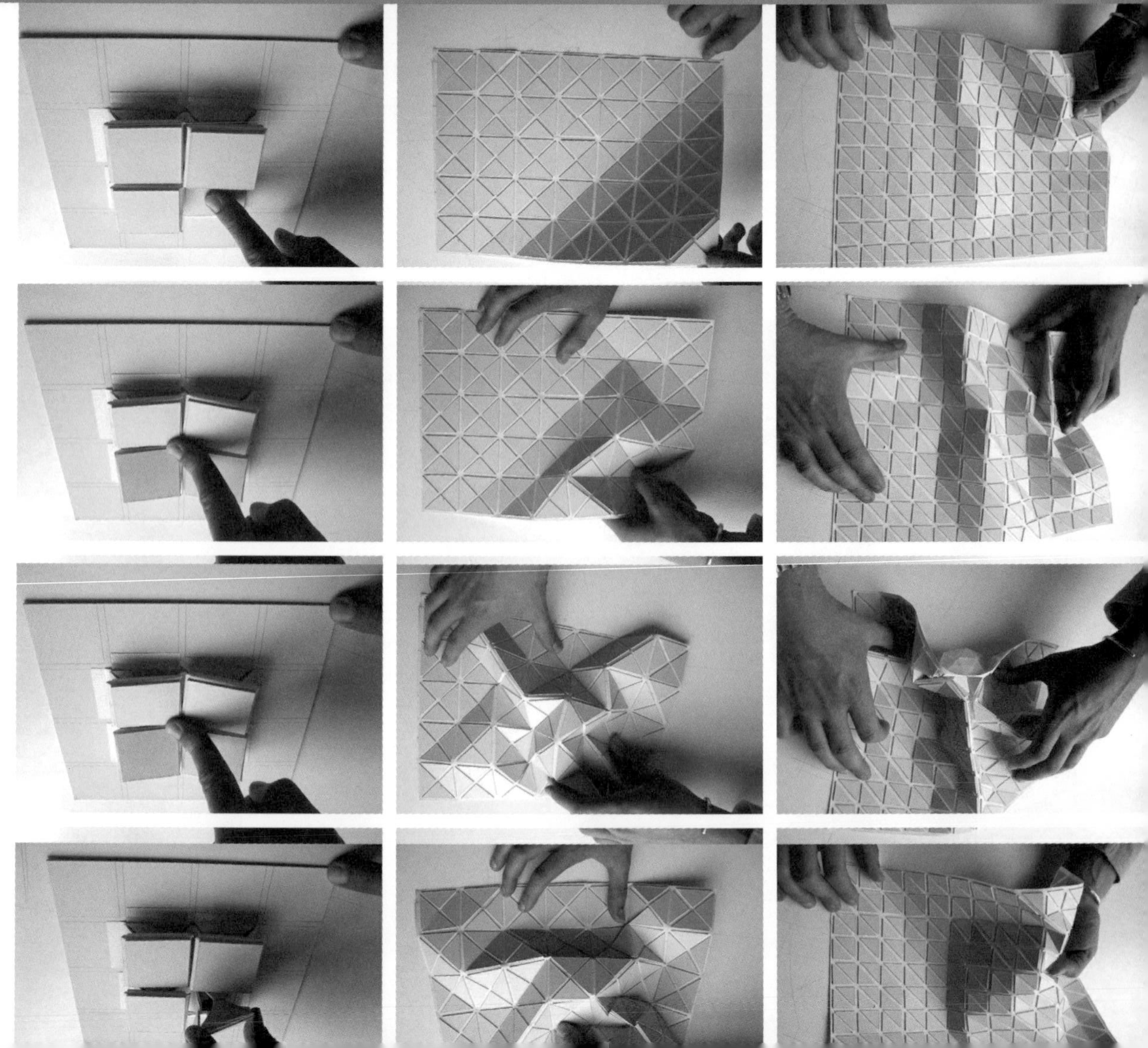

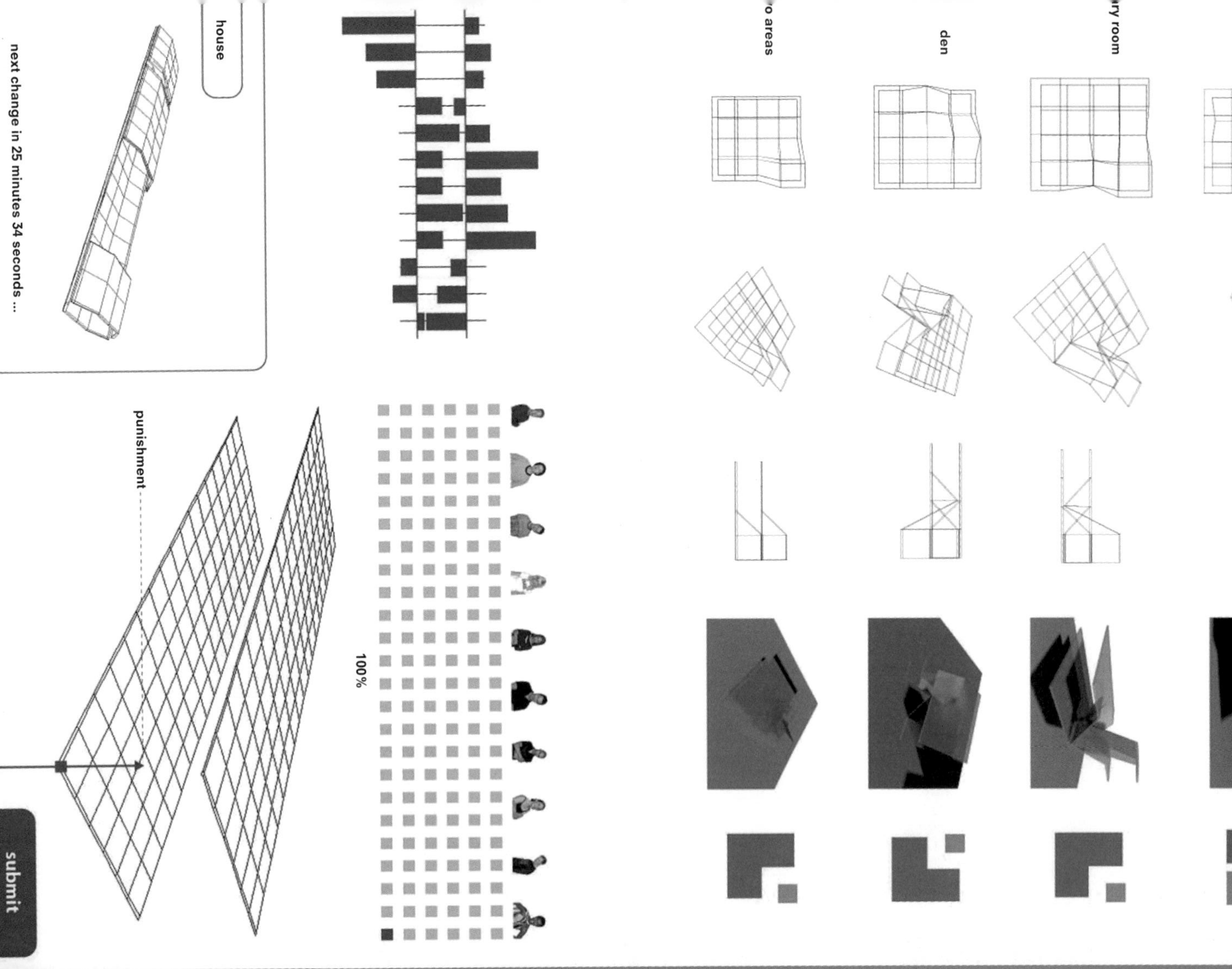

Noe Golomb Punishment and Reward

In the new Big Brother house a language of reactions is designed to change the parameters of domestic space. Every action of the contestants has, as in life, a reaction. The audience has complete control over the house configuration – each module is triggered by online votes. The correct physical alignment of the modules provides a reward – easy living. The misalignment of the units acts as punishment – complex, inconvenient spatial arrangements.

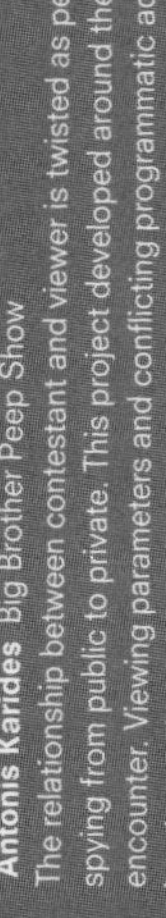

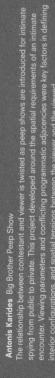

Antonis Karides Big Brother Peep Show

The relationship between contestant and viewer is twisted as peep shows are introduced for intimate spying from public to private. This project developed around the spatial requirements of an intimate encounter. Viewing parameters and conflicting programmatic adjacencies were key factors in defining interior configurations, and spatial tensions between the viewer and the viewed.

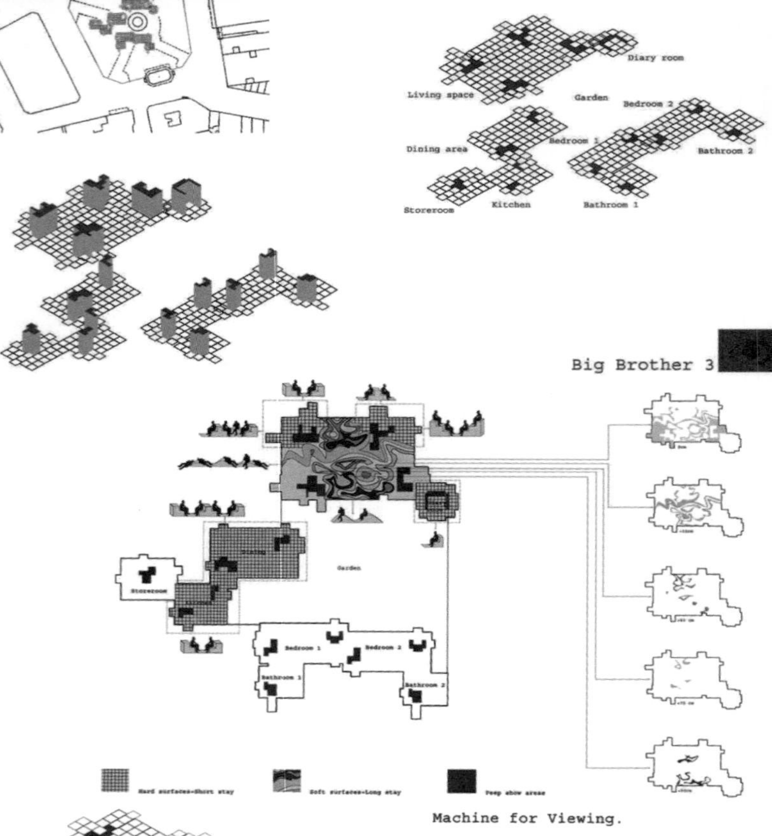

Machine for Viewing.

A further movement of units to accomodate Peep show areas.

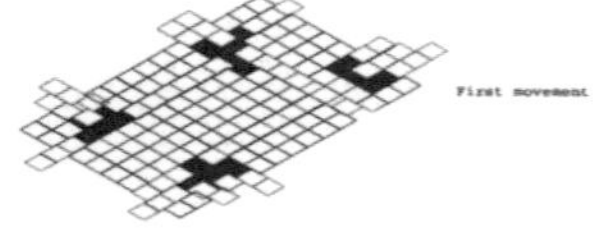

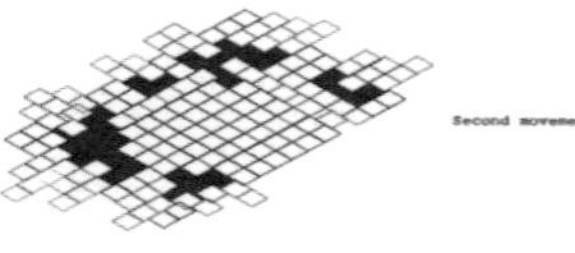

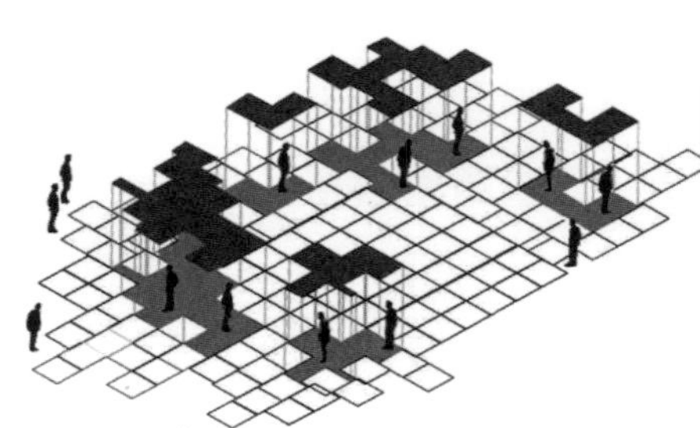

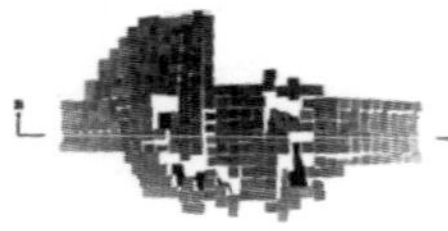

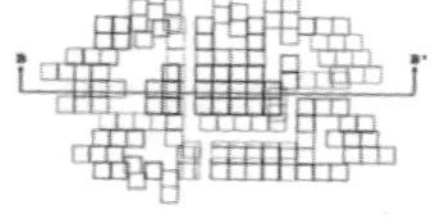

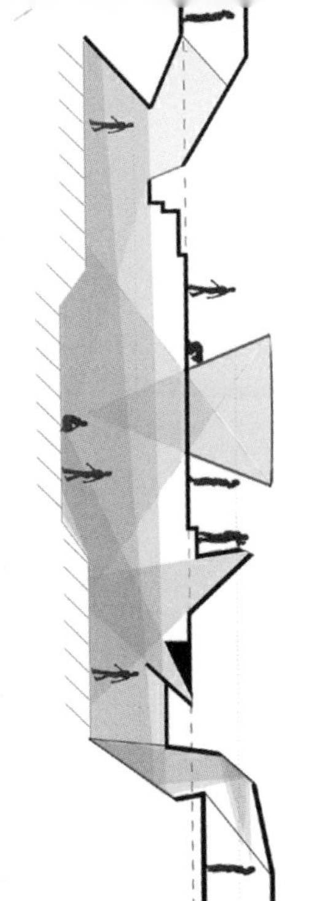

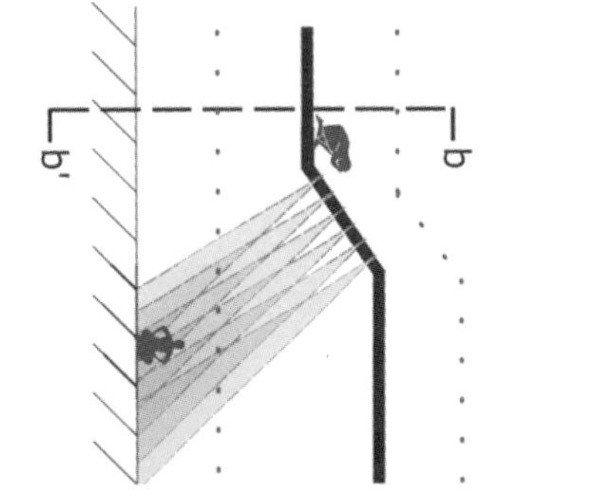

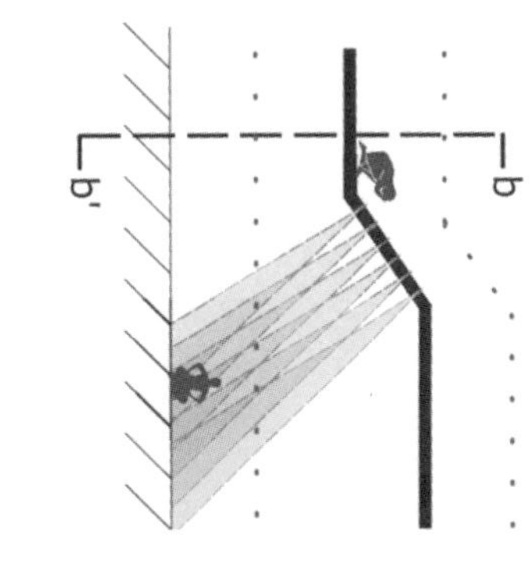

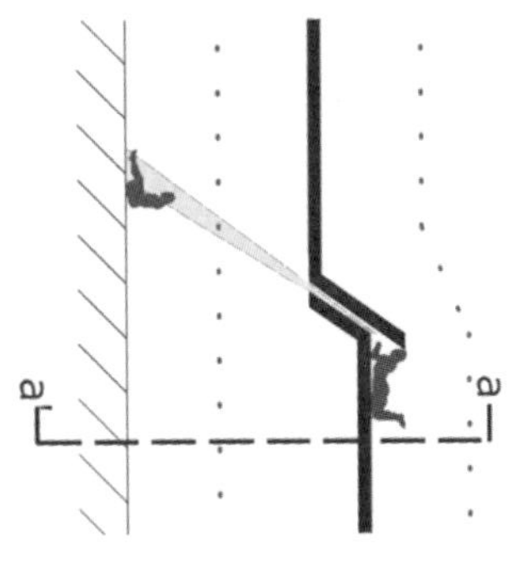

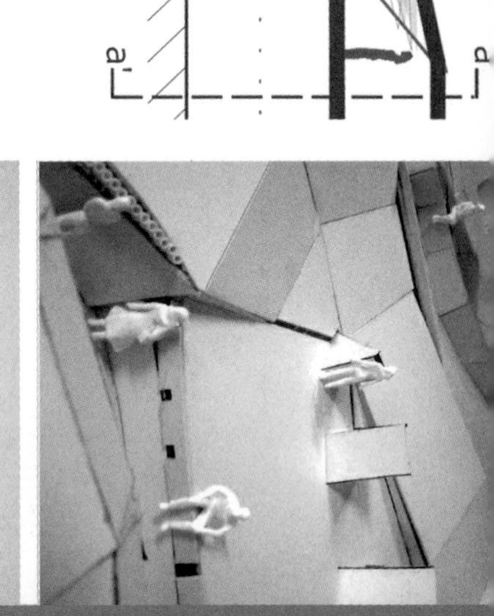

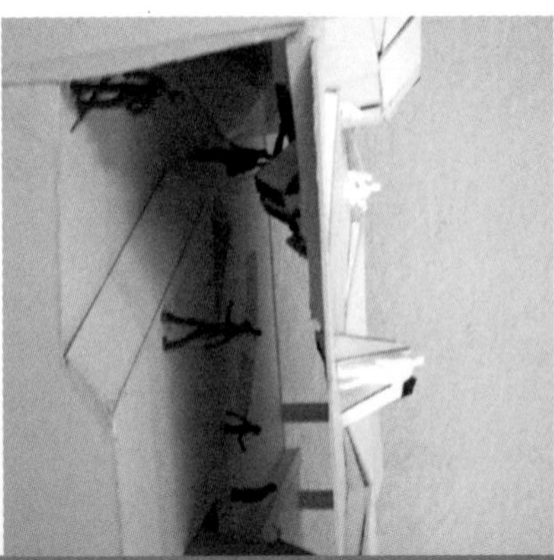

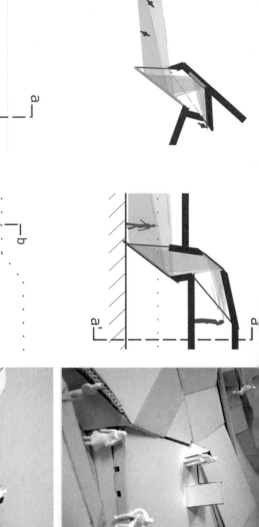

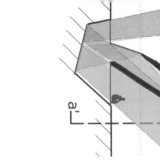

Nausica Gabrielides View Constructs
This project explores the possibilities of a landscaped visual theme park. By developing a series of constructed views that effectively operate as lateral and sectional periscopes, unexpected spatial connections were developed between disparate entities. With the Big Brother House buried under Leicester Square, the ground-level surface evolved into a complex landscape that allows the public to survey the interior.

The Book

An important part of the unit work was the production of a comprehensive project document – this year in the form of a book. Students used the books to move from the standard portfolio format to a more thorough volume that catalogues not only the project work but also essays, thought processes and precedent research. Each of these books is a stand-alone document on permanent access in the AA Library.

Ashley Littlewood Pick 'n Mix Lifestyles
Mark Tynan Disposable Lifestyles

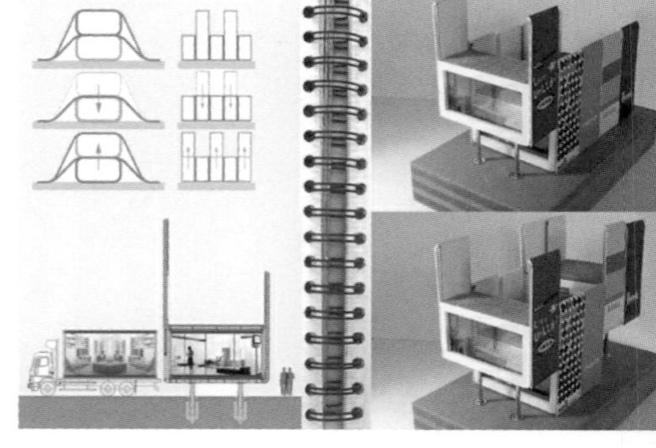

Nausica Gabrielides
Reflections
Antonis Karides
Big Brother Peep Show

Antonis Karides
aFlexi_Walls
Christos Malekos
Folded Flexibility

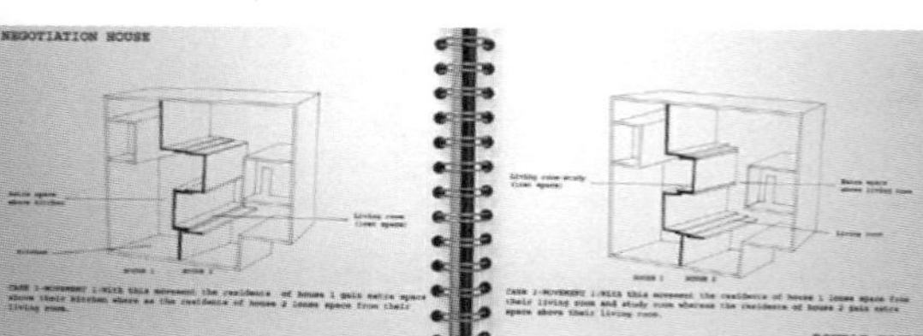

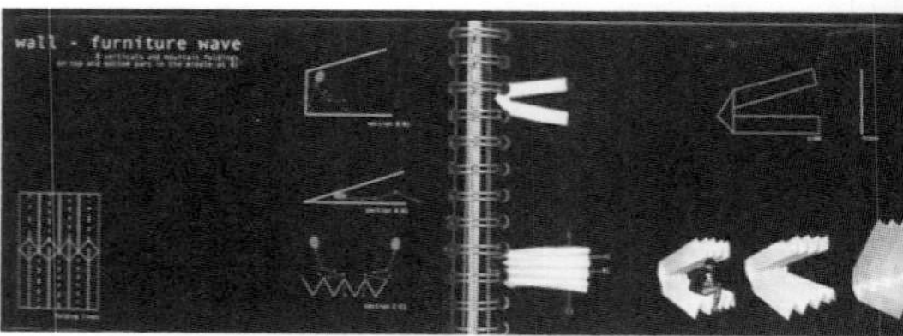

Nausica Gabrielides
View Constructs
Adam Cossey
Transformable House

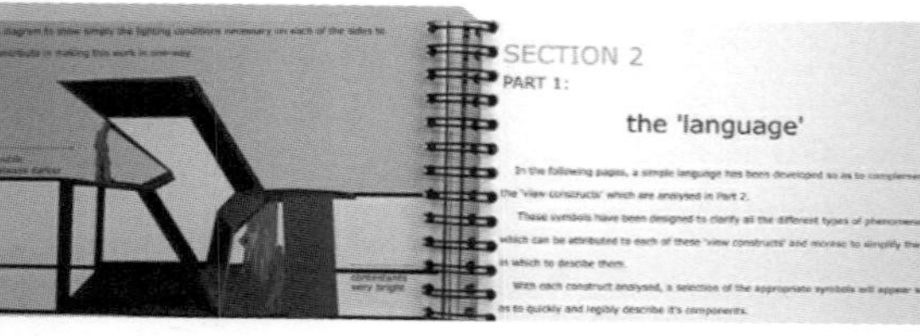

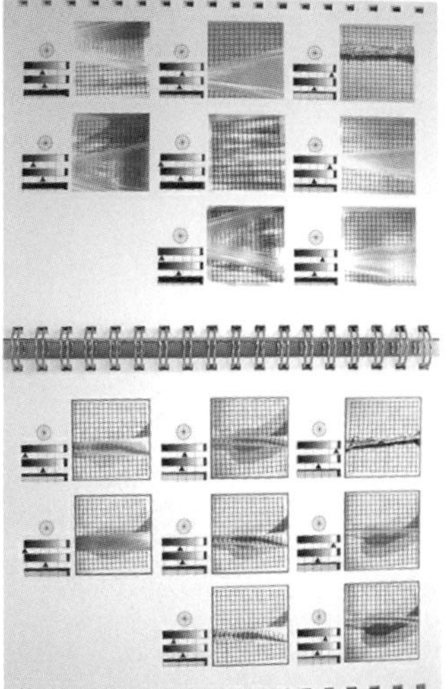

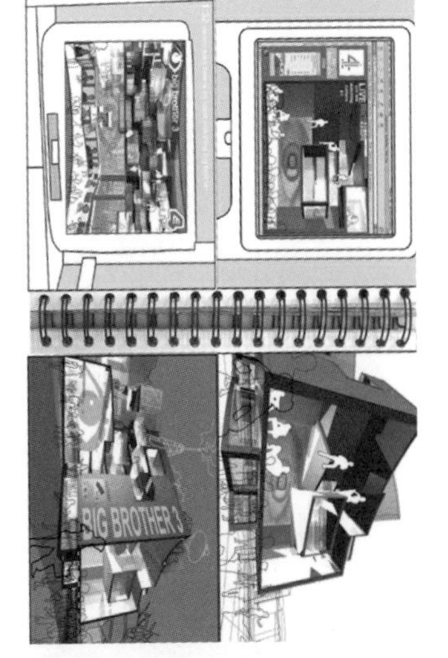

Noe Golomb Water Laboratory
Ashley Littlewood Panopti*Vision*

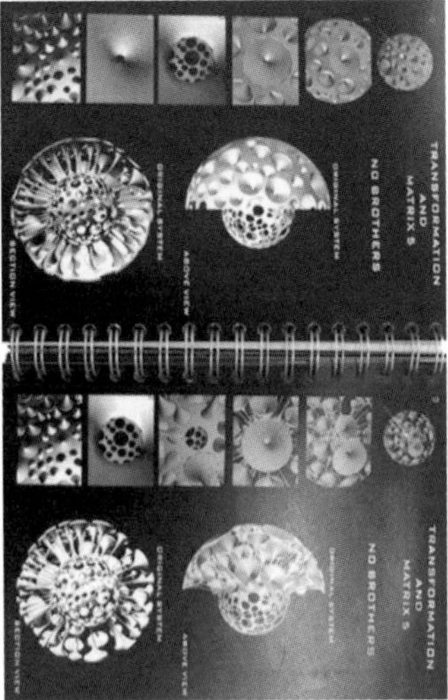

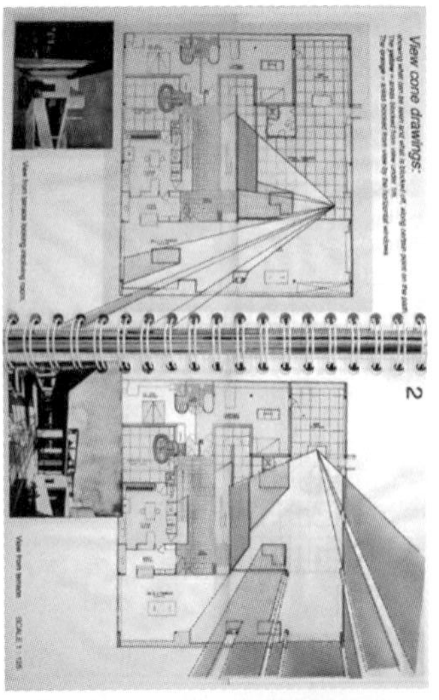

CNan-Kuei Lin Collapsible House
Sara Castilho Constructed View

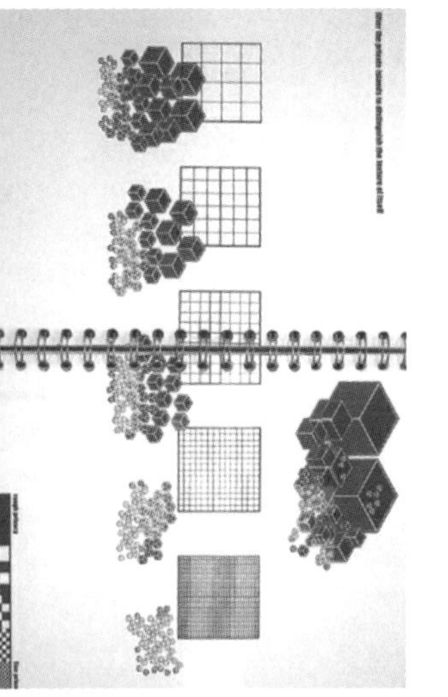

Jun Kawamata Visibility Gradients
Mitsuhiro Tokuda Twisting

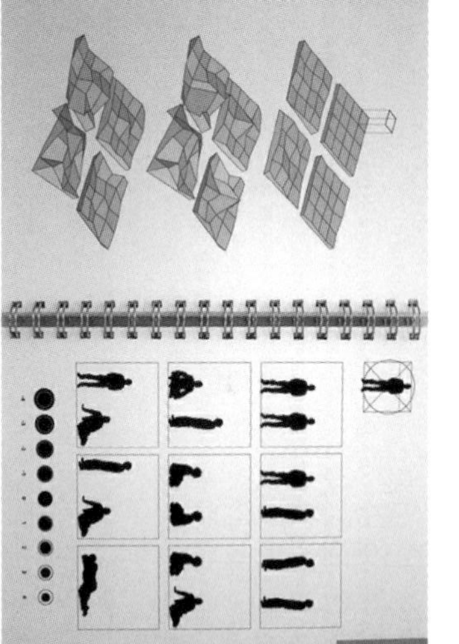

Christina Liao Viewing Machines
Noe Golomb Punishment and Reward

Absolutely Prefabricated

The theme of research this year has been housing and prefabrication. Catalogues and material samples have been used as references and givens, students chose from a list and developed designs according to the criteria and opportunities inherent in the selected material. As usual, Inter 4 has been concerned with closing the gap between conception and construction, pursuing a 'reverse' design path – from the particular to the general, and back again.
In this unit no distinction is made between design and technical explorations; in architecture there can be no imagination that is not technical.

Students were expected to endow one material with the apparent properties or characteristics of another: from weak to strong; flat to 3D; cheap to chic; and banal to beautiful (or vice versa).

Unit Masters
Alex de Rijke
Philip Marsh
Sadie Morgan

Students
Omar Al-Omari
Ema Bonifacic
Toshio Fukuhara
Panayiotis Hadjichristofi
Anna Kubelik
Rita Lee
Christina Leung
Emu Masuyama
Ayako Mizuma

Invited critics
Tim Atwood
Peter Beard
Giles Cherry
Victoria de Rijke
Jenny Jones
Fred Manson
Natasha Sandmeier
Helge Solberg
Charles Tashima
Mike Tonkin
David Van Handel
Roger Zogolovitch

With thanks to
Kingspan/TexHaus
Hans Lensvelt
Ben Morris
Lucy Musgrave
Abe Rogers
Will Russell
Fred Scott
Jeff Thomlinson
Jeremy Till
Sheffield University
Print Studio
Paul Grover

Rita Yen-Chun Lee LenoTec Town – 'Tailor-made Housing

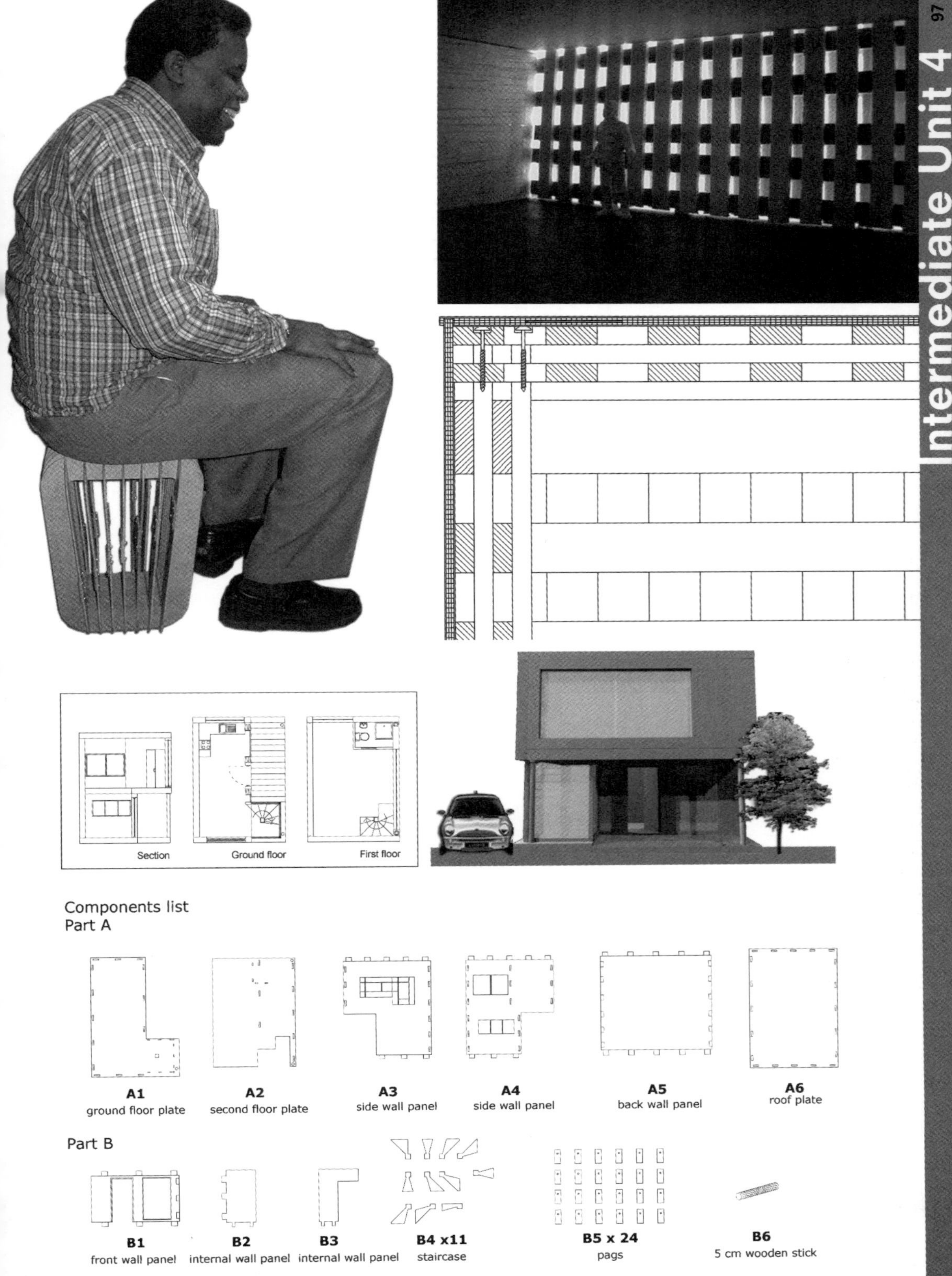
Section
Ground floor
First floor
Components list
Part A
A1
ground floor plate
A2
second floor plate
A3
side wall panel
A4
side wall panel
A5
back wall panel
A6
roof plate
Part B
B1
front wall panel
B2
internal wall panel
B3
internal wall panel
B4 x11
staircase
B5 x 24
pags
B6
5 cm wooden stick

Circle 33 /Architecture Foundation National Housing Competition
Winner: Ema Bonifacic
From Park Hill to Hardwick Hall to Zip-Up House to WoZoCo to Golden Lane/Barbican to Yorkon to AVL-Ville, etc.

Working with 'givens'. **After an analysis of housing typologies, Inter 4 made study tours to existing housing in Britain and the Netherlands, and looked at associated factory manufacturing and organising methods. The understanding of typologies, organisational principles, density and prefabrication issues had to be aligned with chosen materials. Students then made a retrospective random choice of one material with which to develop a competition scheme. The question of site characteristics and constraints was then tested off-site. Thus material invention is forced into a catalytic encounter with individual proposals.**

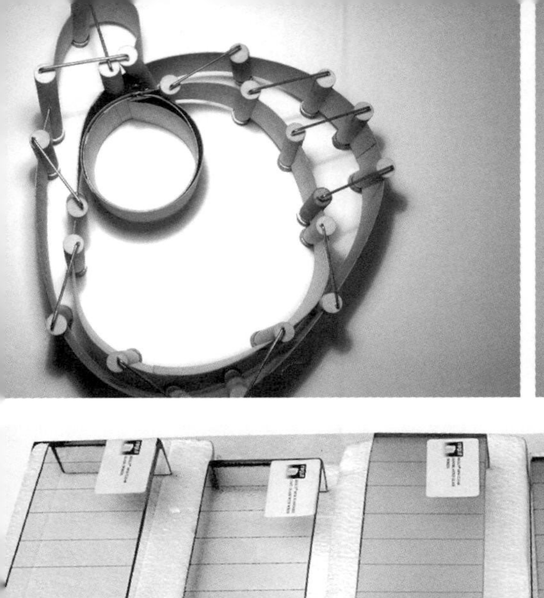

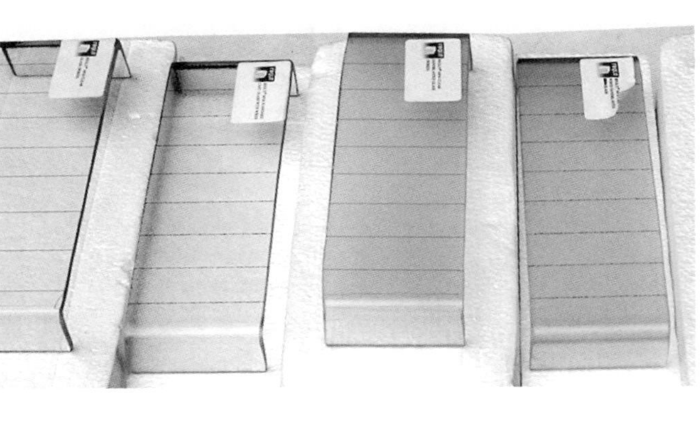

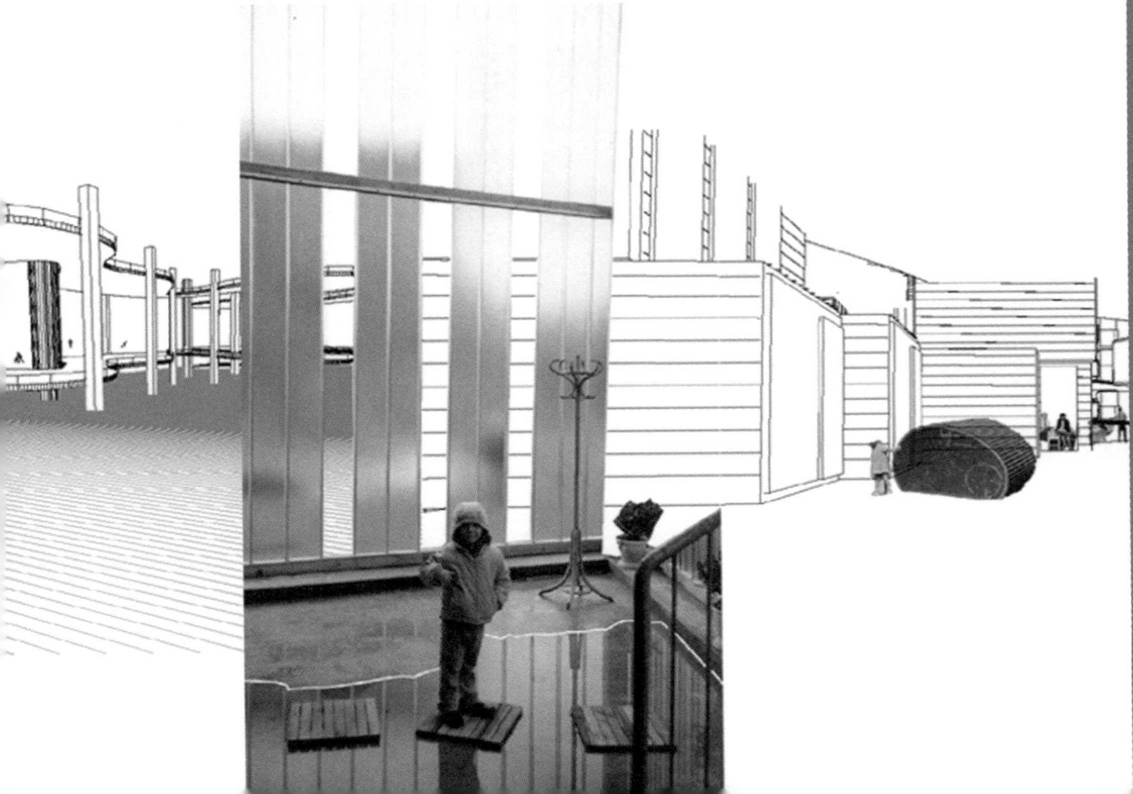

05 VARIABLE SKIN

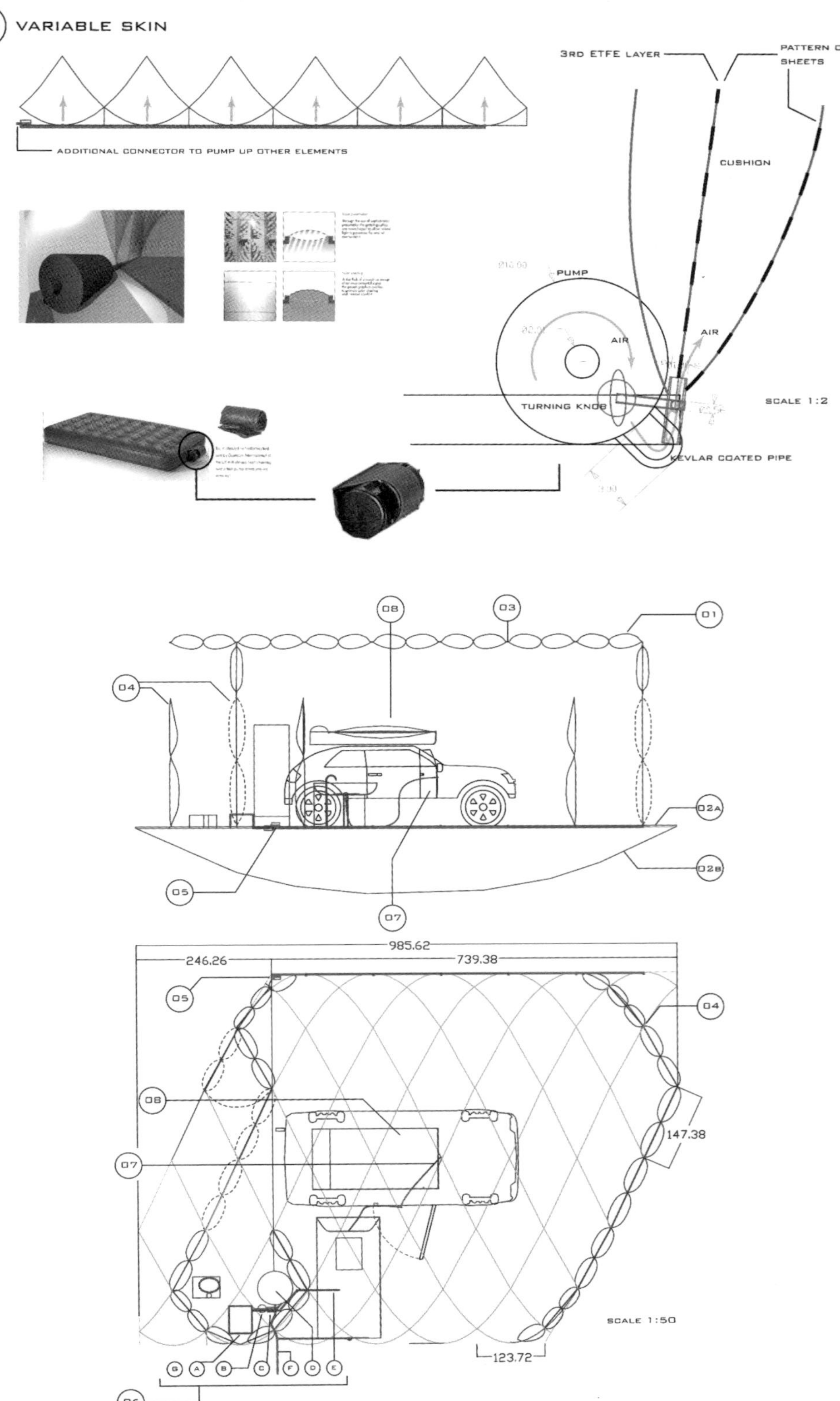
ADDITIONAL CONNECTOR TO PUMP UP OTHER ELEMENTS
3RD ETFE LAYER
PATTERN ON SHEETS
CUSHION
PUMP
AIR
AIR
TURNING KNOB
SCALE 1:2
KEVLAR COATED PIPE
08
03
01
04
02A
02B
05
07
985.62
246.26
739.38
05
04
08
147.38
07
SCALE 1:50
123.72
G
A
B
C
F
D
E
06

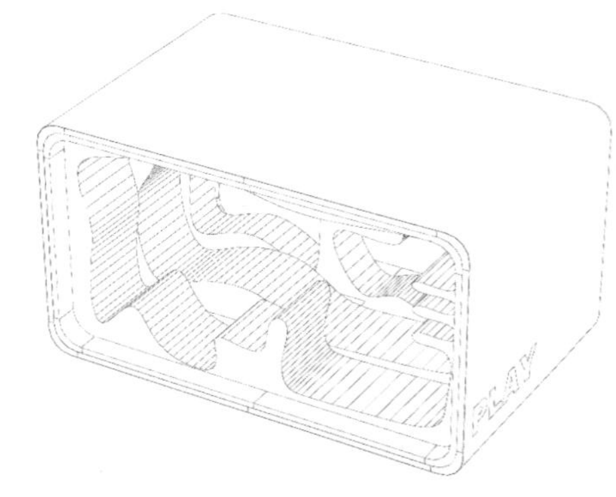
PLAY

EAT
SLEEP

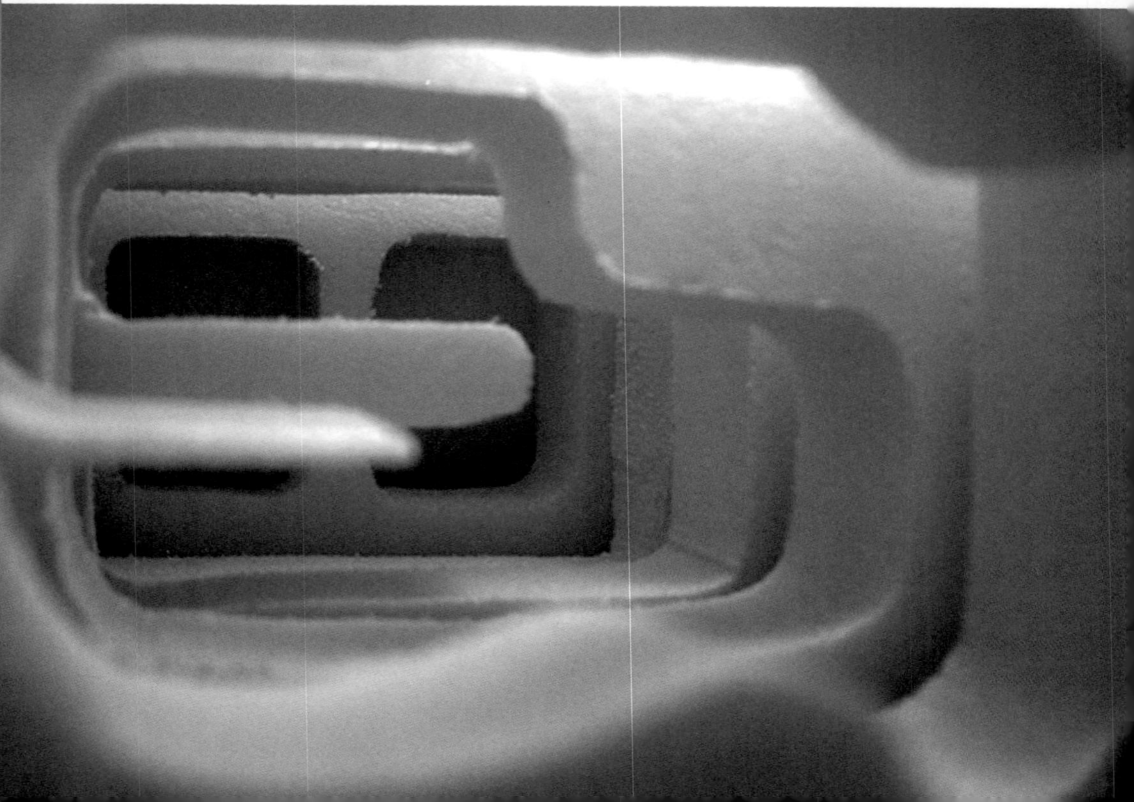

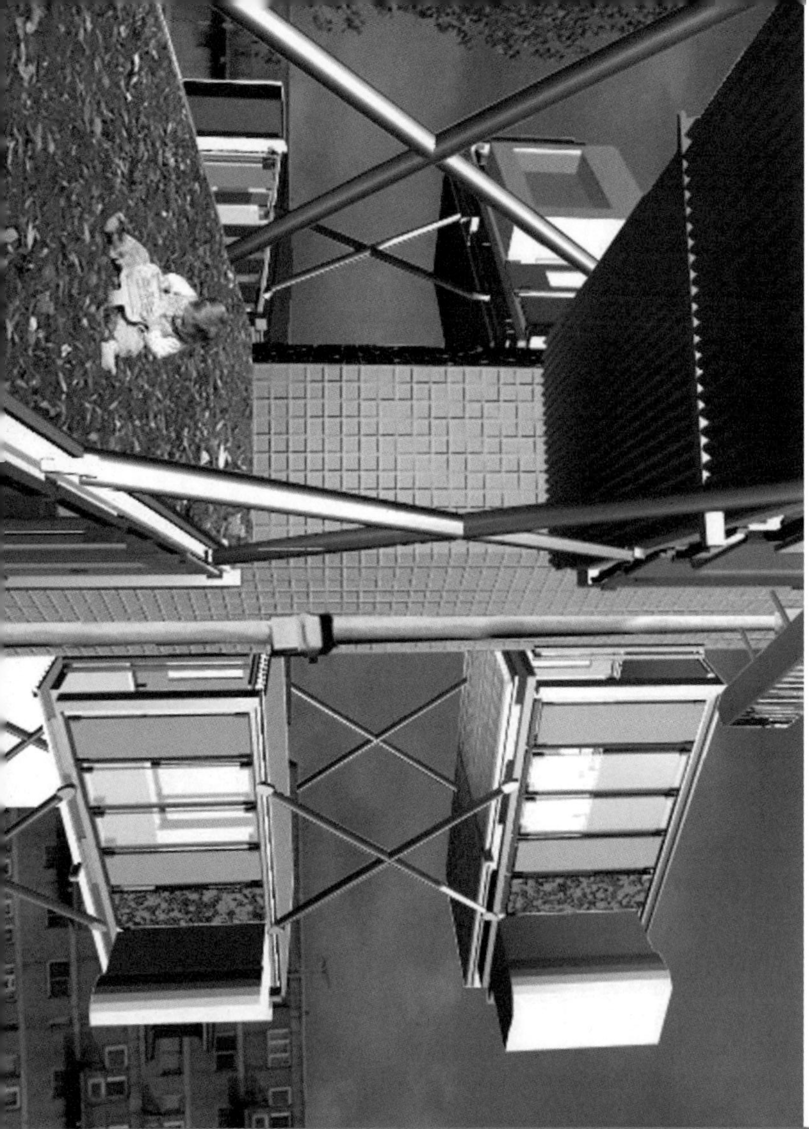

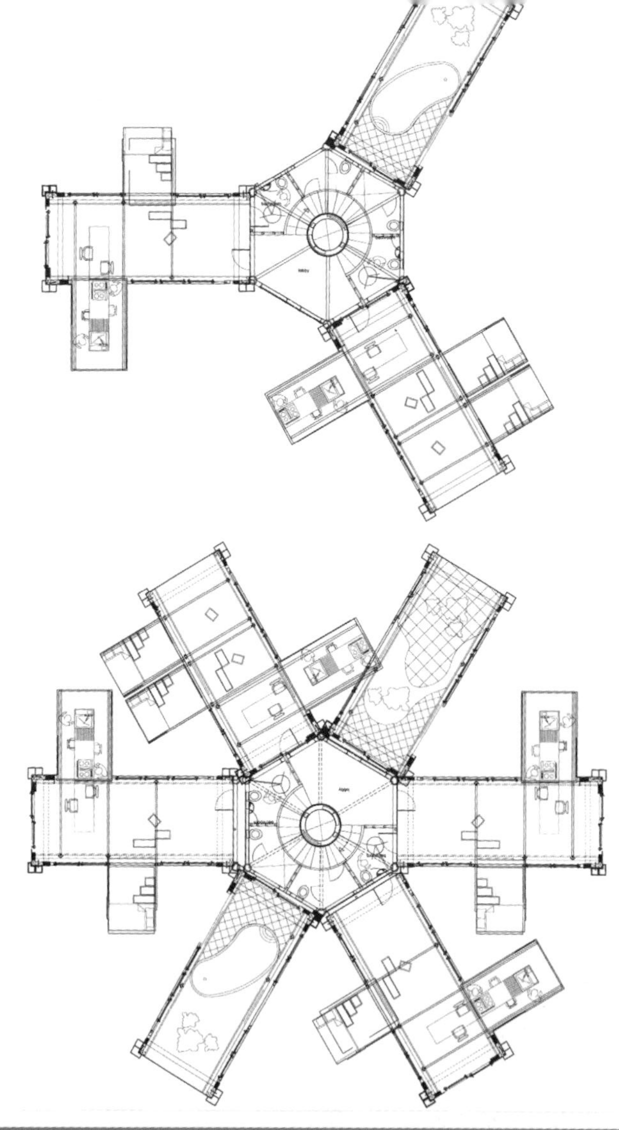

Spaces in _ between

Between the material and the immaterial, the public and the private, the temporary and the permanent, the solid and the fluid, the seeable and the unforseeable.

The personal: Unit 5 began the year with four short projects, self-contained episodic pieces about a spatial memory – a moment in time, the making and the materiality of an affinity object, the occupation of a non-place (1:1), and finally the construction of a small spatial fragment (1:1), to define a specific relationship between the inside and the outside.

These short projects helped define a way of looking at things and a kind of personal theme. The focus was on trying to find methods to translate specific immaterial, phenomenal observations into different forms of materiality, which were then analysed and rationalised through drawing.

The final 1:1 constructed fragment established the raw idea for a specific spatiality that was carried into the next project. This started in Istanbul, with the capturing and definition of an everyday urban event – another moment in time.

The public: Back in London the Istanbul event became the guide and the tool for finding and defining a site in Kingsland Road. By overlaying special qualities of the site with the extracted themes from Istanbul, rules were established, tested, discarded and reinvented towards the proposal for a small public space in between.

Unit Staff
Katrin Lahusen
Jamie Fobert

Students
Farah Azizan
Alex Chalmers
Diego Garcia Scaro
Therese Hegland
Suk-Kyu Hong
Ruth Kedar
Kun Min Kim
Marie Langen
Hoi Chi Ng
Spencer Owen
Tania Rodriguez

Critics
Miraj Ahmed
Carolina Bartram
Peter Beard
Valentin Bontjes van Beek
Javier Castañon
Shin Egashira
Jonathan Sergison
David van Handel
Mark Hemel
Takuro Hoshino
Andreas Lang
George Liaropoulos-Legendre
Ana Liu
Duncan Macaulay
Mohsen Mostafavi
Irénée Scalbert
Goswin Schwendinger
Charles Tashima
Mike Tonkin
Mike Weinstock

Special thanks to:
Petra Marguc
Chris Pauling
Diana Periton

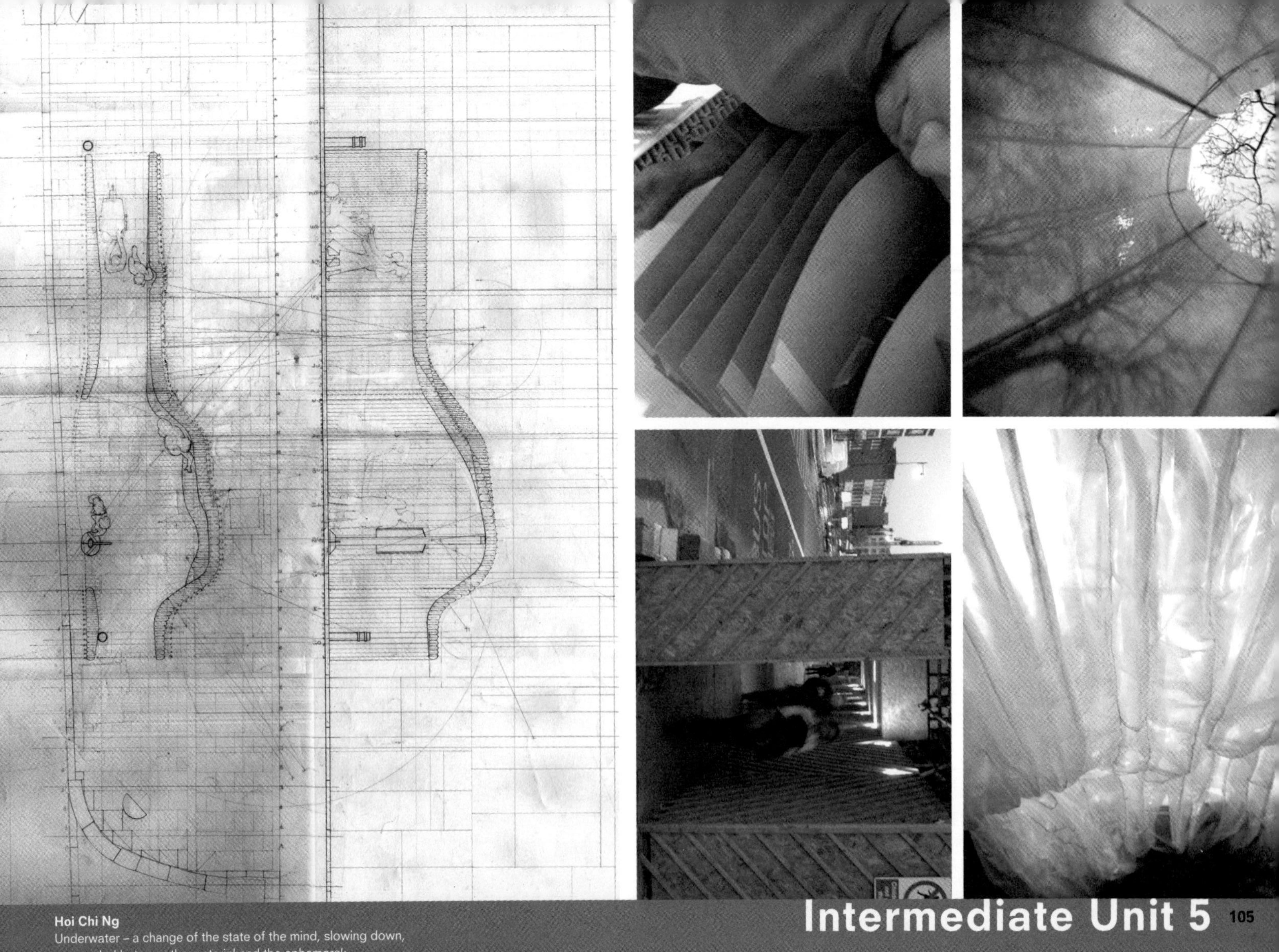

Intermediate Unit 5

Hoi Chi Ng
Underwater – a change of the state of the mind, slowing down, suspended between the material and the ephemeral;
the inflated bus stop – a space which could be there and not be there, a space which creates a moment of intimacy in Kingsland Road between waiting for and getting on the bus

Ruth Kedar
A process of rearranging, of digging, casting and layering the movement of the earth defines the next location for one of the small gathering places – gathering rooms fitted into the ground like tea glasses into the hand

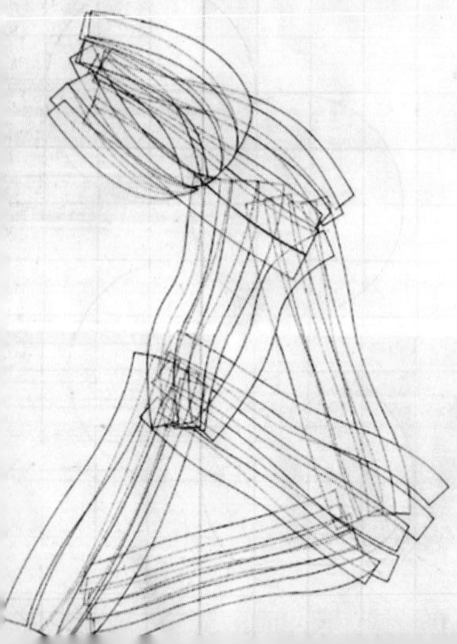

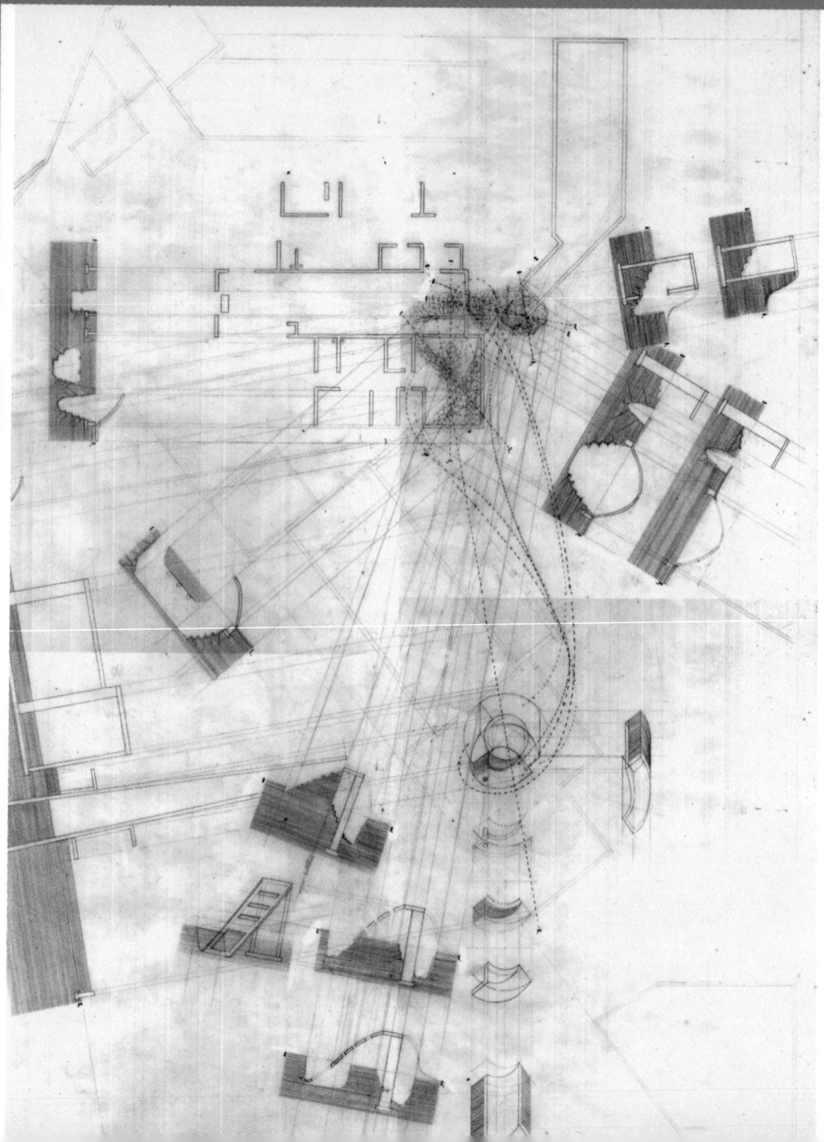

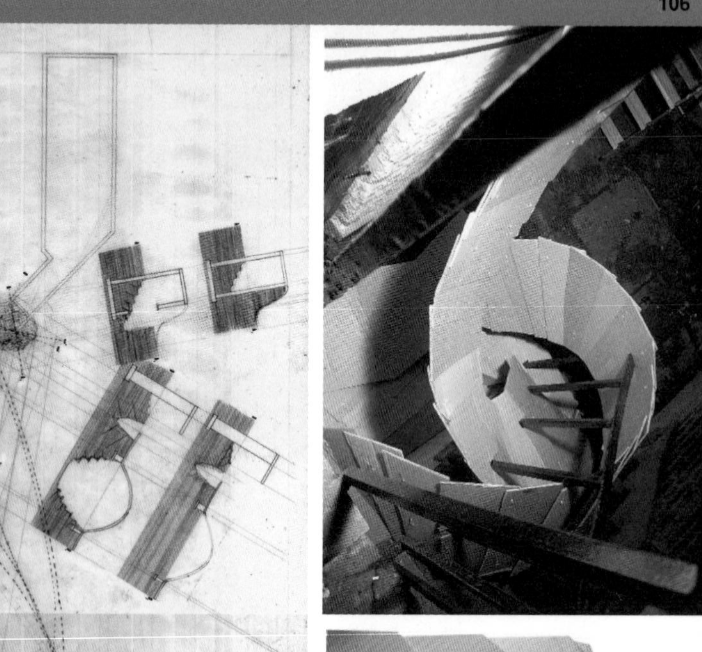

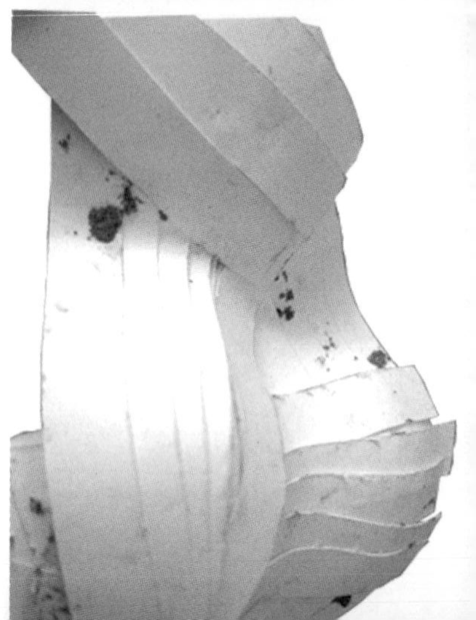

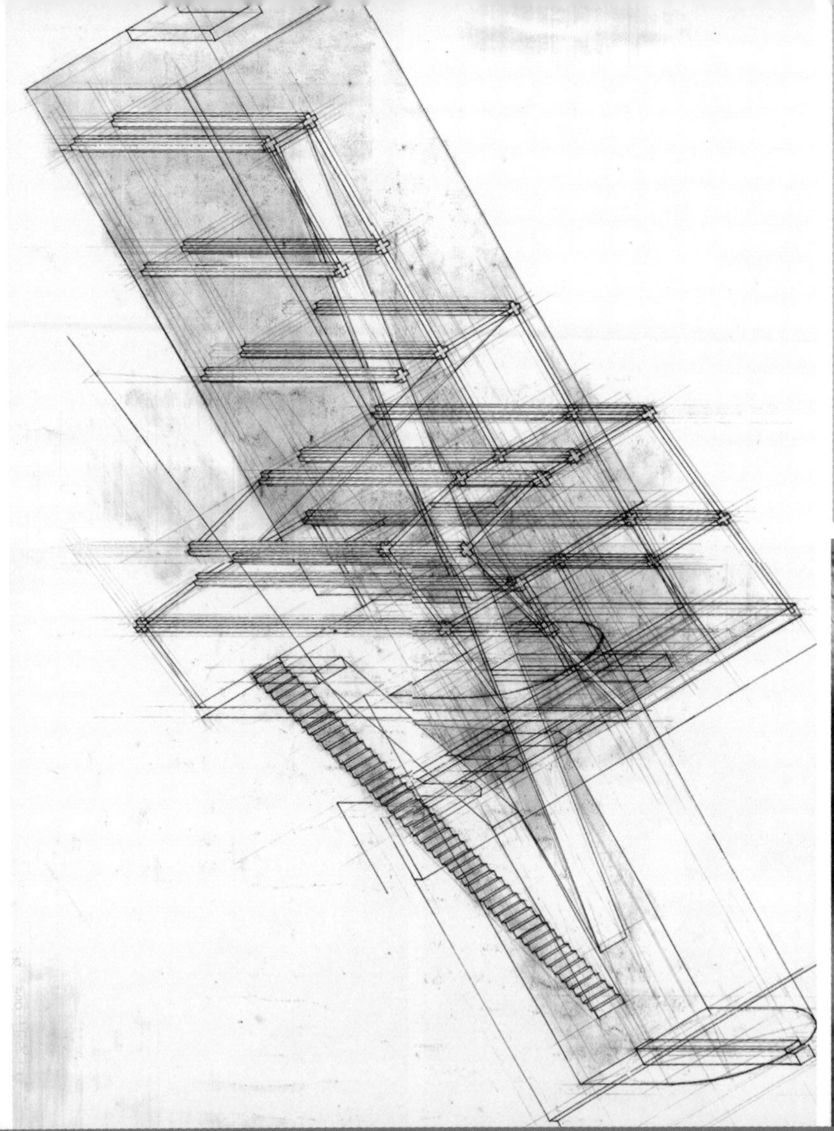

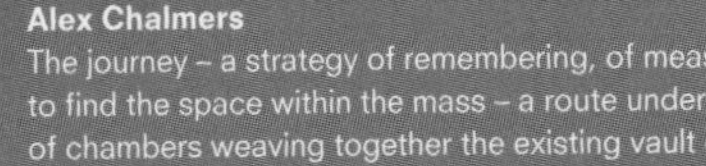

Alex Chalmers
The journey – a strategy of remembering, of measuring and of cutting to find the space within the mass – a route underground, a sequence of chambers weaving together the existing vault of the street, the church and the black room

Tania Rodriguez
Stability and presence of the form through a balance of forces,
gravity and tension balanced and frozen through time;
the final form becomes the trace, the memory of this process
like the memory of growth still visible in the fossil

Kun Min Kim
A web of balcony/bridgelike connections between existing rooms; small half-public enclosures and pathways for sitting, meeting, talking, a potential, temporary extension of private space

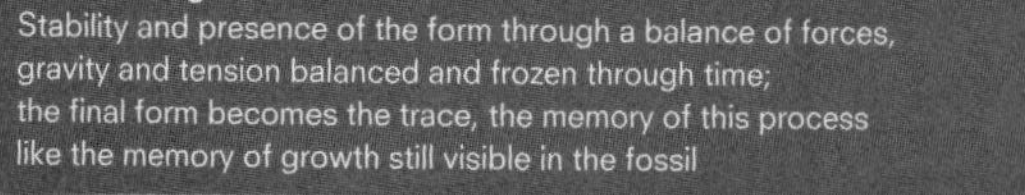

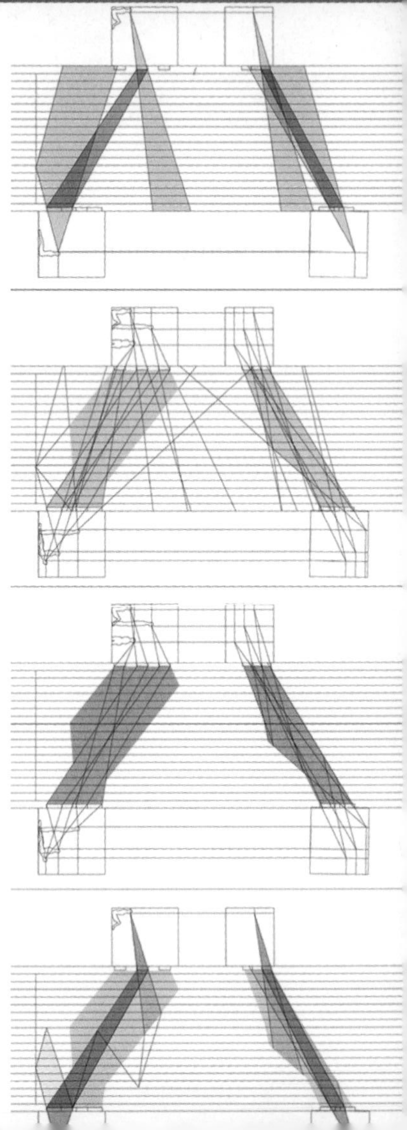

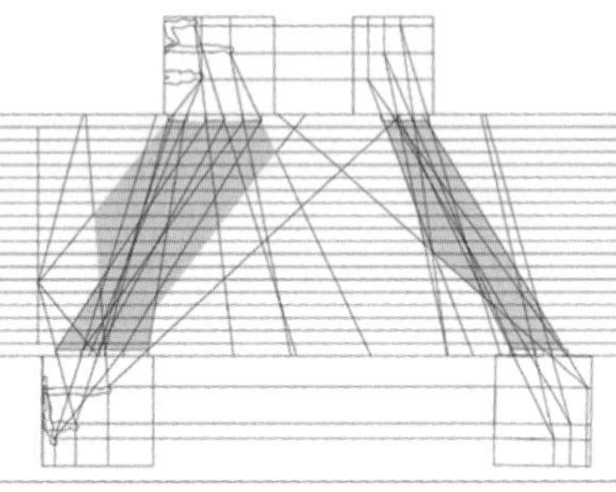

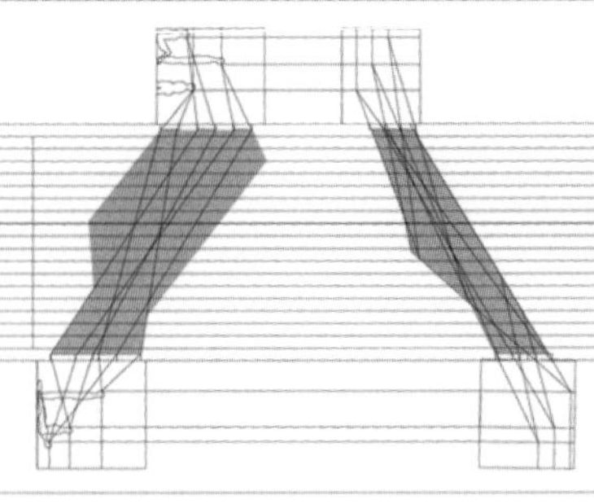

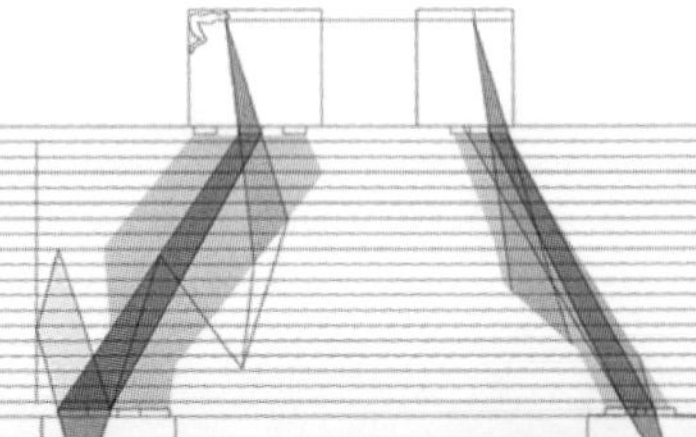

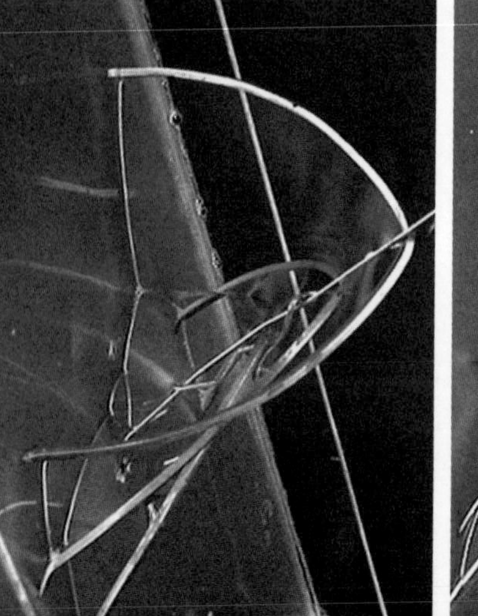

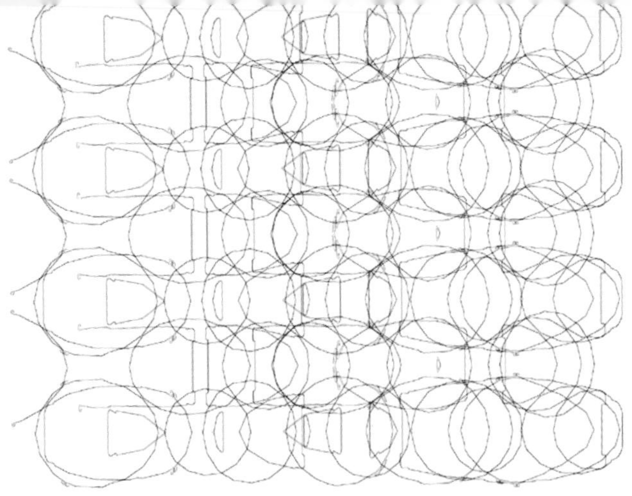

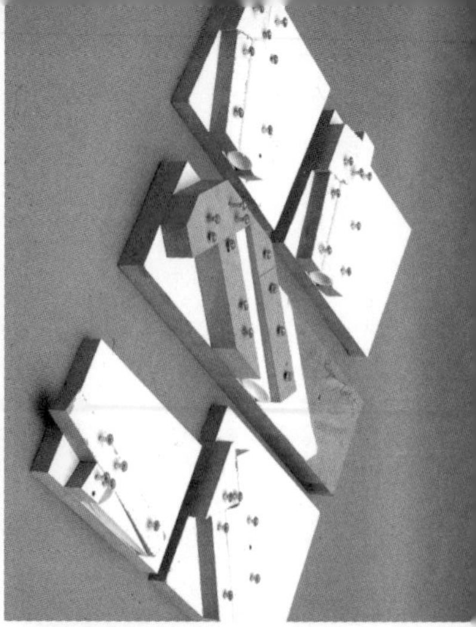

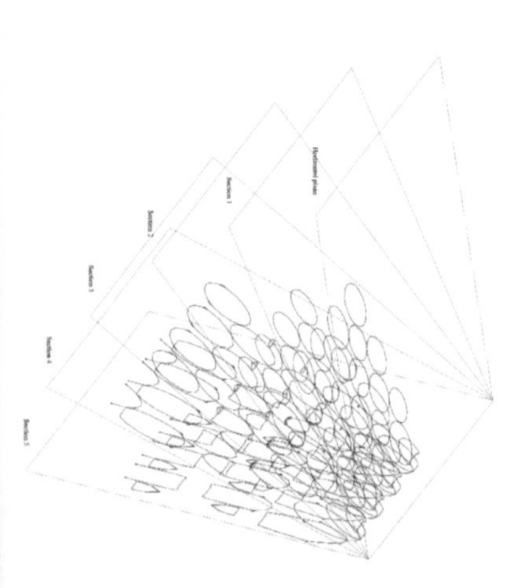

Suk Kyu Hong

A dream – liquid wax in flowing water, a frozen moment
the object of immeasurable spatial complexities
pipes and cups; raw material for testing strategies of cutting,
assembling and overlaying towards a complex structural system

Farah Azizan
A threshold – an urban 'paper' bag, a vessel of light echoing traces of urban life, a 'folded skin', suspended between the viaduct and the abandoned building

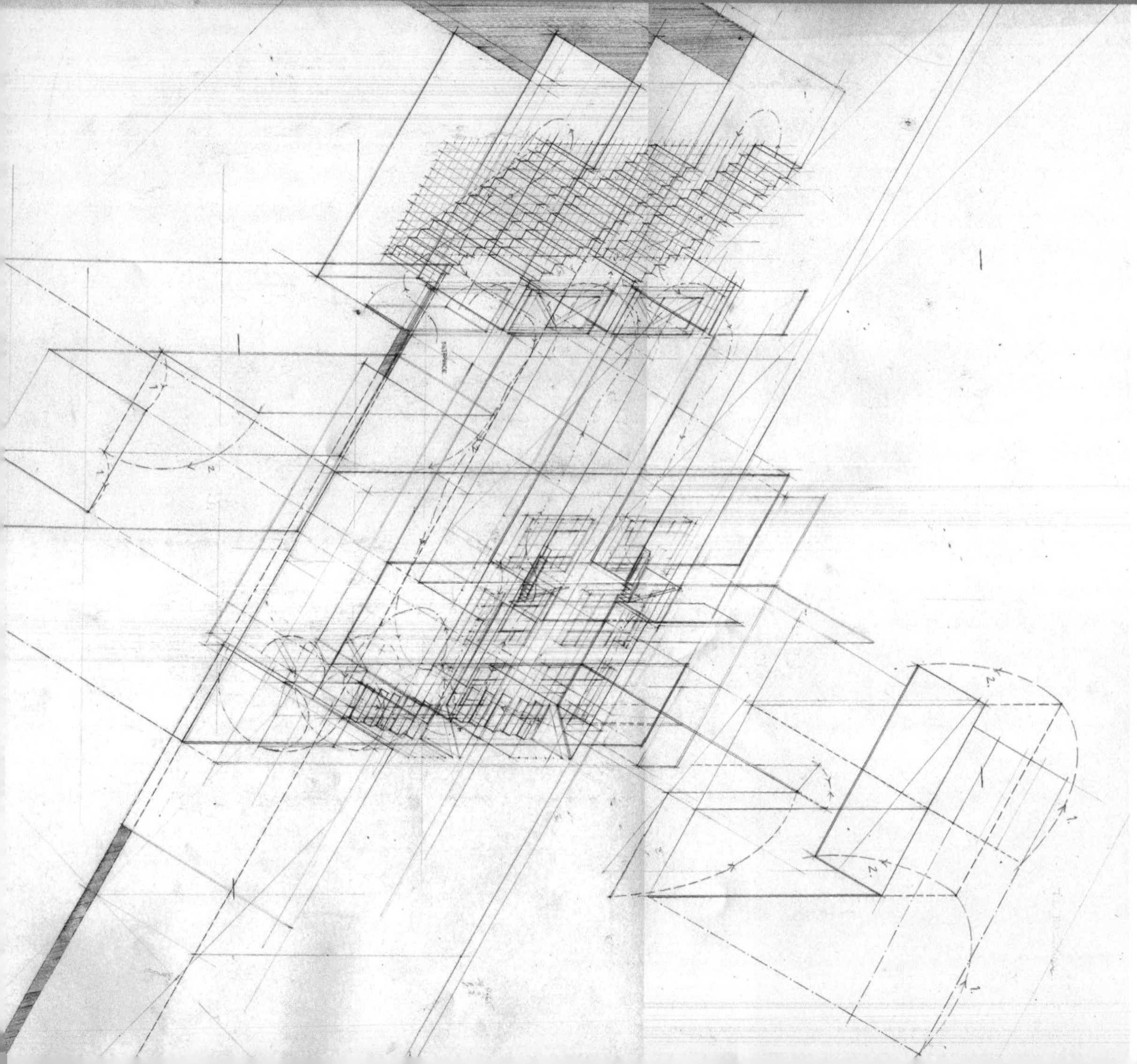

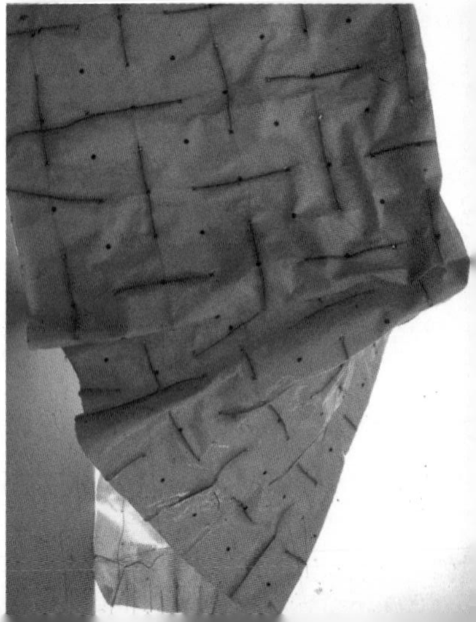

Marie Langen
A sequence – a double door, the urban void, the wax room – solidified light, a warm and quiet, half-open chamber suspended between the bridge and the canal

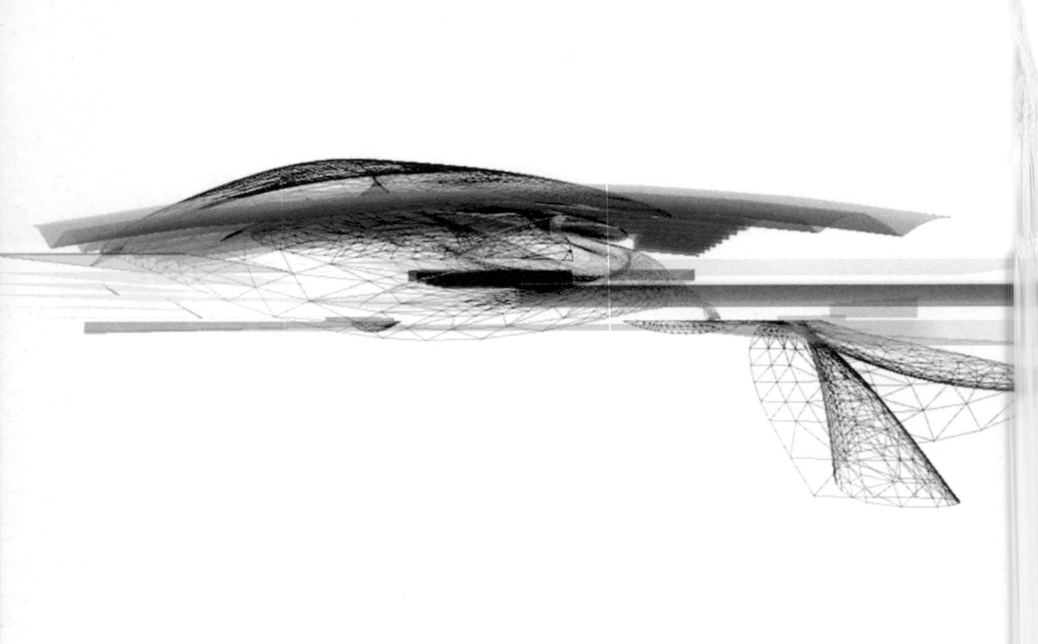

Emergenc[i]es: Territories and Agendas

Introduction

The core research of the unit is in developing new approaches to architectural design. Our attempts a underpinned by two main contentions; that architecture should be conceived using three-dimensional media and that form and programme should develop simultaneously and interactively. The use of digit media is not an end in itself for the unit; it is predominantly a pedagogic tool. Through creative engagement with modern technologies, which we believe to offer the greatest area of opportunity for t contemporary designer, we hope to develop a better understanding of our decision-making processes d through this understanding extend our effectiveness as architects.

Discussions that bear on whether or not an approach is process-driven are common in architectural education. We would like to think we infiltrate both territories; the most apposite summati f the unit's strategy was set out by A N Whitehead, writing in 'Process and Reality' on art and architectur 'Order is not sufficient. What is required, is something much more complex. It is order entering upon novelty; so that the massiveness of order does not degenerate into mere repetition; and so that the nov is always reflected upon a background of system.'

Process and Technique

The unit works through observation, recording, datascaping and synthesis, which are conceived as me whereby multiple fragments of each project are developed simultaneously in a dynamic system. Digital technologies are employed from the outset of each project, allowing seamless interplay between multidimensional inputs and outputs.

While computer based tools can facilitate the production of work that would be prohibitively difficult to accomplish by any other means, students are encouraged to take a critical position with resp to their chosen means of production and media of display. We take the view that all modes and mechanisms of production and representation are themselves sites; for instance, the operating ideologi that inform the development of the software applications we use present particular difficulties in this regard, being based, in the main, on crude approximations of physical processes. In order to move beyc

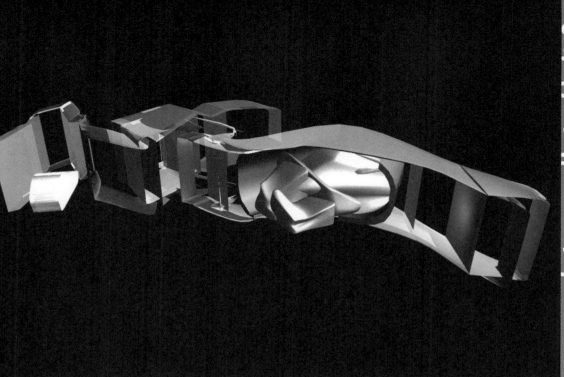

Vanessa Poon

Unit Staff
John Bell
Theo Lorenz

Technical Tutor
Aran Chadwick

Students
Chi-Kit Cheung
Teresa Cheung
Nicolas Durr
Federico Ferrari
SoonTak Joo
Justin Lau
Paula Nascimento
Charles Peronnin
Vanessa Poon
Yee Seng Tan
Stephanie Talbot (Term 1)
Michel'angelo Ziccarelli

The unit would like to thank
Shumon Basar
Adam Covell
Jon Goodbun
David Greene
Charles Holland
Nathaniel Kolbe
Gunther Koppelhuber
Haruo Morishima
Mohsen Mostafavi
Joel Newman
Keith Priest
Kevin Rhowbotham
Charles Tashima
Kim Thornton
Filip Visnijic
And anyone else we may have forgotten...

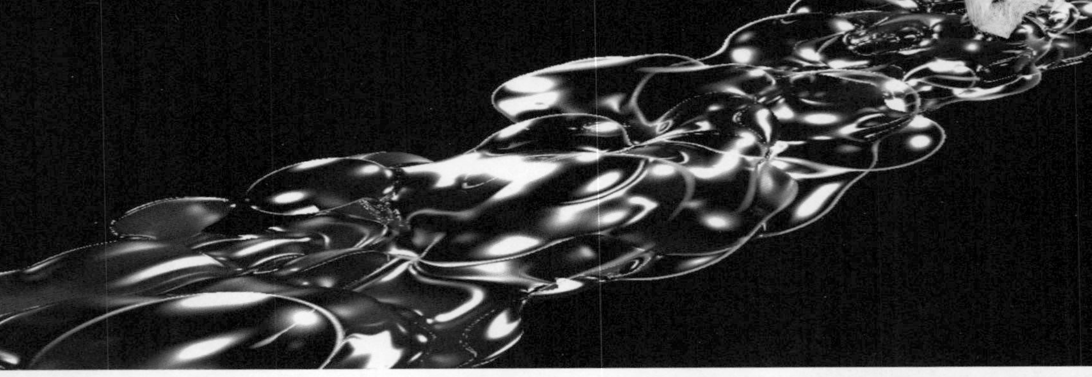

Yee Seng Tan

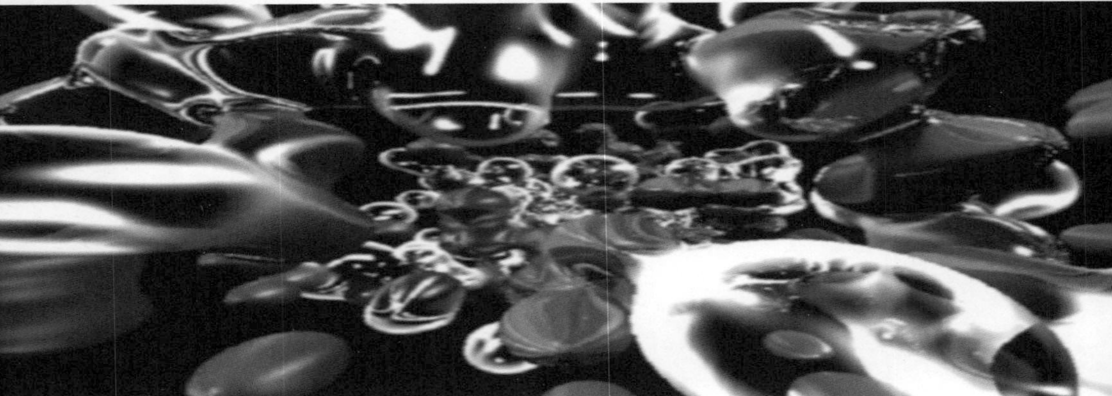

Yee Seng Tan

the restrictions of 'proper' operation, we encourage the creative misuse of all available information systems.In that anyone with a modern laptop is now able to transform constellations of temporal, vector, textual and bitmap data simultaneously and with relative ease, critical and pedagogic approaches in the unit bear upon the points of emergence of propositions. As we must make proposals that are fixed in some way out of a nonhierarchical set of geometric, programmatic, technological and cultural information, outside of fixed relation or position, choice is immanent: each member of the unit is encouraged to develop their own protocols in order to be able to operate in these conditions of continual flux.

In this second year of the unit, we continued our interest in design development through the construction of a multimedia machine, a generating device where formal and programmatic outputs become the metadata of the emergent proposal. As it is pivotal to understanding the work produced by the unit, we have set out the process in some detail here.

Students first constructed a piece of work that presented their site survey information in an interactive form. The content of these surveys was varied, but centrally comprised video journeys around or to the airport, photographic recordings of aspects of the life and function of the airport, text and diagrammatic materials that individuals had chosen as starting points of interest (these being derived from observations of the processes, rituals and apparent requirements of entering or occupying airside). We discussed this post-passport-control area as a 'third place', revisiting a term we had initially appropriated from computer-game advertising, though finding other resonances in anthropology. First interpreted as a space of unfranchised occupation in the urban play project, which began the year, it was now extended to begin to define the space of geotemporal and political ambiguities we were researching.

Utilising the fact that, in organising data, we privilege in time and space those things that we consider, for whatever reasons, to be of greatest interest or import, and capitalising on the operating paradigm of Macromedia Director as a two-dimensional stage upon which sprites play out preprogrammed or interactive operations, we first reviewed the interactives as objects in themselves. This criticism was intended to begin a discursive elaboration of each individual's points of interest and engagement with the site. We then returned to the proposals and began an interrogation of their structure. When an interactive presentation is seen as a collection of sets of x-y data, with each set extended along its own z axis of time, it becomes possible to use this data in many ways to construct form.

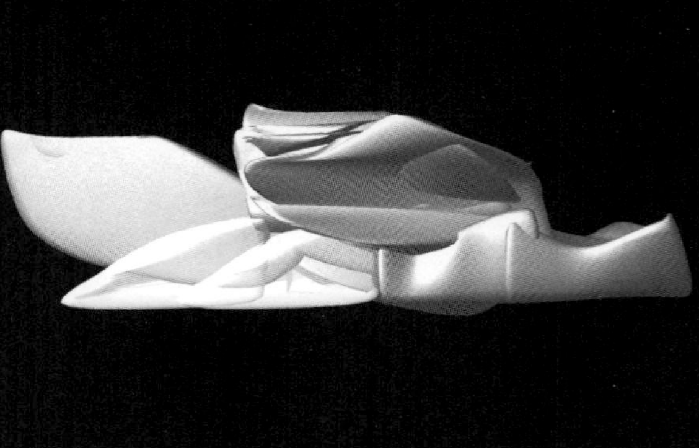

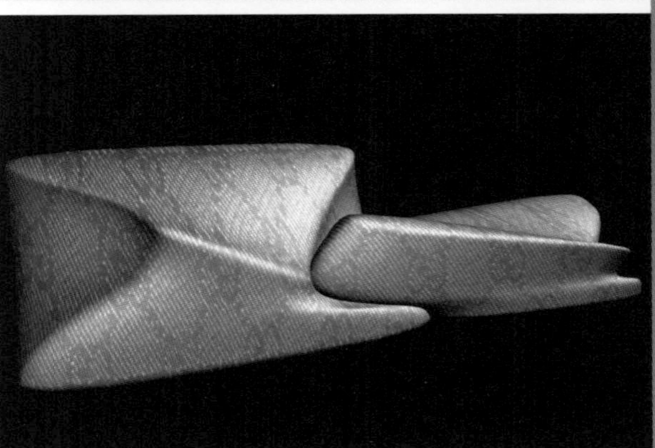

Paula Nascimento
Vanessa Poon

The main technique for the next iteration of the process was the time-based section. We exported frames and timelines into Lightwave 3D, a modelling and animation application most commonly used in the film and broadcast industries. We then set cut frequencies and orientations through the body of the now fully spatialised multimedia object. The conceptual driver was to take a deliberately warped vision of this paradigmatic modernist projection as a starting point, which introduced discussions on the place and type of drawing in architecture in the expanded field of digital operations. This model was then interrogated using the Lightwave virtual camera in a process of recursive visualisation, which facilitated a return to discussions about projective geometries and cinematography, begun in the first term, but now with particular emphasis on animation, metrics and motion dynamics.

Work was then examined, and modified by the use of sampling techniques; as all operations were nondestructive, this process should not be seen as merely convenient attenuation, but rather as a means of interpreting data and finding new possibilities in each construction. The sampling method we used was based on point sampling, a technique commonly used in biological surveys, where a grid overlaid on the site creates intersections at which to record information. This data can then be used to construct an understanding of the informational surface as extrapolation of sample frequency. The act of sampling in this context resonates with the technique as used in modern music; the sampled trace retains a sense of its prior context and is potentially 'legible'. These resonances and extrapolations are employed as generators within the design process of each project.

Students were encouraged to interpret their production as a surface from which productive directions could arise at any point. These vectors could then be recombined into the developing project, which was itself the product of many such recursive operations.

Conclusion

These operations can produce high levels of formal and programmatic complexity, which we contend are commensurate with minimum conditions for entering into any form of architectural design. The exact techniques and protocols used by each individual were not set in advance. The ability to shift the production of primary form into a process that conflates morphology and use, simultaneously developing both strands through shape-based elaboration, capitalises on what we believe to be the architect's bias

Justin Lau

towards the visual while avoiding premature conceptual or architectonic closure. Objects produced by these processes offered rich surfaces for subsequent interrogation and development. It is important to note that the final projects are not direct transcriptions of their generative diagrams, the distinctions between metadata, data about data, and the more familiar architectural diagram, were identified as the intersection of pretectonic and architectonic working. The site of production is, then, always the transforming site-object dyad, lodged within a very particular notion of contextualism. Possibly, and despite appearances, there is no tabula rasa here.

The Projects

The year was structured around two projects, Urban Play and Airside. The first project also acted as the vehicle for introducing the software applications, which are the primary design tools in the unit. The second afforded the opportunity to implement newly acquired skills in a more extensive and ambitious proposal.

Urban Play

'We must not forget that an object is the best messenger of a world above that of nature: one can easily see in an object at once a perfection and an absence of origin, a closure and a brilliance, a transformation of life into matter (matter is much more magical than life) and in a word a silence which belongs to the world of fairy-tales.'
Roland Barthes, 'Mythologies'

Proposals were developed for ludic activity outside the ambit of conventional urban planning and architecture; an acknowledgement of our irrepressible desire for apparently pointless fun. Proposals ranged from a device for making people temporarily invisible to a game played over wireless networks along bus routes. The notion that play gave access to a 'third place' was considered; a place of temporary autonomy, where, for a moment people might find themselves freed from the vicissitudes of day-to-day routine. This project concluded in Percent for Play, a public presentation with fxv.org at the Architecture Foundation, as part of the London Calling project.

Airside

'I suspect that the airport will be the true city of the 21st century. The great airports of the planet are already the suburbs of an invisible world capital, a virtual metropolis whose faubourgs are named Heathrow, Kennedy, Charles de Gaulle, Nagoya, a centripetal city whose population forever circles its notional centre, and will never need to gain access to its dark heart.' – J G Ballard

The desire for unmediated contact – seeing with one's own eyes – provided the initial impetus for this project and its site: airside.

We researched the airport environment with particular emphasis on two groups: the business traveller and the tourist. Despite the best efforts of the proponents of broadband communications, virtual presence and the multimedia teleconference, business travel remains an obstinate fact. Being there is still perceived as a necessity for much commerce, with the immateriality of telepresence still a poor second. Given the persistence of the frequent flier, of real rather than virtual distance, the limited velocity of a passenger plane and the body's homeostatic love affair with circadian rhythms, the certainty of jet lag becomes a significant factor in the experience of transcontinental relations, with obvious penalties for the traveller involved in any commercial process. Although the physiological effects of long-distance travel are of less critical moment for the leisure traveller or tourist, they still pertain. We have considered the present conditions and possible future design of airside as a leisure facility, and assessed the possibilities for life there in terms of dwell time, activity and experience. For both sectors of our study, certain questions emerged as key issues. These were summed up as centring on the nature of our chosen site as a particular and identifiable place, and its status with respect to local and global time: where is airside, and when, exactly, is it?

Students were free to choose the airport. The site for educational or hypothetical architectural projects is, of course, always more than a geographical location; it might be seen as a territory across and through which information flows – cultural, technological, institutional, temporal – and possibly only then geographic.

Final proposals include a permeable agora for Chep Lap Kok; art space and dynamic retail and transfer environments at Heathrow; and a peripatetic event space.

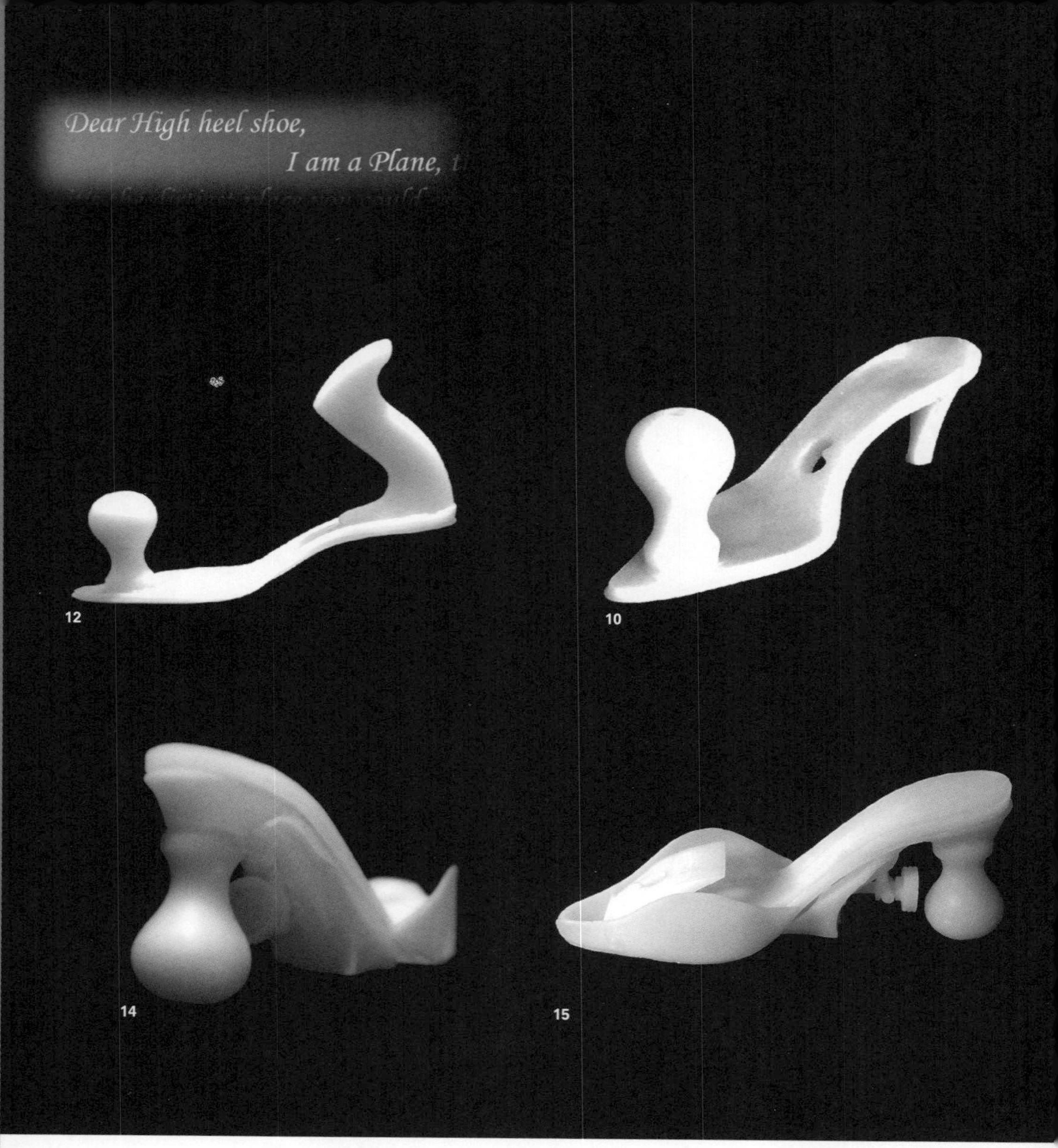

The Catalogue of Transplantation
10 Untitled: A subtle way to repress the idea of subvert. It depicts the idea of how to transplant the essential moment.
12 Planeshoe: Assembling the form. Impressive with the context of the subvert idea, but creativity is restricted.
13 Right Plane: Literally transplant the component of the plane to the shoe. The image shows the strong impact of subvert but is too obvious.
14 Angle's Shoe: A link to continue the idea of narrative.
15 Round Heel Shoe: Aside from the appearance, it also subverts the function. It is a summary of all the subvert ideas.

Dear High heel shoe,

I am a Plane,

12

10

14

15

Unit Tutors
David Racz
Andreas Lang

Students
Francesco Brenta
Anuk Chayapak
Marija Gonopolskaja
Maria Kalapanida
Maria Kouloumbri
Henry Leung
Eiichi Matsuda
Satoshi Nishio
Tom Smith
Yuka Suganami
Eldon Tam

Intermediate 7 would like to thank
Mohammad Baktashian
Sue Barr
Carolina Bartram
John Bell
Valentin Bontjes van Beek
Celine Condorelli
Sandra Denicke
Chris Dondorp
Tak Hoshino
Mark Hemel
Michael Hensel
Johannes Käferstein
Torange Khonsari
Habib and Minu Khonsari
Katrin Lahusen
Marcellus Letang
Petra Marguc
Mohsen Mostafavi
Chris Pauling
Diana Periton
Natasha Sandmeier
Goswin Schwendinger
Rassa Sheikh and family
Charles Tashima
Michael Weinstock

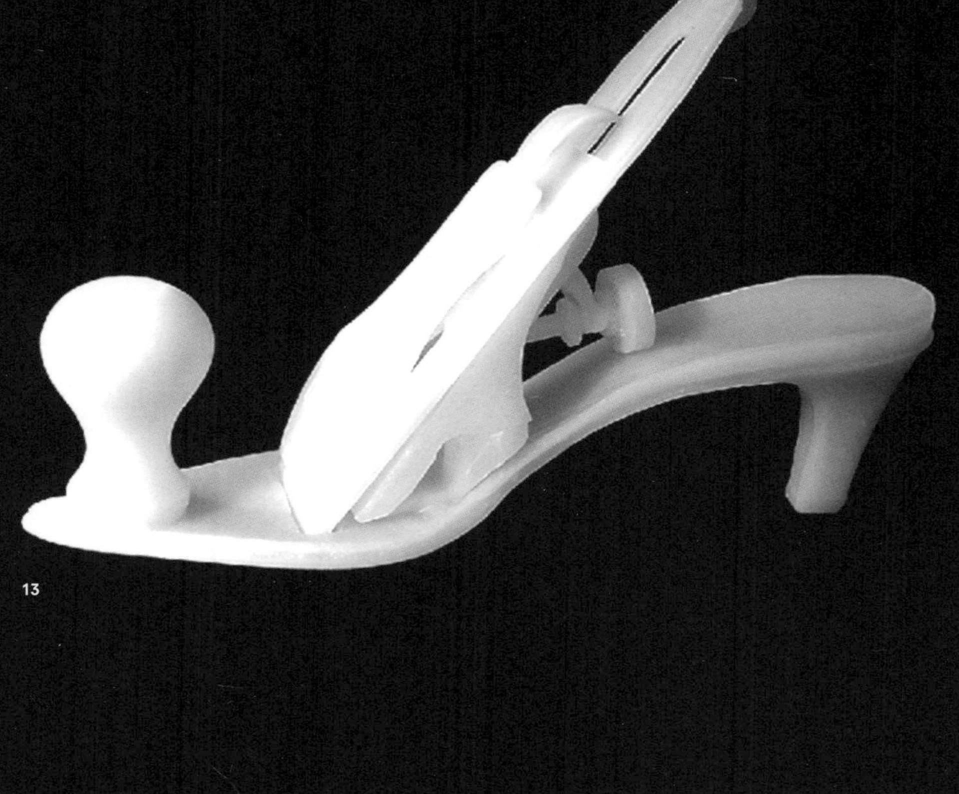

13

The primary concern of the unit programme has been to encourage students to develop a central issue in their work to help focus and relate different elements within the projects. Students have also been strongly encouraged to pursue an independent direction within the overall framework. This year the unit work has been structured around two major projects.

In the first project, the students selected an action from a list (embed, misregister, invert), chose an object that had accrued a value over time (for example, a wood plane or an espresso machine) and then subverted a value or characteristic of the object. Initially the object was drawn accurately to describe its qualities or functions. Then, using only the technique of casting, students made a series of objects. These could either be constructed from cast elements or used to explore the limitations of the process. The students gained control of the technique to embody their thoughts. The focus was on drawing, making and establishing the groundwork for the second half of the programme. The final project was located between a disused railway and Kingsland Road in Hackney. Students chose a site and developed a proposal for a performance space using criteria they had isolated either from the casting project or the unit study trip to Iran.

Unit trip to Iran, February 2002

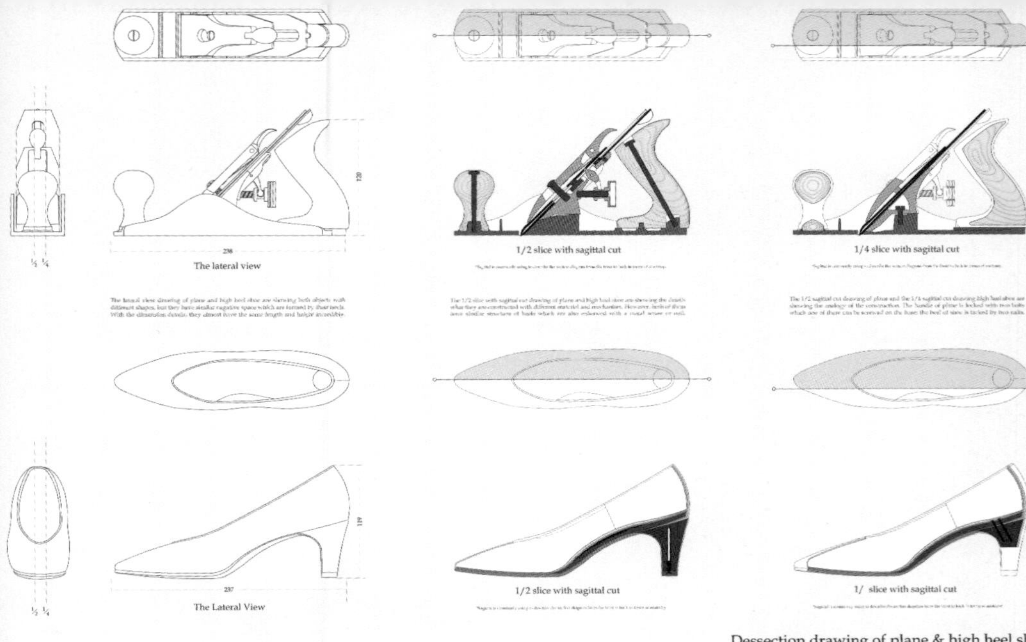

Dessection drawing of plane & high heel shoe

Studying the analogy in terms of their sizes, structures and materials

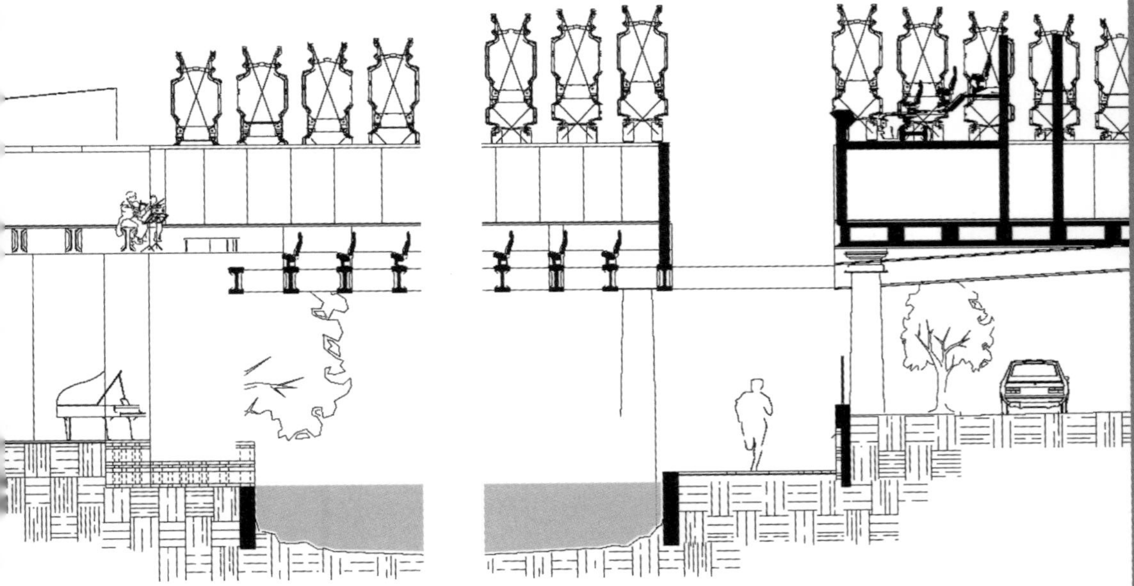

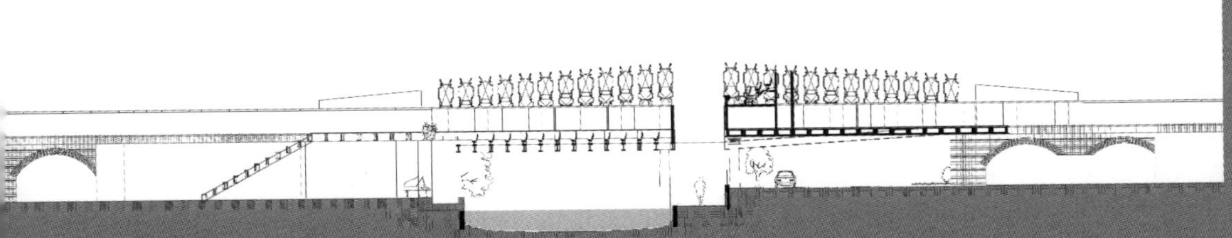

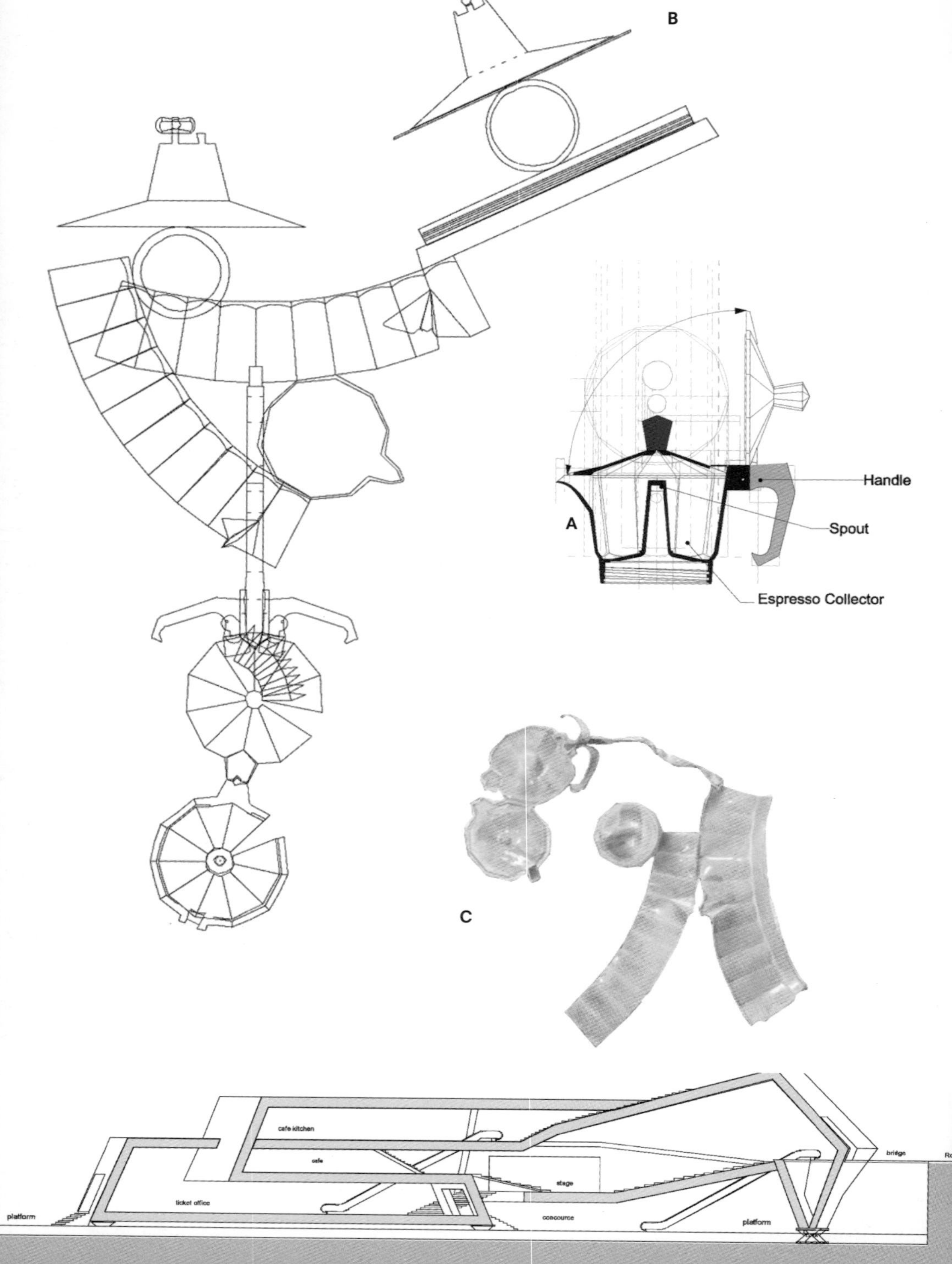
B
Handle
A
Spout
Espresso Collector
C
cafe kitchen
cafe
stage
ticket office
platform
concourse
platform
bridge

A original object: espresso maker
B unfolded surface of espresso maker
C unfolded silicon rubber register of original surface
D translation of surface onto unfolded klein bottle
E unfolded surface of station theatre
F refolding of surface

D

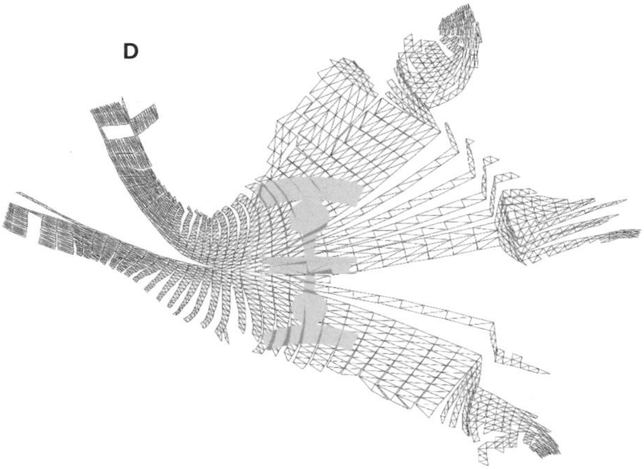

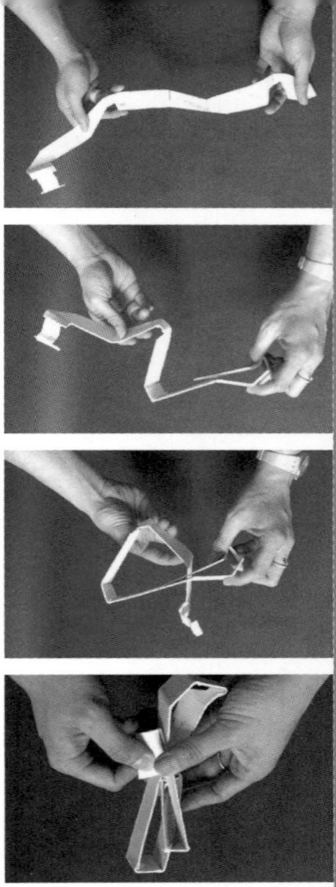

F

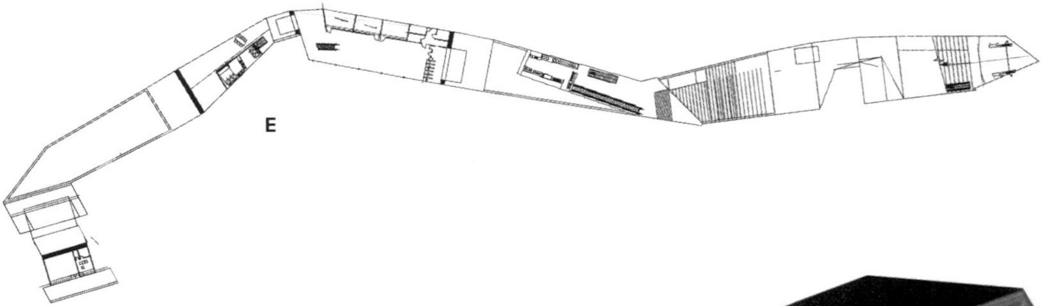

E

A Embed through folding

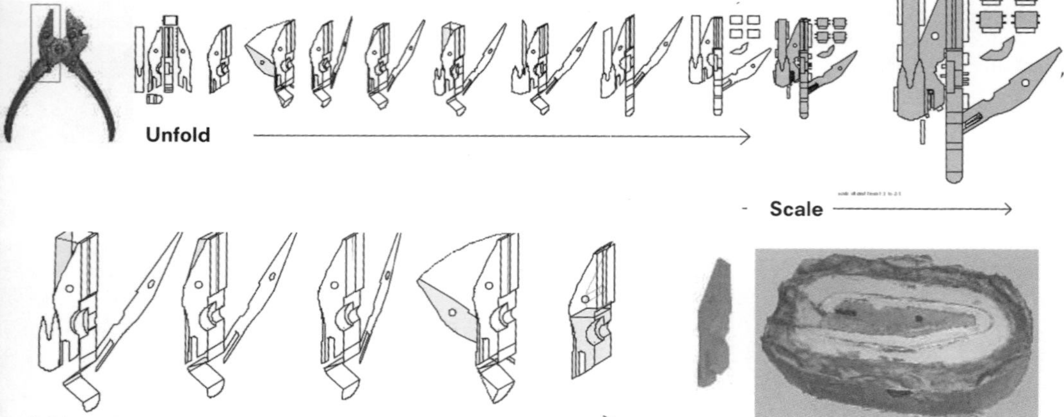

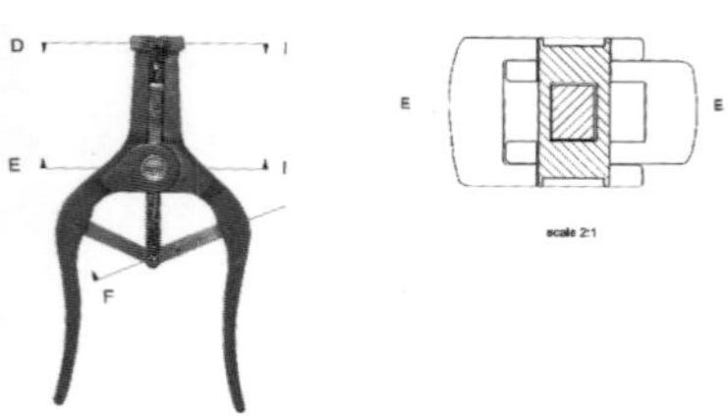

C Dynamic Embedding

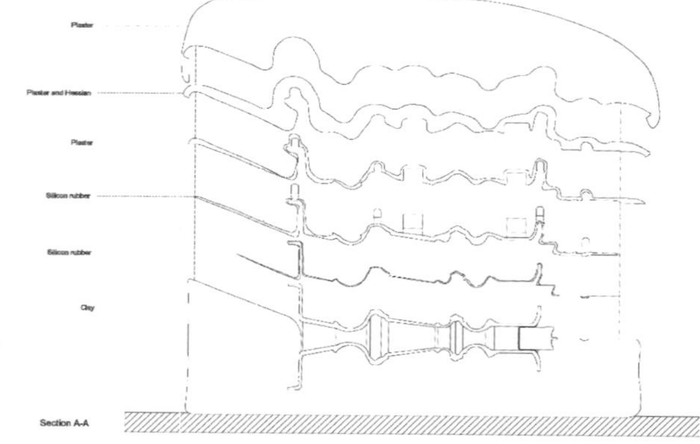

B Embedding through

A

B

C

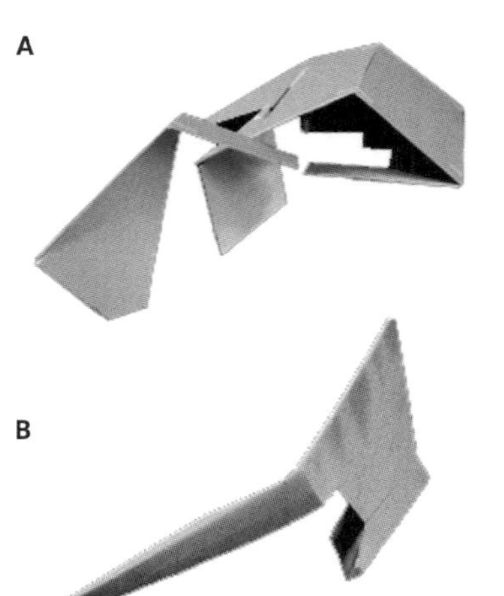

Embed,
You operate ambiguously and assertively
in the fluid realm of communication.
You are omniscient in the space between objects.
You embrace, you seal and you reject.
You bear the burden of information with alacrity.
You defy the proscriptions of scale.
You are pitifully dependent.

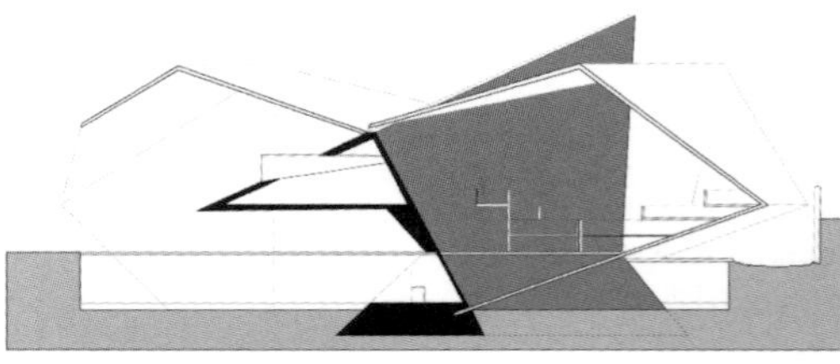

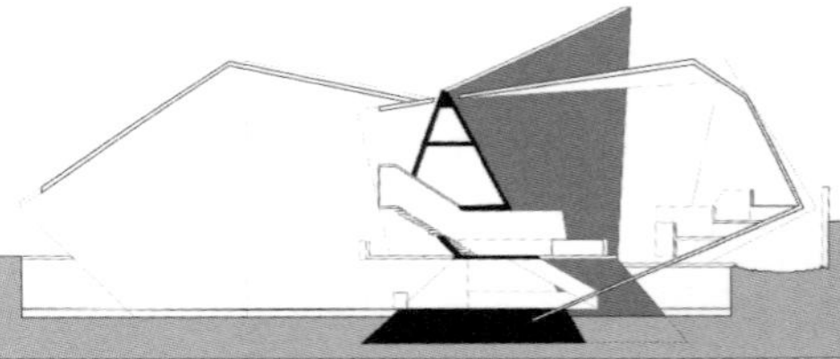

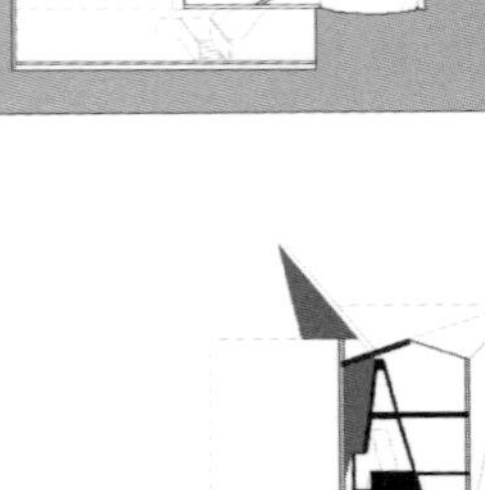

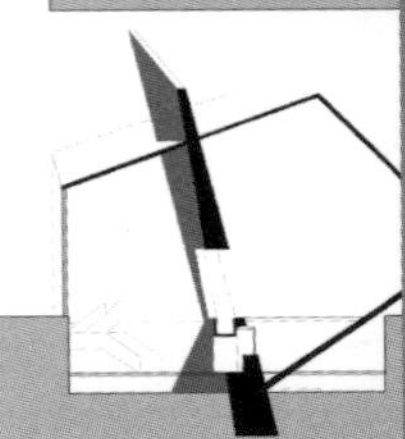

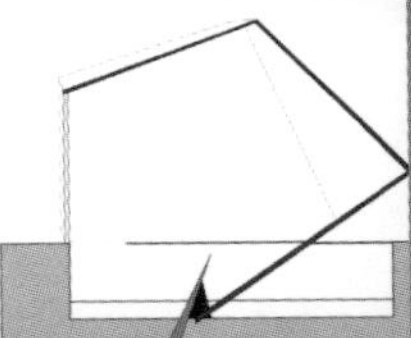

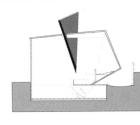

Embed,
I meekly follow your footprints
across the topography of registration.
I am confounded by your tendency to corrupt.
I am filled with admiration for your passivity.
I fear for your mishandling.
I am sceptical about your claims to interiority.
I commend your celebration of materiality.
I am most affectionately yours.

The work of the unit seeks architectural invention via strategies initially establishing imaginary, complex, and generic 'spatial structures' or fragments that emerge from an abstract game-like system called here a Topographical Fiction. As a general concept, the Topographical Fiction is any environment exhibiting a characteristic pattern of relations that is used projectively as a design tool. As a device, it is a process-driven, time-based game that is constructed via the incremental accumulation of multiple, independent strategies governed by both objective and subjective criteria. Similar to a game, these invented topographies are comprised of a 'field of play' or gameboard within which a series of programmes and events simultaneously interact. Once fabricated, fragments of the topography assume a second role – what originates as a simulation of urban processes later become generic sites or environments of 'spatial structures'. In process, students defined and tested a series of abstract terms and rules that were continuously re-articulated throughout the year. Instead of developing along a single all-encompassing 'idea', projects simultaneously integrated multiple rules and design criteria within a complex of relations. Similar to the layered development of the Topographical Fiction, particular interest was placed upon both coincident and independent investigations of two or more systems enabling not only their individual development but also the possibilities for recombination and conflict.

In the second half of the year architectural fragments were elaborated in collusion with a complex urban situation in Strebeniotis, Thessaloniki. This second site was not to be understood as the raison d'être of a design project but, rather, as yet another layer installed within the incremental process of the year. This deactivated military training area is one of a series of five large urban voids at the periphery of the city currently undergoing integration into the dense city fabric. To date, this site is the only one to be developed, but in a manner that has been no more than an ad hoc collection of public programmes which include schools and sport facilities. With a set of design tools in the form of rules and spaces, each student defined an architectural brief within the programme of sport. Issues within this programme included, among others, the spanning of large spaces, complex circulation systems, as well as the technical problem of defining large flat surfaces within a sectionally difficult topography. Despite addressing problems of the site and programme within the scale of 1:200, the ultimate motivation for the work was to produce generic architectural structures and strategies that could be adapted in other, future sites. Throughout, the notion of play affirmed the importance of various modes of architectural thought, fluctuating from moments of uncertainty, reflection, evaluation and reconfiguration; for rules are written within continuous processes of negotiation.

Unit Master
Charles Tashima

Students
Stefania Batoeva
Katrin Eliasdottir
Flavia Foguel
Hongbin Lu
Patty Lui
Joana Pacheco
Isabel Pietri Medina
Valeria Segovia
Adiam Sertzu
Phivos Skroumbelos
Yeojoong Yang

Visiting Critics
Peter Beard
John Bell
Peter Carl
Javier Castañon
Jean Michel Crettaz
Martine De Maeseneer
Alex de Rijke
Jamie Fobert
Ines Geisler
Ludo Grooteman
Jenny Jones
Johannes Käferstein
Joe Kerr
Neil Leach
Regine Leibinger
George Liaropoulos-Legendre
C.J. Lim
Theo Lorenz
Wolf Mangelsdorf
Julia Mauser
Florian Migsch
Spela Mlakar
Robin Monotti Graziadei
Michel Mossessian
Robert Mull
Ciro Najle
Dominic Papa
Annabelle Perdomo
Natasha Sandmeier
Pascal Schöning
Patrik Schumacher
Luis Viu Rebes
Caroline Voet
Eyal Weizman

Special thanks to
Charis Christodoulou
Vilma Hastaoglou-Martinidis
Marina Lathouri
Morten Ludviksen
Tino Schädler
Eva and Kostas Skroumbelos

In memory of
Yorgos Simeoforidis

Group Work
Site 1: Topographical Fiction III
7 of 11 layers from 8 panels

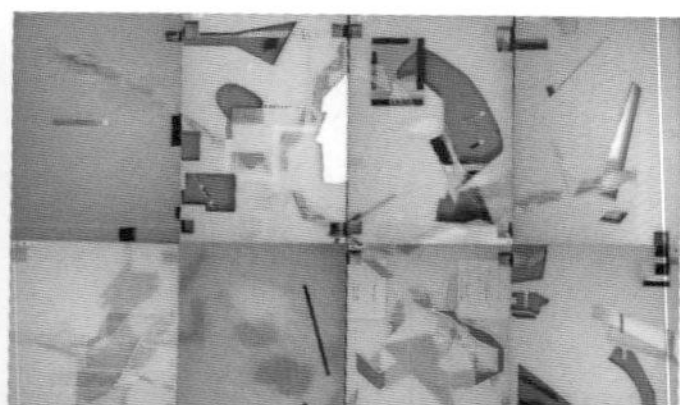

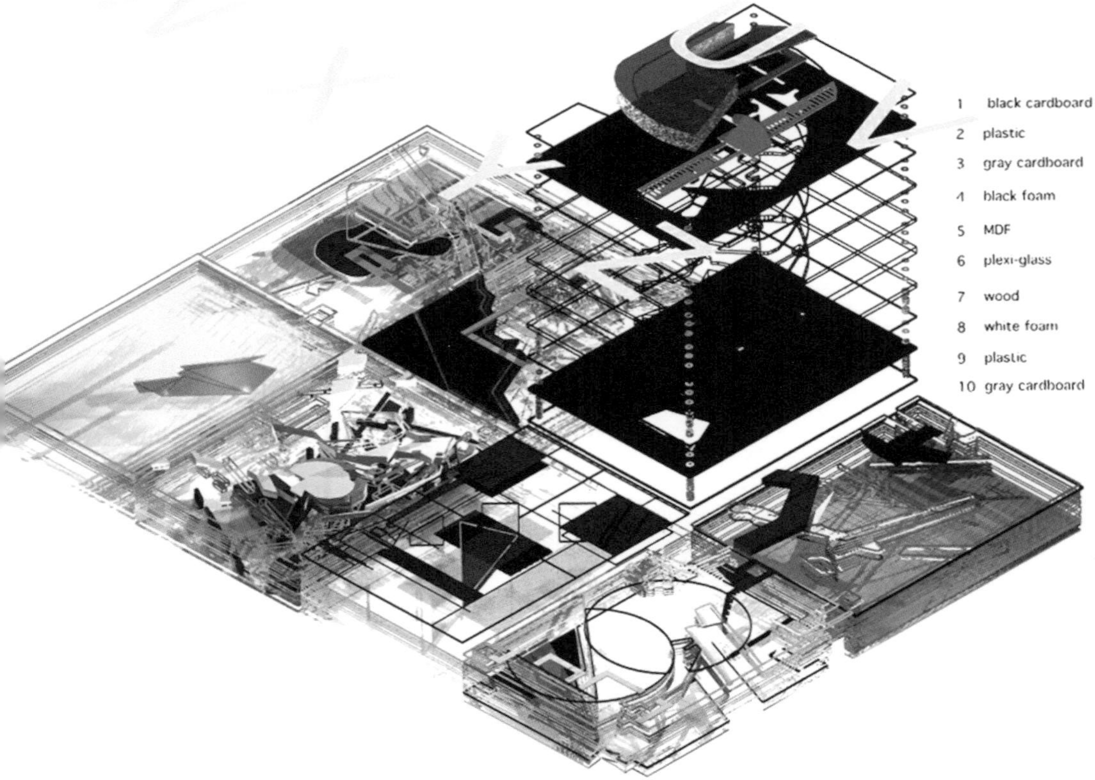

1 black cardboard
2 plastic
3 gray cardboard
4 black foam
5 MDF
6 plexi-glass
7 wood
8 white foam
9 plastic
10 gray cardboard

Phivos Skroumbelos
Axonometric overview of Topographical Fiction III

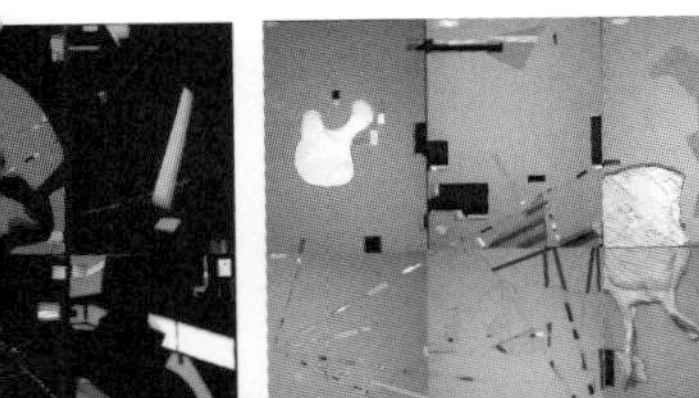

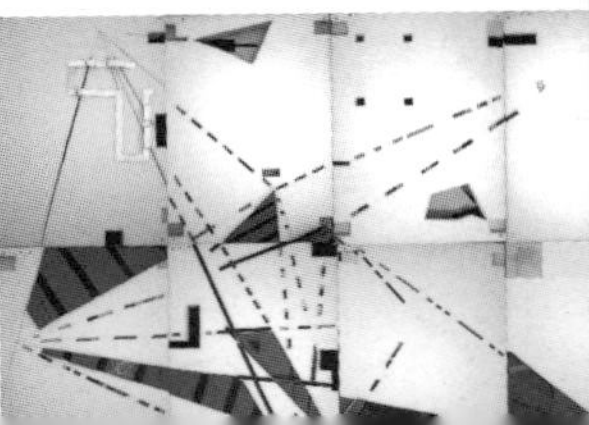

Joana Pacheco Growth Model
Section and plan of urban simulation within
the Topographical Fiction

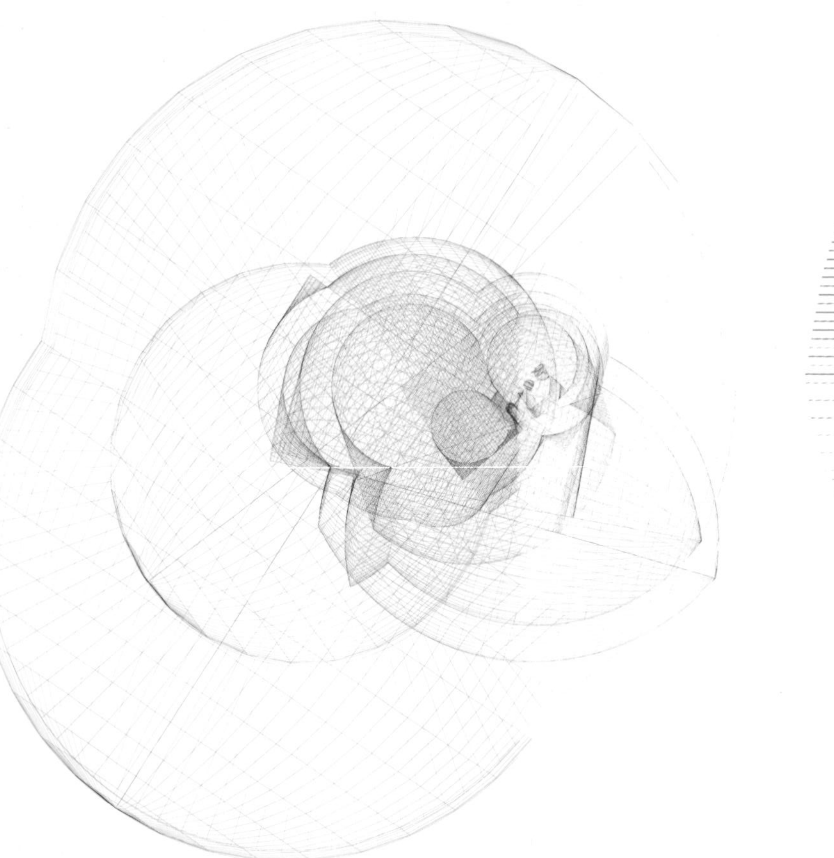

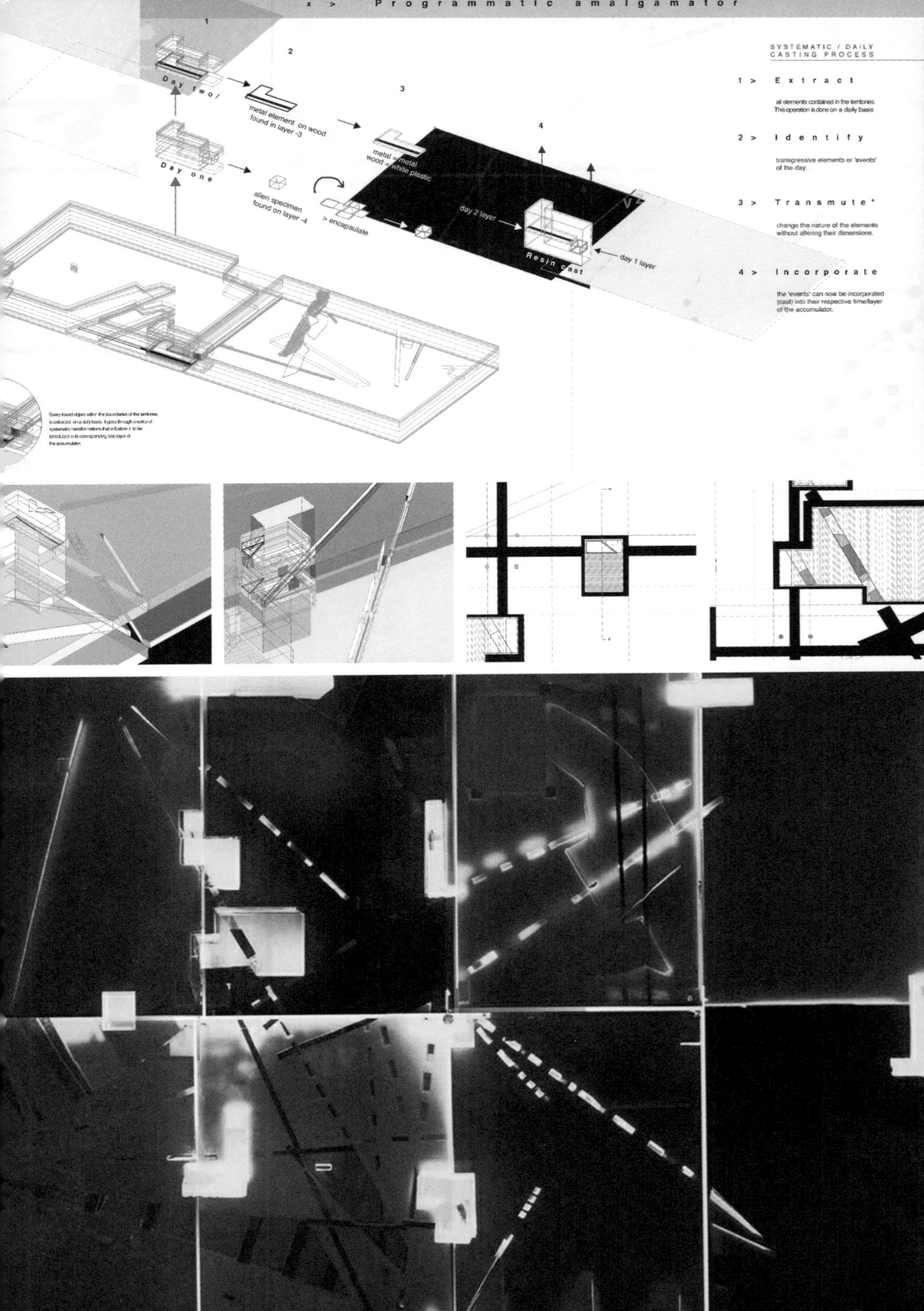

x > Programmatic amalgamator
1
2
3
4
Day two/
Day one
metal element on wood found in layer -3
metal = metal
wood = white plastic
alien specimen found on layer -4
> encapsulate
day 2 layer
Resin cast
day 1 layer
SYSTEMATIC / DAILY CASTING PROCESS
1 > Extract
all elements contained in the territories. This operation is done on a daily basis.
2 > Identify
transgressive elements or 'events' of the day.
3 > Transmute*
change the nature of the elements without altering their dimensions.
4 > Incorporate
the 'events' can now be incorporated (cast) into their respective time/layer of the accumulator.
Every found object within the boundaries of the territories is extracted on a daily basis. It goes through a series of systematic transformations that will allow it to be introduced in its corresponding time layer of the accumulator.

Isabel Pietri Medina Urban Voids
Construction of spatial fragments via time-based accumulations

Valeria Segovia Tracks and Zones
Incremental and layered negotiation of three bicycle tracks within a zoned site

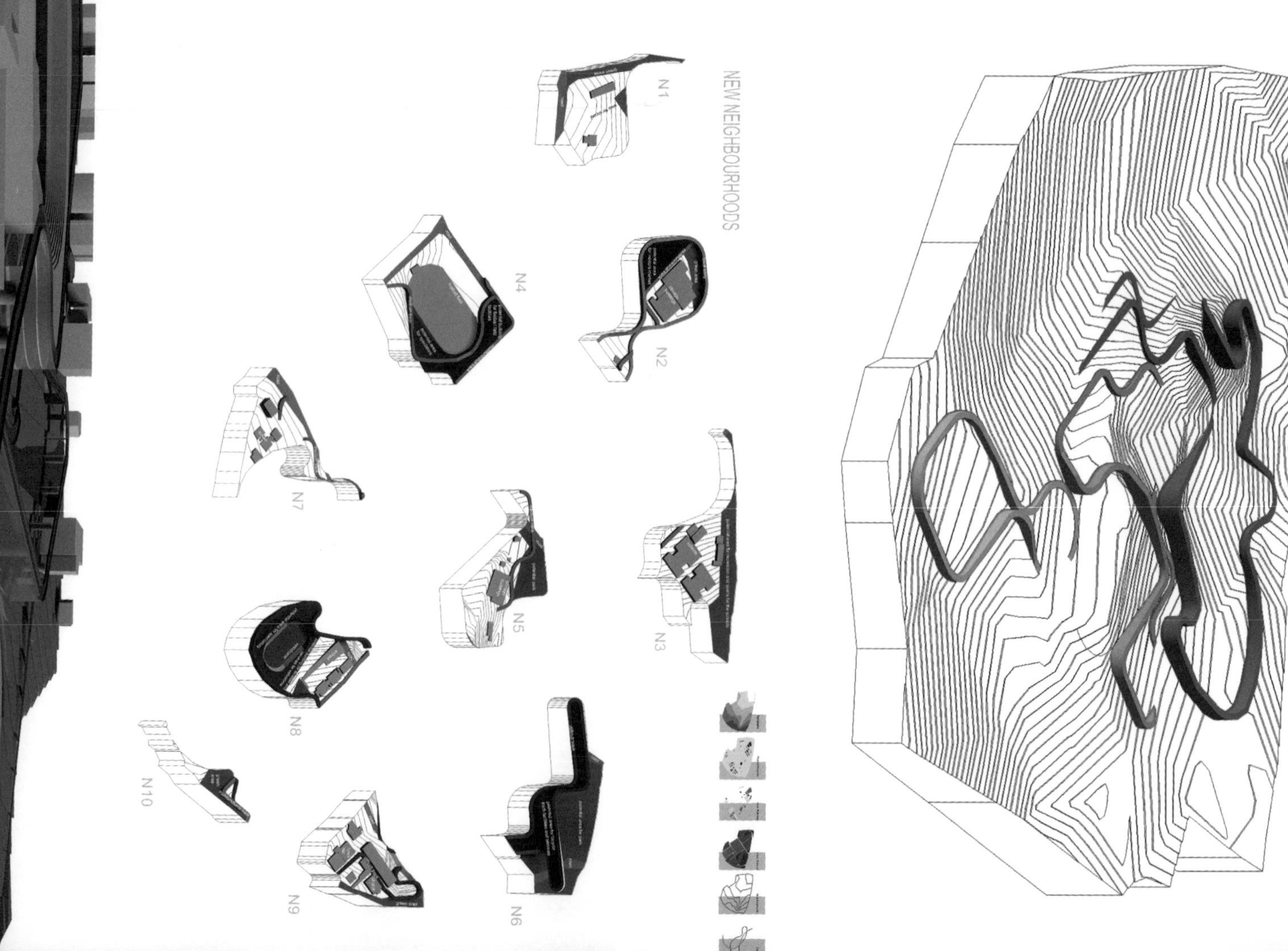

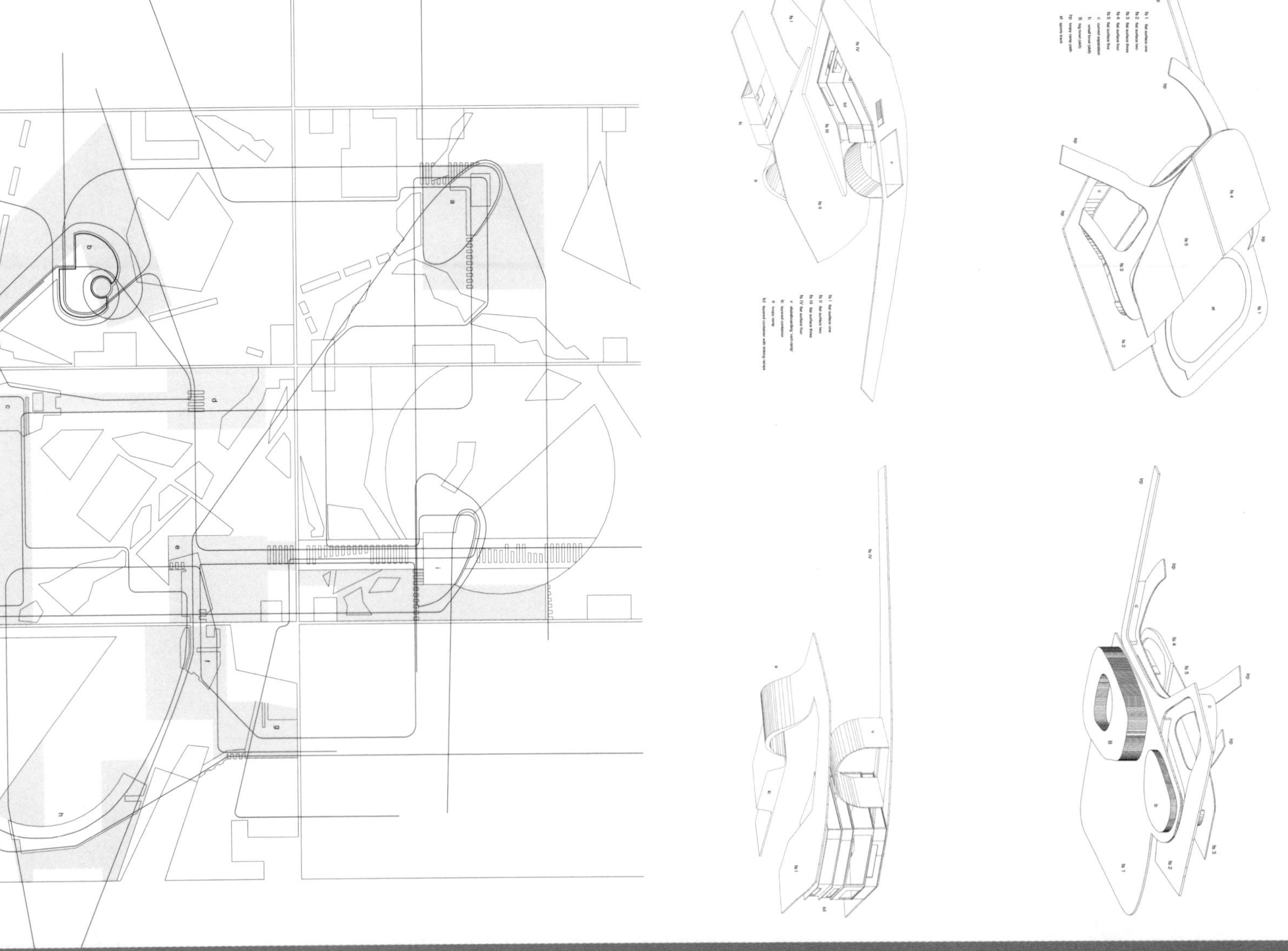

Stephania Batoeva Urban Stations
A series of event stations/links to accommodate multi-use sports facilities

Hong Bin Lu Fragment Elaborations
A process 'building on' and 'building off' to produce spatial structures

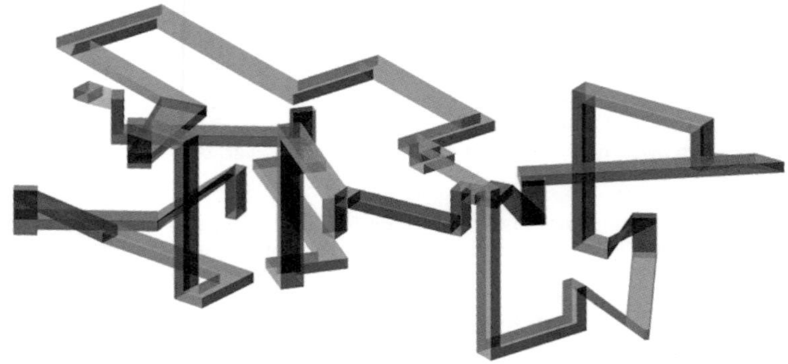

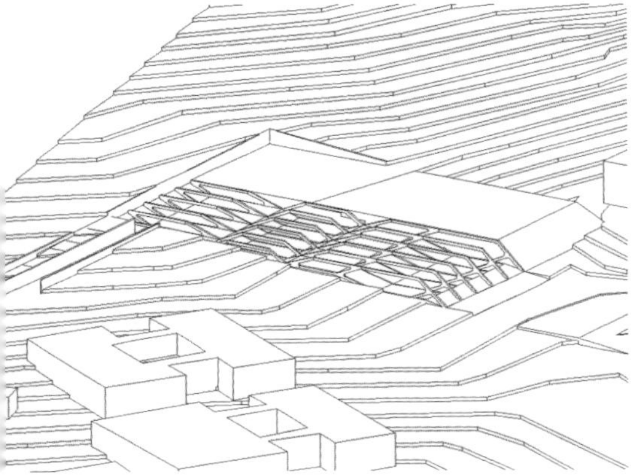

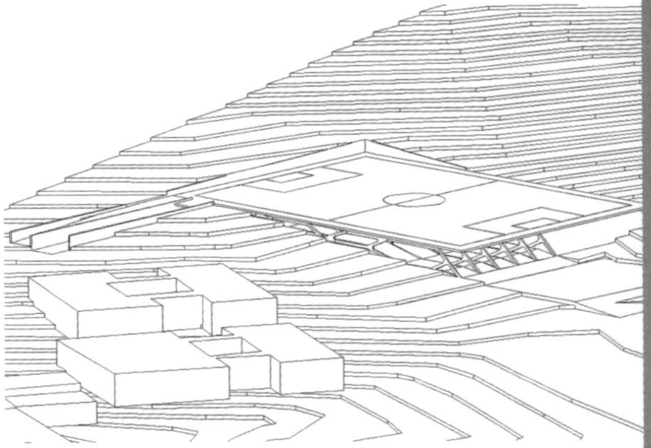

Flavia Foguel Meandering Lines
Elaboration of a series of lines structuring the landscape and programme

The Delirium Of Seduction

The last decade has seen a profound mutation of the art museum typology. If historically the museum performed as a fundamental organ of intellectual reverie and social discourse, the contemporary museum is subject to a more pressured array of economic, symbolic and mediatised demands that catalyse the mutation into unknown areas.

One reaction to this mutation is outrage or despair. More productive, perhaps, is an active, nonperjorative realisation that the increasing functions of the contemporary art museum – aesthetic, commercial, urban – require an equal reconfiguration of both its institutional role and, reciprocally, its physical locus.

Museology **refers to the unit's collective effort to address these issues. An initial project introduced the students to contemporary art practice and the significance of the site of its production. The major project took place in London and envisioned a new Guggenheim to script diverse future museological scenarios.**

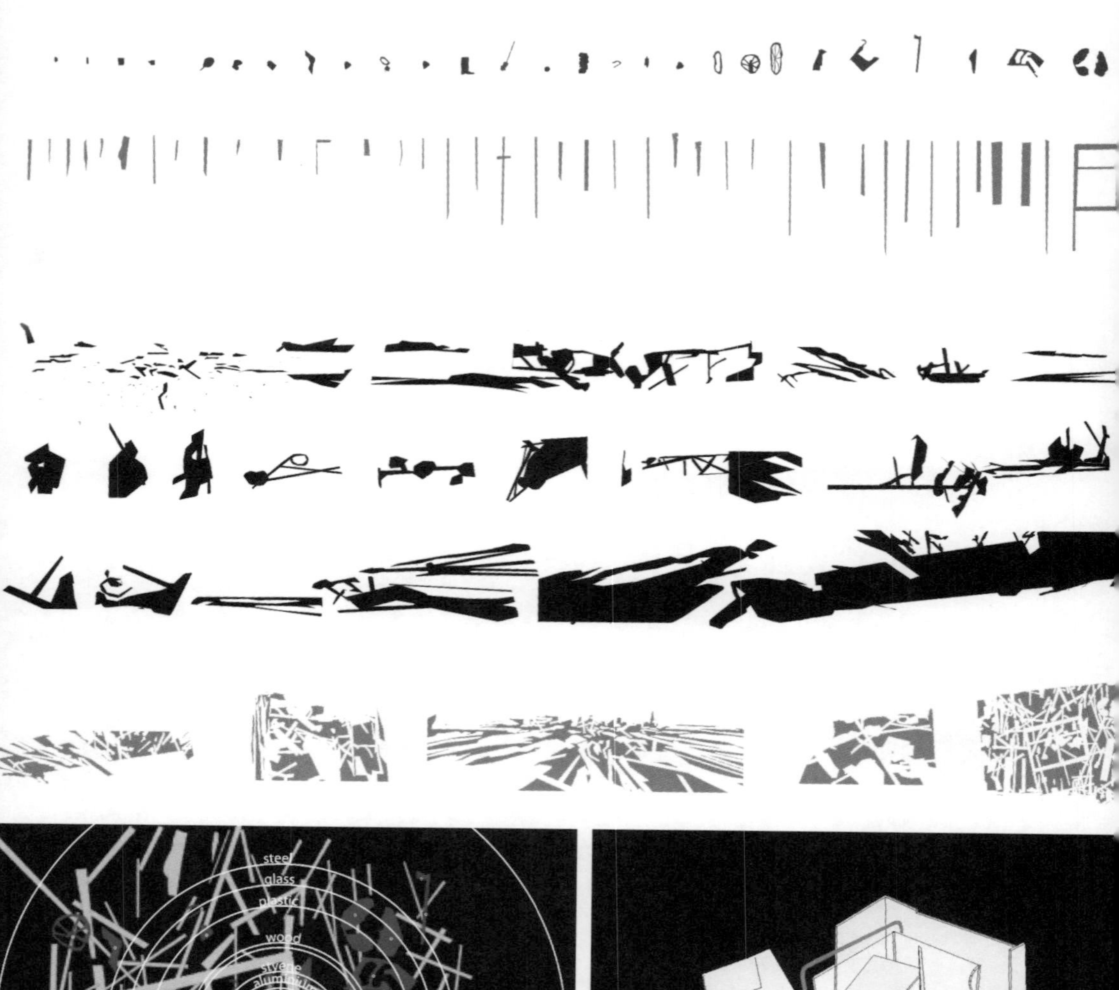

Chihiro Nakagawa Cornelia Parker

The Artist's Studio: Production in Reverse

'Of all the frames, envelopes, and limits which enclose and constitute the work of art (picture frame, niche, pedestal, palace, church, gallery, museum, art history, economics, power, etc.) there is one rarely even mentioned today that remains of primary importance: the artist's studio.'
Daniel Buren, The Function of the Studio **(1971)**

An artwork is the result of a process of manufacture. This might vary from something that has been manipulated physically to something that has evolved through several conceptual propositions until it reaches the (perhaps arbitrary) 'final' form. Some artwork is better than others at concealing the process and location of its production. All artwork signifies something – materially or indexically – that alludes to a locus of origin that may either be actual or fabricated.

Each student chose a contemporary artist and a celebrated work from their oeuvre. Individually, the students interrogated the relationship between the artwork and the possible, imaginary site of its production. Less an exercise in actual detective work, the task was to dream the space around an item that was rich with personal, material and symbolic connotations. Rewind the tape and press play.

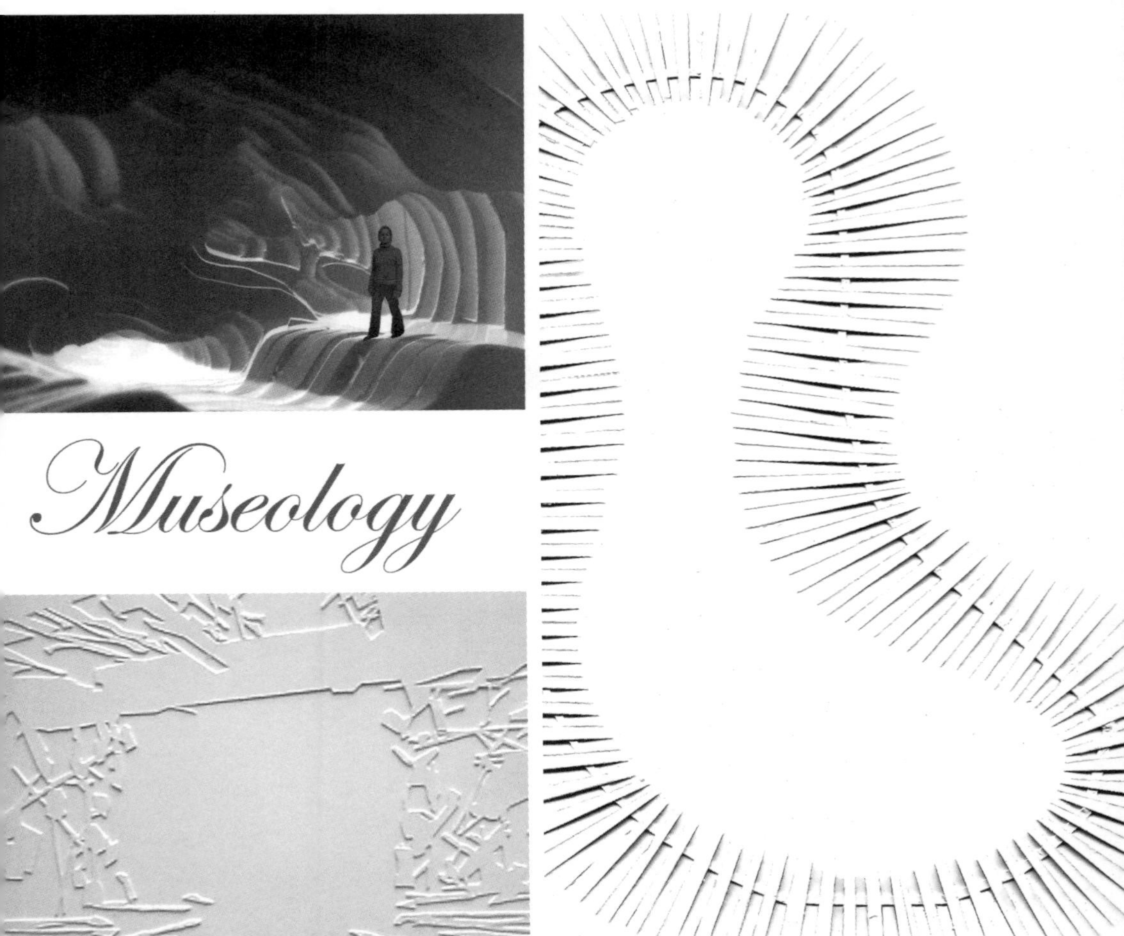

Tiffany Beriro Tony Oursler
Nazaneen Roxanne Shafaie Richard Deacon

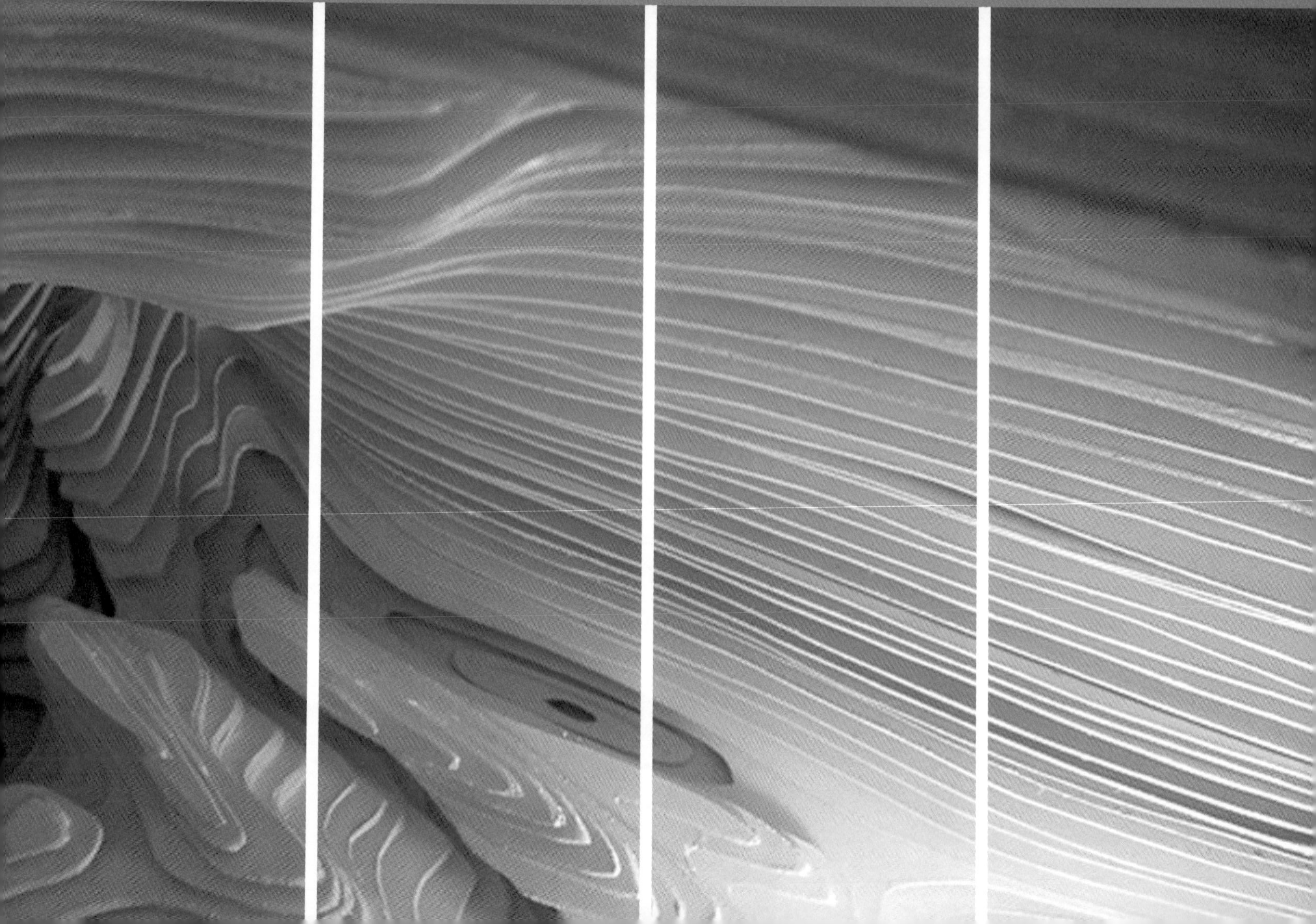

Museologise!

Programming

The contemporary art museum gradually swallows more and more programme that has less and less to do with exhibiting art. Instead, the programmatic mixture begins to resemble small patches of urbanity, neatly presented under one cultural headline.

Collecting, Naming, Making Monsters

Students employed the museum mentality by refining and accelerating chosen programmatic contents into new, monstrous constellations, on the basis that the museum envelope is to programme as the gallery is to objects: it affords new categorical status to existing orders of things. The smoothing out of ostensible differences gives rise to new realms of possible interpretation and experience.

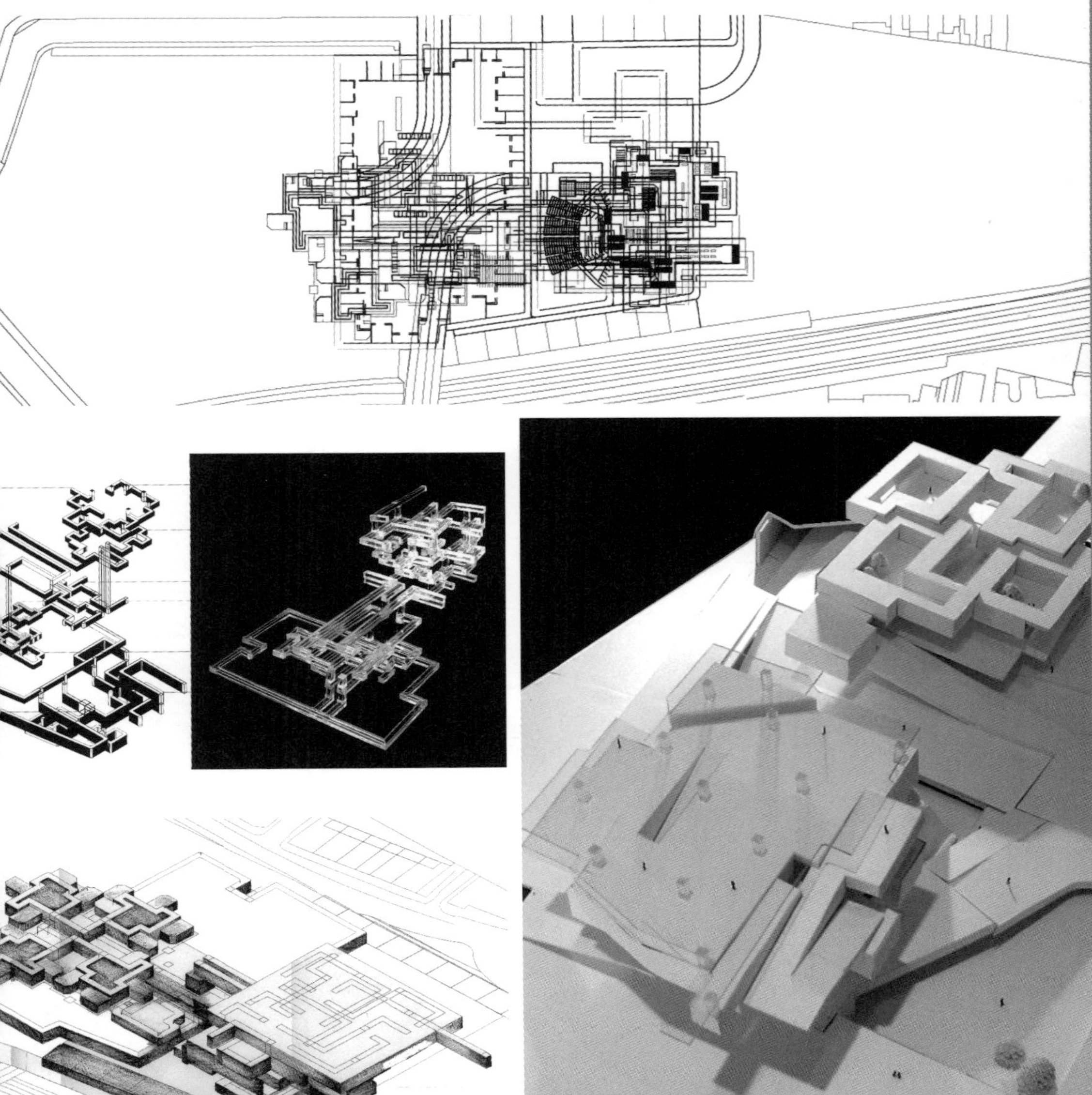

Nazaneen Shafaie The Art Filter
New and old works move through the building mechanically, entering and inhabiting various urban programmes, such as a market, a hotel and a multifaith chapel. The speed of the art's movement is related to the programme it is situated in. The public decides how long a work should remain, and the level it attains in the art-route hierarchy. Winning pieces reach the very top, where they remain for a period of six months. Unpopular works are simply ejected from the system.

Not a Place of Dead Things

Viewed as a performing body that produces vital (and not ossifying) effects, the contemporary art museum must begin to explore in detail the specific roles it might now play. Each student was asked to define such an identity – a set of institutional ambitions – and predict the ramifications of such a radical shift in direction.

Curator, Where Art Thou?

What if the architecture of the museum participated more instrumentally in the curatorial process of selecting, instigating or rejecting art? What if the architecture calibrated the relationship between the experience of art and all the museum's 'other' events in more strategic ways than mere denial? In expanding the repertoire of the new museum, students have developed their own performative architecture. This becomes the tool and measure of deviation from traditional typologies.

The Ackermuseum, Los Angeles
As part of a unit trip to LA, we visited a number of esoteric museums. One of the most fascinating – and strange – was Forrest J Ackerman's house-cum-collection of sci-fi and B-movie memorabilia. Latex masks, puppets and props decayed in front of you – paradoxically animating the space of the museum from dead to alive.

Tiffany Beriro Guggenheim24
Existing artwork is newly classified according to the attention span required to view it and the correlative movement this attention span would infer. For example, Jeff Koons's floral 'Puppy' becomes a nodal point in a 60-second route experienced only by car, while Douglas Gordon's '24 Hour Psycho' requires visitors to stay overnight in special hotel rooms that allow you to fall asleep as the Hitchcock classic is projected outside. Associative programme is thus distributed according to and around the nodes and ribbons of artwork-duration. Here, Jubilee Gardens becomes a knotted freeway of cultural consumption.

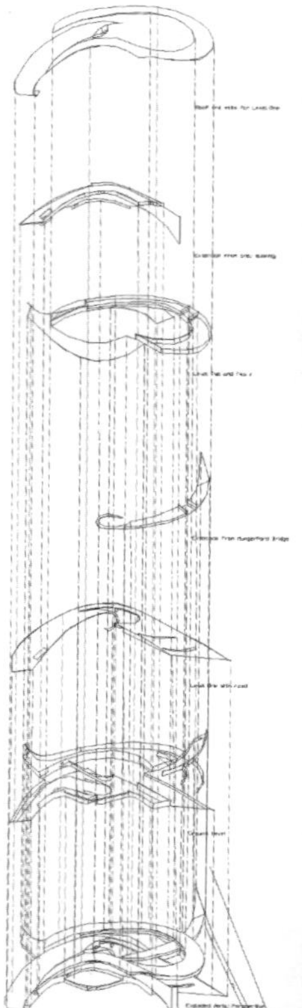

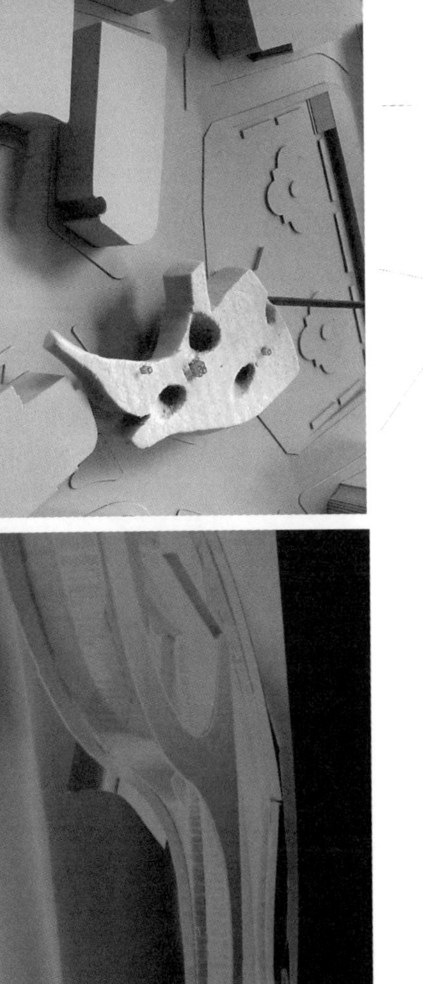

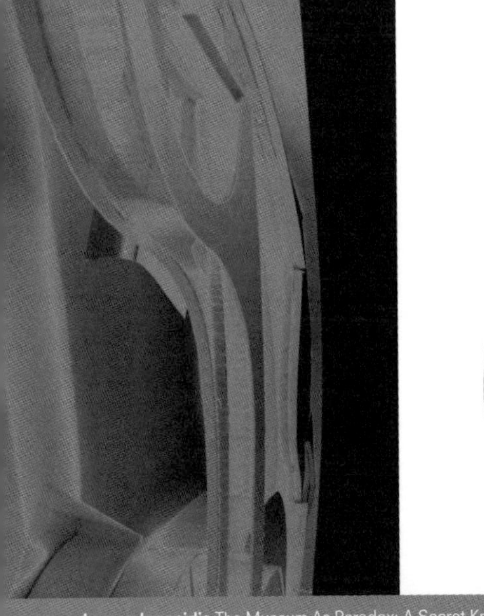

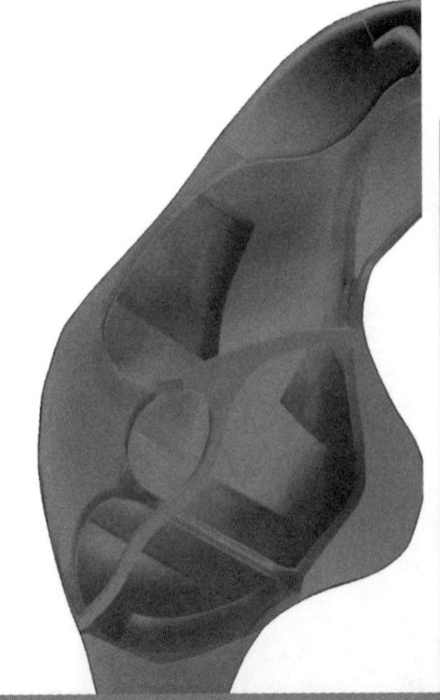

Ioanna Ioannidis The Museum As Paradox: A Secret Known to the Whole City.
Under Trafalgar Square, not the beach, but sinewy tunnels, pockets of programme and mythical excavation.

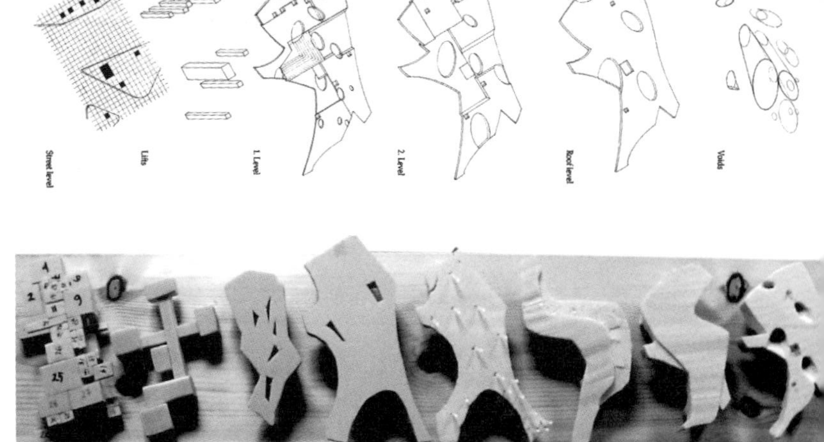

Sara Camre The Art Factory
A celebrity machine for success-hungry artists, floating above Trafalgar Square. Visitors witness the development of both the artists and their work, selectively, day by day.

Staff
Shumon Basar
Oliver Domeisen
Michelangelo Spinelli
Natalie Waters

Students
Tiffany Beriro
Sara Camre
Eugene Chung
Ioanna Ioannidis
Patrick Klugesherz
Chihiro Nakagawa
Gabriel Sanchiz-Garin
Nazaneen Shafaie
Lirong Soon

Jurors
Peter Beard, John Bell, Maria Bennis, Javier Castañon, Susanne Clausen, Shez Dawood, Tom Emerson, Masoud Golsorki, Jim Heverin, Chris Hight, Jenny Jones, Joe Kerr, Charlie Koolhaas, Ana Liu, Theo Lorenz, Petra Marguc, Mohsen Mostafavi, Diana Periton, Urs Primas, Mark Rappolt, Natasha Sandmeier, Graham Snow, Brett Steele, Charles Tashima, Mike Tonkin, Jacqueline Uhlmann, Madelon Vriesendorp

Thanks to
Abake, Forrest J Ackerman, Tom Barker, Herwig Baumgartner, Mark Cousins, Helene Furjan, Zaha Hadid, Shirazeh Houshiary, Jeff Koons, Maria Martin, Neil Wenman, and Antonia Loyd, Belinda Flaherty, Matt Kelly and Joel Newman at the AA

Special thanks to
Jee-eun Lee

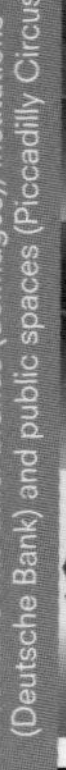

Michelangelo Spinelli
The Guggenheim London as a network of deployable insertions into other brands (Selfridges), institutions (Deutsche Bank) and public spaces (Piccadilly Circus).

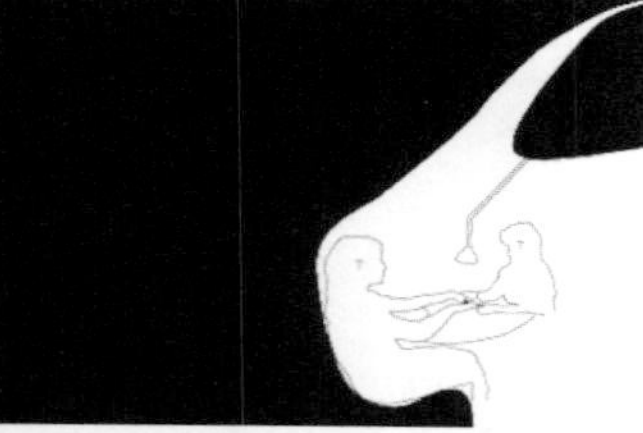

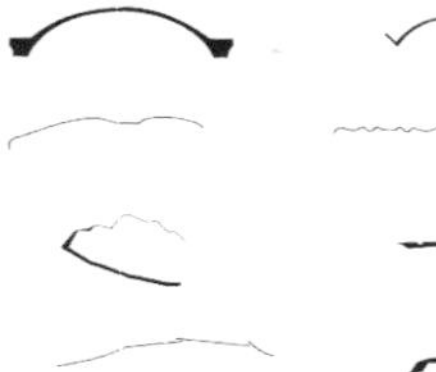
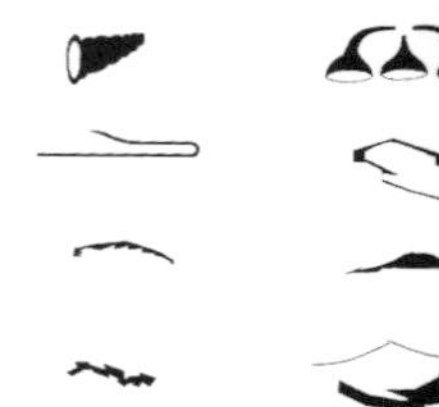

WIFE1: Something going on? BEAUTY CONSULTANT: You know, there's an opening next Friday. We're fully bo
Are you going? WIFE1: Oh right, I don't know. BEAUTY CONSULTANT: I think its a big event, I see some fa
people booked in for next week. I'm doing Sam Taylor-Wood on Thursday. Oh, what a pretty bracelet! WIFE1: Oh
you! I hear she's great friends with Elton John. Saw it on this BBC program. Artists are celebrities nowaday
BEAUTY CONSULTANT: I guess no more starving artists. I can name a handful that come here regularly. Well, let'
you started. We'll begin today with a deep tissue massage on your hands PUBLIC 1: Do you hear something? PU
2: I don't know, wait, I just heard something. PUBLIC 1: I hear a murmur, where is it coming from? PUBLIC 2: W

Eugene Chung
Inspired by the art market's dependence on rumour and gossip, an ecology of acoustic situations constitute the museum's architecture. Rich wives, bankers and the public overhear and are overheard throughout.

Natalie Waters aMUSEUMent Park
Two serpentine routes – one trashy, the other rarefied – twist round each other, providing the visitor with constant distractions.

On the Make

Intermediate Unit 10 focuses on the craft of making as a vehicle for the construction of ideas. The conceptual approach undergoes formal transformation through fabrication, confronting the laws of quality and character that are part of being material.

We work along physical lines of thought, and we use a process of making and unmaking. We create tools to produce new tools that enable us to establish our conceptual path.

A series of interdependent 'makes' become our set of personal tools for commuting across borders. The first make is an Installer Tool that defines the student's identity throughout the year, granting access to desired areas.

Intermediate Unit 10 considers the making and its unmaking to be the driving force towards architectural articulation, tectonic invention and tactile poetics.

Covering to Reveal

'The fireplace reveals in its new appearance an unexpected presence and identity within the room. The act of covering is a semiotic operation; it shifts our perception, from a preconceived understanding to a new and unknown meaning. It operates on a phenomenological level, affecting us as well as the object.'

Hotel Weisses Kreuz

The dialectical tension between the making and the unmaking is intrinsic to the physical line of thought, carrying our efforts towards a hotel project in the Swiss Alps that brings apparent contradictions to a synthesis of intellect and emotion, engineered structure and alpine landscape.

After establishing our path through the making and unmaking of installer tools, we have turned towards the village of Bosco/Gurin in the Swiss Alps, where we are implementing the Making Tool to introduce a hotel.

In consultation with local planners, we have chosen three sites. We are using our toolboxes to determine materials and structure while travelling along the conceptual paths.

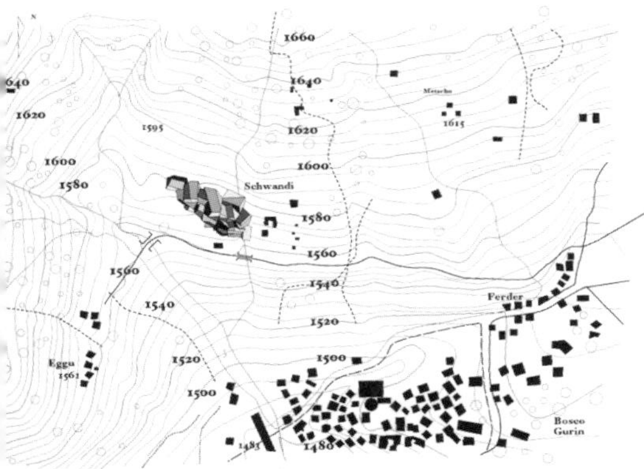

Camouflage

noun. **1a. The disguising of military vehicles, aircraft, ships, artillery and installations by painting them or covering them to make them blend with their surroundings**
1b. such a disguise
2. the natural colouring of an animal which enables it to blend in with its surroundings
3. a misleading or evasive precaution or expedient
verb. **hide or disguise by means of camouflage**
French, from camoufler 'disguise'

Stefano Rabolli Pansera Falcon Hunter Hotel (top); Hunted Space (bottom)

1. Installer Tool

Identify yourself through making. Two relevant materials will be crafted into a furniture-object. One will be connecting, the other connected. Disrespect everything you think you know. Respect what you discover through experimentation and observation. Record process with a camera. Think about yourself, about scale and appearance within a room. How is it used? How does it influence its environment?

2. Reinstaller Tool

You are involved in the process of identifying yourself through making. Reveal the essence of your Installer Tool by unmaking it. Start establishing a physical line of thought by a process of making and unmaking. Recognise the inherent rules of your first make. Introduce conceptual thought into your work. Create tools that enable you to establish your conceptual path. Record process with a camera. Map your transformation lines. Think about scale.

Hunted Space

'Camouflage is one of the criteria for relating site and body: to not be seen and to disappear into the landscape, or to be covered, as an object between other objects, on the "dead ground"; the form of the land is reflected in the display of the masses. Camouflage is a behaviour and an artifice used equally by the hunter and the hunted.'

3. Echo Door Tool

You have created a key. You have unmade a lock. Open the now-unlocked door. Listen to the echo of space. Record this echo through remaking, **drawing, printing, photographing. Verbalise your conceptual thoughts.**

4. Desired Area: Forged or Real

Search for and create an interior environment for your makes. Use photography to represent your three makes and their line of thought. Bring yourself into this environment as the instigator and victim. Regard your representations as the fourth make, being consistent within this series of makes. Think about the contained environment in a photographic representation. Consider the positive and the negative path, the visible and the invisible object-subject. Work with moods. Your installation will be photographed with a 5 x 4 camera.

7. Echo House Model Tool

The making is the foundation of our course. How far is making informing your hotel project? You will be building a hotel model at scale 1:50. Choose materials that join hotel and installer tool conceptually. Work with sections and spacial sequences, tectonic dramaturgy and rhythm. Your construction principles and the specific use of materials shall be visible, clearly presented and subject to discussion.

View from the sky
Plan of the roofs

5. Bosco Gurin

Three sites have been identified in Bosco Gurin and its vicinity. Use your photographic material, videos, maps, sketches and memory to choose one of these sites. Which site does your conceptual path lead you to? Which site do you feel attracted by? Create a volume and its environment on the chosen site in 'Einklang' with your series of makes. Do not think about programme – yet. Make drawings, collages and models. Rework your furniture and portfolio.

6. Weisses Kreuz

Hotel Weisses Kreuz: 30 rooms with bath, dining room, salon, terrace, reception, kitchen, mountain-gear-and-ski-storage area, swimming, ice skating, curling ... Provide for long-term lodgers and hikers. Define tourist profile, control relationship between landscape and building, consider the path as movement through landscape towards a building. Articulate the tension between base and topography, translate traditional building materials and construction methods.

Unit Staff
Johannes Käferstein
Goswin Schwendinger

Students
Carol Aoun
Eduardo Ardiles
William Chen
Robert Gluckmann
Abraham Gordon
Charlie Hui
Sibylle Lienert
Asa Nilsson
Anna Ohlin
Stefano Rabolli Pansera
Ana Saboia
Alicia Tan
Alexander Trimboli
Max Von Werz

Special thanks to
John Andrews
Shumon Basar
Peter Beard
Valentin Bontjes van Beek
Javier Castanon
Jean Michel Crettaz
Shin Egashira
Simon English
David van Handel
Takuro Hoshino
Kei Ito
Katrin Lahusen
Andreas Lang
George Liaropoulos-Legendre
Markus Lüscher
Urs Meister
Mohsen Mostafavi
Erica Overmeer
Muck Petzet
David Racz
Natasha Sandmeier
Irénée Scalbert
Teresa Stoppani
Tony Swannell
Charles Tashima

four cell structures in plastic cups
by **Patrick Pei Pin Ng**, and clothes pegs
Esi Carboo

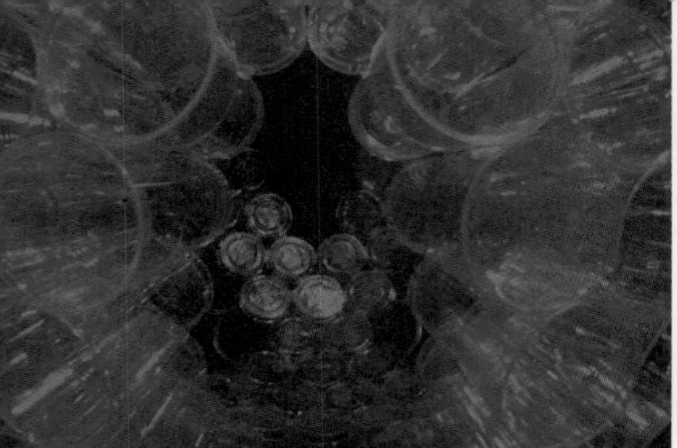

Primal Patterns
Seven people began by asking questions.
The questions yielded a string of associations free from logic.
These were treated as clues through which seven stories emerged.
The stories constructed spaces, and the spaces constructed fantasies.

Ticket Office Leicester Square

Glow is our natural attraction to light, from the moth flying to the moon to the crowd that flocks to the neon. We began by observing the patterns of light and characters that inhabit Leicester Square. Proposals were made for a glowing information and ticket space.

Cell Structures

Grow is our power to multiply, from cellular patterns in nature to the sprawl of a city. Beginning with the body's dimensions, a cube is filled with an emotion at 1:10. Looking at cellular patterns in fruits, in the work of Escher, and in building construction, an everyday lightweight object is chosen to form a three-dimensional pattern of structure and growth.

Singing Space Leicester Square

Flow is our desire for movement, from migrating birds to the psychology of the individual in the crowd. Beginning with questions about patterns of behaviour in crowd, swarm, and public space, stories were written about an imaginary scenario in the Square. The final project was a space for mass gathering, dedicated to the most primal form of expression, singing.

Students
Johannes Beaujolin
Esi Carboo
Hadiza Gwadabe
Kun-Wook Kang
Smita Khanna
Patrick Pei Pin Ng
Takumi Sugimoto

Stories
The cave of whispers
The day the beating of their wings rose as a cacophony of sound.
A sweet sound of strings echoing
The three tunnels of memory
The oceans on the land now unknown to man
The bat that heard, saw, and began to sing
The trees that grew from the traveller's songs

Tutors
Anna Liu
Mike Tonkin

Thanks
Antonia Loyd
George Procakis

Critics
Shumon Basar
David Bothwell
Mary Branson
Javier Castañon
Oliver Domeisen
Thomas Heatherwick
Gwyn Lloyd Jones
Richard Land
Jay Merrick
Tom Mival
Sadie Morgan
Mohsen Mostafavi
Adriana Nacheva
Diana Periton
Matthew Priestman
Natasha Sandmeier
Peter Thomas
David Ward
Michael Weinstock

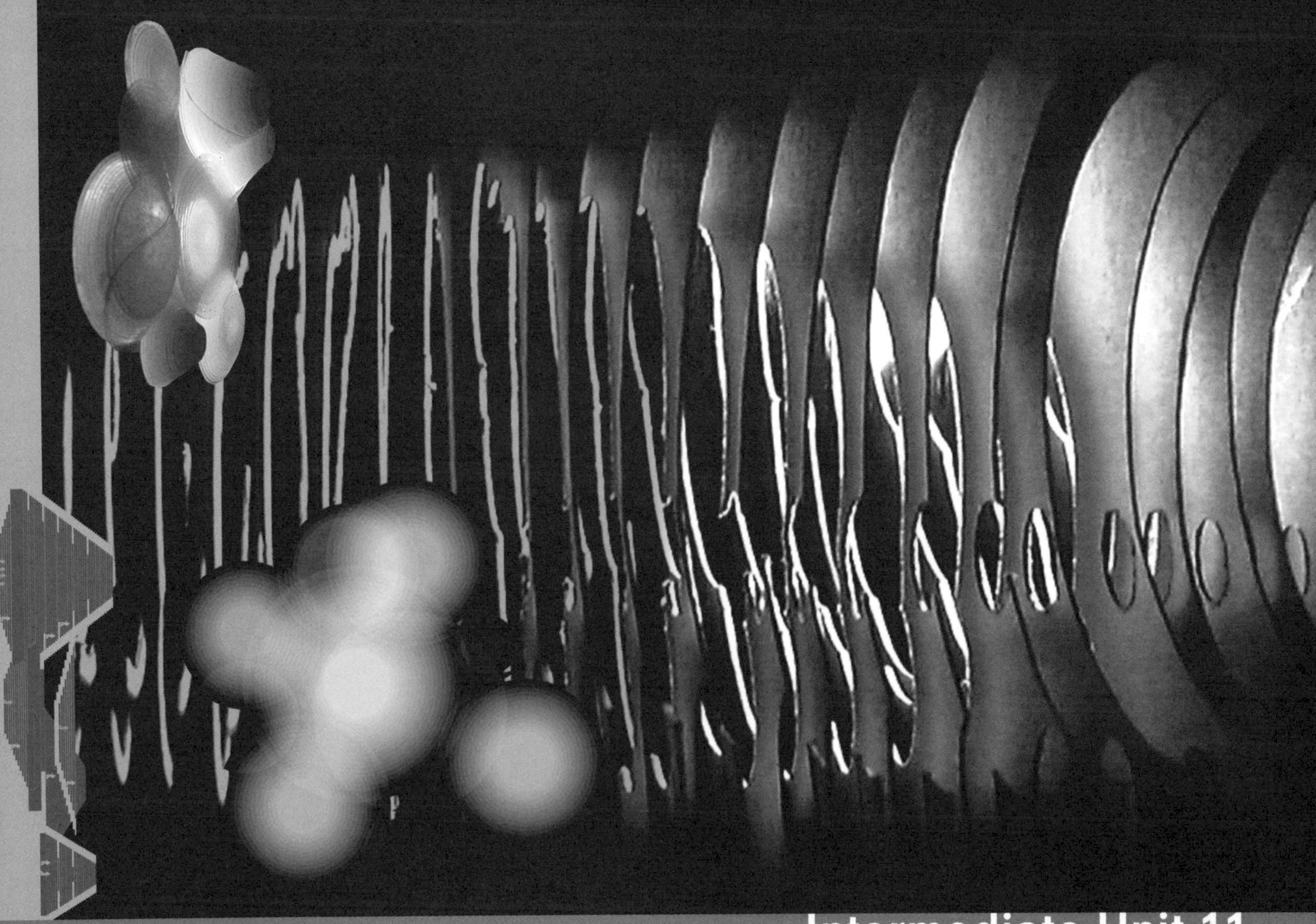

No one heard it. And no one saw it.
But he heard it. And he saw it.
And he began to sing. Then they heard it.
Then they saw it too. And they left singing.

Patrick Pei Pin Ng E-W section across Leicester Square, Schematic plan, Bat's view,Glazed soundscapes

Intermediate Unit 11

This whispering
where did it come from?
Outside.
This village.
Those hollow words
He had to go back to the cave
and speak those echoes.

Jahannes Beaujolin Diagram plan, Section through Leicester Square, View of Cave of Whispers

On the happiest day in the land now unknown to man
the oceans danced
high high high – so high that they could not be seen
they never came back down
So on the water in the land known to man
are shadows that are almost real

Smita Khanna String section, String plan, Painting of connecting oceans, Internal view of House of String

In the grassy field was a sweet
sound of string echoing.
In a short time he came upon
a black box.
He then removed one face of the box and
discovered the sound was coming from within.

Hadiza Gwadabe Cups and string, Plan in Leicester Square, Elevation of chambers, View of Sound Garden

On the hottest day of the year
the colony emerged from
the Lumino shafts.
The beating of their wings
rose as a cacophony of sound

Esi Carboo Plan, Section, Cartoon, The Beating of the Wings Rising, View of Lumino Layers

When she opened her eyes,
around her had appeared
three tunnels,
each with a different song and
light coming towards her.

Kun-Wook Kang Internal view of tunnels, Crossing tunnel's model, Model in Leicester Square, Sound block section

When the traveller sang,
plants and flowers grew.
The day that the storm came,
the roots of the trees grew,
with the traveller's singing,
into a shelter where
everyone was safe.

Takumi Sugimoto Plan, Section, Double stage, Leicester Crossing, Cartoon, Tree Shelter
View of Leicester Crossing

Work assembled for a Diploma Unit 12 jury.
Photograph Chris Fenn

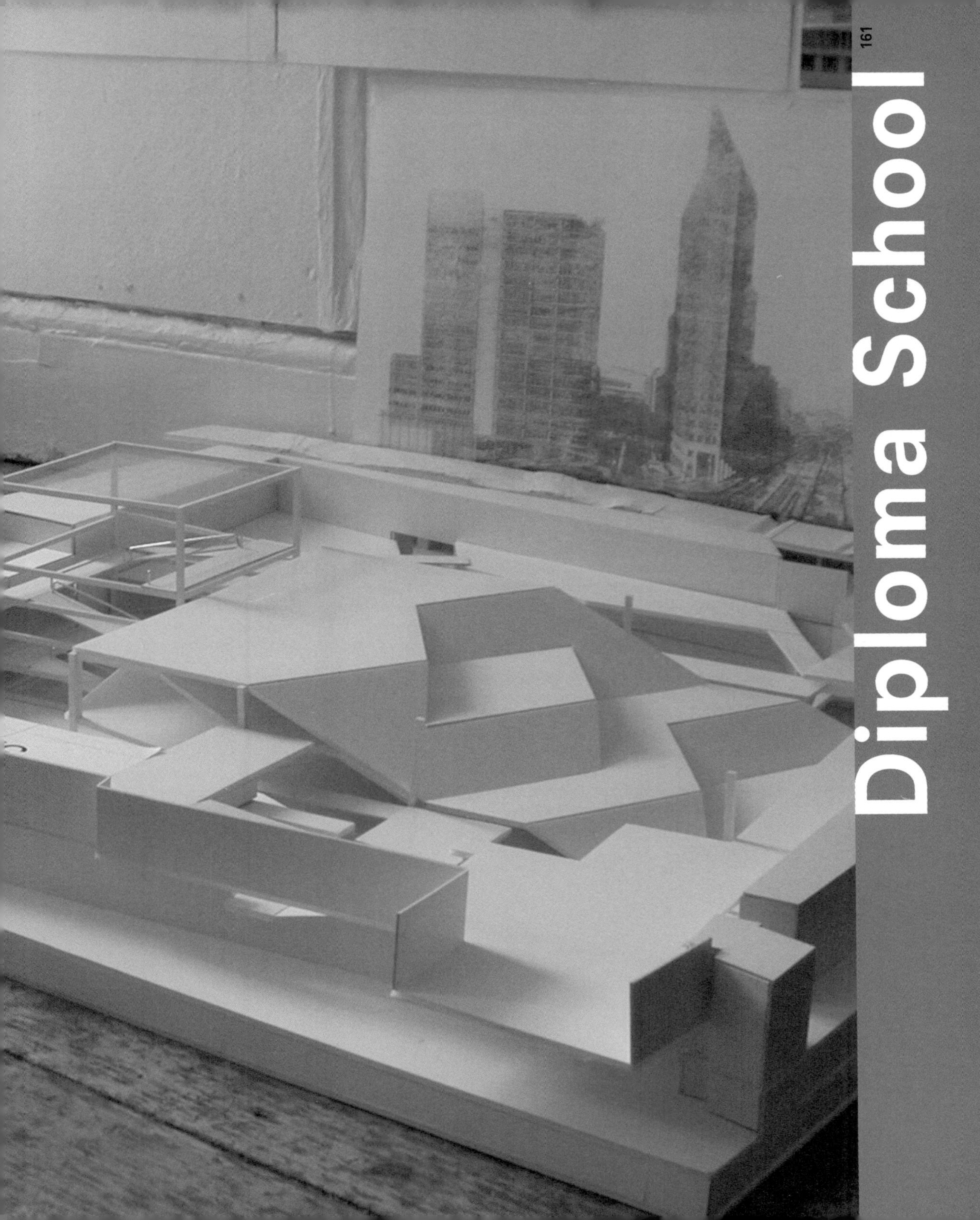

Diploma School

Opera Mundi – Corpus Mundi

Opera Mundi **outlines the year's unit programme. The research is led by the objective of developing a design method for a proposed new opera house in Copenhagen. The conception of design criteria is largely informed by the human experience of opera – by the response to the drama of mortality, as conveyed through the human voice. Our work takes up the challenge of defining spatial scenarios that provide an immediacy of experience and reflect conditions of cultural and economic development within a globalised society.**

Globalisation **outlines emergent conditions from which we cannot escape. Being part of a larger entity challenges traditional policies of containment; finite boundaries are being replaced by new networks of connections. The basis for the unit's approach is an acknowledgement that an essential generator of change in a responsive built environment is our internal wellbeing, which is inseparable from external conditions.**

Architecture is the material dimension of a boundary system. The mediator between inside and outside space, it defines the role of space as a negotiating, fluid and adaptive body – not as an autonomous machine, as stated by the some modernist architects. In the same way that in politics responsibility has shifted from corroding power structures to the individual, decision-making methods in architecture have shifted from control-driven devices to tools of direct environmental negotiation. Consequently, the success rate of any proposed structure is ultimately measured by its ability to thrive under new conditions.

The concept of architecture as part of an eco- and supra-system addresses modes of mutation and adaptation. Internal structures reflect external conditions; equally, the complexion of the exterior is shaped by the disposition of the interior. Thus architecture becomes an emerging life form as opposed to a mechanism of singular operative modes.

Life forms **outlines dynamic structures that are able to thrive and develop within the globalised conditions of our living environment, and defines the site for our proposals.**

ROH**, the existing Royal Opera House in Copenhagen – small, provincial, stuffy and struggling for survival – has been challenged by a move to build a rival second opera house. Money for the project would come from a large Danish company specialising in containerised shipping trade, which poses the conundrum of how industrial and globalising forces can successfully be brought together with cultural activities.**

Corpus Mundi **embraces the tool for developing the thesis topic. The preparatory project stage investigated issues of sensory experience through work with performance space. Body-specific attachments and extensions initiated negotiations and transitions between the body and its immediate environment. Hearing, touching, breathing, seeing and related modes of sensory experience were observed and mapped. Stage work with a choreographer and contemporary dance artists provided an inspiring platform for the design of a new species of opera.**

Proposition. **The principles developed through this experimental work were subsequently applied to new large-scale scenarios to form the basis for the opera house design. The project data was produced during two trips: a continental opera tour, and an intense ten-day workshop held in Copenhagen in collaboration with the Architecture School of Aarhus. Cooperative design tools were introduced to maximise negotiation and adaptability, properties crucial to the formation of a new species of opera.**

The resulting Opera Mundi propositions are based around a design method that incorporates both external conditions and internal organisational principles. They reflect our attempts to develop an architecture that is capable of acting as an incorporation of inner energies, life forms and globalising conditions.

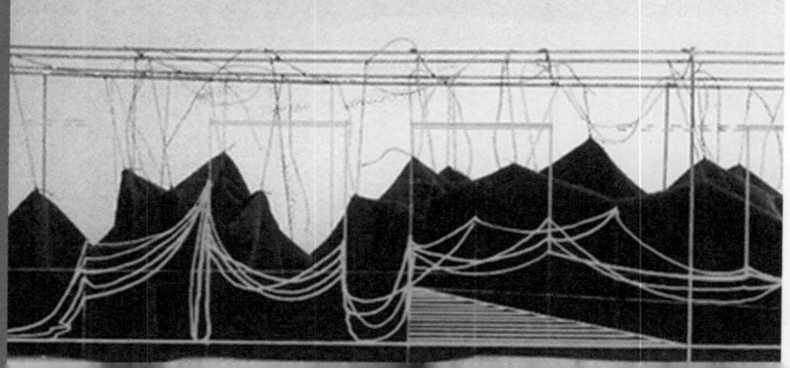

Opera Face **Asma Zeenni**

The fabrication of a latex mask as the Corpus Mundi object provided a tool for the manipulation and construction of specific modes of expression, making it possible to trace and observe the impact of programmes and spatial scenarios on a given face and matrix.

A critical analysis of the archetypal opera house set-up revealed its limitations of expression. The Danish Opera displays a tired face, isolated by infrequent use, socially outdated rites, lack of space and scarcity of connections with its social and cultural environment. The challenge of the Opera Mundi proposal lies in the construction of a vehicle for a new operatic expression. Site-specifically, the proposal employs various urban programmes to coalesce opera production with the urban environment and reinstate the broad spectrum of traditional opera culture. The architectural proposition embodies three horizontal datums: the ground-related matrix negotiates opera-specific functions as well as daily and seasonal programmes, the upper plane accommodates 'light' opera activities, while the lower level serves the industrial requirements. The interrelated choreography of the different planes and the external environment provides the basis for an adaptive opera face, a new form of urban staging.

Opera Stage **Christina Pappa**

The Corpus Mundi project explores the outer skin as a means of expression, simultaneously creating a differential between body and garment. Where the garment transfers the body's expression, the in-between space of body and garment probes an intimate space transitional to the boundary condition between body and skin. This analysis led to the manipulation of expressions by correlating the body–garment performance and by generating an intimacy of in-between spaces.

Economic considerations make it difficult to justify devoting a large amount of space exclusively to backstage use. Coupled with the public's growing interest in visiting the spaces pertaining to opera production, this factor gave rise to a proposal in which all opera functions become components of a single large-scale stage. A double-layered translucent fabric, suspended from a supporting steel structure, dresses the stage. Mechanically operated, this 'garment' can adapt its form, allowing the space inside to respond to specific environmental conditions and to the particularities of the opera programme, the choreography and dramaturgy of operatic space at an urban scale.

Opera Fleet **Maria Exarchou**

The Corpus Mundi project reassembles coded flat-screen projections of human body parts into perplexing and mystifying chains of new entities that challenge conventions and order. The traditional opera house is an idiosyncratic assemblage of opera components bound by convention and limited by geographical constraints. Inbreeding has resulted in a weakened and predictable format, with all its resultant states of ennui both within and as a response to performances.

The Opera Mundi proposal presumes the necessity to revitalise creative power by cross-breeding with other species. A new form of opera body emerges through the process of reassemblage of coded opera body parts and the shipping industry. Employing the Danish-based Moller-Maersk fleet, reconstituted opera body parts organised within container spaces and shipping logistics travel around the world from port to port. Shipping programmes provide the subordinate logistics and codification, fragmentation and reassemblage of the new opera house model. The interweaving of opera inventory with commercially shipped goods around the world develops a new opera house hybrid unfolding at designated port locations. Opera performances take place in the container ships and are set in between unloading and loading supporting temporary performance scenarios.

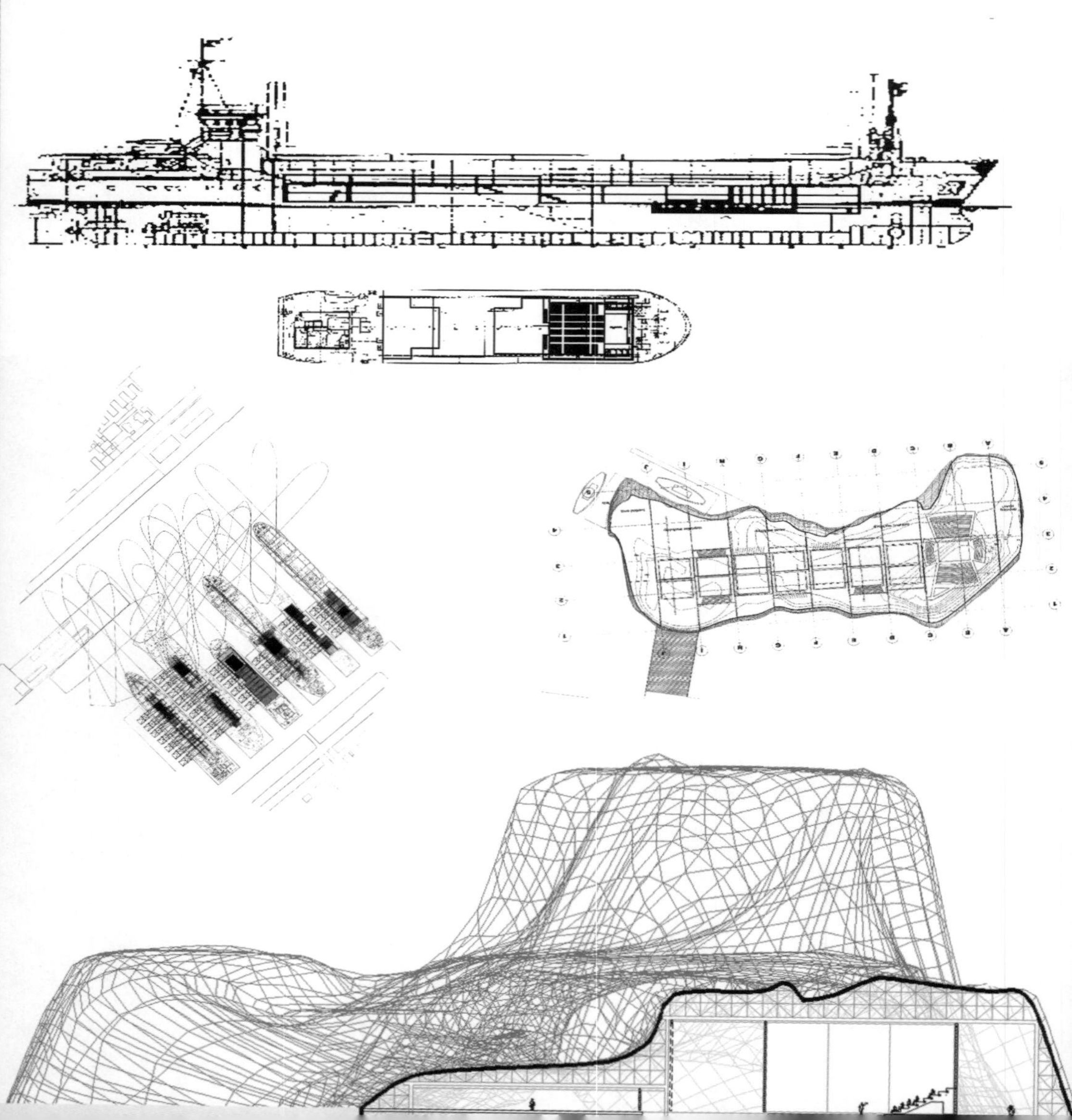

Opera Tail **Jennifer Pedtke**

The Corpus Mundi, a tail-like extension, explores the symbiotic equilibrium between body and environment. A negotiating tail requires room to operate; space restrictions become apparent, new modes of movement emerge, and spatial organisation requires recalibration. This approach generates a tool for analysing the traditional, formal opera experience, and particularly its restrictive spatial organisation.

The proposal for an Opera Park sets the new framework, a large, empty canvas for the reinvention of an operatic programme. The result is an operative landscape that responds to redefined programmatic requirements. Open-air and sheltered areas accommodate and support the new facilities on an expansive sloping plane. Set upon the grassy hill are opera beach huts, dining facilities and open zones. Opera stage rafters, loaded with each opera act in sequence, are towed into location and set into a new time-based programme. The opera moves, whereas the audience sets its own pace and place. Set against an urban backdrop, the opera experience is re-staged as a horizontal experience defining new relations to scale, audience and city.

Casting Opera **Sharon Givony**

In the Corpus Mundi project, anatomical parts are cast into shell-like forms and employed to camouflage and dissimulate their origins in the body. The new figures require mapping, followed by reappropriation and experimentation by means of performance.

The exclusion of a wider audience from the current opera form makes it essential to rethink the image of the opera, yet it appears unnecessary to change the body of the opera in its entirety. The method of separating body and image is applied, leading to the reassemblage of opera forms, functions and spaces. What emerges is a mound of initially pre-empted, shell-like objects requiring reidentification and reappropriation. A rigorous rational organisational principle had to be developed in order to recompose the opera's functions. The proposal embraces a double-skinned structure with curtain-like partitions providing an ever-changing new operatic body and space.

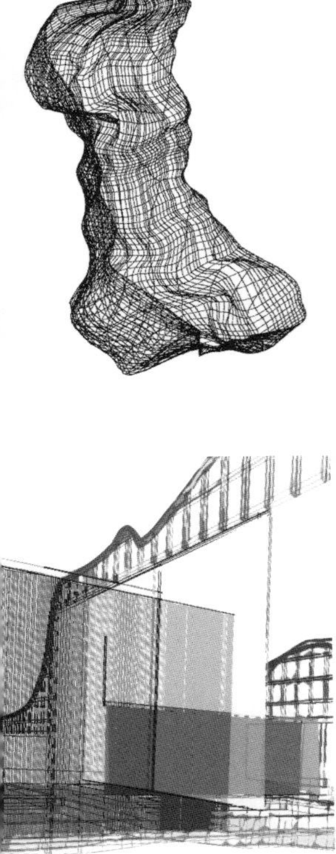

Opera Park **Hiro Nishizawa**

A study of the respiratory system of the lungs, with their fluctuating air capacity, led to the construction of a body-related rib cage creating an environmentally responsive diaphragm. The Corpus Mundi project provided the ground to test flexibility and adaptability of the body object together with the characteristic motion of an embracing shell. This fuzzy body boundary accommodates external conditions within the interior and extends the internal outwards, resulting in fluctuations of resources and adaptability of capacity. The project thesis evolves from these given principles, investigating the capacity of organisms to adapt to fluctuating environmental conditions.

Observations of the Danish Opera House revealed wide seasonal fluctuations in the number of visitors linked to the influx of tourists to the city. Although there is a variation in type and size of opera performances by different opera companies, the rigid installation of the existing opera house does not accommodate these variations, resulting in a considerable amount of dead space and waste of resources. Conversely, Copenhagen's Tivoli Park and its changing park programmes provided a workable model for seasonal programme-related adaptability.

The Opera Mundi proposal introduces an interlaced operatic park into the site. The dynamic nature of the programmes, together with the full use of such an expansive space, affords the realisation of a large-scale operatic landscape fusing opera and park. The building, made from structural mesh concrete and structural silicon membranes, negotiates the programmatic fluctuations between park experience, opera performance and opera production while disregarding accepted notions of interior and exterior.

Opera Supra **Nicolo Stassano**

The Corpus Mundi object explores body-boundary conditions generated by the respiratory system and defined by the exchange of the body's energies and fluids with its environment. The study led to the construction of an anatomical appendage in the form of an artificial lung system, the inflating and deflating air chambers articulating the amplitude of energy transactions. At performance stage the instrument exposed the notions of body boundaries, leading to an exploration and negotiation of object and environment reflected on the exchange of energy.

The Opera Mundi site, a former Naval Yard, advocates water as one of Copenhagen's most dominant environmental materials. The proposal encroaches on the vicinity of precedence and reinstates the opera performance as a water-related scenario. The site is flooded, and the water from the river and sea employed as heat-regulating mass. Water spaces and large-scale semienclosed glass structures work as regulating air chambers, reducing overall energy consumption in terms of maintenance and opera performance. The form of the opera house is thus transmuted, leaping from an antiquated cult of excess to an environmentally interlaced form of urban culture. The proposed floating opera components are staged as exterior and partly interior activities that optimise seasonal and programmatic conditions and capitalise on the available resources. The redefinition of opera culture and experience within global and local environmental conditions underlines the attempt to generate a new entropic economy of energy in direct relation to the development of operatic culture.

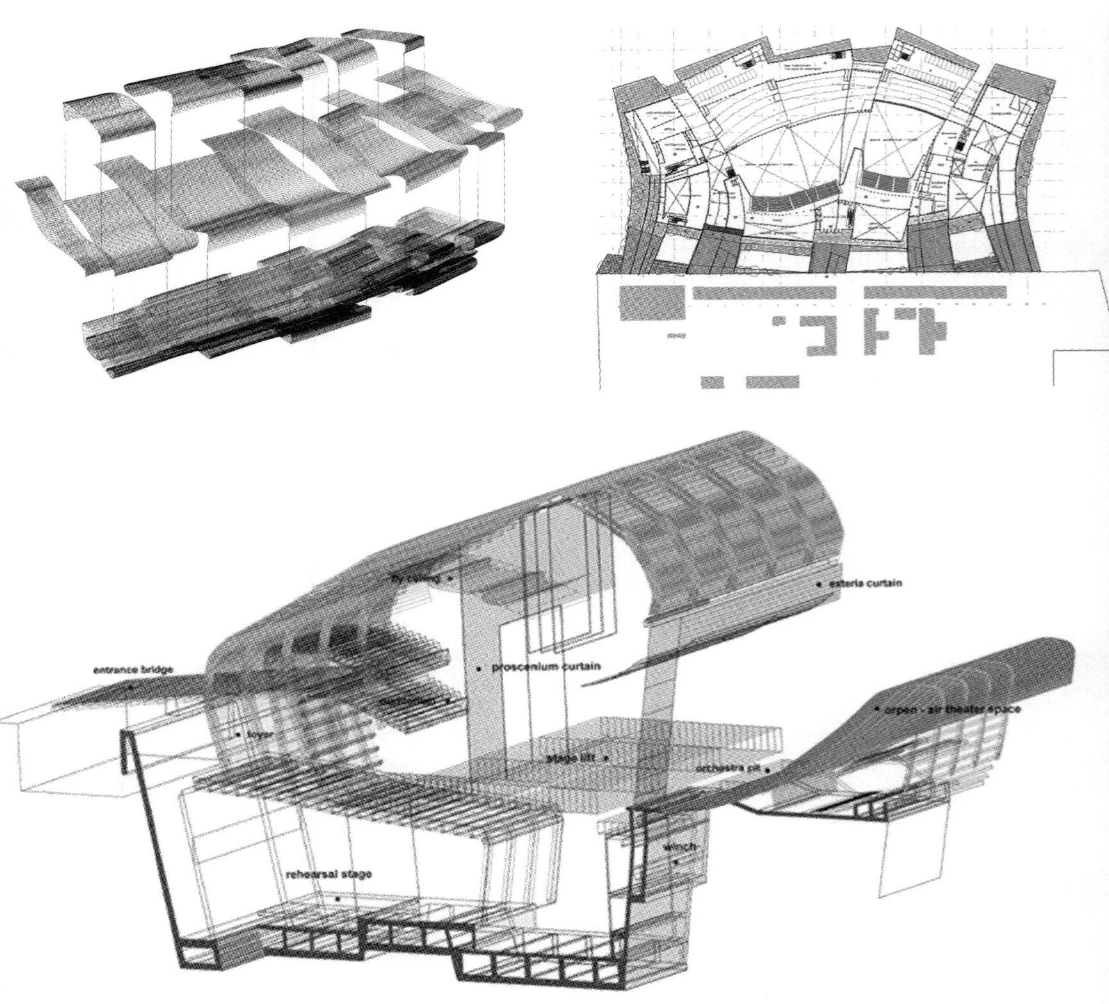

Operatic Memory **Sabine Frei**

The Corpus Mundi object is conceived as a navigational helmet fracturing visual information into labyrinthine structures. In order to be useful, any given information requires reconfiguration while lost information challenges the urge for rediscovery, re-use and rewriting.

The opera analysis looks at the complexity of the human drama embodied in opera narratives. The memory operates like a Daedalian structure with surrealistic readings occurring through cross-references and event/time overlaps. In current opera practice, scenery and stage material become waste due to the lack of storage space. The Opera Mundi proposal fuses organisational principles of re-use and storage with reassemblage of information leading to the reconstitution of opera fractals. A rational and logical warehouse structure is proposed whereby categorised props and scenery, stored according to subject and size, ready to be hired and shipped, are adapted to new configurations of use. The rational layout of the warehouses is intersected with pathways cutting through the park, storage and game rooms convoluting into a maze of memories, dreams and operatic spaces. The opera experience is one of consideration, reassemblage and construction of personal memories set within a framework of artefact interweaving the virtual with the physical.

Opera Ear **Lawrence Ler**

The project addresses the question of listening. Corpus Mundi, an oversized membranous auditory device, extends the communication space of the ear and, with it, the space of the performance.

In a traditional opera set-up, audience size is limited by the auditorium's accessibility and acoustic qualities. The new opera house addresses these constraints, introducing a peripatetic opera programme that reaches a wider audience through the appropriation of shipping logistics. A production hub in Copenhagen and is connected to the worldwide sea and land shipping despatch system of the Moller-Maersk fleet, with container ships, aeroplanes, railway, trucks, etc. The new opera is defined as a take-away model, marketed as a low-cost cultural imported product. The proposal is developed accordingly: ethereal origamilike objects using membranous and fibrous textiles, lightweight foldable structures, as well as infrastructural containers that can be deployed as temporary opera spaces wherever the operatic company disembarks.

Unit Master
Jean Michel Crettaz

Tutor
Takuro Hoshino

Assistant Tutor
Tamar Jacobs

Students
Fifth Year
Hiro Nishizawa
Christina Pappa
Nicolo Stassano
Asma Zeenni

Fourth Year
Maria Exarchou
Sabine Frei
Sharon Givony
Lawrence Ler
Jennifer Pedtke
Anthony Anderson (Term 1)

Special thanks to
John Andrews
Josephine Bacon
Peter Beard
Valentin Bontjes van Beek
Simon English
Jason Griffiths
Peter Hasdell
Johannes Käferstein
Neil Leach
Barbara Loyd
Peter Moore
Adrian Robinson
Pascal Schöning
Goswin Schwendinger
Charles Tashima
Michael Weinstock

Improvisation Dance Workshop I
Liat Shinar-Ogden
Improvisation Dance Workshop II
Sue Maclennan and the Choreography class students
The Place-London Contemporary Dance School

Denmark
Morten Daugaard, Claus Peder Pedersen, Peter Hemmersam, Aarhus School of Architecture
Kent Martinussen, director of the Gammel Dok, Danish Architecture Centre

House

This year began with a critical study into forms of housing construction, in addition to case study research into a series of small houses with very different material and constructional agendas. This included a collaborative workshop with Diploma 11 led by Bill Dunster, architect of BedZed, the new zero-carbon-emission housing development recently completed in Sutton. The workshop introduced concepts of embodied energy and investigated the environmental costs of differing approaches to construction. Based on these preliminary studies, students were asked to speculate on how they might approach these issues in their own work, relating methods of construction to a specific project: test-case studies for the development of the Ancoats area of East Manchester. The site is currently a patchwork of derelict buildings, vacant sites and low-density postwar housing projects. It has been identified in reports of the government's Urban Task Force as an inner-city area in urgent need of investment and support.

Some of the unit's projects propose a tabula rasa approach with extensive demolition of existing building fabric. Others work to intensify and clarify latent urban figures by working around existing housing terraces and blocks. We have tried to address issues of high-density mixed-use settlement, and all of the projects speculate on provision of uses other than purely residential: city farms, schools and playgrounds, workspace, and Sainsbury's Locals. In the latter part of the year we were lucky to work with the Swiss architect Valerio Olgiati in a series of three extended working sessions with the unit. We would like to offer him very special thanks for his high energy, attention and commitment.

Unit Staff
Peter Beard
Jim McKinney

Students
Lorenzo Alvarez
Ting Na Chen
Athanassios Economou
Thomas Goodey
Seijiro 'Bibo' Hayashi
Aidan Hodgkinson
Amanda Ku
Patrick Lewis
Henrik Lønberg
Valeriy Petrushechkin
Eleni Stika
Etsuko Ueda
Amilia Zainudin

With additional thanks to
Lawrence Barth
Stephen Bates
Bill Dunster
Shin Egashira
Diego Ferrari
Ines Geisler
Susannah Hagan
Brian Hatton
Lorens Holm
Gillian Horn
Andrew Houlton
Katrin Lahusen
Neil Leach
Antonia Loyd
Mohsen Mostafavi
Valerio Olgiati
Adrian Robinson
David Ward
Michael Weinstock
Jonathan Woolf
and also to **Jane Pickering of the East Manchester Environmental Resource Centre**

Aidan Hodgkinson Photo-portrait

Etsuko Ueda Site document and strategic proposal sequence

From above;, left to right Views of new public spaces by
Athanassios Economou, Ting Na Chen, Amelia Zainudin, Amanda Ku

Aidan Hodgkinson Cross-section of new mixed-use building

Val Petrushechkin Part of study sequence looking at techniques of tilt-up concrete construction middle, early scheme for single-storey houses. below, sectional study for new mixed-use buildings.

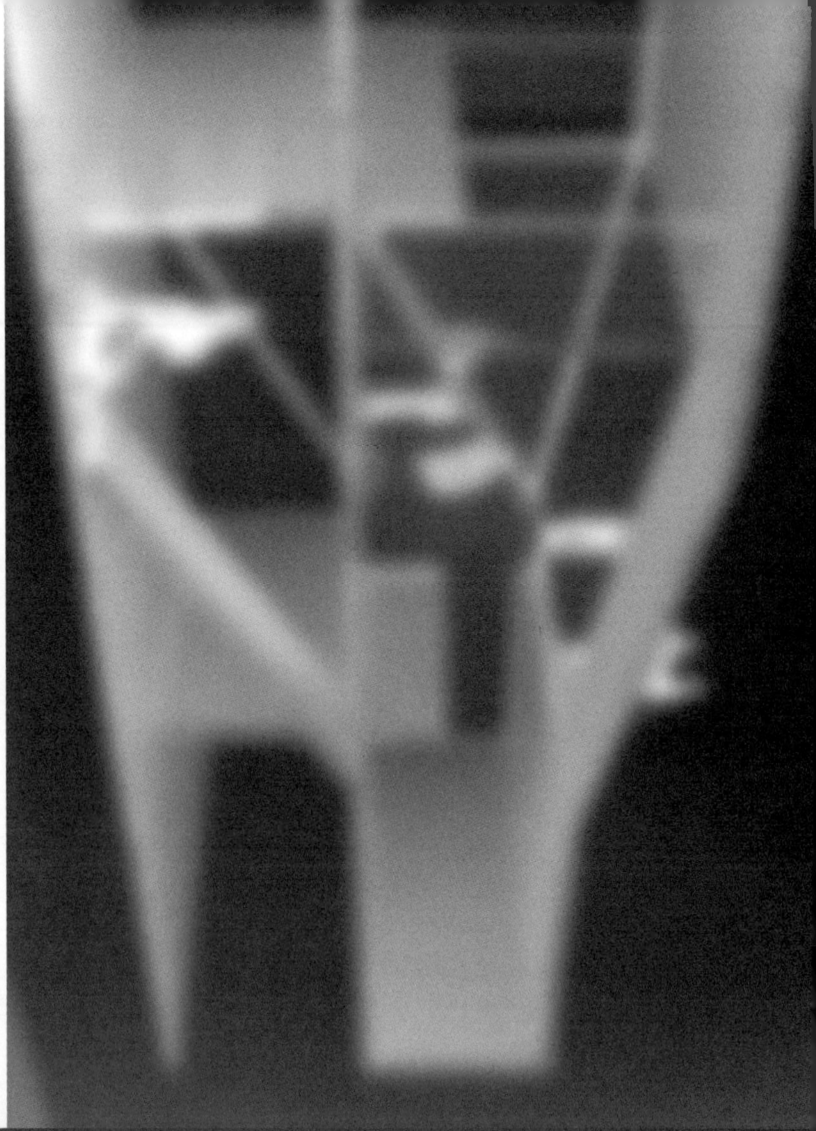

Eleni Stika Sectional model study for courtyard house

Henrik Lønberg View of three-storey 'house' shell, contractor and indication of three levels of finish – shell, diy, and key-in-door

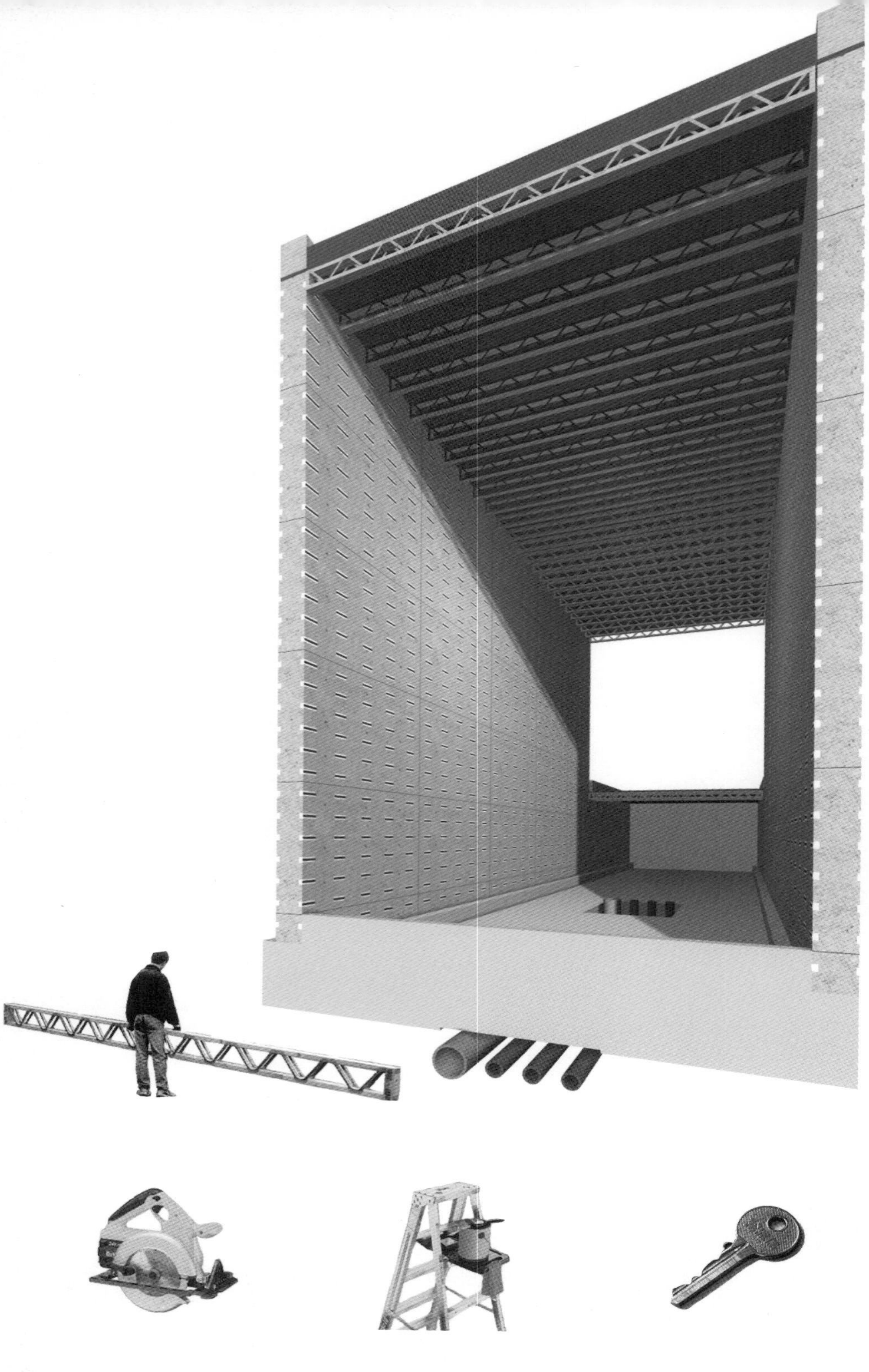

Bibo Hayashi Collaborative workshop proposal – integration of rammed earth wall and dual combustion wood-fuelled stove

ANARCHITE

CTUREPOEM

How to design seduction

This is a breakwater, it protects the shore from the sea, sometimes it is something else...

Daniel Flower

Architecture Is a Bed in Which to Rest

Cities are very good at avoidance. They bury everything in time, whereas confrontation leads back to intimacy.

The ruin is embedded within the folds of a fabric like a body seeking intimate comfort and escape within the sheets of the bed. Within these new folds lie the pools of dream, the route of lost escape. An ignored site is exposed by covering.

Mattias Ekman

Wishing to Leave to Be Able to Stay

Why is it impossible to get up from the streets? What do you hide behind the houses, on the rooftops?

Could these places complement the streets as a domain for the community?

Leisure and recreation; a retreat from your busy and dusty city.

Expansion within yourself, opening up to the inside.

Oriel Zinaburg

Ring City

This scheme is intended not only to restore the urban fabric but also to create a physical basis for social interaction. What follows is a speculative proposal to inspire a denser and more integrated society. At the same time, a resistance is created to spatial fragmentation and division. The Ring City would provide a circulation of common experience and markers or transit stations. This would assist in building a mental map of the city with a coherent set of landmarks that would highlight important nodes located in districts around the central core. In this way a person's sense of orientation would be greatly improved. Moreover, previously separated parts of the city would be united.

Palermo Mondiale
con molta seduzione la terra non trema piu

The architecture of appearing physicality – drawing the line of thought.

Palermo, which one doesn't want to leave, but has to: surrounded by land and water – but not enough water for the land.

Palermo, which welcomes but doesn't offer a home: beautiful palaces – but not enough to live on.

Palermo, which is so beautiful to see, but not to live in: gentle atmosphere – but ungentle living structure.

Where to house yourself in an inhospitable condition, how to inhabit Palermo, where to go when you want to stay?

The students had to develop their own theme, their own narrative, then develop that into their own architectural speculation and creative conclusion. Books and films document individual interpretations, in which aspects of temporality and adaptability are important criteria.

The unit deals with the problem of housing one's own identity in relation to an acceptable 'urban identity' on both a mental and physical level. We see memory as important in generating, developing and concluding a project, because memories are always related to physicality, defining its dynamic value. Within this research procedure and transliterative meaning of materiality, space and time processes play an important role.

Breathing Space
Palermo is suffocating. How could you tell? What does breath look like?

Exchange only happens between the surfaces of the old city maze. Towards the harbour, where vital plasticity is expected, breathing appears unconscious. Freedom of movement is denied by protecting walls and fences, and the link to the sea is nonexistent. Imagine a space that takes on the existing qualities of enclosure but translates it into a breathing space that is both programmatic and architectonic. Emptiness, air, the absence of programme, together with imaginary enclosing surfaces, sometimes impenetrable, sometimes porous, sometimes transparent, sometimes opaque, define a gradient sequence of spaces informed by local intensities that lead from the city towards the sea. Paradoxically, vertical surfaces, once a barrier, now become the threshold to the consciousness of breathing.

Kyoko Kobayashi

Unboxing Water

Thanks to 'the golden valley' created by rivers, the sunniest city, Palermo, was developed as a port. Yet as the sun dried up the rivers, the sensation of water was lost, and the city dried up in turn. Does water come back to moisturise the city again? From the abundant seawater around the city, a box generates water to return the missing element to the city.

Christopher Dukes

A Ruin Collapsed Under the Weight of Its Memory

By displacing my domestic objects in various situations, I discovered a boundary condition between the public space of the city and the private space of the house; I took temporary possession of one of Palermo's ruins between the harbour and the city. An architectural speculation has followed on how this may be rehoused in terms of its perceived and reversed value.

Sylvia Ng

Un senzacasa con molte case

It all began with a name. The duality in my name leads to another name – the city that bears my name defines my own place in the world. Names replace objects; naming is a desire for the object. Being homeless, without objects, I travel to names as a longing to find the right name, the right home, the right object. On the contrary, homeless without space is the presence of too many objects, where these 'memory objects' are a hindrance to home and living. The foundation is to recover home through actively using memory objects in a house, from structural mechanisms to appliances, to 'home' inhabitants with personal meaning.

Simultaneity

Simultaneity, a temporal instant, confronts you with the awareness of the surrounding and the nearby, constituting spatial and temporal realities.

Simultaneity is not a merging of differing modes, but rather a wakefulness between them, accommodating them, feeding a moment for break-off.

The device is the instrument to the event. It mediates atmospheres, then suggests functions as such. It negotiates between the overall event and the subject, accommodating your immediate motivations. It never imposes a perimeter to keep the influx going.

Julian Löffler

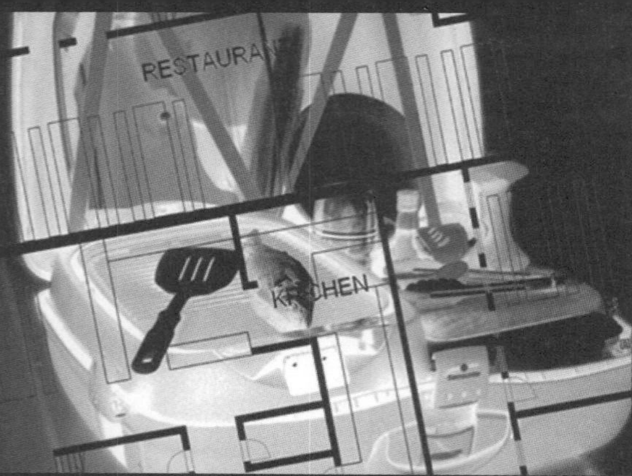

Uncannable

One-hour suitcase architecture – a tool for the transformation of space. My suitcase, full of ready-mades, carries a potential temporary building. It travels on a global route in a state of camouflage, until it suddenly unfolds, merging with a local situation and transforming it into something new.

Andy Meira

Speed Is a Scooter But Not a Jumbo Jet

Speed is an exhilarating sensual experience, but isolates the subject through interventions of safety and efficiency. The inhabitants of slow space need an escape from their defined boundaries: a lane of sensory volume.

The breakwater is a very specific functional structure. It protects the shore against the sea, but sometimes, when it is not being used as a protective device, the breakwater stays in its position – static like the women waiting for the men at sea. This is when it is a house. The house develops around the breakwater as mental interiors, temporary shelters for dreams. At the breakwater, everything is possible. In Palermo I found my house at the breakwater.
It is not only the usefulness of the breakwater that makes it interesting. It is specially its geometry and materiality, which create all kinds of different space conditions that attract people there. The breakwater seduces because of its mysterious passages and gaps. The house at the breakwater exists; the proposal is to create a new city by giving another dimension to the breakwater. My breakwater works in opposition to the existing functional one.

Unit Staff
Pascal Schöning
Thomas Durner

Students
Rubens Azevedo
Christopher Dukes
Mattias Ekman
Daniel Flower
Kyoko Kobayashi
Julian Löffler
Andy Meira
Sylvia Ng
Peter Staub
Roman Wittmer
Oriel Zinaburg

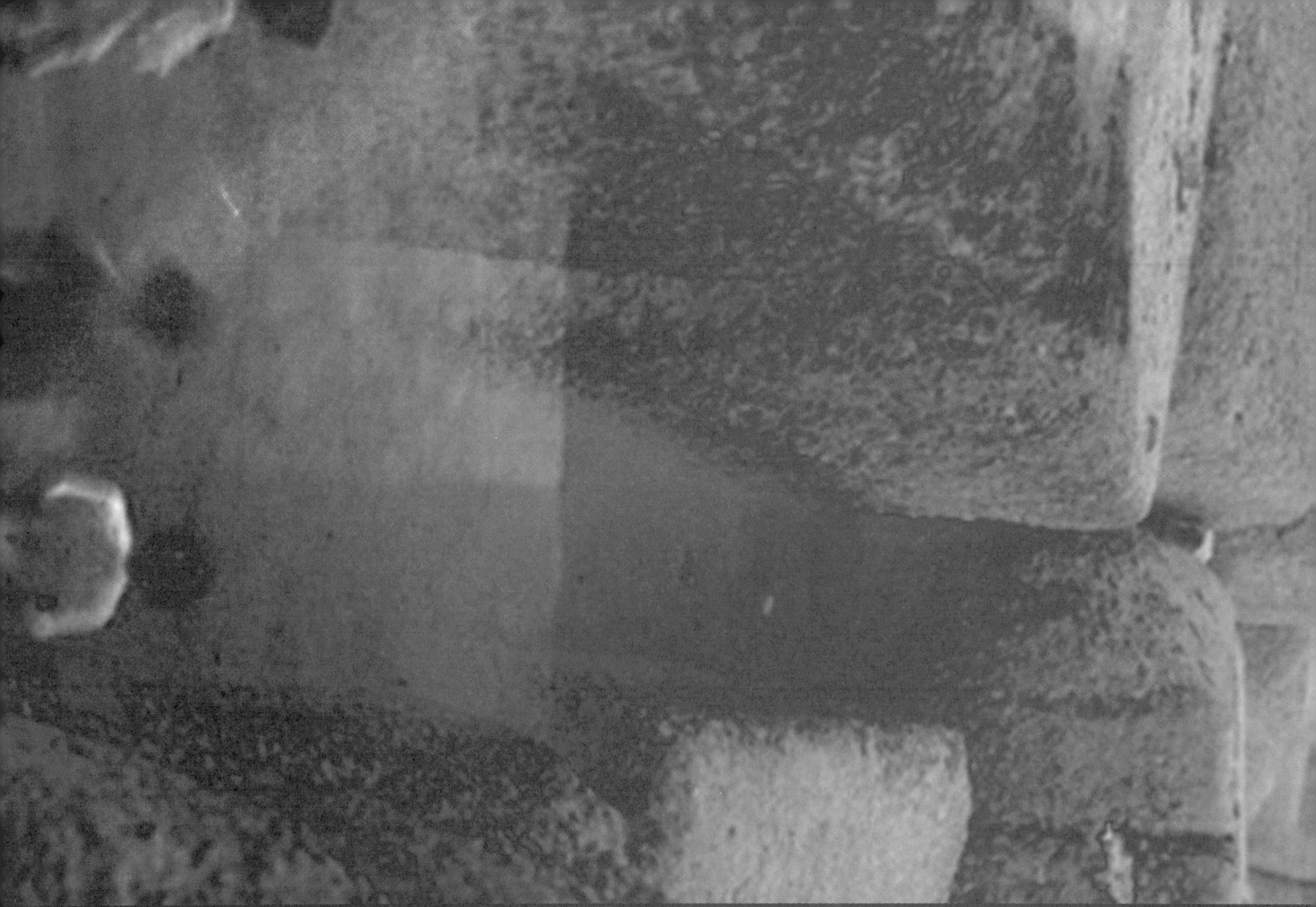

Humanity is faced with a double perspective: in one direction, mystery, seduction and dreams – precisely the perspective of architecture - and in the opposite direction, that of control or the real world of utility. Only the useful, the real, has a serious character. Use has rights over us; I prefer seduction. And we must respond to something, which not being God, is stronger than every right, the physicality to which we accede only by forgetting the truth of all these rights. (More or less Georges Bataille, adapted by Rubens Azevedo)

Lip-khoon Chiong, Morten Gregersen, Achim Menges (this page) and **Nasrin Kalbasi and Dimitrios Tsigos** (opposite page)

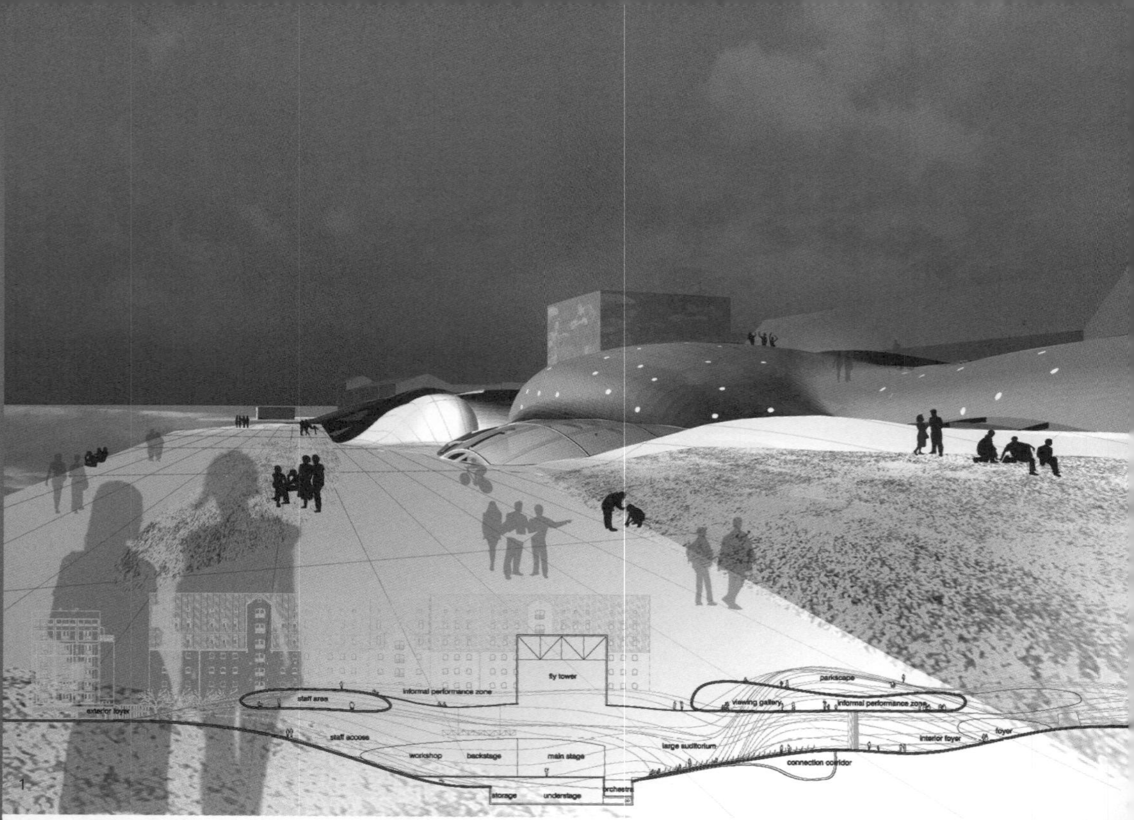

1

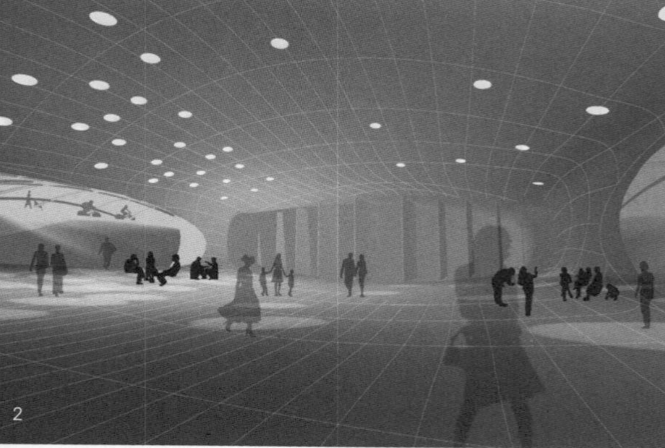

2

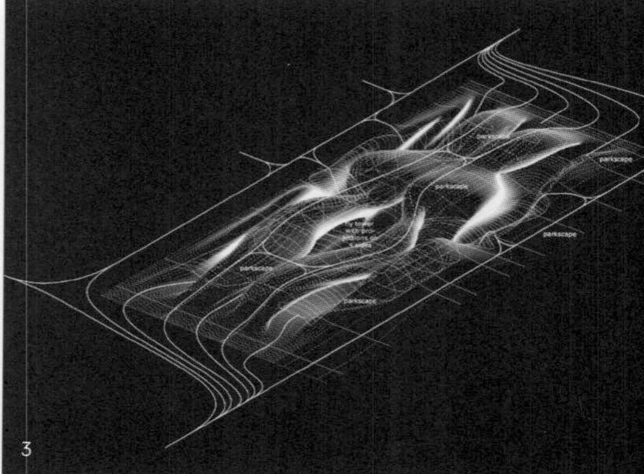

3

Becoming Architecture[s]

'Nothing retains its own form.' – *Pythagoras*

Dip 4's architectural agenda is based on the notion that architecture is about the articulated transformation of the human environment and thus, inherently, about change. This notion calls for a time-based approach to design, and for design techniques and a technical agenda that facilitate a dynamic articulation and experience of the built environment. This year the unit undertook two projects: a competition for the new playhouse for the Royal Theatre in Copenhagen and proposals for the transformation of the Dutch countryside. The two Copenhagen entries explore differentially articulated building schemes as highly permeable experiential public landscapes that provide for both formal and informal theatrical performances and cultural events. One scheme does so by employing a continuous surface tectonic, in which intersecting surfaces articulate a fluid theatrical space and provide for structural capacity [figs 1–3]. The second scheme employs a striated tectonic, with each strip morphing in dimension and geometry, from primary structure to furniture provision, while at the same time regulating visual transparency and circulatory permeability [figs 4–6].

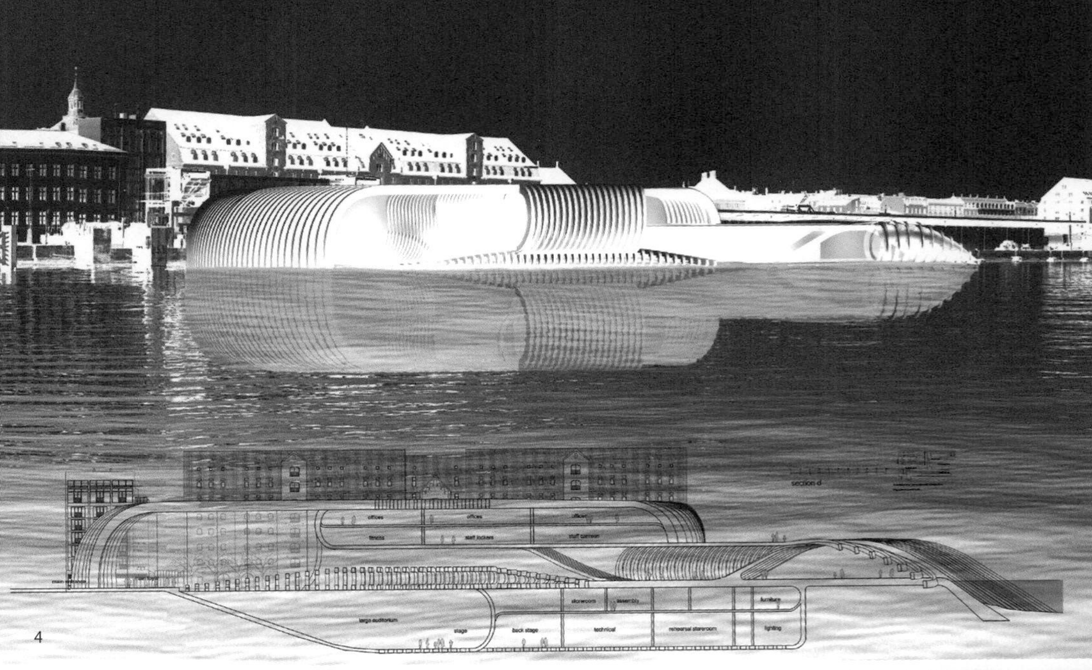

4

5

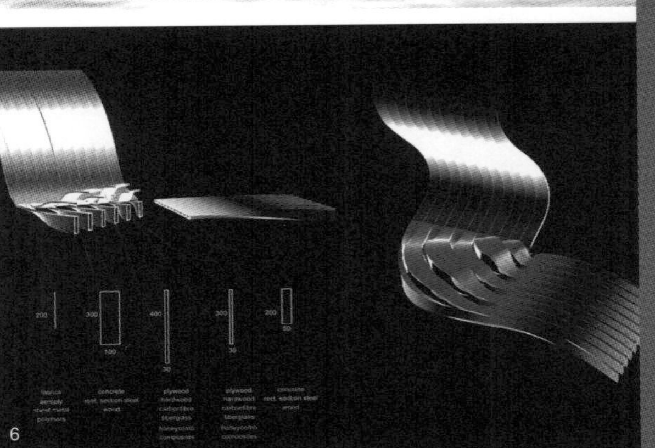

6

Unit Masters
Ludo Grooteman
Michael Hensel

Students
Lip-khoon Chiong
Morten Gregersen
Jethro Hon
Alessandro Isola
Nasrin Kalbasi
Jieun Lee
Morten Ludviksen
Supriya Mankad
Achim Menges
Kayoko Ohtsuki
Kenzo Osuga
Adrian Priestman
Michael Shevel
Dimitrios Tsigos

Technical Consultants
Michael Weinstock
Tim Lucas
Chris Carroll and
Michele Janner
Wolf Mangelsdorf
Hanif Kara

Thanks to
Jan Broeze
Helen Castle
Jan De Wilt
Pierre De Vries
Chris Hight
Hugo Hinsley
Igor Kebel
Prof. Steinar Killi
Willemijn Lofvers and
Jago Van Bergen
Ben Morris
Sandra Morris
Mohsen Mostafavi
Ciro Najle + Dip 14
Joel Newman
Pascal Schöning
Birger Sevaldson
Kivi Sotamaa
Peter Trummer
Jeff Turko
Carlos Villanueva Brandt
and especially
Michael Weinstock for
continuous support

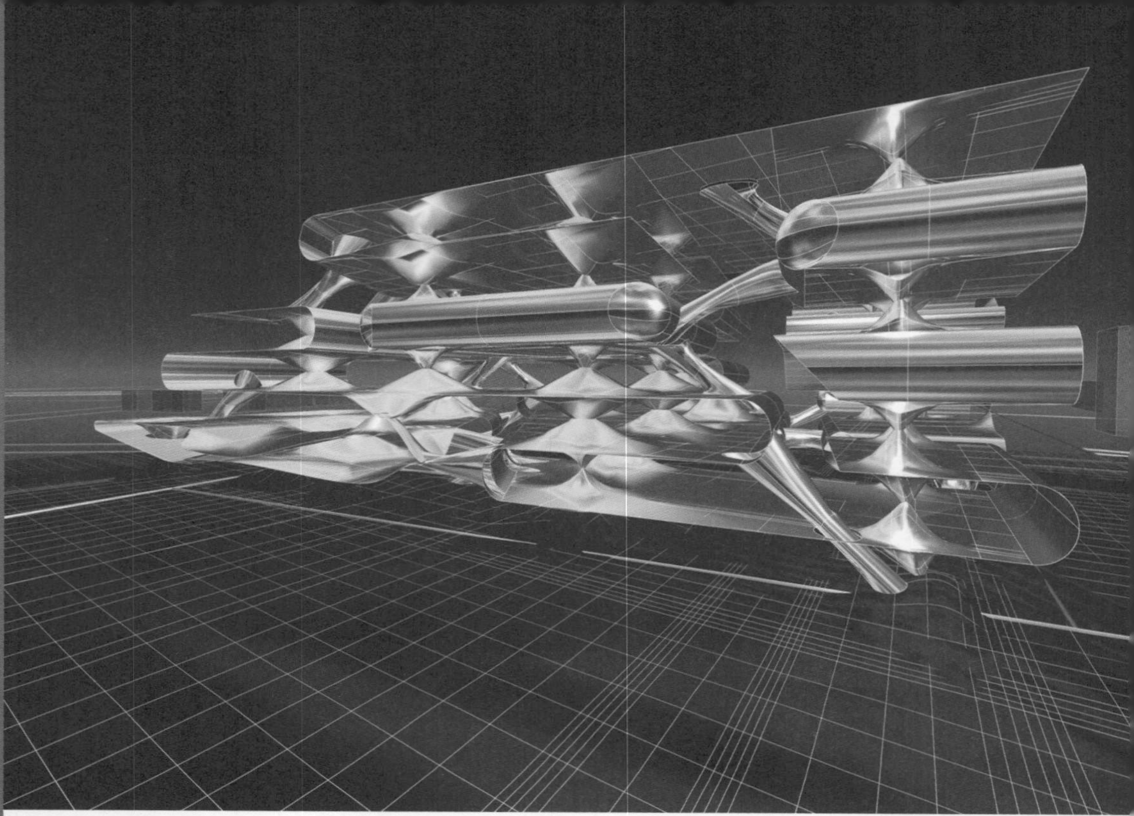

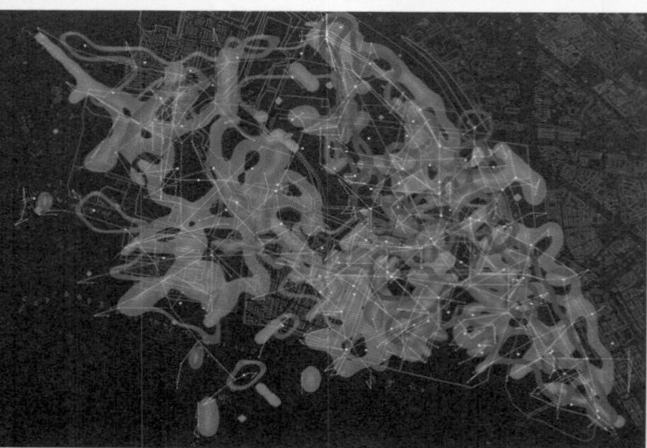

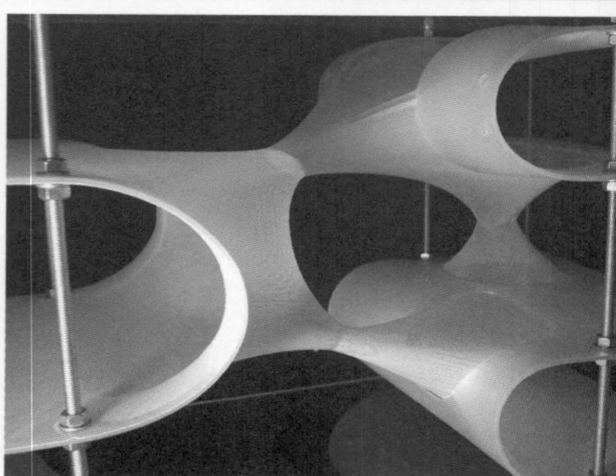

Rethinking [sub?] Urbanisation **Lip-khoon Chiong**

30,000 houses and 700,000 sqm of office space are to be built in the former agricultural area of Leidsche Rijn, near Utrecht. The existing master plan projects a monotonous density of homogeneous building types for housing, business and industry. An analysis of the planned infrastructural network and distance of facilities from the dwelling areas revealed an overdependence on the automobile and a highly unequal distribution of facilities, showing that daily engagement networks of work, leisure and consumption are not well provided for. The project proposes an urban growth strategy based on working with, rather than against, multiple claims on land use, multiple cores for intensive programming and a differentiated densification scheme. The urban growth strategy is paralleled by the design of a multidatum urban fabric for dense multiuse areas. Differential structural and circulation cores based on minimal surface geometries enable a high degree of connectivity and a dense distribution of infrastructural and engagement networks in three dimensions. The densification scheme helps to reserve land for a continued agricultural production or green leisure areas.

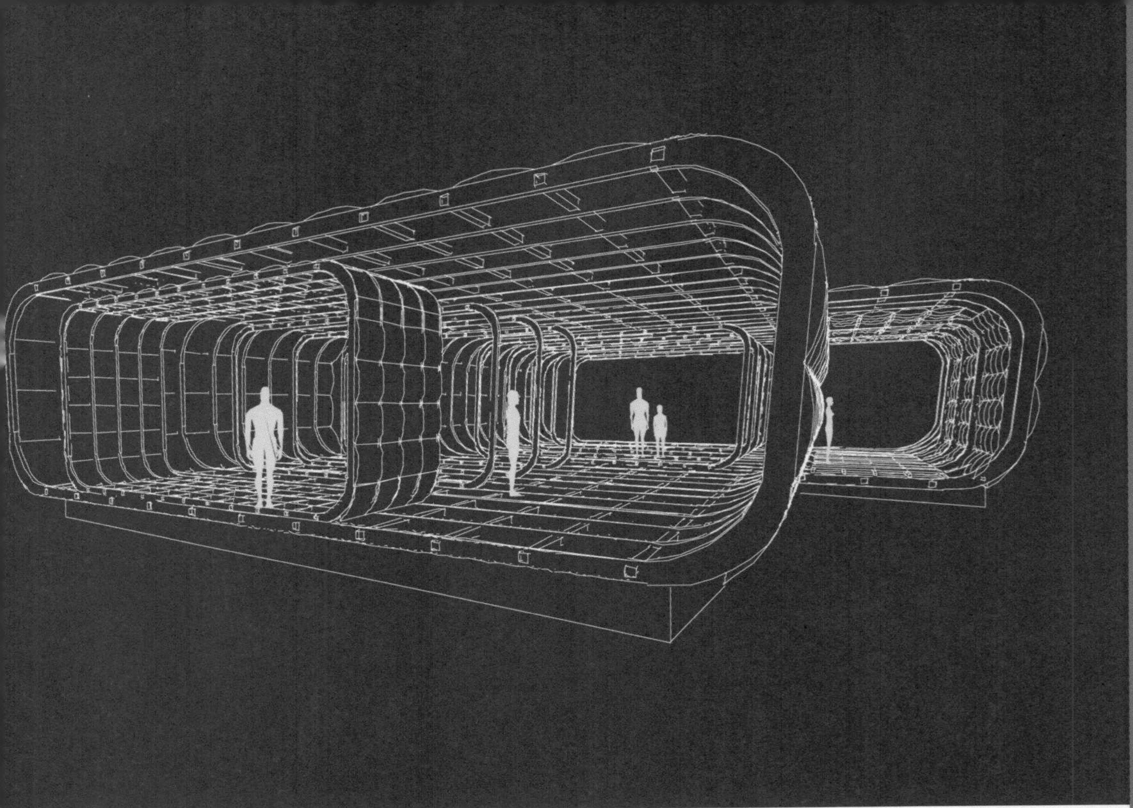

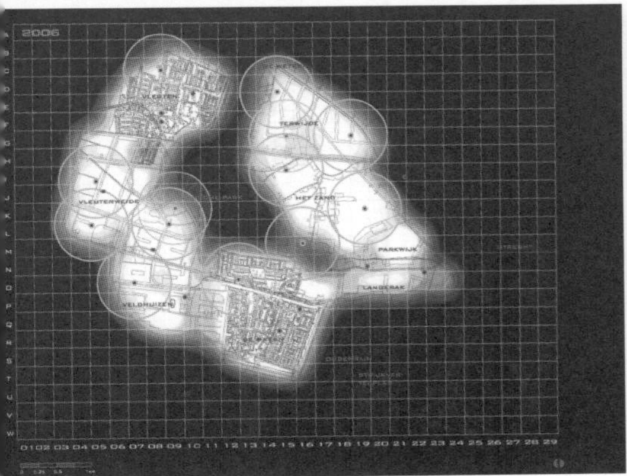

Re:assemblage **Nasrin Kalbasi**

Leidsche Rijn awaits the construction of 30,000 new homes between 2002 and 2013. The current master plan for the site provides exclusively for single-child middle-income households. Changes in the site's demographic composition would thus lead to problems with respect to the adequate provision of public institutions and amenities, such as nurseries, schools, libraries and shopping facilities. This project therefore aims at a responsive and adaptable urban and architectural scheme that can accommodate changes in needs by providing and distributing relevant institutions and amenities at the time, location and articulation they are needed. By means of a modularised striated structural system, each building can be (re)located, adjusted and articulated according to plot size and footprint, spatial, programmatic and ergonomic requirements, access and communication spaces, and visual connection and transparency. Every assemblage then becomes recognisable as part of a family of transparent striated objects giving identity to locations as sites of public life, while demographic and ergonomic needs articulate and activate the human environment.

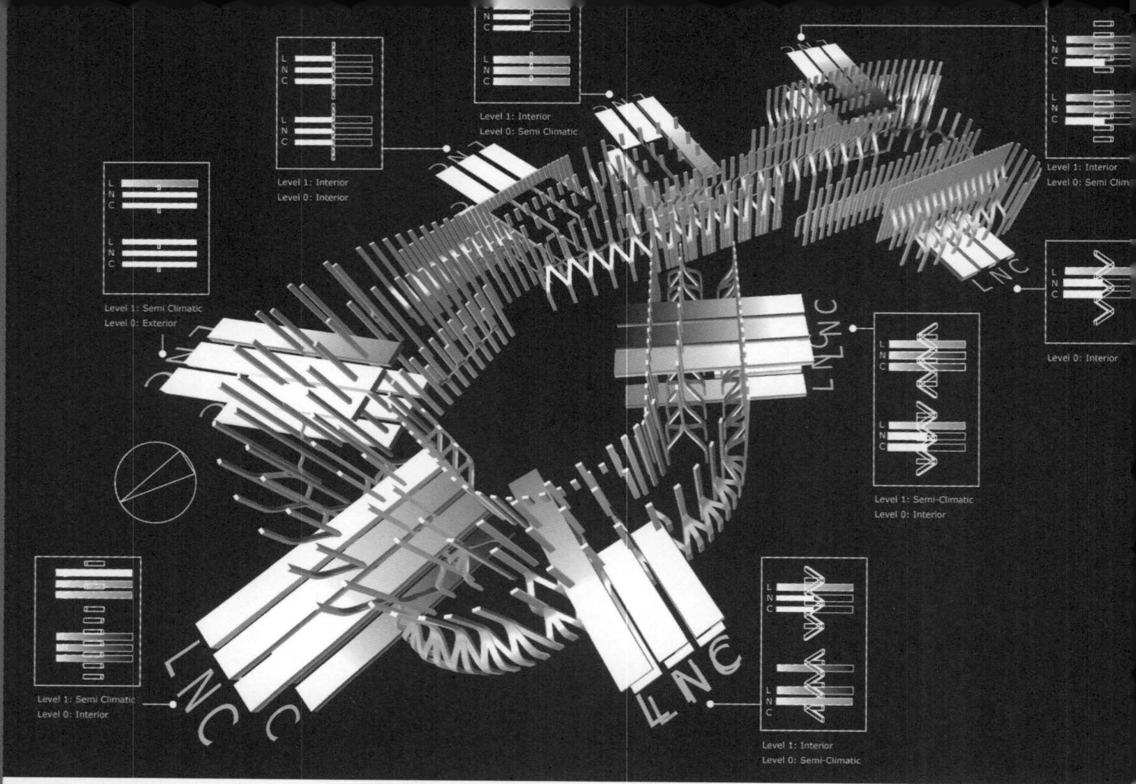

Level 1: Interior
Level 0: Interior

Level 1: Interior
Level 0: Semi Climatic

Level 1: Interior
Level 0: Semi Clim

Level 1: Semi Climatic
Level 0: Exterior

Level 0: Interior

Level 1: Semi-Climatic
Level 0: Interior

Level 1: Semi Climatic
Level 0: Interior

Level 1: Interior
Level 0: Semi-Climatic

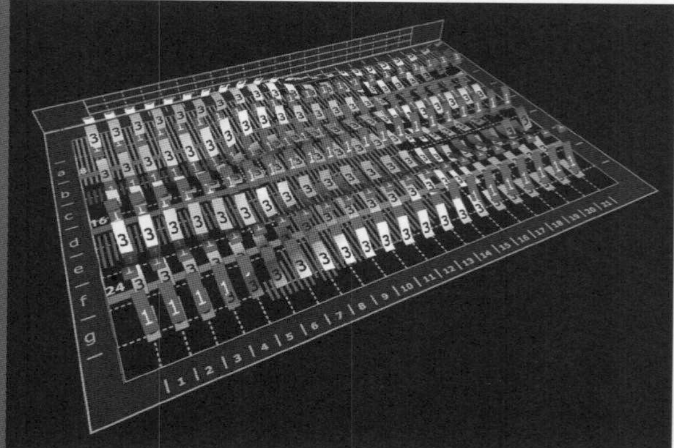

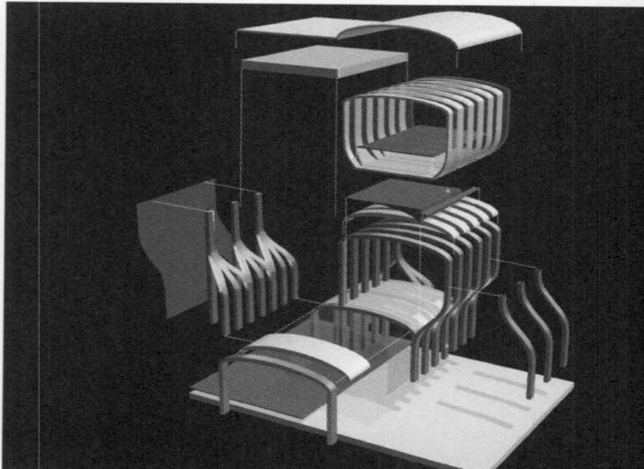

More or Less Planning **Morten Gregersen**

Current developments are leading to the transformation of the agricultural production areas adjacent to the Dutch Randstad into large suburban housing areas. This project investigates an alternative to this kind of homogeneous, monoprogrammatic urban fabric, proposing a revised urban growth strategy that commences with a merger of infrastructure and activity zones as a catalyst for site development. This requires a highly differential articulation of infrastructure according to mode and velocity of circulation, as well as a redefinition of the material threshold that mediates between proximity to infrastructure and performance criteria. A modularised system of branch columns and beams serves to articulate thresholds as spatial transitions and atmospheric gradients that provide for the conditions needed for each activity zone. The possibility of organising infrastructure and programmes in much closer proximity allows for compaction of land use, reserving the gained surface area for future developments.

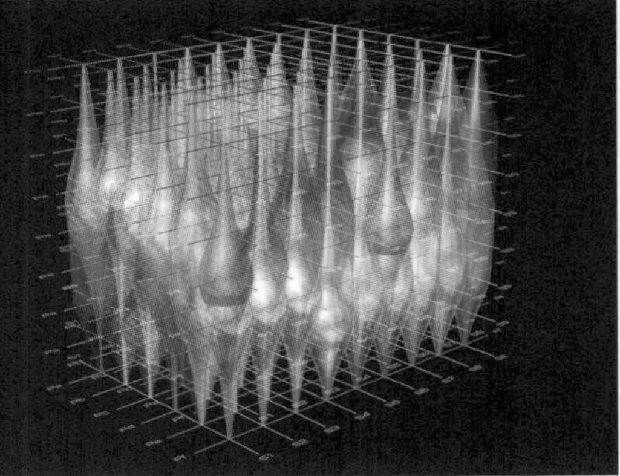

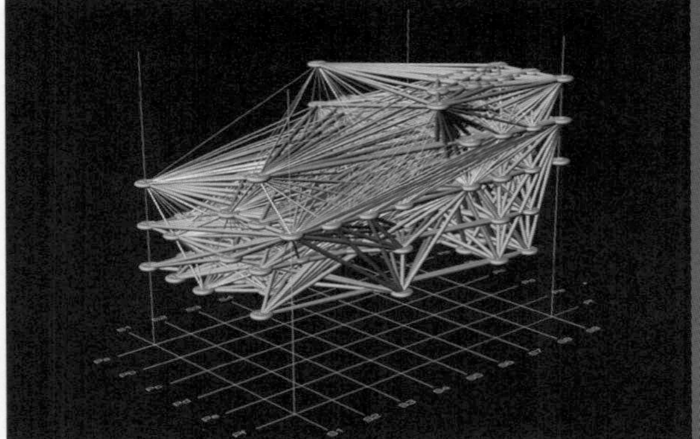

Postagriculture **Achim Menges**

Located in Westland, the biggest and most dense Dutch greenhouse area, the project undertakes a revision of agroproduction in the Netherlands, to create an environmentally and socially sustainable food production. The project aims for an open and responsive organisation that treats agricultural production as an inclusive, mutable and highly urban programme that can be hybridised with leisure programmes for the Hague area, thus negotiating regional and national development aims. The project deploys a differentiated layered pneumatic structure in order to facilitate and regulate a dynamic microclimatic organisation.
The type and treatment of the surface material regulates light, temperature and smell conditions over time. Software that combines digital form-finding with structural analysis and the possibility of determining cutting-pattern facilitated the design of the differential pneumatic structure. Through this approach, the project provides for varied and dynamic microclimatic conditions that suit agroproduction and leisure activities with similar requirements in each sublocation of the deep structure. This constitutes a shift from a static, unit-based architecture to a performative, condition-based environment.

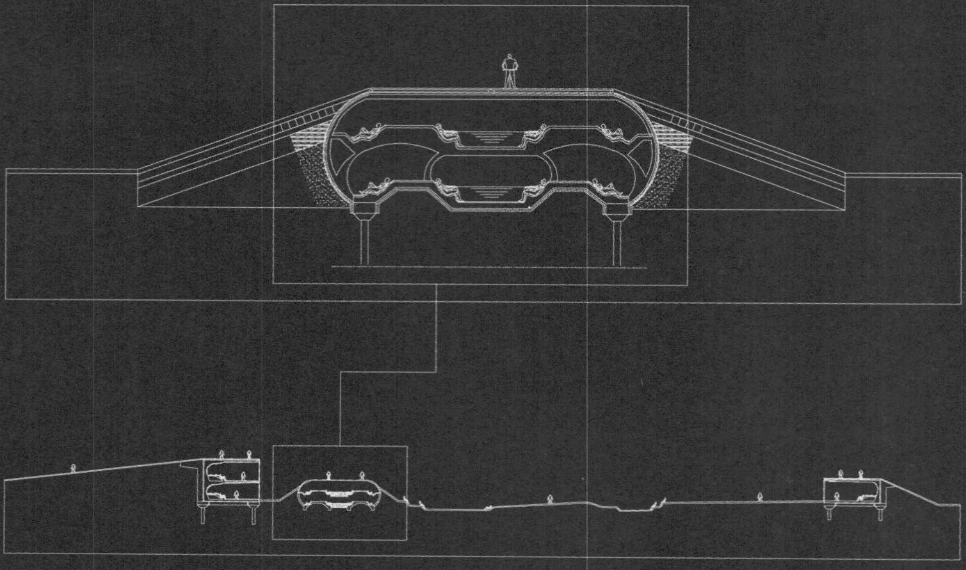

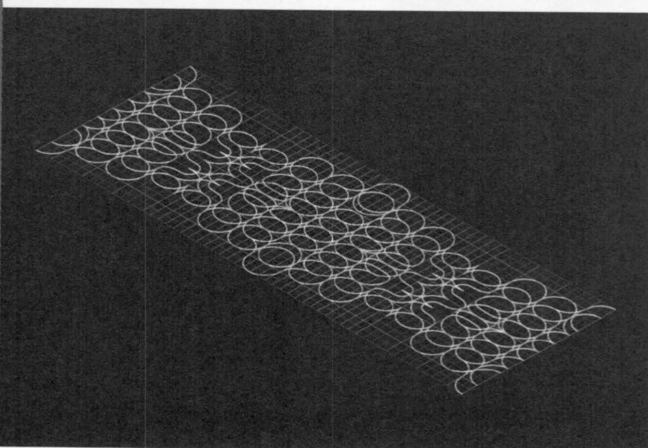

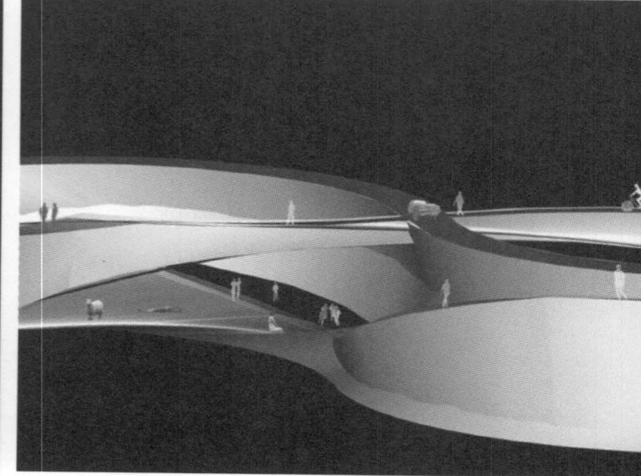

LandFormations **Kayoko Ohtsuki**

The inhabitants of Alblasserwaard, a traditional agricultural polder landscape, are under pressure to sell their lands to urban professionals seeking country homes or to transform them for leisure use for the Utrecht and Rotterdam areas. In either case, it is generally assumed that the site will have to undergo a reparcelling of the land and a revision of the related drainage and infrastructural networks. The land is currently being drained in order to stabilise the peat soil for agriculture, a system that would become redundant under any proposed changes in land use. In sites undergoing similar development, such as Leidsche Rijn, a 1-metre-thick layer of sand is laid over the land, erasing the particular characteristics that make these traditional cultural landscapes special and attractive. This project investigates the possibility of introducing multiple land use but reorganising land parcelling, drainage and infrastructural networks according to the logic that already governs their presence. This is done through curvilinear landscape-engineering structures that articulate continuous programme bands, leaving the majority of land unchanged or available for other types of development.

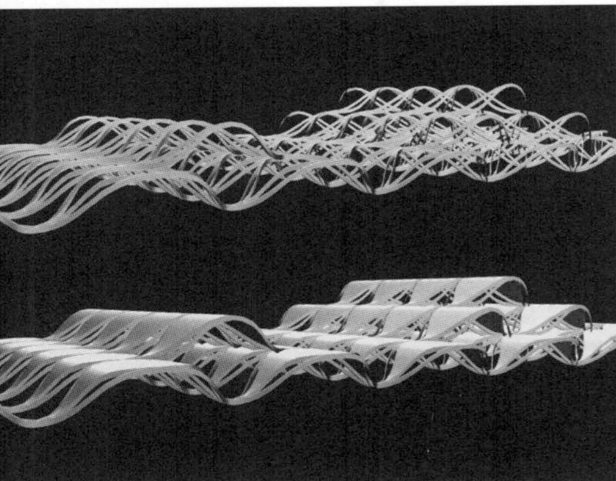

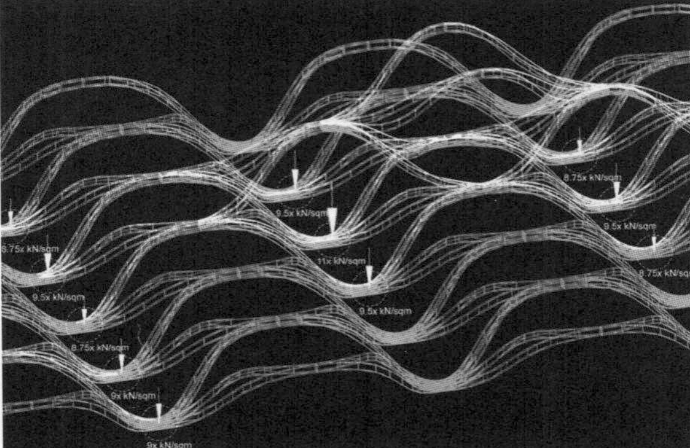

Evolving Landscapes **Jieun Lee**

As a typical Dutch polder, Alblasserwaard lies below water level. The peat soil of the area is stabilised by the high water-table, the height of which is controlled by the water boards in order to reconcile agricultural use with stabilisation of the soil, which would otherwise begin to subside. The question with respect to the future of the site is whether it would be possible to work with these soil dynamics as a developmental and environmental dynamic that can suggest alternative ways of conceiving and organising land use over time. The scheme is based on the development of a three-dimensional wave-form structural lattice that is laid over the site. This flexible, jointed lattice forms a thick carpet of inhabitable spatial corridors, enclosable pockets and top surfaces. Through its articulation, the lattice retains the horizontal character of the polder, leaving the ground datum and water-soil dynamics intact. Wherever spaces need to be added, the lattice can be vertically thickened. As large occupiable surface areas within and on top of the lattice are inclined, new forms of surface occupation were strategised, based on an elaboration of Claude Parent and Paul Virilio's notions of habitable circulation and oblique space.

Anatopism

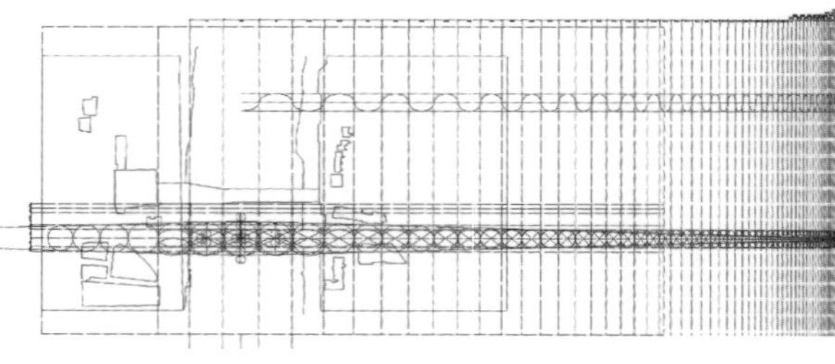

Bobby Jet Wai Wong
Nausicaa Voucalis
Sandra Piesik

Substance

Idan Schein
Spyridon Kaprinis
Harry Paticas

Schmuck

Amrit Marway

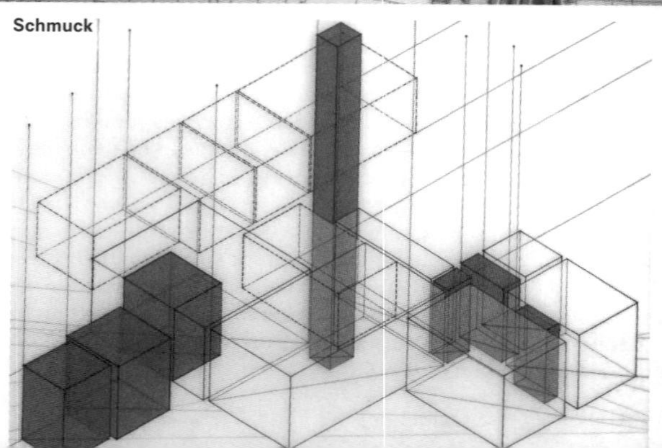

Unit Master
Christian Kieckens

Tutor
Caroline Voet

Students
François Chambaud
Dan Eliassen
Andrew Gancikov
Spyridon Kaprinis
Amrit Marway
Harry Paticas
Sandra Piesik
Geoffrey Poon
Tomas Ramos
Idan Schein
Nausicaa Voucalis
Bobby Jet Wai Wong

Visiting Critics
Martine de Maeseneer
Shin Egashira
Mark Hemel
Barbara Kuit
Cedric Libert
Mohsen Mostafavi
Rik Nys
Richard Padovan
Charles Tashima
Li Mei Tsien
Tom Verebes

Special thanks to
Tom Barker
José Géal

London

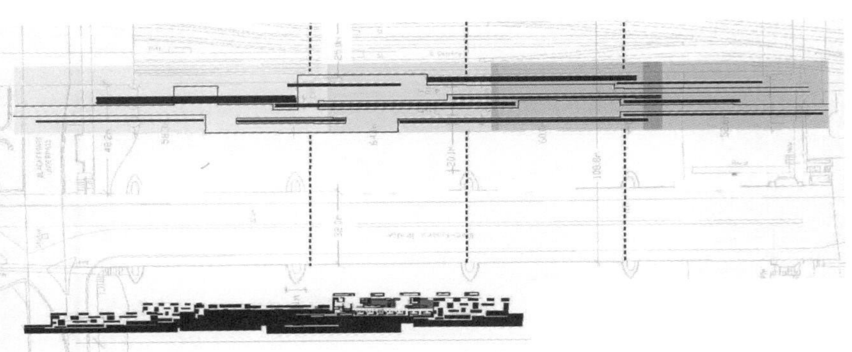

Brussels

Vienna

Each architecture possesses an obvious absent presence and a present absence.

Within the city, infrastructural systems are separated from housing because of environmental concerns about noise and pollution. Bridges in London are seen mainly as infrastructure, crossing over and connecting roads, rivers, highways or train tracks. Because of their scale, the only 'housing' that faces them on an equal level is freestanding highrise. Within the city itself, bridges offer many small-scale in-between spaces, gaps in the urban fabric. We introduce a new type of house/haus that grows within these in-between spaces.

The focus is centred on the structural properties of the bridge and its place within the urban fabric. To build up a profound understanding of the main structure, as well as its transformations and changes, we added a supplementary volume and/or replaced it with a new structure.

An investigation of typical bridge structures, such as the 'Vierendeel-ligger', enabled us to transpose meanings between infrastructure, structure and house. An analysis of the methodology and

Spyridon Kaprinis
Amrit Marway
Harry Paticas and François Chambaud

Bobby Jet Wai Wong
Sandra Piesik
Nausicaa Voucalis

Spyridon Kaprinis
Harry Paticas and François Chambaud
Andrew Gancikov and Tomas Ramos

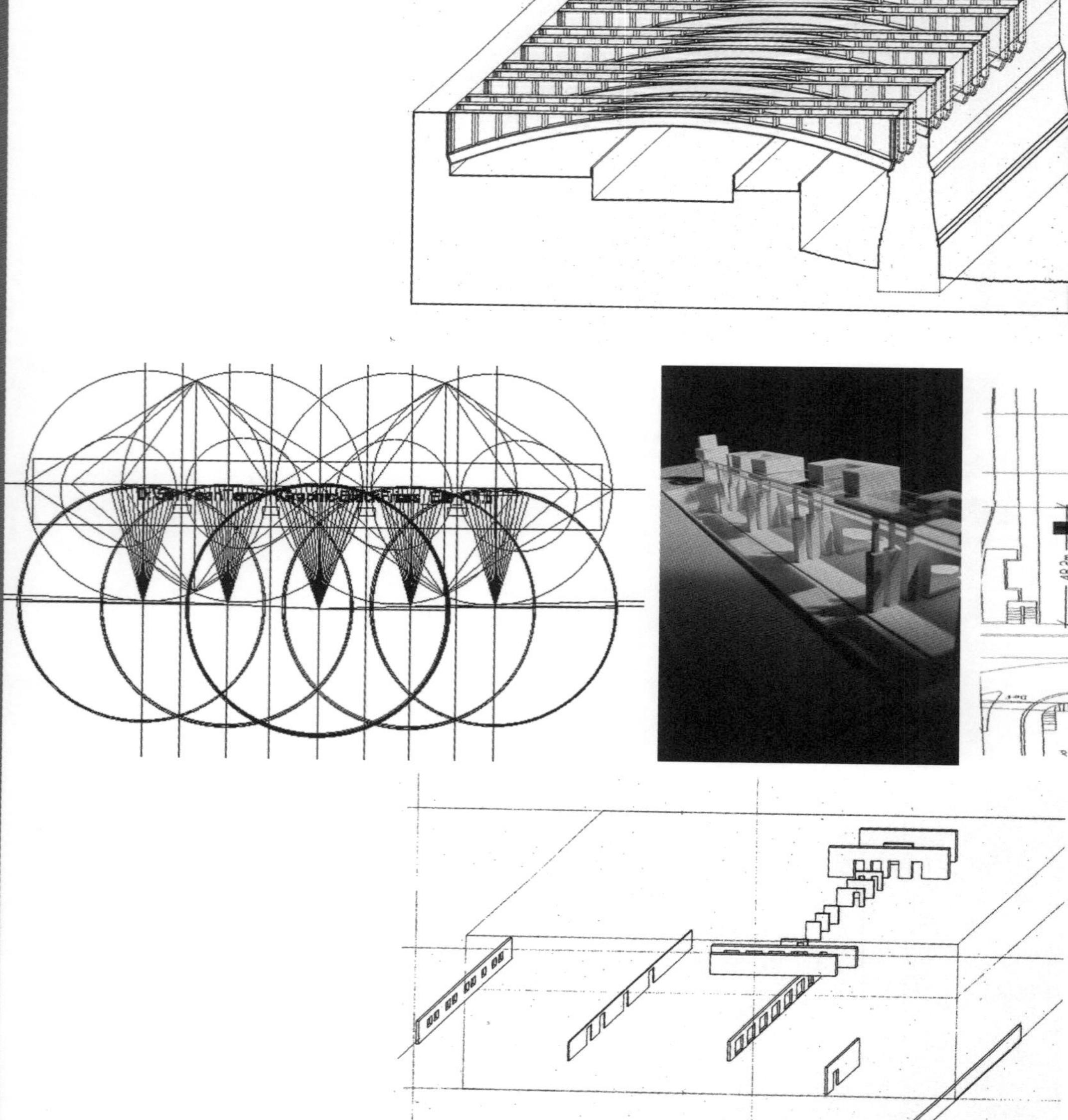

proportional systems of Peter Zumthor, Ludwig Wittgenstein, Dom Hans van der Laan and Francesco Borromini revealed their architectural meaning and indicated a possible starting-point.
This unit investigates how the act of urban development can contribute to a new topos in historic city centres. The main concepts of context / content / perception are linked to new architectural meanings as displacement / substance / appearance through two different research projects.
From a diagrammatic analysis of basic theorems from architectural history, new techniques are developed to balance contemporary urban situations in London and Brussels.

1. Searching On The Haus / Next 2
Term 1 concerns the development of house/haus**, using an existing bridge structure in the City of London as the site of a new intervention.**

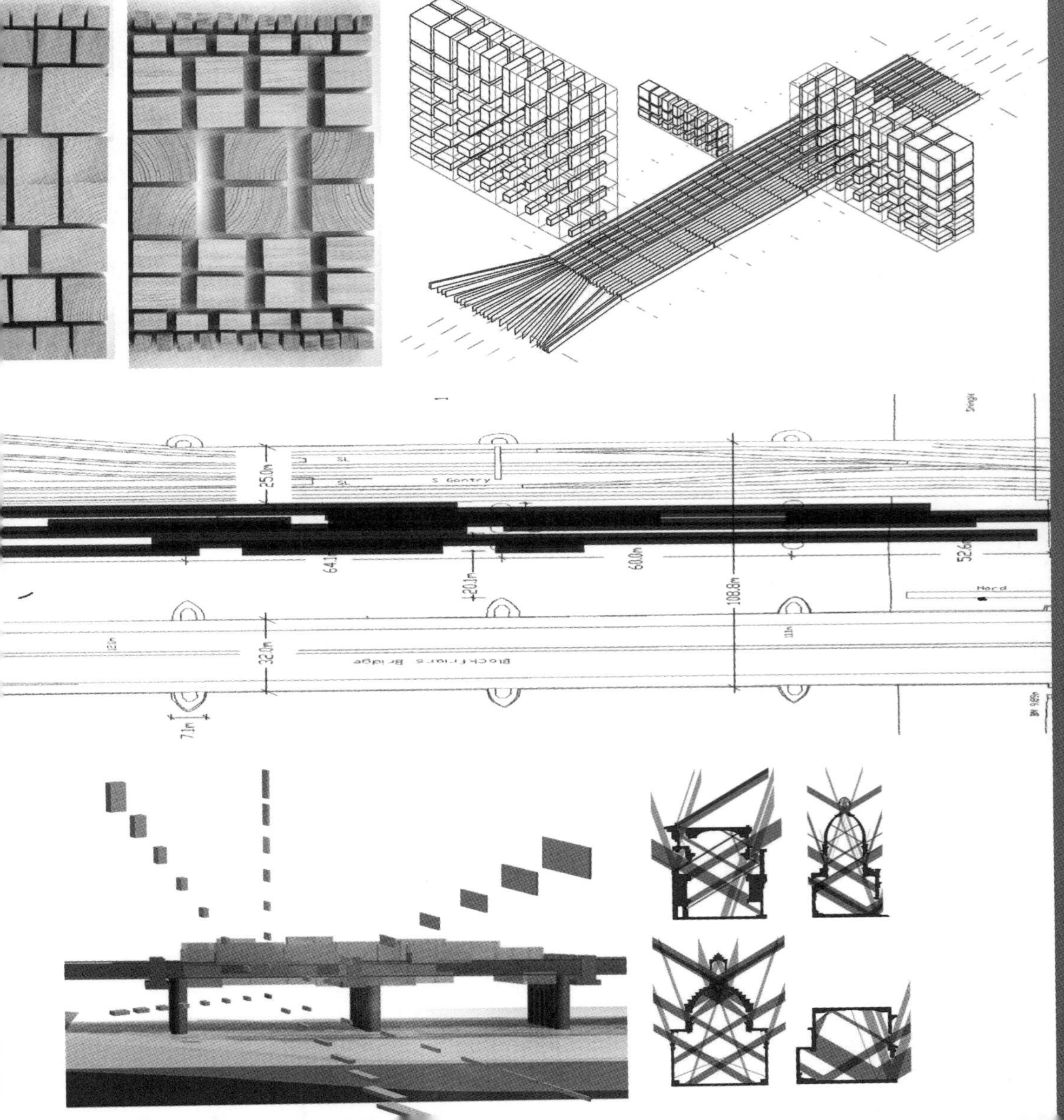

2. Thinking about the city / haus-ing

The second and third terms address the way in which the historic city, as a preserved image, as scenery, is embedded in a high-tech, contemporary urban fabric, thus perpetuating the duality and co-existence of redundant spaces.

A site in the very heart of Brussels, an empty plot of the same size as Belgium's biggest historical attraction, the Grande Place, provides the *topos* for new interventions connecting all contemporary urban needs into a single structural complex with a range of new programmes and in-between spaces.

Spyridon Kaprinis

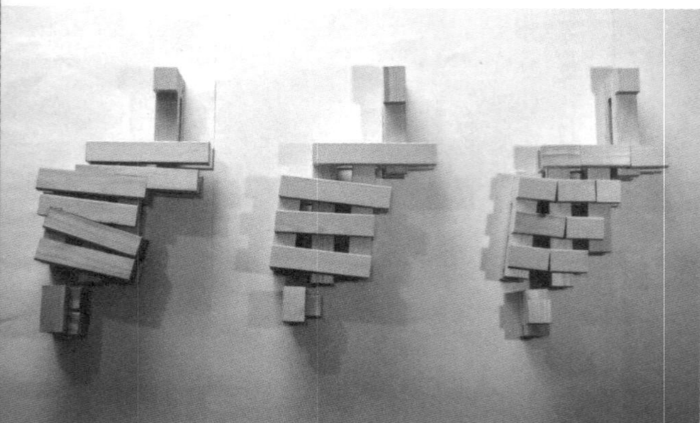

Bobby Jet Wai Wong

Harry Paticas

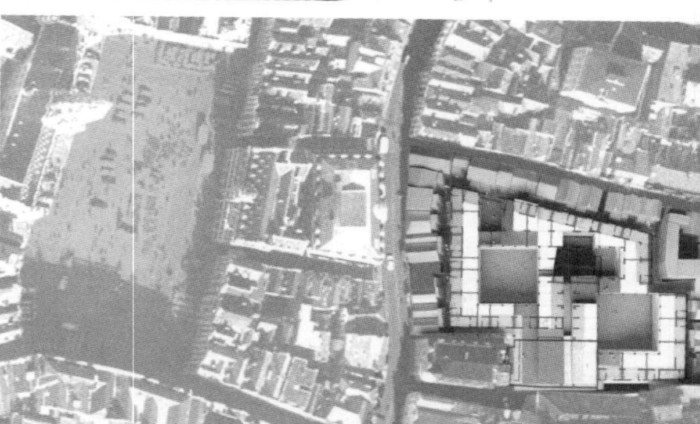

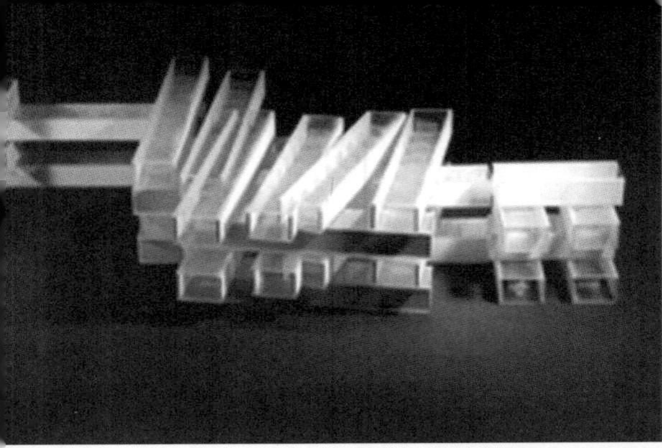

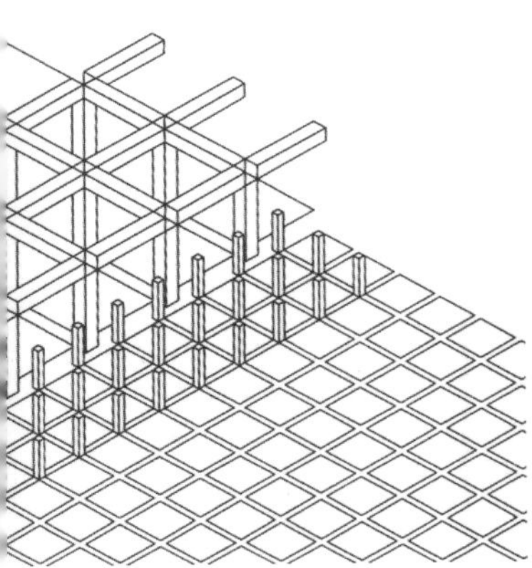

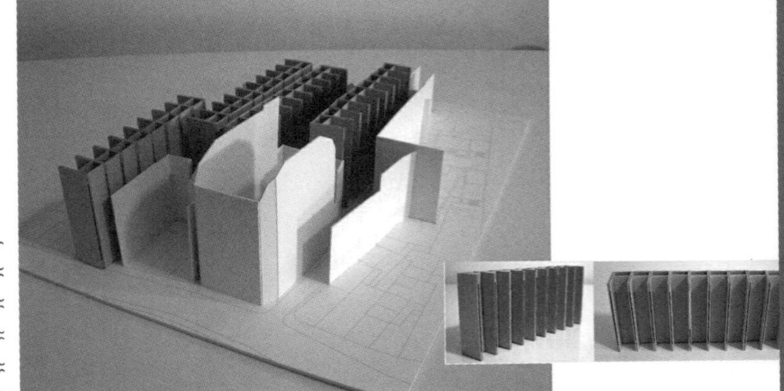

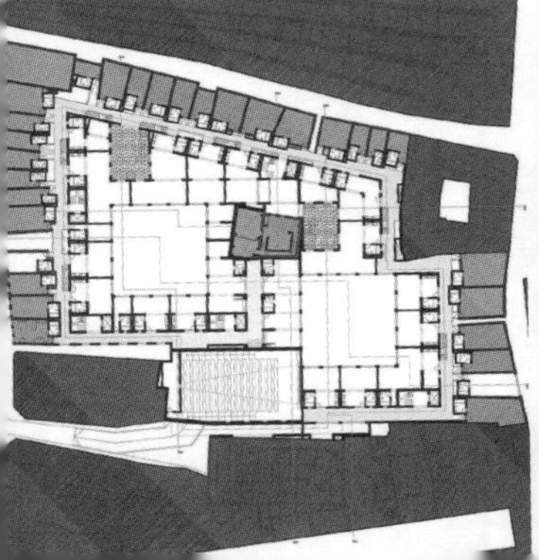

Geoffrey Poon
Nausicaa Voucalis

François Chambaud

Amrit Marway

Andrew Gancikov
Idan Schein
Sandra Piesik

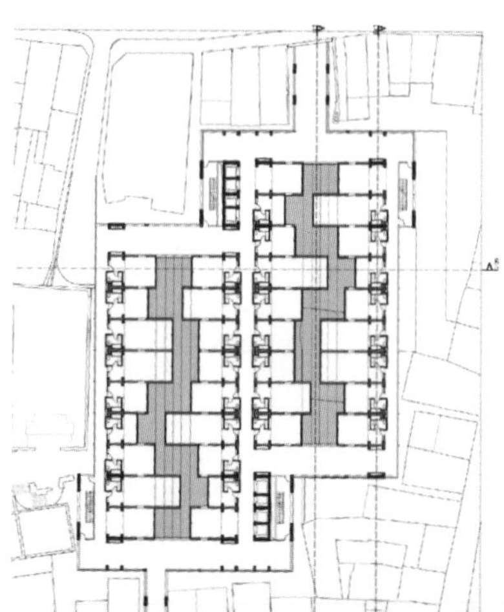

How does one work within the city's heritage, not from behind the scenes but by taking up the challenge of confrontation? How does a city like Brussels create its own contemporary character (as it did in the past, with art nouveau structures)? What new strategies can be developed for facades and screenings, and how can we achieve an understanding and acceptance of them that goes beyond every form of subjectivism? How do recent building regulations deal with 'monuments', and how can they be altered? How do we approach the standardised versus the monument, the rule versus the exception? The final proposals are based on the reality of 'construction', which links the building with a contemporary economic realm, based on the understanding of structure and the need for materialisation and appearance.

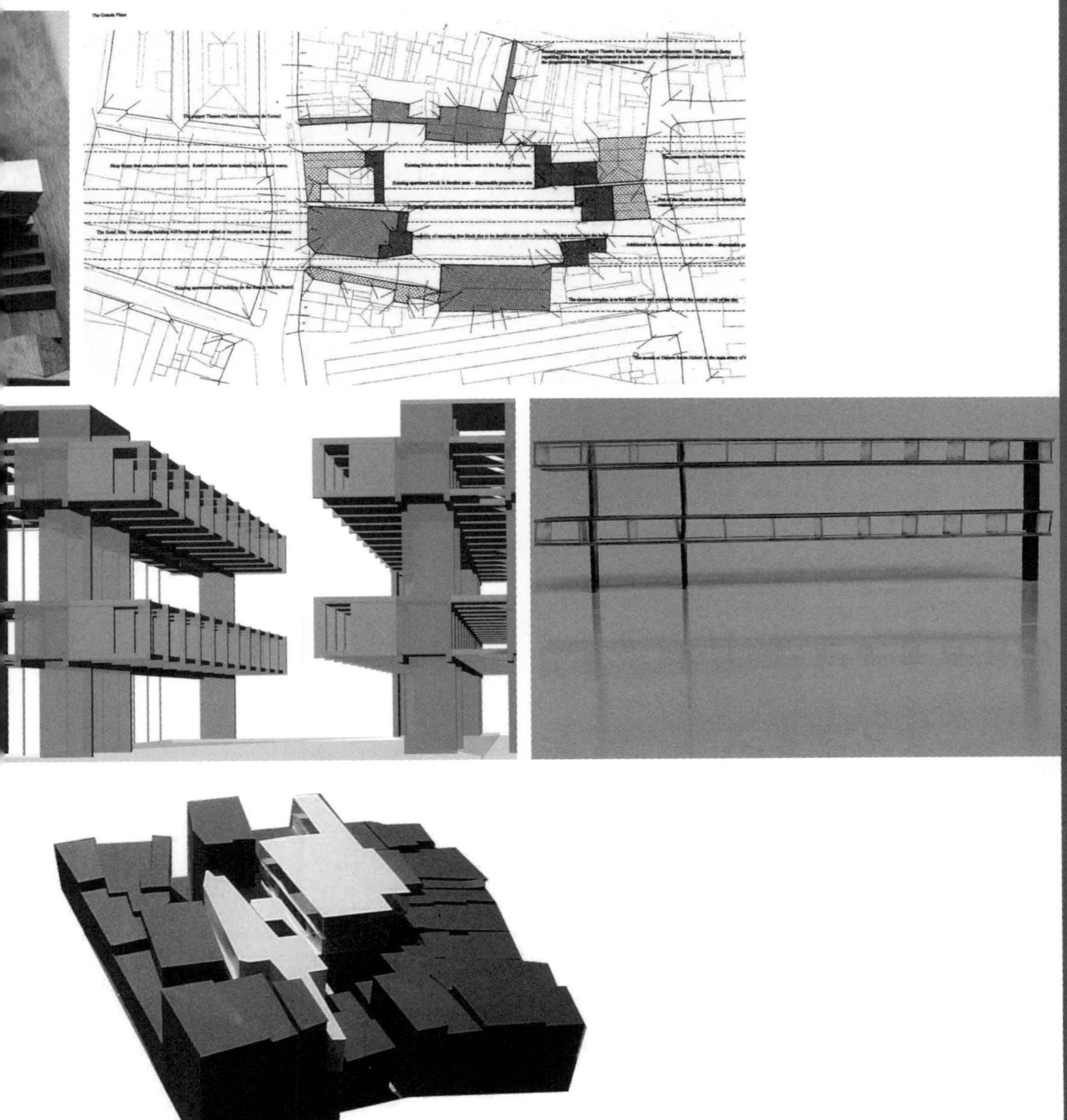

An Architecture of **Weak Form**

Philosophy

Architecture is dominated by a number of key formal paradigms, the most significant of which is the Miesian credo of a reduced, even classical, mechanism. Traditionally, this approach stands opposed to naturalism, to a bewildered and bemusing organicism in which the contrived geometries of an ethical mechanism give way to fatalism. Emergence (so called), by which is meant some predestined consequence of as yet unforeseen natural phenomena, is only the least distasteful of its deified products. Between these two polar limits of the machine metaphor and the organic metaphor the formal landscape of architecture is periodically reconfigured. Both approaches remain primarily formal and singularly myopic, preferring the trivial ground of form-making to the politicised territory of programmatics. They reappear cyclically in the history of modern architecture and continuously re-present an empty formalism as but the latest in a very attenuated line of inappropriate solutions to unrelenting social and economic problems.

Diploma Unit 6 realigned its points of engagement with design practice by rejecting this iconographical and egocentric approach, refocusing on pertinent contemporary issues such as communicability, accessibility, broad appeal, and the establishment of core social values in the organisation of space. This refocusing presented an opportunity to construct an architecture of weak form**, precisely a** weak architecture**, disinterested in the resisting and closed geometries of the Miesian aesthetic paradigm; an architecture driven by a much more flexible response to programme. Plural, inclusive, complex and formally pliable, such an approach constructs an architecture based on the needs of a broadening and more variegated social mix, and in terms of the conditions of an unprecedented social mobility and economic variability. It pursued a relevant, unselfconscious aesthetic, formulated from these conditions and from these conditions alone, on the basis of an inventive economy and practical execution.**

Social Enclave: Economic Ghetto

Programme

In order to sketch the conditions for the occupation of the contemporary urban core, Diploma Unit 6 students studied a discrete urban enclave, a social gathering place, in which key social programmes, demographic groups and specific economic conditions are concentrated.

Issues

Continuing its research into the demographic basis of social structures, projects focused on the consequences of several key contextual conditions and their influence on changes in the patterns of urban occupation. These included:
the nature of emergent social and demographic groupings
shifts in social identity, ethnicity and sexual orientation
the spatial distribution of emergent social patterns
the reconfiguration of economic localities
the contraction of social space in time.

Method

Design has shifted towards a more bespoke condition, a more tailored approach. The demand for a much more specific definition of user behaviour and requirements has emerged. From demographic analysis to weak architecture the unit has taken advantage of contemporary methods of social analysis and market definition to identify the specific nature of user groups and how they perform within the metropolitan core. These analyses determined the parameters for a highly specific architectural response.

Site

This year's studio concentrated on a number of sites within the London urban core. Studies focused on the London Borough of Tower Hamlets and the London Borough of Hackney, specifically Shoreditch. This offered itself as a productive site for the observation of emergent programmes, most interestingly the relatively new programme of live–work. Although a cliché of estate agent cant, there is little understanding of either the nature or future development of this programmatic type.

Students concentrated on a number of issues that emerged from this study. They were:

Space Compression in Multioccupancy Dwellings

The building types proposed multioccupation of the live–work type, allowing the development of programmes that eliminated the repetition of utilities typical of the bourgeois apartment block. The concentration of social facilities, together with the reduction of private space to a minimum, established what came to be known in the unit as the 'Big Brother' programme. Strictly private activities (urination, defecation, fornication, sleeping, dressing, etc) were divided from sociable ones (dining, working, playing, etc) – in contrast to the bourgeois apartment, in which all programmatic fragments of bourgeois dwelling are repeated in every unit. As with the Big Brother example, programme was polarised between strictly private and strictly social spaces.

The Prop

What has emerged from this is the 'Prop', a programmatic apparatus used to facilitate the delivery and concentration of utilities within the social sphere. Water, sewage, power, telecommunications, IT and their respective delivery devices are concentrated into a single article. Space for the enactment of social programmes is then 'attached' to the Prop.

Unit Master
Kevin Rhowbotham

Technical Tutor
Yousif Albustani

Students
Igor Gottschalk
Joseph Grima
Nicholas Hayhurst
Phil-Soo Kim
Asaf Mayer
Sebastian Nau
Jonathan Nicholls
Nader Seraj
Tim Sudweeks
Danny Sutresna
Kerem Turker

Visiting Critics
David Panos
John Buck
Dominic Cullinan
John Bell
Nic Clear
Adam Ogilvy
Ken Hin Teo
Henry Kong
Debbie Sher
Clive Sall

Special thanks to
Cedric Price
Diane Lewis
Paul Finch

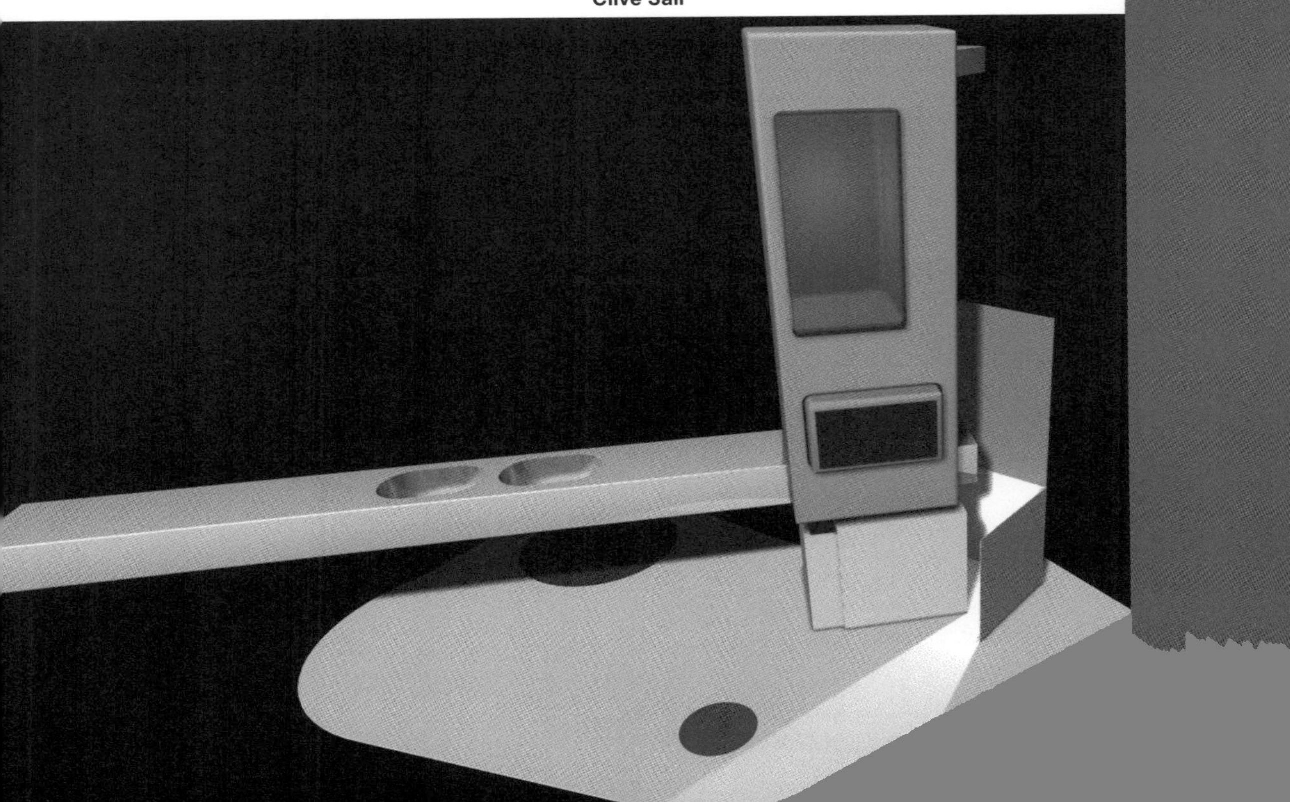

Chinese Take-Away Architecture
An Architecture that Aims at Promoting Conscious Consumption

Whilst sociologists maintain that society is becoming increasingly fragmented as community groups become less clearly defined, global companies – through sales and branding – have developed a new analysis of community based on consumption. Society's dependence on image and the perceived value of goods has provided the product developer with unprecedented control over consumer choice. Previous speculation on market trends has been transmuted into the creation of real consumer groups.

To predict (or rather create) these future consumer groups, the product designer relies on market research and the perpetual creation of consumer taxonomies. The current British housing market supplies a product that neither addresses the issues of the individual consumers nor influences their demands. The house-building industry is defined by a traditional and financially rationalised construction process and not by an understanding of the market as a dynamic condition. Streamlined production that favours repetition rather than innovation has resulted in standardised environments.

A dynamic market challenges architecture in a way that can only be addressed through a strategy of meaningful user control.

It would make sense for the construction industry to borrow from the field of product design and its 'understanding' of the consumer. Market research could then take on a new role, allowing the architect to address the specificity of the consumer.

In the past, industrialisation in the construction sector has only been attempted through the reduction and standardisation of form and programme. The evolution of industrial technology has created the potential for mass-production to meet mass-customisation. A restructuring of the design process would cause a major shift to occur with respect to the way control is exercised over the urban condition. The architectural profession, with its elitist and hierarchical structures, would be challenged; control of architecture would be surrendered to those who use it.

Themes of aestheticisation in today's postmodern society reflect the increasing role of consumption as an art form. Youth culture, in particular, consciously mixes different products in search of the unique combination. A new consumer type – the 'fluxus' consumer – has emerged. Multiple selection and combination of 'dishes' allows a unique dining experience, the parameters of which are the ingredients (materials) and cooking methods (production techniques) – the architecture of the Chinese take-away.

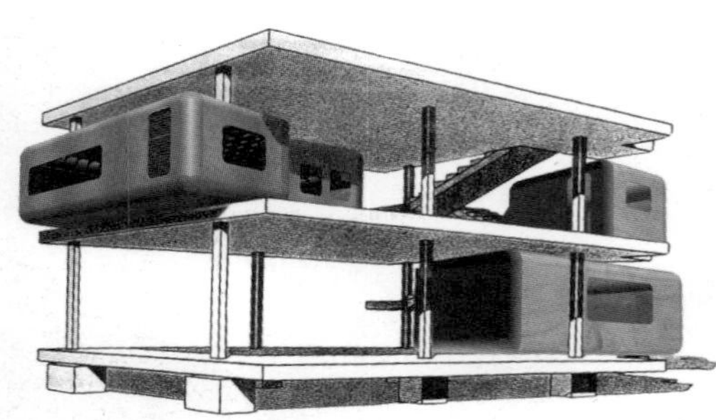

Joseph Grima
Jonathan Nicholls
Nicholas Hayhurst

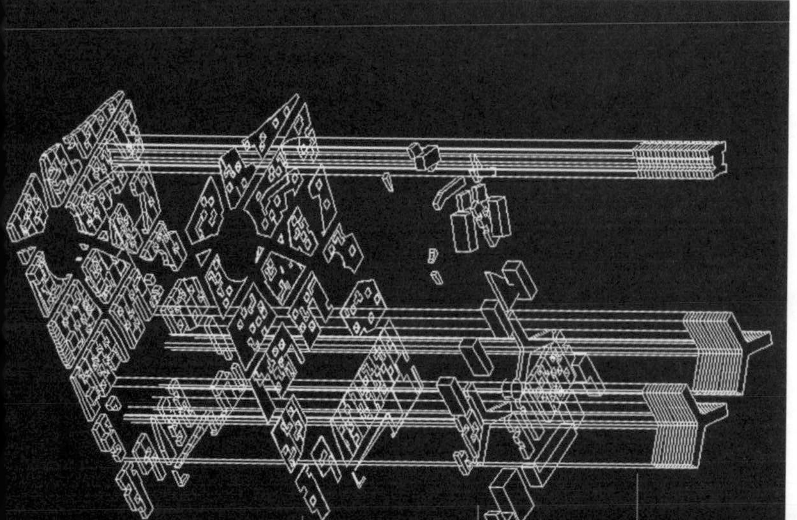

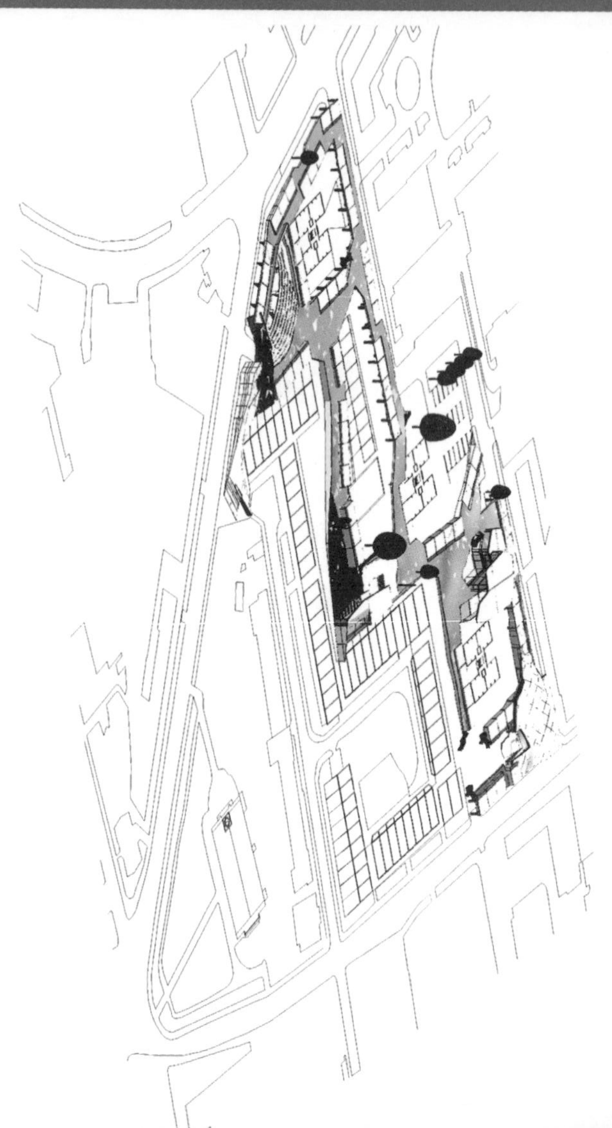

Asaf Mayer

Sebastian Nau

Nicholas Hayhurst

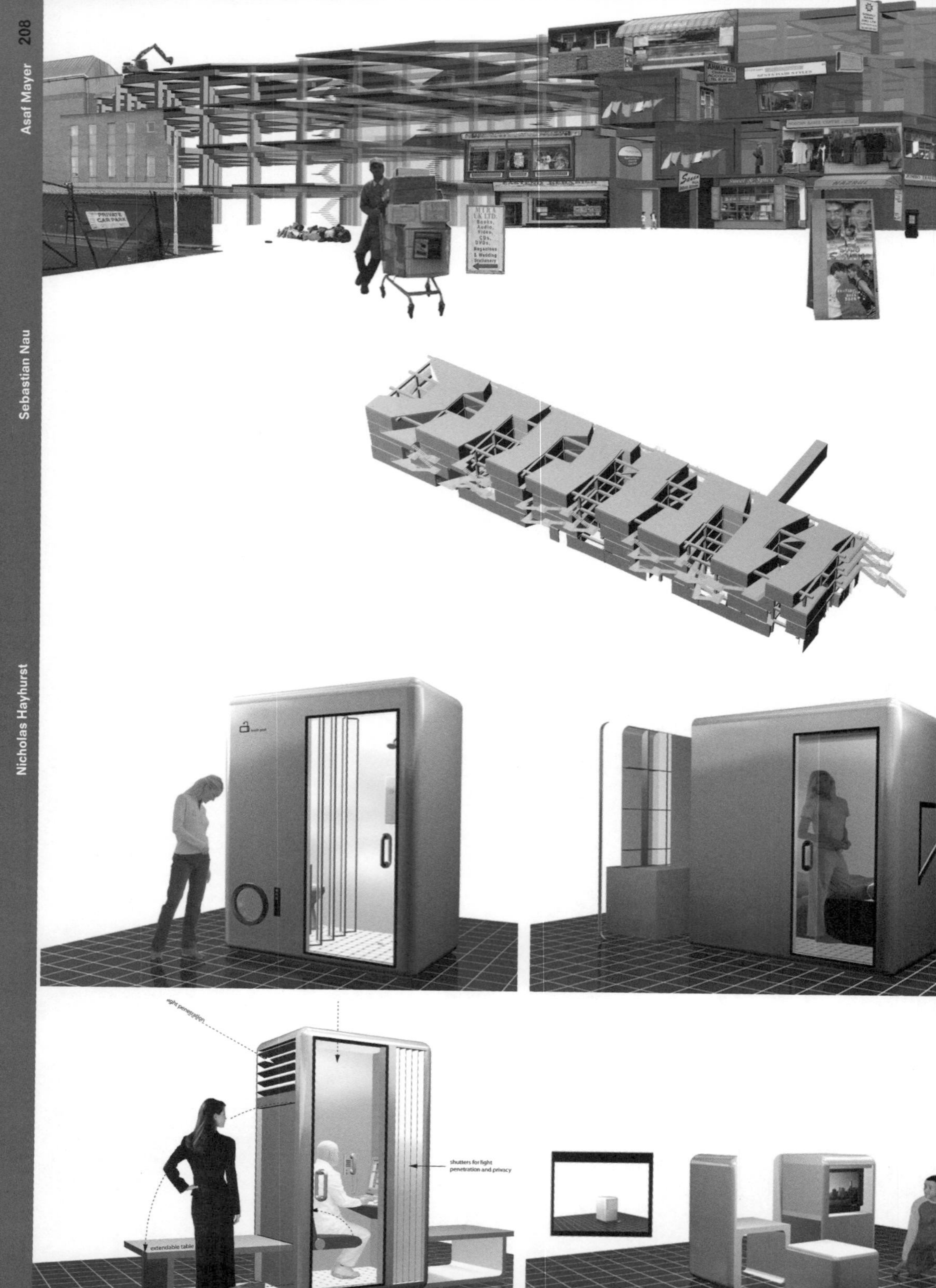

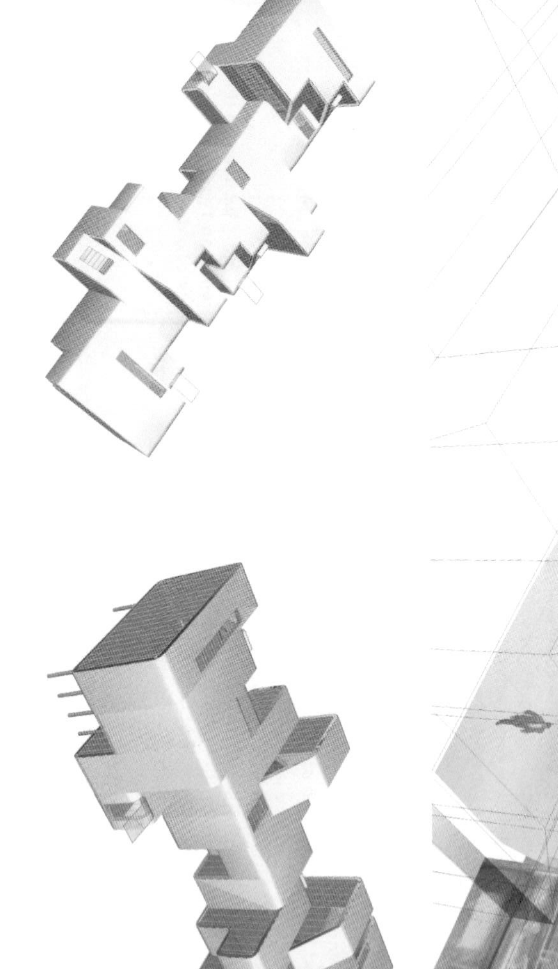

Tim Sudweeks

Phil Soo-Kim

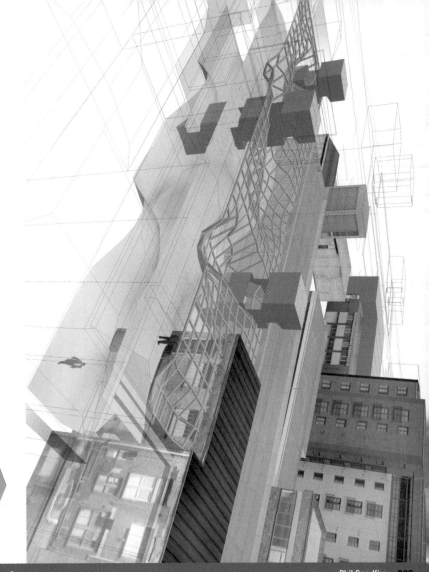

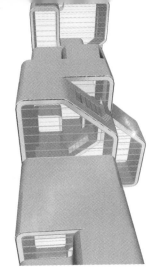

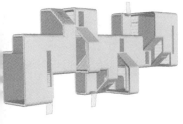

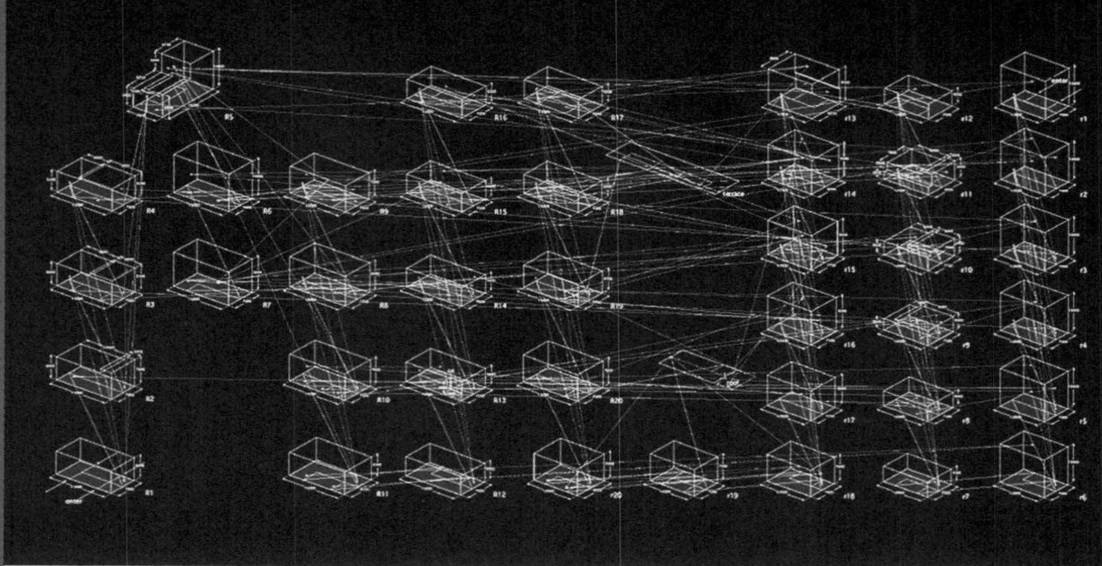

Opening and Closure

The increasing autonomy and self-reference of art led to the construction of an architectural paradigm: the white cube. Yet the boundaries of the white-cube system can be questioned: on the exterior, by social and economical forces; on the interior, by art practices that incorporate external phenomena. The goal of Diploma Unit 7 is to investigate the architectural implications of these border conflicts in order to develop new models of an autopoietic system and ways to define opening and closure.

Site or Non-site

Urban research on art institutions focused on the contradictory status of the site. On the one hand, the white cube seems to exist without context, as a systemic model producing a non-site condition. On the other hand, galleries and museums become strategic instruments of urban planning and politics that aim at reactivating entire cities or specific sites. The terms for the identification of a strategic site (or non-site) were developed through a series of workshops, supported by visits from museum experts and curators.

Inside and Outside the White Cube

The unit explores the internal and external modes of architectural space. The internal logic focuses on the relationship between exhibitions and their containers, between architectural coherence and programmatic openness, between an architecture of background and foreground. The investigation of external relations clarifies the possibilities and limitations of contextualisation.

Materialities and Tectonics

Material elements (like walls, ceiling and floor) are interpreted as interfaces between system and environment, as boundaries between opening and closure. Research into material tectonic detail concretises different conditions: modes of visibility and perception, degrees of differentiation and temporal duration.

Unit Staff
Nikolaus Hirsch
Makoto Saito

Students
Ariel Ariel
Gilles Chan
Valentina Giacinti
Thomas Katsibas
Makoto Kishino
Neng-hung Lu
Hiromasa Makino
Yuko Nanno
Benny Ng
Azlina Raja Azwa
Igor Sabara
Borja Lopez Santamaria
Joseph Tai
Silvio Tonolli

Experts/Visiting Critics
Peter Beard
Jessica Coates
Soren Grammel
Neil Leach
Finn Geipel
Kaye Geipel
Brian Hatton
Takuro Hoshino
Wolf Mangelsdorf
Jim McKinney
Phil Misselwitz
Michel Müller
Ciro Najle
Carsten Nicolai
Brett Steele
Charles Tashima
Peter Thomas
Carlos Villanueva Brandt
Mike Weinstock
Markus Weisbeck

Reconfiguring the White Cube **Hiromasa Makino**

Based on an investigation of the John Soane Museum as a programmatic and spatial countermodel to the white cube, the project develops a gallery that focuses on physical and visual connectivity. Hierarchies of exposed and hidden spaces are replaced by a system that shows cultural production as a whole (exhibit, artist in residence, curatorial practice). Organised in a double loop, a system of 36 individual cubes allows a variety of reconfigurations and links.

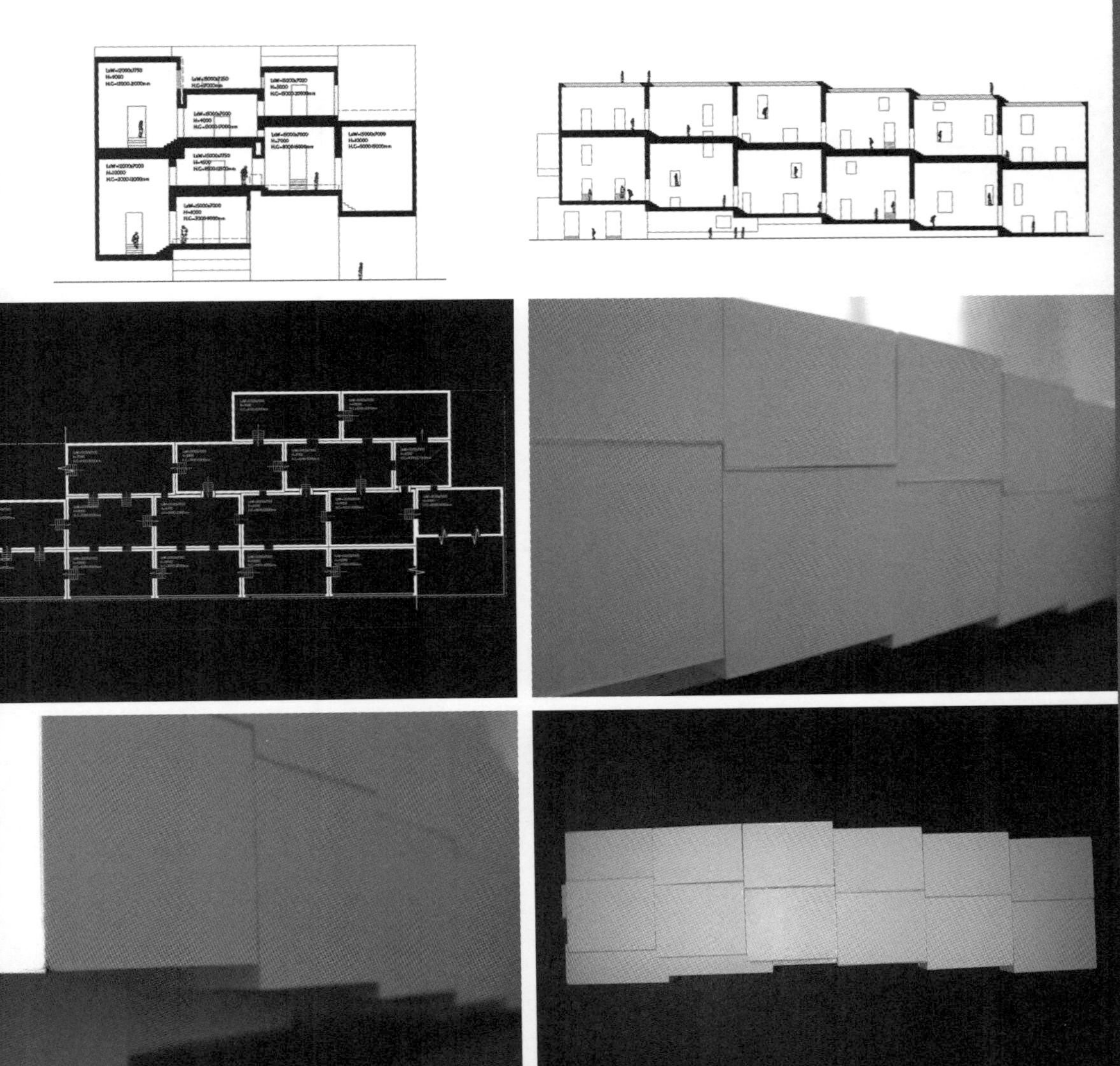

Boundaries **Azlina Azwa**

The art institution questions its autonomy and redefines its boundaries. By weaving it into the complex tissue of a Berlin block the gallery becomes a building without facade. As the nucleus of an urban redevelopment it creates a journey of different light conditions: informal areas with direct light and – as the main structural support of the building – enclosed cubes with controlled light conditions.

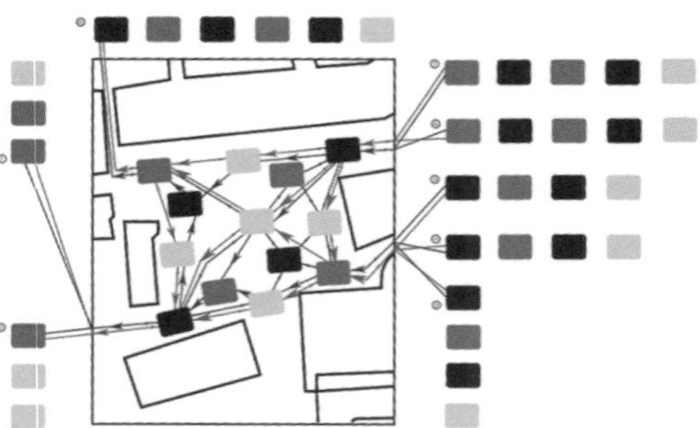

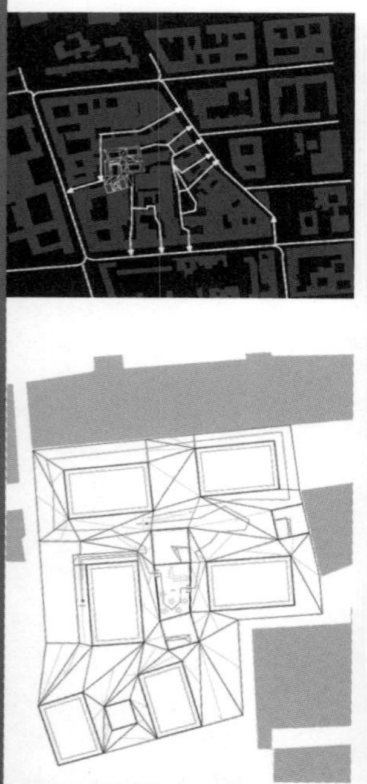

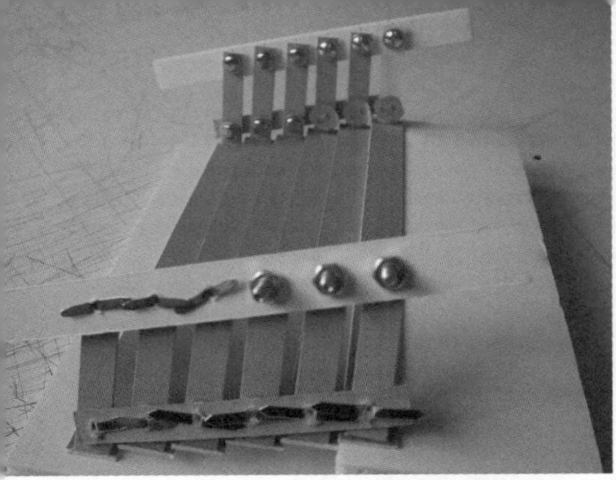

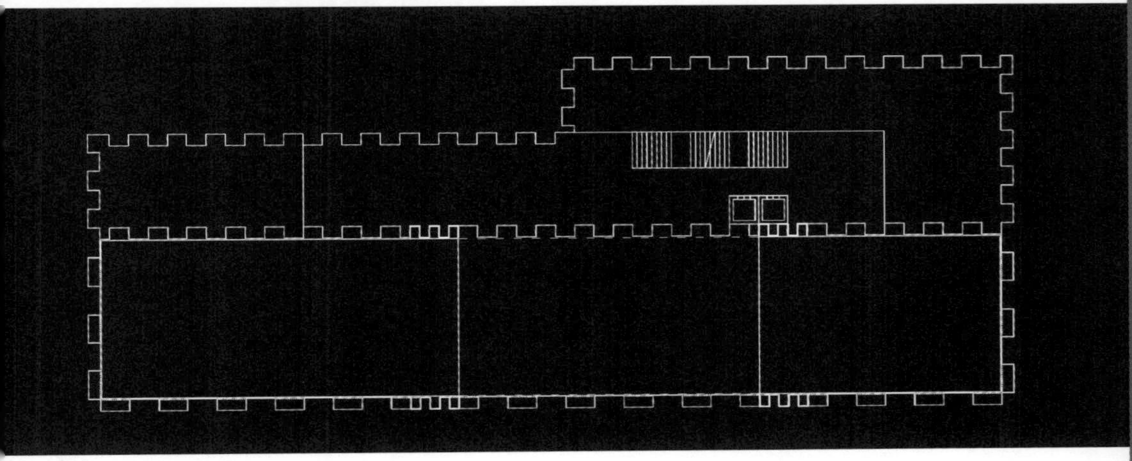

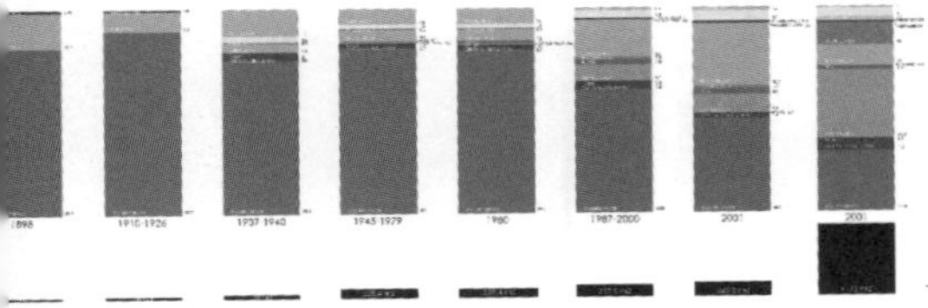

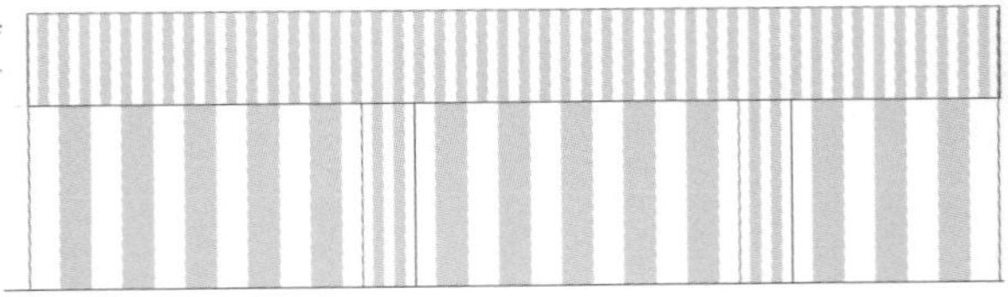

Programmatic Shifts **Joe Tai**

The history of museums and galleries is characterised by programmatic shifts. The tendency to decrease exhibition areas and – reciprocally – increase commercial activities is at the basis of an approach that intensifies temporal rhythms. The art institution is organised in zones of varying structural and programmatic stabilities – determined and undetermined areas, partial hingeing elements – allowing dense series of programmatic reconfigurations.

White Cube and Vacancy **Gilles Chan/Thomas Katsibas**

A nomadic art institution questions the role of architecture in cultural and urban politics (with respect to something like the Bilbao-effect). Institutionally stable but spatially unstable, it uses the leftovers of urban development. Art leaves the neutrality of the white cube and moves to vacancy, a temporarily neutralised yet site-specific status. In a process of constantly shifting locations, architectural coherence is maintained by an adaptable structure and a self-sufficient energy and information system.

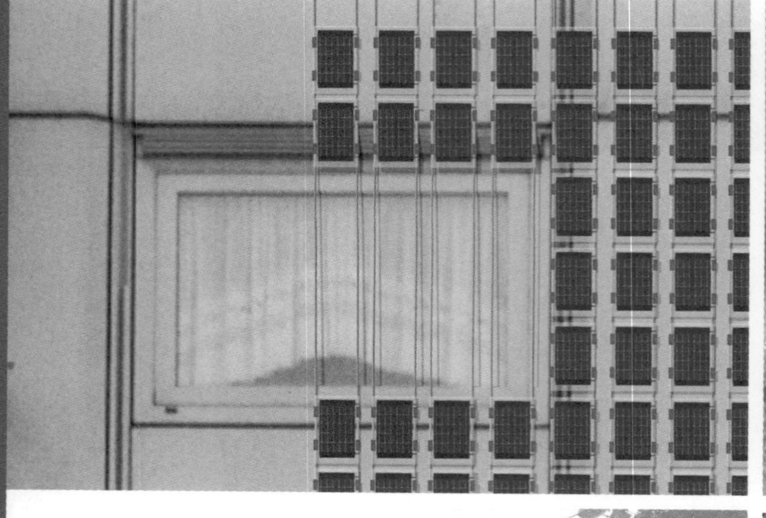

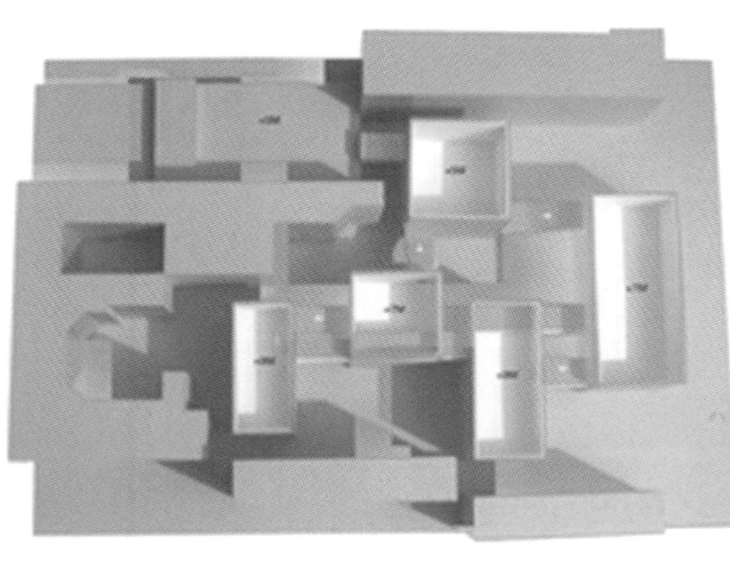

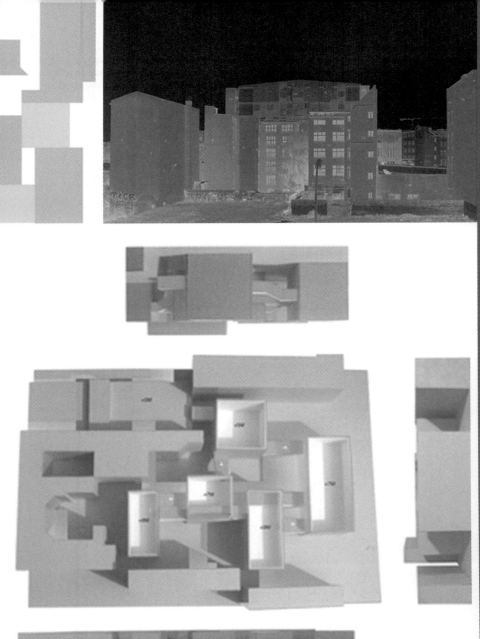

Enclosed and Open Spaces **Yuko Nanno**

Using the material condition of a fragmented block typology the project introduces a logic of interior and exterior conditions. Open spaces are part of a constant reinterpretation of public space, enclosed spaces are areas of control (light and climate). The wall, as the main element of art space and its ideologies, follows a material logic of inside and outside: from smooth layers and surfaces to rough, always changing, compressed concrete.

Distraction and Contemplation **Makoto Hishino**

Analysing the relation between movement and perception the project develops a gradation of spatial conditions: from highly exposed urban situations to zones of extreme intimacy. In a linear movement from exterior to interior the material elements (wall, ceiling and floor) generate increasing degrees of physical control (light, sound, etc).

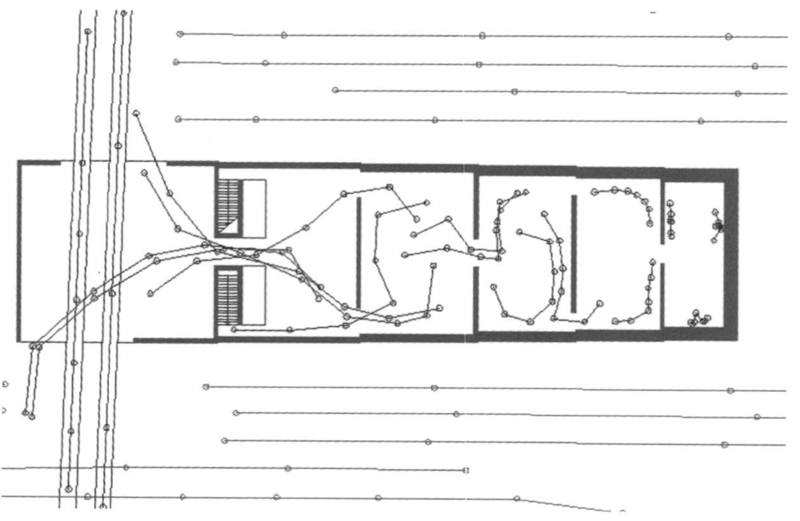

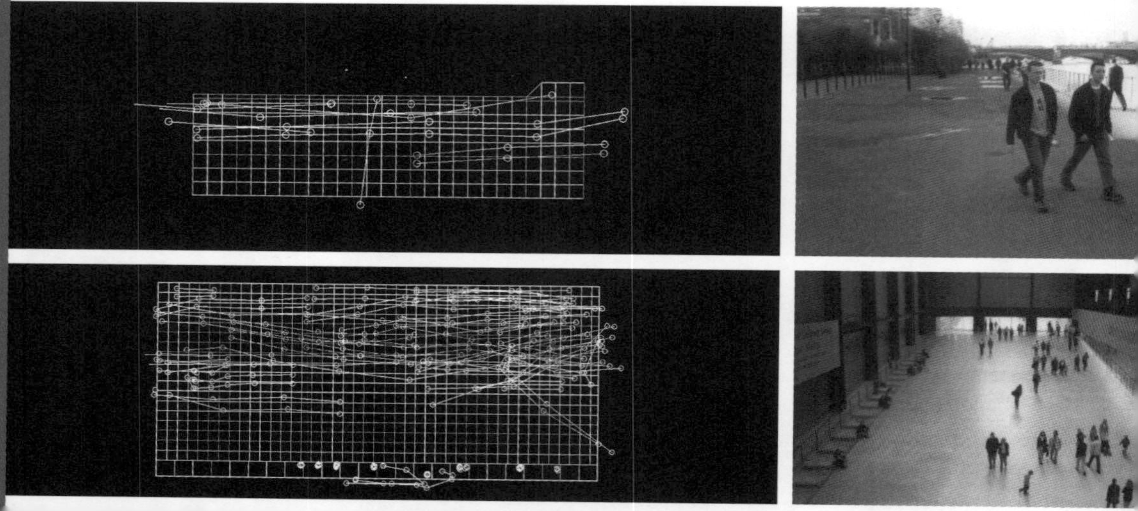

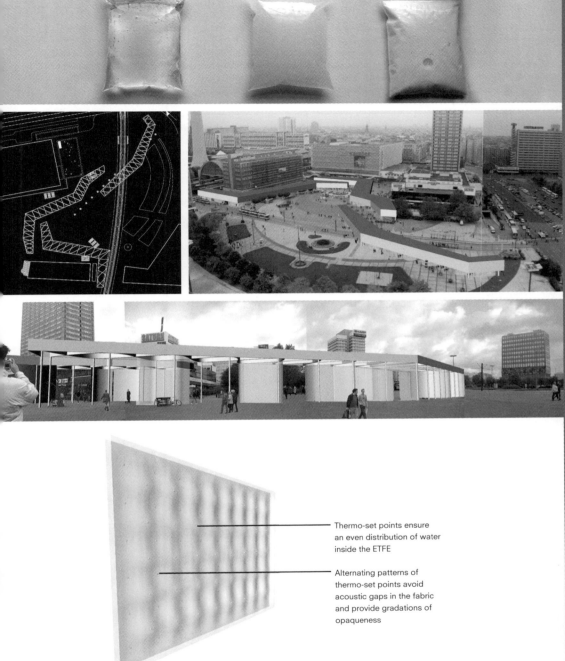

Thermo-set points ensure an even distribution of water inside the ETFE

Alternating patterns of thermo-set points avoid acoustic gaps in the fabric and provide gradations of opaqueness

Wall Conditions **Borja Lopez Santamaria**
The boundary between the art institution and its urban context is a parameter that establishes degrees of opening and closure. In Alexanderplatz, one of the most public areas in Berlin, the project provides a structure that defines art spaces as zones of constant negotiation. A curtainwall system of water cushions creates different configurations (continuous, fragmented, porous) and various visual and acoustic conditions.

We used the means of production as a way of inspiring a built form, which was measured in terms of appropriate architectural solutions to real problems.

Economic globalisation has left the architectural possibilities for regional redevelopment in the UK devoid of purpose. We looked at industry, from farming to heavy chemical production, and considered its relation to the community. In a world of digital satisfaction, how do communities in which 40 to 50 per cent of the population are unwaged reinvent the identity of the workplace as something desirable?

We worked in Middlesborough, where North Sea oil comes in and money flows out, where the Sydney Bridge was built and where the estuary is filled with slag from the former heavy iron foundries which, having become landfill, now support a new diaspora of chemical works, nuclear power plants and container terminals caged in discreet pens.

We worked in Dorset, where the farms are barely breaking even and the economic sustainability of food production is seriously questioned, where the influx of commuters and the grey pound is seeking to redefine the role of the countryside forever.

We went to a pub and saw a social mechanism that could give us the tools to create space from behaviour. A mirror to nostalgia and an alcohol-fuelled formica swoosh through the immediate future in interior decoration.

These three slices through social dysfunctionality were paired with an investigation of the material qualities involved to give us a unique overview.

Unit Staff
Mark B Prizeman
Peter Thomas
with **Kevin Shepherd**

Students
Stefanie Berchtenbreiter-Overbeck
Amanda Friedman
Daniel Fagerberg
Keb Garavito-Bruhn
Maria Haralambidou
Sherri Harvey
Nigel Height
Matthew Lynch
Alexandros Marcoulides
Carlos Peña Ponte
Barbara Perez Marina
Il Hoon Roh
Stefan Rydin
JooEun Sung
Alastair Townsend
Daniel Tsoi
Junko Yanagisawa
and
Lena Nalbach
Daniel Pitman

Visiting Critics
Chris Booth
Carlos Villanueva Brandt
Thomas Coward
Julian Cripps
Brian Hatton
Mohsen Mostafavi
Katherine Shonfield
Sven Steiner
Mike Weinstock

Special thanks to
Chris Booth
Victor Crutchley
Anderson Inge
Gemma Nesbit

Alexandros Marcoulides The farm

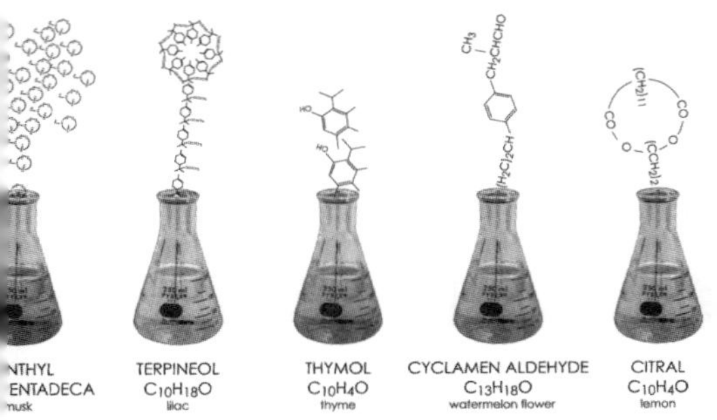

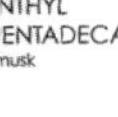

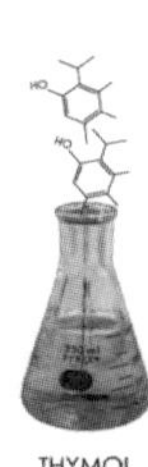

JooEun Sung Joy car racing **Daniel Pitman** Pithead sanatorium
Above: **Amanda Freidman** Perfume industry

20 0
91
100

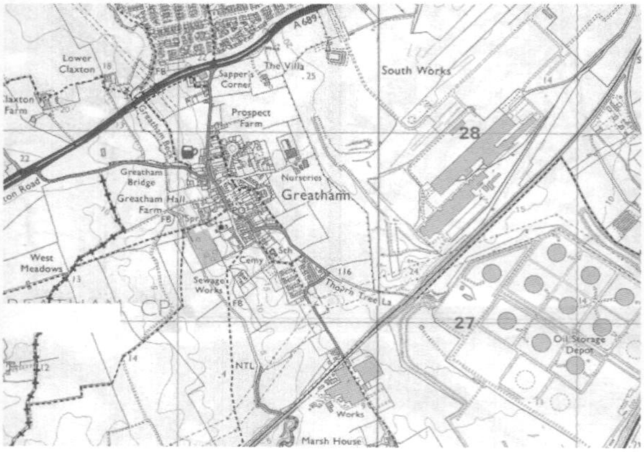
A689
Lower Claxton
Claxton Farm
Sapper's Corner
The Villa
South Works
Prospect Farm
28
Greatham Bridge
Nurseries
Greatham
Greatham Hall Farm
West Meadows
Sewage Works
Cemy
Thorpe Tree La
27
Oil Storage Depot
NTL
Works
Marsh House

20 0
100 100

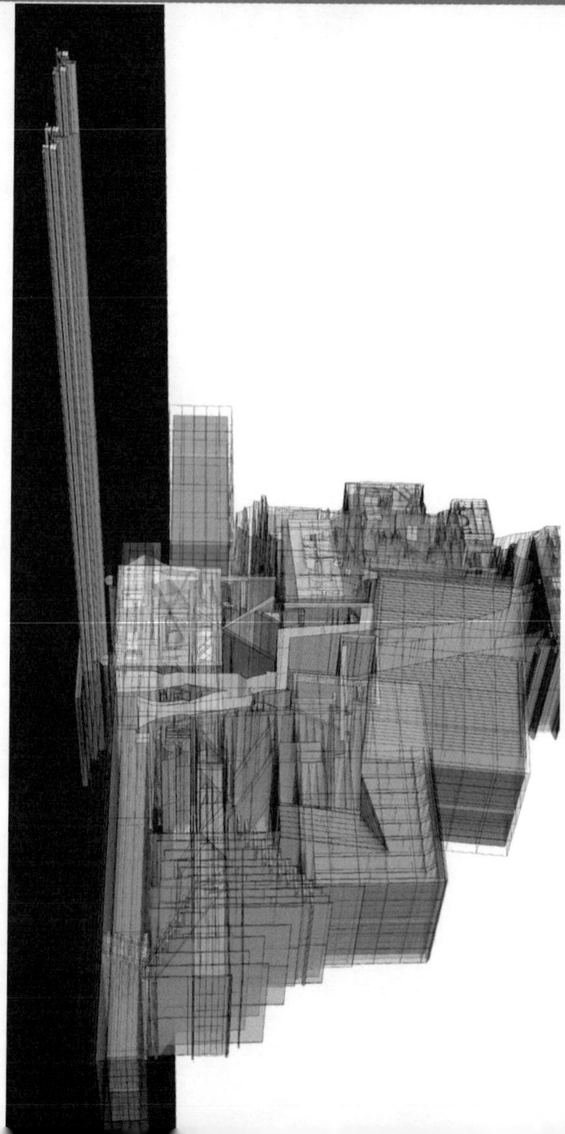

Alexandros Marcoulides Makeshift town à la Cité de la refuge, a moving ancillary building serves hostel blocks

Barbara Perez Marina Using vacuum-laminated panels for sound reduction in home industrial facility

Alaistair Townsend Car deconstruction plant

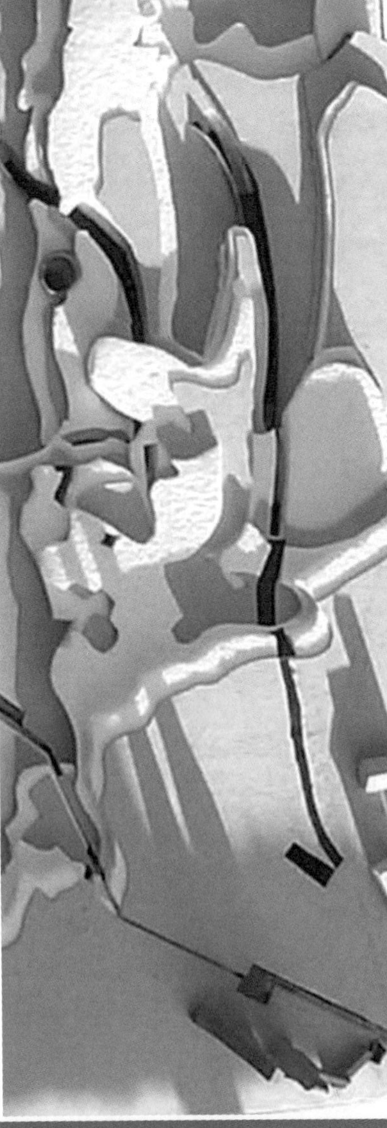
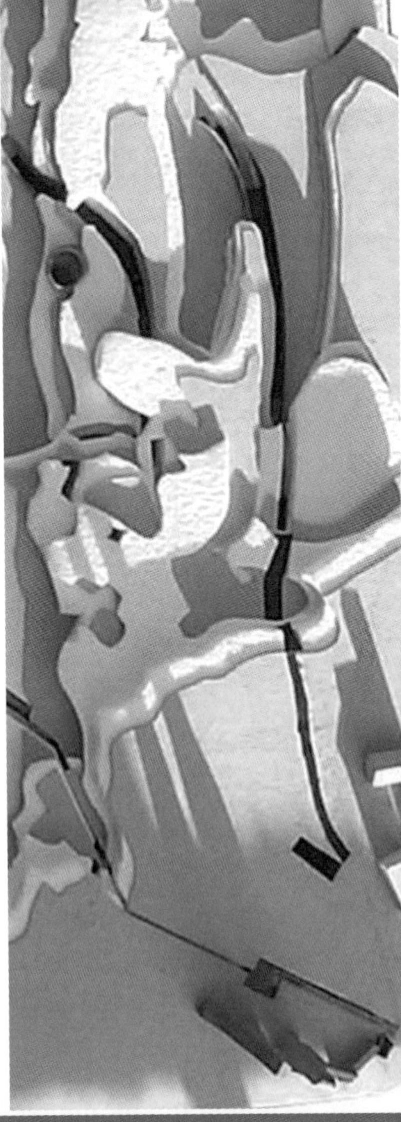
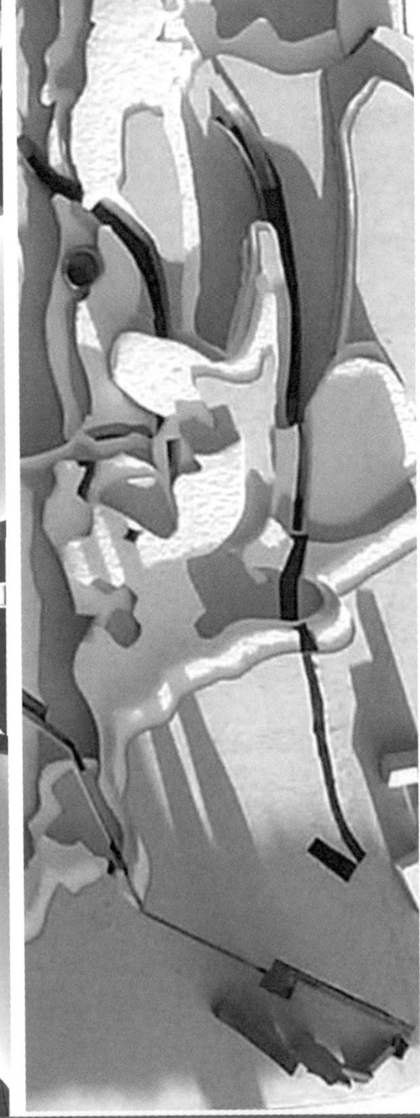
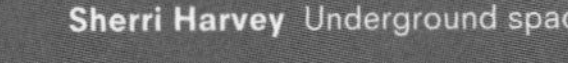

Sherri Harvey Underground space

Alaistair Townsend Terraced public house in quake 111

we had to gather what we could for the future...

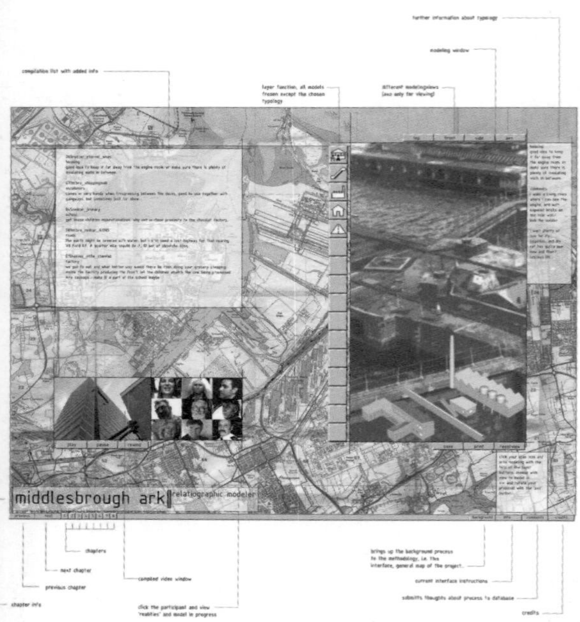

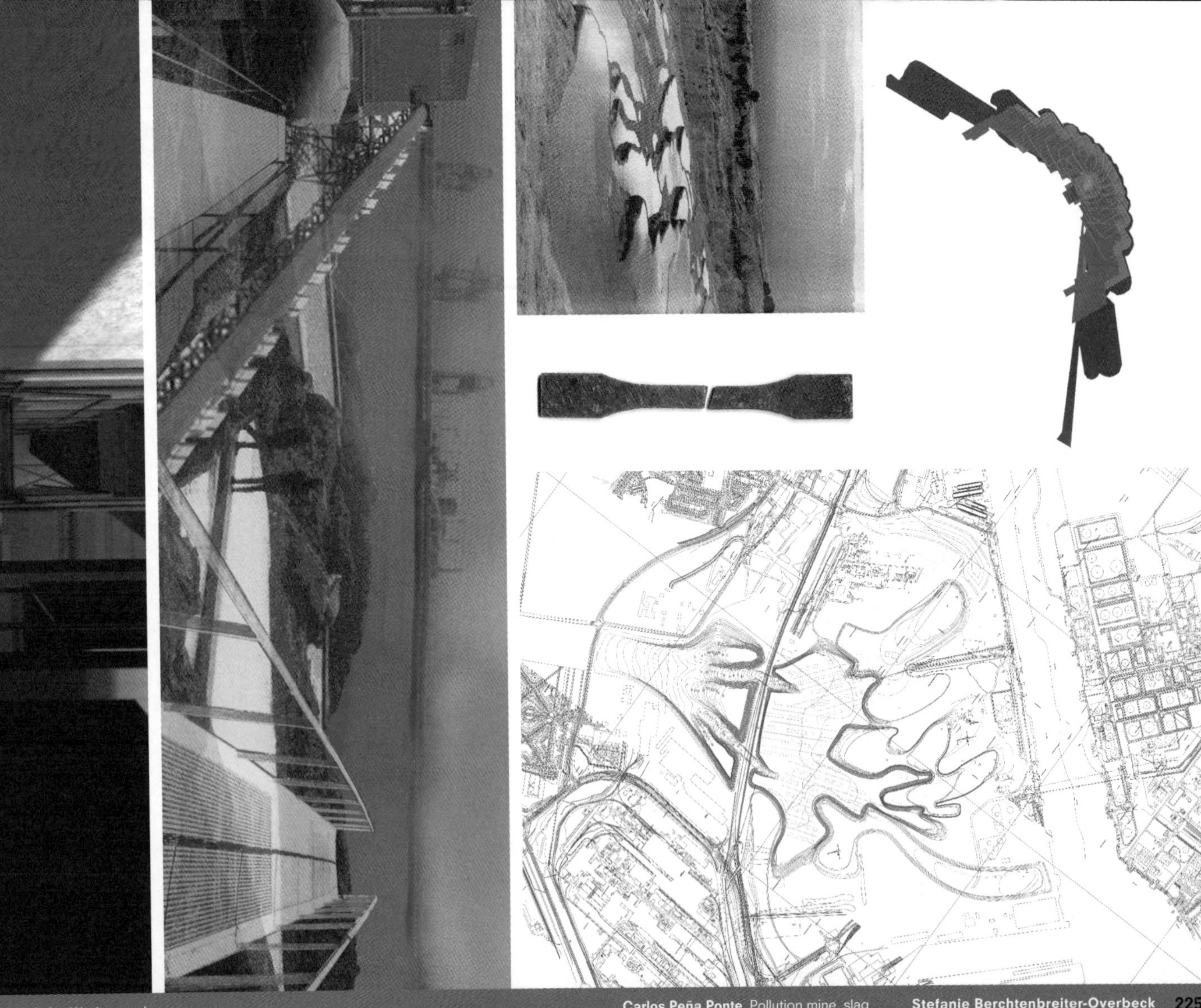

Nigel Height Workers pub

Carlos Peña Ponte Pollution mine, slag landscapes reformed using biodegradable plastic formwork and informal labour

Stefanie Berchtenbreiter-Overbeck Elevated healthcare wings

From Aldgate to the Blackwall Tunnel, the A13 has been transformed by Diploma 10 into a territory of action. Through immersion and direct involvement, we have set up a new series of service structures that address the ambitions of the GLA's east London development corridor. We have reconsidered public services in order to activate this corridor and have altered the fabric of the city at the urban, social and architectural scales. We have proposed physical and social structures in the form of service infrastructures and service architectures and then combined them into active urban interventions. These range from events such as the 'Penalty Shoot-out' or the 'Temporary Cinema', through infrastructures such as the 'Recycling Caretakers' and the 'Space Search Engine' to new structures such as 'Recycling Plants', 'Service Paths', 'Service Courtyards' and 'Service Intersections'.

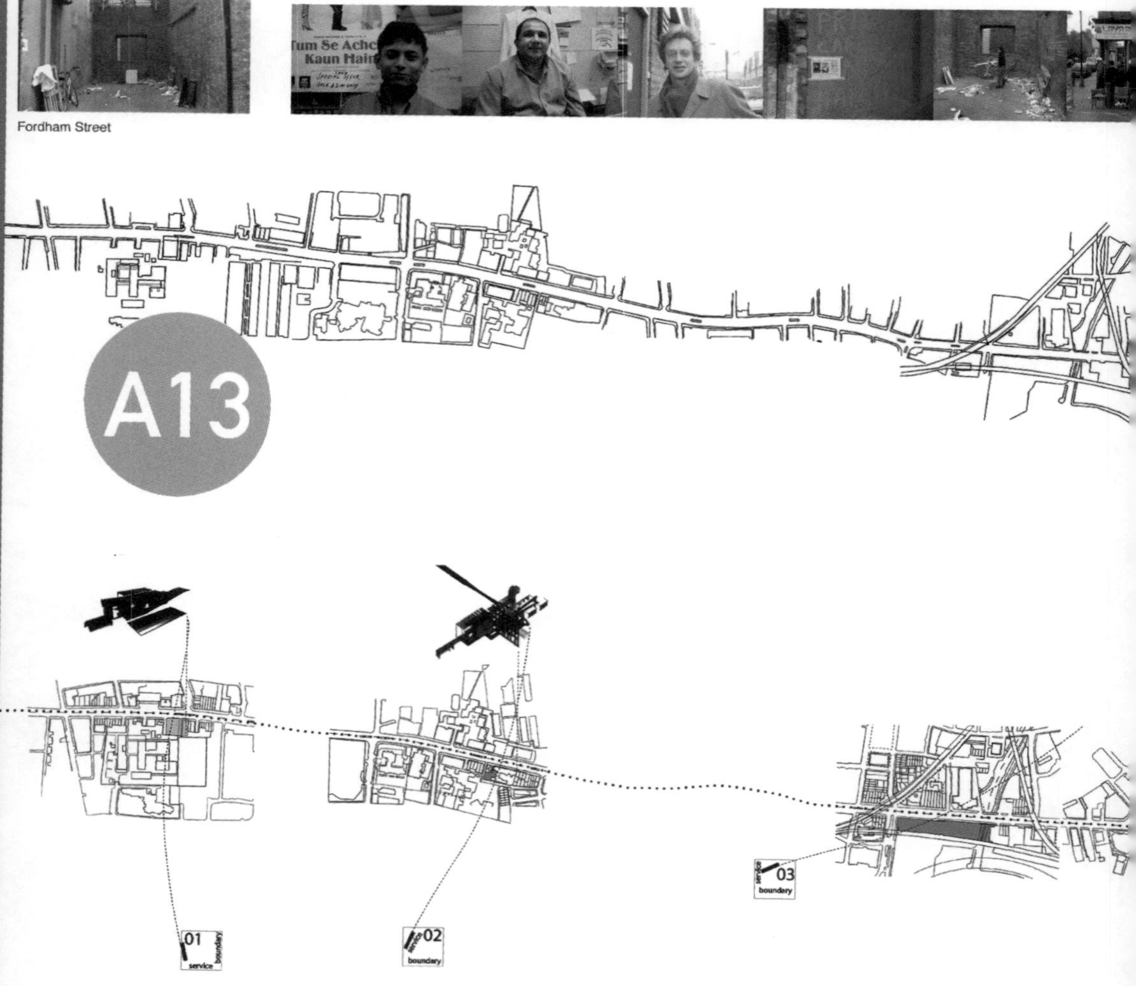

Fordham Street

Shu Zhen Lee
Two distinct time-scales are to be found on the A13: one 'slow', relating to the waterways, and the other 'fast', relating to the road. At present, the road and waterways are completely unconnected but this situation is readdressed by means of 'Service Overlaps' that bring together the initiatives of the Blue Ribbon Plan and the GLA's development corridor into combined slow-fast spaces, designed around existing services along the A13.

Luisa Sanchez Cleves
The line of the A13 is defined by the events that take place around it. This concept – further refined through an understanding of the criteria that lead to what the police refer to as urban 'hotspots' – is used to propose positive event-based interventions servicing the territory of the A13. At the architectural level, the 'Temporary Cinema' was proposed for a derelict site and successfully constructed as a one-night event. And, at the urban level, a series of orchestrated events, 'City Event', is proposed as an urban strategy.

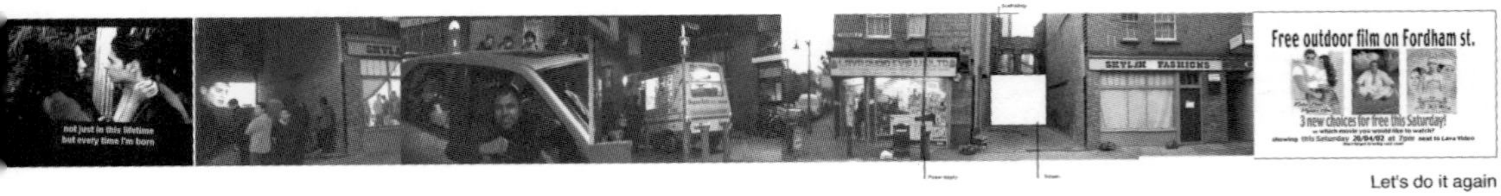

TOWER HAMLETS

not just in this lifetime
but every time I'm born
SKYLINE FASHIONS
Free outdoor film on Fordham st.
3 new choices for free this Saturday!

Let's do it again

A13

The roof garden
- connected to the rock wall
Office workers during break times, students during PE.
Adults coming for evening and night classes.
bridge
- connecting to the Cheviot House
Spaces and Planes (platforms) to house events like
- an eating place
- classrooms for adult improvement skills.
The Rock Facade
- rock climbing wall
It gives a distinctive character to the new addition.
Also acting as the connecting element for the boundary space.
connecting events and activities, causing a merging and blurring of boundaries, betweent he existing svchool grounds and the new interventions.
A13
The Social Club.
A13 Club House
section across the road

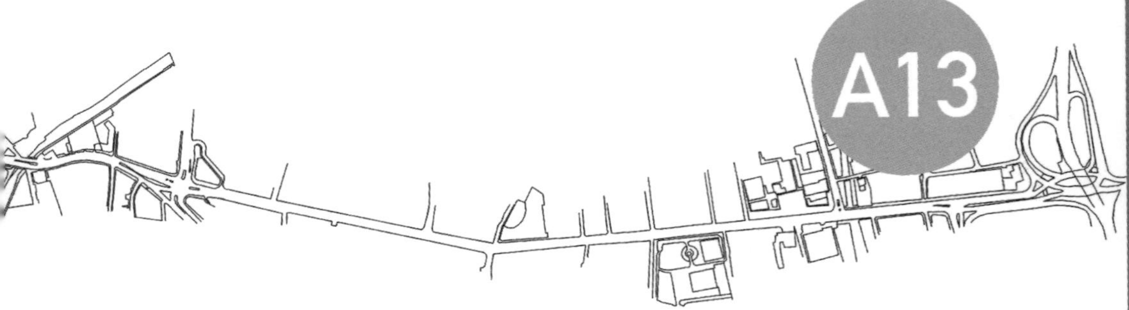

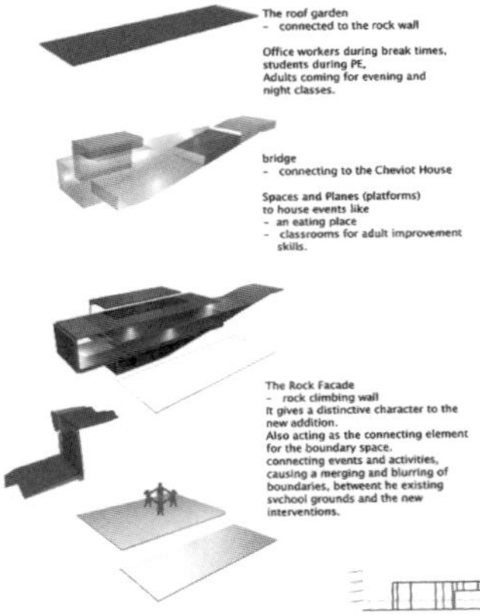

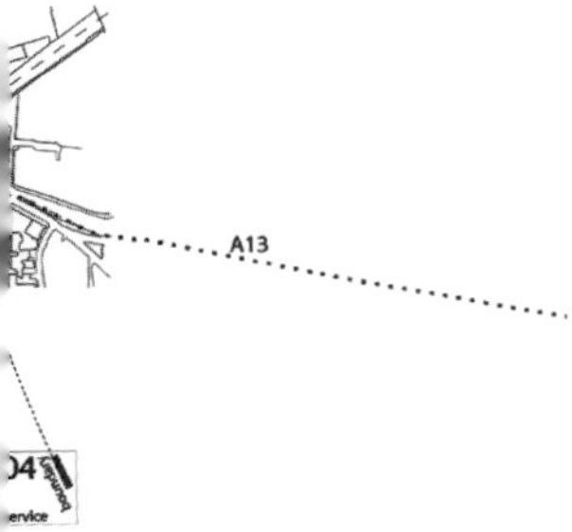

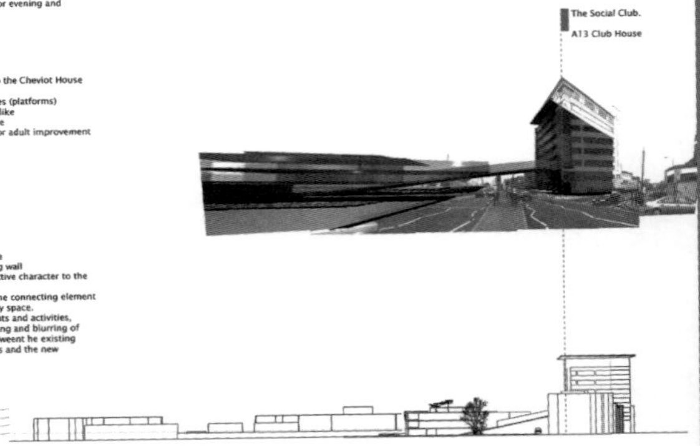

Unit Master
Carlos Villanueva Brandt

Workshops
Sandra Denicke
Torange Khonsari

Students
Mohammad Iskandar Abdul Razak
Simone Shu Yeng Chung
Carolin Hinne
Shu Zhen Lee
Jin-Seok Park
Key Portilla-Kawamura
Luisa Sanchez Cleves
Irina Velkova
Gabriella Zauberman

27-11-01, bus stop of route 15/115 eastbound, Commercial Road/ Lukin Street

11.00am
Buying the books in a book discount shop on Charing Cross: I choose three classics, from a cheap edition, books I could imagine myself flicking through at a bus stop. (Something I probably would not have the patience to read completely but a few pages could be interesting...)
The books will be hung on cables that can be cut easily on site. The purpose is not to secure the books so that they will not get stolen, but to hang them in order to give them a certain status of being public. I decide to leave a note book so that people can answer to my question, maybe I will get some feedback.
My question on the back of each book:

Read while you wait.........

The other day I was looking for a book store in Tower Hamlets.
I couldn't find any.
So I had to go all the way to Charing Cross to buy these books.

Where do you go to buy books?

If you would like to answer this question or if you have any comments about my action, please leave them in the notebook beside.

these books have been provided by:
busstopbooks@hotmail.com

3pm
I start setting up the books, observed by some teenage school girls who are waiting for their bus.
They are guessing and ask me if I was promoting books ("people start reading and get interested and then they want to buy them...").
As I tell them that I am putting up the books just to see if anybody would be interested in reading at all, one of them says that she would, if she was bored waiting for the bus.
But they are warning me I should have laminated them, people would start tearing pages, ripping etc.
Or they might take "Romeo and Juliet", as they have to read that in school.
When they buy books, they go to Waterstones in the center of the city.
Waiting for the next bus, another groups of girls gets interested. They are also warning me that if I want to leave the books over night, people would come and burn them..

3.30pm
The books are up and I cross the street to observe the busstop from inside of the phone box opposite.

3.35pm
A **young black man** comes to wait for the bus, sits down, but does not seem to even have noticed the books.

3.42pm
A **young black woman** comes to wait for the bus. She not seem to notice the books either. She has not at all looked back into the bus stop away fromthe street.

3.45pm
Two teenage schoolgirls are a book into their hands, readir note on the back of the book.

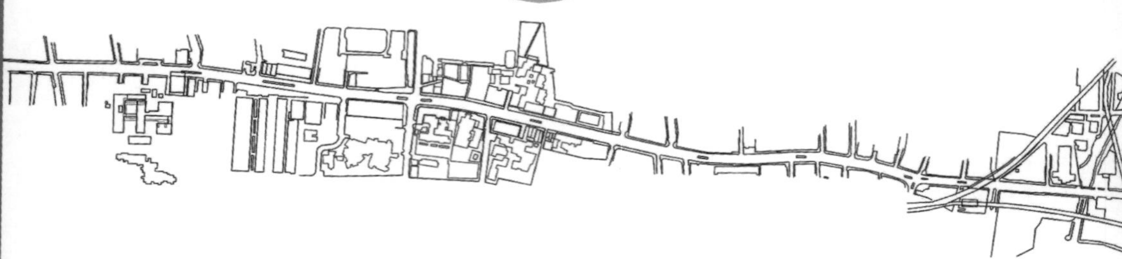

Gabriella Zauberman

Two particular sections of the community, old ladies and schoolchildren, reveal the inadequacies of existing public space. The old ladies, with their shopping trolleys, delineate their own service territory ranging from their homes to the Bingo Hall and in the process demonstrate the strength of social adaptability. Using them as an example, a constructed situation, the 'Penalty Shoot-out', was set up to bring schoolchildren together in a redundant space. A similar approach is proposed, at the urban scale, to create interventions that reclaim restricted and underused public spaces.

Carolin Hinne

Services are dislocated, removed from their habitual context and repositioned in public space. Books are placed in a bus stop in order to transform it into part of the library. The spatial boundaries of existing services are questioned by the displacement of either objects or spaces and the economic boundaries are rearranged by altering the balance between public and private.

them write into the
eft:
n in Chrisp Street".

3.48pm
One girl alone, does not look at books at all, **Asian woman** sits down and does not take notice of books either.
A **mother with young child** come, mother looks briefly at books, but does not take them in her hands; child becomes curious and mother and child are looking at book closelier, taking it into their hands, child writes his name into the note book.

3.50pm
One **black woman** briefly looks at my message on the back of a book, two other people are waiting for bus, but do not look at books at all.

3.51pm
Six independent people are waiting for the bus now, none of them except for the black woman has looked at the books at all. They do not seem to notice them, one woman only checks them from far.

3.55pm
A **gang of teenage school boys** are looking at the books and then they are standing around the note book for a long time (a couple of minutes, everybody leaving some message.
They all left their names, one page for each name, some drew a face, only one senseless phrase with "fucking..."
I am surprised that it took them so long just to write their names, I was expecting a lot of dirty drawings etc.

4pm
I cross the road to pretend I am waiting for a bus, because I am curious to look at the notes that people left. I am just casually looking at the books...
over hearing the conversation of the only two guys from the group that are still there: "What do you think?"- "What?" - "The books"-"Shit".......Then their converstaion ends.
I take the next bus.

5pm
I return one hour later to the bus stop: all the four books have been cut off, the cables hanging lonely from the busstop. There are no traces of the books having been destroyed, somebody must have taken them.

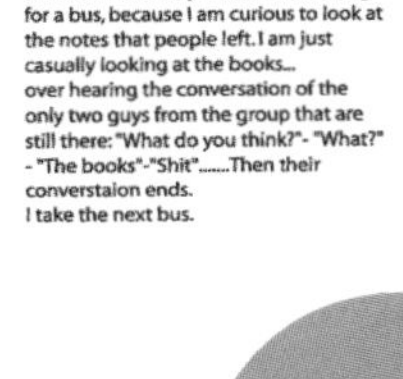

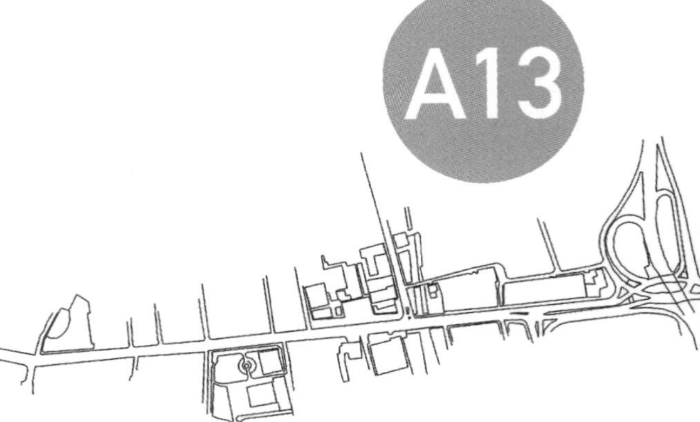

Mohammad Iskandar Abdul Razak
The culture of the market is celebrated, amplified and modified into a flexible service structure. Existing market territories are linked by means of the proposed A13 roadworks, so creating a backbone for the provision of informal services.

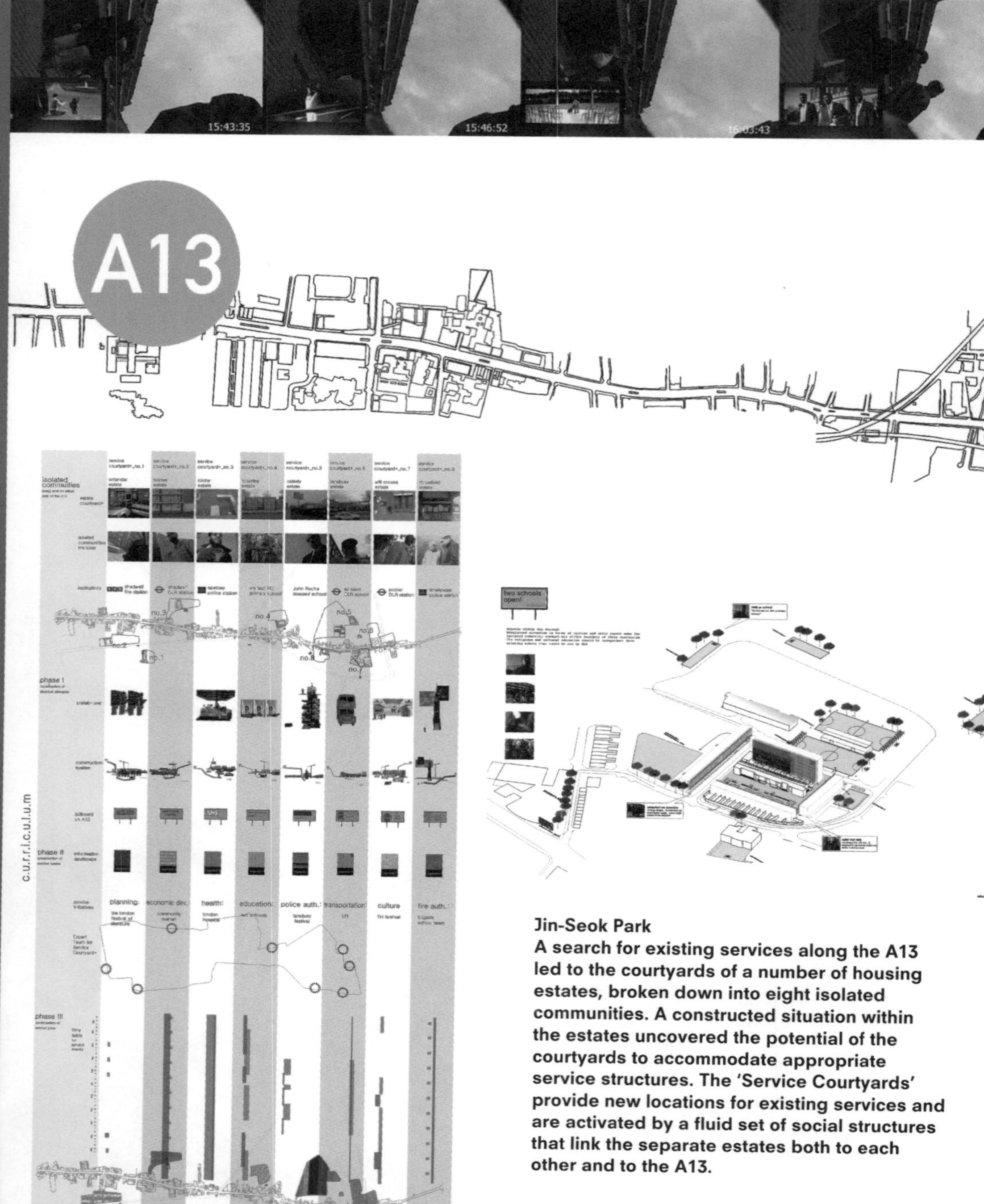

Jin-Seok Park
A search for existing services along the A13 led to the courtyards of a number of housing estates, broken down into eight isolated communities. A constructed situation within the estates uncovered the potential of the courtyards to accommodate appropriate service structures. The 'Service Courtyards' provide new locations for existing services and are activated by a fluid set of social structures that link the separate estates both to each other and to the A13.

Irina Velkova

The perception of space in relation to the fear of crime is categorised in three ways: psychological, factual and fictional. All three directly influence the way in which the city is used and control the experience between the home and public space. The 'Service Intersections', sited at the existing transport interchanges, relocate services in varying configurations and readdress the territory between the A13 and the existing housing estates.

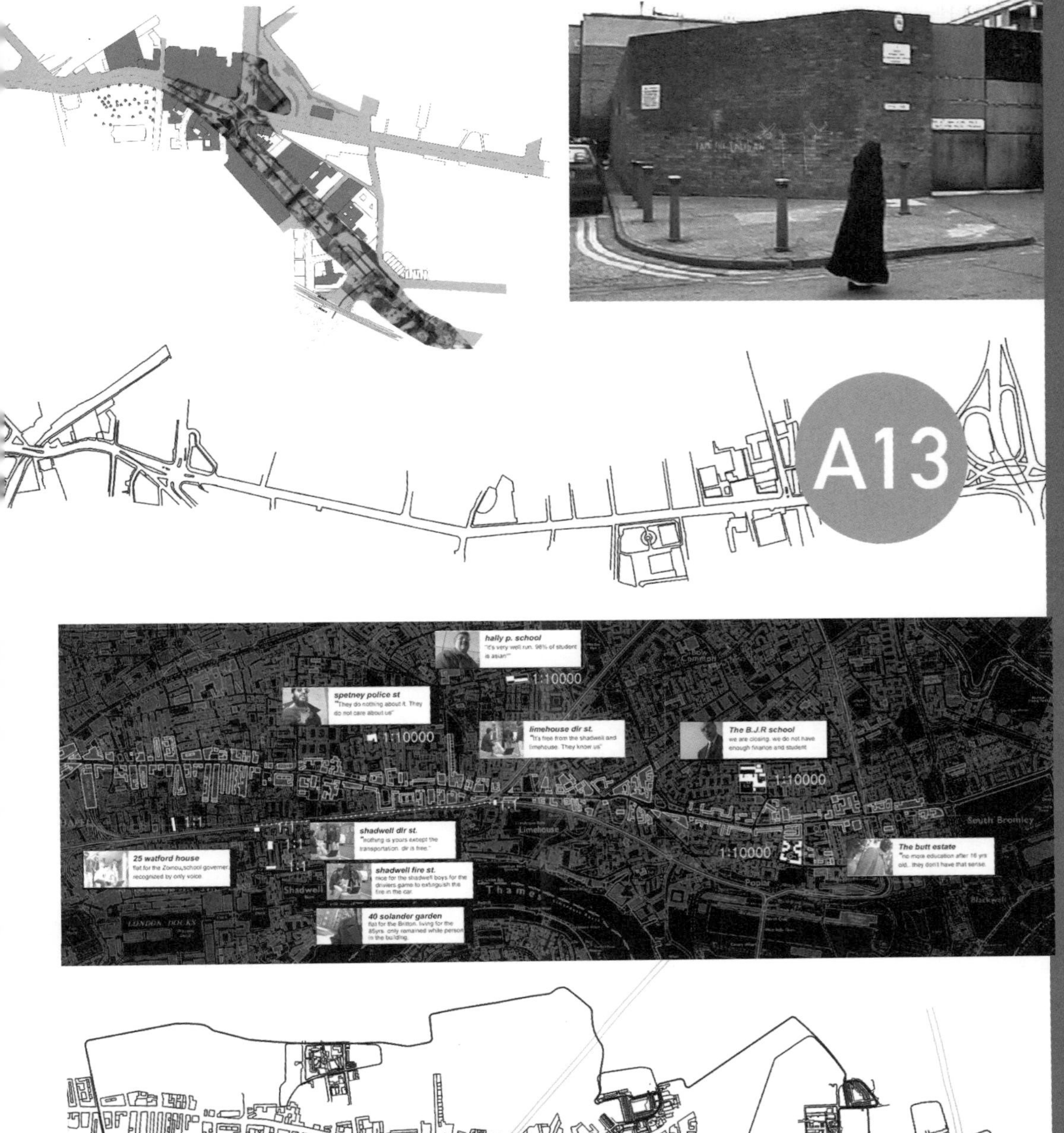

Simone Shu Yeng Chung
The A13 needs to be recycled, both physically and socially. At the level of waste, physical and social structures are closely inter linked and the process of recycling is proposed in two ways: social conditions will be actively monitored by 'Recycling Caretakers', and physical waste will be dealt with by strategically located 'Recycling Plants'.

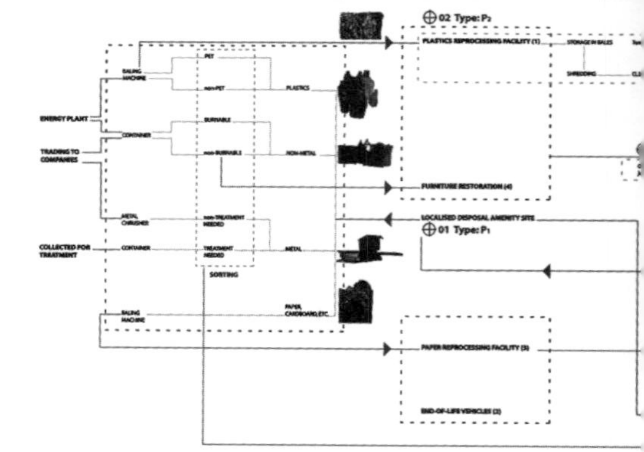

PHYSICAL RECYCLING: PHYSICAL STRUCTURE

A13

7 months

30 years

74 years

9 / 2002

4 / 2003

9 / 2003

3 / 2004

how does the network operate?
junctions

1. service programme network
a drop-in-service building on the junction between each path of action and the A13 provides the link to other paths¥ services.

2.transport network
the new express bus service A13x allows a fast connection along the route, stopping only at the junctions with the paths of action. it may also alleviate the demand on public transport derived from the congestion charge plan.

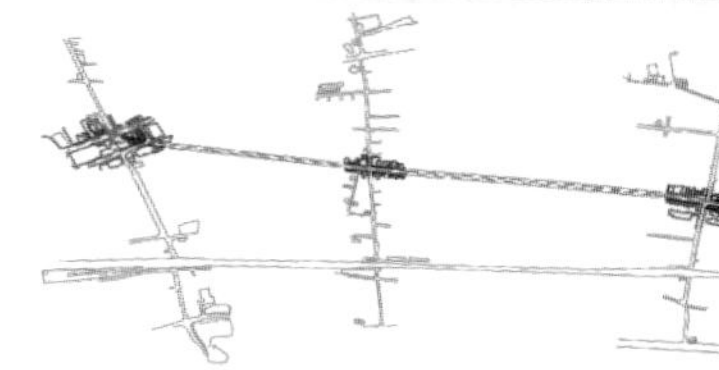

Key Portilla-Kawamura
Citizenship is interpreted according to the following categories of time: 7 months, 30 years, 74 years. The provision of services is to vary in relation to these overlapping timetables of inhabitation. Territorially the services are distributed randomly by the 'Space Search Engine' and formalised by means of a phased process along the 'Service Paths'.

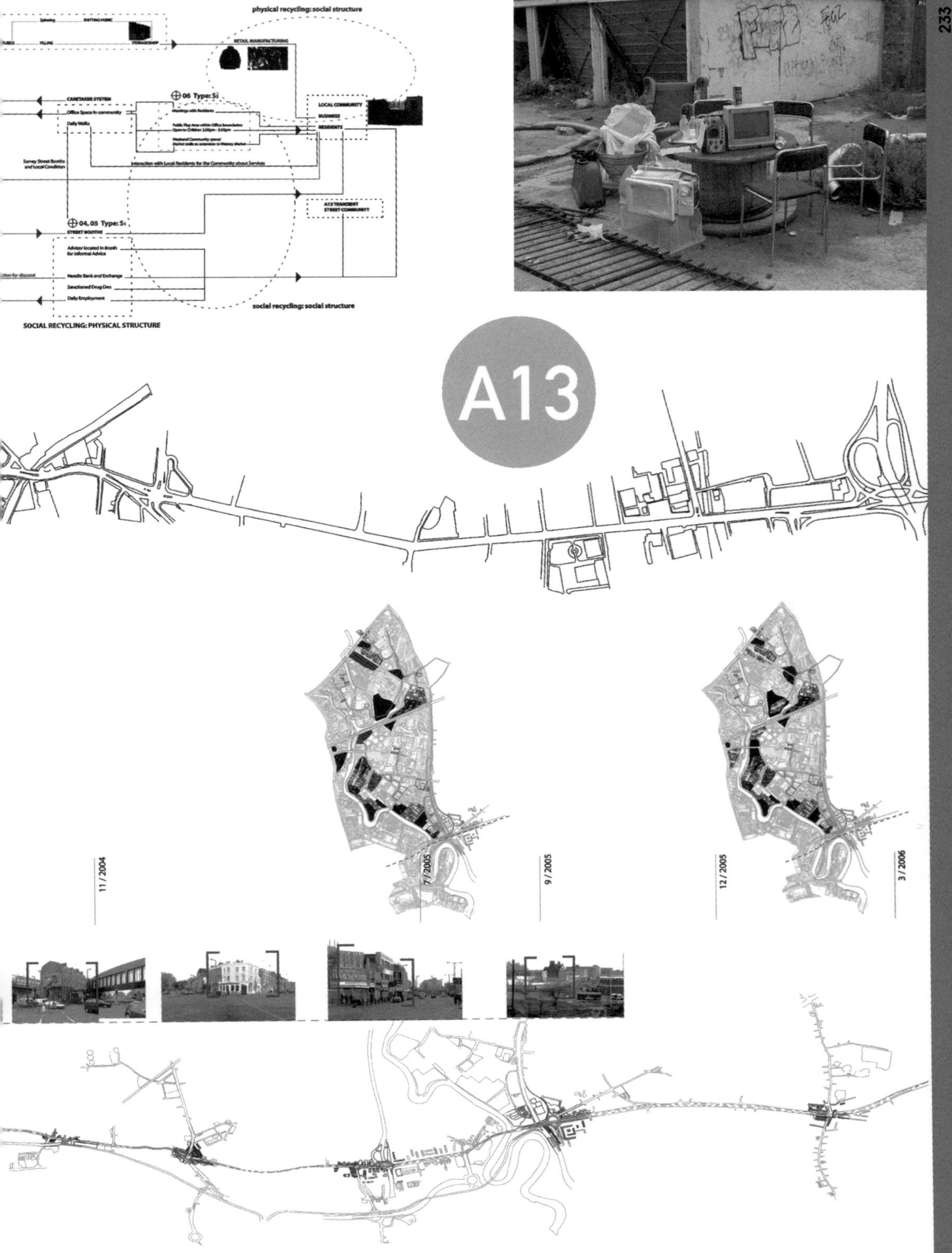
physical recycling: social structure
RETAIL MANUFACTURING
06 Type: S2
CARETAKER SYSTEM
Office Space in community
Daily Walks
LOCAL COMMUNITY
BUSINESS
RESIDENTS
Survey Street Booths and Local Condition
Interaction with Local Residents for the Community about Services
A13 TRANSIENT STREET COMMUNITY
04, 05 Type: S1
STREET BOOTHS
Advisor located in Booth for informal Advice
Needle Bank and Exchange
Sanctioned Drug Den
Daily Employment
social recycling: social structure
SOCIAL RECYCLING: PHYSICAL STRUCTURE
A13
11 / 2004
7 / 2005
9 / 2005
12 / 2005
3 / 2006

This page, clockwise from top: **Yoichiro Akiba** Sustainable Television; Pendulum; **Takashi Nishbori** Body-Skin; Earth-Digging Tools; **Tom Raymont** Breathing Backpack. Opposite page, clockwise from top left: **Yoichiro Akiba** Sustainable TV components; **Pedro Jervell** Composting Energy Generator; **Ayesha Aziz** Earth-Softness Testing; Earth Samples; **May Tang** Site Analysis; **Takashi Nishibori** Earth Samples

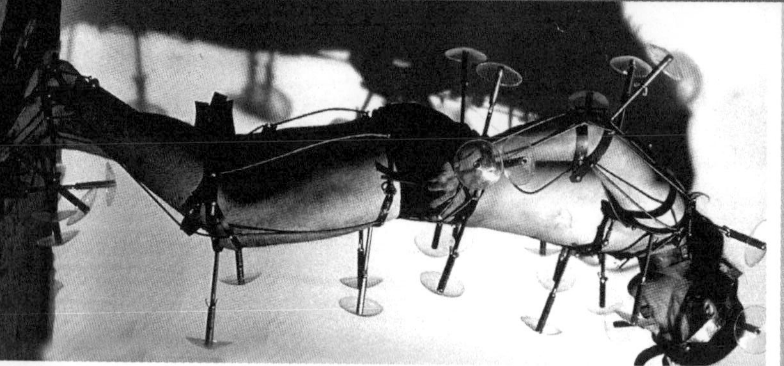

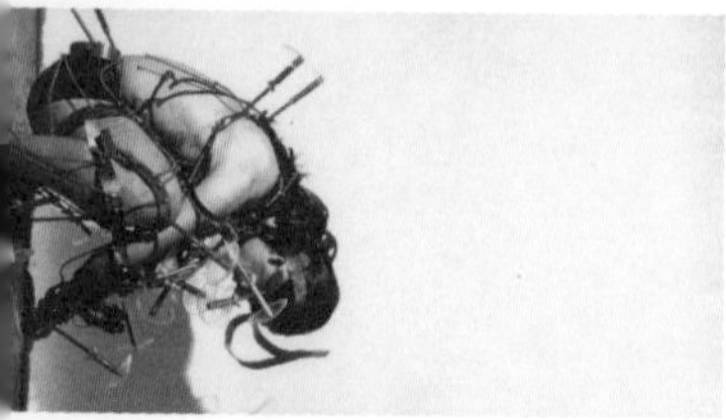

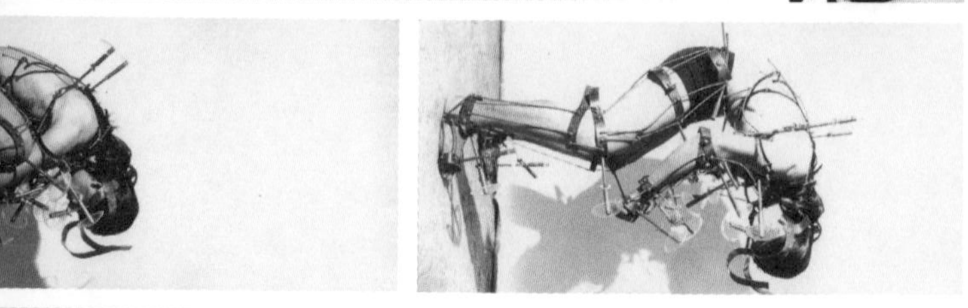

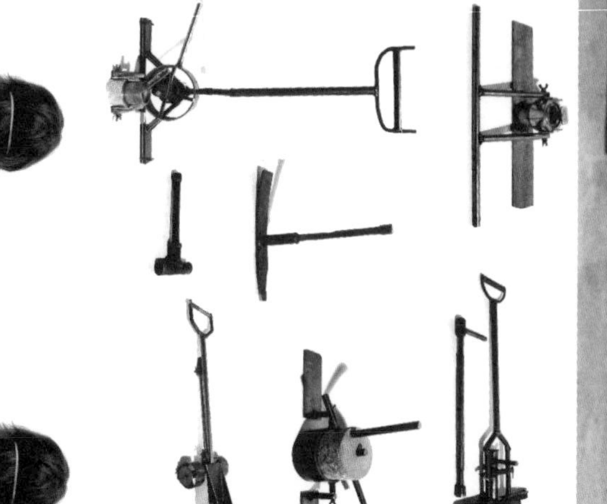

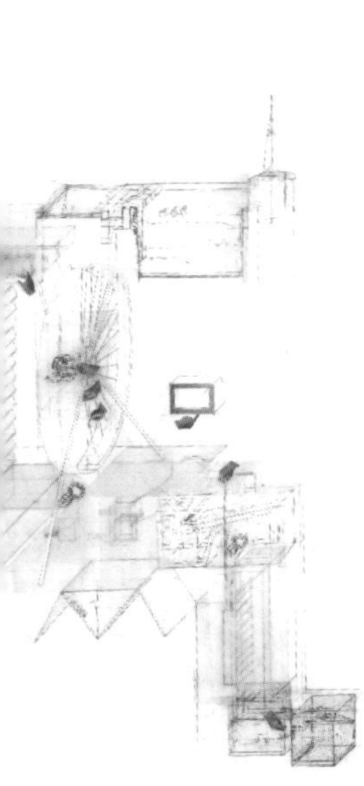

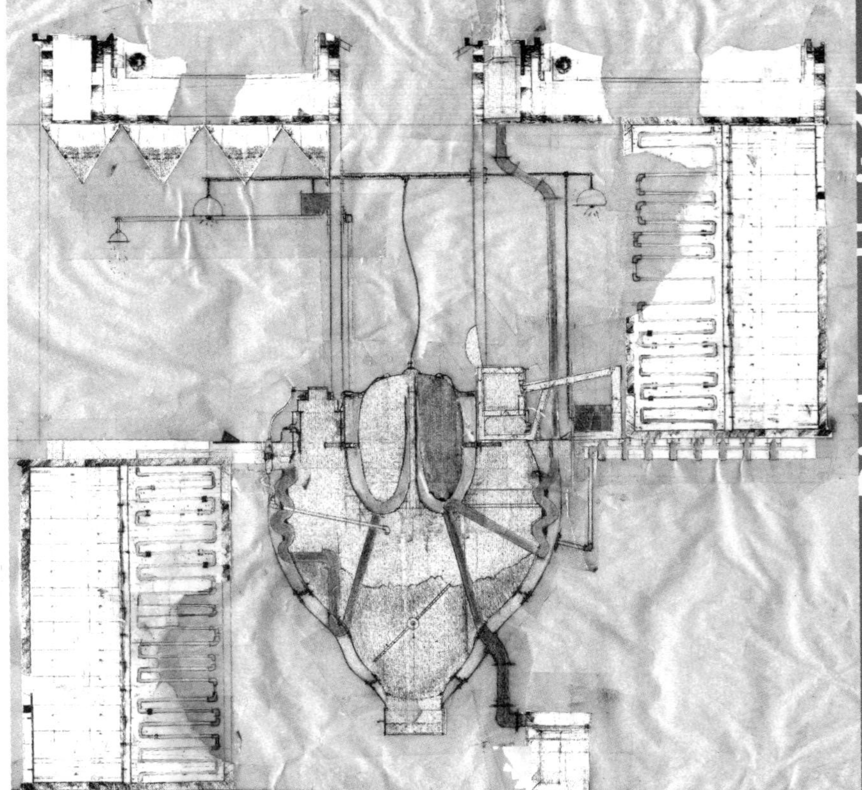

Through the construction of full-size prototypes, Diploma 11 put details at the very heart its working method. This year, the notion of the 'body power plant' led to initial full-size prototypes, in which the body was considered as a small industrial object, its space, chemistry, topology and machine acting as extensions of its architecture. The work then shifted to the domestic realm, via a workshop with Diploma 2 and Bill Dunster, the themes and agendas of whose work – biomass, embodied energy, air, water and heat circulation – infused our own. We began by accumulating objects, constructions and drawings that represented components closely associated with the body but also applicable to housing; these ideas were then taken to the small village of Tannan, in Taiwan. The collaborative construction of a set of interrelated urban fragments was made possible during the two-week workshop, jointly run with students from Taiwanese universities. A bench/gas holder, water compound, stove, composting station, fat and soap filter, and rainwater collector were developed and then combined as forms of local stations for a postearthquake community.

This page, clockwise from top left: **Kensuke Nisho** Clay-Compressing Machine and Components; Topographical Structures from Combinations of Bricks; Brick Samples and Molds; **May Tang** The Hanging Wall; Sectional Model of Hanging Dwelling Prototype; Hanging Clay Sample.Opposite page, from top left: **Walter Guidry** Orchestrated Movements; Sectional Model of Archive Passage; **Yeuk-Yi Li** Clay and plaster casting process; Interior Space, void–solid–void; **Walter Guidry** Archive Passage

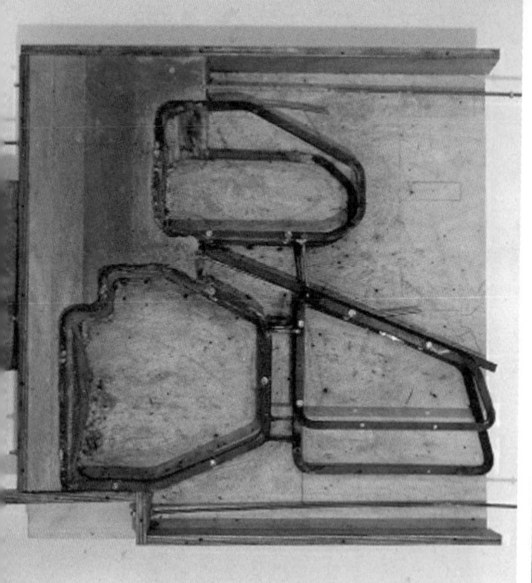

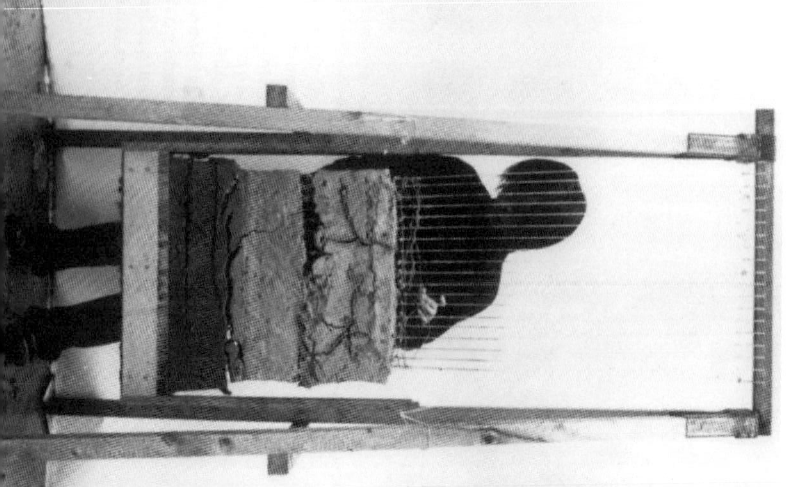

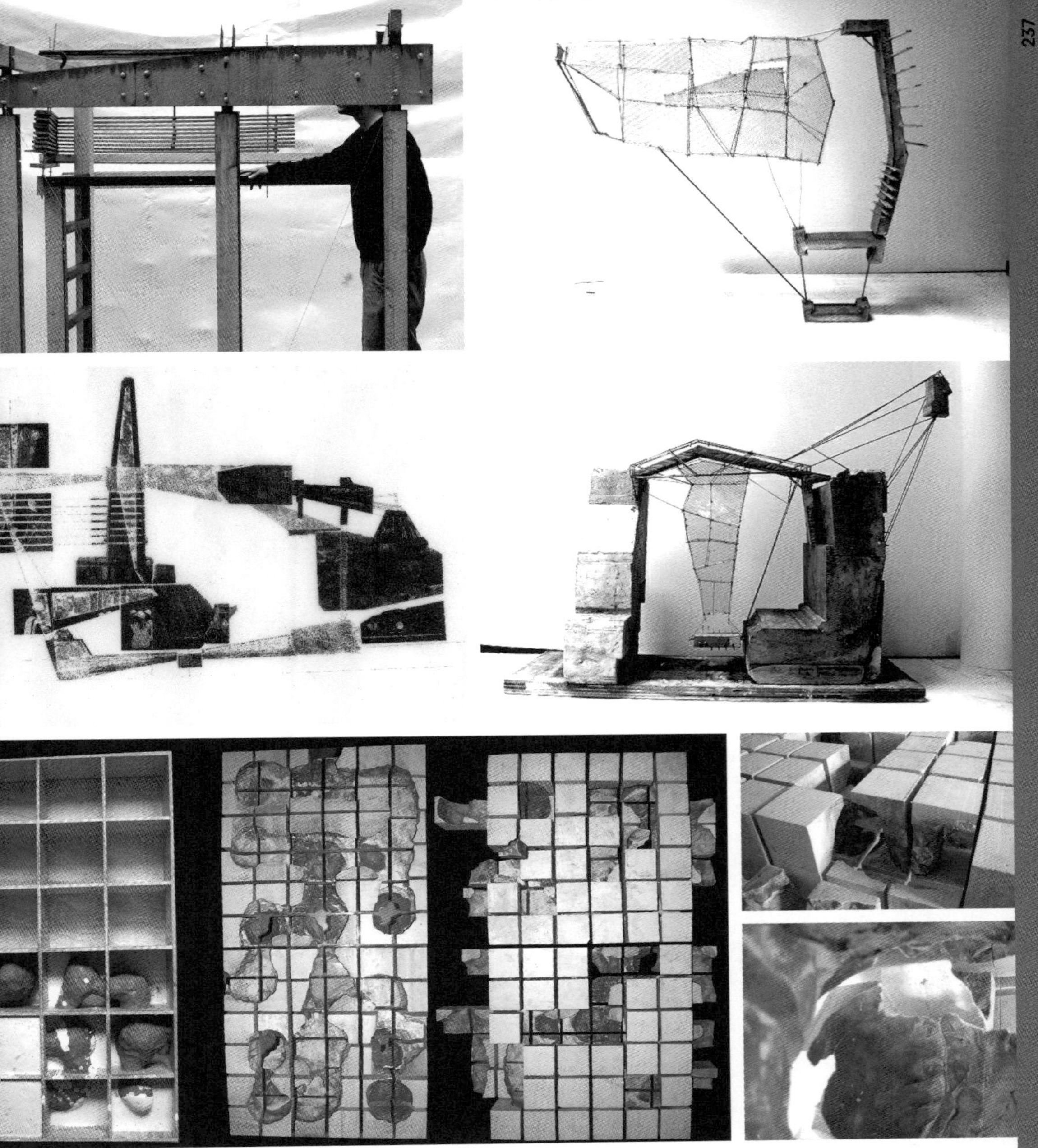

Returning to London, we examined two peripheral sites, 17 and 70 km from the city centre, as key moments in the city's consumption and construction. One is the Brent Cross scrap yard, where timber is collected from all over London, chipped and then exported to board manufacturers. The other was Stewartby Clay Pits (London Brick), where Lower Oxford Clay is dug, ground, pressed and fired into bricks. The landscape at Stewartby, near Bedford, is a startling mosaic of craters, some filled with water from previous clay extraction, and some still occupied by draglines and conveyor. This became the site of the main project.

This page, clockwise from top: **Yoichiro Akiba** Model of Flywheel; **Takashi Nishibori** Section of Earth-Digging Tools; **Sharron Lee** Working Elevation, Watercress Pumping Station; Models of Pumping Station; **Yoichiro Akiba** Elevation of Flywheel; Model of Flywheel. Opposite page, clockwise from top: **Pedro Jervell** Section Collage of Composting Generator; Model of Generator; **Takashi Nishibori** Section of Earth-Digging Tools; **Pedro Jervell** Section Collage of Composting Generator

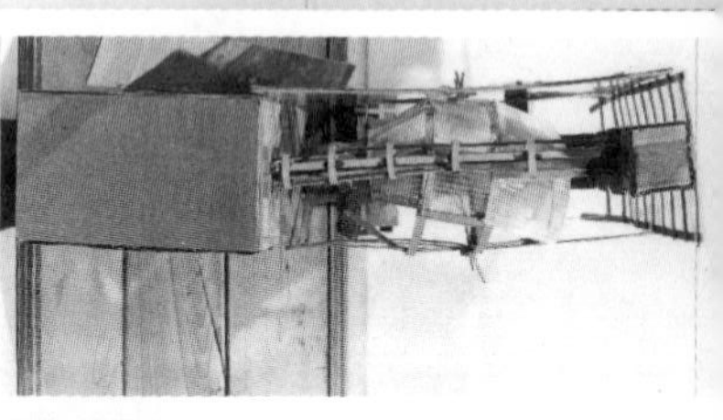

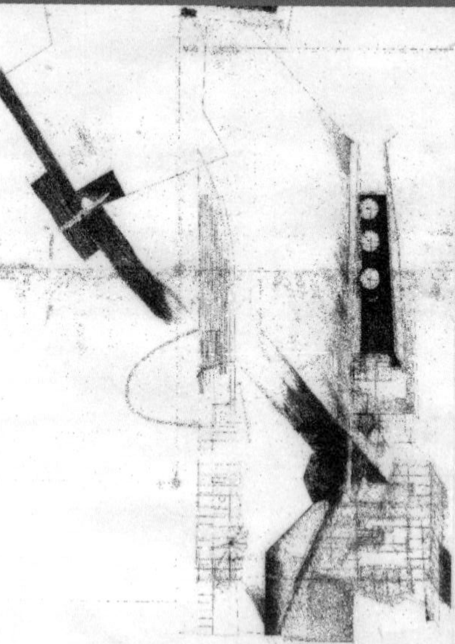
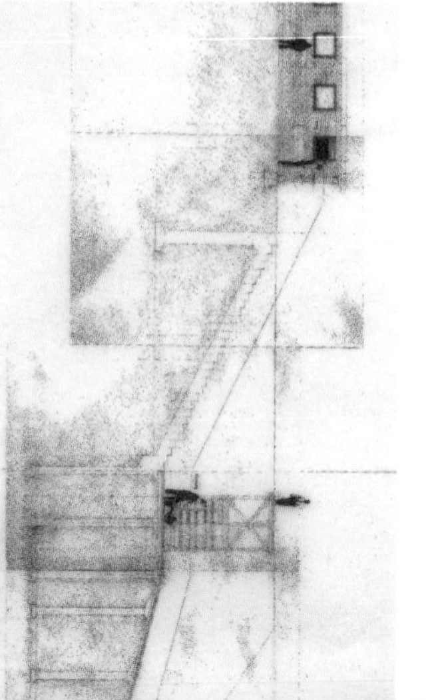

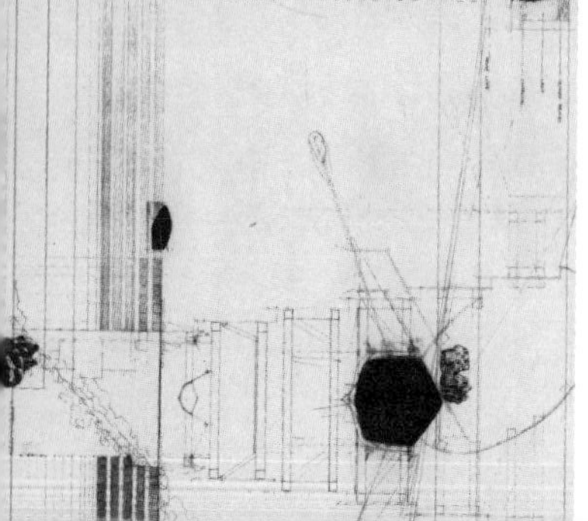

Initial prototypes were explored and developed as forms of dwellings. In this landscape of large industrial behaviour, the body can be seen as catalyst or perhaps a missing counterpart, an enclosed system within the open system. Conjunctions between small-scale industries and dwellings were proposed within the landscape. Further speculation focused on the landscape's texture as an alternative pattern for the transformation and re-covering of the exhausted skins of the postindustrial terrain – an interior landscape.

This page, clockwise from top left: **Ingrid Frydenbø** Simultaneous Extraction–Construction, Phases 1–6; Section Through Ceramic Workshop and Mushroom Farm; Interior of Mushroom Farm; **Tom Raymont** Tile Factory/Moss Farm; Callow tipping sequence; **Ingrid Frydenbø** Land-Formation Diagram Model. Opposite page, clockwise from top: **Kai-Ping Yang** Catalogue of Details, Caretaker's House; Axonometric of Charcoal-Making, Fish Smokery and Coppicing Areas; Plan of Caretaker's House and Coppicing Workshop; Model of Caretaker's House and Coppicing Workshop

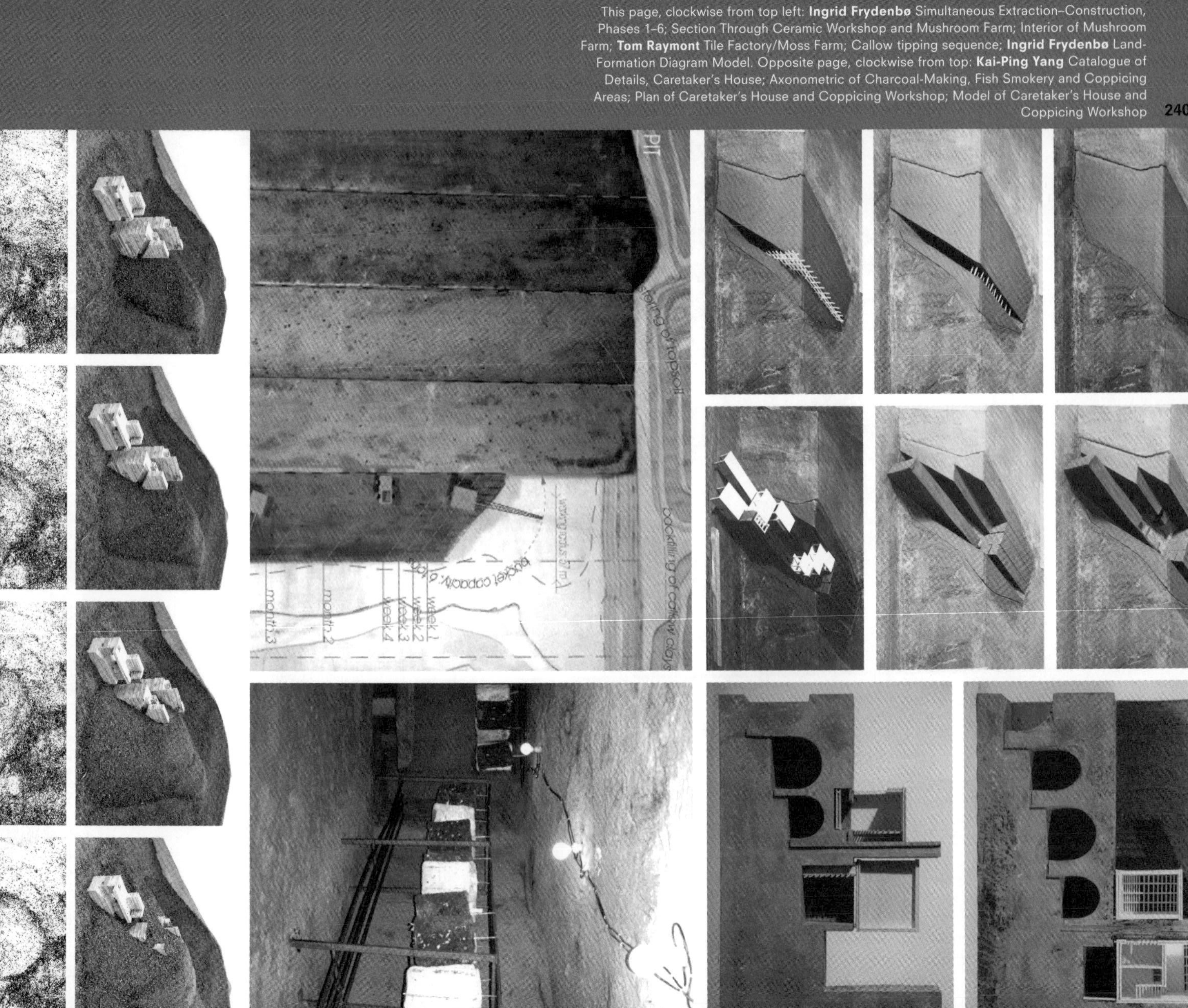

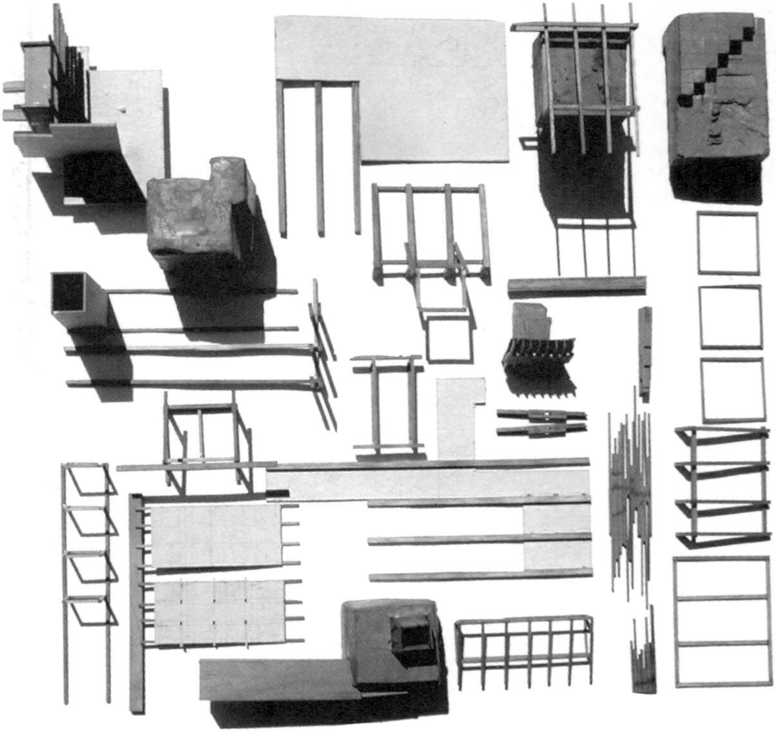

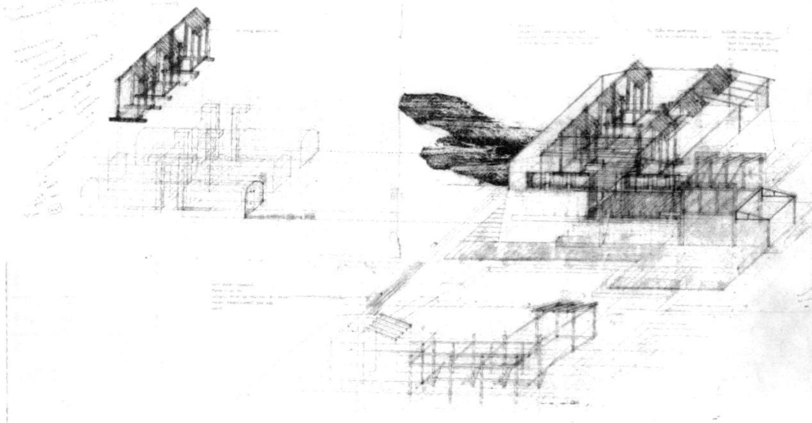

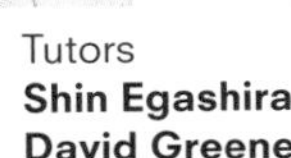

Tutors
Shin Egashira
David Greene

Students
Yoichiro Akiba
Ayesha Aziz
Ingrid Frydenbø
Walter Guidry
Pedro Jervell
Sharron Lee
Yeuk-Yi Li
Yoko Murakami
Takashi Nishibori
Kensuke Nishio
Tom Raymont
May Tang
Kai-Ping Yang

The unit would like to thank:
Bill Dunster for his workshop
Wei Tseng for supporting the Taiwan Workshop
Hanson Brick Company for supporting our field research

Free Agents, Free Agendas Double

The aim of the unit was to study spaces of changing identities and to enhance these transient spaces through an architectural intervention.

In the first term, students looked at a specific form of contemporary public space: the London Underground. The Underground is supposedly a space of endless displacement, with individuals merely passing hastily through, but it also contains spaces full of hidden opportunity. This unit focused on the changing agendas or identities of these infrastructural spaces. The intermediate zones of Underground stations, particularly the transition space between the platform and the street, were of primary interest for the study of human gestures and relationships. In a further exercise, students were asked to enhance or intervene in the moment when one situation suddenly flips into another. The idea was to plan a scenario that would make people act subliminally against their routines. With the emphasis on the possibility of switching identities of place and space, form was not important. Rather, the interest lay in a kind of manipulation of our mental maps.

This first task was accompanied by a series of theoretical readings on heterotopias, political space and the concept of the everyday. In an attempt to go beyond the much-cited and simplified concept of heterotopias and allow for a more meaningful investigation, a contemporary myth was incorporated into both the analysis and the design process. In order to catalyse this process and challenge the investigated situations, different fragments, such as film scenes, texts and landscapes, were tested.

Strategies to find a certain sensibility with regard to urban procedures brought about different project themes and narratives. Following an unknown person from the Underground into Leicester Square, only to find oneself in turn watched by CCTV cameras broadcasting live on the internet, turned the act of watching into the awareness of being watched. The idea of the project then was to reverse the control of the virtual community. In another project, using the Underground as a place to read was a means of rethinking its use as purely one of transport. The Underground was understood as a spatial network mediated through reading – the Circle Line turned into a library. Another idea understood the Underground network as a labyrinthine space in which to stage theatre.

In the second and third terms, studies shifted from the London Underground to Berlin's network of almost-forgotten subterranean structures. Caverns, air-raid shelters and railway tunnels, some long out of use, others never used, are spread in a random pattern over the entire municipal area.

The objective of the project was to find a possible use for a combined network of tunnel sections often located far from each other. Somehow the task of the first term became reversed; now it was an issue of finding a use for reduced and excluded spatial situations, and to enrich them through an architectural intervention. The concept was now to bring light into the dark and to create a connection between above ground and below.

The tunnels of Berlin were imagined as hubs in a kind of network. Here a play on words – *route – tourist – truism* – opened another dimension: rather than a tourist route, which would again fall into the trap of heterotopias, students developed the idea of a routing. Such a conceptual routing, which could be either a narrative or a concrete functional project, was intended to open up new spatial and human relationships, and to enhance the sublimity of the everyday. Hence the emphasis on a design process in which the construction of narratives and myth occupies an important role.

The idea of this project was to access the numerous blind tunnels of Berlin through 'reading rooms'. The reading room is imagined to reside between forgetting and remembering. More than a space for reading, it is a place where books and personal artefacts can be stored and, to a certain extent, subsequently forgotten. But it is also a place where the many facets of the city, including its personal stories, could unfold. The train tracks, acting as a mnemonic device for the storage shelves and the reading rooms, recall images of farewell and arrival, of rest and excitement, images of forgotten and fashionable places in the city. Tzeh Bin Cheong

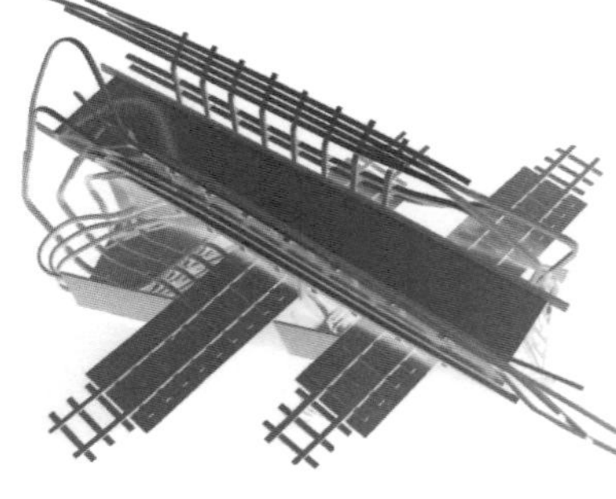

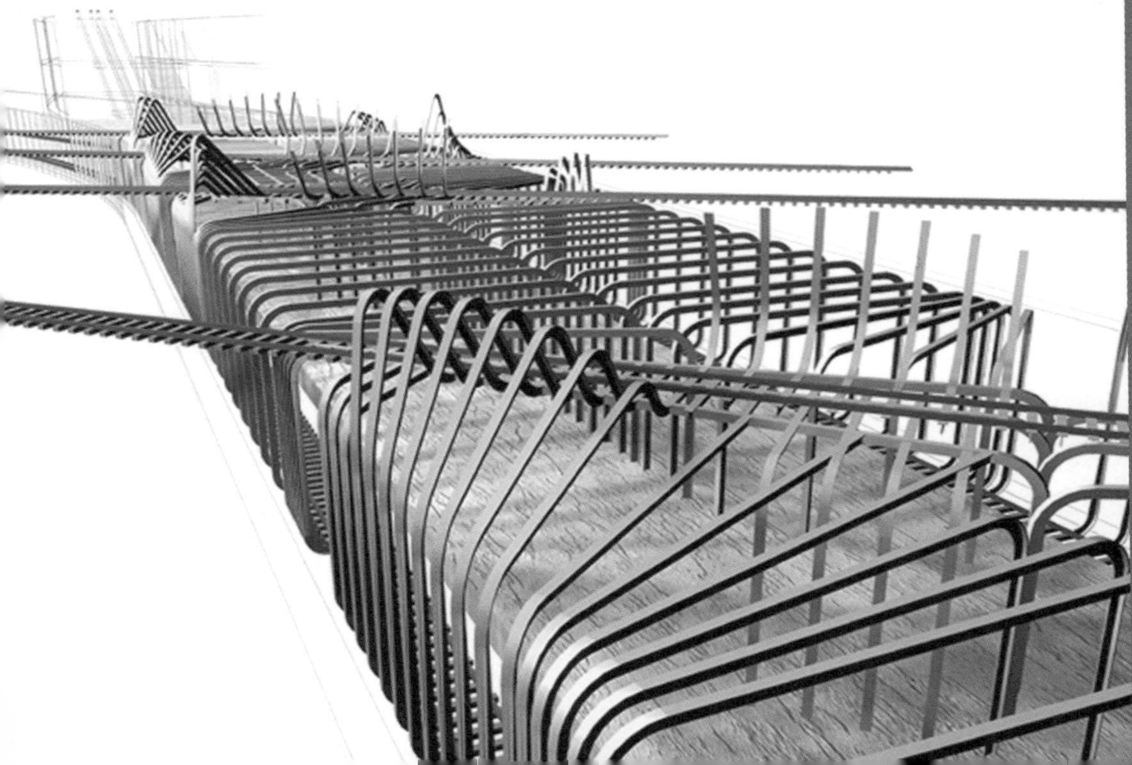

Developed from a historical study of the many different faces of Potsdamer Platz, this project sought to create a place of encounters. Investigations into the practice of encounters led to the study of the five phases of love. Overlaying the attraction, recognition, interaction, arousal and resolution phases with a spatial equivalent led to a new narrative, forming a 'journey of encounters' through the Potsdamer Platz. The realisation of the project involved the development of nonstatic structures and strategies that can offer a flexibility of programmes as well as encourage changes in distance and gaze relationships. Timothy Tan

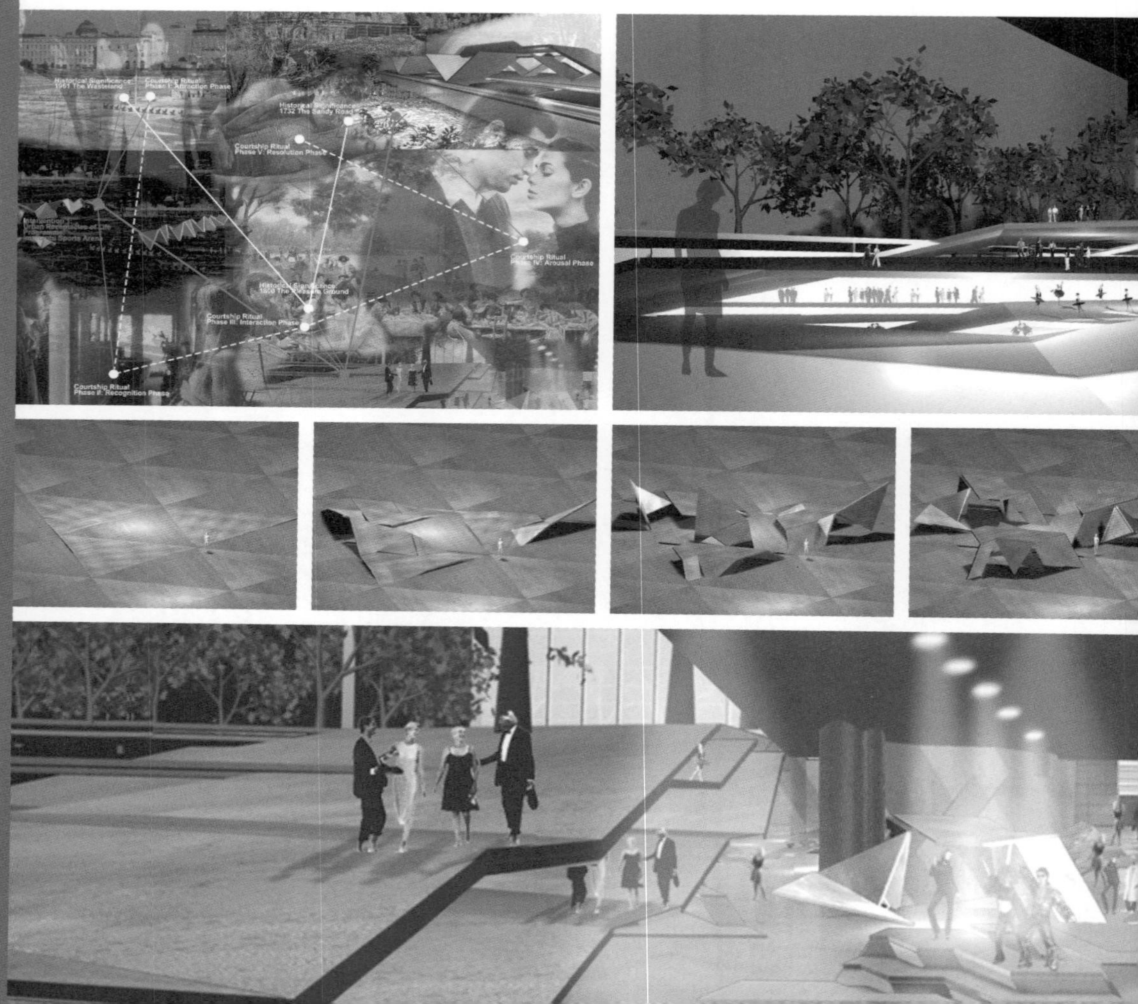

This project further developed the project of a 'tracescape' in the London Underground. A 'moving wall', designed to accommodate the relaxed postures of waiting, was adapted to an urban planning project in Berlin. Here a flexible structure was developed, aiming to keep a remaining segment of the Berlin Wall intact, and using no more original plans than the former block fabric. The new topographical fabric provides a slightly elevated green footpath with space on the inside for public facilities. Jaihyuk Lee

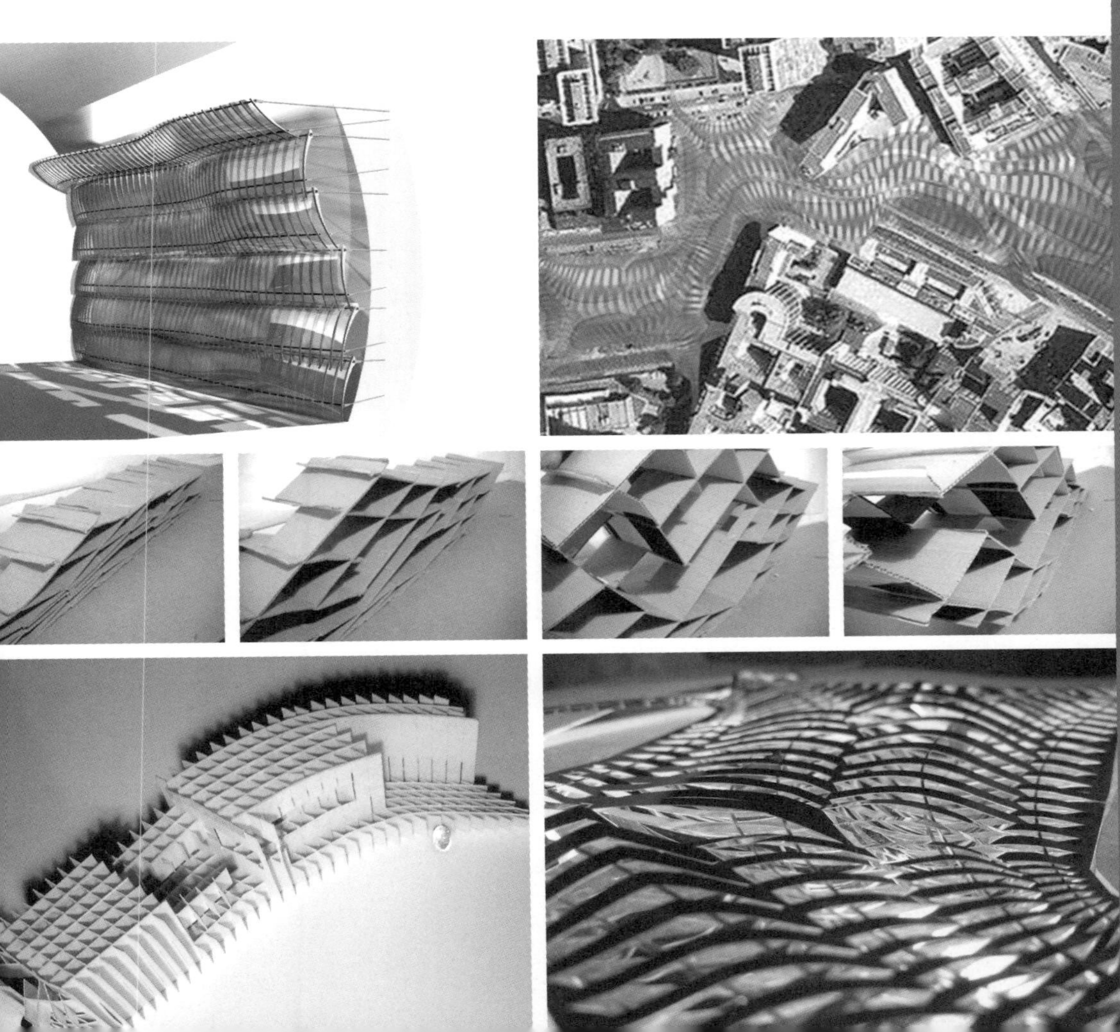

The project of the urban cemetery responds to Foucault's concept of heterotopias, in which he explains how, from the 18th century on, the cemetery was increasingly excluded from the experience of the city. Reacting to the urban voids and empty lots still characteristic of Berlin, the project aims to reintroduce cemeteries into the city, intertwining with other everday programmes. The investigations launched in the course of this study aimed to redefine the relationship between the living and the dead, and propose a scenario where the two may coexist. The employment of various rhythm instruments seeks to integrate different levels of silence into the rhythm and noises of the city. Jason Lai

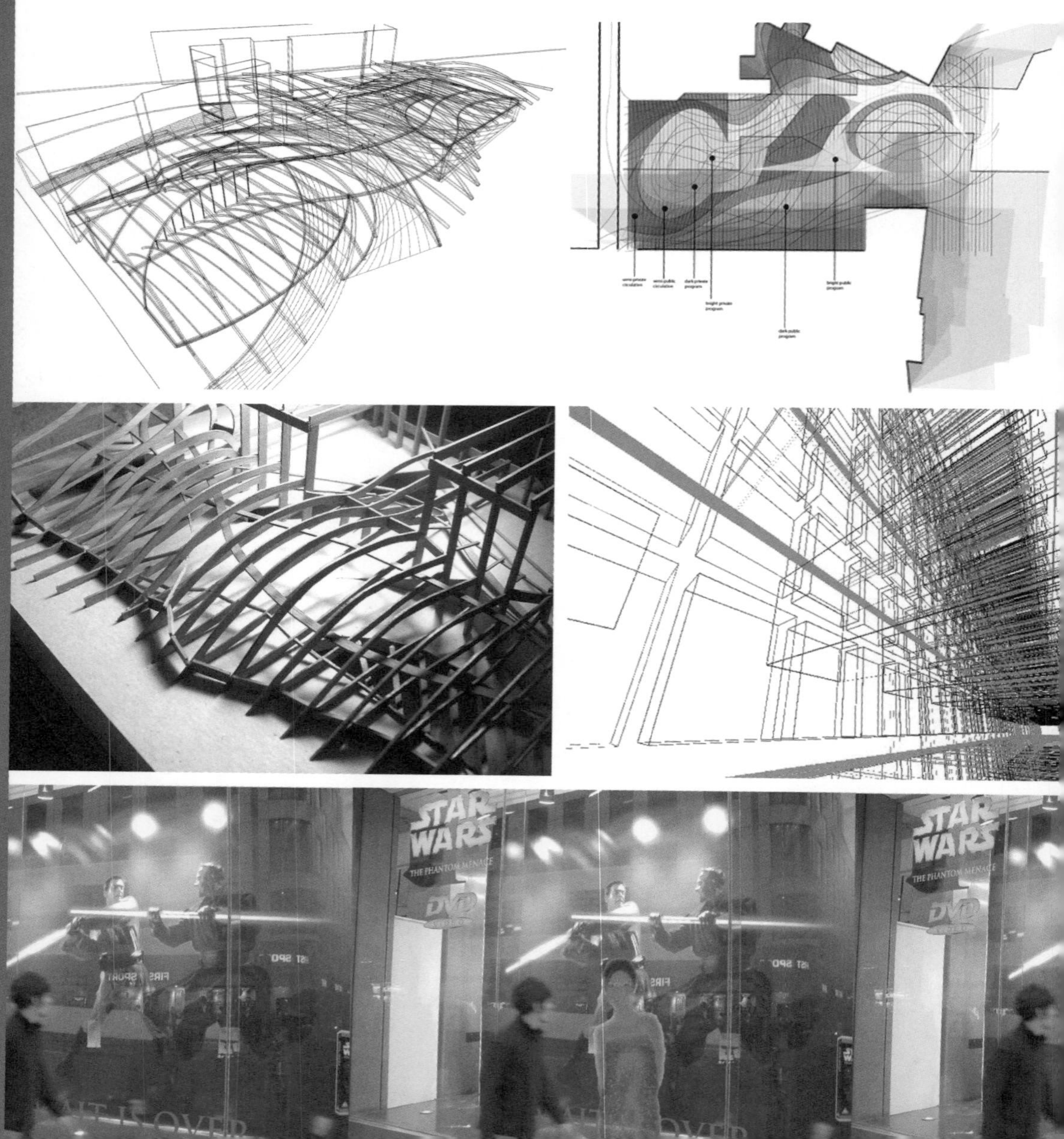

The aim of the project was to intervene in the everyday routine of waiting, providing a critical counterpoint to the flimsy spatial rules of personal etiquette and myths of queuing. Its intention was to 'build with people' – to form an intelligent, informed crowd that could participate in the functioning of the city and even contribute to a form of branding. The project adopted the logic of the game of dominoes, assigning its figurative combinations to the randomness and short duration of moments of waiting. Starting with a basic set of 28 stones, it tested a 'sensitive pavement' in front of the Reichstag, visitors now moving in nonlinear queues and leaving slowly disappearing 'traces' on the site. Colin Priest

A man walking in the streets is unaware of being watched; he seems free in this space to ignore the world around him. But this freedom is countermanded by the power of surveillance. Capturing an image is a two-way process between observer and observed. The question now is how to establish a balance between them. This project located its case study in Berlin's Friedrichstrasse. An empty lot was used to amalgamate the loot of a tourist raid through this street, forming a building consisting of 'copied' places. The formation of cone-shaped volumes piercing the building create viewing paths that can be captured neither by the panopticon gaze nor by digital surveillance. Ioannis Orphanos

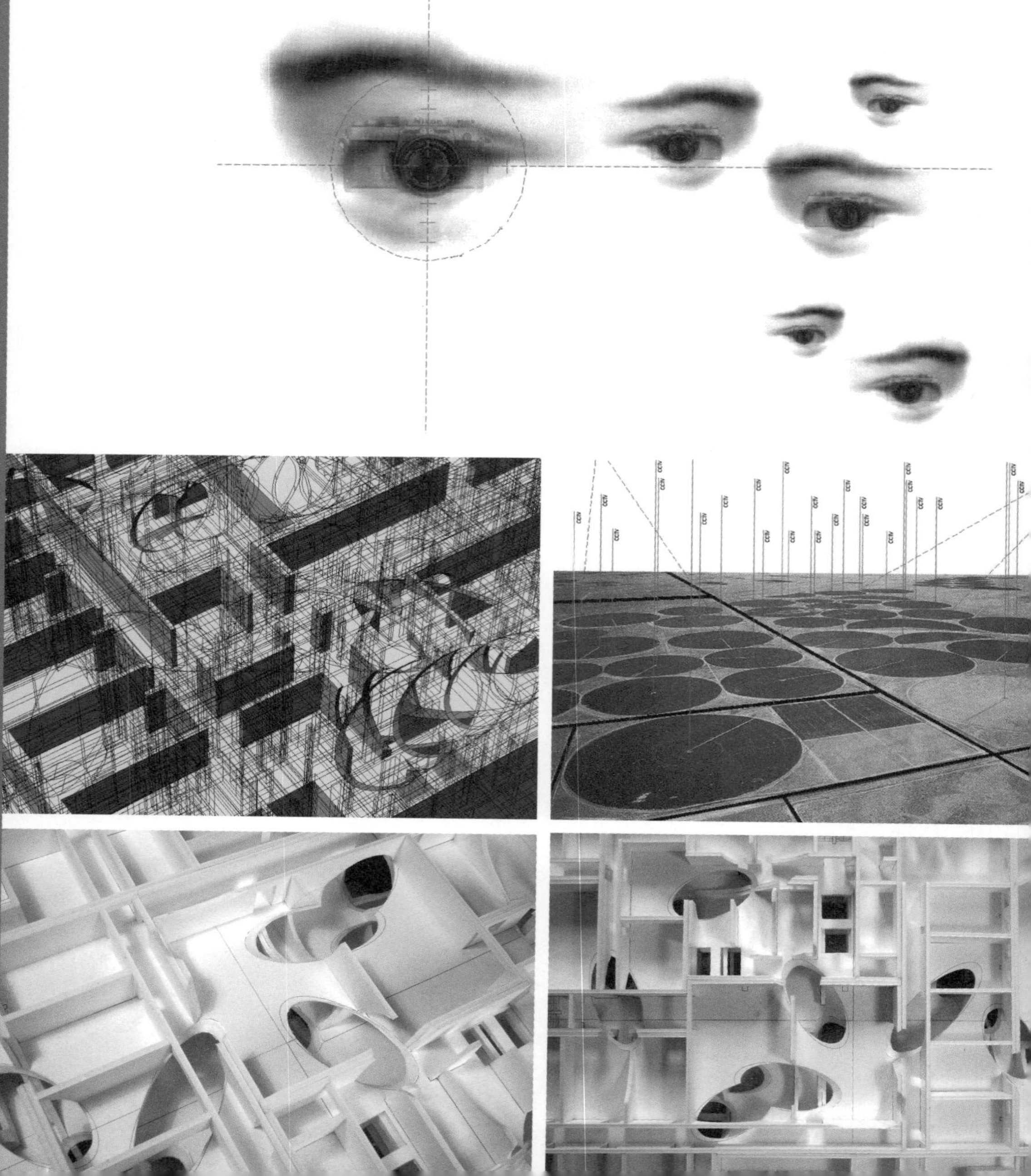

Like the investigation of the Underground as library, this project for a 'water landscape' on Potsdamer Platz is concerned with the relationship between events above and below ground.

The construction projects undertaken over the last twelve years in Berlin have attempted, on a massive scale, to shift and isolate the new buildings from the surrounding water. As a reaction to this, the project proposes to flood the disused tunnels in the city. In a case study located on Potsdamer Platz, it investigates forms of manipulation of above ground and below ground, examining how rainwater can be collected and how pedestrians can experience and interact with the new water landscape.
Wan Sophonpanich

Unit Masters
Martine de Maeseneer
Ines Geisler

Students
Sarah Akigbogun
Tzeh Bin Cheong
Jason Chon Yin Lai
Jaihyuk Lee
Mum Choen Lee
Ioannis Orphanos
Colin Priest
Wan Sophonpanich
Timothy Yit Ching Tan
Swee-Puan Tung

Special thanks to
Dietmar Arnold
Peter Beard
Mark Cousins
Gunnar Degerlid
Philipp Oswalt
Matthias Reese
Kai Vöckler

Visiting Critics
Francesca Hughes
Peter Lee
Ciro Najle
Lina Stergiou
Eyal Weizman
Tobias Zettler

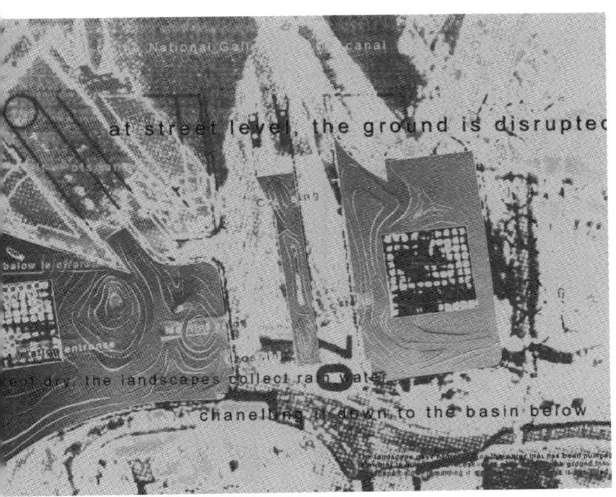

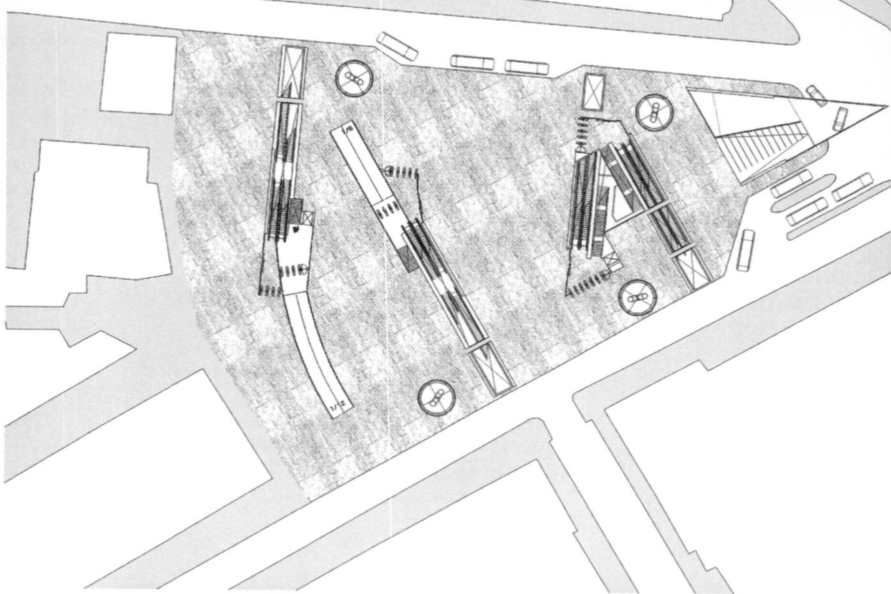

The Architectural Approach

The unit aims to take account of each student's potential regarding approach, process, style and design. Dip 13 researches architecture as a multi-layered artefact embracing a diversity of issues: environment, metropolis, transport, ecology, structure, construction, function, beauty, etc.

The Technology

The combined approaches of architect and engineer form the unit's basic structure. Together they question the making of built form: is form a result of function, of structure, of digital analysis, of metaphor, of idea? Technical integrity is considered an enriching part of the design process, and exterior influences like soil, water, light, sound, air and heat provide valuable guidelines for design, as do user patterns, people flows, etc. All are blended into the construction and contribute to the development of the idea.

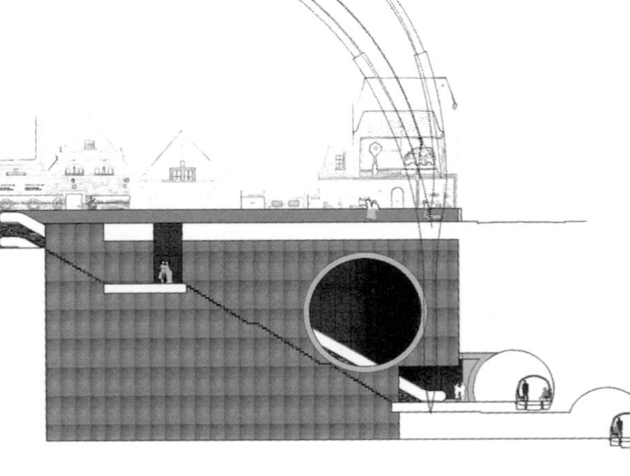

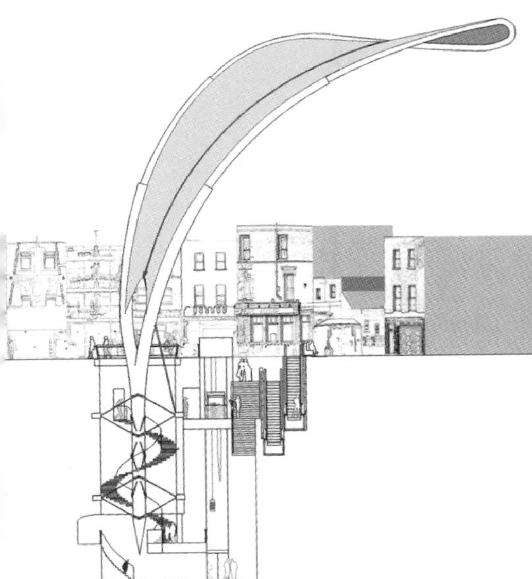

Tomonobu Hirayu
The Station Square

The Holistic Urban Oasis

The project will be a medium to work the body and stretch and calm the soul. You are going to provide places for continuous activities, where people can gather to lounge, eat, drink; talk, sing, act, play music; dive, climb, swim, skate; think, read, meditate, contemplate. You should consider the extreme as well as the mundane, reach high, low and wide with swimming pools, rock-climbing walls and scuba-diving tanks; with steep dance floors and sinking music halls. You will be encouraged to provide 24-hour refreshment in multi-storey restaurants and liquid bars. You should also design simple cells for solitary thought and meditation and large spaces for spiritual gathering. Along the east and the west of your site flow numerous bus routes. To the north is Camden Lock and its culture of youth, craft, music, the bazaar, the canal; on and under our site is Camden Town Underground station. You will have to understand the need for quiet and calm as much as for noise and the bustle of activity.

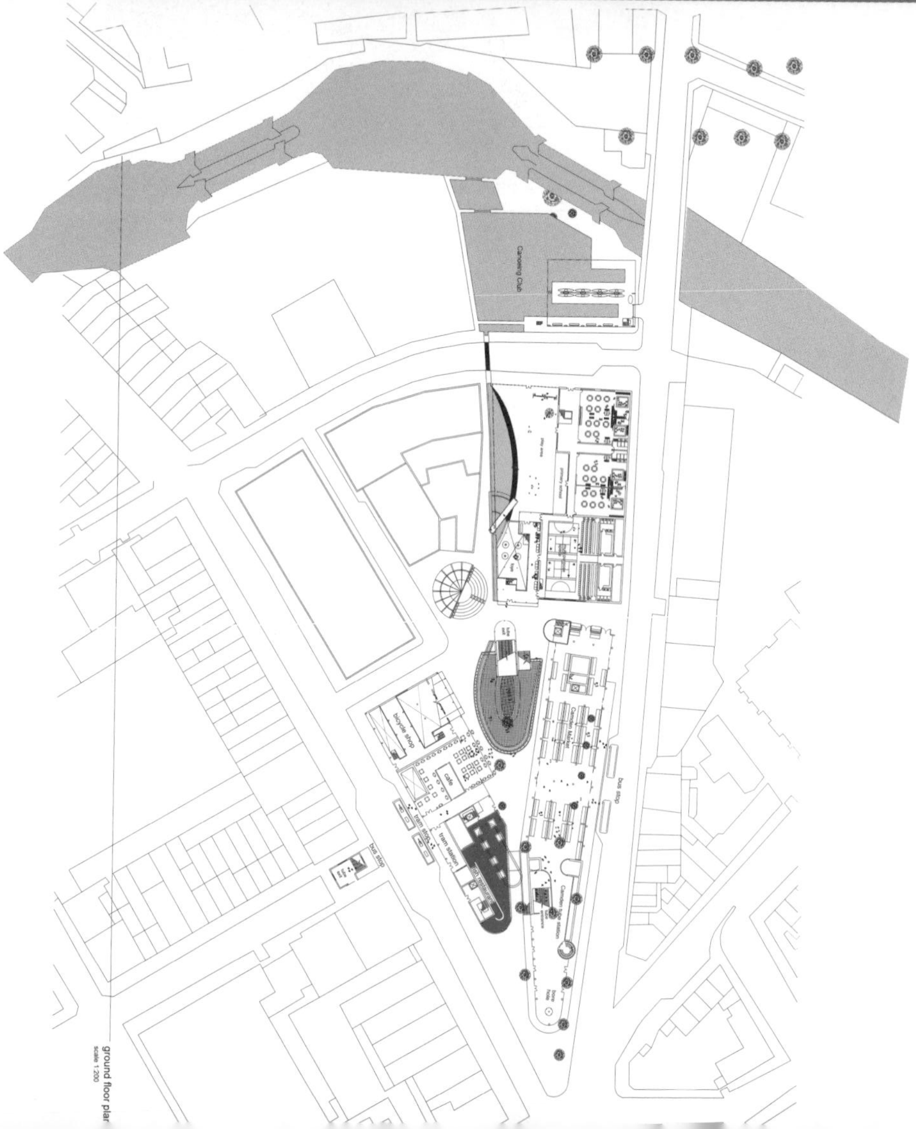

Sarah Mackie
Moving Water in Camden

bus stop
Camden Market
Camden tube station
bore hole
primary school
play area
Canoeing Club
cafe
bicycle shop
tram station
tram stop

ground floor plan
scale 1:200

Hackyub Jang
Read, think, swim at Camden Square

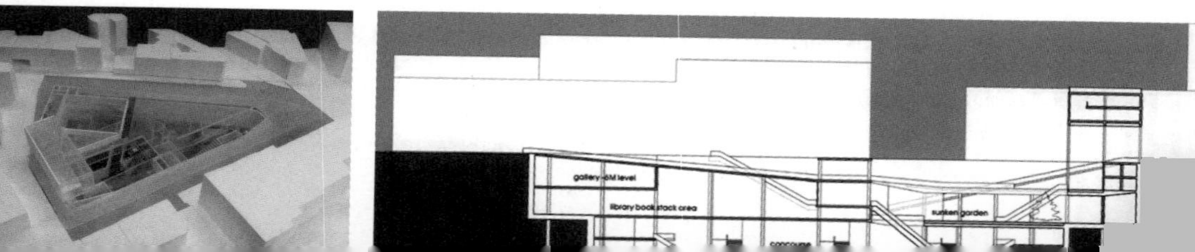

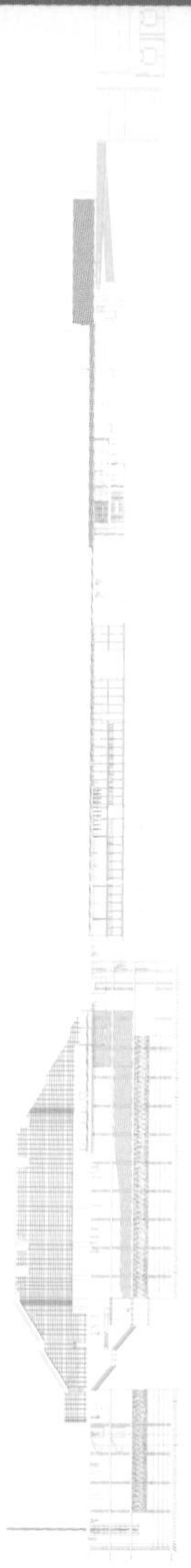

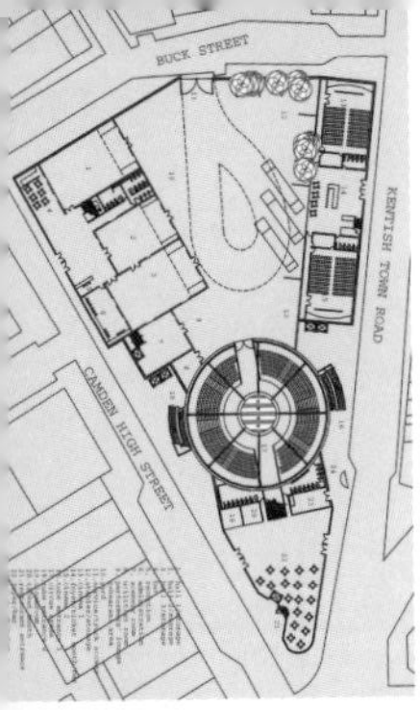

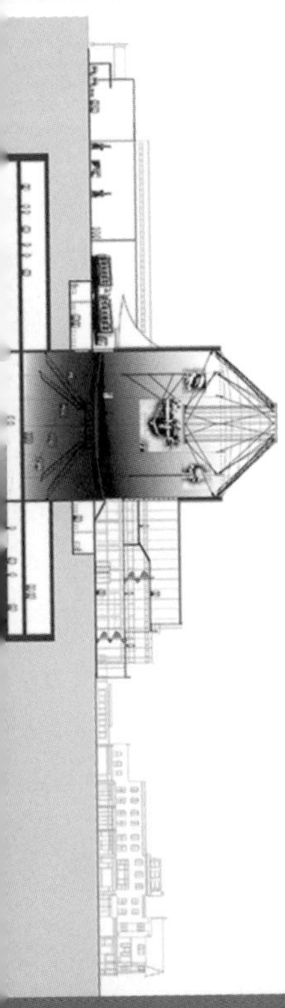

Peck-San Chan
Camden Circus School

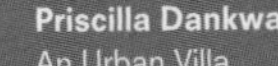

Priscilla Dankwa
An Urban Villa

Chang yil Han I-Ching Huang

Spiral down to the Station Swimming Station

250

<NORTH—SOUTH>

ACCESSABLE PLATFORM

BRIDGE / GROUNDLEVEL
LINK BOTH SIDES OF SITE

OUTDOOR CASCADE

ENTRANCE

INDOOR SWIMMING POOL

▽-3.00

PLANT ROOM

LIFT

EXIT ONLY

ATRIUM

LEVEL OF PLATFORM 1&3 ▽-15.00

LEVEL OF PLATFORM 2&4 ▽-18.14

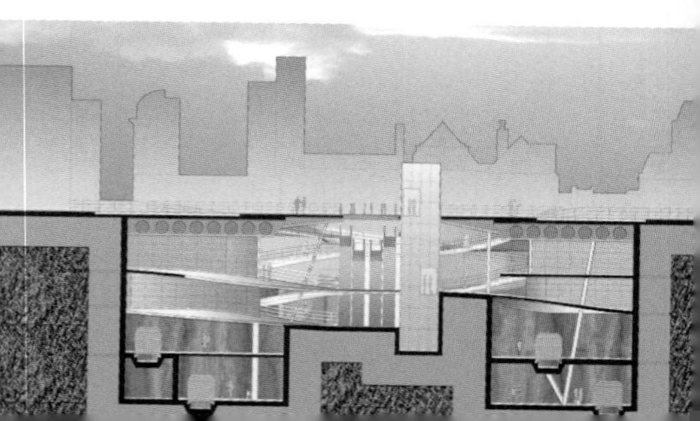

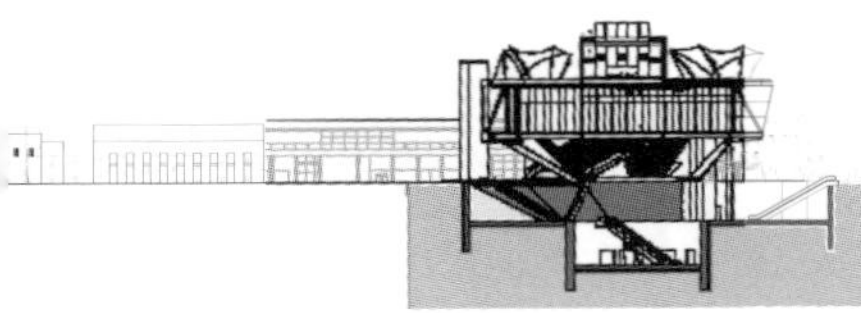

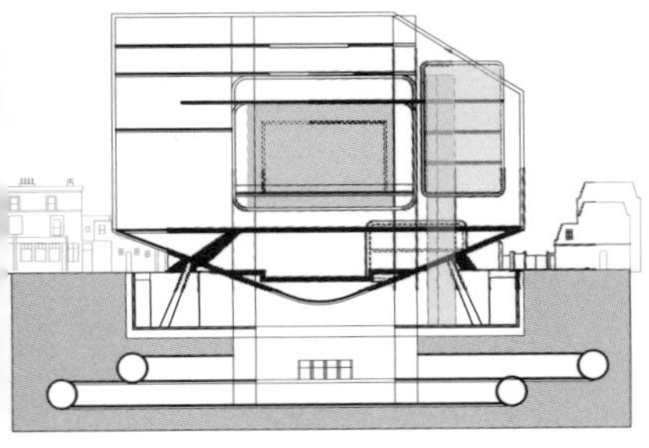

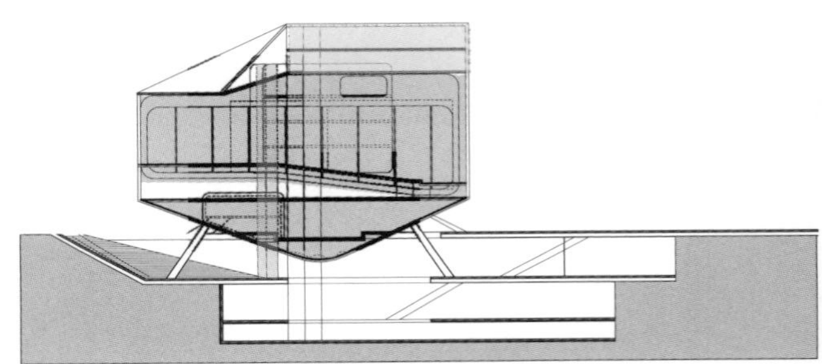

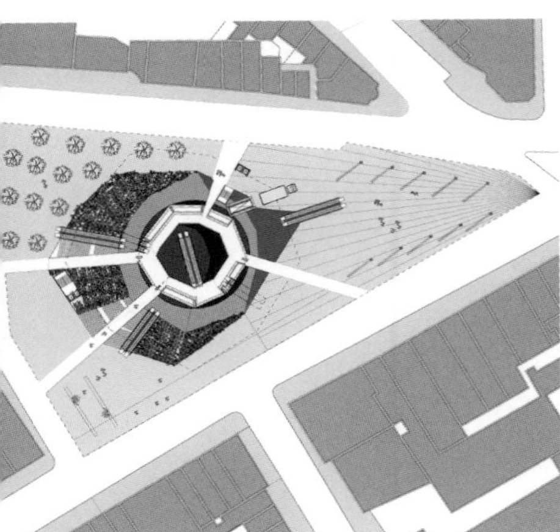

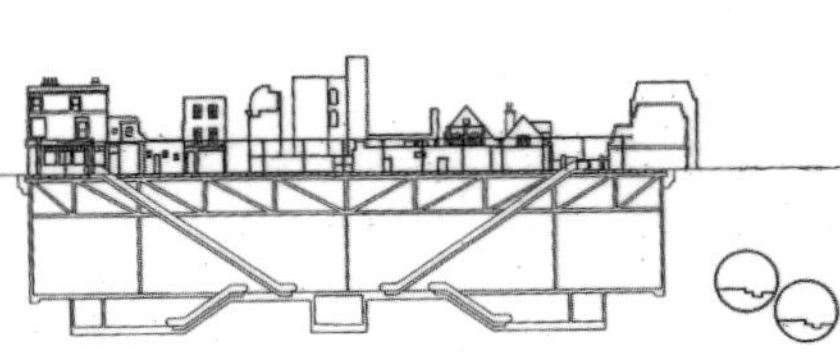

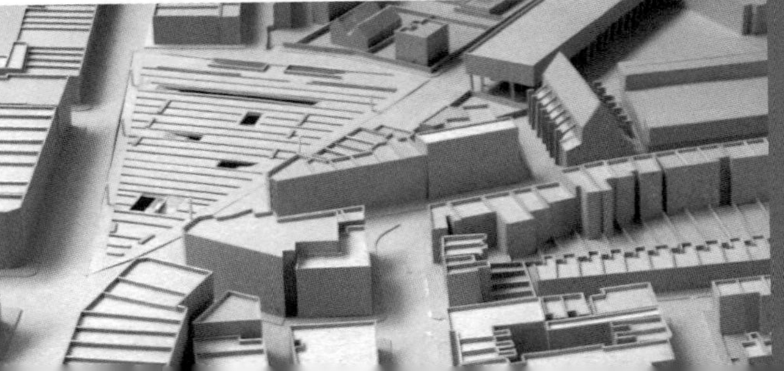

Tanyawat Worathonghchai Railway Museum

Jung Whang Vertical Square

Jason Ho — **Irineos Charitou**

Shopping interchange — Houses above the station for swimming, praying and meditating

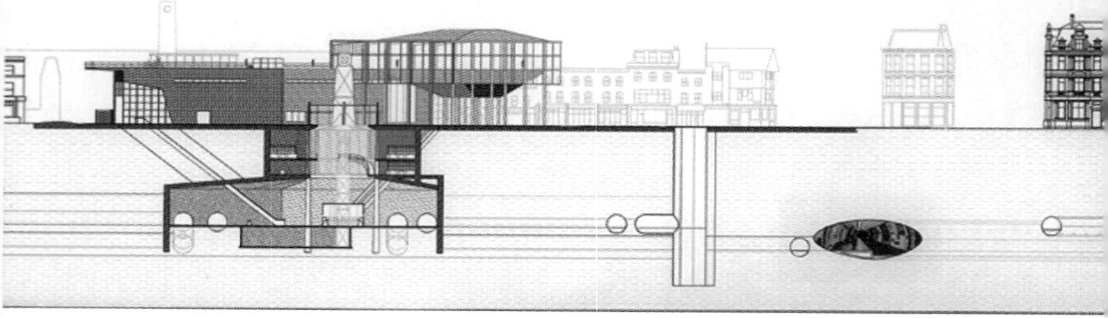

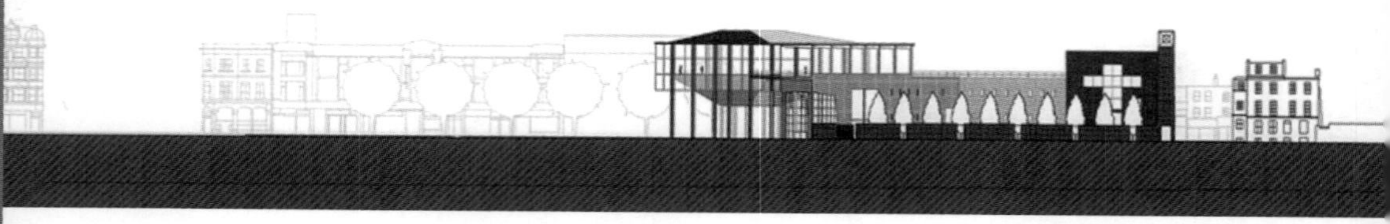

ROAD

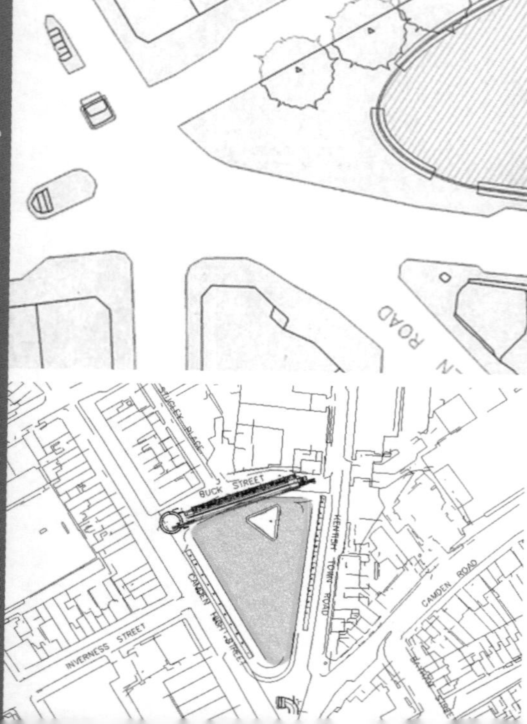

BUCK STREET

CAMDEN HIGH STREET

KENTISH TOWN ROAD

CAMDEN ROAD

INVERNESS STREET

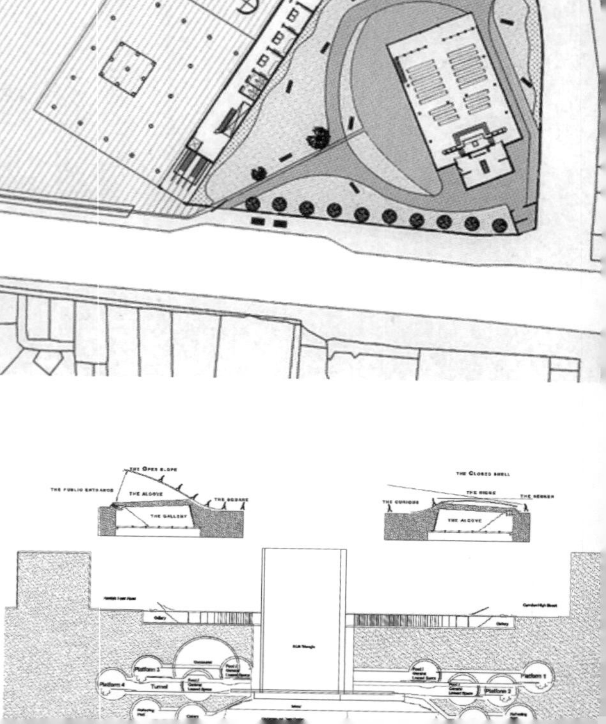

THE OPEN SLOPE

THE PUBLIC ENTRANCE

THE ALCOVE

THE GALLERY

THE SQUARE

THE CLOSED SHELL

THE CURIOUS

THE BRIDGE

THE SEEKER

THE ALCOVE

Platform 3

Platform 4

Tunnel

Platform 1

Platform 2

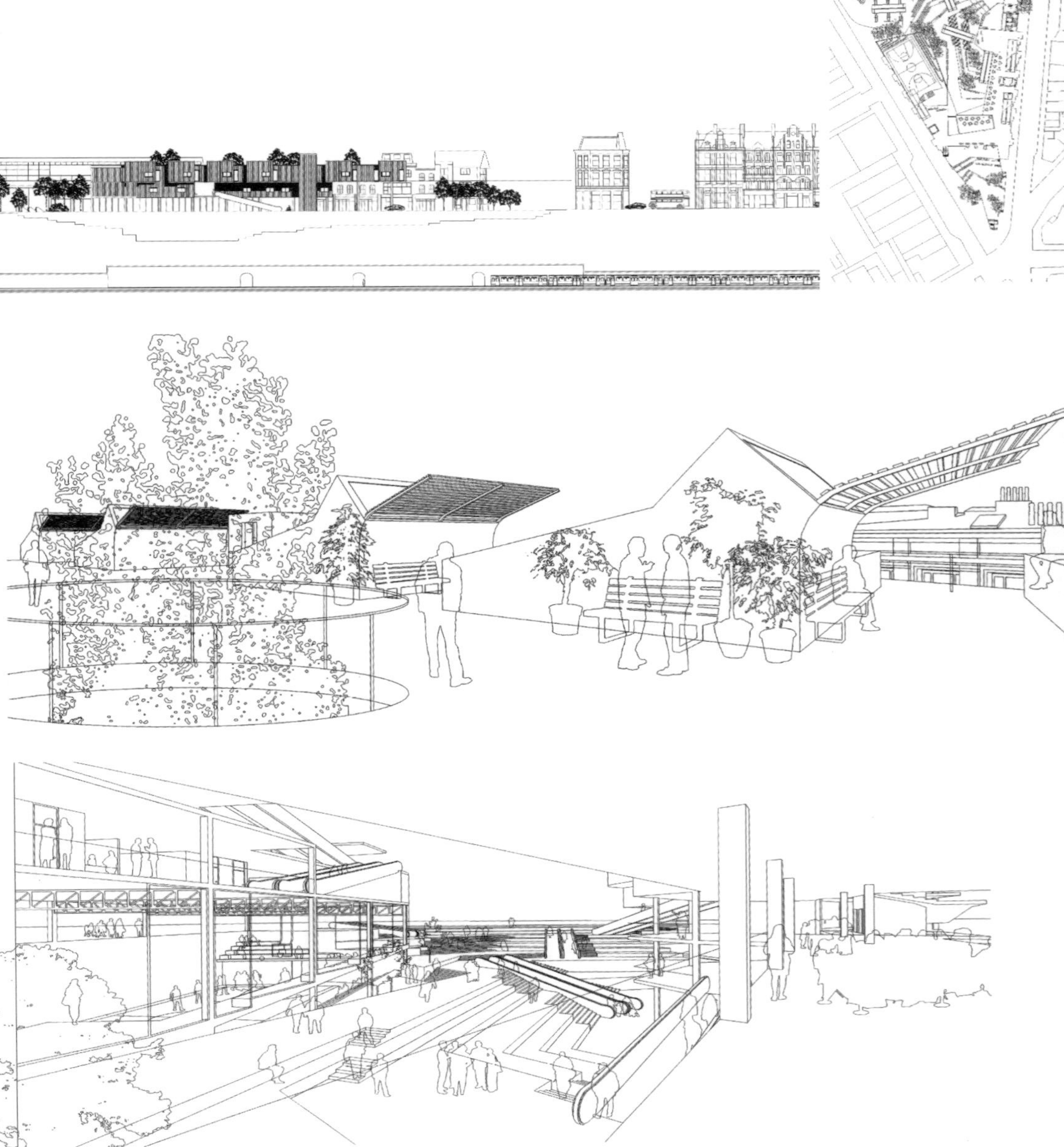

Artur Carulla
Health care for the body and mind

Unit Staff
Götz Stöckmann
Jane Wernick

Students
Artur Carulla
I-Ching Huang
Peck-San Chan
HackYub Jang
Irineos Charitou
Essicka Kimberly
Priscilla Dankwa
Sarah Jane Mackie
Chang-Yil Han
JungHun Whang
Tomonobu Hirayu
Thunyawart Worathongchai
Jason Wei Loong Ho

Special thanks to
Andy Groarke
for construction advice
Chris du Lake and
Mohsen Zikri
for technical advice,
as well as
Larry Barth
Sophie le Bourva
Robert Maxwell
David Dunster
Ciro Najle
Paul Finch
Kimberly Paumier
Thomas Fietz
Jan Kavan
Matt Salenger
Rita Lambert
Tony Lang
Sarah Wigglesworth
Helen Mallinson

Life Engineering 2: Crowds **The Performance Shed**

Transport Interchanges

Diploma 14 understands the practice of architecture as a problem of material organisation, aligned in principle with the most genuine, straight and established modern agenda. But rather than rooting its materialism in the mechanistic paradigm, it endeavours to open it up to a generative life. The unit works on the expansion of the organisational condition of architecture, to the point of curving it. Or better, to the point of recognising that its straightness is a particular and extremely aestheticised case. We assume that any material organisation participates in many scales of order, which are systemically continuous although conventionally segregated by expertise and decision-making. We also assume that this multiplicity of scales unfolds in a manifold of coexisting temporal processes. Diploma 14 produces material organisations as a stabilisation of this machinic environment. We recognise the need to construct a prearchitectonic machine that operates as if it were previous to the project, as if the project were its material sediment – the simulation of a kind of disciplinary prearchitecture, a mode of material life.

Diploma 14 understands the material itself as organisation. We see materials as nonfigurative series of relationships operating at a certain virtual level (at certain scales, across certain domains, in a certain temporal stage). The projects engage a set of systems and establish a bunch of attributes and performances in an attempt to engineer a regime of sensitivity (parameters, intensities, ranges and limits) with the capability of integrating energy exchanges and internal weaknesses into organised matter. We breed materials with potentials; we increase their robustness; we plan their ability to mutate and their capacity to codevelop with the environment without collapsing. The role of the architect is here continuous with that of the engineer, in that the two are interested in working on the performance of systems of relations. Such an artificiality requires the construction of a dynamic attitude capable of avoiding at the same time the efficiency-based model of the traditional western engineer and the ideology-based model of the traditional western architect. This attitude iteratively forces the collaboration between structural redundancy and architectural significance. Five kinds of work are unfolding:

1. The absorption of techniques from other disciplines with the capacity to handle contingency.
2. The constitution of resilient operative systems (relationships between segregated levels of organisation).
3. The construction of regimes of responsiveness (cause-effect ratios between a system and its environment).
4. The emergence of novel materials (new structural assemblages emerging out of extreme performances).
5. The integration of disparate material behaviours, isolated fields of work, diverse domains of power.

Along the lines of research of previous years, Diploma 14 has investigated the effects of nonlinearity in the extreme conditions where intense determination engenders indetermination. The paradigms of the collective research that Diploma 14 is developing have evolved from questions of rigour and relevance to questions of vigour and robustness. Treating materials and processes as collective organisations opened the possibility of engaging directly with problems of performative redundancy through abundance and excess, beyond our previous impulses towards material richness and refinement. The search for stiffness and toughness as driving forces in the process of material organisation have mutated into more complex modes of material life, where simultaneous qualities and performances coexist. A kind of ubiquity has emerged more dramatically this year from the projects: their megalomania has proliferated and been absorbed in the virtuality of the process of production. Procedure has often become a field of negotiation, open to changes in the environment but also assuming or forcing them. Although Diploma 14 continues investigating ways to engineer this process, it has begun to accelerate it to a point of immediacy where new forms of production are emerging. Based on rigour, yet beyond it, the systematisation in the projects is becoming increasingly intuitive.

This year, the unit has focused on collectives: crowds of people and matter. Proposals were developed in the format of system projects. Lineages of differential prototypes for transport interchanges were generated through the engineering of precise modes of differentiation of structural fields as they traverse collective trajectories in various economic, environmental, social and cultural contexts. The proposals investigated the possibility of constituting comprehensive operative systems through which many projects could be produced: sets of specific cause-effect relations that enrich and expand a generic potential. The development of particular cases of interchanges between transportation networks, linked to the students' professional horizons, was often taken as a sample to test the capabilities of these systems. Apart from the tutorial routine, the course involved formal and informal collaboration with engineers from AKT, a series of talks from diverse architectural and engineering practices, a two-week cooperation with First Year 2, joint juries with Diploma 4 and Diploma 12, a weekly seminar during the first term with Neil Leach, workshops with Frven Lim and Sebastian Khourian, and the Giro d'Italia lecture series given by Roberto Lombardi ('Rigidity and Tectonics: On Connection and Position', 'Structure: On Continuity and Differences of Degree', 'Joints: On Changes of Class', 'Configuration and Material: On Actions and Resistances', and 'Transposition: On Figures and Places').

Ifeanyi Oganwu POW

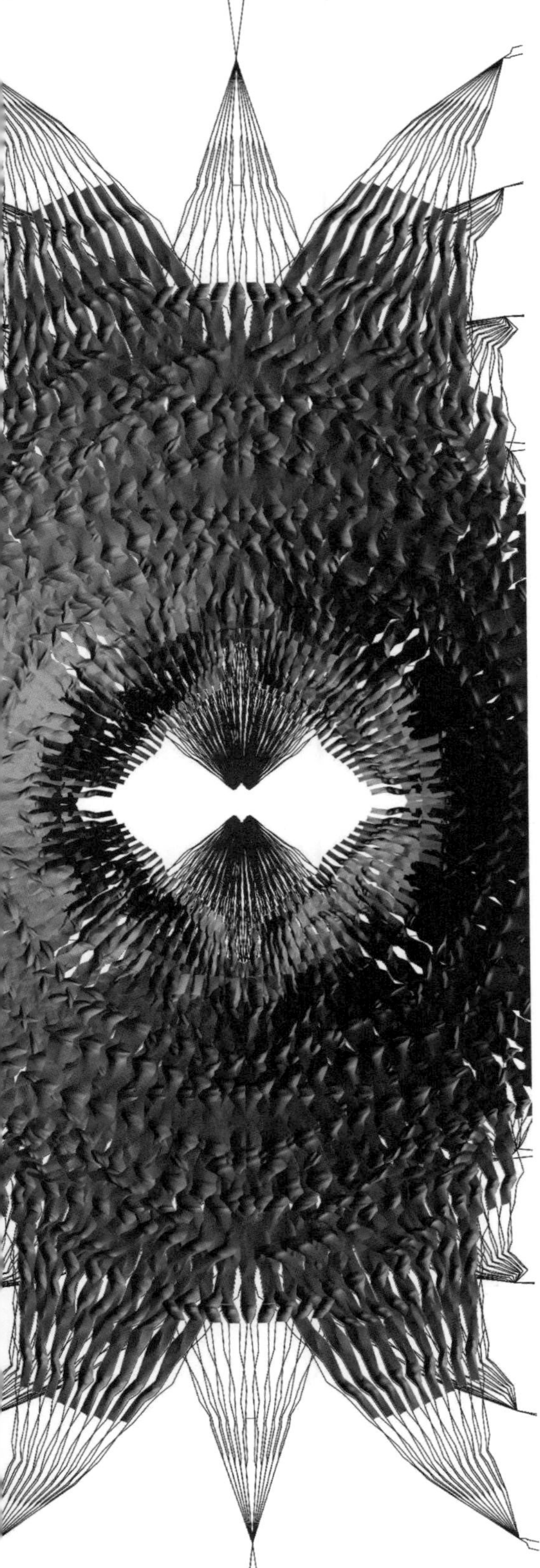

Unit Masters
Ciro Najle
Hanif Kara

Students
Christian Hutter
Lea Katseli
Raymond Lau
Chiang-Tat Lee
Kevin Lim
Ifeanyi Oganwu
Jordi Pagès Ramon
Rodrigo Rada Jaman
Eva Scheffler
Jinbok Wee

Consultants
Reuben Brambleby
Jessica Brew
Paul Earwalker
Alex Johnson
Stephan Reuter
Paul Scott

Workshop Directors
Mark Hemel
Sebastian Khourian
Nate Kolbe
Frven Lim

Visiting Critics
Leyre Asensio
Simona Bencini
Katharina Borsi
Santiago Bozzola
Bhupinder Chawla
Martine de Maeseneer
Juan Frigerio
Ines Geisler
Ludo Grooteman
Marco Guarnieri
Michael Hensel
Chris Hight
Nikolaus Hirsch
Sebastian Khourian
Marcia Krygier
Neil Leach
George Liaropoulos-Legendre
Roberto Lombardi
Friedrich Ludewig
Robin Monotti
Irénée Scalbert
Tom Verebes
Lluis Viu Rebes
Michael Weinstock

Lecture Series
Roberto Lombardi

Special thanks to the students of First Year 2, Diploma 4 and Diploma 12

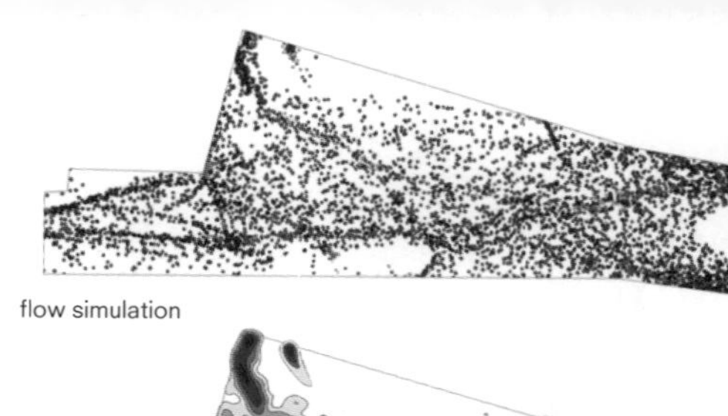

flow simulation

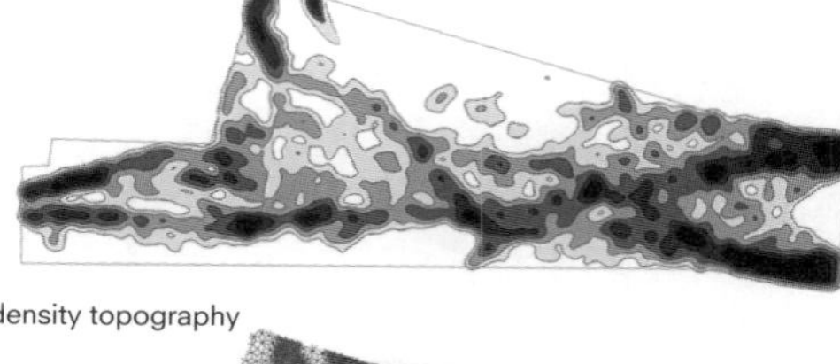

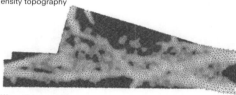

density topography

differential space frame

capacity of peak flow

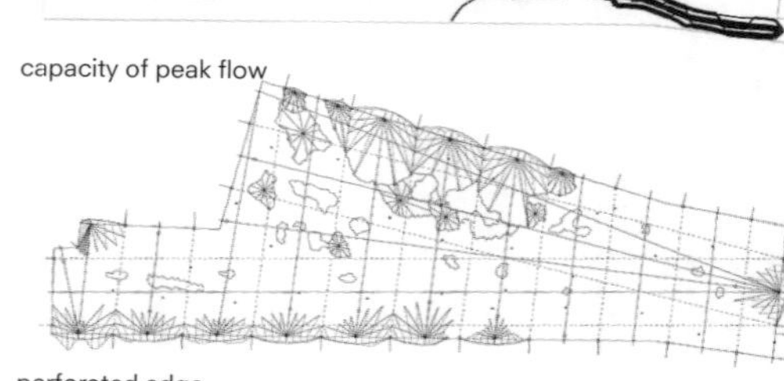

perforated edge

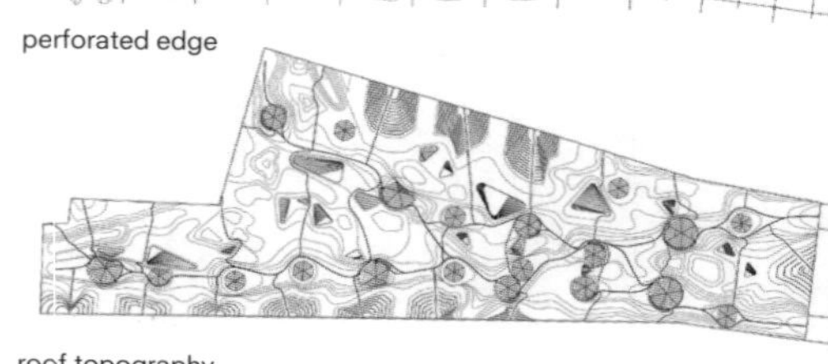

roof topography

degree of surface softness

ground plan marinas

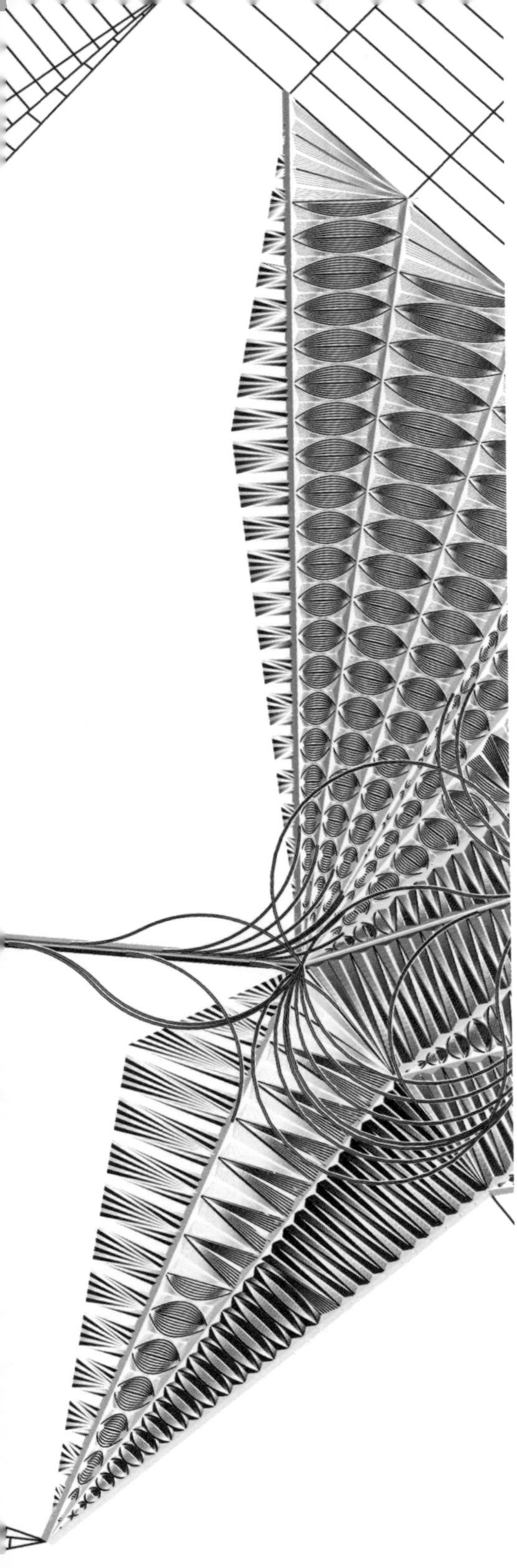

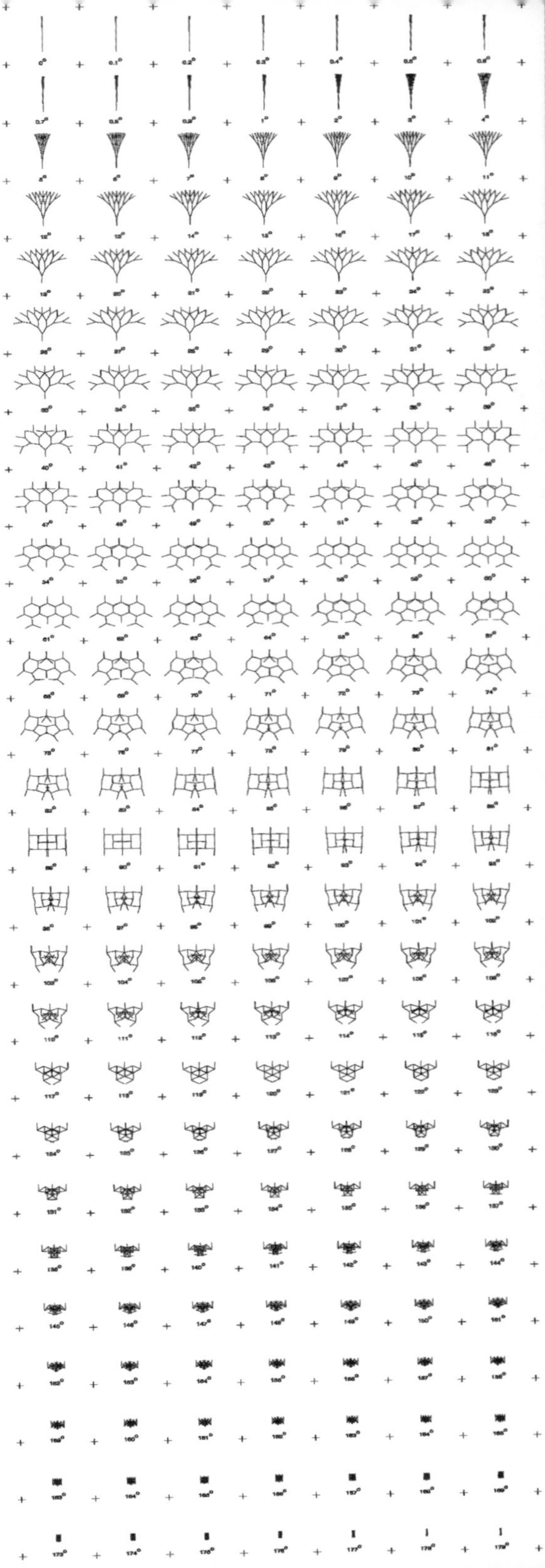

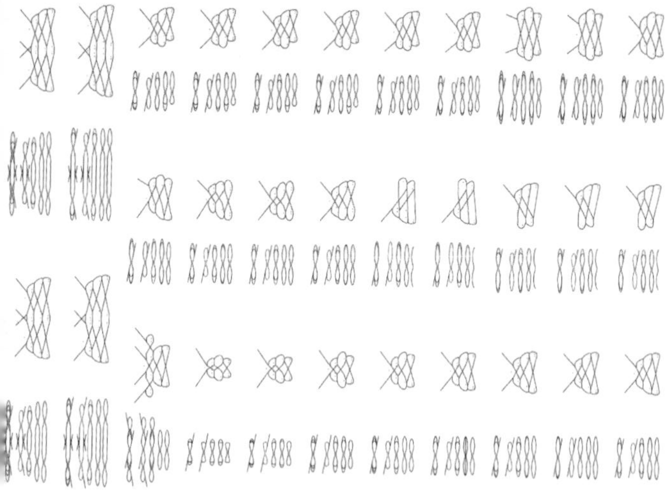

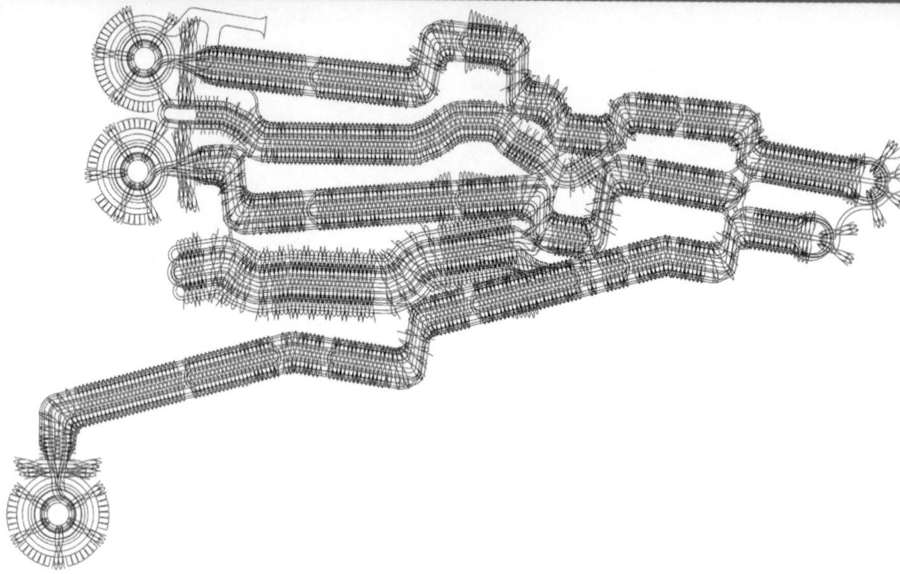

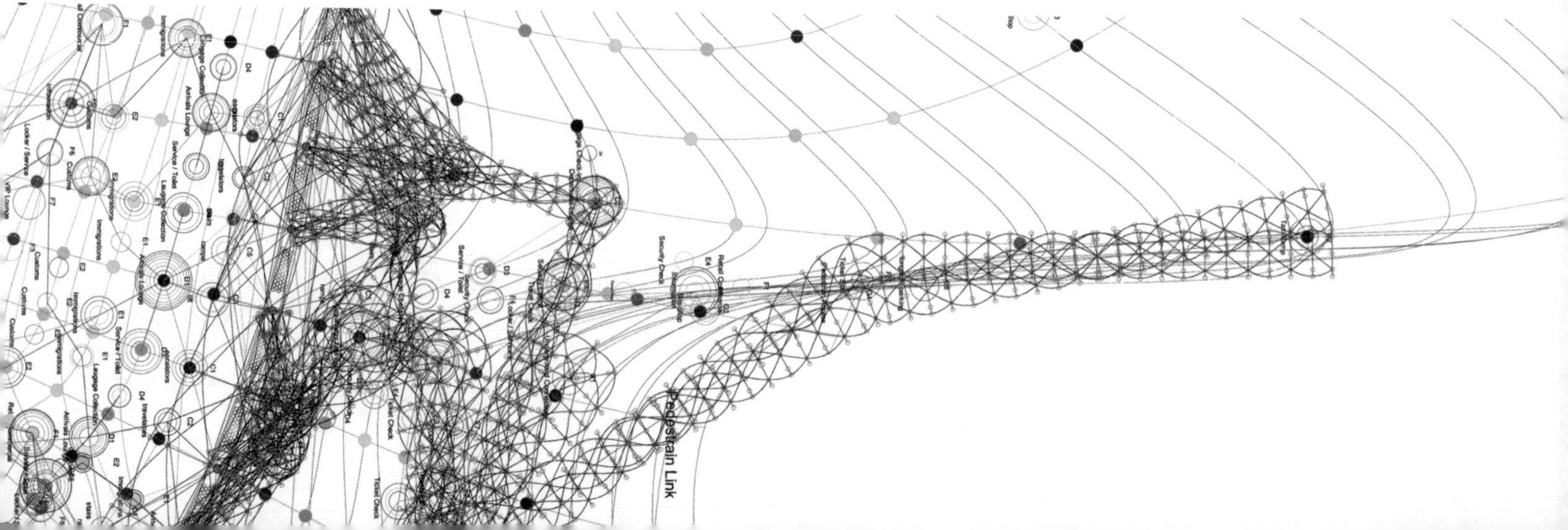
Pedestrain Link
Security Check
Ticket Check

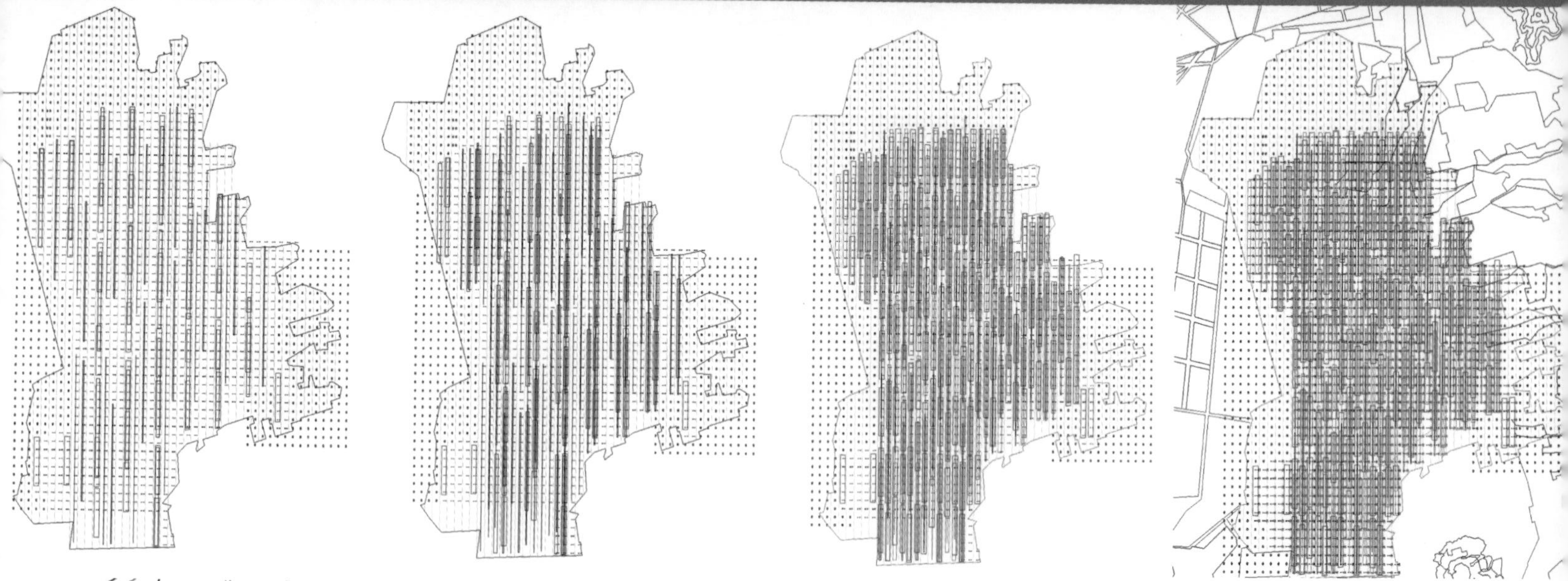

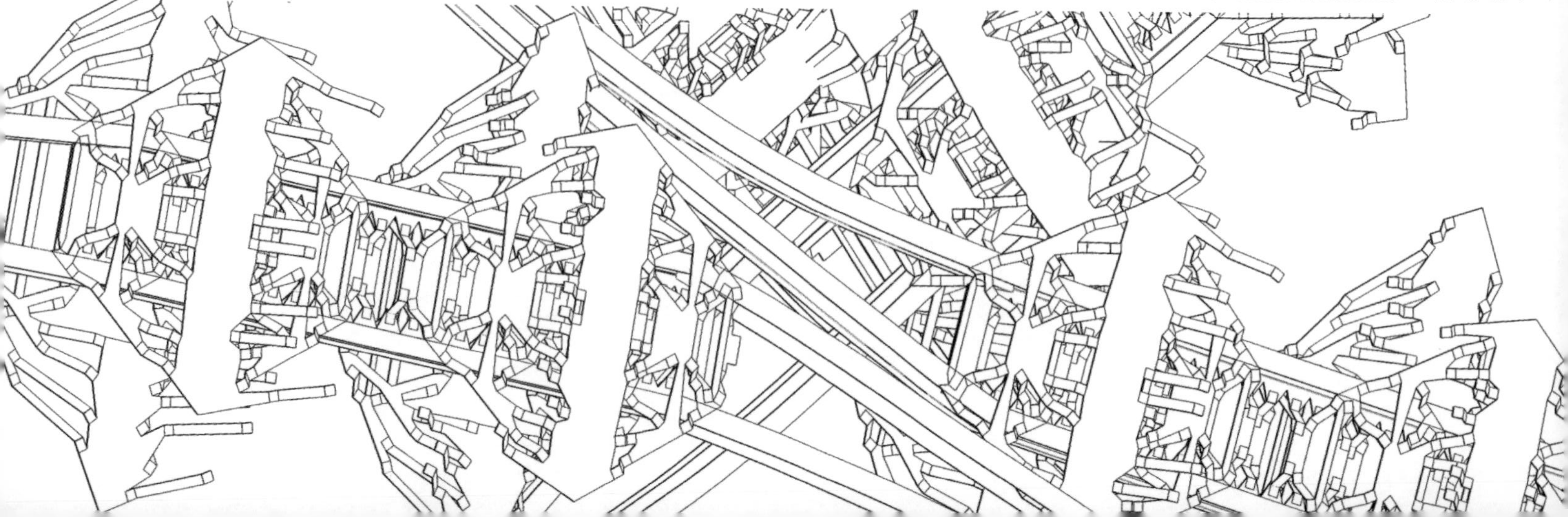

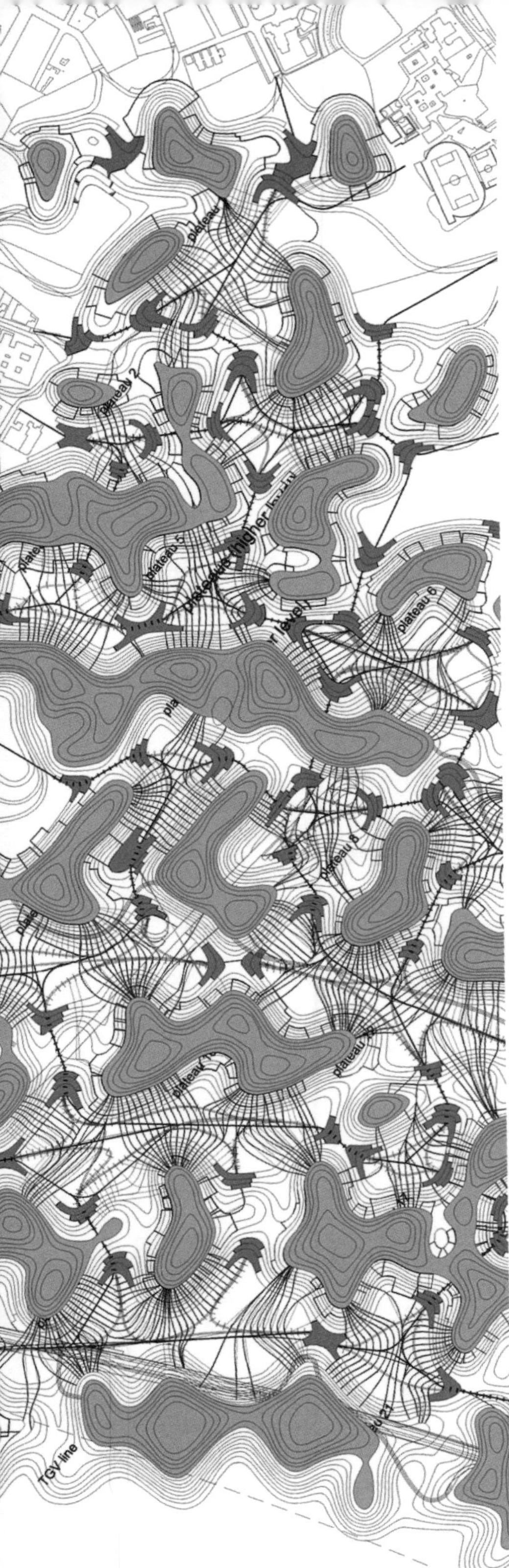

Transpiratron: The Leaking Airport **Christian Hutter**
The development of the maximum growth potential of an airport provides a field of latency for the restitution of the drained lake of Mexico City. Transpiratron elides the antagonism between natural and economic resources by satisfying both. It assumes that infrastructures, including nature, are mutually reinforcing.

POW **Ifeanyi Oganwu**
Deployed on the membrane of Lake Michigan, a surface thickens in order to float, doubles to accommodate a public arena, bundles to drive the circulation of the masses and blows up to provide public furniture.

Supernova: Biomachinic Orbits **Rodrigo Rada Jaman**
The interchange for the Stratford International Terminal is spread in a field of urban potentials as a collective of strands of double-helix structural orbits that circulate around user-based trajectories of arrival and departure.

Urban Sponge: Differential Porosities **Eva Scheffler**
A differential space frame provides for a time-based field of negotiation of circulation, shopping and noncommercial spaces. The omnipresence of shopping malls in Hong Kong is rethought as a porous terrain interwoven with informal activities.

22 Plateaus: Girona Networks **Jordi Pagès Ramon**
The insertion of the TGV into the Spanish transport network will provoke massive migrations between cities. 22 Plateaus is a system by which the city of Girona can address its impending urban transformation and mediating between the needs of community and developers.

Stressed Car Parks: Vertical Interchange **Jinbok Wee**
Deformations are a nonlinear output of stresses, and stress is used as an active force to generate deviations from conventional car-park typologies. The car park 'strains' existing programmes and 'tenses' new ones in a mix of uses at the gates of Canary Wharf, London.

Meshland: Land Reclamation by Branching **Chiang-Tat Lee**
Branching structures are used as a means of land reclamation that mediates structural and infrastructural systems and incorporates diversity of services distributed in linear fields, configuring the structural ground on top of which new skyscrapers can be built on Hong Kong Bay.

Public Ground: Elevated Infrastructural System **Kevin Lim**
Stratified circuits for bicycles, motorcycles and tuk-tuks are merged into an elevated transport system to mediate the pedestrian trajectories exiting from Bangkok's Sky Train and to regenerate the street activity of the city.

Axquaponiac: Terra Nova **Raymond Lau**
Axquaponiac uses the neutral ground of the sea to encourage collaboration of economic development between countries. Axquaponiac transforms the potentials of surplus in the mainland and the energy in the sea into a new territory of commodities.

Redundant Bottleneck: Multistation **Lea Katsely**
Efficiency of evacuation is used to generate economic inefficiency and opportunity for growth. A redundant circulation system proliferates between the various levels of transportation at King's Cross and grounds a mixed-use development.

The Workshop extends out into Ching's Yard
Photograph Sue Barr

Required Courses

The TS programme is based on the premise that Technical Studies must be sensitive to the local demands of unit agendas, but must also stand as a complete education. It is developed from detailed discussion with lecturers, all of whom are drawn from leading engineering practices and research institutions. Students are encouraged to develop a range of skills, from strategic organisation of large constructions to detailed design and fabrication.

The programme continues to evolve, founded on the provision of a knowledge base, developed through critical case studies of current material processes, constructed artefacts and buildings. Lecture courses require the undertaking of specific case studies, and include either critical reflection on these studies or experimentation with the ideas and techniques revealed. Knowledge acquired in this way generates a 'means', a set of precepts capable of negotiating the distinct technical requirements of construction in unforeseen futures and unpredictable contexts.

The technical design work of each student in First Year and Third Year is where the individual synthesis of lecture coursework, workshop experiments and the technical ambitions of the unit takes place. Students undertake design research and experiments to explore and resolve the technical issues of their main project.

In the Fifth Year students choose to submit either a Design Thesis or a Research Thesis. These are substantial individual works, conducted by the student under the guidance of Technical Studies. The chosen topic of this work is individually negotiated through personal tutorials, and reflects the student's central interests and concerns. This may have emerged from current or past design work, or from one of the many lecture/seminar courses that the student has attended during previous years, but is placed into a broader dialogue in which technical and architectural agendas are synthesised.

Master of Technical Studies
Michael Weinstock

Technical Design Tutors
First Year
Brendan Woods
Anderson Inge

Intermediate School
Javier Castanon
Duncan Macaulay

Diploma School
Michael Weinstock
Wolf Mangelsdorf

Selected works of distinction from First Year, Intermediate School and Diploma School
Eric Brett Jacobsen
Dan Narita
Eva Scheffler
Achim Menges

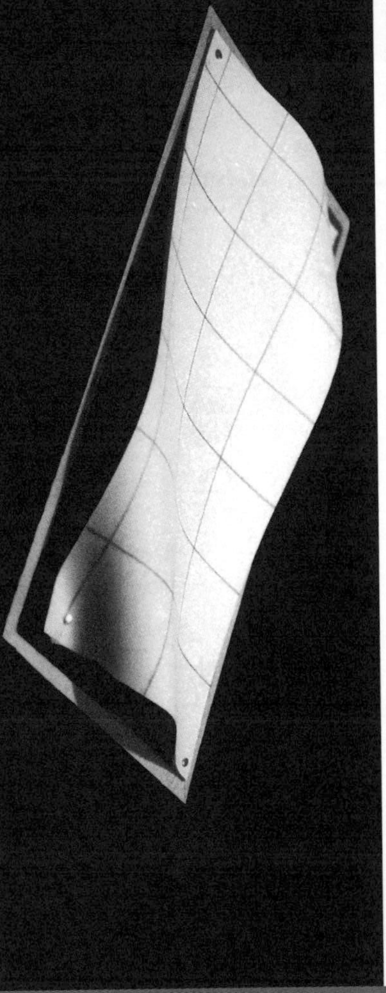

Eric Jacobsen
Surface structure: plywood composite

Dan Narita's project was about inflecting an existing corner of a room to make it inhabitable. The intersection lines of two walls were inflected to generate a step, platform and a shelf.

Techniques considered for the building components:

1. The entire volume of corner will be sectioned. Major sections will be fabricated in plywood using a CNC machine.

2. Volumes between plywood sections will be filled with foam. The foam will have to be sanded to the sections. A hard coat of plaster will have to be applied.

3. The exterior skin of the corner will be a composite of high-density fibreglass and polyester resin. The finish of the composite skin will be considered. In general a glossy resin finish is not desirable.

4. Ideally, the exterior skin should be made in one piece. However, this seems impossible to achieve. The surface will have to be fabricated in sections. A system for bolting surface sections together will have to be found. Bolts should not be exposed.

Structural stability and test loading

Considerations for test loading of one vertical section through platform:

1. Platform can be compared to the nose of a surfboard. Surfboards are built up in timber/foam sections and painted with resin; a composite action of sections and resin skin occurs.

2. For the mock-up of the plywood section it is important to test load at the board and not lateral fixtures. The plywood section should be fixed only on the floor.

Comparison of model and 1:1 structure:
Thickness of material 25mm
Density of plywood 1,5 kN/m≈
A= 0,148 m≈

$$R = \frac{W}{EL^2}$$

$$Wp = 0{,}025 \times 1{,}5 \times 0{,}148 = 0{,}00555;\ 5{,}55\ N$$

$$R = \frac{5{,}55}{9000 \times 83^2} = 8{,}9515 \times 10^{-8}$$

$$\frac{Wm}{5000 \times 0{,}005} = 8{,}9515 \times 10^{-8}$$

Results from test loading: 1:5 model, foot was badly made. Result from test loading of 1:2 model: 12 mm plywood was used therefore R was not necessary. In the model, the first split occured with 80 kg; thus it is likely the 1:1 structure might start to split with 160 kg.

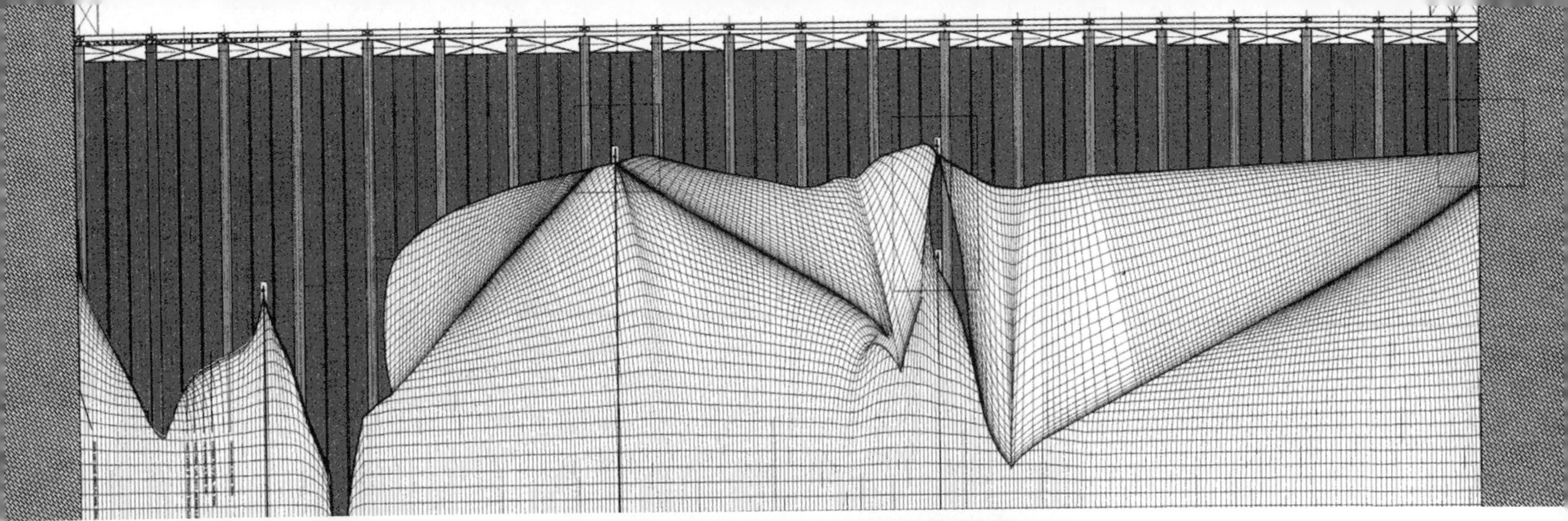

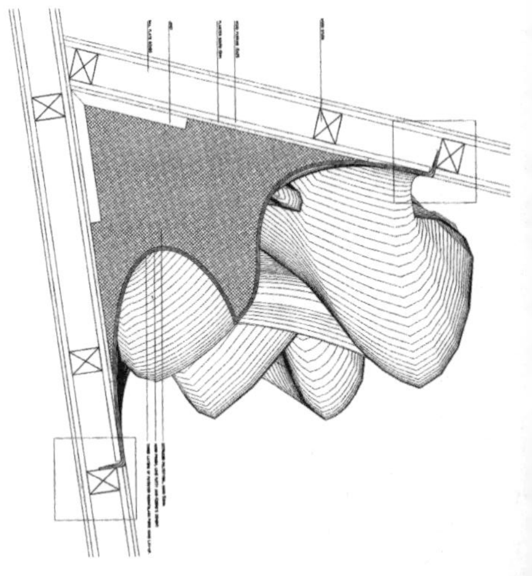

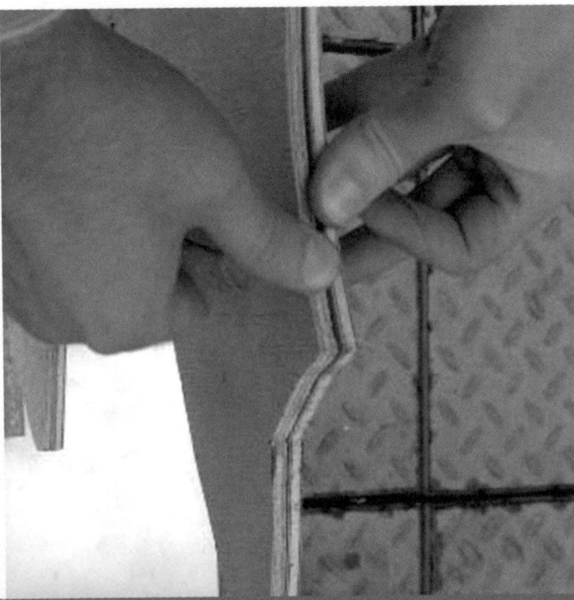

Eva Scheffler

This page, from above: opening and concentration of structure, expansion and contraction of vertical spaceframe members, differential spaceframe structure responding to density of flow
Opposite: physical test model

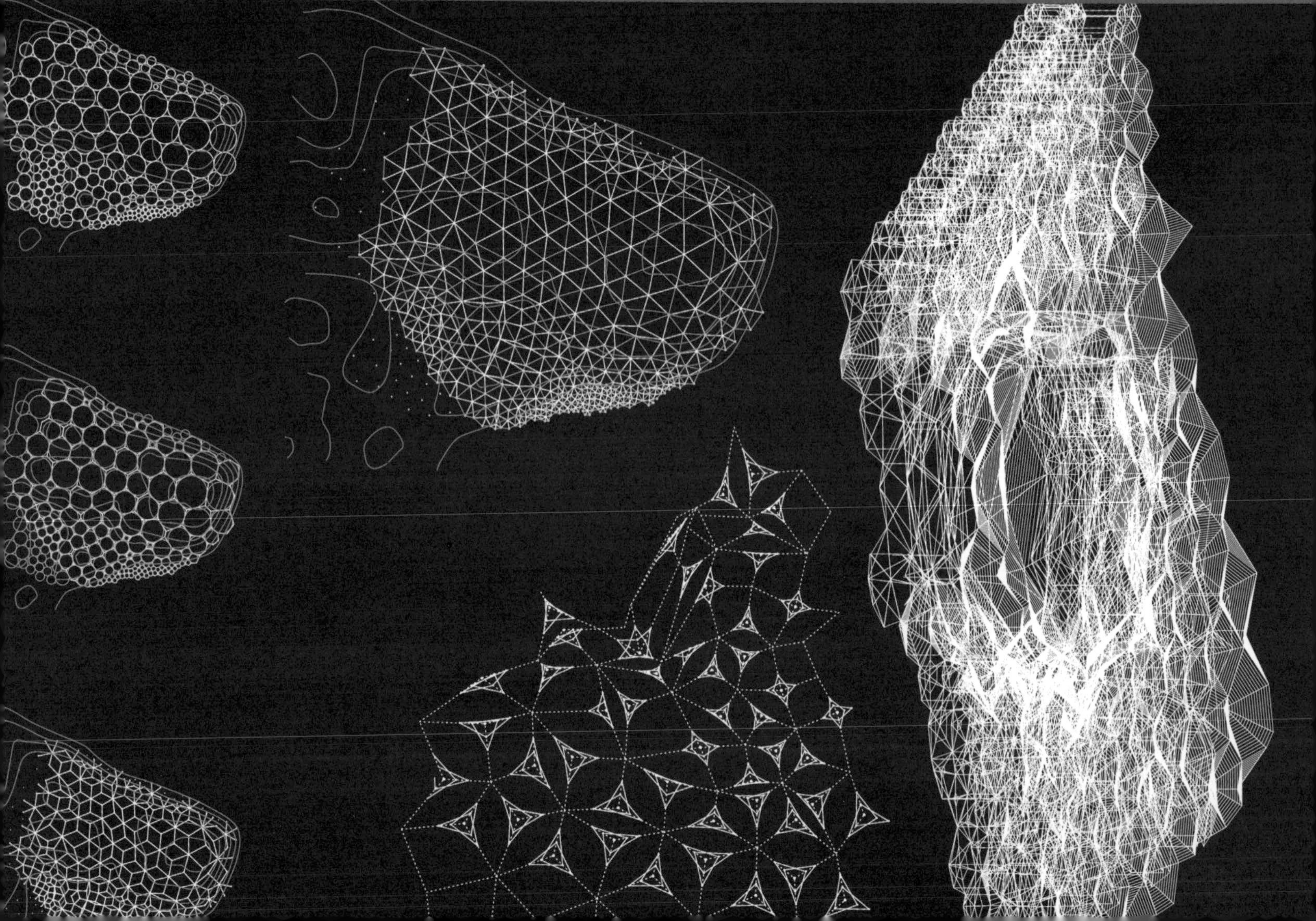

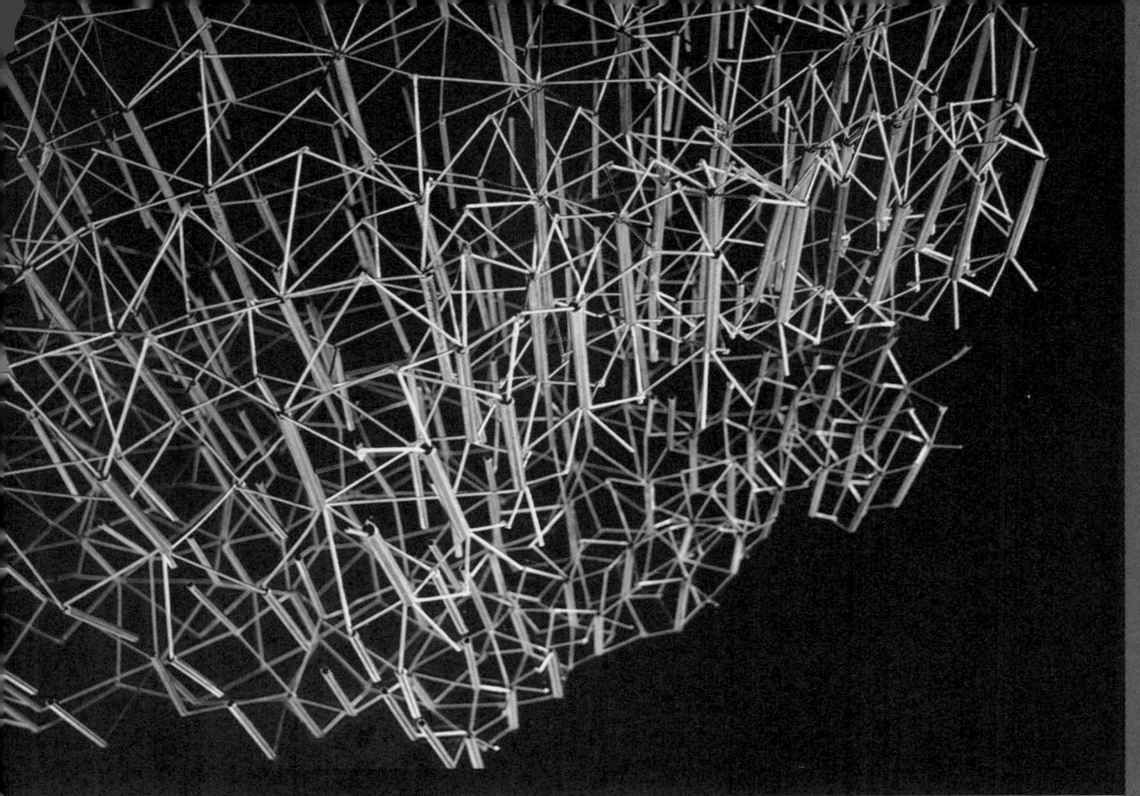

Eva Scheffler's Technical Design Thesis explores the potential of spaceframes in the context of urban-scale structures with extra-wide spans. The structure must be multi-layered, be capable of being internally occupied, support changing loads and be suitable for implementation for a land-reclamation strategy.

The investigations were organised to examine the different scales at which the structural behaviour of a spaceframe could be designed to accommodate different programmatic and ambient conditions, and provide appropriate spaces. Strategies were developed from these investigations that utilised structural differentiation, a complex variation of the scale and density of the spaceframe elements to produce a sponge-like structure.

The vertical and horizontal grouping of structural members was studied, and by relating the scale of members to the density of their deployment in any area, a three-dimensional global system was developed that has many local variations. These variations allow spatial definition, including large enclosed and semi-enclosed urban spaces.

The material surfaces of these spaces have a number of different inclinations, so that different walking-speeds can be organised. Surfaces are further developed to provide furniture and extended to make connecting surfaces between levels.

Where the programme requirements permit a very low level of loading, large openings penetrate to sea level. These openings are designed to bring light deep into interior spaces, and to manipulate passive environmental engineering effects.

Achim Menges

This page: physical models of surface component

Opposite: proliferation of surface component

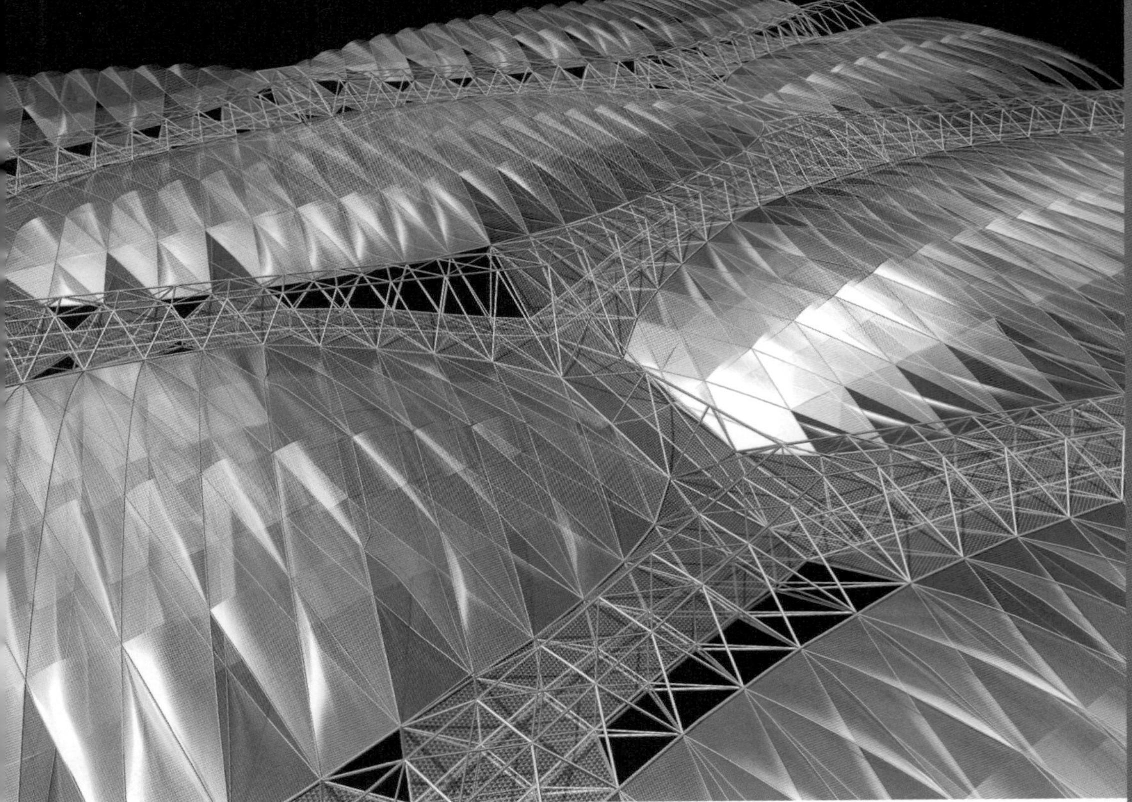

Achim Menges's Technical Design Thesis explores the potential of pneumatic structures in the context of a complex, multi-layered, and very wide-span structure of an agricultural scale. The structure must satisfy highly differentiated light and climatic conditions, as well as changeable loads. By exploiting the non-linear characteristics and states of stability of pneumatic structural systems, Achim has developed a pneumatic component that can be proliferated into a complex structural system.

The design research was conducted on three interrelated scales:

1. The evolution of the component

Starting with a simple inflated cushion and exploiting the basic structural principle of the relations between the applied loads, the pressure of the compressed air volume and the consequent geometry and pre-stressing of the membranes, the component was evolved. The working methodology was based on feedback between different modalities – a digital definition of the boundary points and the related cut patterns produced in engineering software, physical modelling, digital form-finding and digital structural analysis.

2. The prototype component

Multiplying the evolved 'single cushion' component allowed Achim to articulate the prototype of a multi-chamber surface component. In response to the dynamic relation between structural stability, surface geometry and internal air pressure the boundary definition points were animated. This provided the input for differential digital form-finding process that enabled the production of a physical model. The model has a number of forms and pressure states in which it is stable.

3. The proliferation of the component

The developed surface component was proliferated into a complex and differentiated structural system by the deployment of structural parameters such as the internal pressure, the depth of the 'pneus', and the reinforcement of the seams to provide extra stress reaction material. Each parameter has variations, and this allows the development of a number of local geometries within a global system, made necessary by the requirements of a complex programmatic system, changing load-bearing capacities and evolving light and climatic conditions.

The Workshop provides students with the opportunity to deal, at first hand, with a broad range of materials and techniques. The work produced, often in tandem with the model workshop, varies in scale and type – from small site models to large conceptual pieces.

The Workshop provides a unique setting in which design and its application can be combined. Students are encouraged to explore the properties and application of materials in order to increase their capacity for lateral thinking and problem-solving.

During the past year the Workshop has engaged with twenty-first-century technology, following the introduction of a CNC routing machine that enables professional up-to-date production techniques to be married to traditional craft skills. A link has been created between the Computer Room and the Workshop, which has given a new dimension to the process of model-making.

The Workshop epitomises the philosophy that order is achieved through chaos. Often hectic but always creative, the Workshop has a unique atmosphere and is an essential resource within the AA.

Staff

Manager
Marcellus Letang

Assistant Manager
Trystrem Smith

Technician
Anthony Beckett

Object Fabrication (Model Workshop)
Chris Pauling

Workshop Tutors
Shin Egashira
Valentin Bontjes van Beek

Student Assistants
Alex Chambers
Panayiotis Hadjichristofi

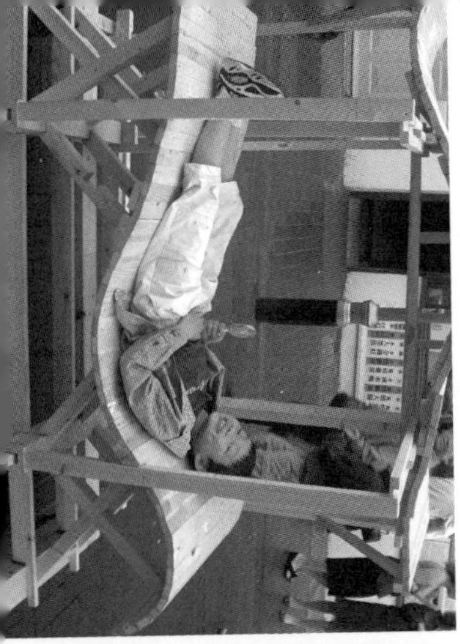

Workshop

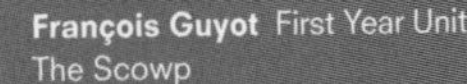

François Guyot First Year Unit 4
The Scowp

Farah Ghanim First Year Unit 2
Andrea Marini First Year Unit 1

CNC

Nimish Biloria Emergent Technologies
Ting Na Chen Diploma Unit 2

CNC

Igor Gottschalk Diploma Unit 6
Sherri Harvey Diploma Unit 8

Model Workshop

Yoko Murakami Diploma Unit 11

Model Workshop

Hoi Leung Intermediate Unit 4
Marie Langen Intermediate Unit 5

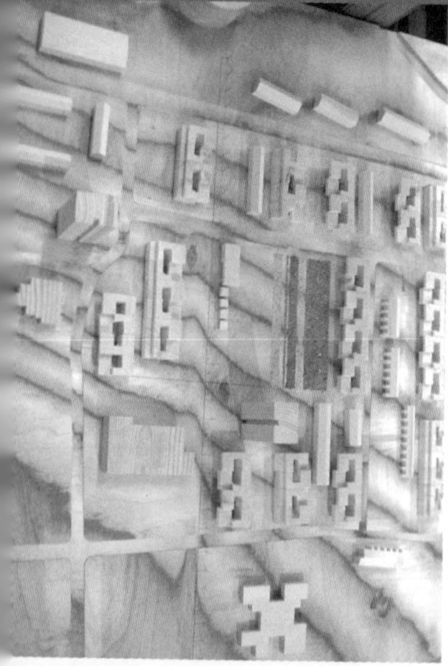

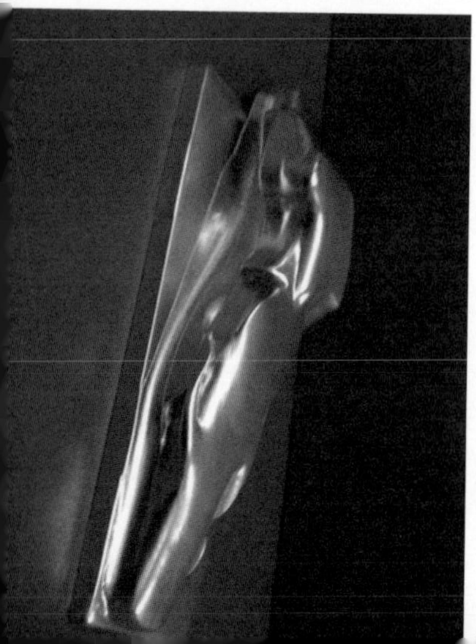

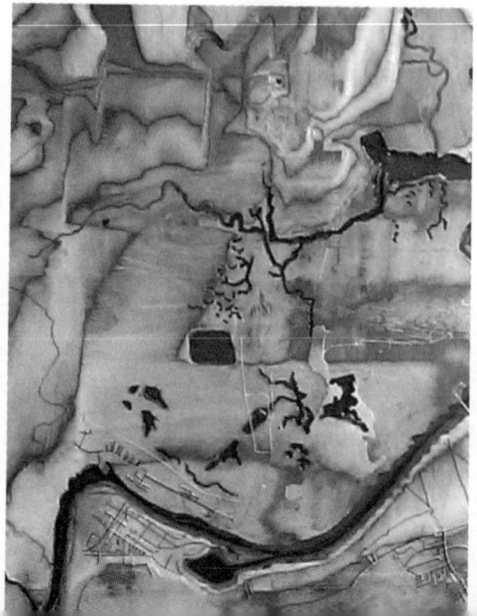

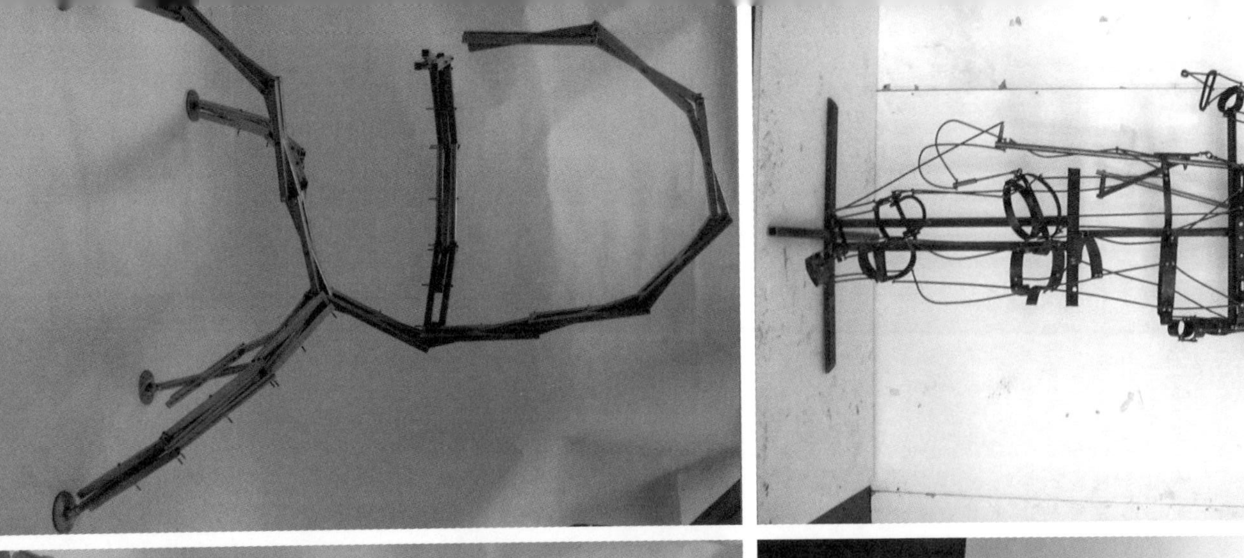

Workshop
Dan Marks First Year Unit 2

Workshop
Takashi Nishibori Diploma Unit 11

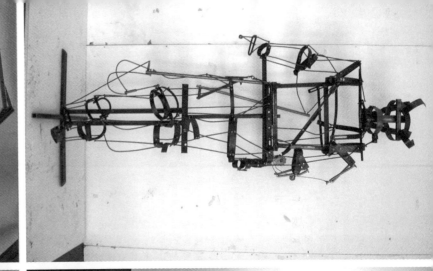

General Studies seeks to help students engage with the field of architectural debate and criticism. The first three years explain the framework within which this debate has developed, and provide tools with which to question its terms and values. The Diploma School courses broaden the scope of the debate and explore its relationships to other disciplines. They also allow for a detailed study of specific topics. We reflect below on the courses which took place this year, but no reflection would be complete without an acknowledgement of the extraordinary efficiency and good humour of the General Studies coordinator, Belinda Flaherty, who knows more about the programme than any of us.

First Year Term 1: Architects on Architecture

Irénée Scalbert, Timothy Brittain-Catlin

Buildings are not neatly aligned in the minds of architects, as they might be in a book of history. Architects know buildings by a name, one or two photographs, perhaps a visit, or drawings and publications. These buildings constitute a rather shapeless collection: like a small and sparsely constructed town -- a town hall here, a museum there, two or three beautiful houses, a handful of monuments – by and large it is empty. We think of this collection not as the environment in which we live, but as 'Architecture', as a stock that defines its tradition. For architecture, history begins with historians who put buildings on the map by writing about them, but this remains a dead letter until architects notice and discuss specific works, until they imitate and transform them. In this introductory course, architects, including Florian Beigel, Neave Brown, Richard Burton, Nicholas Boyarsky and Nikolaus Hirsch, were invited to talk about the work of another architect, in order to demonstrate how history works.

Term 2: Modernism

Irénée Scalbert, Diana Periton, Helen Thomas

Students are often assumed to have a familiarity with seminal buildings and moments of the Modern Movement that they do not necessarily possess. This course charted the progress of Modernism from its eccentric beginnings in the bohemian avant-garde, to its constitution in the International Congress for Modern Architecture (CIAM), to its near hegemonic power. Further lectures described how its programme became undermined in the 1950s -- as much by changing ideas in architecture as by the very affluence to which Modernism itself had contributed. Over the last 40 years, histories of modern architecture have emphasised specific buildings and their artistic qualities. We set this against the collective, politicised and practical attitudes that characterised Modernism, and through which it attempted to make lives more equal, more comfortable and sometimes more free.

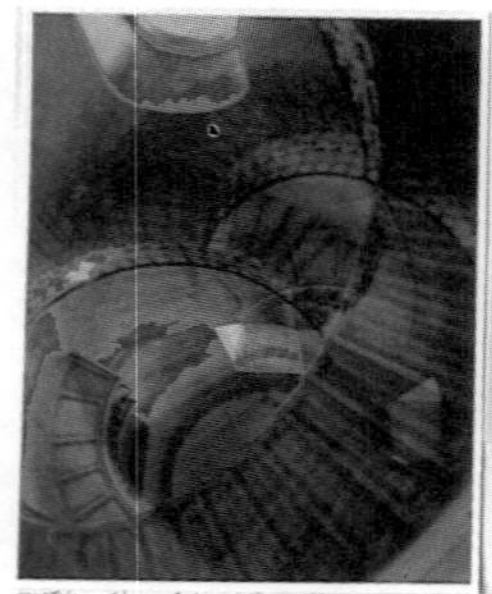

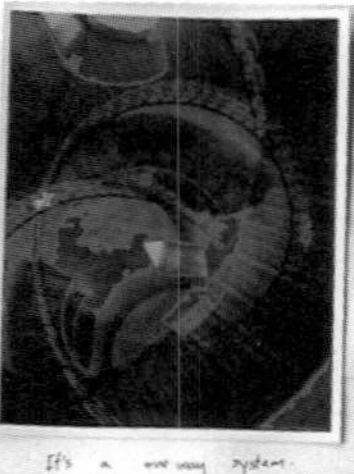

(photos: st. paul's bell tower's stair case)

Second Year Term 1: Architectural Themes of Modernity

Diana Periton, Vittoria Di Palma

The second year courses seek to introduce students to the ideas, ideals, values and assumptions that lie behind the ways we think about and judge architecture. The topics discussed throughout Term 1 (scale, fragment, ornament, type, artifice and surface) were intended to explore the contingencies and conditioning of our modes of experience and description, and to question the ways in which they are conceptualised and manipulated in architectural practice. The course began with a simple exercise: we visited well-known buildings (St Paul's Cathedral, Syon House, St Pancras Hotel, Tate Modern) and students described their experiences in a short text illustrated with one image. The responses were rich and varied: some wrote personal accounts, others produced more distant, seemingly objective observations; some focused on details, others constructed more general pictures. A debate at the end of term raised broad questions concerning the practices of theorising and making, seeking to encourage a dialogue between General Studies and the design work of the Intermediate School units.

Term 2: Media and Meanings

Vittoria Di Palma, Renée Tobe

In the second term, two options were offered: 'Media and Meanings' and 'Construction'. The principal goal of 'Media and Meanings' was to provide a theoretical and historical grounding in issues – perspective, shadow, framing, etc. -- central to a number of representational practices including photography, film and computer modelling. In addition to attending lectures on these topics, students presented samples of their own work that engaged with or used one of the selected themes. With its focus on viewing and framing, this course particularly attracted students from Intermediate Units 1, 3 and 10.

Construction

Mari Hvattum with David Dernie

Many of the Intermediate School units at the AA emphasise the process of making. Yet throughout history, architects have understood this process in very different ways, from the interpretation of divine revelation, to efficient problem solving. Are we to rely on 'rational' and objective analysis, on intuitive sparks of inspiration, or on something else altogether? This was the principal question that lay behind a series of examinations of the meaning and materiality of architectural making, from the importance of prehistoric creation myths to the role of the computer in the distribution of materials. The term concluded with a combined session, which included a visit to London's only surviving surgical amphitheatre near London Bridge. Confronted with images of dissection, students from both Second Year options discussed the interrelationships between making and representing.

Third Year Term 1: Modernism versus Modernity

Mark Cousins with Benedict O'Looney and Ines Geisler

Students were presented with two options, each focusing on the city. This course concentrated on the rise of the nineteenth-century city and the practices and discourses which attempted to regulate it. One of our approaches was to read the transformation of medicine at the end of the eighteenth century in relation to urban planning strategies. We argued that the idea of an 'organism', derived from a reformed conceptual understanding of medicine, together with that of 'public health', had changed the understanding of the city. 'Function', a key term in both medicine and urban planning, had introduced criteria that allowed a territory to be mapped by isolating and excluding that which could be considered non-functioning, disturbing or deviating. Records of symptoms and diagnostics of disease became integral to the administration and infrastructure of the city. Lectures were accompanied by visits to typical nineteenth-century institutions, such as a board school and a pumping station, as a means of illustrating the way divisions of function are related to everyday conduct and find their reflection in the architectural organisation of the city.

Twentieth-Century Cities: Imagined Communities

Helen Thomas, Ellis Woodman

Imagination and vicarious experience are essential to anyone expecting to write convincingly about a city. This year we have sought methods by which to visualise and animate the realities, both contemporary and historical, of cities as diverse as Vienna and Brasilia. Articulations of time have been especially important. First, with Dalibor Vesely, we looked at how discontinuities in form and meaning arise from the slow accrual of dense urban fabric. We went on to look at how history was used as a means of validation in the construction of postcolonial modern cities, aided by Valerie Fraser's insights into Brasilia. Then we examined how this was challenged in Utopian alternatives to establishment polemics, such as the Grupo Valparaiso's journeys across the Atacama Desert and the deflowering of El Pedregal in Mexico City. Finally, we looked at the usefulness of ruins, visiting several sites in East London that exploit ex-industrial glamour to great effect.

Term 2: Theory

Marina Lathouri, Diana Periton

This 'Theory' option proposes that architectural theory is a mode of practice, an integral part of making which cannot be treated as an independent discipline. Not all of the students readily agree and our weekly discussions constantly questioned the role of theory in suggesting methods, providing explanations or elucidations, or connecting different fields of activity. A brief survey of architectural theory of the last 100 years led to an exploration of its involvement with criticism and history (past and future), and to an examination of changing attitudes towards the evaluation of products and the importance of processes. In the essays written as part of the course, many of the students explored works (whether built, written, painted or filmed) which allowed them to interrogate their own assumptions about the relationship between thinking, making and the made. In the end-of-term debate, held jointly with the second elective option, 'The Real World' (described below), theory and practice became increasingly indistinguishable.

The Real World

Irénée Scalbert, Tim Brittain-Catlin

Great practitioners like Norman Foster attach little importance to theory. Conversely, the theories proposed by people such as Peter Eisenman are increasingly impractical. But this situation is changing. FOA, for example, speak like Eisenman but act like Foster. They are awed in equal measure by Deleuze and by the thrill of large building sites. Pragmatism has become desirable and architects today seem interested in practical theories, in practical ideas that deliver.

For several decades, more value has been attached to Le Corbusier's unbuilt Plan Voisin for Paris than to his plan (largely realised) for the city of Chandigarh. A lot has been said and written about Mies's Barcelona Pavilion, but little has recently been heard about the Seagram building, even though this last project was imitated throughout the world. Such priorities make sense if one expects buildings to play a significant role in culture. Arguably this expressive burden placed upon architecture can be better satisfied elsewhere. Buildings could then get on with performing the job assigned to them in the real world. And so could architects, whose attitudes towards land, people, money and construction form the subject of this course.

Stefano Rabolli Pansera's essay, written as part of the Second Year course, 'Architectural Themes of Modernity', grew from a description of Juan Muñoz's 'Double Bind' at Tate Modern. It discusses Muñoz's dissolution of perspective into a 'contemporary sublime'. Extracts from the essay appear below:

Muñoz and the Paradoxical Representation of Postmodernity

… the thesis that I will explore is that there is no non-problematic use of perspective. In his work, Juan Muñoz takes this traditional tool of representation to its most extreme possibilities in order to reveal the crises, the contradictions, that use of perspective faces when required to express 'our' world …

'Double Bind' occupies the east end of the Turbine Hall and is structured in three levels – the viewer is forced to move physically around the installation to gain the full experience of it. The upper level is the most 'pictorial' … the viewer is constrained by a handrail in front of it. He looks out across a horizontal grey surface, its expanse the same grey as the concrete walls of the Turbine Hall which suggests that the walls do not terminate it, but just frame or intersect it. There are holes that break the expanse, or perhaps they are trompe l'oeil holes, which imply a homogeneous and infinite space in three dimensions … The two lifts, which arrive from the lower ground level, are empty: they are transformed into pictorial presences because they lose their physical weight. They don't alter the space, but just pass through the surface … Commentators have suggested that this work was influenced by Tiepolo's ceilings, but here, the illusion is concentrated on the floor … Unlike the frescos of the late Baroque, there is no attempt to … create a spectacular image of the transcendent miracle, just a 'manifesto' of the infinite space suggested by perspective.

The intermediate level is the proper focus of the representation, but it is the only level where the viewer cannot place himself. It is a heterogeneous space: there is no continuity, no homogeneity, between the sculpted scenes which it contains … An abyss of darkness separates all these moments of 'life-like' representation. All the elements displayed at this level speak of 'human-ness' – the fragments of buildings, the mannequins, the actions and movements of these figures. But ... life situations are presented through allusion, and 'life' is absent. From this representation, the viewer is able to grasp a new image of society: the postmodern world and the reduction of everything to images. This simulation is the loss of dialectic categories, the destruction of boundaries. There is no original and copy, no reality and image,

but instead, something that is in between and which mixes the identity and transparency of our intellectual divisions …

The definite crisis of the perspective system is at the lower ground level … Muñoz uses light and shadow, an 'extra' for theorists of perspective, to express the feeling of a contemporary sublime …

In the gloom, light creates vertical columns that mirror and define the illusionary scenes of daily life above. As the viewer walks around the space, he is influenced by the asymmetric disposition of the light …

The space is characterised by discontinuity ... in contrast to the upper level, with its perspective order, where the viewer has a panoptic vision. Here one is able to pass through heterogeneous pools of possibility; at the upper level, one is part of a neutral, quantifiable emptiness. The contemporary sublime is not the epiphany of transcendence, there is no miracle, but, in the metamorphosis of simulation, the viewer enters the realm of the visionary. The experience of the sublime is not an apotheosis, but a melting of mental categories. Order lies on the edge of chaos and darkness highlights our human fragility and the way in which our lives are suspended between these incommensurate entities …

In the Diploma School, students are offered a large selection of courses from which they may either choose three, or take one while pursuing their own research towards the preparation of a thesis. Most students who elect to take the second path elect to write on a topic which is close to issues raised in their design work in order to develop their ideas and to present them in a more public discourse.

Courses on offer this year covered topics ranging from the architectural model and perspective, to ecology, fashion and architecture, and the space of military action.

Alessandra Como
Traces of Landscape: Roman Sites and Sixteenth-Century Italian Villas and Gardens
Mark Cousins
Aesthetics in Art, Architecture and Landscape
Paul Davies
Tourism, Place, the Media and You
Susannah Hagan
The 'Sustainable City'
Sophie Hampshire
To Hear and Back Again
Brian Hatton
Studying Sterling/Reading Rohe
Andrew Higgott
Books and Building: British Architectural Culture in the Twentieth Century
Paul Hirst
The Spatialisation of Military Power
Lorens Holm
Architecture + Perspective
Neil Leach
Surface Culture
Sandra Morris
Water-Landscape
Benedict O'Looney
Workspace: The Way We Work in Cities
Doina Petrescu
Informe
Teresa Stoppani
Manhattan and Venice: Paradigm Islands of Anti-Modern Space
David Ward
Space, Place and the Role of the Viewer
Elizabeth Wilson
Dressing

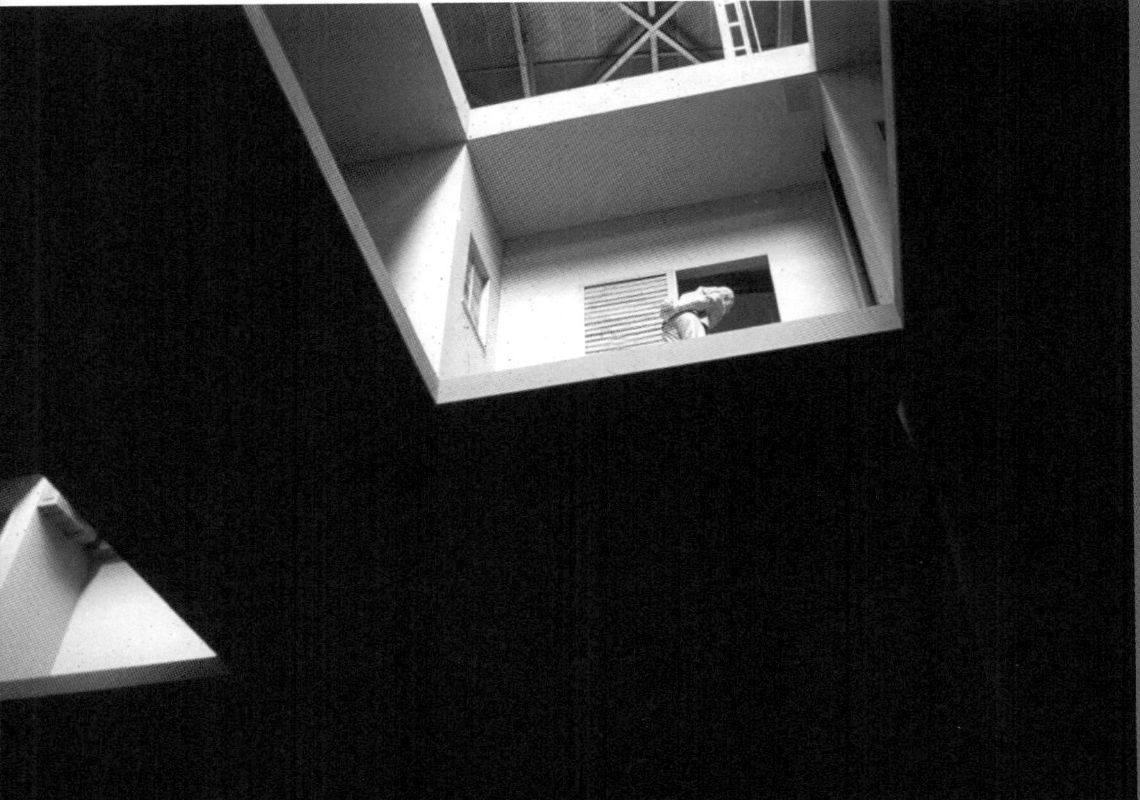

Communications is an instrument of negotiation. It is based on skill and methods of articulation, and is fundamentally political.

A focused operativity defining the progression of ideas requires a variety of well-developed skills. Besides the obvious technical methods of constructing thought and argument, the skill to develop and materialise ideas and the ability to engage with a larger audience are key requirements for the successful development of an architectural proposition and the communication of its intent.

These skills are taught through a variety of studios. Communications is at no point treated as solely a technical matter. Its courses are all aimed at providing participants with instruments for the design of architecture.

Recent developments in the Communications programme have placed increased emphasis on experiential values, on the use of colour and choice of materials, and on cooperative teaching structures. Tutors from different subjects have collaborated in a series of new courses, resulting in unexpected combinations like scenario staging (Figure & Site in partnership with Colour Photography) and dynamic structures (Digital Film with Object Fabrication). Others focused on sound and space, exploring the world of sound in relation to architectural programme and spatial scenarios, analysing, translating and articulating environmental transmissions and sounds of specific actions into space-defining tools. Another new course, Site Specific, provided the opportunity for a reflective critical discourse exploring the relationship of site to idea and proposal, thus extending the depth of theoretical discourse within the programme.

The third term was engaged in communicating the year's body of work to the School community. A three-stage exhibition, curated by Joanna Maggs, was held over a period of six weeks and showed the works produced by the 18 Communications courses. Installed in the main stairwell and at various other locations around the School, the exhibition provided a valuable reflection on Communications' intense and vivid culture of production.

Courses
Object Fabrication
Sonics
Figure & Site
Virtual Space
Drawing I
Drawing II
3D Drawing
Video
Print Installation
Photography
Interactive Multimedia
Intermedia
Digital Film
Digital Film & Object Fabrication
Colour Photography
Figure and Site & Colour Photography
Site Specific & Digital Print
Drawing Collaboration

Course Master
Jean Michel Crettaz

Coordinator
Joanna Maggs

Course Tutors
Sue Barr
Enrico Benco
Simon English
Pete Gomes
Denise Hawrysio
Mark Hemel
Katrin Lahusen
Antoni Malinowski
Peter Moore
Joel Newman
Chris Pauling
Goswin Schwendinger
David Ward

Object Fabrication **Term 1**
Katrin Lahusen & Chris Pauling
Students: Eldon Tam, Panayiotis Hadjichristofi, Henry Ki Cheong Leung, Ioanna Ioannidis, Phoivos Skroumbelos

Object + Place – Materiality
We made a series of quick, inventive small-scale fabrications and experiments, testing the specific structural and spatial qualities of cheap, everyday materials, defining the rules for transformative processes in relation to a specific spatial situation. We tried to work with a minimum of tools and equipment and concentrate on one or two chosen materials.

Sonics **Terms 1 & 2**
David Ward
Students, Term 1: Kun-Wook Kang, Max von Werz, Nazaneen Shafaie, Nausica Gabrielides, Emu Masuyama, Robert Gluckman, Maria Martin, Federico Ferrari, Peter L. Knutson, Sandra Piesik, Muge Belek
Term 2: Eir Saemundsdottir, Sibylle Lienert, Chris Dukes

Sonic – Speed of Sound from Latin *Sonus*: 'Sound'
The course introduced a wide range of sound experience through context-setting seminar sessions. Students worked on the development and production of their own sound projects, supported by tutorials and technical advice. Course sessions included an introduction to the mythological, historical and modern backgrounds of sound and radio, including recorded and cinematic sound; an exploration of the voice, ambient sound and spatial and acoustic experience using recorded and available sound; and an investigation of a range of artists involved with sound, from the music of John Cage and Glenn Gould to the contemporary sound works of Tacita Dean and Janet Cardiff. Students were introduced to a range of sound media, including digital recording and computer editing, analogue recording and live sound production.

Figure & Site **Term 1**
Simon English
Students: Daniel Coll I Capdevila, Smita Khanna, Hideki Oka, Pavlos Sideris

'The Dot's Day Off'
The Soft Room was converted into an incident room from which to track the Sunday afternoon leisure pursuits of a couple who never existed. Who, what, when, where and why were just some of the questions raised by the students, who worked both individually and in groups. We set up an inquiry team to investigate and retrieve the accoutrements of the couple's private life and give them a new context in art and architecture. The brief was to design and make a large drawing based on the recreational apparatus they may either wear, operate or perform within or on. The final drawing was exhibited alongside a dossier profiling the couple and a set of operational guidelines relating to the performative use of the object-structure. We worked with a range of media, drawing alongside model boxes, prototype object simulations, location shots, models-performers, text and video to help actualise the drawing process. While in the past Figure & Site introduced drawing as a means by which to instigate performance within the context of the body or architecture, in this project it proposed to use performance as a means of instigating drawing.

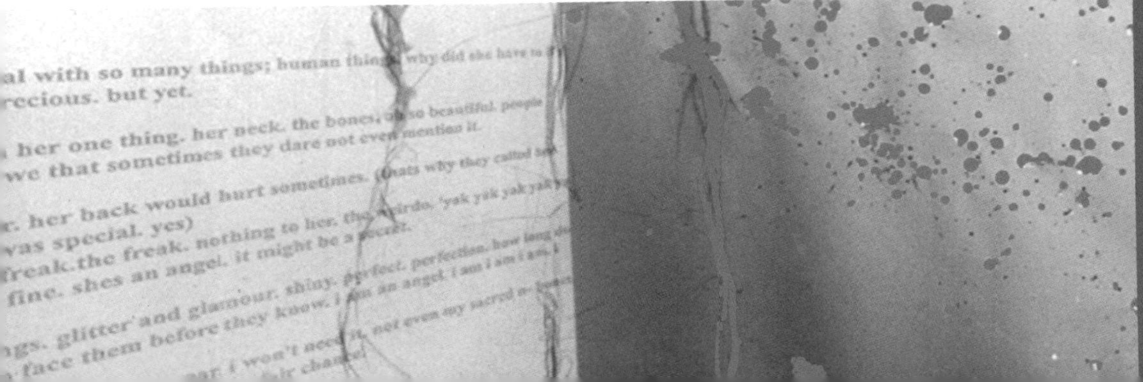

Virtual Space **Terms 1 & 2**
Peter Moore
Students: Anthony Andersen, Antonis Karides, Nilufer Kozikoglu, Lawrence Ler, Nan-kuei Lin, Christos Malekos, Jennifer Pedtke, Samuel Thoma

A practical exploration of the impact of digital values on architecture, this course addressed the impact of the digital revolution on architecture, exploring new ideas in the context of inevitable and sweeping change. Looking into the future, we foresee a much greater integration of technology into our lives, and an increasing awareness and acceptance of its implications. Patterns and structures will change. New existential concepts will emerge. Physicality will change its shape, its nature.

Students used internet technology to stimulate, express and document the development of new ideas arising from the digital revolution within architecture. Projects explored the nature of virtual space and collectively aimed to articulate the way in which it can be manifested in a physical dimension. Projects were hosted on the internet and were included in, or formed part of, other coursework.

Drawing I **Term 1**
Antoni Malinowski
Students: Joshua Ishan Goh, Tom Smith, Michelangelo Spinelli, Satoshi Nishio, Claudia Pasquero, Adrian Priestman, Anna Kubelik

'From 4D to 2D and Back Again'
This course focused on drawing as the simplest way to translate four dimensions into two. Drawing with pencil, charcoal or brush is the most direct means of materialising an idea. Drawing exercises the connection between the mind and the hand; it is about scrutiny and economy; each line drawn by hand is different. Architects concern themselves with large-scale projects, most often drawn at small scale. Yet there are differences in the perception of a work at different scales. Towards the end of the course, the work was developed to produce a final piece – a wall-size drawing.

The aim was to encourage individual working methods within the medium of drawing using the simplest means; to strengthen personal vision through the development of the poetics of drawing; and to translate a visual concept into a large scale in order to encourage pictorial questioning. The emphasis was on the movement between two and four dimensions – between pictorial space and the time-space of everyday reality.

Drawing II **Terms 1 & 2 Katrin Lahusen**
Students, Term 1: Stefania Batoeva, Edouard Cabay, Sara Camre, Therese Hegland, Kun Min Kim, Marie Langen, Asa Nilsson, Gabriel Sanchiz-Garin, Tania Rodriguez
Term 2: Joo Han Baek, Jae Hyuk Choi, Carl Fraser, Farah Diab Ghanim, Francois Guyot, Andrea Marini, Danny Marks, Elidq Cing Geo Ong

'Mind Mapping'
Fictional space or a moment in time lies somewhere between documentary and fiction. We constructed a sequence of drawings that tried to record what takes place between the moment of looking and the moment of drawing a line. We observed, analysed and imagined a film space through drawing, in order to

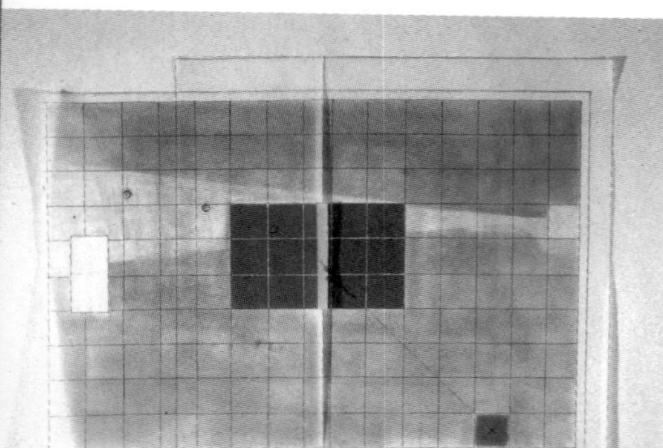

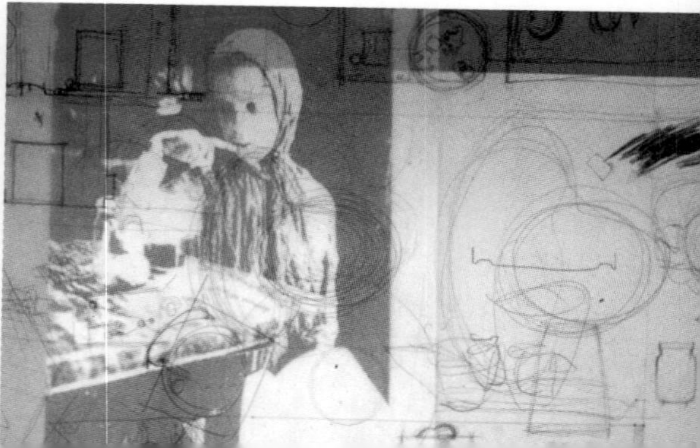

test and realise the possibilities of transforming a space through processes of construction: layering, adding, subtracting, cutting and distorting. We then made a sequence of multiview drawings by working with precise pencil and ink drawings, different types of projections (orthogonal, perspectival) and collage and photographic processes.

3-D Drawing **Terms 1 & 2**
Mark Hemel
Students, Term 1: Megumi Sakamoto, Mariko Sakuma, Patrick Klugesherz, Bart Schoonderbeek, Ho Min Kim, Omar Al Omari, Kelvin Chu, Maria Kouloumbri
Term 2: Christopher Thorn, Nikolay Shahpazov, Seung Joon Oh, Erik Brett, Jacobsen, Raphaelle Heaf, Jason Cheung, Federico Ferrari

In this course the focus alternated between the processes of space- and form-making. In a virtual environment, space is only a graphic illusion. Is space, therefore, subordinate to form? Does space merely follow form, or can it be the determinant? We investigated the space–form relationship through the making of a computer model. Animation and perspective are the usual techniques for translating characteristics of space onto the flat screen of the computer. Choosing for our virtual site a scaleless cube of space, we used these techniques to capture our individually developed concepts of the interdependence of space and form.

Print Installation **Term 1**
Denise Hawrysio
Students: Valeria Segovia, Adiam Sertzu, Maria Kalapanida

'Mark, Light and Space'
The aim of this new elective was to experiment with and expand the concept of what defines 'the print' and to develop these expanded concepts through an installation. The class is concerned with exploring and recognising process in art, investigating the semiotics of meaning within mark-making and working collaboratively to produce a collective installation. The primary elements of the installation are the light and space and the mark.

From this class, three main projects developed: *The Solid Integrated Circuit* stamp project, a printed-cup project called *A Discreet Mark,* and an installation called *The Forest.* As well as expanding notions of the print, all three projects necessarily involved a social engagement with processes of repetition. For the stamp project, a microchip stamp was created and stamped on people as they entered the AA. For *A Discreet Mark,* 400 cups were individually printed with each student's fingerprints, signed and dated, and then left to take their place among the social fabric of the AA bar. Their subsequent movements traced human activity and brought awareness to the residual marks – visible and not – we leave behind. *The Forest* connects these various approaches to installation in a new hybrid form. As in American action-painting, gestures and marks are a key element, here recording the action of blowing up balloons. This activity occurs while students and tutor drink wine. *The Forest* becomes a collective installation made up of various individual pieces, and finally it disappears. The balloons are dispersed and only the residue remains.

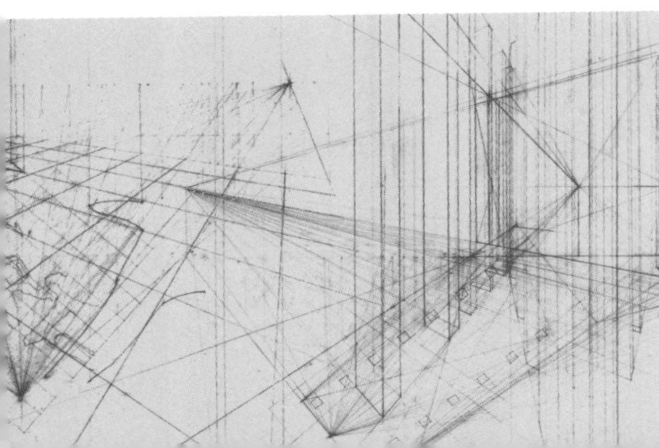

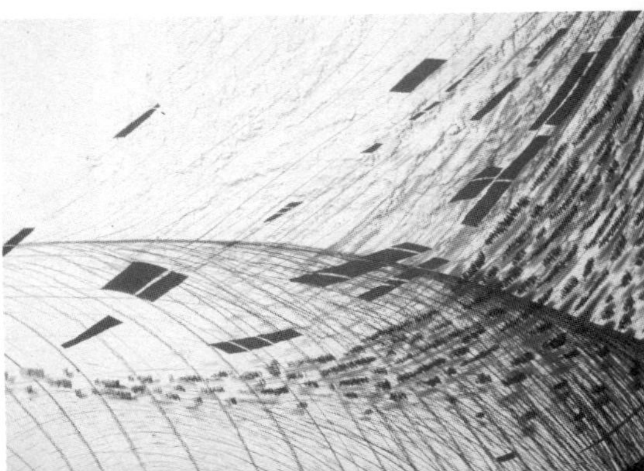

Photography **Term 1**
Sue Barr
Students: Ayako Mizuma, Toshio Fukuhara, Eir Saemundsdottir, Lirong Soon, Patrick Ng

This course investigated the ideas of narrative and sequence in photography. Rejecting the notion that there is a decisive moment that expresses the essence of a situation, and experimenting with combining, montaging and repeating images, students produced a single photograph or photographic series that illustrated ideas of light, space and time. A thorough introduction to the basic principles of black-and-white printing and camera controls were included for students with no previous experience.

Interactive Multimedia
Terms 1 & 2: Enrico Benco
Students, Term 1: Vanessa Poon, Nicolas Durr, Dan Narita, SoonTak Joo, Sibylle Lienert, Esi Carboo, Charles Peronnin, Steve Gastright, Dongkyu Lee, Ariane Sphikas
Term 2: Anuk Chanyapak, Toshio Fukuhara, Eiichi Matsuda

This was a crash course in multimedia production. In eight weeks, the module covers both the theoretical and technical aspects of designing and programming an interactive presentation. The aim is to provide students with the skills required to present their work in a nonlinear digital format. Through tutorials and workshops, the course addresses issues ranging from planning, project management and content creation to interface design and implementation. At the end of the term, students are required to submit a complete interactive project.

Video **Terms 1 & 2**
Joel Newman
Students, Term 1: Nazila Maghzian, Alex Chalmers, Hongbin Lu, Suk Kyu Hong, Justin Lau, Ruth Kedar, Kevin Petersen, Regan Shields
Term 2: Keita Tajima, Jze Yi Kuo, Mario Gottfried, Tim Den Dekker, Madeleine Adlercreutz, Kun Wook Kang, Yoon Jeong Han, Hoi Ying Leung, SoonTak Joo

The Video course allows students of all abilities to start developing methods of combining their own architectural practice with varying formats of time-based media. Emphasis is on the nonlinear editing environment, allowing the user control of experimentation in a near-abstract digital loop.

The group is required to watch examples of narrative and non-narrative work, and asked to make submissions in the form of finished video pieces. The subtext of the course is to question video-making as a valid means of architectural investigation and representation. Given that the digital realm supposedly offers endless possibilities of image and sound manipulation, are we starting to lose a sense of truth?

Digital Film **Term 1**
Pete Gomes
Students: Sara Castilho, Noe Golomb, Johannes Beaujolin, Marija Gonopolskaja, Beatriz Minguez de Molina, Eduardo Ardiles, Hadiza Gwadabe, Takao Shimizu

Video cameras are part of our everyday world, used in entertainment, infotainment, leisure, security, work, news and in documenting our own histories.

On September 11, in New York, a single moment in time was revealed to the world from multiple viewpoints. Nonsequential, fragmented and descriptive, each recording was a single component in an overall picture that could never have been achieved from a single viewpoint. Buildings in the urban and suburban environments now have cameras attached to them, inside and out, that are designed to comprehensively record and describe spaces. They are fixtures of the city, with buildings acting as hosts.

In Mike Figgis's recent films *Timecode* and *Hotel*, four digital video cameras were used to describe a single moment in time within a split-screen format.

These ideas and references formed starting points for the course. We explored the possible uses of multiple cameras and multiangle DVD, alongside the possibility of creating 'parallel narratives' using multiple simultaneous video streams.

Digital Film & Object Fabrication Collaboration
Term 2 Pete Gomes & Katrin Lahusen
Students: Catherine Saethre, Roberto Marsura, Takamasa Kikuchi, Samuel Lam, Katrin Eliasdottir

Object + Place – A Dialogue
Carrying on from Term 1's Object Fabrication course, we investigated materiality, processes of making and their latent spatial qualities. To achieve this, we used video to test how objects appear in space, and how they might become something different according to how and what we see. To conclude, we made a short video clip documenting the brief dialogue between the place and the object, which was then revisited, manipulated and edited until it became a new piece of work in itself.

Intermedia **Terms 1 & 2**
Pete Gomes
Students: Adam Cossey, Abraham Gordon, Charles Hui, Jun Kawamata, Tokuda Mitsuhiro, Alicia Tan, Mark Tynan, Max von Werz, Michel'angelo Zicarelli, Michael Davis

The concept of wireless internet access and mobile computing is changing the way we perceive networks – what we can do with them, how we shape them. This project was run in conjunction with the AA computer lab and dek.spc in southeast London. Dek.spc is an independent technology-access space that is at the forefront of Consume – a growing independent and maverick wireless-internet group using pirate-radio technology to transmit internet data. Working alongside dek.spc, we set up an antenna on the roof of the AA in order to transmit material to everyone within a two-mile radius. We looked at the conceptual implications of wireless technology for cities and created the first material to come from an AA channel. This was coordinated via a software program called the Frequency Clock, which allows users to schedule and sequence audio and video material like an internet jukebox.

The students worked to gain an understanding of the wireless technology concepts and encoding technologies. They looked at how information and wireless might affect architecture, learned how to schedule material using the new software and prepared a series of ideas to apply to their own work and the AA. There are no rules, so don't follow them.

Colour Photography **Term 1**
Goswin Schwendinger
Students: Carol Aoun, Stefano Rabolli Pansera, Eugene Chung, Flavia Foguel, Anuk Chanyapak, Daniel Koo, Christina Liao, Farah Azizah, Katrin, Eliasdottir, Hoi Chi Ng

'Identification and Transformation'
This course involved dismantling and analysing the films of Michelangelo Antonioni while focusing on the development of themes of space and character. Both diagrammatic and emotional means of investigation were required in order not only to understand and re-explain our points of interest but also to identify with the psychological structure and patterns of behaviour of selected protagonists within the space of the films. We examined Antonioni's language and found that it owes more to silence than to verbal communication, more to stasis than to action.

In the second stage, each student wrote a detailed script for a personal reinterpretation of a chosen film sequence. This script was used as the basis for a photographic setting, which enabled us to become at once producer, actor and director. We worked on a fixed number of still images, acting out personal interpretations. Using the properties of photography to produce a precise image of our ideas allowed a shift from our own personalities towards those of the protagonists.

Figure & Site and Colour Photography Collaboration **Term 2**
Simon English & Goswin Schwendinger
Students: Krasimir Kotsinov, Antonis Karides, Aurelia Teneze, Charles Hui, Gabriel Sanchiz, Noe Golomb

'A Streetcar Named Desire'
When choosing the contents of the course, *Ghostbusters* was thrown to the wind, and the car became the vehicle of our attention. Goswin showed me a photo of a woman clambering, skirts lifted, into the back of a car, and said, 'I really want to get into this'. 'The car?' I asked. 'The car', he insisted, continuing, 'well, a charged space, a space with energy from the moment you open the door'. I flicked the proverbial mint and thought for a bit it had to be a streetcar named desire.

Clichéd or not, we were now hooked, the car was connected to all our lives. It was indeed a rich seam of memory and desire. Once we started, we couldn't stop, fuelled by stories of vice, crime, sex and death, as well as long bored waits and family disputes.

We span into road movies and looked at the car in art, from Sarah Lucas's gyrating Capri to Matthew Barney's Pan-Portation. We returned in the back of Nan Goldin's cab and squeezed Martin Creed's balloons into a packed Lada.

The course was set, and the ad read: 'Students are invited to implant a desire in or on the car of your choice. 6 weeks to rehearse, 3 to shoot, 1 to reflect. Models, performers, cameras and drawing tools provided. Prepare to photograph the tableau of your dreams. Meet us on Tuesday afternoons in the Soft Room and at a garage near you.'

Site Specific Digital Print Collaboration **Term 2**
Denise Hawrysio & Sue Barr
Students: Mika Iwazaki, Celia Imaz, Mariko Sakuma, Megumi Sakamoto, Asa Nilsson, William Hai Liang Chen, Stefano Rabolli Pansera

This project involved creating, in the form of a digital photographic print, a direct response to ideas and concepts relating to students' individual unit work, exploring the duality between the actual site and the representation of that site. How the work altered our perception of the space or site was an important aspect of the project.

In approaching this project, we analysed and exploited the differences between realistic and artistic photography, the first social in its goals, the second more appropriate to affirming a new kind of identity. We further encouraged the exploration of the aesthetic potential of emergent postmodern media, incorporating etching – a technique of the past – with the digital world, thereby enabling the 'resingularisation' of mechanically mediated means of expression, and the resulting hybrid compositions. Such hybrid works should self-consciously interweave past and present aesthetics, creating not so much instances of contamination or chaos but the integration of the old and the new within 'changing creative realms'.

Drawing Collaboration **Term 2**
Antoni Malinowski
Students: Joshua Ishan Goh, Smita Khanna, Daniel Kin Kay Koo, Hadiza Gwadabe, Nausica Gabrielides, Daniel Coll I Capdevila, Pavlos Sideris

'Colour Me Moves'
The course aimed to create an ownership of the ideas of space and colour, movement and space, and movement and colour by practical exercises involving the students experiencing their habits of perception in a neutral way, thereby equipping them to explore, witness and rotate the world in these terms.

It facilitated an understanding of the dynamics of space and colour through exposure to, and experience of, pigment and its use in relation to other objects and pigments, and created an ability to recognise the role that colour can have in our daily lives in terms of product selection, choice of route and reflexive ocular response.

Students developed a sensitivity to the use of colour in relation to the dynamics of space and movement, and created an instinctive notational system that was sensitive to space, time, density, age and type of person, and used colour and quality of mark made.

Students were introduced to the sensibility and materiality of pure pigments. The focus was on colour as matter, teaching how to make paint from pigments and to apply and test it on different surfaces. In a series of practical workshops, the students were encouraged to analyse the various aspects of human movement in an urban environment. Those observations were translated into 3D choreographic notations, with colour as an integral part of the final installations.

To look at the use of colour in architecture, the group went to Venice, which has a unique tradition spanning from Byzantine to the modern projects of Carlo Scarpa. This allowed students to gain a different perspective on their research and to test their work in the Venetian context.

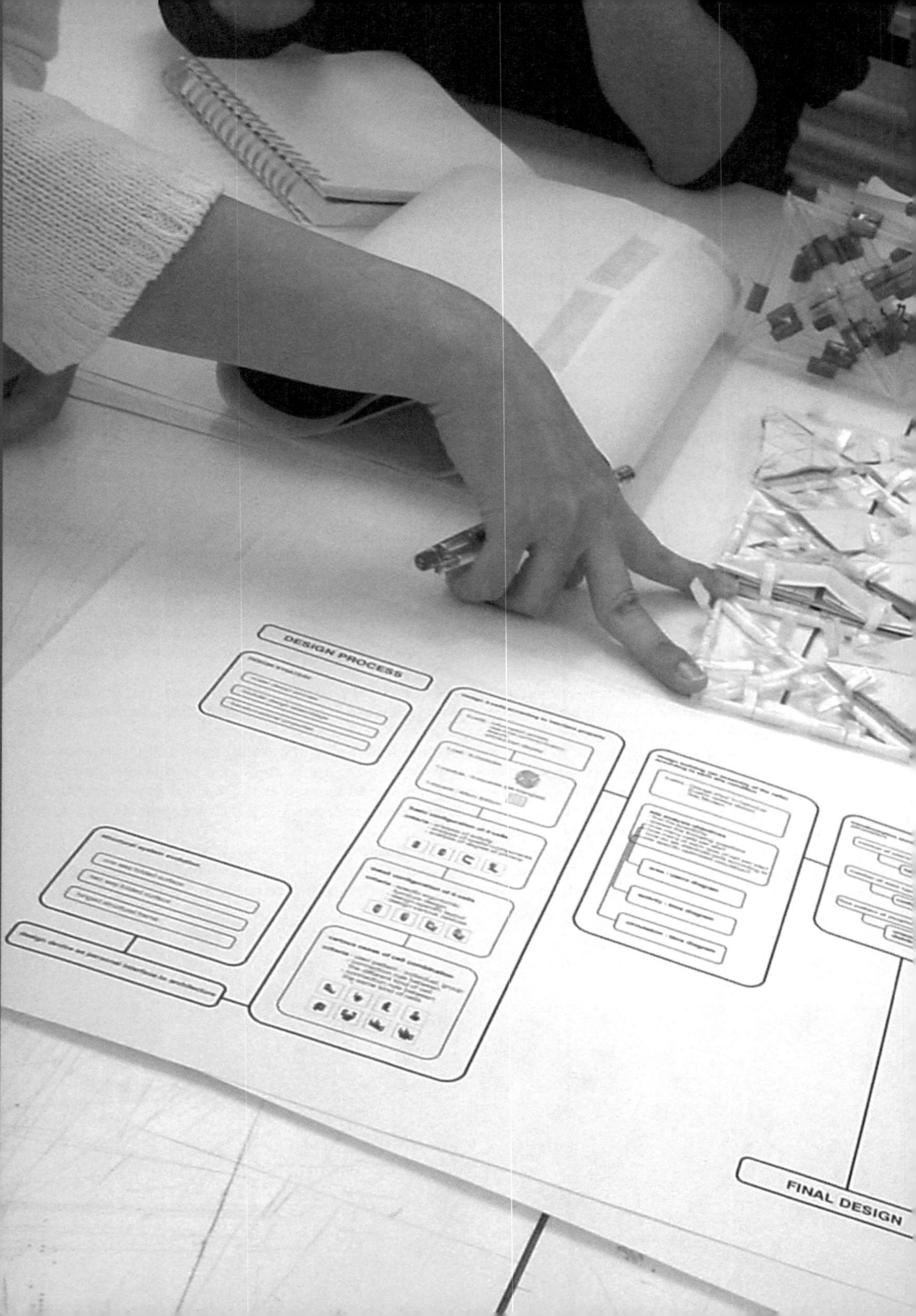
DESIGN PROCESS
FINAL DESIGN

Graduate School

The Histories & Theories programme is designed to provide students with a critical understanding of contemporary architectural discourse. We aim to do so by thoroughly considering and questioning particular architectural, theoretical and methodological approaches. Tutors take an interdisciplinary and varied approach to study, drawing on the humanities and social sciences, and on a range of analytical frameworks, including aesthetics and psychoanalysis. An exploration of themes in modern and contemporary architectural theory, landscape and urban form, is complemented by close examinations of twentieth-century architectural practice.

The programme attracts a wide variety of students and this year was no exception – students were drawn from Australia, Germany, Brazil, Turkey, Greece, the United States, Portugal, Britain and China. Some were architects wishing to take a year to reflect upon some of the theoretical implications of their design practice, some came to take the first steps in an academic career, while others hoped that the programme would contribute to future careers in architectural journalism, exhibition curating or other related fields.

The study trip to Athens in December offered students a unique opportunity to explore the Acropolis, including the restoration work on the Parthenon, in sub-zero temperatures; to participate in a discussion with students and professors in the architecture programme of Athens University; and to contribute to a public debate with architects, academics, and members of the wider community on architecture and nomadism, held to mark an exhibition of competition winners in the new Syntagma Square metro station.

This year, in addition to Aesthetics: Art, Architecture and Landscape, Modernism in Architecture, Narratives of Modernism, Modernism after Modernism, Modern Architecture and its Myths, Space and Politics, Surface Culture**, and** Psyche and Architecture**, we offered two new classes in landscape theory –** Toposophy **and** Wasteland **– as well as a one-week workshop on postwar British architecture.**

Staff

Mark Cousins
Lawrence Barth
Katharina Borsi
Vittoria Di Palma
Hilde Heynen
Paul Hirst
Marina Lathouri
Neil Leach
Robert Maxwell
Dalibor Vesely

Visiting Critics

Andrew Benjamin
Iain Boyd-Whyte
Peter Carl
Alan Colquhoun

MA Students

Robert Curtis Anderson
Carolyn Bennett
Elizabeth Goodfellow-Zagoroff
Yuki Gottschaldt
Huey Ying Hsu
Rosemary Lamont
Edward Leyva
Martin Neilan
Georg Rafailidis
Pedro Filipe Vieira
Mariangela Verotti Zanini

PhD Students

John Abell
Manuela Antoniu
Maria Benitez
Marcelo Espinosa Martinez
James Karl Fischer
Ines Geisler
Derin Inan
Nuttinee Karnchanaporn
Nikolaos Koronis
Pablo Leon de la Barra Vargas
Hua Li
Kijchot Nuntanasirivikrom
Nikolaos Patsavos
Enrique Walker

1.

2.

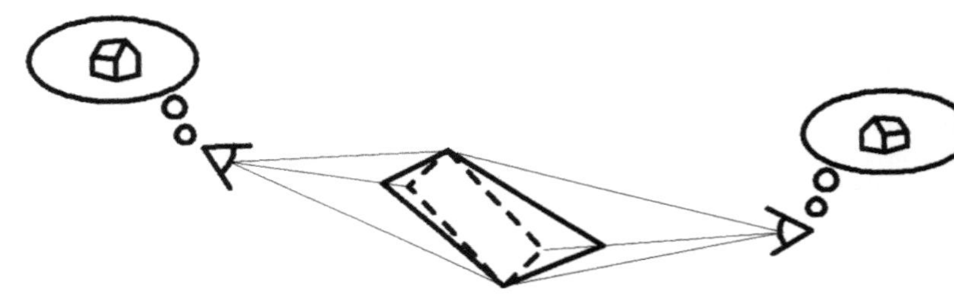

3.

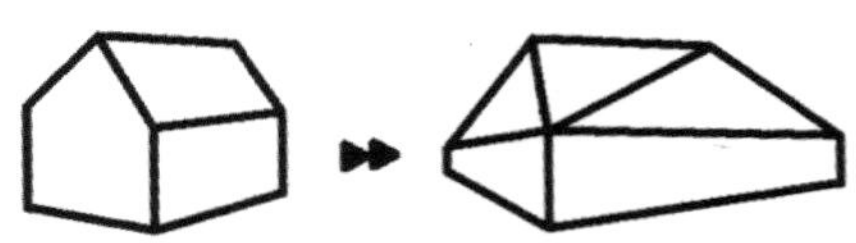

4.

"private"
"common area"
"common area"
"private"

5.

"common area"
"private"

Edward Leyva

It is common within the architectural milieu to contrast the activities of design with the activities of history and theory. It is less common, however, to contrast the activities of history with those of theory, and to consider the unexamined dialogue between them. Narratives of Modernism**, a core course in the MA programme, provides an opportunity to observe how, for example, the historian traces the evolution of a theoretical debate, thus generating a very specific articulation of it, or the way in which a particular historical narrative is constructed from the vantage of theoretical engagement. Reflecting the composition of its students – and acknowledging the diverse interests that inform architectural production – the course, and the programme in general, also encourages analyses derived from 'a range of disciplines in the humanities and social sciences'. It was these two aspects that suggested a critical reading of Aldo Rossi's** The Architecture of the City **as a quasi-metaphysical text, using the motif of negative theology to analyse Rossi's characterisation of the city's architectural pedigree, especially the influential concepts of analogy, locus and the type. Grafting onto an architectural terrain the theologian Maimonides' declaration, 'every time you establish by proof the negation of a thing in reference to God, you become more perfect, while in every additional positive assertion you follow your imagination and recede from the true knowledge of God', the essay examines how Rossi's text, if somewhat reluctantly (and unwittingly), constructs a theory of architecture based principally on what architecture is not, his critique of naïve functionalism being only the best-known example of the many negative claims in** The Architecture of the City**. Understood as a corrective to the positivistic, empiricist ideologies of early Modernists, Rossi's text struggles to promote that which is ultimately ineffable, anticipating those 'spaces that defy measurement' that Rossi would later dwell on in** ***A Scientific Autobiography*****. Drawing on the religious writings of thinkers as diverse as Maimonides, Pseudo-Dionysius, Aquinas, Kant, Kierkegaard and Wittgenstein, the essay attempts to parallel Rossi's theoretical polemic with the Modernists alongside the theological debates between the linguistic rationalists and logical positivists at the turn of the last century. It suggests Rossi's thought is, in the end, situated restlessly between the Kantian impulse to go beyond the limits of reason and Wittgenstein's sober recognition of the impenetrable bounds of those limits. And it is the metaphysical ambiguity generated by this tension, the essay concludes, that accounts for the widespread and impassioned, though multifarious and even contradictory, endorsement of** The Architecture of the City**.**

Martin Neilan

My decision to pursue an MA in Histories & Theories at the AA was formed with some ambivalence. Besides being a return to the sort of writing I had not done for a long while, I had experienced very little of the sort of cultural climate one might associate with a major city such as London – indeed, it was going to be my first exposure to study overseas.

In coming to the AA I was struck by how ideal this environment was, not just for the exchange of ideas between diverse groups, but also for the manner in which people from all over the world can so easily assimilate this place as a sort of second home. The course trip to Athens presented most of us with the perfect setting in which to understand each other's sense of enjoyment of architecture. Eventually the entire group was to find a certain bond that made lectures and discussions both challenging and rewarding. The potential to participate in other courses within the School is a distinct advantage. The Histories & Theories programme presents a rare scenario, allowing one can to tap a vast (and at times conflicting) array of ideas and commentaries. In this sense, the course has the potential to provide, for willing students, the kind of expert and often unexpected input that one may not find elsewhere.

Georg Rafailidis

The 'Most Wanted Building'. The course Aesthetics **offered a brief but intense introduction to the development of thought on the subject since antiquity. It was particularly relevant to a consideration of the following observations: firstly, the current avoidance of, or mistrust with regard to, aesthetic discourse (take, for example the last biennale slogan** Less Aesthetics More Ethics**) – an ostensible rejection of the aesthetic question that is undermined by a hidden fetishisation of it; and, secondly, the notion of aesthetic experience introduced by Kant which seemed interesting to me in that it contains a line of thought, emphasising the disinterestedness of the subject, that would allow one to escape from consumerist behaviour. In the context of the latter, I analysed Peter Zumthor's Thermal Bath in Vals, a spa whose pools are too small for swimming in and whose main purpose seems to be to provide an aesthetic experience of architecture. In this sense it is an example of how one moves beyond consumerist behaviour. An investigation of Zumthor's own description of the design process revealed an unexpected twist: the origin of the design was an advert for the mineral water of Vals.**

Advertisements are the result of opinion polls, the main instrument of analysing and constructing desires. In that sense the Thermal Bath in Vals can be compared with Alex Melamid and Vitaly Komar's work The Most Wanted Painting, **for which the duo carried out opinion polls in order to paint a work for each country. They are conscious that the most wanted painting is in itself a paradox according to Kant: 'Everyone must allow that a judgement on the beautiful which is tinged with the slightest interest, is very partial and not a pure judgement of taste. One must not be in the least prepossessed in favour of the real existence of the thing, but must preserve complete indifference in this respect, in order to play the part of judge in matters of taste.'**

Liz Goodfellow Zagoroff

Being a generation older than most of my fellow students, and coming not from architecture, but from a landscape background (where historical studies generally petered out at the end of the nineteenth century), the programme was especially exciting and challenging for me. The spectrum of studies, together with extra-curricular events and activities, allowed me to find my place. Apparently unconnected lectures provided unexpected cross-references and understandings – if I was struggling to 'get it' one way, chances were it would come to me in another. Happenstance conversations over lunch or in the bar at the end of the day provided many insights and inspirations. One such encounter led to an essay topic that examined eighteenth-century aesthetics from both a landscape and an architectural point of view.

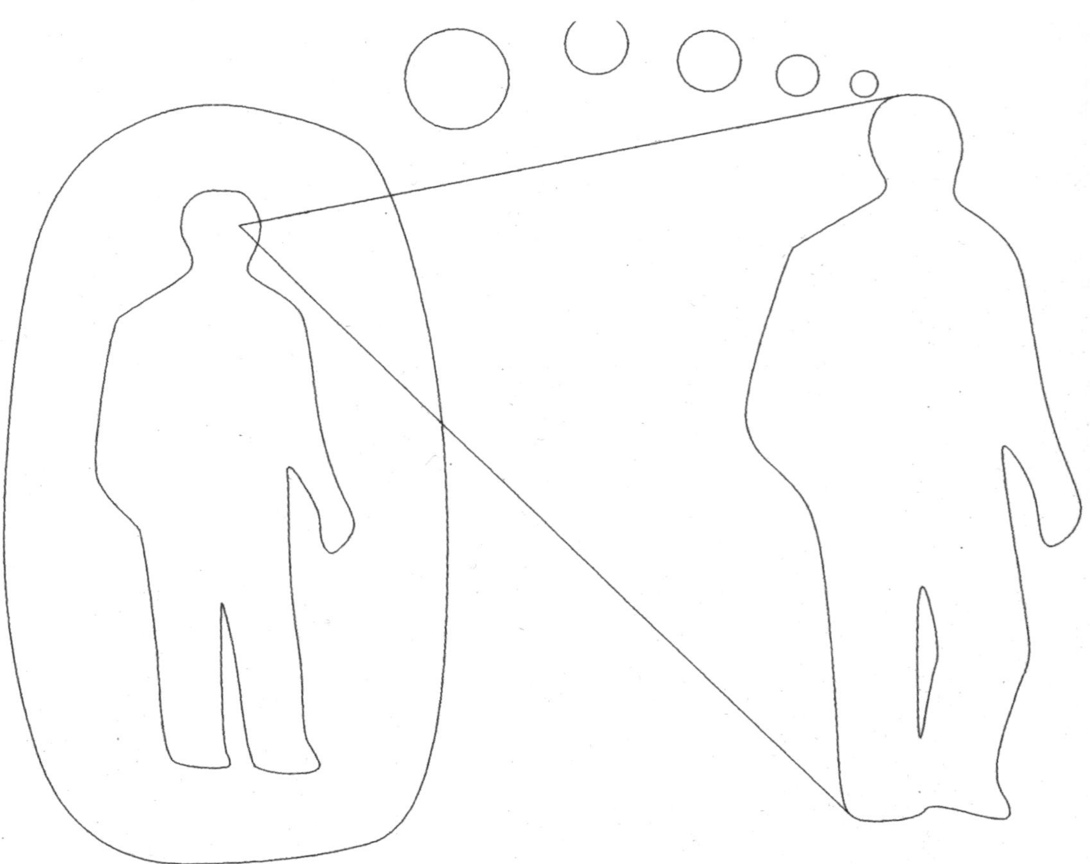

Georg Rafailidis Black and Blue

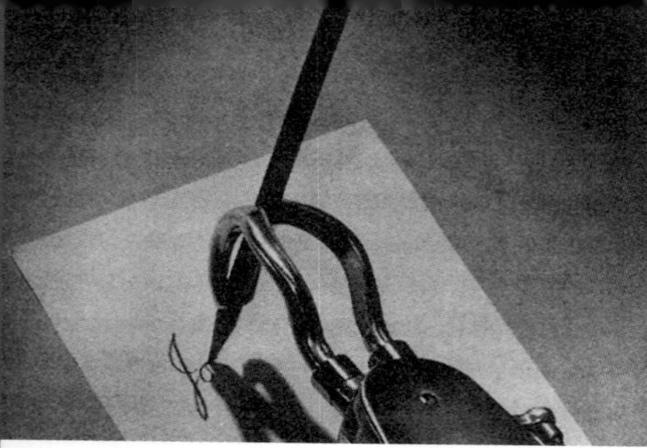

Left: Mechanical hand designed by Henry Dreyfuss (1904-1972) in collaboration with psychiatrists, engineers, materials experts and amputees. Henry Dreyfuss Collection, Cooper-Hewitt, National Design Museum, Smithsonian Institute
Right: Photo of Keeling House by Robert Curtis Anderson and Huey Ying Hsu

The Prosthetic Discourse of Architecture **Edward Leyva**

Since antiquity, the image of the human body has served a primary, if often naïve, role in the discourse of architecture. From Vitruvius to the Modernists, the Humanist conception of the stable, unblemished (male) body found recurrent expression within the shifting concerns of architectural theory. For Le Corbusier, the universality of the human body – epitomised in his Modulor – elicited standardised design praxis concerned firstly with 'the extension of our limbs'; decorative art was merely the 'totality of human-limb objects'. Indeed, the notion of architecture as prosthesis became a common Modernist trope. However, following the demythologising wave of post-structuralist and feminist critique in the1960s and 1970s, the archetype of the universal, originary body was compellingly refuted, in effect irrevocably dismembering a principal model for architecture. With this destabilising lack, an amputee architectural theory turned toward interdisciplinarity to find new 'modes of legitimation', rearticulating the boundaries of its own 'body' in the process. Through the concepts of identification and appropriation, this essay examines the Modernist notion of a prosthetic architecture, its eventual eclipse, and the discursive supplements sought by a prosthetised body of architectural theory in response.

One Man's Garden: Domesticity and Individuality in a Suburban Garden **Carolyn D Bennett**

The small, personal back garden of suburban London (c.1900) was an integral part of a family's demesne. Yet, because of its size, inaccessibility, and ephemeral nature it has never been studied. One book, The Story of My Old-World Garden and How I Made It in a London Suburb **(Swinstead, 1910), chronicles through photographs, sketches and prose the making of such a garden. This paper will analyse the Swinstead garden in an effort to explore how he infused a sense of domesticity and individuality into his garden, why that was important, what it meant, and how this fits into the broader societal context.**

Herman Munthe-Kaas and Gudolf Blakstad: Functionalism and the Invention of Tradition in Norway **Robert Curtis Anderson**

At the beginning of the twentieth century, Norwegian architects hid behind the guise of National Romanticism, believing that it furthered Norwegian traditions. As such, the notion of an 'invented tradition' of architecture, based on Eric Hobsbawm's book of the same name, became the catalyst for my discussion of the transition from National Romanticism to Functionalism in Norway. Functionalism, which grew out of the International Style, was seen to be the much-needed break from nationalistic tendencies. However, it is much more plausible that Functionalism was a continuation of architectural trends in Norway and could thus be seen as yet another 'invention of tradition'.

The Banqueting House **Rosemary Lamont**

The Banqueting House by Inigo Jones (1619–23) was the first fully Italian classical building in England and was part of the complex of late medieval buildings of Whitehall Palace. The King's request was to replace a timber Masqueing House that had burnt down, but when completed (with Rubens's ceiling) the new building was too precious to stage smoky masques. Was it an audience chamber constructed with anterooms or withdrawing rooms – or simply the grandest spare hall in Christendom? What was it that the King had really asked for and what was it that was built?

Construction of the Singular Subject **Huey Ying Hsu**

The topic of the urban singular dwelling has produced many fascinating projects in modern architecture – Mies van der Rohe and many contemporary architects have presented sketches of who they think single

dwellers are and how they should live. From the housing census we see a steady increase, over the past 50 years, in the total number of people who live alone, however here we are given a very different image of the persons who actually live alone, the majority of whom are the poorest, oldest and the most vulnerable. This thesis examines the reasons behind modern architecture's construction of a fictional singular subject, its living condition and our adoption of the dwelling type in modern life.

The Transparent Modern Family **Martin Neilan**

The proposed research paper looks toward the sociological theories of both Nikolas Rose and Jacques Donzelot in an effort to further interrogate the Modernist glass-wall house and to provide a series of possible re-readings. It directs attention towards what part such an architectural statement might play in the deployment of technologies of governance that contribute to the formation of the modern family and those individuals within it. In that these technologies of subjectivisation are viewed here as being intrinsic to a certain internalisation, the idea of the glass wall is regenerated as though a screen for the projection of all kinds of desires framed within a schematic framework of normativity.

Through investigation and conjecture, the intention becomes that of illustrating the largely unproblematised nature of a critique that addresses both the idea that the 'private' ever existed, and also that the publicisation of the private was really as significant an interpretation of transparent architecture as some would like to make out. The notion of the 'open' and 'closed' home is hopefully rendered with a greater complexity than previously.

London's Burial Ground Gardens **Liz Goodfellow Zagoroff**

This thesis looks at more than 130 ancient burial grounds, throughout metropolitan London, which were closed during the 1850s due to overcrowding and disease, and later laid out as public gardens, providing open space in densely populated areas. It examines their history and the circumstances of their closing; the events and philanthropic endeavours that led to their reopening as public spaces; the reason for their survival into the twenty-first century; and their future as open space, as historical heritage, as something that gives a community its sense of place and continuity.

The Subversive Copy **Georg Rafailidis**

I am examining the need for fictive origins, the resulting role of retroactive narratives, and the role of built architecture in this process as a 'taking of evidence'. I am interested here in the copy without original or, better, an active copy that produces its original. In other words, the subversive copy. The thesis analyses the discourse about the origin(al) and examples where conscious or unconscious errors make copies productive. The Stalinallee in Berlin will stand as one example for its ability to 'prove' the most contradictory narratives and its failure to function as a self-fulfilling prophecy for its first fantasy: the superiority of socialism.

Shifting Grounds: A Critical Analysis of Concepts of Nature in Architecture **Yuki Gottschaldt**

With architecture being ambiguously positioned between culture and nature, recent architectural discourse has increasingly embraced varying concepts of nature, justifying this both from an environmental and from an often diametrically opposed aesthetically expressive perspective. In tracing the shifting meanings of the term 'nature', both as a material reality and as a cultural construct, the thesis examines the way differing concepts of nature have informed recent cultural and aesthetic discourse. Subsequently, it questions how far contemporary architecture(s), while embracing these concepts both ethically and/or aesthetically, have found or, possibly, can find satisfying answers in the way they relate to these complex and challenging ideas of nature.

The Garden City-Hellerau and the Dalcroze Institute **Mariangela Verotti Zanini**

The goal of the thesis is to understand the reasons and effects of the theatre as an element of cultural life in the garden city of Hellerau. The Hellerau project reflected the apprehension aroused by the expansion of industrial civilisation in Germany at the end of the nineteenth century, a mood that resulted in the 'Reform of Life Movement', which sought the renewal of human existence through the practice of a new hierarchy of cultural values. It was a self-reform achieved by renouncing the artificiality of metropolitan life, rediscovering the healthy energy of nature, applying principles of community cooperation and self-management.

The Disappearance of the Everyday in East Germany since 1989 **Ines Geisler**

It is now widely recognised that the reunification of Germany at a legal and political level created a kind of cultural and urban vacuum in the former GDR. This thesis tries to chart the process through which reunification robbed former GDR cities of their physical and institutional marks of 'everyday life' and replaced them with the imposition of those of the ex- Federal Republic. This process, which has not been systematically studied through the particular consideration of the urban imagery, is argued to be a major source of the eastern population's sense of estrangement from the new Germany.

Modern Mexican Style **Pablo Leon de la Barra Vargas**

Modern Mexican Style exposes selected episodes of the urban, architectonic and contemporary art context of Mexico City, while questioning the adaptations to modernity and globalisation in the Mexican context. As such, it analyses the creation of a dominant national cultural identity which excludes many of the existing phenomena, while at the same time signalling the risks of the aestheticisation of the existing singularities and their appropriation and transformation into new forms of exoticism.

An Architecture of Knowledge: The Ideology of Greek Architectural Education **Nikolaos Patsavos**

This investigation concerns architectural education in Modern Greece. Starting from a description of the present condition, and analysing the relation of architectural education to architectural practice and the academic system in general, the research continues by attempting to trace its main paradigms in the way different Modernisms have been historically applied to the field. Working on the interaction between a nation's modernisation projects and a discipline's theories of progress is expected to provide some answers to questions of both a general or exemplary nature and those that are more idiosyncratic.

Modernity in the Production of Contemporary Chinese Architecture **Hua Li**

In the last two decades Chinese architecture appears to have developed a kind of hybrid style, distinct from both Western and Chinese traditions. This phenomenon responds to diverse social and political forces and a diversity of perceptions of modernity and modernisation in China. Although the notion of modernity is borrowed and imported from the West, it achieved a complex Chinese architectural interpretation. This thesis attempts to explore that complexity over the last 20 years through case studies.

Monumental Discrepancies in the Architecture of the Modern Capital: Ankara **Derin Inan**

The thesis addresses the current architectural condition of Ankara. Its goal is to highlight the dilemmas in its struggle to attain the desired modern image that will fit the ideology of the new republic. Ankara is the primary site of a revolutionary spirit and a collective and monumental celebration of the new. The research will concern new notions and instruments, and their functions and perceptions as pragmatic tools to highlight the gaps and challenges in the epistemological formation of Turkish architecture.

Photo of Shanghai by Yu Yu
Opposite: Photo by Nuttinee Karnchanaporn, fear as a cultural phenomenon in Thailand

Architecture of the Negative – The Representation of Negative Entities in Contemporary Architecture
Marcelo Espinosa Martinez
Architecture has always been considered as a totality. From the end of the nineteenth century through Modernism, it has been concerned mainly with the organisation and the manipulation of space. Nevertheless, in the recent production of architecture, space itself has become a qualitative object. To talk about Negative Entities is to talk about differentiation in space and about qualitative conditions, conditions of presence and absences within architecture. The concept of differentiation within production and form allow us to establish relations to the subject (Negative Entities) and that of architecture. Holes, or Negative Entities are not a significant part of architecture as long as the process of construction is not within its architectural focus. The question of Negative Entities is posed as an issue within the construction of the physical realm.

Fear as a Cultural Phenomenon in Thailand and the Spatial Relations of Domestic Architecture
Nuttinee Karnchanaporn
This thesis problematises the spatial practise of domestic sanctification (i.e., domestic remedies, rituals of house building and spatial conduct) applied within the contemporary Thai domestic sphere in Bangkok as possessing a 'double-edged' characteristic. It lends the house spiritual protection, while at the same time, potentially causing domestic misfortune. The thesis focuses particularly on the extent to which domestic sanctification could subtly induce a conflict in the use of domestic interior and, to an extent, portray the familiar space of one's home as a site of horror and fear.

On Space, Transparency, and the Freudian Subject **John Abell**
Lacking a theoretical model of the subject that accounts for the unconscious, architecture exhibits philosophical and technological extremes when interpreting subject–object relations as a basis for the experience and production of space. To address this shortcoming, the thesis reinterprets modern conceptions of architectural space on the basis of the spatiality of the Freudian subject. Architectural conceptions addressed in the thesis are spatial coherence, surface character, composition, simulation and the programmatic event.

The Housing & Urbanism programme addresses a terrain between politics and the building of cities, and we locate our work where there is the challenge of political dispute and the opportunity for significant change. This work cuts across the moment of design, critically reflecting on the patterns of reason running through urban architectural production and comparatively assessing the results of the city-building process. The courses are designed to interlink and to cover a broad range of issues, so that recurring themes and topics will be approached through different disciplines and references throughout the year. Project work focuses on current problems within urbanism, and each year engages with a particular 'live' development in London and a shorter workshop elsewhere, this year in Mexico City. Course work broadens and deepens these primary investigations through an engagement with historical materials and transnational comparisons.

The programme offers a one-year MA and research degrees at MPhil and PhD level.
The MA course has a balance between theoretical reflection and the pursuit of practical design solutions, with design projects providing an arena in which to test ideas and illustrate current problems and strategies within urbanism. We engage in three types of work:

1. Lectures and seminars, which explore current theoretical and historical approaches to housing and urbanism; courses were:

Cities in a Transnational World
The Reason of Urbanism
Shaping the 20th-Century City
Critical Urbanism
Housing and the Irregular City
Themes of 20th-Century Housing

2. The Design Seminar and workshops, which offer the opportunity to investigate urban areas and test design strategies; projects were:

The Spitalfields Market
Elephant & Castle redevelopment
Mexico City urban renewal
Netherlands study trip

3. Thesis work, which allows students to develop an extended and focused study within the field.
A selection of titles of this year's work:

New Design and Construction Approaches to Housing
Public Domain as Urban Strategy in Tokyo
Social and Private Housing in Shen Zen, China
Public Spaces as a Regeneration Frontier
Organisation and Perception of Space in the Information Society

The Elephant & Castle redevelopment site: public land holding.

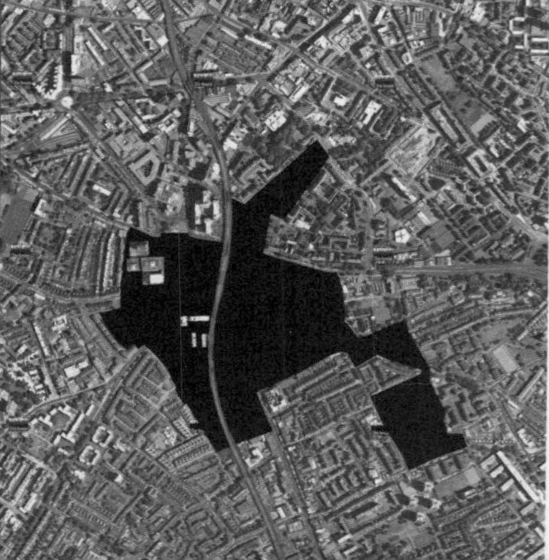

Responding to the Inner Periphery

The challenge always facing urbanism is how to respond to the embedded trends and conflicts that configure the urban fabric. Problems that knot themselves around a particular site present the traces of general conditions, including the forces of globalisation. Today, London's strategic planning is caught between two counterposed trends in the contemporary urban process. On the one hand, the densification of the inner city follows the growth of international finance and business services, coupled with an increasing demand for inner-city housing. On the other hand, job creation, especially in manufacturing and lower-level services, along with overall residential demand, continues to disperse outside the major cities. The recognition of these trends intriguingly provides support for each side in the continuing debate around the pursuit of the compact city. Many of the answers depend upon whether we find sound spatial solutions for what we might call the inner periphery, that blurred and heterogeneous terrain wrapping itself closely around London's teeming corporate and entertainment core. This inner periphery is where we have located our design work this year, both with the short workshop at Spitalfields Market and the major

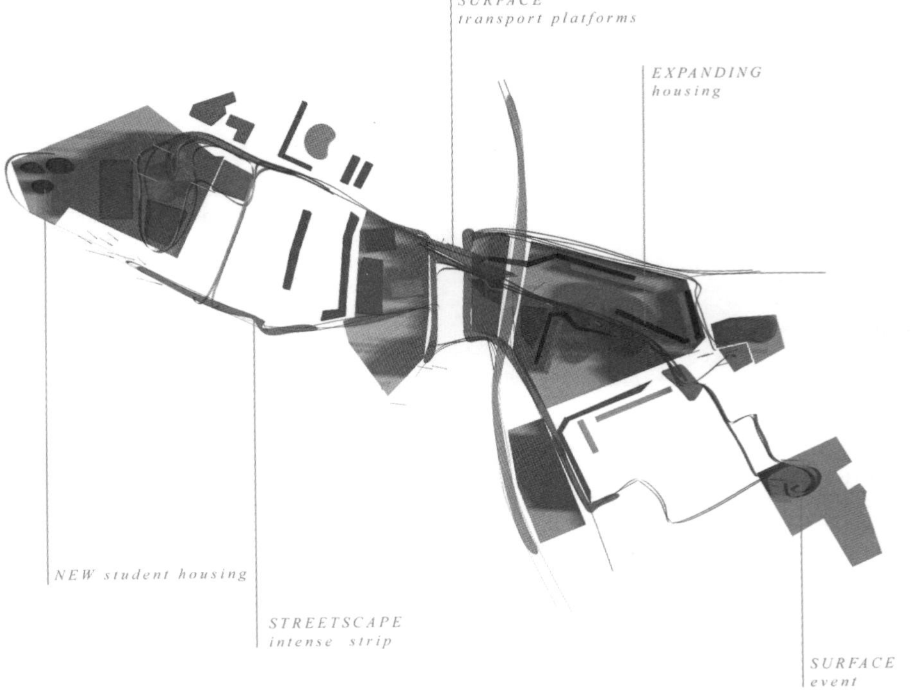

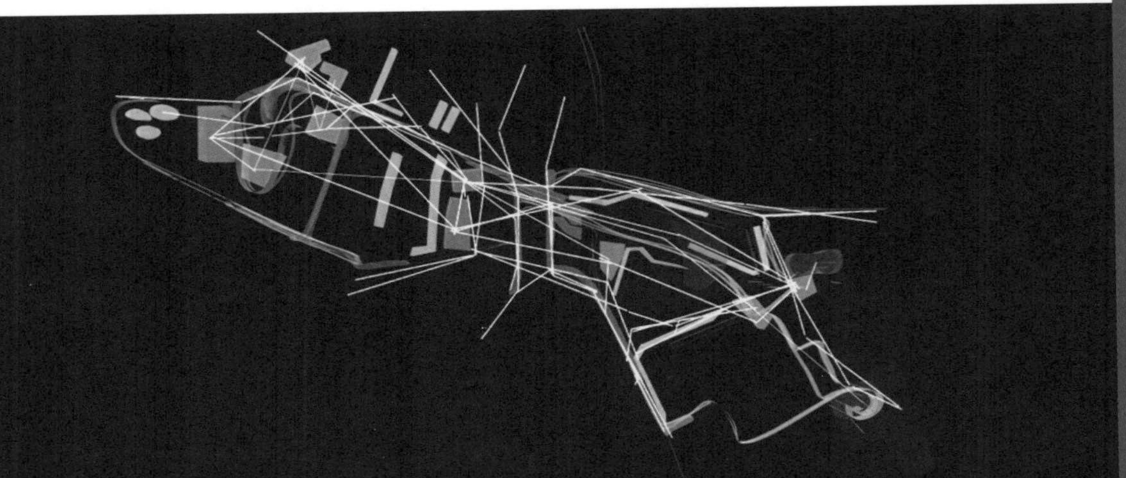

The area of intervention is seen as much wider than in the current proposal, stretching east–west across the central area. The project grows through programmatic exchanges of existing and new spaces, starting from the wide range of institutions in the area, and through integrated design for the streetscapes (managed through a Community Development Trust). The large slabs of the Heygate are retained and have parallel new housing and commercial structures which link into other areas.

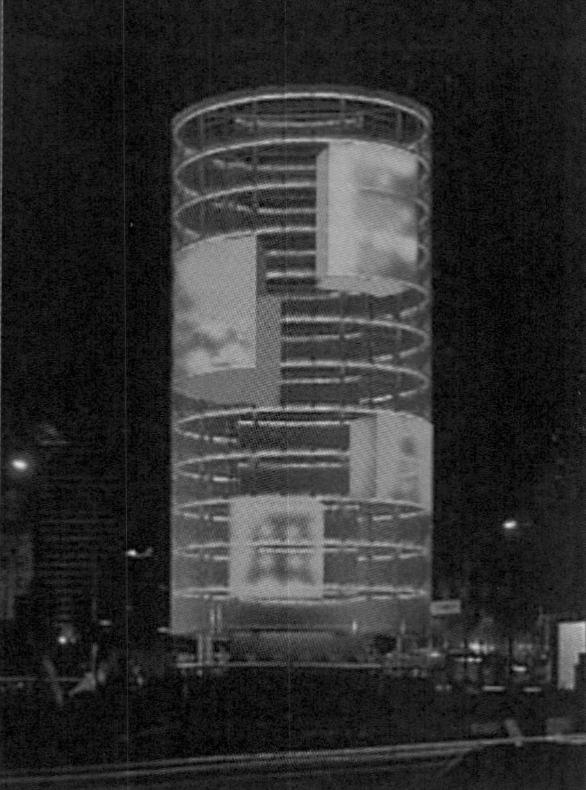

investigative project at the Elephant & Castle. Infrastructurally, these sites contain major pieces of London's transport capacity, and concentrated development of an appropriate mix here would seem to offer a vastly more efficient 'London of transport nodes'. To achieve this, however, urbanism must reach beyond the developmental stasis which plagues this terrain and create well-tailored spatial solutions on a number of scales. This 'tailoring' implies a broad range of investigations into the urban process, but analysis in itself will not show the way forward. Instead, meaningful strategies must take the form of a spatial argument graphically responding to existing patterns and intensities. Teams in the Design Seminar were required to confront and respond to several key questions, of which two may be mentioned here. The first is concerned with the centrality of the Elephant & Castle within the fabric of South London. Tightly concentrated new office development and market housing would have to be balanced against a desire for porosity and integration, which is difficult to achieve in an area dominated by poverty and social housing. Can convincing urban solutions be found, or should a less highly concentrated programme of development be sought?
A second question addresses the relation between new market housing and the pursuit of a richer infrastructure of urban services. As inner-city residences close to work become more attractive for those employed in an office economy, the demand for a broad range of services, from supermarkets to schools and sports centres, increases. An urban strategy for inner periphery sites should indicate the impact this demand will have on the spatial development of the existing infrastructure.

The Pursuit of Housing as Urbanism

Any path to effective urban transformation in the inner periphery must pass through the issue of housing as an urban element. At the Elephant & Castle, social housing presents a dominant feature of the physical and socio-economic landscapes. It is not only an issue of the proportion of local people who depend upon social housing, but also a matter of the formal and spatial qualities of the Heygate Estate, which commands an inner quadrant of the local urban fabric. A once reasonable response to the Elephant's position in a road-dominated transport infrastructure for Greater London, the Heygate's imposing slabs present an optimistic face of the welfare state towards the traffic while protecting what amounts to a vestigial image of neighbourhood. This ambivalence toward the road, part enthusiasm and part fear, is one of many contradictions which have left the Heygate paralysed for so many years, unable to press ahead

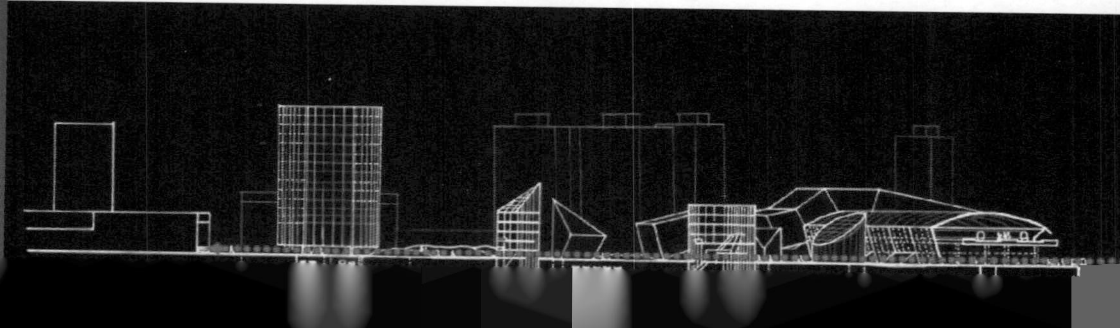

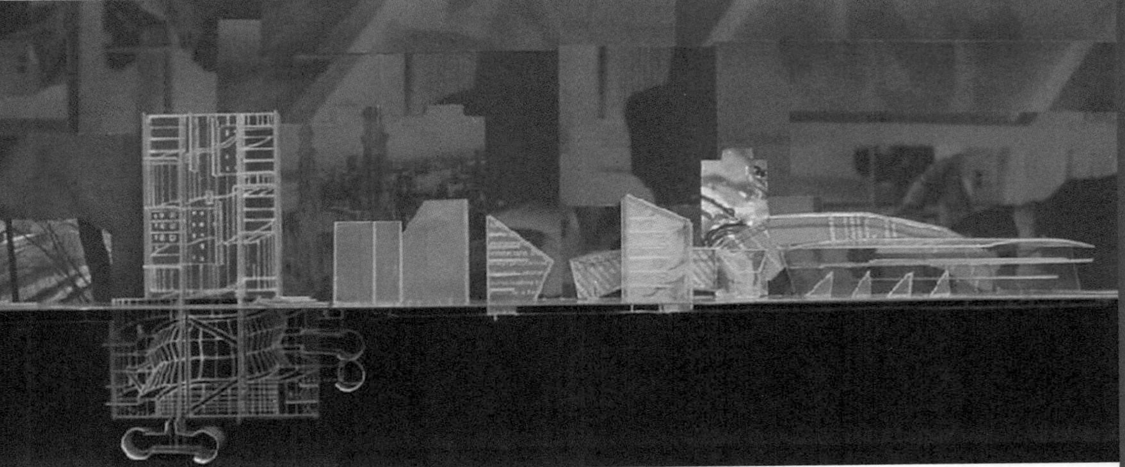

Mapping at local and city scales reveals fragmentation which is seen as an opportunity. An 'urban staircase' will link levels of tube, road and rail into a continuous territory which will be a unique urban space. New shopping will be linked with existing activities along Walworth Road, and new 'short-use' offices and hotels will provide space for international travellers using Waterloo station. The Heygate is rebuilt as low-rise high-density housing for mixed tenures.

with the changes demanded by new conditions. Its insistence upon programmatic uniformity fundamentally contradicts the close relationship between residence and retail street that typically characterises London and is also a central feature of the ideal neighbourhood unit plan. Similarly, its socio-economic homogeneity rejects the urbanity that is desired in so much of inner London. These problems and others, combined with more prosaic practical difficulties of renovation, such as asbestos removal, have suggested to many that the Heygate be demolished. Considering this question allowed us to investigate a range of socio-spatial strategies. Demolition encourages one to consider how housing might be freshly composed within a pluralist strategy, while retention offers the exploration of smaller steps towards a more intensified ground and more diversified slabs. In either case, housing solutions must respond with greater clarity and attention to the complexity of the urban process. This is not about a shallow diversification of forms, responsive only to today's deepening sense of individualisation. Rather, through our course work we have read this trend in the architecture of housing as the flip-side of the narrow focus on domestic and personal life that has underpinned mass social housing. A richer reworking of the place of housing in the fabric of the inner periphery begins with a deeper reflection on the internal politics of the home within the urban process.

The Strategy of Infrastructure

Serious proposals for inner periphery sites cannot avoid a programmatic questioning of the transport infrastructure, for two reasons. Firstly, the pervasive impulse to intensify the use of these sites suggests an increasing burden on the existing transport system. Secondly, and perhaps more interestingly, the pattern of disinvestment from the inner periphery has led to the neglect of the area's transport infrastructure. This is yet another unfortunate outcome of the rationality of urban renewal, although it appears to conform to the dispersal of manufacturing outside the city. Plans for the regeneration of these sites continuously encounter neglected or disused elements of an older infrastructure which pointedly pose the question of their refurbishment or adaptation to new uses. As soon as the question is seen in this light, the transport infrastructure emerges as one aspect of a larger set of issues concerning the broader strategy of infrastructural development, which might easily include the system of public spaces. The network of streets, paths, parks and urban atria together make up an infrastructure for movement, concentration and integration, generating a platform for both local economic growth and the cultivation of diversity. While it is

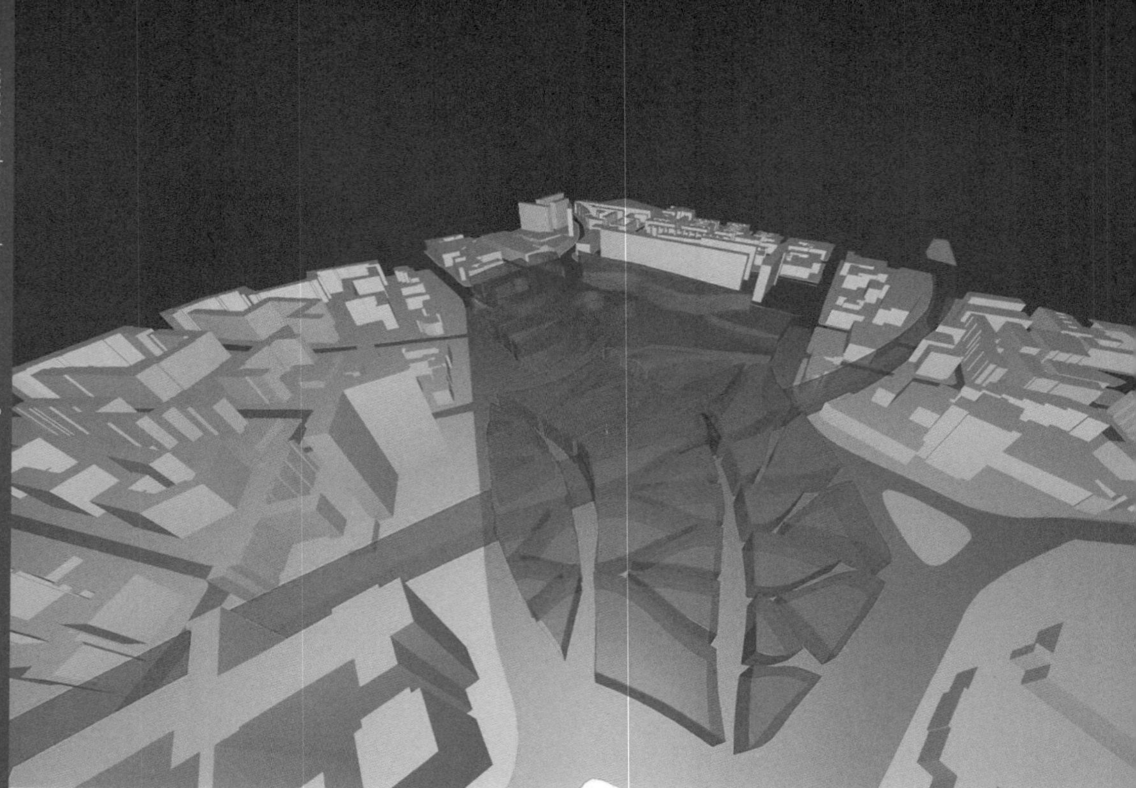

A key to the first stage work is traffic and parking generated by being on the boundary of the proposed 'congestion zone' for central London. By fragmenting, distributing, and linking the existing infrastructure, we create a field of interaction to increase the activity in the intensive and extensive thoroughfares. We develop a study of appropriation of sites out of which evolves a secondary structure of shortcuts and a set of urban rules. The different site areas created can be developed according to the interests of the private and public sector.

easy to notice that this network is as important at the local scale as transport is at the district and metropolitan scales, what is often missed is that the performance of the two are intimately interconnected. At the Elephant & Castle, for example, neither the significant expansion of the transport infrastructure nor the development of a major interchange command attention without a concomitant development of local flows. Many of our teams this year approached the two issues as part of a linked infrastructural strategy. In this way, public space ceases to be simply a static domain for expressing personal difference, as it is so often described in urban literature, and instead becomes an occasion for action and decision.

Scaling the Response

Proposals for the redevelopment of the inner periphery tend to be pursued as large, integrated projects. In London, this has been the experience at Docklands, Paddington Basin, Kings Cross, and with Southwark Land Regeneration's recent proposals for the Elephant & Castle. There is a noticeable reluctance to invest in the inner periphery at all until there is a clear promise of coordinated development of a critical mass. This inherent tendency in the urban land market is exacerbated by the long-standing instruments and policies of urban renewal: the decision to invest depends on large-scale governmental commitment to the transformation of the area. This pattern has pushed commercial development of the inner periphery toward ever larger projects with faster programmes of change. The difficulty this poses for strategic planning is that the long-term spatial and economic patterns of an area are suddenly subjected to dramatic upheaval, with less predictable results than either local government or developers would wish. In this way the operation becomes rather speculative, rendering the decision-making process unwieldy. It is this problem which stands behind the recent breakdown of the proposals for the Elephant & Castle, postponing once again meaningful and necessary improvements for the area. The major projects that have gone ahead, however, have often lacked imagination and flexibility, substituting standard typologies and secure programming for innovative responses to complex conditions. While satisfying the desire of developers and local governments for sufficiently predictable outcomes, this rarely presents a forward-looking response to local complexities. For these reasons, our project work has pursued a line of reasoning which values ongoing diagnosis and flexibility in the context of far-reaching plans and strategies.

The Design Seminar

Research themes for the Design Seminar are the concepts of renewal, restructuring and regeneration; the values of 'public' or social spaces and questions of their scale and design; the issues around density and mix of uses which have currently resurfaced as the 'compact city' debate in Europe; and the recent questioning of divisions between domestic and work space. These themes all have spatial, social and political dimensions, requiring complex responses.

The main work of the Design Seminar was in London, a city which illustrates very powerfully in its debates and its physical projects the forces at work in urban change. The work focused on the issue of large-scale redevelopment, based on proposals for the Elephant & Castle area. This, together with a shorter project in Spitalfields, allowed us to explore the dynamics of urban change at different scales, and the potential of architectural and urban design in such situations.

Spitalfields: Central and Marginal? (Term 1)

Through the disputed site of Spitalfields Market, a few minutes' walk from the Bank of England but in an area with a long history of poverty and marginalisation, we explored the forces of change and the conflicting needs of inner-city redevelopment. Groups made proposals for the site that were both design and policy responses to the needs of the area and its urban landscape. They explored the tensions between the formal and the informal uses of space, between the needs and interests of rich and poor citizens, and between the existing buildings and spaces and the demand for new uses and built space. This was a joint design workshop with Diploma Unit 10.

Elephant & Castle (Terms 1 & 2)

The main work this year has focused on the Elephant & Castle in South London, long neglected as a 'poor relation' of North London. The current proposals for its regeneration illustrated for us key questions about the scale and programme of such projects, and about who will benefit from the complex changes they produce. The recent breakdown of negotiations between the local government (the major land-owner) and their preferred developer demonstrates the fragile nature of such necessary collaborations. The local government must safeguard public assets and produce widespread benefits, but needs (and is encouraged by current government policy) to collaborate with private investors who have the necessary skills and finances to undertake such large projects. The aims of the two parties may not be

Spitalfields Brewery site – part of a network of restructured spaces.

This project aims to benefit the local population and regenerate the Heygate area by using its strategic position in relation to the transport network system in the city of London as the 'propeller' of change. Interpreting the existing conditions of the site to generate a new landscape guided by desire lines, in relation to social interaction, degrees of appropriations, degrees of privacy, human scale, phasing, permeability, mobility and connectivity.

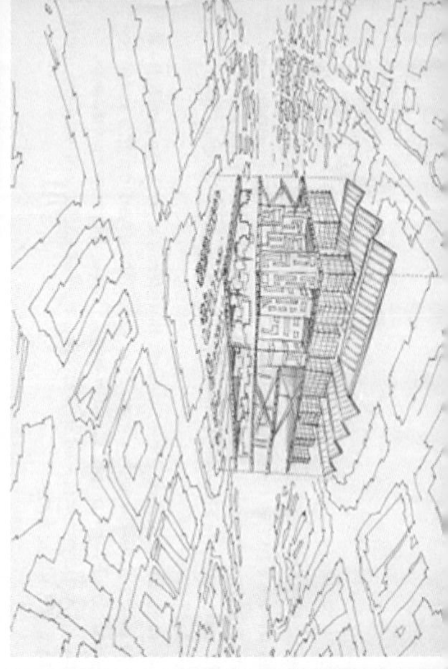

Spitalfields Market and Brewery: a network of restructured spaces.

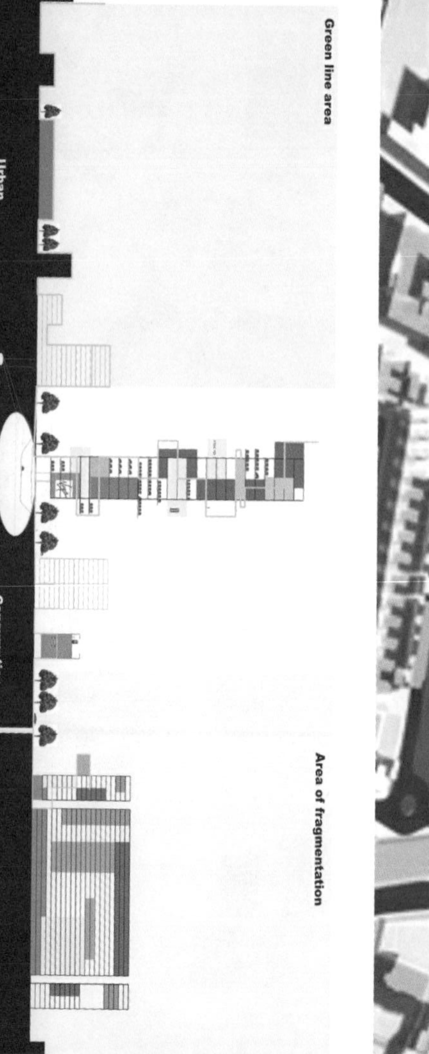

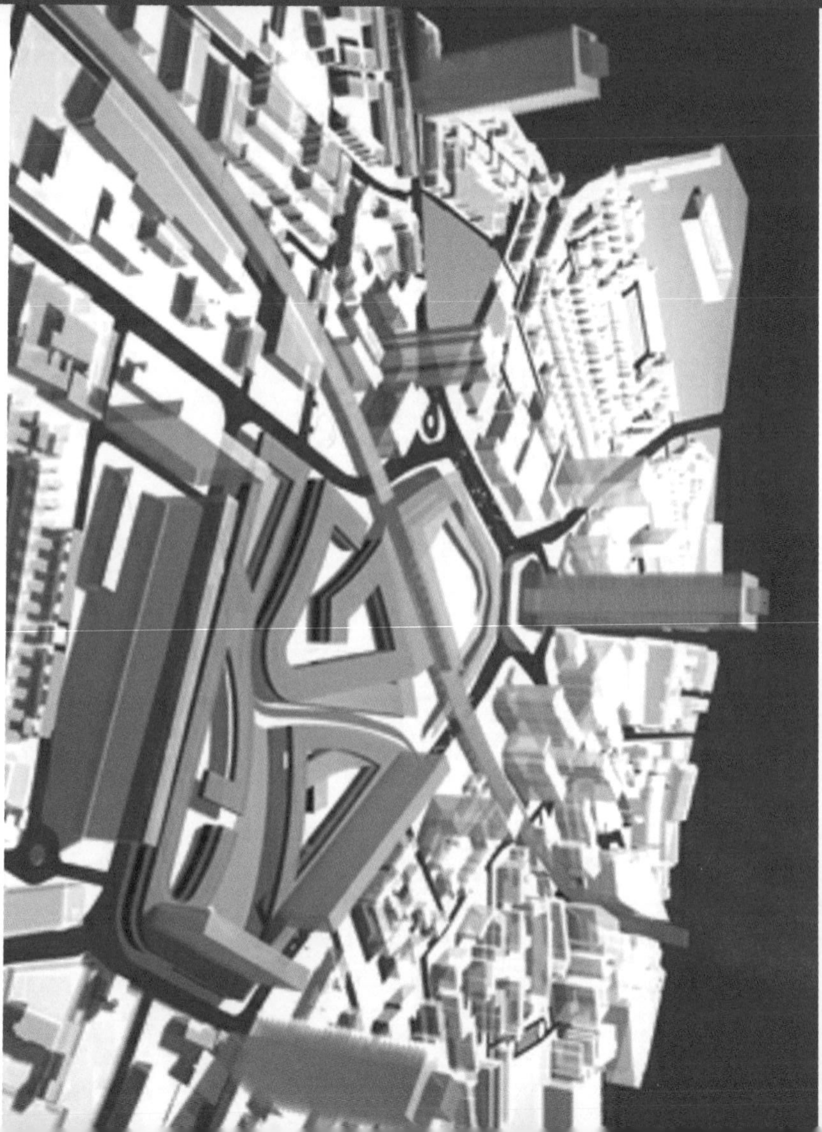

always contradictory, but the models adopted in terms of strategy and design are often crude.

Our awareness of this real-time negotiation led to questions about who should initiate change and how; who controls the process; who is investing what, and what risks the different actors are taking. What might be other appropriate strategies for 'regeneration' of the area in terms of process, programme and design? We researched the background and tested emerging ideas through discussions with the planning team of Southwark Council and the urban planner working for the Community Forum.

As our teams' proposals developed we organised an intensive workshop with Professor Joan Busquets from Barcelona. This focused on strategies and time-frames for change, and on issues of quality and impact (where do you spend the first £1 million?), as well as on the meaning and values of public space.

Mexico Workshop

A different focus on methods of intervention was investigated in a two-week design workshop in Mexico City, in collaboration with the School of Architecture of the Universidad Iberoamericana. The workshop examined issues of densification and inner-city housing provision where significant population loss in the central city, and the opportunities offered by old industrial sites, raise the possibility of a redevelopment providing major new housing and integrating a fragmented area of the city.

Netherlands Workshop

There is much interest in the recent housing and urban projects in the Netherlands and we spent a week in Amsterdam, Rotterdam and Groningen, visiting many projects and meeting architects and urbanists.

For more details of Design Seminar project work visit the H&U website: www.aaschool.ac.uk/hu

Staff
Jorge Fiori
Larry Barth
Nicholas Bullock
Hugo Hinsley
Irénée Scalbert

Visiting Staff
Joan Busquets
Chris Moller
Dominic Papa
Ed Robbins
Carlos Villaneuva Brandt

Contributors
Jon Abbott
Katharina Borsi
Michael Hensel
Elizabeth Lebas
Emilio Martinez de Valasco
Michael Parkes
Peter Thomas
John Turner
Ruysdael Vivanco de Gyves

MA Students
César Bernardes-Wagner
Santiago Calva-Maisterrena
David Enrique Cordoba
Manuel Figueroa
Galia Galili
Rita Graca
Stephan Matthias Kehrer
Maura Rogers
Toru Saeki
Massimo Santanicchia
Samuel Thoma
Holta Turku
Kathleen Van de Werf
Bin Wang
Cristian Wittig
Li-Hsuen Yeh
Hong Yin
Kirill Zavrajine

Research Students
Ludwig Abache
Wafa Al-Ghatam
Claudio Fodrigo Araneda
Marco Bianconi
Jose Brandao
Pedro Ressano Garcia
Sarah Morgan
Elena Pascolo
Gerardo Puente
Paulo Rizzo
Komson Teeraparbwong
Jose Zavala

Claudia Pasquero & Marco Poletto
Site analysis for library project on Tourel site, Lisbon
(see 'Magical Skin' Project)

The AA Graduate School's MA, MPhil and PhD programmes in Environment & Energy Studies explore the issues of sustainable environmental design at the levels of the city and the individual building. The one-year MA programme introduces environmental criteria as parameters in building and urban design, provides knowledge and skills for lessening dependence on nonrenewable energy and combines training in environmental research with field studies and building design projects. The MPhil and PhD programmes combine taught components with advanced research projects over two and three years respectively.

Principles

We define sustainable environmental design as the technic (perhaps, increasingly, a 'techne') for achieving thermal and visual comfort in buildings and outdoors by modulating nature's energy sources and sinks by means of architecture. Described in many textbooks, the fundamental principles may appear simple, but the underlying physical processes are complex. More important, the temporal interactions between occupants, building and environment are counterintuitive, as well as difficult to predict. In architectural design, the starting point for any environmental consideration must be the building programme, in particular the function and occupancy of individual spaces. From these we determine the environmental conditions that will suit the activities envisaged, as well as the rate of internal heat generation, which will have such a strong effect on the building's comfort conditions and energy requirements. Occupancy, activity, location and time are critical factors for the environmental performance of buildings and urban spaces. They are not yet widely seen as such, which is why close scrutiny of most major new buildings that claim to be environmentally friendly shows large discrepancies between expectations and the built reality. In city centres, wide microclimatic differences and discontinuities in the urban fabric further accentuate such discrepancies. The development of an environmentally sustainable architecture now depends on three complementary faculties, which we name as cognitive, experiential and analytic. The cognitive faculty is that which allows us to translate environmental principles into architectural concepts and forms; the experiential is informed by direct observation and measurements in occupied spaces; and the analytic provides the means for predicting a building's likely environmental performance at the design stage and later, for comparing prediction with reality. Jointly, these three faculties will produce an informed environmental intuition on which to base design decisions. Without them, it is easy to fall for the wrong models. An environmentally sustainable architecture can hardly be taken for granted or plucked off the shelf; it is an evolving concept that has to be redefined and reassessed each time.

MA Programme 01-02

Following from these premisses, the MA programme has combined lecture courses on the theories, principles, tools and practice of sustainable environmental design with cross-course projects and workshops. This year's first-term project focused on studies of recent London buildings and open spaces. The project aimed to develop students' observational skills and ability to ask and answer questions using the knowledge, scientific instruments and analytic tools provided by the taught programme. This was supplemented by theoretical essays and technical studies on related topics. In the course of a study trip to Lisbon in early January, three sites were selected for our second-term project, which focused on the development of a variety of building programmes and design proposals around the theme of a 'magical skin'. At the beginning of the third term, MA students presented their proposals for dissertation projects that will be continued over the summer, for submission in September 2002. Presentations on current and recent MA and PhD projects were given this year at the Technical University of Lisbon, and at the PLEA 2001 and 2002 international conferences.

Gonzalo Echarri & Juan Carlos Sanabria
Peckham Library: Ventilation paths based on stack effect and site wind conditions; axonometric shows proposals for improving daylighting in the building.

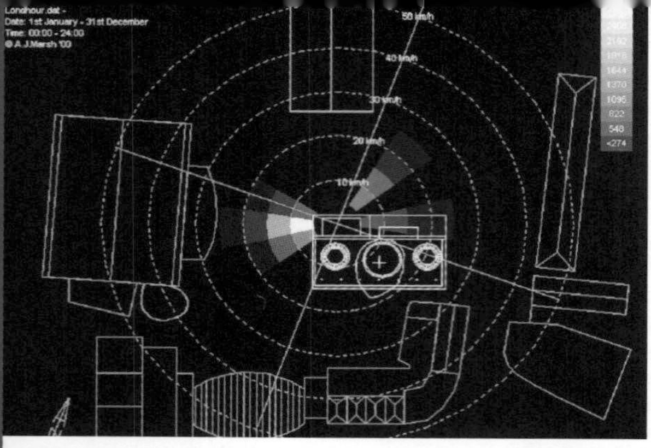

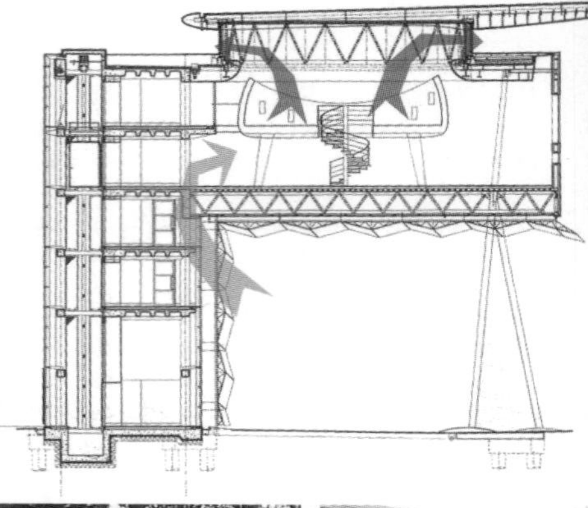

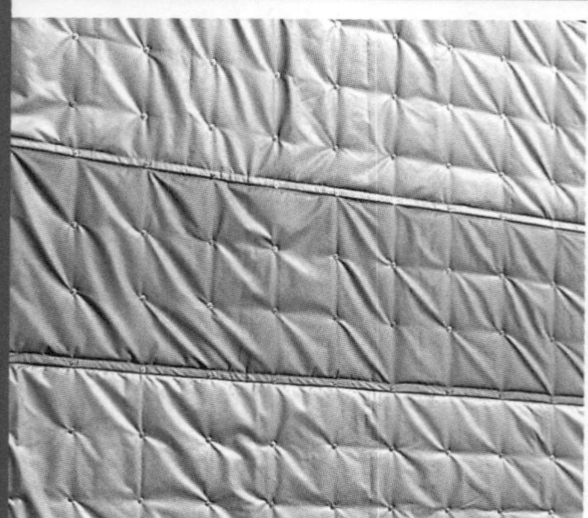

MA Dissertation Projects

Hector Altamirano-Medina Feasibility of Improving the Thermal Performance of Social Housing in Chile
Konstantinos-Thorvald Barlas Environmental Retrofitting of the Urban Block in the Contemporary Greek City
Alexandre Blouin A Sustainable Prefabricated House for the Southeastern Canadian Climate
Gonzalo Echarri Nighttime Cooling Effect and Complementary Cooling Strategies for the Climate of Madrid
David Goldman Relocatable Classrooms
Alice Hsieh Dynamic Wind Towers in the Urban Microclimate
Sophia Karagiannaki The Present and the Past: Retrofitting a Listed Residential Building in Athens
Lara Martins Recycling
George Papagiannopoulos Passive Downdraught Evaporative Cooling: Experiment and Application in Greece
Claudia Pasquero The Time Variable on Organic-Inorganic Systems: How Building Typologies Can Evolve
Marco Poletto Computer Modelling of Space Evolution Under the Influence of Environmental Variables
Ignacio Riutort Rossello Interaction Between the Natural and the Built
Juan Carlos Sanabria Small-Scale Housing Prototype for the Climates of Costa Rica
Ruben Sepulveda Chapa Climate-Responsive Improvements to Social Housing in Monterrey
Yasemin Somuncu The Educational Role of Buildings in Energy and Environment Issues: A Case Study in Turkey

PhD Projects

Dulce Marques de Almeida Environmental Design Guidelines for Pedestrian Areas
Luciano Dutra Design Process and Environmental Information
Solange Goulart Thermal Inertia and Natural Ventilation
Benito Jimenez Alcala Environmental Aspects of Hispano-Islamic Architecture
Carlos Miranda The House: Energy Efficiency and Architectural Expression
Helena Massa Urban Aerodynamics
Raul Vilaça e Moura Thermal Comfort and Environmental Quality in Social Housing
Guilherme Quintino Environmental Aspects of Traditional Building Techniques in Southern Portugal
Abeer Shaheen Dynamic Visual Representation of Environmental Performance of Buildings with Special Reference to Bahrain
Joana Gonçalves Environmental Issues of Tall Buildings

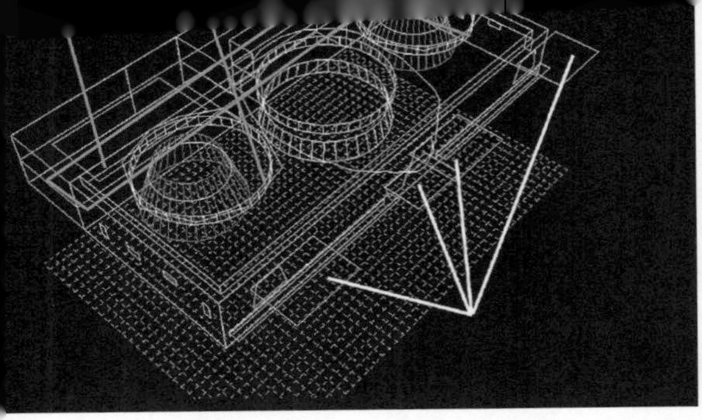

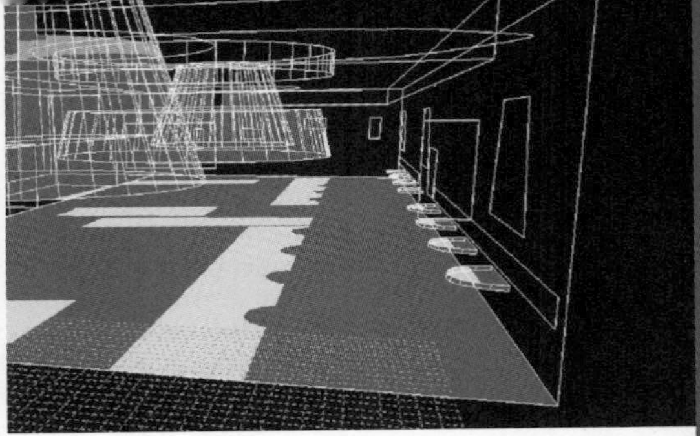

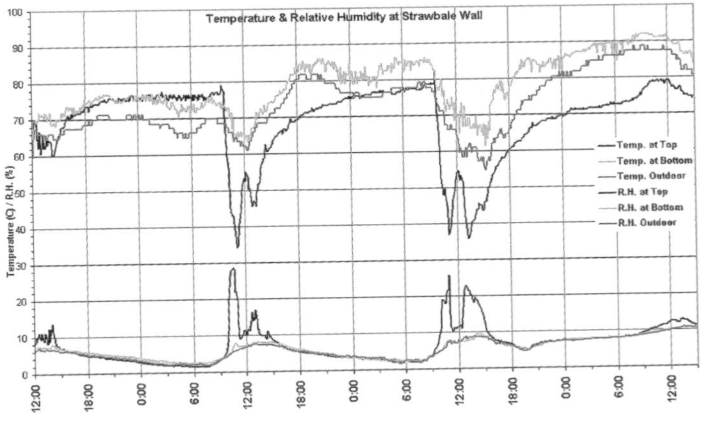

Alexandre Blouin & David Goldman
Architect's house and office, London: Materials used on building, installation of sensors into the air cavity of straw-bale wall, and temperatures and relative-humidity values showing warming and drying in wall.

Building Studies, Term 1

Using on-site observations and measurements, as well as comparative performance data and calculated results, this project provided training in the undertaking of a critical appraisal of the environmental design attributes of contemporary buildings. The seven London schemes selected by the student teams this year included an architect's office and house, a university campus, a public library, a riverside open space between two buildings, a secondary school and a large residential complex. The selected buildings formed the basis of a series of investigations driven by testable hypotheses arising from site analysis and fieldwork. Work on this project was in teams of two or three students.

The 'Magical Skin' Project, Lisbon, Term 2

The second-term project provided a vehicle for applying the knowledge and tools introduced by the taught programme to a building design programme in an urban context. The project brief called for a mixed-use building on one of three sites visited in Lisbon during January. The formulation of functional and environmental design requirements formed part of the project. Lisbon has a mild climate and plentiful supply of sun, wind, water, vegetation and other natural resources. One key aim of the project was to invent a 'magical skin' to exploit these resources and make the proposed buildings independent of nonrenewable energy. Development of this magical skin required exploring the interdependence of programmatic and environmental objectives, the specificities of climate and site, the environmental attributes of building form, the properties of building materials and the potential of renewable energy technologies. Students were expected to draw upon historical or contemporary precedents, as well as use appropriate analytic tools to test design hypotheses and inform design decisions. Fourteen schemes were developed for three different Lisbon sites; a few of these are briefly illustrated here. The building programmes chosen varied from leisure, sports and ecological parks on the Tourel site (a green hilly patch) to art workshops and galleries, residential units and offices on the Alecrim site (a long, narrow central site) and commercial development for Praça Espanha (a large, noisy intersection).

Claudia Pasquero & Marco Poletto
Proposals for urban park and leisure activities on Tourel site, Lisbon; topological analysis of environmental variables

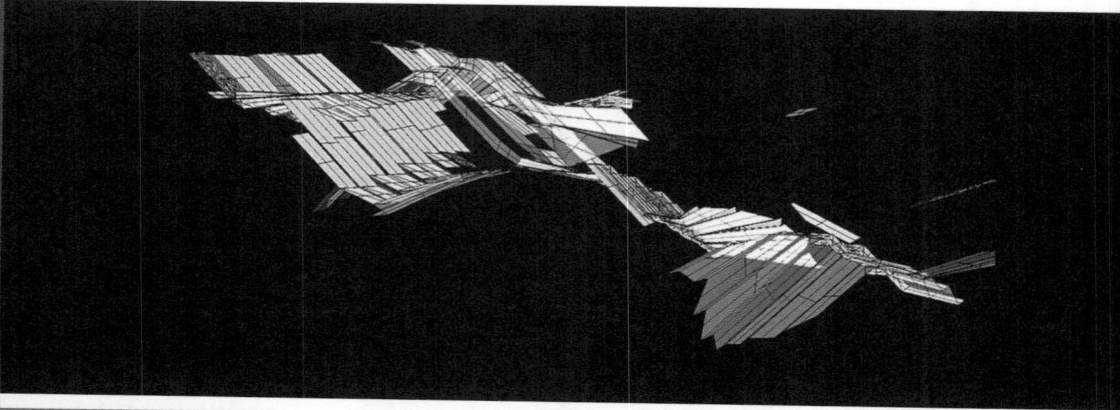

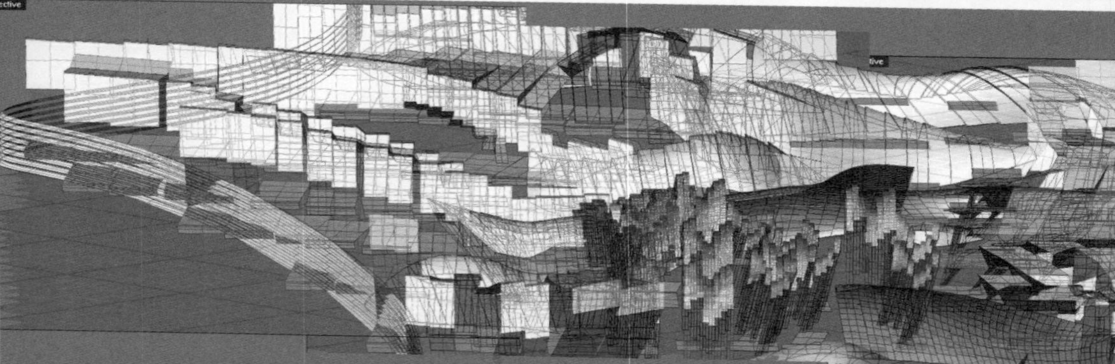

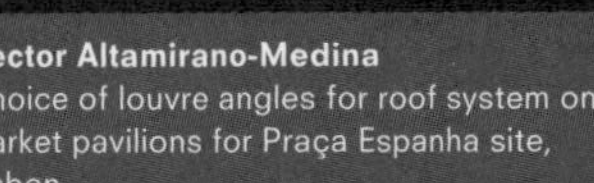

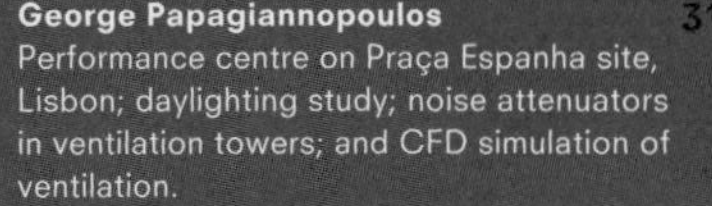

Hector Altamirano-Medina
Choice of louvre angles for roof system on market pavilions for Praça Espanha site, Lisbon.

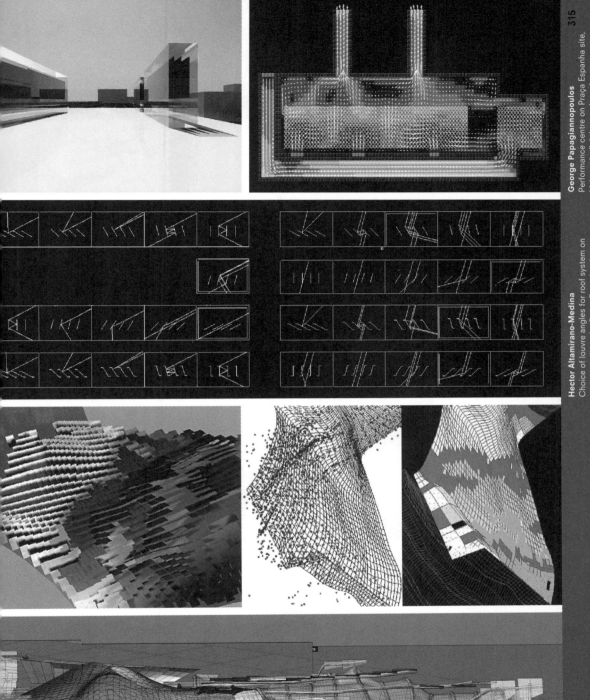

George Papagiannopoulos
Performance centre on Praça Espanha site, Lisbon; daylighting study; noise attenuators in ventilation towers; and CFD simulation of ventilation.

Alexandre Blouin
Office development for Praça Espanha site, Lisbon; section and details of double envelope and vegetal screen on western elevation.

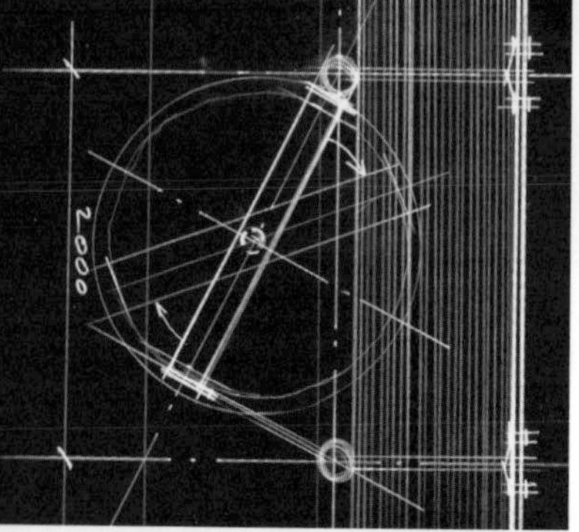

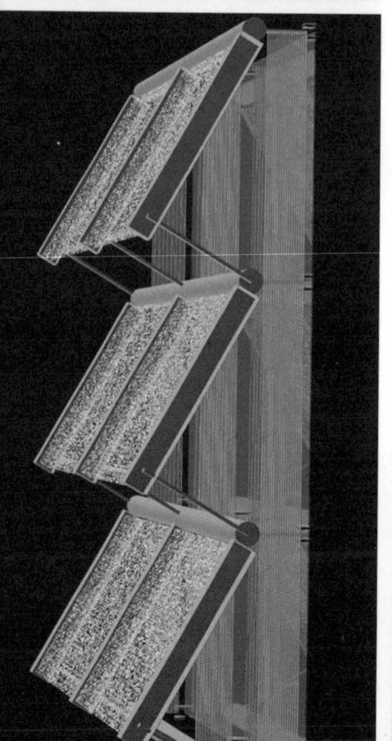

Ignacio Riutort Rossello
Proposals for an ecopark on Tourel site, Lisbon.

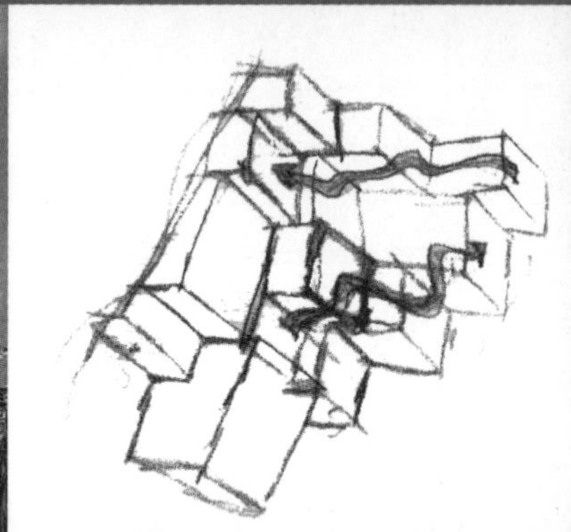

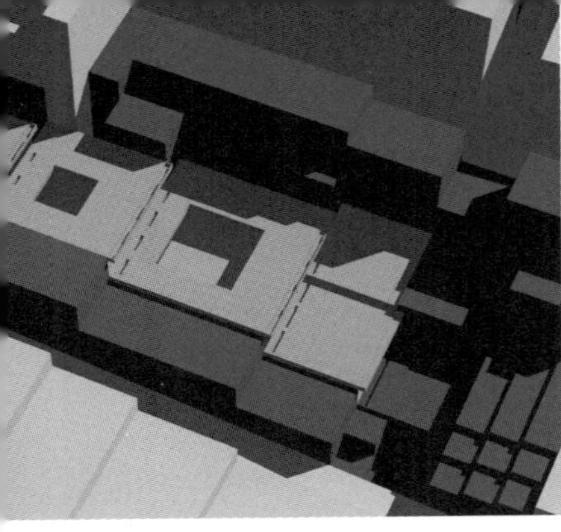

David Goldman
Evolution of proposal for an arts cßentre on Alecrim site, Lisbon.

Staff
Simos Yannas
Susannah Hagan
Peter Sharratt

Visiting Lecturers and Critics
Jane Anderson
Peter Beard
Matthew Brundle
Peter Chlapowski
Mariano Ciccone
Richard Cochrane
Mario Cucinella
Brian Ford
Catherine Harrington
Mark Hewitt
Ben Humphries
Andrew Marsh
Ciro Najle
Cristiana Paoletti
Jean-François Roger France
Derek Taylor
David Turrent
Andre Viljoen
Mike Weinstock
Marc Zanchetta

External Examiner MA
Phillip Jones

Research Assistant
Georgios Skourtis

London Building Studies
Will Alsop Architects
Ove Arup & Partners
Battle McCarthy
Edward Cullinan
Foster & Partners
Whitby Bird & Partners
Sarah Wigglesworth and Jeremy Till

UK Study Trips
Bill Dunster Architects
BEDZED
Proctor Matthews
Greenwich Millennium Village
Nick Martin & Nick White
Hockerton Housing Project
Jenny Kirby and Terry Dix
Arup Campus, Solihull
James Fisher, BRE
Building 16
Caroline Rock
Lanchester Library
Bennetts Assocs & Lou Carroll, Powergen HQ

Lisbon and 'Magical Skin' Project
Rui Barreiros Duarte
Klaus Bode
Duarte Cabral de Mello
Paula Cadima
Maria Clara Mendes
Raul Moura
Jorge de Novais Bastos
Jorge Ribeiro
Luis Rosmaninho

Students

MA
Hector Altamirano-Medina
Konstantinos-Thorvald Barlas
Alexandre Blouin
Gonzalo Echarri
David Goldman
Alice Hsieh
Sophia Karagiannaki
Lara Martins
George Papagiannopoulos
Claudia Pasquero
Marco Poletto
Ignacio Riutort Rossello
Juan Carlos Sanabria
Ruben Sepulveda Chapa
Yasemin Somuncu

PhD
Benito Jiménez Alcalá
Dulce Marques De Almeida
Luciano Dutra
Joana Gonçalves
Solange Goulart
Helena Massa
Carlos Miranda
Raul Moura
Gui Quintino
Abeer Shaheen

Course Staff
Patrik Schumacher (Course Director)
Brett Steele (Course Director)
Tom Verebes (Course Master)
Christopher Hight (Course Tutor)

Guest Critics

Phase I
Ove Arup BG 4
Tom Barker
John Bell
Eva Castro
Steve Hardy
Mark Hemel
Michael Hensel
Jenny Jones
Theo Lorenz
George Liaropoulos-Legendre
Jonas Lundberg
Detlef Mertins
Ciro Najle
Andreas Raptopoulos
Lindy Roy
Natasha Sandmeier
Stephan Silver
Lars Spuybroek
Jeff Turko
Mike Weinstock

Phase II
Andrew Benjamin
Ben Van Berkel
Mark Cousins
Marcelyn Gow
Bob Lang
Martine de Maeseneer
Frederic Migayrou
Chris Perry

External Examiner
John Worthington DEGW

Workshop Tutors & Assistance
Dirk Anderson Modelling, Scripting
Nicola Bailey & AA Print Studio Documents
Sue Barr Darkroom
Andrew Benjamin Diagrams
Valerie Bennett Photography
Matthew Bielecki Network
Christian Bodhi 3D Web
Clement Chung Scheduling
Pete Gomes Wireless Networks
Marcelyn Gow, Chris Perry & Oliver Bertram Elastic Archive
Marcellus Letang CNC
Margaret Marshall Coordination
Joel Newman Video
Felix Robbins Modelling, Scripting
Thilu Schmutat Maya v. 4.0

Engineering Tutors
Tom Barker Materials & Structures
Bob Lang & Ove Arup BG4 Structures

Phase I Research Teams
5subzero:
Delphine Ammann Switzerland
Karim Mualem Lebanon
Robert Neumayr Austria
Georgina Robledo Mexico
b.SHOPPING.net by vorTEX
Naina Gupta India
Kazuyuki Nagasawa Japan
Manuel Vizcaino Mexico
d_RIVE:
Michael Davis NZ
Steven Hatzellis Australia
Anat Stern Israel
EF.Fields:
Florian Busch Germany
Wissam Mansour Lebanon
Electra Milkelides UK
Pim Van Wylick NL
HC2O:
Chiao-Ming Chen China
Yu-Hua Chung Taiwan
Xiao-Jiang Huang China
Sherman Ou Canada
Leisur.ATOR:
Nilufer Kozikoglu Turkey
Marco Pastore Italy
Valentina Sabatelli Italy
Pablo Velazquez Mexico
MUMA by Log.0:
Muge Belek Turkey
Frederico Fialho Portugal
Felipe Loayaza Ecuador
Jaime Noriega Peru
PCSC:
Alexander Britt Switzerland
Zhao Lan China
Lucia Pflucker Peru
Yu Yu China
PINKTRAP
Mirco Becker Germany
Siriyot Chiamnuay Thailand
Ramon Gomez Mexico
Maria Jose Mendoza Mex
SOHOtel:
Jens Borstelmann Germany
Yosuke Hayano Japan
Simon Kim Canada
Cyril Shing China
transFOUR:
Niraj Doshi India
Vladimir Kalinowski Peru
Abraham Koshy India
Spiros Papadimitriou Greece

Phase II THESIS Teams
Emergen-C:
Christiane Fashek USA
Margarita Flores Mexico
Cesare Griffa Italy
Yasha Grobman Israel
Yanchuan Liu China
inter.ACTIVE.arch:
Byungwook Jeon S. Korea
Sophia Park S. Korea
Yi-Chang Tsai Taiwan
Jiann-Jyh Wu Taiwan
Camia Young USA
Network_Living:
Fillip Innocenti Italy
Zetta Kotsioni Greece
Debora Laub Brazil
Sarah Manning USA
Maurizio Meossi Italy
RAMTV:
Aljosa Dekleva Slovenia
Manuela Gatto Italy
Tina Gregoric Slovenia
Robert Sedlak Germany
Vasilis Stroumpakos Greece
Smart Strata:
Jeongsu Eun S Korea
Derek Renata Kawiti New Zealand
Jyong-Ki Min S Korea
Elke Stauber Germany
Urban_RE.sort:
C Fernando Perez Mexico
Marco Ortiz Perez Mexico
Marco A Velazquez Mexico
Cesar Villarreal Mexico
V_Living:
Alan Furlong Ireland
Paul Loh Malaysia
Lawrence Sassi USA
Lorenzo Viola Italy

Open Source Networks

The AADRL embraces the design potential inherent in today's widely distributed and networked ways of working and thinking about the forces currently reshaping architecture and urbanism.

All team-based design research in the AADRL is developed and then distributed across networks that are treated as essential design resources and not just the material memory of all current and past studio work. All projects and their related research are made accessible across these networks in the form of shared folders containing coursework and resources, data, diagrams, design documents, animations and videos. Individual participants within the AADRL maintain and update this resource, a model based on open-source, peer-to-peer-programming movements already transforming design cultures.

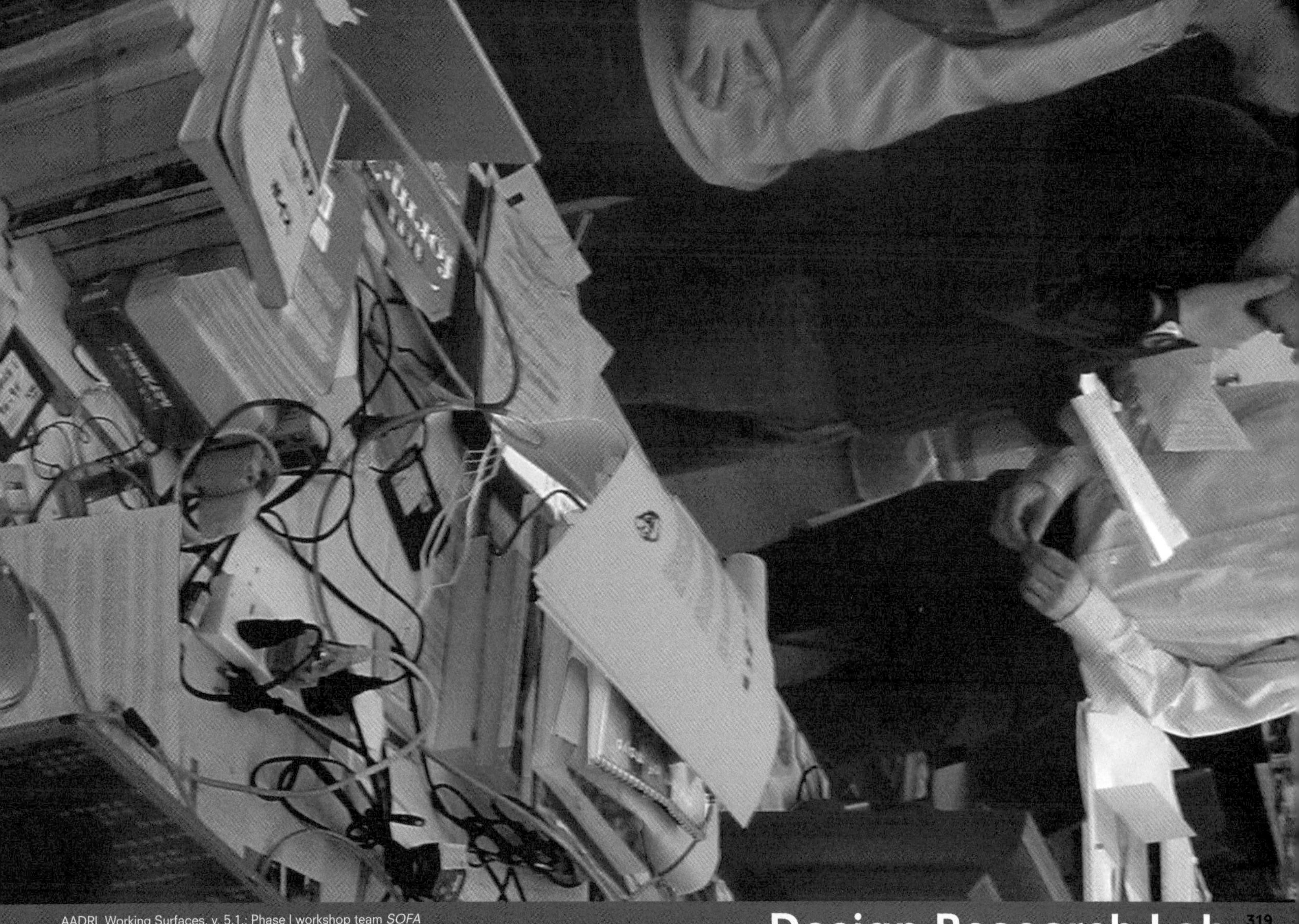

AADRL Working Surfaces, v. 5.1.: Phase I workshop team *SOFA* coordinating software installation

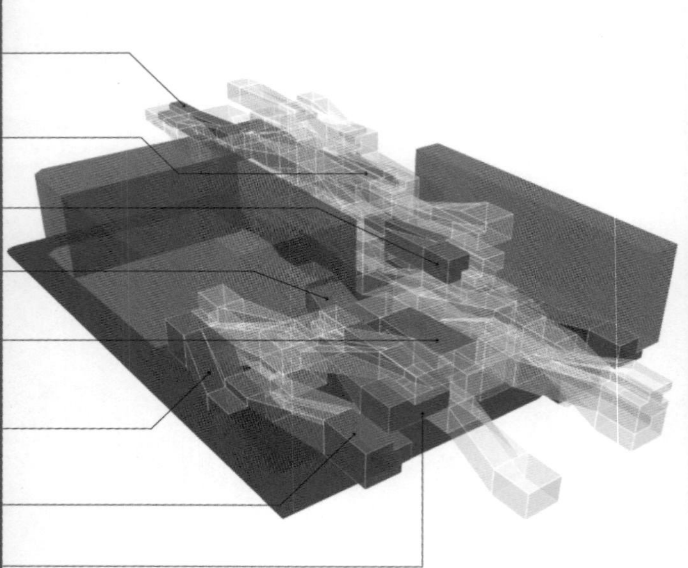

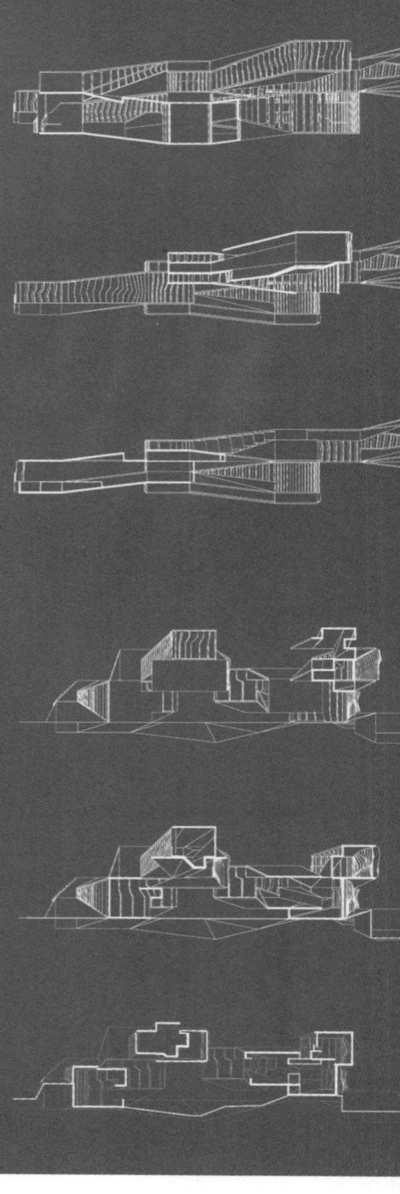

Phase II: Excerpts from final documentation of Level-3 Mass Customisation Strategies, Responsive Urban Housing proposal and Negotiate My Boundary, by RAMTV

Design as Research

The AADRL encourages the proliferation of emergent and distributed approaches to shared design tools, techniques and processes. This work demands clear, rigorous, systematic thinking, including the design of constraints within these processes able to limit, and so control, the outcomes of the design systems. Architecture is currently preoccupied with celebrity and signature styles. It's not entirely surprising that graduate design studios around the world continue to promote an endless invention of individual, idiosyncratic students. In such a world, professional identities and their artificial differences have created a kind of grotesque design excess, which the AADRL seeks to deflect by pursuing instead the design project as a form of open, accountable research.

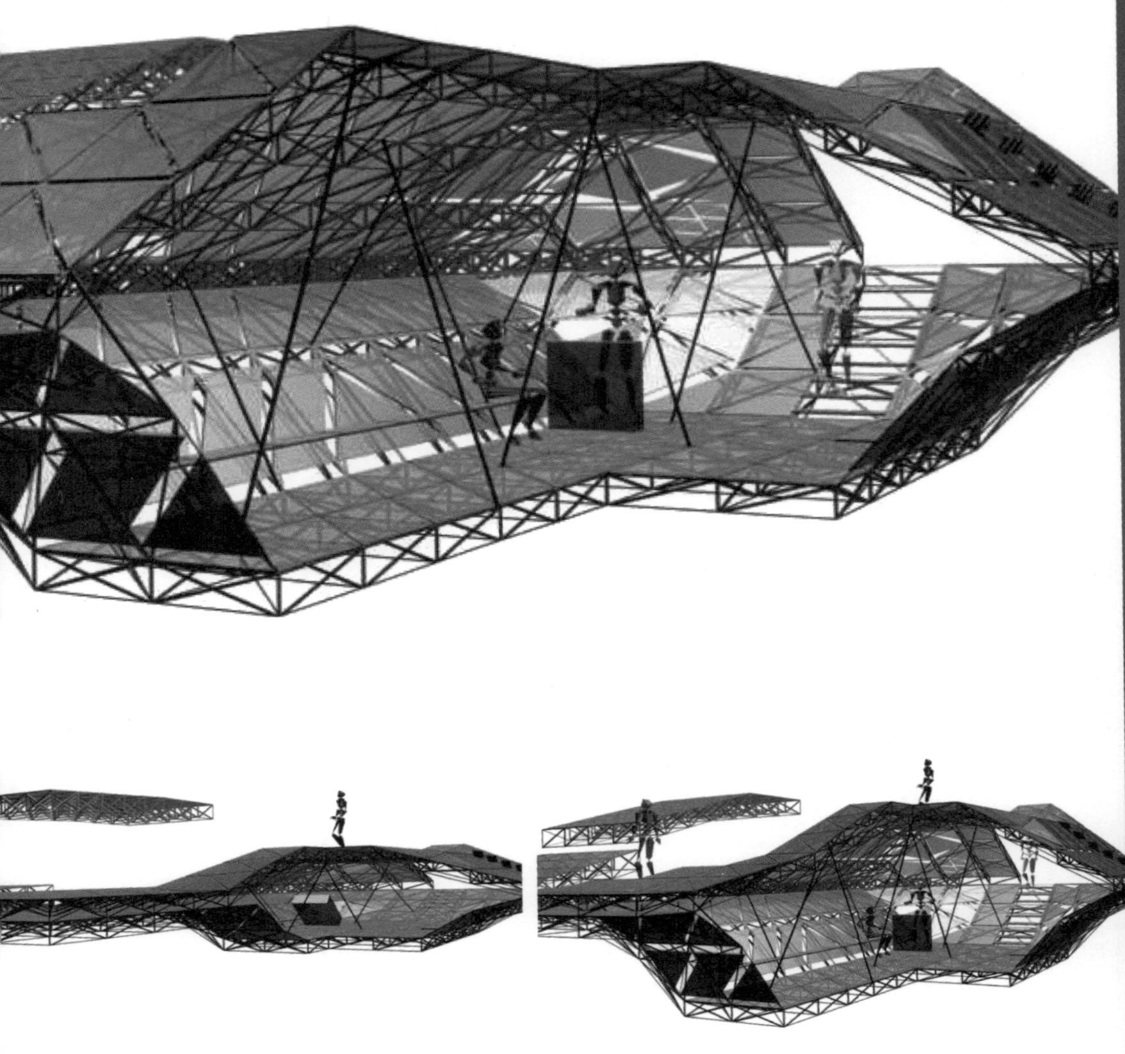

Responsive_Environments

This year the AADRL initated a new three-year agenda for its design studios, workshops and seminars, which will systematically investigate the ways in which architecture is able to provide intelligent interfaces connecting spaces, users and performance criteria. The potential for this connectivity challenges long-held assumptions about architectural materials as passive arrangements, bringing architecture closer to many other forms of information.

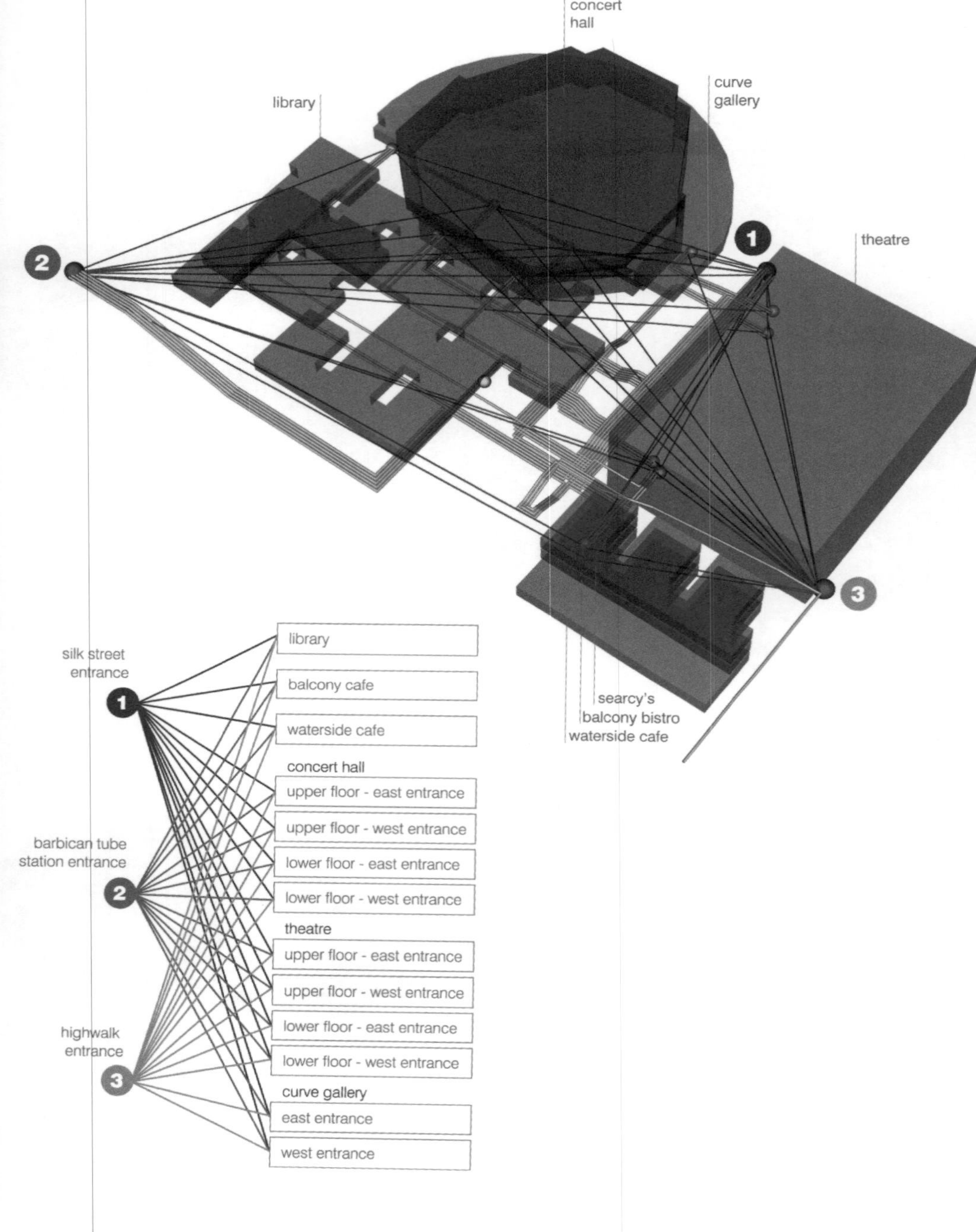

Adaptive Urban Surfaces: Animation stills from transegrity surface project by team *5subzero*, showing programmable, interactive floor structure installed within existing Barbican Centre lobby spaces

Parametric Scripts

The AADRL extended its work into networked design tools by focusing on a systematic introduction of scripting techniques prior to beginning any of the year's other research and projects. The rule-based, heuristic sensibilities of design processes approached this way emphasise, above all, iterative testing of design results in order to form working conclusions about how design outcomes relate to specific procedures and their parameters. In such a setting, design projects are not just necessary to test the research guiding their development: they are necessarily experimental.

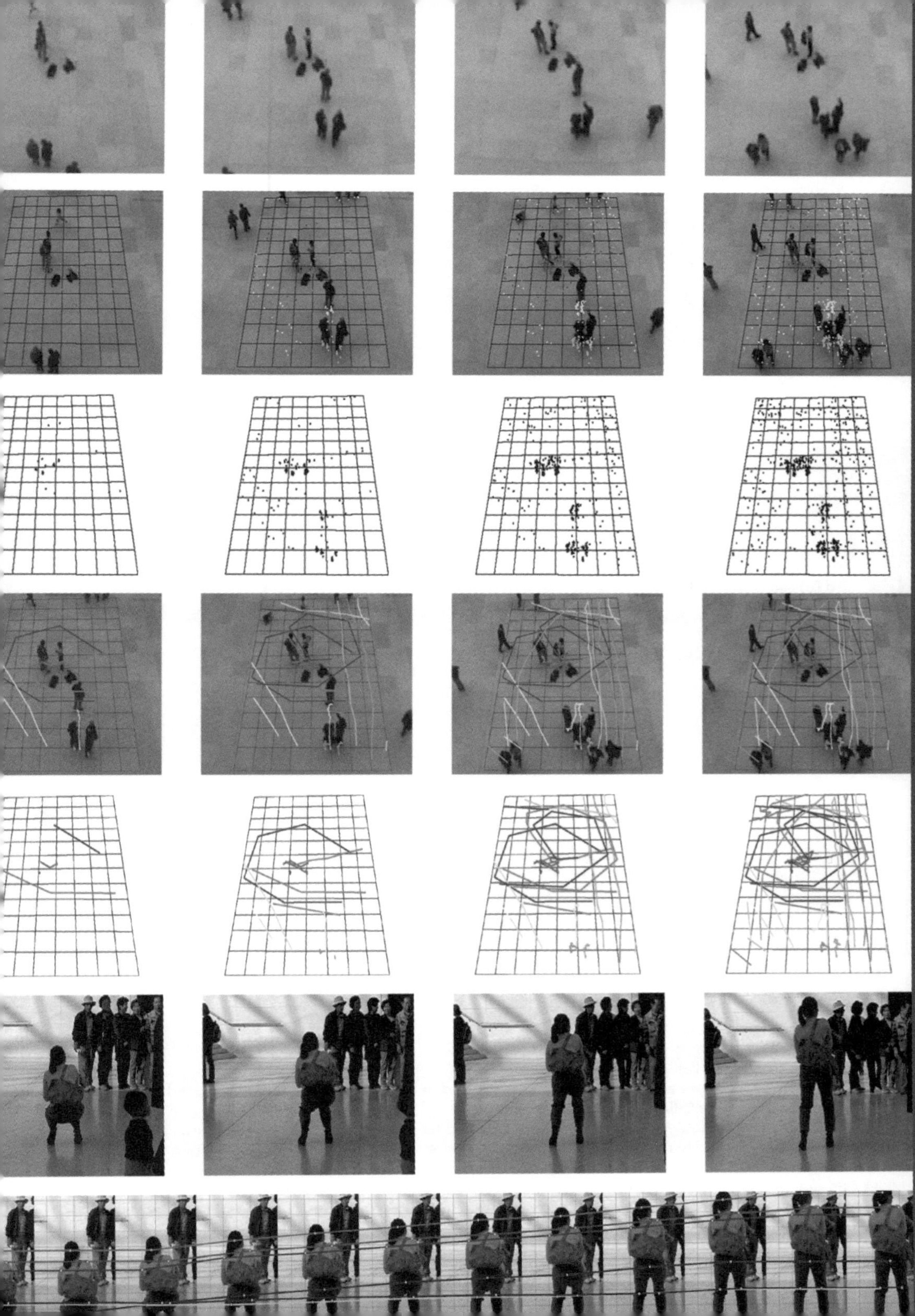

Data Structures, this page and bottom opposite: Interactive lobby prototypes and performance models – RoboCurtains. Opposite page, top: Elastic Archive workshop catalogue of configurations

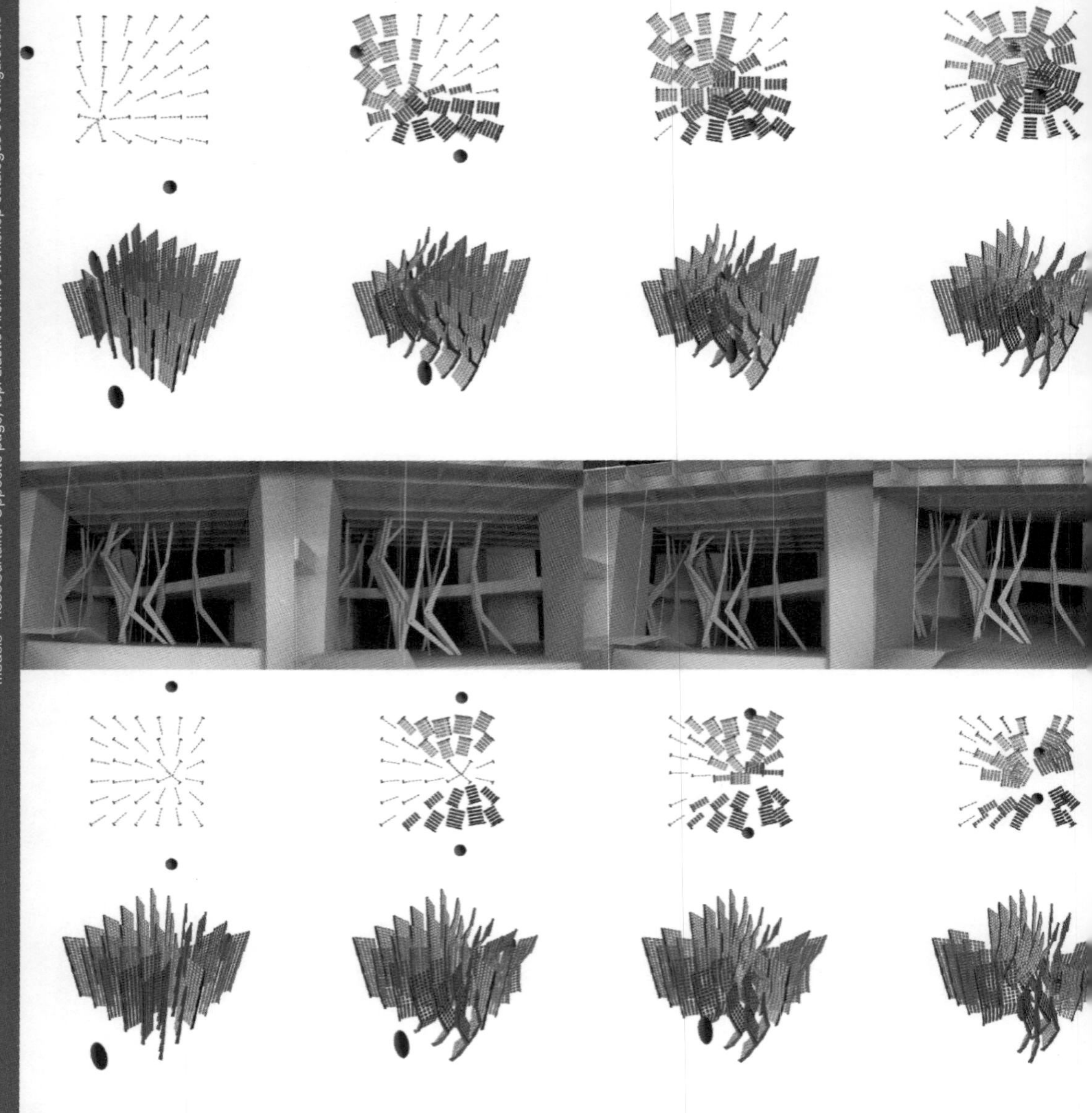

Machinic Installations

Arrays of switches, sensors and input devices embedded in otherwise dead building materials transform architectural space into intelligent operating systems.

These occupiable interfaces make it possible for architecture to anticipate and react to the habits guiding their use. This year's Phase I Studio Projects developed yearlong prototypes for such systems within the context of barren existing public spaces in London's Barbican Centre. The goal of this work has been to assemble prototype installations of intelligent, adaptive structures. Initial scripting formed the basis for further developmental models then pursued as larger, more complex buildings and structures, which are being carried forward in 2002-3 as exhibition installations in Athens, Italy, London and Graz, and as Phase II Thesis Projects that will be presented at the AA in January 2003.

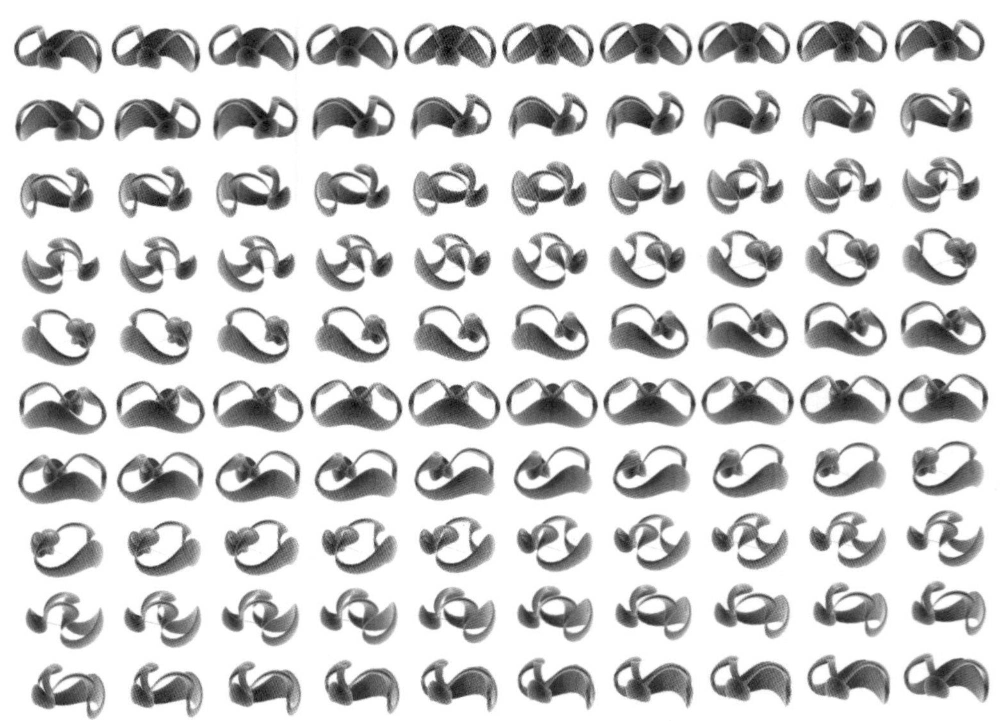

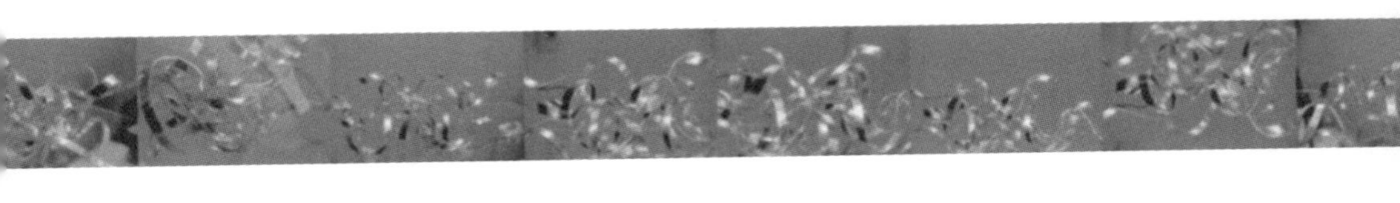

Serial Nano_Structures

This year's Phase II Thesis Projects extended research begun last year into the new forms of subatomic, highly integrated urbanism implied by smart-material microscales. These precisely controlled serial structures adapt to the forces and flows defining the city today, employing woven material frameworks that behave more like flexible nets than fixed, stiff structures. These meshes are able to accommodate programmatic changes as effectively as they can distribute three-dimensional structural forces. Like the research undertaken in workshops last year, structures like these were developed in the studio this year within multidisciplinary teams that included the AADRL's outside structural and new-material tutors.

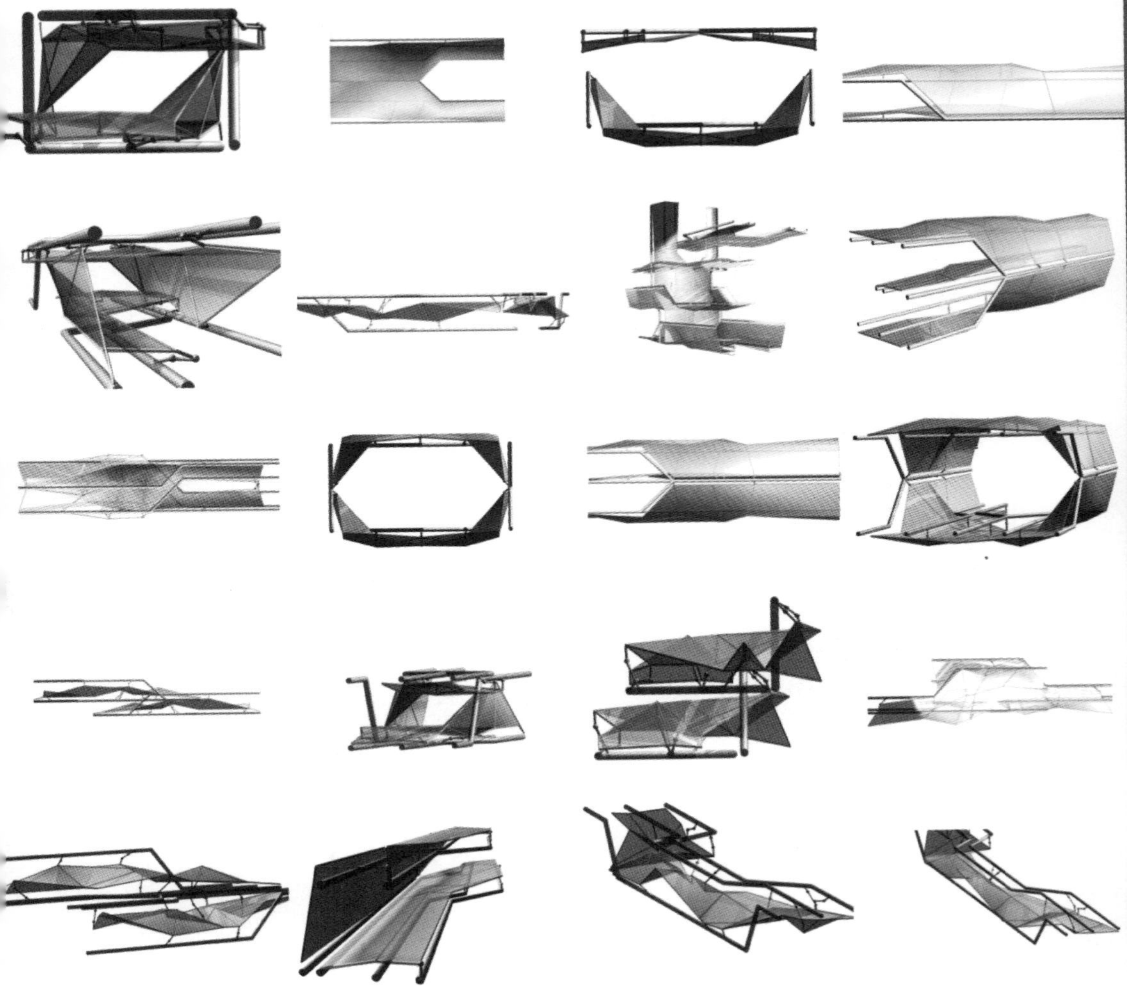

Information Modelling

Today's parametric software tools are able to record the performance and appearance of architectural space, a profound addition to modelling tools used to describe space.

These performative, informational models are the means by which architects can initialise design projects from the earliest stage as strategic alterations to, rather than arbitrary interventions within, existing spaces, sites and programmes. During Phase I, all AADRL projects begin life as extended diagramming exercises circulating between team members, which seek to capture the habits, flows and oscillations of our clients' sites, briefs and urban surroundings. These early exercises in data-mining and information-mapping promote the invention of tools and techniques then made available across the studio's networks for the projection of new forms of responsive, interactive, urban and architectural space.

Emergen-C Phase II Thesis Design Brand Gallery: Logo and image surface, aerial view

Interfaces as Infrastructures

Selected Phase I & II work carried forward recent AADRL projects addressing London's most aggressive forms of 'brand space', including the ways in which today's hypervisual branding strategies continue to radically transform architectural space into extensions of modern advertising's single greatest invention: brand-name recognition. Working with London-based companies like Virgin, Tate Bankside and Orange Mobile Telephones, AADRL teams first recorded information-based models of these companies' presence in urban spaces, and then transposed these diagrams into new kinds of active, highly strategic display structures.

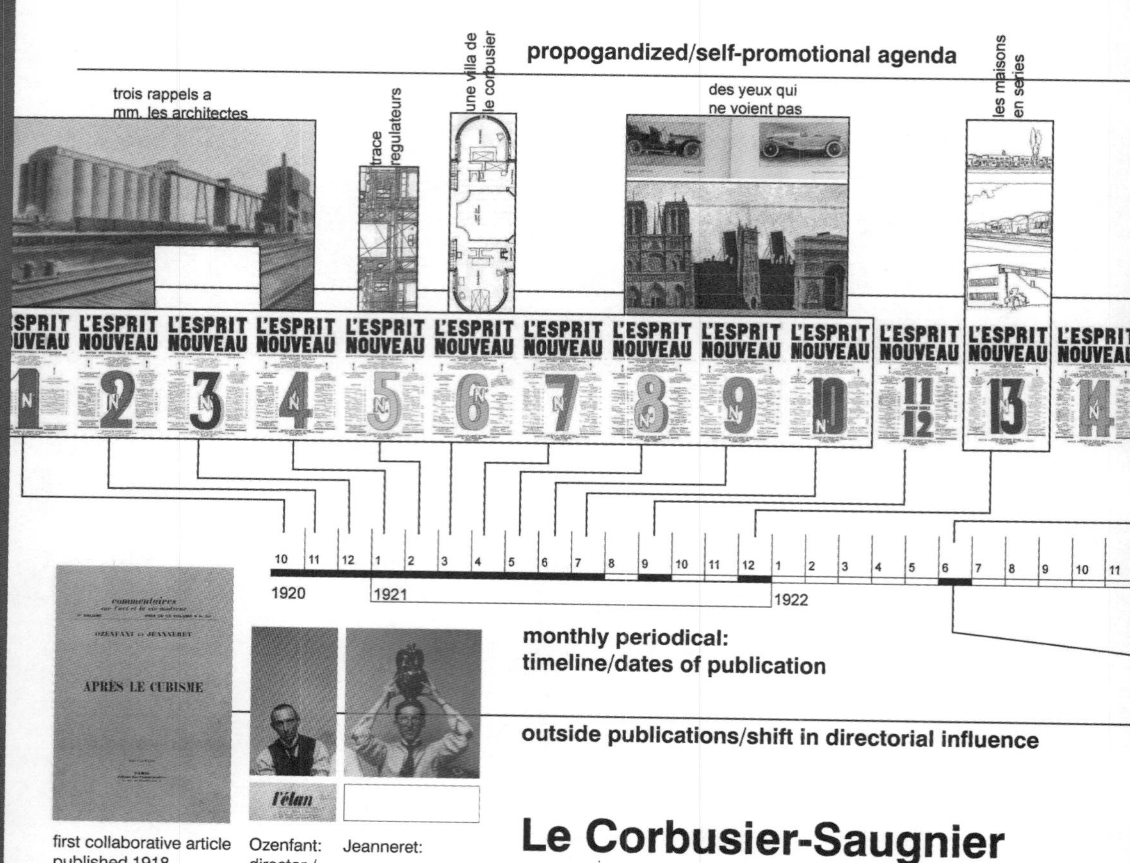

first collaborative article published 1918

Ozenfant: director / producer of L'Elan 1915-1916

Jeanneret:

Elastic Archive

This year a workshop led by Marcelyn Gow and Chris Perry, with the assistance of Oliver Bertram, used the AADRL's own network as the site for generating limited short-term design proposals. Scripted modelling applications were used to initialise group design processes that were then distributed across the network to team members, who undertook specialist tasks related to the projects and their online data structures. This form of production was also extended beyond the boundaries of the AADRL studio, and included CNC equipment in the AA Materials Workshop and stereo lithography model fabrication done in the United States in parallel with the development of the workshop projects on the studio's networks.

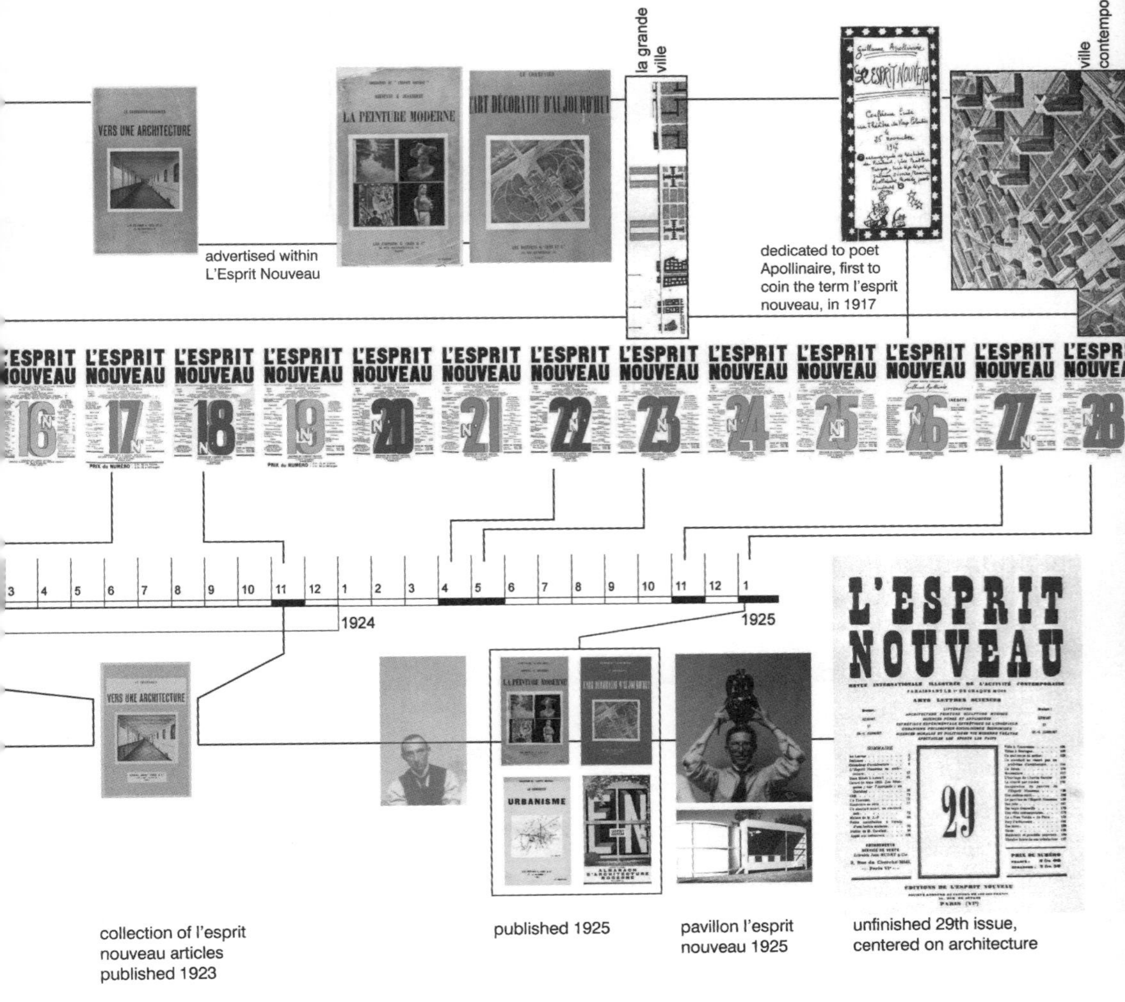

Monography v. 2.0: Diagramming Architectural Magazines

The AADRL's three-year Monography project focused on architectural magazines and the ways in which their serial spaces disseminate architectural projects, products or personalities.

Following last year's work on the monolithic singularity of ten influential twentieth-century monographs, this year's seminar, led by Brett Steele, studied the information structures of architectural periodicals whose serial patterns of change have long escaped historical or theoretical description. Beginning with early pioneers like L'Esprit Nouveau **or** De Stijl **and carrying forward through leading European or North American examples, including** Domus, Casabella, Perspect, Oppositions **and contemporary lifestyle magazines like** Wallpaper*, **case studies analysed their general influence on modern architectural discourses, examining content, contributors, design, appearance and circulation.**

Phase I Studio Session, this page: Urban.Resort interim tutorial meeting with T. Verebes. Phase II Thesis Design Project, opposite page: Team meeting and structurall modelling session

Self-Organizing Teams

The AADRL recognises and promotes the sort of unstable, contingent forms of production characterizing today's most-advanced design cultures. Just as these new forces have changed the way design professionals work, so too they challenge existing models of teaching and learning.

The AADRL treats these new realities as the genuine forces for the creation of new kinds of architectural projects as well as a new form of graduate design studio: one where its own organisational design embodies the topics, tools and techniques guiding its projects. The single central feature of the AADRL is its shared, team-based approach to all teaching and learning. This work is pursued deliberately and provokes its students to coherently link the cumulative results of their various studio, workshop and seminar courses in the form of a single, comprehensive design research project.

The Landscape Urbanism MA programme is a twelve-month studio-based course designed for students with prior academic and professional qualifications. Landscape Urbanism constitutes a collective endeavour to construct a new mode of practice where techniques and modes of operation historically described as landscape design can be integrated within the domain of urbanism. For urbanism, landscape offers a double opportunity: both to reframe urban problems and to recontextualise the practice in general. It introduces a context of immensity: a context so large that urban complexity is made simple. It introduces a varying context that can reframe urban problems contingently and that can be increasingly complexified. It introduces a temporal context based on non-physical determinations. It introduces an active context with a life of its own. It introduces a context that is at once pre-existent and simultaneous to an actual urban condition. These five contexts offer the conditions for a different perception and understanding of the temporal dimension in the logics of urban developments. But, beyond the simple recognition of these new logics, Landscape Urbanism seeks to engineer new operative capacities for the discipline through the exploration of adequate techniques, according to the corresponding contexts: multi-scalarity; cross-scalarity; pre-physicality; performativity; and intensive coexistence.

Landscape Urbanism also attempts to construct a practice that can overcome the persistent and still dominant segregation of domains of production, based on standardisation and repetition, independence or – at best – interdependence. Rather than accepting the conventional view of distinct fields of expertise, the practice of Landscape Urbanism contructs a system of abstract relations that bring together disparate areas of knowledge. In this system, where all relationships are intensive and malleable, time can be collapsed or expanded as if it were infinitely flexible and available. This overexpressive mode of operation is controllable only circumstantially and in principle; as a whole it is multidirectional and unpredictable. The landscape works as a metainfrastructural net, holding together disparate domains, fostering organisational interactions, destabilisations and consolidations, and grounding the generation of new urban materials.

Exhibition, AA Front Members' Room
February–March 2002

Final Review, AA Lecture Hall
September 2001

Coastlines

Landscape Urbanism establishes an annual research project on the management and development of European coastlines. Adopting a collaborative approach, we develop Generic Coastal Substrates through which to investigate methods, tools, strategies, tactics and technologies that aid the implementation of an Integrated Coastal Zone Management (ICZM) in Europe. Without segregating domains, a series of Action Plans are proposed to unfold the extensive scales of production potentially present in activities that are currently seen as mere environmental threats. Increasing natural resilience by artificially breeding new buffer capabilities into European coastal areas as a response to the increasing pressure of an urbanised population and in anticipation of the impact of climatic change, the Studio aims at tracing and exploiting the potentials emerging from the dynamics of this complex field. With a particular focus on tourism as a territorial practice, prototypical organisations are tested on local conditions and then meshed in networks of different levels, times and scales of implementation as a way to promote resilient, adaptable and responsive modes of urban growth. The Studio proposes the Action Plan as an operative alternative to the Master Plan.

Dynamic Substrates Studio Term 1 Ciro Najle, Sebastian Khourian, Chris Fannin, Mohsen Mostafavi

During the first term the Studio concentrated on the generation of prototypical ground propositions to reinforce, attenuate, accelerate or proliferate existing environmental pressures on specific costal segments of Europe. Five European landscape types, dependent on predominant substrate, slope and tidal regime, were studied and dynamic conditions simulated as a series of systematic performances.

Reverse Indexing Studio Term 2 Ciro Najle, Sebastian Khourian, Chris Fannin, Mohsen Mostafavi

During the second term the Studio was subject to two fluctuating processes: a fast mode specifying organizational structures and their reverse engineering; and a slow mode reindexing the proto-urban landscape infrastructures developed during the first term. The generic substrate prototypes acquired material, spatial and programmatic specificity by incorporating normatives, physical constraints, local habits, developmental strategies and management tactics, and construction technologies.

Franchising Urbanism Studio Term 3 Ciro Najle, Sebastian Khourian, Chris Fannin, Mohsen Mostafavi

The Studio geared towards the creation of a European Network of Infrastructural Franchises in the context of the European ICZM. Studio projects entered an expansive movement as they proliferated into a collective organisation. They developed the capability to manage prospectively their effects as a network, by codifying, regulating and documenting potentials and systems of growth, as a viable strategy for sustainable development. Franchising was understood as the opportunity to expand the potential of a single urban operation into a system of transformation of the territory at a continental scale.

Action Plans: Design Thesis Studio Term 4 Ciro Najle, Sebastian Khourian, Chris Fannin, Mohsen Mostafavi

Intrinsic to the concept of the Action Plan is the notion that for something to happen, certain forces, resources, concerns and negotiations must unfold in a temporal frame, introducing mutual feedback and progressive learning. The fourth term aimed at establishing the dynamic rationale under which the projects operate. The focus was on recognising the contexts of the project and on demonstrating how the projects cope with them through the instructions of their operative systems, the contextual variables to which they are responsive, and the material organisation of their by-products.

Staff

Ciro Najle
Mohsen Mostafavi
Sandra Morris
Christopher Fannin
Sebastian Khourian
Ian Carradice

Students

Ilaria Di Carlo
Magdalena Cuanda
James Haig Streeter
Juan Pablo Porta

Guest Jurors, Lecturers

Pierre Baillargeon
Larry Barth
Florian Beigel
Simona Bencini
Katharina Borsi
Santiago Bozzola
Martin Cairns
Mark Cousins
Paul Davies
Ines Geisler
Neil George
Iain Gunn
Joshua Gutman
Zaha Hadid
Greg Haigh
Mark Hemel
Hugo Hinsley
Takuro Hoshino
Peter Jacobs
Ed Jones
Nate Kolbe
Makoto Saito
Mick Van Marken
Clon Ulrick
Julian Varas
Tom Verebes
Michael Weinstock

Vertical Landscape
Magdalena Cuanda

[re]bordering Mediterreranean
Juan Pablo Porta

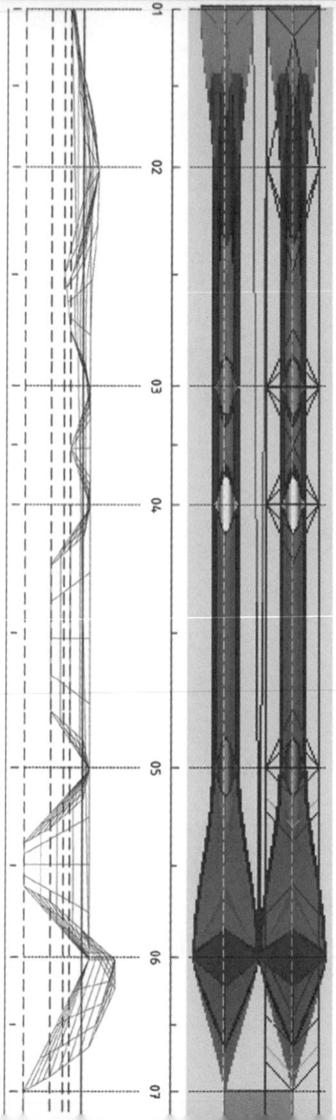

01 02 03 04 05 06 07

Netted Dunes
Ilaria Di Carlo

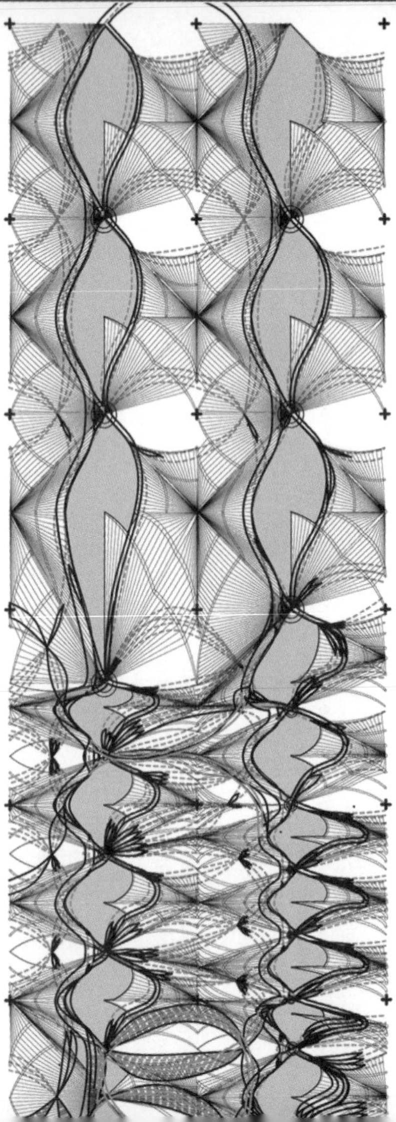

Autogenic Landcsape
James Haig Streeter

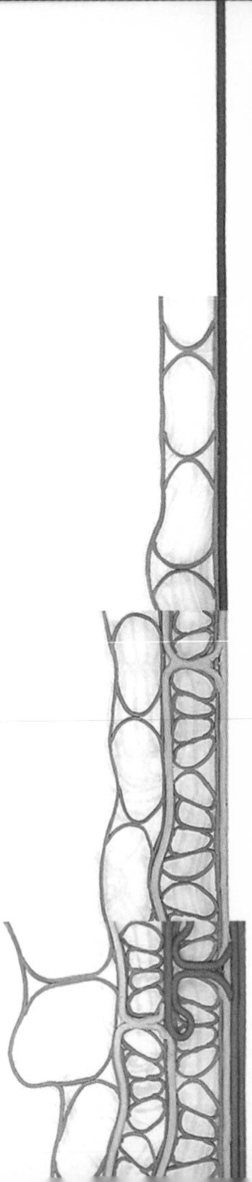

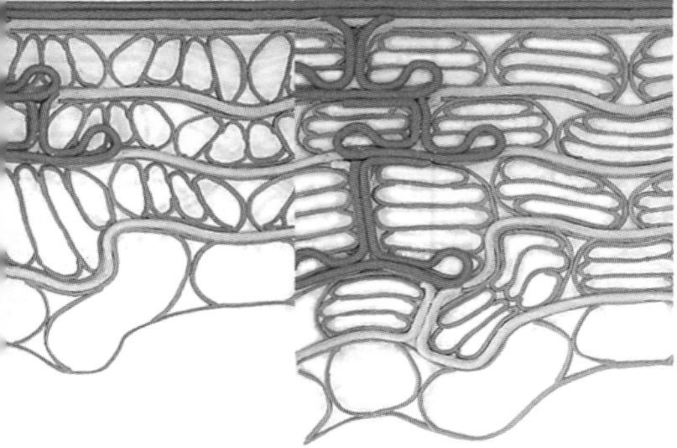

Autogenic Landscape **James Haig Streeter**

The artificial manipulation of coastal dynamics, resulting in a shifting of sedimentation equilibriums, enables the autogenesis of new coastline morphologies tailored to specific human requirements. Autogenic Landscape is a temporally responsive mechanism, synthesised through the interrelated accretion of land, infrastructure and programmatic demands.

Netted Dunes **Ilaria Di Carlo**

A system of artificially stiffened dunes, multiple infrastructures and generic programmatic pockets are set up in an energetic autotrophic field of connections between the land and the sea.

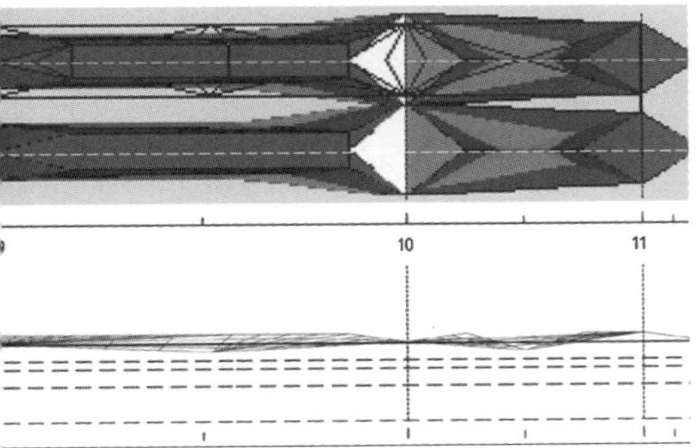

[re]Bordering Mediterranean **Juan Pablo Porta**

Structural topographies are joined, aligned and networked configuring a field with a large variety of leisure systems – from ponds to piers, from parking infrastructure to buoys. The Mediterranean becomes an open continent for the unfolding of an extensive moving ground.

Vertical Landscape **Magdalena Cuanda**

The dynamism of erosion in hard rock cliff systems and their topographic formations allow for the construction of a ground for urban expansion towards the sea. Positions and performances of the body and its extensions when climbing, running, biking or sailing are used as a distributed pattern of anchors through a vertical landscape. New urban organisations adapt to the topography to exploit its difficulties as opportunities.

Vertical Landscape
Magdalena Cuanda

[re]bordering Mediterranean
Juan Pablo Porta

Netted Dunes
Ilaria Di Carlo

Autogenic Landcsape
James Haig Streeter

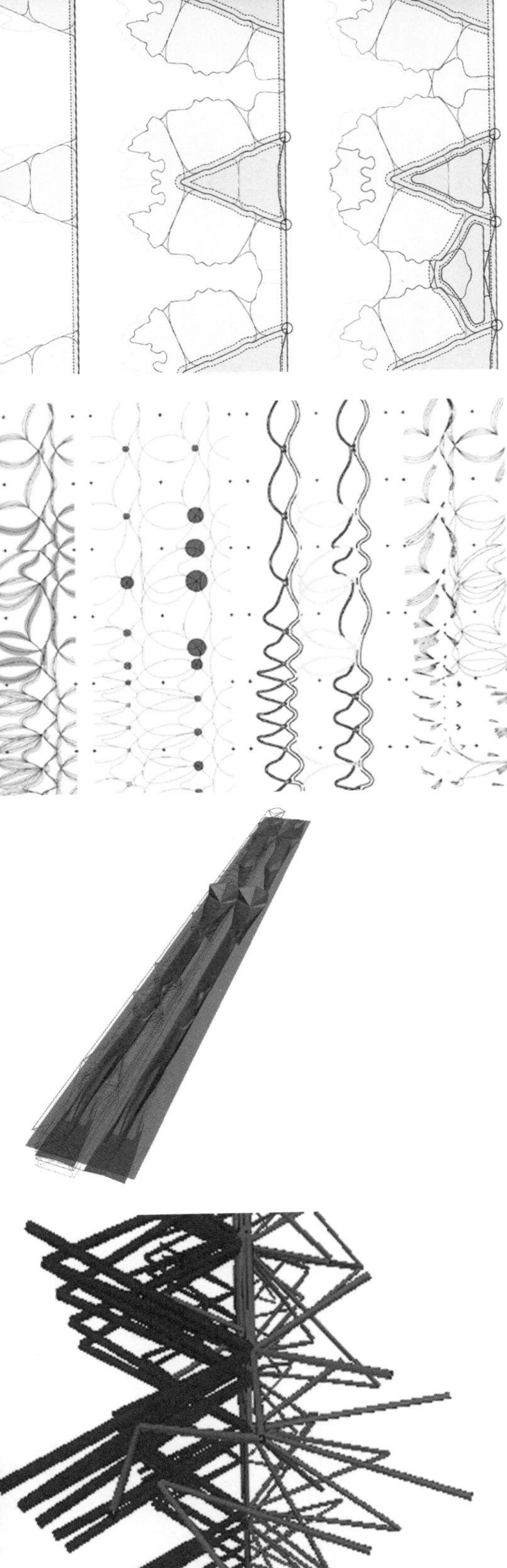

During 2001–02 a series of workshops, lectures and fieldtrips supported and challenged the continuity of the projects' development. Following the Studio assumption that the design, planning, implementation and construction of an urban development can be understood as the programming of an evolutionary process, the Breeding By Modelling **workshop consisted of the construction of a test-bed for the studio projects coupled with an ongoing tutorial on Maya 4.0 (Sebastian Khourian, Ciro Najle). The** Direct Interventions **workshop series made physical studies and mappings of the European Coast, and produced direct interventions that challenged the understanding of place (Chris Fannin, Sandra Morris). The** Tourism Management and Development **lectures gave an overview of the typological structure of the tourism industry – from market analysis to funding, implementation and post-construction ramifications – aiming at incorporating these logics as productive restrictions to the way urban projects are conceived (Chris Fannin with Ian Ohan, Duncan Thomas, Pierre Baillargeon and James Soane). During the first term, a series of short** Field Trips to the Coast of the UK **were arranged in order to introduce students to different coastal conditions and developments on the South Coast, Norfolk Coast and Dorset Coast (Sandra Morris and Chris Fannin). A ten-day** Field Trip to Las Vegas **aimed at the construction of taxonomies of material organisations and palettes of operative rules through the study of their evolution in time. It included investigations into recent hotels and resorts and visits to the desert, the Hoover Dam, the Grand Canyon and LA (Ciro Najle). The** Models And Modalities I **seminar was based on the assumption that a recent theoretical bifurcation in architecture culture is linked to an emergent kind of materialism detached from the mechanistic paradigm (Ciro Najle, Mohsen Mostafavi, Julian Varas).** Models And Modalities II **investigated models of fast urban transformation by recognising their implicit development rules, their complex economy and potentials (Ciro Najle,Mohsen Mostafavi, Paul Davies). The** Contemporary Landscape Projects **seminar studied the ways in which landscape has been used as an urban tool to regenerate public space and infrastructure during the last twenty years, particularly in Paris, Barcelona, Lyon and the Netherlands. During the first two terms, it studies both strategic and material levels in their economic and social contexts (Sandra Morris). Finally, the** Ecology and Environment **lecture series, given by Ian Carradice and experts from Ove Arup introduced environmental concerns via a wide range of techniques for the sustainable management and design of coastal areas under various types of environmental pressure.**

Field-Trip Term 2
Las Vegas
Ciro Najle

Field-Trips Term 1
UK Coast
Sandra Morris , Chris Fannin

Workshop Term 1
Direct Interventions Tour Series
Chris Fannin and Sandra Morris

Workshop Term 1
Breeding By Modelling
Ciro Najle, Sebastian Khourian

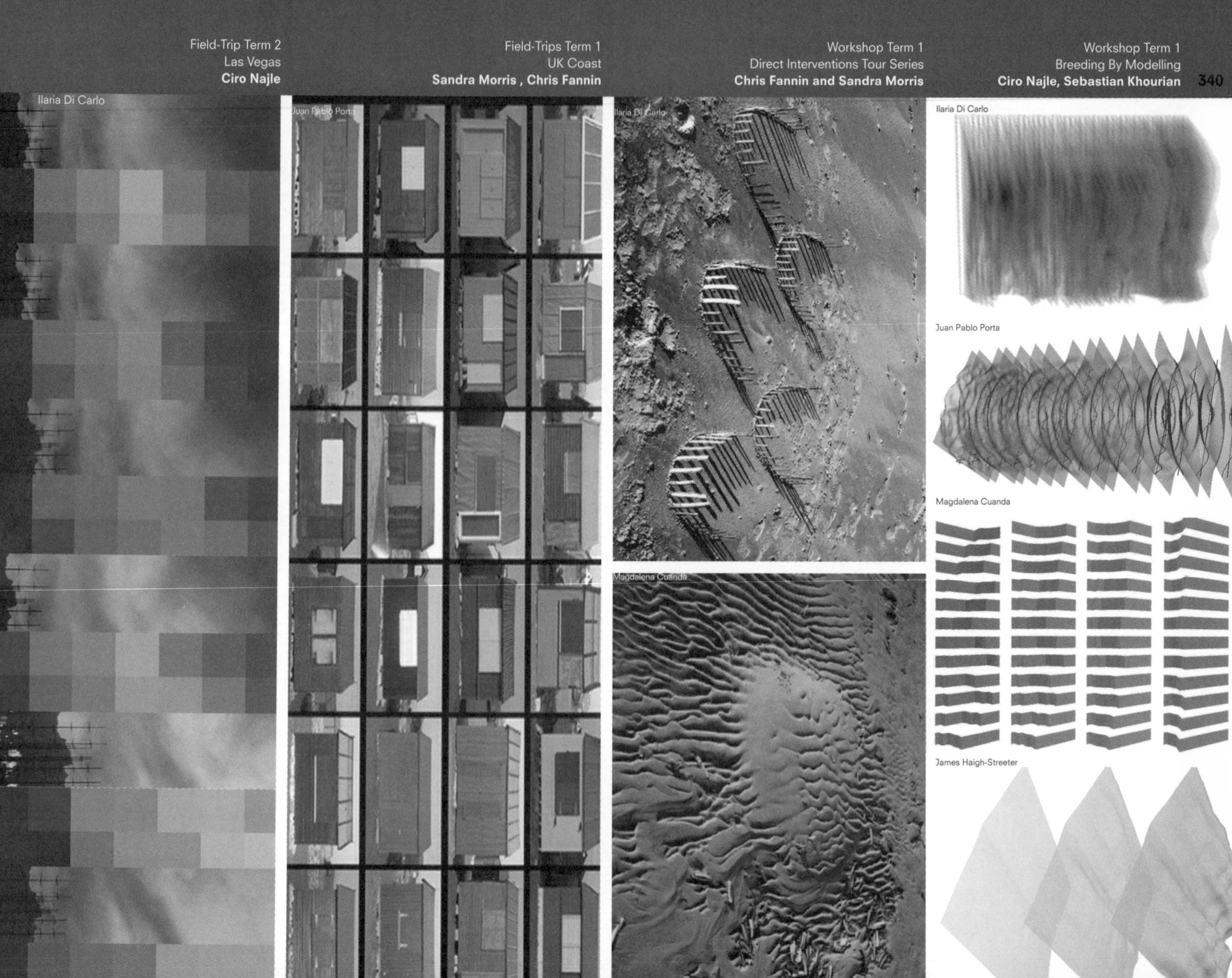

Ilaria Di Carlo

Juan Pablo Porta

Ilaria Di Carlo

Magdalena Cuanda

Ilaria Di Carlo

Juan Pablo Porta

Magdalena Cuanda

James Haigh-Streeter

A Genealogy of Movement **Ilaria Di Carlo MM1**
An analytical journey through the differentiation and repetition of the prototypical. Nine models occur in the history of thought in a cycle: flow, wave, atom, spiral, line, circle, ellipse, variation and mathematics.

Operative Evolution **Juan Pablo Porta MM1**
A primitive is a virtuality actualised by differentiation. Differentiation is selective, its transformation occurs through a machinic process. An abstract machine generates a plane of consistence. A plane of consistence is a plane of differentiation. Actualisation is differentiation, and differentiation is creation.

Concepts and Time **Magdalena Cuanda MM1**
Based on Deleuze's What is Philosophy?**, the essay discusses the temporality of concepts. It bridges theoretical arguments using empirical evidence.**

The Made and the Born **James Haig Streeter MM1**
A web-based matrix of philosophical and scientific terms and ideas aims at examining interrelationships between the mechanical and the lifelike, the 'made' and the 'born'. www.vivisystems.com/glossary

Persuasive Urbanism **Magdalena Cuanda MM2**
The essay explores the mechanisms of manipulation though persuasion: innovative ways to control people's behavior through visual guidance and sequences of optical devices.

On the Lack of Boundaries **Ilaria Di Carlo MM2**
Las Vegas interiors reorganise and reset the concept of boundaries. Interior spaces are made according to a chromatic hierarchy of the exterior space, rather than mimesis. It is a refined mode of emulation.

It's all about Control **Juan Pablo Porta MM2**
Las Vegas is a surface of maximum interface for forces developed from the economic and social conditions in America. Las Vegas's surface is a space of flux and oscillating conditions.

Xtreme Ecology **James Haig Streeter MM2**
A [re]learning from Las Vegas, this essay examines the interrelated mechanisms that generated the forms that fascinated the Venturis, framed within a current understanding of system dynamics.

Barcelona 2004 **Ilaria Di Carlo CLP1**
Barcelona has built up considerable expertise in the renewal of large areas of the old cityscape. These skills have been successfully incorporated in both public and private urban development schemes.

Curitiba: Third World City **Juan Pablo Porta CLP1**
While other cities are busy designing their master plans, Curitiba is taking steps to extend services and solutions to its entire metropolitan area: mobility, density, instability.

Ecotourism and Agriculture **Magdalena Cuanda CLP1**
Having existed since the Aztec Empire, Chinampas are agricultural fields based on water. Xochimilco is under pressure from massive tourism and the rapid population growth in Mexico City.

The Radiant City **James Haig Streeter CLP1**
The 'Radiant City' has been seen by many as avant-garde and progressive. But could the contrary be the case? Do these schemes represent a return to a retrogressive and outmoded philosophical construct?

The Voice of the Dunes **Ilaria Di Carlo CLP2**
What kind of relationship is involved in the notion of sound as a raw material? How much does this relationship change between an enclosed and an open space?

Building under the Sea **Juan Pablo Porta CLP2**
Human activities and natural disasters have caused a reduction in natural reef systems. Artificial reefs provide of a shelter structure, while creating waves to improve human activity in the coastline.

Epoxy Resins **Magdalena Cuanda CLP2**
The paper reviews the advantages and disadvantages of epoxy resins in the construction area. The Crack Injection system is seen as a system for new applications in landscapes.

Environmental Prosthetics **James Haig Streeter CLP2**
This essay investigates the material properties and applications of geosynthetics, framed in a context of their similarities to internalised human prosthetics.

Emergent Technologies, or Emtech, is a new one-year MA programme at the AA, inaugurated in October 2001 and directed by Michael Hensel and Michael Weinstock.

'Emergent' is defined as that which is produced by multiple causes, but which cannot be said to be the sum of their individual effects. It has been an important concept in biology and mathematics, in artificial intelligence, information theory and computers, and in the newer domains of weather and climatic studies, the material sciences, and in particular biomimetics engineering. Commonplace terms such as 'self-organising structures' and 'bottom-up systems' have their origin (and perhaps their deepest meaning) in the science of emergence, and are encountered in fields as disparate as economics and urbanism. Emergent behaviours are demonstrated by the culture of production at large, a dynamic interaction of diverse forces that follow local rules rather than imposed, higher-level instructions. Larger coherent patterns, or macrobehaviours, are discernible, arising from material productions that are localised by author, time and geography.

Dialogues that involve the characteristics of materials and ideas about nature have always been central to architectural theories. Materials themselves have been revised by new technologies enabled by the science of emergence, extending beyond refinement of traditional materials to the design of new materials. New composite materials are designed and produced at the molecular level, and in this arena biomimetics plays a significant role.

It is axiomatic that the radical changes that have occurred in the design and production of aerospace, maritime, automotive and consumer artefacts will, in time, have similar effects on the production of architecture. Our field of work is to trace those revisions that are relevant to architecture, to locate their theoretical, historical and critical relations, and to advance design processes that proceed from the new production dialogues.

Course Directors
Michael Hensel
Michael Weinstock

Students
Nimish Biloria
Mariano Ciccone
Ifat Finkelmann
Jose Louis Jaspeado
Manika Koshla
Abraham Papakirillo
Carlos Segovia

Teaching Staff
Timothy Lucas
Director of Special Structures, Price & Myers Consulting Engineers
Chris Hight
Member of the Teaching Staff of the Design Research Laboratory, Doctoral Candidate in Cultural Studies and the Humanities, the London Consortium, University of London
Professor George Jeronimidis
Director of the Centre for Biomimetics, Reading University, Department of Engineering
Michael Stacey
Brookes Stacey Randall Architects
Cecil Balmond
Advanced Structural Geometry Group, Chairman of Operations Board, Ove Arup & Partners
Dr Chris Leubkeman
Codirector of Research and Development, Ove Arup & Partners
Wolf Mangelsdorf
Team Leader and Associate Designate, Buro Happold
Professor Birger Sevaldson
Vice Rector of the School of Architecture, Professor of Industrial Design, University of Oslo
Professor Stefan Behling
University of Stuttgart

Manika Khosla
Dynamic glass tube/louvre system

The boundary between the natural and the manufactured has been reconfigured by biomimetic engineering. This part of the Emtech programme is intended to introduce students to the thinking that has led to the evolution of new materials, particularly composites, that may play a significant role in shaping the future of our built environment. It examines the conceptual foundation and organisation of 'smart' or adaptive structures. Analysis of the biological means of achieving complex 'emergent' structures and performances from simple components is combined with an exploration of current architectural and industrial component design, prototyping and production. The goal is to develop the potential of a radical bottom-up programme for architectural design. Reproduced below is a selection of texts written by Mariano Ciccone for thesis preparation and seminar projects.

Active Multiple Layer Systems in Nature

Natural forms, patterns and structures are analysed to reveal principles, mechanisms and operational systems for a new approach to the material technologies of architecture. Nature is not wasteful; its systems are self-designing, self-evaluating and constantly developing and adapting, orientated towards change and redundancy. What were once thought of as purely human technological systems, such as hydraulics, pneumatics and cellular structures, are all present in nature. Examples are:

Growth patterns of bones show stress patterns in their buildup that relate directly to the loads applied to them. This is produced by mineralisation of the collagen and the mineral is deposited only when needed. Bones develop under continuous load, both that imposed by our movements and that of the general condition of a structure steadily growing larger over time and under gravitational load.

Tropism is the internal movement in plants: certain types of plants are responsive to touch. They move because water is transferred under osmotic pressure, a hydraulic system that is related, in principle, to another common natural mechanism, pneumatics, the movement of air under pressure to realise structural rigidity. Such systems are able to adapt, reacting to stress and producing optimal solutions in order to resolve it.

Professor G Jeronimidis explains that 'cellulose walls of cells are flexible in bending but stiff in tension; the structures are the cells themselves, and they maintain their shape with the biologically active

membrane that can control the passage of fluids in and out of the cells; the energy source is the chemical potential difference between the inside and the outside of the cells. These systems are essentially working as networks of interacting minihydraulic actuators, liquid-filled bags that can become turgid or flaccid and that, owing to their shape and mutual interaction, translate local deformations to global ones and are also capable of generating very high stresses. Therefore, nonlignified plants are entirely dependent on control of turgor pressure inside the cells to achieve structural rigidity, prestressing the cellulose fibres in the cell walls at the expense of compression in the fluid. Similarly, in the flexible skins of animals such as the worm, hydrostatic skeletons where the prestressing of fibres in tension is balanced by compression in water is used.'

Multifunctionality Instead of Monofunctionality

Technology transfer occurs between different fields of research that can yield synergistic benefits from their integration. Functional integration is a key factor. In natural structures, each 'component' has to fulfil several tasks in cooperation with other components in order to optimise the organism. For example, the structure of the shell of the bluebottle egg is coated with a membrane made out of chitin, which has to meet a number of requirements that are very dissimilar from each other. These are:

- a basic structural stability
- an elasticity for local deformations to allow shape reestablishment
- a selective permeability to water, to allow vapour, but not fluid, to get through
- an ability to exchange gas for oxygen, and vice versa
- a thinness that permits as many eggs as possible to be produced from a limited amount of material.

What is extraordinary is the way in which the response to those differing requirements is achieved with one building material only, chitin. The internal structure of the chitin has relatively thick columns in the lowest layers, a mesh network that narrows upward and gradually mutates into a very fine lattice system towards the outer layer. This type of geometric organisation ensures that dripping water cannot spread by capillary action and therefore cannot penetrate the shell boundary. At the same time, the external lattice openings are structured so that gas and water vapour can get through, but bacteria and particles of dirt cannot. The overall structural configuration combines this system further to produce the required stability and elasticity.

Mariano Ciccone investigates the temporary use of space within urban sites that are in the process of redevelopment. He proposes an alternative to the building industry's existing conventions of modular systems, in which the repetition of similar components results in envelopes that are rigidly deterministic. This research explores, through design case-studies and experiments, the possibility of achieving spatial differentiation in order to enable multiple activities to take place over time. The goal is to generate gradient conditions between programmatic boundaries, consequently triggering interaction between what are conventionally separate public and private zones. Within the design process, the instrumental analysis focuses on human movement and orientation in space over time. Programmatic trajectories are unfolded; spatial effects and mechanisms that offer the potential for spatial reconfiguration are investigated.

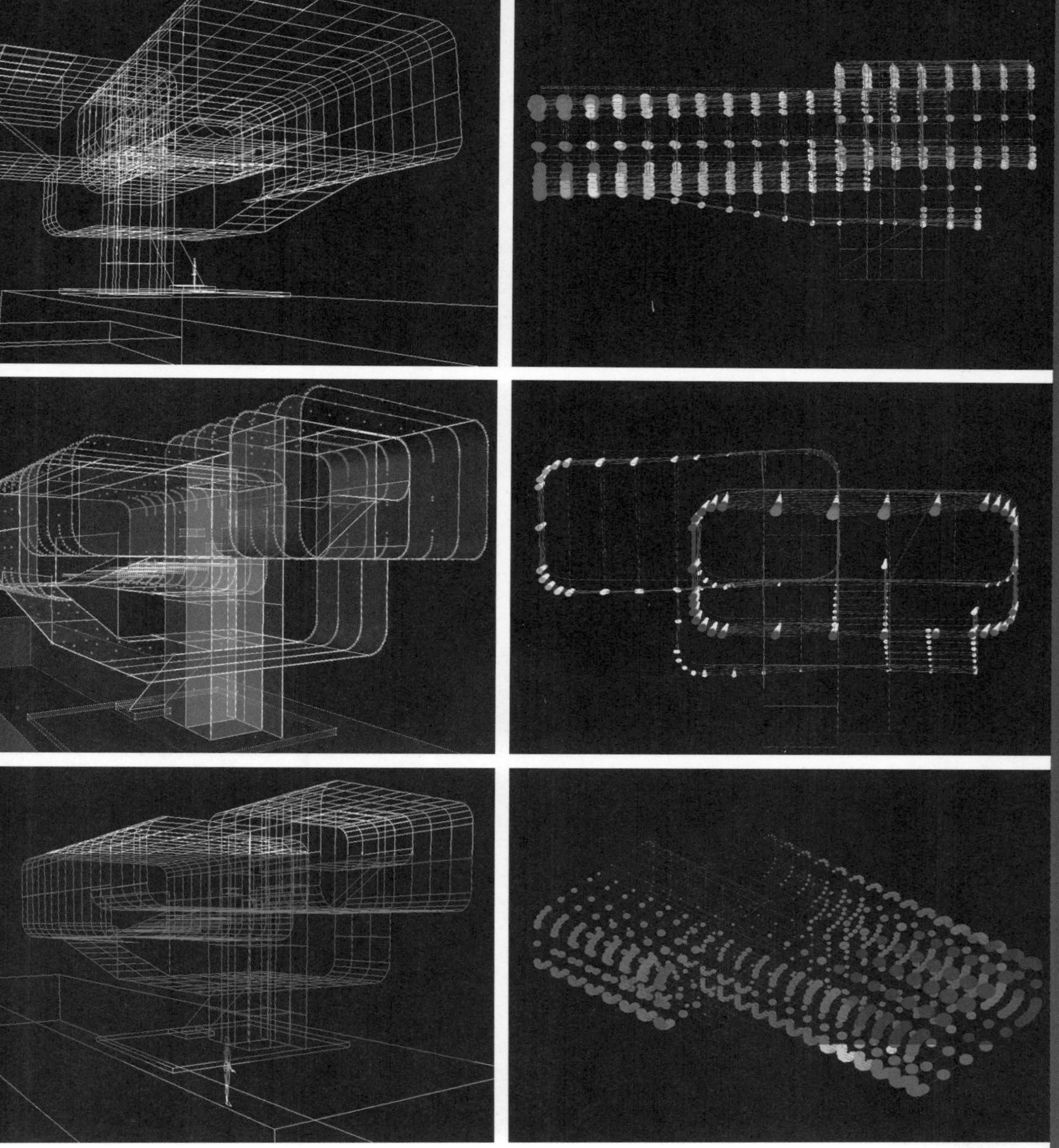

A close relation to industrial manufacturing methods facilitates adaptation to changing conditions, both within the design and manufacturing process and according to different site locations. Digital technologies, including parametric modelling, are essential for these design experiments. Advanced structural analysis is used to investigate material and physical behaviours of the project components and their assembly into a structure that has modules (each with their own programme) cantilevered from a central core. The images show an extract of the finite element analysis (originals in colour) that examines the stiffening of the load path within the building structure. Material properties have been kept constant, and the shaded areas refer to different degrees of surface deflection. The dots show different degrees of node deflection.

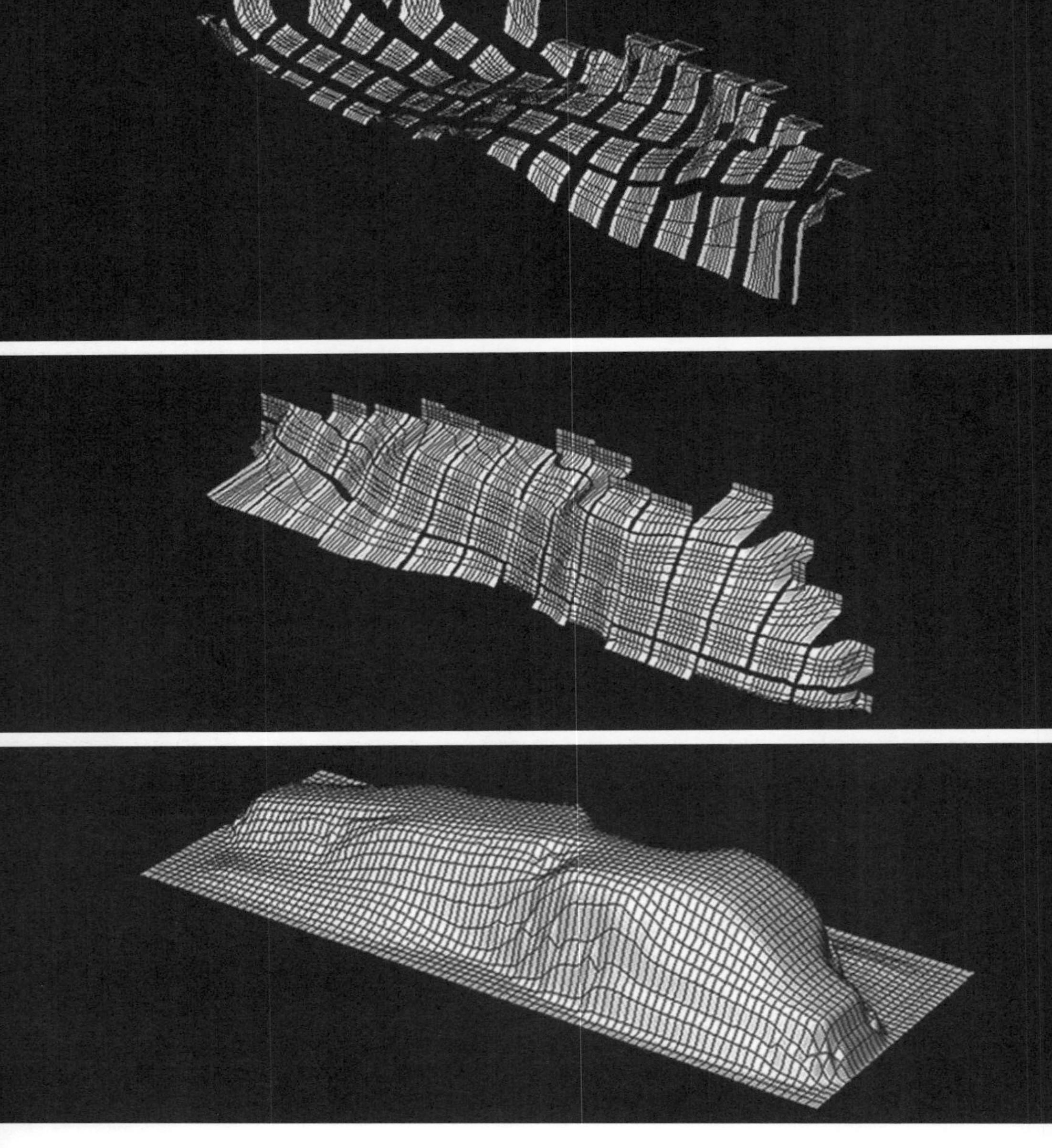

Material and production technologies have undergone a substantial revision, which is at last becoming available for architectural speculation. Recent developments in the understanding of biological systems, and the transfer of these concepts into material systems, pose a critical reassessment of contemporary architectural space. The primary concern of Nimish Biloria's project is to extend computing beyond the screen space and to draft possibilities of deploying computational processes, capacities and effects into everyday objects, such as furniture, walls and windows. The project is based in Leicester Square, London, and posits an enhancement of spatial qualities of the existing TKTS (ticketing centre) booth.

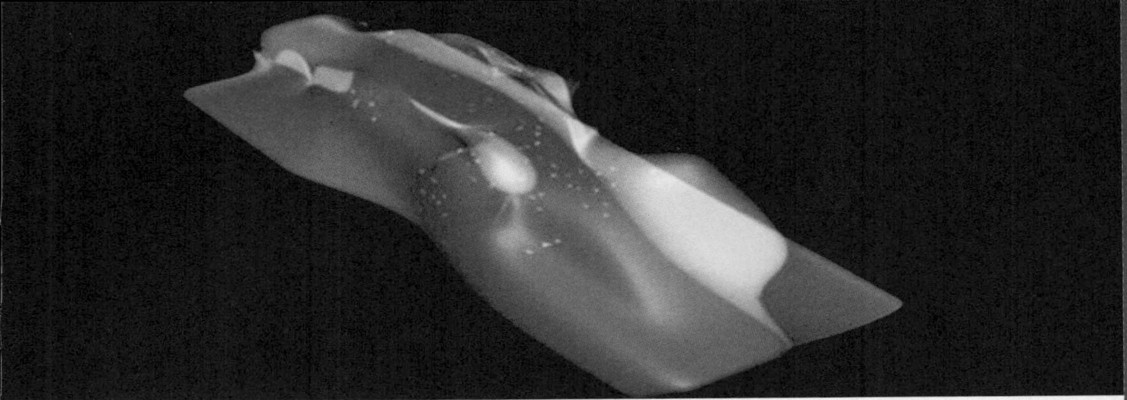

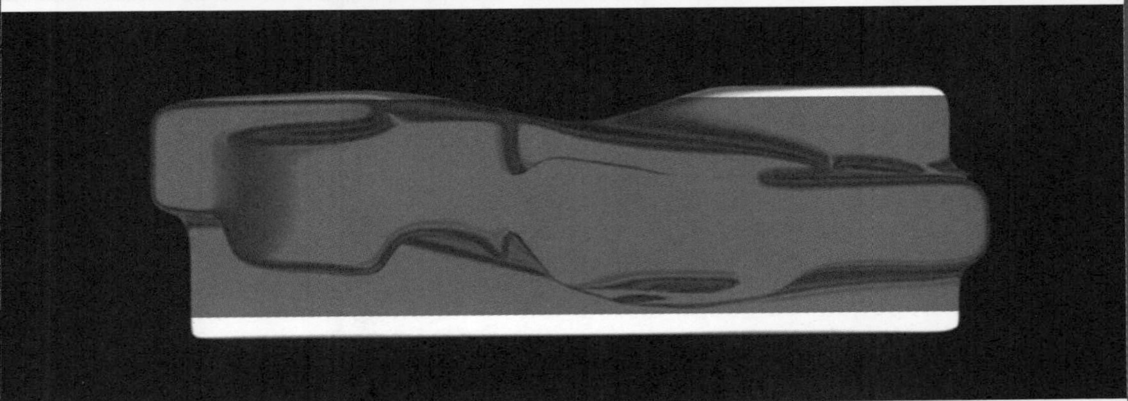

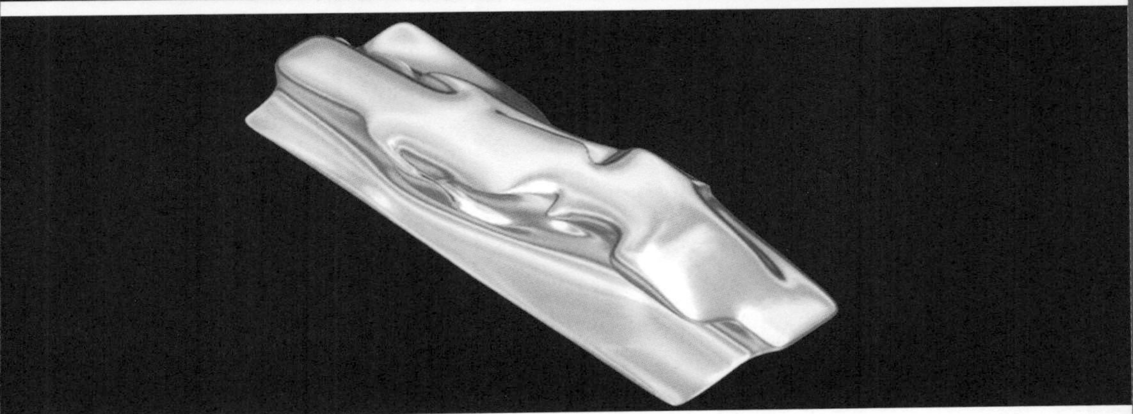

This project is to be accomplished by integrating new media tools into the architectural form. The complex geometry achieved by fusing programmatic components was materialised by CNC modelling. The external surface is proposed as a coating of light-transmissive films over foldable LCD panels. The coated panels can display information utilising 'green screen' technology within the projected silhouettes of the spectators. The skin possesses a dual character of being transparent from certain angles while being an information surface from other viewpoints. The project pursues the development of newer object 'types', architectures appropriate to contemporary programmes and their requirements, and responds to changing definitions of reality, presence, privacy and space.

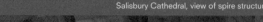

Salisbury Cathedral, view of spire structure

Ely Cathedral, lead work to lantern

This year's work continues to develop the postgraduates' awareness and skills in the core subjects of:

Historic knowledge and cultural appreciation
Research and report writing
Philosophy of conservation
Traditional building materials
Structures of historic buildings
Fabric deterioration and repair
Building investigations, inspections and assessments
Conservation and design in modern, urban contexts

As well as the necessary wide range of knowledge concerning historic buildings of all periods there is a heightened emphasis of these, including those of the twentieth century, in association with the current political and social issues or urban redevelopment, change and sustainability.

Statements by the Government and English Heritage regarding urban and metropolitan area development led us to choose, as the destination for this year's UK visit, the city of Birmingham, which is undergoing major redevelopment for the third time since the 1950s. In the same visit we visited Lubetkin's buildings at Dudley Zoo and the Odeon Cinema at Dudley.

This year's international visit is to Prague looking at the historic core as well as the Modern Movement buildings in the city.

Staff
John Redmill
Alan Greening
Sue Blundell

Visiting Lecturers
Bridget Cherry
The Middle Ages and their built record
Richard Halsey
The Medieval church and the way it was used
Eric Robinson
The Geology of Building Stones
Jacques Heyman
The Stone Skeleton
Ian Bristow
Historic Colour and Paint
Rosemary McQueen
Planning and Listed Building Legislation
Clive Richardson
Structural Movement
Richard Harris
Timber-Framed Buildings, Structure and Form
Sharon Cather
Wall Paintings and their Conservation
Roger White
Classical Architecture in Britain
Sam Price
Cantilevered Stairs
Robert Thorne
Nineteenth-Century Building Types
Sarah Stainforth
Environmental Controls
Alan Frost
Somerset House and Windsor Castle
Diane Kay
Twentieth-Century Buildings
Tony Walker
Repair of Modern Materials
Julian Harrop
Services

First Year Attendees
William Batley
Emma Bradley
Mary Cleary
Philip Crew
Stuart Ellis
Kate Graham
Murray John
Tobius Lumb
Ian McInnes
Julia Thomas
Amanda White

Second Year Attendees
Tony Barnard
Robert Collingwood
Tom Cromwell
Carolyn Dolgenos
Fred Gardner
David Gullick
Tim Nicholson
Nicolas Pope
Edward Rutherfoord
Dougal Ticehurst
John Woodcock

Cressing Temple Barley Barn

Trips to Old Sarum, Dublin, Hampton Court and Orford Castle

Lectures are reinforced by visits to current projects or to locations reflecting current issues.

Weekend study tours to Suffolk are offered in the First Year, one visiting churches and the other inspecting medieval domestic buildings and castles.

Visits to workshops and studios included:

Goddard and Gibbs, London – Stained-glass conservation
CEL, Peterborough – Lead-casting and metallurgy
The Stained-Glass Museum –Stained-glass collection
The AA – Lime workshop

In the Second Year visits have been made to:

St Paul's
Greenwich and the Queen's House
Chiswick and Marble Hill
Chatham Dockyard
Somerset House
Soane Museum
Victoria and Albert Museum, British Galleries
British Museum
Art Deco cinemas
Eltham Palace, restored Art Deco mansion of Stephen Courtauld

This year's Thesis submissions are:

Tony Barnard Life After Death – A Study of the Repairs of Nunhead

Robert Collingwood Plecnik at Prague Castle – Making History?

Tom Cromwell Open-Air Museums – A Critique

Carolyn Dolgenos 3, The Terrace, Richmond – Concepts and Misconceptions

Fred Gardner Norman Stonework – Beak Moulding

David Gullick The Works of Edward Pugin in Ramsgate

Tim Nicholson The Chapter House at Southwell Minster – Philosophy, Nature and Stone-carving

Nicolas Pope The Construction, Renovation and Ongoing Completion of the Second Goetheanum at Dornach

Edward Rutherfoord The Conservation of the Multicultural heritage of St Kitts and Nevis

Dougal Ticehurst Horse Engine Houses of the North York Moors – A Study of their History and their Place in the Modern Built Environment

John Woodcock The Buckler Family – A Study in Nineteenth-Century Attitudes to Medieval Buildings

Elaine Wren Went House, West Malling, Kent

The AA's two-year day-release Graduate Diploma is the UK's foremost postgraduate course in the conservation of designed landscapes and gardens, providing a solid foundation in historical skills and conservation. Its graduates have gone on to take up leading roles in the field in the UK and abroad. In 2002, validation was received for a full-time MA course, sharing the taught units with the Diploma, starting in October. It is also possible for qualified architects, planners, landscape architects and others to attend units of the course as part of their Continuing Professional Development. Students are encouraged to participate in the activities of the School and to attend lectures and symposia. The course also has its own programme of lectures, interspersed with day visits to gardens, parks and landscapes of particular interest and importance. In addition to attending the course units on a regular basis, students are expected to undertake associated projects and reports, together with a 10,000-word thesis in the second year.

Course Units

The principal areas of study are divided into modules, detailing specific themes for each term's teaching and learning. In 2001–2 changes were implemented in the teaching of history: beyond the study of garden history for its own sake, an emphasis was placed on linking ideas to practice. A Form and Style module was also introduced this year; it explored the connections between design ideas and intentions on the one hand, and the resultant designs on the other. On the conservation side, the pattern of teaching and learning followed the established sequence of survey, research, evaluation, planning and implementation, as in the two previous years, except for a Conservation in Practice module that rounded out the second year. This gave specific recognition to current issues, including, for example, urban parks and the holistic approach to conservation.

Staff
Edward Fawcett, Thesis Master
David Jacques, Programme Director
Sandra Morris, History Master
Jan Woudstra, Conservation Master
Clement Chung, Coordinator

Students
Sian Brown
Slaine Campbell
Judy Cligman
Adrian Cook
Louise Cooper
Tamar Ecclestone
Sarah Green
Eve Guinan
Consuelo Oppenheim
Sandra Nicholson
Ian Read
Cherrill Sands
Jane Seaborn

Course Tutors
Sarah Couch, Conservation Tutor
Brian Dix, Survey Tutor
Axel Griesinger, History Tutor
Elizabeth Lebas, Evaluation Tutor
Hugh Prince, Research Tutor

Guest Lecturers
Alan Barber
Charles Boot
Susan Campbell
Kate Clark
Richard Clarke
Dominic Cole
Michael Costen
Magdalena Cuando
Susan Denyer
Brent Elliott
Mohsen Faizi
Ken Fieldhouse
Giorgio Galletti
John Glenn
Patrick Goode
Virginia Hinze
David Lambert
Ray Laurence
Brenda Lewis
Jonathan Lovie
Ana Luengo
Lorna McRobie
John Popham
Jill Raggett
Judith Roberts
Marc Schoellen
Paul Stamper
Chris Sumner
Michael Symes
Anthea Taigell
Michael Tooley
Angus Wainwright
John Watkins
Jenifer White
Liz Whittle
Alix Wilkinson